American Government:

The Clash of Issues

Prentice-Hall International, Inc., *London*
Prentice-Hall of Australia, Pty., Ltd., *Sydney*
Prentice-Hall of Canada, Ltd., *Toronto*
Prentice-Hall of India (Private) Ltd., *New Delhi*
Prentice-Hall of Japan, Inc., *Tokyo*
Prentice-Hall de Mexico, S.A., *Mexico City*

SECOND EDITION

American Government:
The Clash of Issues

James A. Burkhart

Professor of Political Science
Stephens College

Henry C. Bush

Agency for International Development
United States Government

Samuel Krislov

Associate Professor of Political Science
University of Minnesota

Raymond L. Lee

Chairman, Department of Social Science
Indiana State College, Indiana, Pa.

PRENTICE-HALL, INC.
Englewood Cliffs, New Jersey

Current printing (last digit):
14 13 12 11 10 9 8 7 6 5

Library of Congress Catalog Card Number: 64-16607

Printed in the United States of America

C-02696

This book is dedicated to the memory of

JOHN FITZGERALD KENNEDY

who saw in the clash of issues their clarification
and in the confrontation with issues
ultimate peace and freedom
for all men.

Introduction

Four years ago, in our introduction to the first edition of this work, we set forth our purpose and our hope. It was our purpose, using a clash-of-issues approach, to confront the reader with a series of unresolved questions spanning American politics. It was our hope that this format would "prod the reader off the sidelines and into intellectual activity concerning government and politics."

The advantages inherent in this approach seem as significant today as they were in 1960. The student must first become involved in the political dialogue of our time. Growing from this involvement are these educational objectives:

a. a recognition that controversy and disagreement are natural parts of the democratic process and that their absence rather than their presence should cause alarm.
b. a realization that even though acceptance of political conditions as fixed or "given" can frequently be bad, the opposite—polarized, irreconcilable standing on principle—is equally dangerous.
c. an idea of how emotionally loaded a major issue is, what makes such an issue, and what courses lead to compromise or stalemate.
d. a personal involvement in many of the issues—if not on an action basis, at least an intellectual identification.
e. an awareness that political practices, rights, and liberties are a function of groups of persons and entail a great deal more than the mere passing of a law.

Our own continued experience with this volume—now involving seven years of use in the classroom—and the reaction to the first edition have been encouraging. This new edition continues the basic pattern, but our objective has required an exhaustive examination of all original articles and a search for live and current problems. Accordingly, our revision includes two new chapters, a dozen or so new issues, and a thoroughgoing revision of the cast of readings.

In this task of re-evaluation we have been greatly aided by comments from users of the first edition. We would like particularly to acknowledge the suggestions of Herbert Garfinkel, Michigan State University, and Edwin Fogelman, The University of Minnesota.

We would also like to take this opportunity to thank those publishers and authors who have granted us permission to reprint. For the most part, the writers represented here are advocates of a distinct point of view and have been selected because of their eloquent, persuasive presentation of that viewpoint.

JAMES A. BURKHART
HENRY C. BUSH
SAMUEL KRISLOV
RAYMOND L. LEE

Table of Contents

IV The Federal System: Instrument of Liberty or Inefficiency? 76

American Government:

The Clash of Issues

I

The State of America

The political life of every nation has a special flavor, in part because of its unique economic, social, and intellectual climate. In this chapter we shall examine the American climate and attempt to put United States politics and government in focus. Although the experts do not fully agree, their identification of trends and problems in our society should give a hint as to the big questions that will face you during the next twenty years.

What's Happening to the Economy?

Unquestionably, the United States has developed—in part happened upon—a system of making, distributing, and using goods and services which is unique. We are eliminating for most people within America the centuries-old problem of poverty. The last several decades have demonstrated that, at least for the foreseeable future, we have a system in which the mass of people near the bottom of the economic heap move up rapidly, and in which there are almost always jobs.

Until about 1939 great economic depressions were followed by great booms and these followed by greater economic depressions. Such a business cycle of boom and bust, boom and bust, was normal. In a depression perhaps as many as 25 per cent of all persons willing to work were unable to get any kind of a job. This cycle has been tamed to a pale cycle of boomlets followed by recessions. The difference is vast in human suffering and personal catastrophe. During our tamed booms we have an "overtime economy." There are more jobs than jobseekers, and prices and wages are rapidly bid up. In tamed recessions unemployment creeps up to about 8 per cent of the total working force. This is decried by Cassandras everywhere, office-holders soon up for reelection worry about voters' reactions, and national and state governments look around for economic hypodermics with which to give this or that lagging sector of the economy a shot in the arm. But the point should be that even when the struggle to earn a living reaches its worst, 92 per cent of all persons wanting work continue to have it. This is the miracle of the American economy. How do we do it? What is it doing to us? How is it changing us? What will it do to us between now and 1980? These economic issues are eventually political questions which are examined here.

Especially are we concerned about the relationship between public and private spending. On the average we're doing fine. Incomes are up. The poor are ceasing to be poor. Nothing like it ever happened before in history. Television sets, food, clothing, household wares, gadgets, new cars, all these we have in amounts almost embarrassing. Yet what do we use it for? Why is the *public* sector of the economy so undernourished? Why, among all our riches, do we have a pressing shortage of policemen, garbage trucks, parks and parking space in the cities? Why the acute shortage of school buildings in rural areas? Why polluted water when engineering and chemical techniques could eliminate it? Why is it we have private wealth yet public poverty?

Finally we are concerned about the impact of the new economy on individual workers. Does the new economy need employees? If so, what kind? Way back in history, back in the mid-1930's, a cynical greeting of New York City college students was: "You went to college! So you work at Macy's?" Meaning there were already too many overeducated persons in America's largest city. That was thirty years ago. Take a look at the want-ads today. "Wanted: computer guidance engineer. Salary to $18,000." "Wanted: O&M man. Must know automatic data processing and small sampling theory." The whole trend is toward "knowledge workers," professionals, technicians. Braininess is in demand, and by 1980 we'll all be electronic wizards or mathematicians or laboratory men, or . . . . Or—What about the 85 per cent of us who haven't got I.Q.'s of 140 or above? Are you becoming obsolete while still in training? What about the unemployed—not in 1970 or 1980 but right now—who are not only unemployed but unemployable?

What's Happening to the Social Structure?

Democracy means more than periodic elections and the right to say who shall run the country. It also means freedom, human dignity, and access to social equality—a chance to be judged on your merits. Americans believe in social equality; there is no doubt of that. But sometimes organizational and technological trends run counter to beliefs. How are trends running—towards more or towards less social equality between men? How free and equal are we?

Optimists declare that in America the rich may drive Cadillacs or Mercedes-Benzes but the "poor" drive Oldsmobiles or Fords, and who can tell the man who earns $50,000 a year from the man who earns $7,000? This is the equalitarian world we have designed. Or are all those equalitarian goods and all personal status to be had only at the cost of rarely being taken seriously, of acting out roles instead of doing things useful, and of "never blurting out the truth"?

The Intellectual Climate: Conformity or Rebellion?

Pessimists feel that the rough and tumble days are over in America. Society is largely set in its mold. The economy is rolling ever onward. Everybody agrees on what is to be done next. At least this is what most young executives and administrators think, according to those who "view with alarm." But such an intellectual climate will run us into the ground in the next decade or so, because our institutions, education, and ideology are obsolete. It may well be that the kind of men we need to think and organize and lead us out of imminent impasses would never pass Personnel.

Much of our concern over the intellectual climate centers on young people—the new generation. Are they soft, spoiled brats, preoccupied with the sensation of the moment? Or are they clear-eyed, far-seeing individuals who have rejected the buncombe of their elders. Not Very Angry Middle Aged Men often bleat that the "kids" are not behaving the way they did. They complain of a "TV generation" while, according to their defenders, young people are reading the latest good book, joining the Peace Corps, seeing the latest out-of-the-way play, and trying to be creative and honest. While their elders talk about property values they talk about justice. But, they say, young people are balked of anything meaningful in life. They sense it and more and more are opting "out" of society as we now run it, or rather as it now runs us.

These, then, are the main economic, social and intellectual circumstances in which American government functions and will continue to function for some decades ahead.

The Political Arena

An examination of the American political arena ends our exploration of the State of America. For in America every problem is eventually political, be it social, economic, or intellectual at the outset. Such diverse questions as those concerning automation, education, and the American character are ultimately drawn into that vortex. College students have been known to survive in the past with only a fuzzy notion of the conflict between Guelph and Ghibelline. But any citizen of tomorrow's world who does not understand the operation of that great decision-making organization—the American governmental system—will experience much the same befuddlement as the tourist in a strange area without a highway map.

1

ON THE AVERAGE WE'RE DOING FINE!*

Average income per family was $7,000 in 1961. Incomes per family are up 70 per cent since 1947! Those at the bottom are moving up in massive numbers. Our income distribution—unlike all others in the world—does not resemble a pyramid anymore, with more at each level below and less at each level above. It is the shape of a spindle, or a chianti bottle, or a middle-aged fat man, narrowing sharply at the top, a big bulge in the middle, especially just below the middle, then narrowing again at the bottom but less sharply than at the top. The biggest number of persons is just below the middle. It is a preponderantly middle-class society. The poor not only become less poor; there are less and less of them. This is democracy in economic distribution!

The average personal income, before taxes were paid, of each American family or "unattached individual" (person living alone) went up by rather less in 1961 than it had in the previous year but the gain was still near $200. Since 1947 there has been an increase of 70 per cent in the income of the average family in terms of current dollars, of 30 per cent in real terms which allow for higher prices. The aggregate of family personal incomes in 1947 was $184.6 billion; in 1961 it was $397.2 billion.

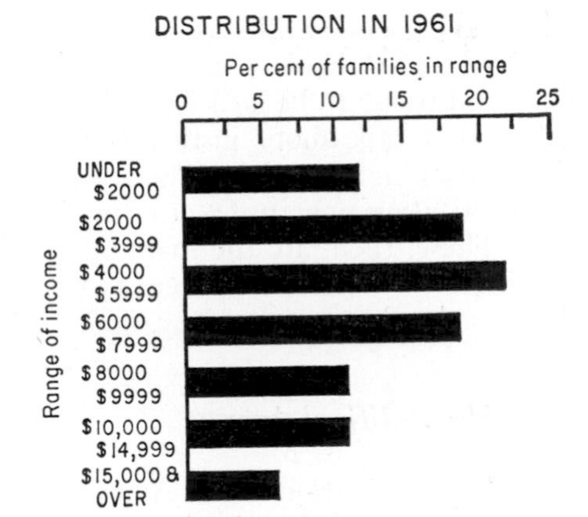

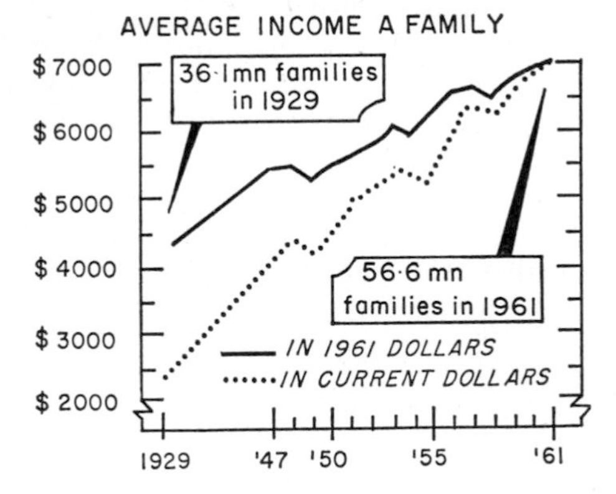

In 1961 the largest number of families (12.4 million) was in the annual income range from $4,000-$5,999, with about 10.5 million families in each of the ranges above and below. In 1947 17.1 million families were in the $2,000-$3,999 range, with 11.1 million in the lowest range of all. Today there are still 6.8 million families with incomes of under $2,000 a year, but 3.7 million have incomes of over $15,000, compared with only 800,000 in 1947.

* *The Economist* (London), September 29, 1962, p. 1197.

2

WE HAVE AN UNBALANCED ECONOMY*

John K. Galbraith

Our economy is world famous and unique in history. In Asia, Africa, or the Middle East you will find reaction is almost everywhere the same: "You Americans, you're rich. You live high." Yet we lack recreation space, we are behind in building schools, short of parking space and almost any other public *facility you name. Do we, in fact, as Professor Galbraith alleges, have an unbalanced economy?*

The line which divides our area of wealth from our area of poverty is roughly that which divides *privately* produced and marketed goods and services from *publicly* rendered services. Our wealth in the first is not only in startling contrast with the meagerness of the latter, but our wealth in privately produced goods is, to a marked degree, the cause of crisis in the supply of public services. For we have failed to see the importance, indeed the urgent need, of maintaining a balance between the two.

This disparity between our flow of private and public goods and services is no matter of subjective judgment. On the contrary, it is the source of the most extensive comment which only stops short of the direct contrast being made here. In the years following World War II, the papers of any major city—those of New York were an excellent example—told daily of the shortages and shortcomings in the elementary municipal and metropolitan services. The schools were old and overcrowded. The police force was under strength and underpaid. The parks and playgrounds were insufficient. Streets and empty lots were filthy, and the sanitation staff was underequipped and in need of men. Access to the city by those who work there was uncertain and painful and becoming more so. Internal transportation was overcrowded, unhealthful, and dirty. So was the air. Parking on the streets had to be prohibited, and there was no space elsewhere. These deficiencies were not in new and novel services but in old and established ones. Cities have long swept their streets, helped their people move around, educated them, kept order, and provided horse rails for vehicles which sought to pause. That their residents should have a nontoxic supply of air suggests no revolutionary dalliance with socialism.

The discussion of this public poverty competed, on the whole successfully, with the stories of ever-increasing opulence in privately produced goods. The gross national product was rising. So were retail sales. So was personal income. Labor productivity had also advanced. The automobiles that could not be parked were being produced at an expanded rate. The children, though

* John K. Galbraith, *The Affluent Society* (Boston: Houghton Mifflin Company, 1958), pp. 251–61, 267–69. Reprinted by permission of and arrangement with Houghton Mifflin Company, the authorized publishers.

without schools, subject in the playgrounds to the affectionate interest of adults with odd tastes, and disposed to increasingly imaginative forms of delinquency, were admirably equipped with television sets. We had difficulty finding storage space for the great surpluses of food despite a national disposition to obesity. Food was grown and packaged under private auspices. The care and refreshment of the mind, in contrast with the stomach, was principally in the public domain. Our colleges and universities were severely overcrowded and underprovided, and the same was true of the mental hospitals.

The contrast was and remains evident not alone to those who read. The family which takes its mauve and cerise, air-conditioned, power-steered, and power-braked automobile out for a tour passes through cities that are badly paved, made hideous by litter, blighted buildings, billboards, and post for wires that should long since have been put underground. They pass on into a countryside that has been rendered largely invisible by commercial art. (The goods which the latter advertise have an absolute priority in our value system. Such aesthetic considerations as a view of the countryside accordingly come second. On such matters we are consistent.) They picnic on exquisitely packaged food from a portable icebox by a polluted stream and go on to spend the night at a park which is a menace to public health and morals. Just before dozing off on an air mattress, beneath a nylon tent, amid the stench of decaying refuse, they may reflect vaguely on the curious unevenness of their blessings. Is this, indeed, the American genius?

In the production of goods within the private economy it has long been recognized that a tolerably close relationship must be maintained between the production of various kinds of products. The output of steel and oil and machine tools is related to the production of automobiles. Investment in transportation must keep abreast of the output of goods to be transported. The supply of power must be abreast of the growth of industries requiring it. . . .

Just as there must be balance in what a community produces, so there must be balance in what the community consumes. An increase in the use of one product creates, ineluctably, a requirement for others. If we are to consume more automobiles, there must be more space on which to operate them, as well as more gasoline and more insurance. Beyond a certain point more and better food appears to mean increased need for medical services. This is the certain result of the increased consumption of tobacco and alcohol. More vacations require more hotels and more fishing rods. And so forth. With rare exceptions—shortages of doctors are an exception which suggests the rule—this balance is also maintained quite effortlessly so far as goods for private sale and consumption are concerned. The price system plus a rounded condition of opulence is again the agency.

However, the relationships we are here discussing are not confined to the private economy. They operate comprehensively over the whole span of private and public services. As surely as an increase in the output of automobiles puts new demands on the steel industry, so also, it places new demands on public services. Similarly, every increase in the consumption of private goods will normally mean some facilitating or protective step by the state. In all cases if these services are not forthcoming, the consequences will be in some degree ill. It will be convenient to have a term which suggests a satisfactory relationship between the supply of privately produced goods and services and those of the state, and we may call it *social balance.*

The problem of social balance is ubiquitous, and frequently it is obtrusive. As noted, an increase in the consumption of automobiles requires a facilitating supply of streets, highways, traffic control, and parking space. The protective services of the police and the highway patrols must also be available, as must those of the hospitals. Although the need for balance here is extraordinarily clear, our use of privately produced vehicles has, on occasion, got far out of line with the supply of the related public services. The result has been hideous road congestion, an annual massacre of impressive proportions, and chronic colitis in the cities. As on the ground, so also in the air. Planes collide with disquieting consequences for those within when the public provision for air traffic control fails to keep pace with private use of the airways.

But the auto and the airplane, versus the space to use them, are merely an exceptionally visible example of a requirement that is pervasive. The more goods people procure, the more packages they discard, and the more trash that must be carried away. If the appropriate sanitation services are not provided, the counterpart of increasing opulence will be deepening filth. The greater the wealth the thicker will be the dirt. This indubitably describes a tendency of our time. As more goods are produced and owned, the greater are the opportunities for fraud and the more property that must be protected. If the provisions of public law enforcement services do not keep pace, the counterpart of increased well-being will, we may be certain, be increased crime.

The city of Los Angeles, in modern times, is a near-classic study in the problem of social balance. Magnificently efficient factories and oil refineries, a lavish supply of automobiles, a vast consumption of handsomely packaged products coupled with the absence of a municipal trash collection service which forced the use of home incinerators made the air nearly unbreathable for an appreciable part of each year. Air pollution could be controlled only by a complex and highly developed set of public services—by better knowledge stemming from more research, better policing, a municipal trash collection service, and possibly the assertion of the priority of clean air over the production of goods. These were long in coming. The agony of a city without usable air was the result.

The issue of social balance can be identified in many other current problems. Thus an aspect of increasing private production is the appearance of an extraordinary number of things which lay claim to the interest of the young. Motion pictures, television, automobiles, and the vast opportunities which go with the mobility, together with such less enchanting merchandise as narcotics, comic books, and pornographia, are all included in an advancing gross national product. The child of a less opulent as well as technologically more primitive age had far fewer such diversions. The red schoolhouse is remembered mainly because it had a paramount position in the lives of those who attended it that no modern school can hope to attain.

In a well-run and well-regulated community, with a sound school system, good recreational opportunities, and a good police force—in short a community where public services have kept pace with private production—the diversionary forces operating on the modern juvenile may not do great damage. Television and the violent mores of Hollywood and Madison Avenue must contend with the intellectual discipline of the school. The social, athletic, dramatic, and like attractions of the school also claim the attention of the child. These, together with the other recreational opportunities of the community, minimize the tendency to delinquency. Experiments with violence and immorality are checked by an effective law enforcement system before they become epidemic.

In a community where public services have failed to keep abreast of private consumption things are very different. Here, in an atmosphere of private opulence and public squalor, the private goods have full sway. Schools do not compete with television and the movies. The dubious heroes of the latter, not Miss Jones, become the idols of the young. The hot rod and the wild ride take the place of more sedentary sports for which there are inadequate facilities or provision. Comic books, alcohol, narcotics, and switchblade knives are, as noted, part of the increased flow of goods, and there is nothing to dispute their enjoyment. There is an ample supply of private wealth to be appropriated and not much to be feared from the police. An austere community is free from temptation. It can be austere in its public services. Not so a rich one.

Moreover, in a society which sets large store by production, and which has highly effective machinery for synthesizing private wants, there are strong pressures to have as many wage earners in the family as possible. As always all social behavior is part of a piece. If both parents are engaged in private production, the burden on the public services is further increased. Children, in effect, become the charge of the community for an appreciable part of the time. If the services of the community do not keep pace, this will be another source of disorder.

Residential housing also illustrates the problem of the social balance, although in a somewhat complex form. Few would wish to contend that, in the lower or even the middle income brackets, Americans are munificently supplied with housing. A great many families would like better located or merely more houseroom, and no advertising is necessary to persuade them of their wish. And the provision of housing is in the private domain. At first glance at least, the line we draw between private and public seems not to be preventing a satisfactory allocation of resources to housing.

On closer examination, however, the problem turns out to be not greatly different from that of education. It is improbable that the housing industry is greatly more incompetent or inefficient in the United States than in those countries—Scandinavia, Holland, or (for the most part) England—where slums have been largely eliminated and where minimum standards of cleanliness and comfort are well above our own. As the experience of these countries shows, and as we have also been learning, the housing industry functions well only in combination with a large, complex, and costly array of public services. These include land purchase and clearance for redevelopment; good neighborhood and city planning, and effective and well-enforced zoning; a variety of financing and other aids to the housebuilder and owner; publicly supported research and architectural services for an industry which, by its nature, is equipped to do little on its own; and a considerable amount of direct or assisted public construction for families in the lowest income brackets. The quality of the housing depends not on the industry, which is given, but on what is invested in these supplements and supports.

The case for social balance has, so

far, been put negatively. Failure to keep public services in minimal relation to private production and use of goods is a cause of social disorder or impairs economic performance. The matter may now be put affirmatively. By failing to exploit the opportunity to expand, public services fall behind private production. We have here the first of the causes of social imbalance. . . .

A feature of the years immediately following World War II was a remarkable attack on the notion of expanding and improving public services. During the depression years such services had been elaborated and improved partly in order to fill some small part of the vacuum left by the shrinkage of private production. During the war years the role of government was vastly expanded. After that came the reaction. Much of it, unquestionably, was motivated by a desire to rehabilitate the prestige of private production and therewith of producers. No doubt some who joined the attack hoped, at least tacitly, that it might be possible to sidestep the truce on taxation vis-à-vis equality by having less taxation of all kinds. For a time the notion that our public services had somehow become inflated and excessive was all but axiomatic. Even liberal politicians did not seriously protest. They found it necessary to aver that they were in favor of public economy too.

In this discussion a certain mystique was attributed to the satisfaction of privately supplied wants. A community decision to have a new school means that the individual surrenders the necessary amount, willy-nilly, in his taxes. But if he is left with that income, he is a free man. He can decide between a better car or a television set. This was advanced with some solemnity as an argument for the TV set. The difficulty is that this argument leaves the community with no way of preferring the school. All private wants, where the individual can choose, are (defined as being) inherently superior to all public desires which must be paid for by taxation and with an inevitable component of compulsion. . . .

. . . The postwar onslaught on the public services left a lasting imprint. To suggest that we canvass our public wants to see where happiness can be improved by more and better services has a sharply radical tone. Even public services to avoid disorder must be defended. By contrast, the man who devises a nostrum for a nonexistent need and then successfully promotes both remains one of nature's noblemen.

3

EVERY MAN AN ENGINEER BY 1980?*

Peter Drucker

The day of heavy manual labor is past according to many forecasters. By 1980 everyone will be a "knowledge worker." Less and less of the national income will be spent for goods: more and more for services. Business and travel will spill over national boundaries. All workers will periodically return to the classroom for more education. They and their families will casually move to the branch office at Dijon or Kuala Lumpur (with TV for the kiddies by Tel Star). And politicians will be worried about "the Ph.D. vote." Peter Drucker, a noted management consultant, suggests many of the above changes in the article which follows.

. . . Already those people whom the Bureau of the Census calls "technical, professional and managerial"—teachers, engineers, accountants, scientists, doctors and medical technologists, market researchers, credit analysts, investment managers and a host of others—outnumber industrial workers. They are also the fastest growing group.

Already, "continuing education"—the general-studies programs of the large universities or the advanced management programs run by or for corporations—is the most rapidly growing part of the educational field. By 1980, teaching, full-time or part-time, will be the largest occupation by far in this country. The teaching vote, rather than the labor or farm vote, may even tip the political scales in key states. . . .

The United States is already consumer-oriented, and services—travel, recreation, medical care, education, etc.—already take a growing share of the consumer's dollar. By 1980, our markets will have become even more consumer-oriented, and services may take 50 cents of each consumer dollar spent. Two million Americans, for instance, now travel abroad each year. By 1980, there should be 15 to 25 million.

The past ten years have seen a good many "specialized mass markets" come into being: for hi-fi sets, for classical recordings, for lawn-care products, to name but a few. Such "specialized" markets rather than the "old fashioned" mass markets, for automobiles or appliances, for instance, are likely to have the greatest growth in the next twenty years.

Only a nuclear war could stop this trend; only a major depression or a very great expansion in defense spending could slow it down. It reflects not only higher incomes. It reflects also the emergence of the knowledge worker, who spends a larger part of his income on services, and needs them more than does the manual worker. Also—a subtle but an important change—material

* Peter Drucker, "The Economic Race: A Forecast for 1980," *The New York Times Magazine*, January 21, 1962, pp. 7, 66–69.

things are not the status symbols for the knowledge worker; they are for the manual worker. A son in graduate school gives him more prestige (and costs more) than a bigger car. . . .

We—and incidentally our challenger Mr. Khrushchev—tend to think that the world economy still consists of two giants: the United States, the old champion, and the Soviet Union, the young and vigorous contender. But there is already a third giant around: the Common Market of Western Europe.

It outproduces the Soviet Union two to one or better. And it is rapidly catching up with the United States. . . . the Common Market already produces as many automobiles, for instance, as we do (though most of them are, of course, smaller than ours).

An *Atlantic* economy, embracing both the United States and Western Europe, would represent a concentration of economic power and economic dynamics beyond anything the world has yet seen—and far beyond anything Mr. Khrushchev has ever dreamed of.

Its total population, by 1980, would be well beyond the half-billion mark. Its production—at least twice that of today—would be so large as to make Mr. Khrushchev's Utopia look like one of the minor economies. It would consume at least one-third more food and twice the minerals, metals and petroleum products now produced by the entire free world. And the standard of life of its poorer classes (such as the Italian workers, for instance) is likely to be not far below that of the American at the World War II when he was the envy and wonder of the world.

Economic necessity will drive the United States toward such an Atlantic economy as President Kennedy implied in his State of the Union message. Western Europe is already among our most important markets (matched only by Canada and Japan). And we sell to Western Europe two to three times as much as we buy from it —manufactured goods, raw materials or foodstuffs. We shall have to increase these exports. To grow ourselves, we shall need sharply higher imports, especially of raw materials. . . .

By 1980, therefore, the American businessman will perforce have become a cosmopolitan—at home as much in the Copenhagen as in the Chicago market. In labor relations, the ability to remain competitive will play as large a role as ability to pay or the balance of power between management and union. In economic policy, concern for our exports, for our competitive position, for our balance of payments and for the strength of the dollar will necessarily weigh as heavily as concern for full employment, for farm programs and for social security.

The young American executive may come to expect to be moved to Sapporo, Dijon or Düsseldorf as he now moves from Chicago to Atlanta. But the foreign businessman is likely also to become familiar with Peoria and Natchez. During the next few years, foreign, especially Western European, businesses may invest heavily in United States industry, start subsidiaries here and acquire American interests on a large scale.

We are some distance yet from the "Atlantic Common Market" of which a good many people talk today. But we are a great deal closer to economic integration of the free world than anybody—politicians, public or businessmen—realizes. . . .

4

THE STUPIDITY PROBLEM*

John Fischer

The rosy projections of most forecasters seem to populate the world of tomorrow exclusively with "brains." By some mysterious process everyone will then be working with slide rules, computers, or other engineering equipment. But is this realistic? The great mass of men are average—mediocre, if you will. Are we perhaps engineering this average man into discard?

It is perfectly clear, to me at least, why . . . [we have not] been able to find jobs for our three or four million unemployed. The human race—or anyhow that sample of it located in North America—no longer fits the kind of society it has to live in. Our society just doesn't have any jobs for certain types of people. If it continues to develop along its present course, the number of such unemployables seems likely to grow rather rapidly. . . .

. . . The chief characteristic of The Overdeveloped Society (if that is the right label) will be a permanent surplus of some kinds of workers, together with a permanent shortage of others. For the assortment of jobs which need to be done is simply out of kilter with the natural distribution of brains.

A few figures show how this happened. . . . If you should pick up a hundred typical Americans off the street, getting a fair sample of our whole population, you would find that about 46 of them would have something close to "normal" intelligence—that is, Intelligence Quotients between 90 and 109. Another 29 would be quite bright, with IQ's ranging from 110 to 139. And one or two would be really brilliant, with IQ's of 140 or above.[1]

On the other hand, 20 people in this group would have to be classed as fairly stupid, since their IQ's would fall between 70 and 89. And two or three, with ratings below 70, would barely have enough sense to come in out of the rain.

From the beginning of history until fairly recently—say, a couple of generations ago—every society in the world had plenty of jobs for low IQ people. They could herd sheep, pick cotton, dig ditches (even the Erie Canal was made with spades), h'ist that bale and tote that load. Indeed, nearly all of the earth's work called for strong backs and weak minds—for drawers of water and hewers of wood. Jobs that demanded real intelligence, on the other hand,

---

* John Fischer, "The Stupidity Problem," *Harper's Magazine*, September 1962, pp. 14–24.

[1] Figures quoted from Lee J. Cronbach, *Essentials of Psychological Testing*, 2nd ed. (New York: Harper & Row, Publishers, p. 172), and based on the standard Stanford-Binet tests. Similar tables can be found in most basic psychology texts.

were strictly limited; most communities had room for only a few doctors, ministers, teachers, lawyers, and captains of industry. Scientists were practically unknown. (As Robert Oppenheimer once pointed out in these pages, quoting Professor Purcell of Harvard, 90 per cent of all the scientists that ever lived are living today.) Government administrators were almost as scarce; Alexander Hamilton could run the Treasury Department with five clerks. As a consequence, thousands of high IQ people lived in frustration, because they could find no work equal to their talents. In many parts of the world this is still true. Some of the brightest people I ever met—in Greece and Yugoslavia—are hauling nets, throwing the shuttle on hand looms, sweeping streets, and winnowing grain with a hand basket.

But in the industrialized countries, as we all know, human muscle has now become almost obsolete. Anything it can lift, a machine can lift better. Practically any task involving repetition of the same motions can be done faster and cheaper by a mechanical or electronic device. So the muscle-worker is out of luck. He can still find a few things to do—collecting garbage, for example, unloading trucks, replacing railway ties—but these are mostly in minor or backward industries which have not yet got around to complete mechanization. And the number of such low IQ chores is dwindling every day.

Farming perhaps offers the most vivid illustration of what is happening. As recently as my grandfather's day, farming was a set of inherited motions, not very different from those used by the Babylonians. As a boy in Ohio, he sowed wheat by hand-broadcasting and harvested it with a scythe. Since neither of these operations strains the cerebral cortex, a youngster who was too dumb for anything else could always make a living on the farm; the demand for field hands was virtually unlimited.

Today, however, a successful farmer has to be a combination geneticist, mechanical engineer, chemist, cost accountant, agronomist, tax expert, and economist; in all likelihood he is a college graduate. While he may still hire some unskilled migrant labor for a few weeks a year to harvest certain fruit and vegetable crops, he can very frequently operate a big farm without any help outside the family. If he does take on a full-time hand, he looks for a smart one; no farmer wants to entrust $40,000 worth of complex agricultural machinery to a dope. . . .

The youngsters who drop out of high school before graduation are a case in point. Most leave school, not because of economic problems, but because they can't keep up with the not-very-demanding work. The Federal Bureau of Labor Statistics has reported that 80 per cent of the drop-outs are lagging by at least one grade; and Dr. Cronbach notes that "the very dull tend to drop out as soon as they reach age sixteen. . . . By the end of high school, almost no one with IQ below 85 is still in school." This is one reason why the unemployment rate for sixteen- to nineteen-year-olds is twice as high as for adults. A few get jobs as messengers, gas pump operators, or dishwashers. Many others drift straight from the classroom to the relief rolls, or to crime. For as our society is now organized, we can't find any use for most of these young dullards—a situation unjust and miserable to them, and to the rest of the community both costly and dangerous.

The counterpart of this situation is a severe and increasing shortage of people brainy enough to man the upper level jobs in our Overdeveloped Society. The design, supervision, and maintenance of automated equipment require a lot of smart, highly trained people—and even now industry can't find enough of them. Did you ever hear of a good computer-programmer who was out of work?

So too with the rest of our society. All the professions which demand better-than-average minds—medicine, law, journalism, teaching, the sciences, advertising, the military—are moaning about their difficulties in attracting enough competent recruits. And as the structure of society grows in both complexity and size, the need for able managers (in business and government alike) grows in almost geometric ratio. Our inability to locate enough first-rate managerial talent in many fields—from college president to corporate comptroller, from regional planner to operations analyst—may yet prove to be the breakdown point in our civilization.

For we have apparently built ourselves, unintentionally and without quite realizing it, a society which calls for a distribution of intelligence entirely different from that which God provided. It remains to be seen whether we can make it work. . . .

. . . We'll have to face up to the fact that all men are *not* created equal, except in the limited political sense which Jefferson had in mind when he drafted the Declaration of Independence. Until we do that, it will be impossible for our public officials to find useful work for the 20-plus per cent of the population with below-normal intelligence, or to train them for jobs they are capable of handling. And it will remain almost equally hard to make the best use of our limited supply of high IQ's.

Right now it is not only unfashionable, but almost indecent, to hint that such a problem even exists. Our educationists presumably know all about IQ distributions, and they are surely aware of the National Education Association's findings that about 25 per cent of Selective Service registrants fail the Army's mental tests. Yet they keep on talking about "slow-learners," "culturally deprived children," "under-achievers"—almost any euphemism to avoid admitting that a lot of children are unable to absorb the kind of education we are trying to push down their throats at such expense.

This is not entirely their fault. It is true that the canonized educational doctrine still puts undue emphasis on protecting the little ego from the harsh facts of competitive life; but this is at least in part a reflection of community pressures. Just suppose that a school principal called a doting suburban mother into his office and told her: "I am sorry to have to report that little Johnny does not have an inferiority complex, as you have always assumed. He is just inferior. He will never get into Yale. He doesn't even have enough brains to pass his final high school examinations. With proper training, however, he might become an adequate bellhop or waiter. I suggest therefore that you remove him at once from high school, thus saving a great deal of taxpayers' money and your own, and enroll him in the Hotel Employees Institute."

The resulting uproar, as we all know, would shake the walls of the Board of Education. And it is not only Johnny's parents who would be affronted. Many of us would feel that it was somehow undemocratic, or at least inhumane, to blurt out such unpleasant truths.

We are even a bit uneasy about giving special attention to especially talented pupils. In recent years there has been a good deal of talk about the gifted child, and the better school systems are experimenting with enriched curriculums. Yet in the great majority of high schools, the really bright youngster is still bored, underworked, and educated far below his capacity.

The social and economic biases in American society are at least partly responsible for this failure to make the best use of our best brains—wherever they may turn up. Wealthier parents, quite naturally, try hard to protect their duller offspring from the consequences of their stupidity. As a result, prosperous communities are likely to spend an inordinate amount of their school money trying to cosset and prop up the mental laggards—to the neglect of the uncommonly able. At the same time, our poorer neighborhoods are likely to have poor schools, where the bright youngster may never be spotted and almost certainly will not get the intensive, top-caliber instruction he deserves. Americans are not yet ready, apparently, to search out the high-potential students—at whatever age their talent begins to show and anywhere they can be found, in slum or suburb—and to say: "This five per cent have the possibility of becoming our future William Faulkners, Robert McNamaras, George Gershwins, and Alfred Sloans. They represent an invaluable asset. Therefore it is vital to the public interest to give them the very best teachers and equipment, and to push them to the limits of their capacity. The second-raters will have to get along with what is left."

Undemocratic? By our traditional habits, it may be. But in the not-so-distant future it may prove to be the only way possible to run the peculiar kind of society we are developing. . . .

5

OUR OPEN CLASS SYSTEM*

Henry C. Bush

For 80 per cent of Americans the widespread distribution of goods and education results in a society that is best called "middle class." But in this "classless" society everyone works hard to "be somebody." No one can depend on birth; to be somebody every individual must merit recognition. There are no permanent members of this class, in which the continuing emphasis is on equality.

Sociologists' studies of class in America, if piled up, would go through the floor; many insist they should. . . . According to these studies, the American "upper class" consists of those whose families are old, honored, rich, and superbly educated. Usually they intermarry; invariably their sons are nurtured in the proper "prep" schools and finished in the Ivy League colleges. And they are less than three per cent of us.

Then there are some 70 to 80 per cent, "the middle class"—all well-off, some with two Cadillacs and a motor-launch, some with one six- or seven-year-old Ford, all dressing and speaking and speaking within the same ranges

* Henry C. Bush, "The Classes in America," *Manchester Guardian Weekly*, November 24, 1955.

of choice, all eating about the same kinds of foods with about the same table manners. Down at the bottom are from 10 to 25 per cent, "the lower class." Most of them are generally described by others as "nice people, good Americans, but poor, dirt poor." They are the underprivileged, who have seen less, read less, heard about less, experienced fewer changes, and who simply know of fewer opportunities. They tend not to bother to vote, not to read anything much, to credulity, bias, and to job records which suggest a lack of talents and a lack of drive. Below them are "the lower-lower class," a fringe outside the American social values, judged by others to be lazy and to lack character, invariably judged by themselves to suffer solely from "being poor" and from "lack of education." Apart from the 10 per cent of our citizens who are Negroes (they have their own pyramid of status), that is it.

The trouble is that almost no marks of class status are valid nationally. For example, in many cities, especially in our older New England and South, we have families who are social history. And money or no money, they rate "upper class." But you can count on the fingers of one hand the old families who are famous nationally. Mid-Westerners and Far-Westerners (who disapprove of "first families" in principle) assert that you can count them on the fingers of one thumb. In a country where four out of five change residence in the course of every seven years who can be gentry? Who stays long enough to admire them?

Then the last fifteen [now twenty-some] years of overwhelming prosperity are making it all but impossible to guess who earn what. Everybody has a car; in one part of oil-rich Texas Cadillacs are so common they carry negative status; the best people advertise their disapproval of this plebeianism by driving Fords, Chevrolets, or M.G.s. Even the last symbol of the rich, the lady's mink coat, has been democratized: someone has invented plastic mink. Taste in sports indicates nothing; everybody drives, nobody rides, anybody may play golf or tennis, or ski; almost everybody follows baseball, and even farmers travel to South Dakota to shoot pheasants each season, at a small fortune per day for the privilege.

Nobody can afford a full-time servant and everybody has an army of mechanical ones, especially in the kitchen. Nobody "sirs" anybody except on the tourist vacation circuit, where all servants "sir" everybody and live handsomely off the tips of the middle-class 80 per cent playing imaginary aristocrat for two weeks or a month each year. Nor is there any continuity from father to son to son's son. The principal ladder upward is formal education, but outside the Ivy League the expense is the taxpayer's, not father's. At our state universities the student pays only 10 or 15 per cent of the cost of educating himself. To attend the excellent municipal college at which I teach one needs only subway fare; even the books are furnished.

So the difficulties of the sociologists with those brass instruments and scales supposed to measure class are that, although you can rank the persons in Yankee City or Jonesville, you cannot rank persons across the United States. And, although in the corporation office you can tell the plant manager by the rug and the private secretary and the mahogany desk so large that a helicopter could land on it, just as you can tell the junior executive by the small metal desk on the asphalt tile floor and the metal box for dictation, you cannot rank them in a bar or a conversation.

Also, any family is likely to have

multiple statuses. Consider the following field report:[1]

The A family apparently has a good deal of money. They have two cars, a nice house. (Score one.) But they don't go to church, they don't help in the Community Chest Drive, and they never go to the Parent Teachers' Association. (Deduct two or three.) But they've all gone to college, they subscribe to a lot of newspapers and magazines and buy a lot of books. (Score at least two.) But you would think that a man with his education would do something better than just be a contractor for building silos and grain storage bins. (Subtract another point.) But not many are inclined to criticize openly because Mr. A has a lot of power in this town—can hire and fire a lot of people and he also has some kind of "in" with the bank. (Add one.)

Almost everybody wants to "be somebody," and almost everybody can be—locally and temporarily. But few can achieve a state of being somebody, so we go on, on, on reachieving, which may acount for the rumor that we are "hard-working." It is the status-conscious yet classless society, but not as Marx anticipated it. . . .

[1] From J. E. Cuber and W. F. Kenkel, *Social Stratification* (New York: Appleton-Century-Crofts, Inc., 1954).

6

THE REVOLUTION OF THE JONESES*

Bruce Bliven

Communist theorists for a century have proclaimed their goal to be a classless society. American capitalism, on the other hand, has never openly accepted this objective, stressing instead an "open society" in which individuals are able to move up or down solely on their own merit. In recent years, however, many observers have detected a trend that, if true, would be one of history's great ironies. According to these analysts, Soviet society has moved toward a new, rigid class structure, while the United States has moved toward a true classless society. Mr. Bliven, in the following article, makes the case for those who believe that the emerging American society is devoid of class lines.

An amazing social revolution is occurring in the United States. Everyone talks about this revolution, but to feel its impact, one should, like me, have been born in the administration of Benjamin Harrison and observe the changes it has made—and is still making.

Here are some of the things that have happened since I first began to notice the world around me, sixty-odd years ago:

The family income of American workers (allowing for fluctuations in the value of money) has increased more than two and a half times.

* Bruce Bliven, "The Revolution of the Joneses," *The New York Times Magazine*, October 9, 1960. © 1960 by The New York Times Company. Reprinted by permission.

Three of every five Americans now own their own homes, as opposed to one in three.

The work week has been reduced by at least twenty hours, or about one-third, and production per man hour has tripled.

Women, formerly one-fifth of all wage earners, now constitute one-third.

The proportion of high school graduates has increased ten times, and of college graduates seven times.

With six per cent of the world's population and seven per cent of the land, we are producing more than one-third of the world's goods.

When the century began, there was—in spite of the Fourth of July oratory to the contrary—a well defined class structure in this country. At the base of this pyramid was the working class and most of the farmers; together they were practically identical with "the poor." Above them was the much smaller middle class, and above it, the wealthy, far smaller still. Each of these sections of the population had its own culture and characteristics; each was uneasy if thrown into social contact with either of the two others.

Today the scene is greatly altered. I don't want to paint the picture with false brightness; class distinctions still exist to some degree, as do artificial snobbery and exploitations of the disadvantaged. Yet, as far as the externals of living are concerned, most of us are really beginning to approach the classless society we were always supposed to be.

The cultural revolution is even more striking than the economic one. Sociologists used to divide our society, especially in the long-settled northeast, into six groups—upper upper, lower upper, upper middle, and so on; today, for most of the country, these divisions are not very realistic as divisions or cultural classifications. A parallel sophistication has been noted by Russell Lynes and others, dividing us into various types of high-, middle-, and low-brow; but here again, the influence of mass communications is blurring the lines of demarcation. More than has ever been true of any other large country in modern times, we are a homogenized population.

The new American society is centered upon the middle-income group, or what used to be called the lower-middle class. Its family earnings begin at about $4,000—the point at which discretionary, or luxury, buying begins—and ends, roughly, at $10,000. Above it, the upper-middle class shades off unperceptibly into the wealthy. But the middle income group is significant as a classification only in a financial sense; culturally, it is rapidly becoming the common denominator of almost the whole nation.

The working class is moving up from below, both financially and culturally. The rich are also taking on the protective coloration of the middle income group, partly because of high income and inheritance taxes, partly because of what Veblen called "conspicuous consumption" has gone out of fashion. It isn't only the automobile that is disappearing as a status symbol (*vide* the amazing success of the new compact cars); all the outward symbols of wealth are becoming less defined. When it is the height of fashion for the sons and daughters of the millionaires to throng college campuses dressed in dungarees like working stiffs, you may be sure that our attitudes have changed perceptibly.

The speed of these changes continues to increase. In the past decade, the median income has risen about 50 per cent—from $3,300 to $5,050. At the end of the Second World War, in spite of high war wages, about a quarter of the population was still earning less than $1,000; today one-half of these have moved up into the $1,000–$2,000 bracket. The lowest two-fifths of the population have gained by 114 per cent and the next two-fifths by 100 per cent; fringe benefits, many of them obtained through union contracts, make these gains even larger. By contrast, the top fifth of the population has gained 59 per cent and the top one-twentieth 38 per cent.

The middle-income group is the "anchor men" in our economy. The Internal Revenue Bureau tells us that in 1957 the 26,000,000 taxpayers in that group had an adjusted gross income of about $156 billion, well over half of the nation's total of individual incomes, now somewhat in excess of $280 billion. The 30,000,000 with incomes of less than $4,000 earned about 62 billion; the 3,500,000 with more than $10,000 received roughly the same amount—about $64 billion. (Of the really rich—$100,000 and over—there are about 23,000, with total incomes of 4.3 billion before taxes. The old gibe of the Marxists—that 20 or 10 per cent of the population owns 80 or 90 per cent of the wealth—is certainly not true today, if it ever was.)

What are the members of the middle class like today? What are they doing and thinking?

I have had an exceptional chance to study them first-hand since, for several years, I have been living in California, in the midst of a vast welter of new suburban developments. As everyone knows, California is the paradise of the middle class. Every new pattern of living occurs a little earlier here than anywhere else, and it seems to emerge a little larger than life-size.

WE ARE MOVING TO THE SUBURBS

In the nation as a whole, 15,000,000 people have moved out of the cities since the end of the Second World War, increasing the suburban population by one-half.

The total in the suburbs will almost double in the next fifteen years. Suburban incomes usually begin a little above $4,000 and slope upward to the wealthy.

It is a familiar story that the move to the suburbs has left the big cities increasingly to the slum dwellers and wrought havoc with the city tax structure. The move is also creating problems in the suburbs; the new communities are growing so fast that neither the physical nor the social organization can keep up. It is hard to get the migrants to take a proper interest in local government, or to vote bond issues for necessary new public services.

WE ARE LOSING OUR INFERIORITY COMPLEX

Those who formerly belonged to the working class are rapidly shedding the remnants of the discomfort they felt when brought into social contact with the middle-income group. This is partly because they have money in their pockets, partly because they now know considerably more about what middle-income living is like.

The public schools have contributed to this understanding, as have new media of communication—above all, television, which offers, among its mediocre dramas, some irresistibly authentic portrayals of "how the other (middle) half lives."

WE ARE UPGRADING OURSELVES CULTURALLY

For generations, the passion of Americans for self-improvement has been one of the wonders of the world. This phenomenon is at its height in the middle-income group today. Our three million college students (they will number six million long before the end of this decade) are without precedent. With a population about three and one-half times that of Great Britain, we have 1,800 colleges to her fifteen.

Mass communication is, again, a potent force in this area, both for good and bad. It brings us millions of comic books, but also millions of color reproductions of the world's great masterpieces of painting. It offers jukeboxes and rock'n'roll, but it also provides hi-fi sets through which the greatest compositions are heard in millions of homes.

While much routine fare on television is sorry stuff, some of it opens wonderful windows on the world. Olivier's "Hamlet" was probably seen by more people in a single showing than saw the play "live" in all the theaters of the world from Shakespeare's day to this. A majority of our third of a billion paperback books are at a pretty low level, but, again, Shakepeare's plays sell more than a million copies annually. The proliferation of new quasi-amateur orchestras and theaters across the country is itself an amazing story.

To be sure, some of our new cultural gloss is superficial, but the point is that it pleases those who possess it and helps remove any lingering shyness *vis-à-vis* those higher in the social scale.

WE ARE PLAYING NEW FAMILY ROLES

With the disappearance of domestic servants, replaced by a multitude of labor-saving devices and products, including packaged, prepared foods, has come a change in the division of household labor. The husband and father has to help in a lot of chores his grandfather would have considered beneath him.

It is a truism to say that "the head of the household" is no longer the sort of petty autocrat that Clarence Day, Sr., represented to his son—a type known to millions of households sixty years ago. New insights into psychology and a new philosophy of education have destroyed the old image. While the reduction of the family tyrant to the status of mother's helper has some bad aspects, it has good ones, too. And anyhow, dictators are going out of fashion—on the national and every other scale.

THERE ARE FEWER TIRED BUSINESSMEN

Our social evolution has caused a tremendous decrease in the relative number of independent enterprises; the trend today is toward salaried employment with big public or private institutions. Elderly employers, not yet reconciled to this change, complain that young applicants for positions now seem more interested in old-age pensions and other fringe benefits than they are in chances to fight their way to the top.

This makes for a new "togetherness" as the center of interest, for the husband and father shifts from his place of work to his family. Margaret Mead has remarked that instead of the tired businessman in the home, we now have the tired family man in the office.

We get a little more conservative. As our income rises, and, especially, as we move to the suburbs, we tend to become more conservative politically. In the anonymity of the big city even the corporation employee can be somewhat to the Left without causing anyone to look askance, but in the goldfish bowl of the suburbs the story is somewhat different: in some of them it takes real courage to register as a Democrat, or to sympathize publicly with trade unions.

Social upgrading also brings some

alterations in church membership, to the advantage of the Episcopal church as opposed to some other types of Protestantism thought to carry connotations of social acceptance.

The sociologists, of course, are wringing their hands at many aspects of the new middle class, especially in its suburban manifestations. They say our moral fiber is rotted with easy living and our young men would not fight to defend their country (the same comment was heard shortly before both the First and Second World Wars). They report that we are "other"- and not "inner"-directed, which suggests that there was a time—perhaps a hundred years ago?—when this was not true.

They worry because the new suburban developments are filled with young people of approximately the same age whose children miss any contact with the old. (The alarmists forget that the whole American continent, from the Alleghenies westward, was settled by bands of people of whom this was pretty true.)

They are gloomy over our obsession with television, the number of broken homes (which helps to produce juvenile delinquency), the use of the automobile by adolescents to escape into a world of their own, the rat-race of more and more installment buying, and the fate of the cities abandoned by so many of their most useful and solid citizens.

While I'm usually ready to wring a hand with anybody, I can't share wholly in the pessimism of these observers (some of whom are intellectuals repudiating their own middle-class origins and, given the chance, would make equally disparaging reports on Paradise). We certainly have plenty of troubles in this country—and shall continue to have them, human nature being imperfect—but my own observation makes me feel that many of the criticisms of the way most Americans now live refer to conditions that are temporary or exaggerated.

Conformism, as I have suggested, is not a new phenomenon; what is new—and hopeful—is the fact that we now bother to take note of it. The high divorce rate is regrettable, just as it is also regrettable when unhappy people who dislike each other are forced for any reason to remain married. But this problem is more serious among the very rich and the very poor than in the middle bracket.

Installment buying also has its dangers, but it is also the foundation for our current prosperity, and there were shiftless, incompetent people, and lots of them, before installment buying was ever invented. More than 95 per cent of the American middle class is demonstrably a good credit risk.

Juvenile delinquency is alarming and exists to some extent in the middle class suburbs, but its real home is in the slums of the big cities. Again, 95 per cent is a good figure for the proportion of young people who behave.

Television presents difficulties, especially in regard to children, but the wild prophecies that school work would be wrecked and the next generation illiterate, heard a decade ago, have all faded away. Dr. Wilbur Schramm, Director of the Institute for Communication Research at Stanford University, writes in *TV Guide*, "none of the studies of the effect of television on children has come up with any evidence of a simple and direct effect that was very important. . . . Television seems to send children to the first grade with larger vocabularies; it fills their heads with a wide assortment of information, some of which is useful and some not. . . .

"The British anthropologist, Geoffrey Gorer, warns us that each time in our century when mass communications have got a new medium, the older people have blamed the new medium for the defects they find in the younger generation. You were corrupted by radio, your parents probably said, and I was ruined by Deadwod Dick."

It is true that the exodus from our big cities is creating a bad problem; but the only real answer is to make the metropolis attractive enough to bring back the middle class or a substantial part of it. (Some countermovement is already beginning to appear.) The great advantages the city possesses in art museums, music, libraries, hospitals, and other necessities and amenities will again exert their appeals, if we can make real progress in solving the problems of living space, smog, noise, dirt, traffic congestion, crime, and vice (to be sure, a tall order).

In short, with all the troubles that still hang over our heads, the American middle class, is I believe, the most resourceful, adaptable, and resilient large group anywhere in the world, with the highest standards in all fields that have ever characterized any major section of the population in any big country. Always allowing for a minority of malcontents, its members are happy where they are: they don't want to go anywhere else, they don't believe that they are in trouble, and, until someone invents still a better way of life, they are here to stay.

7

THE "WELL-ROUNDED" MAN*

William H. Whyte, Jr.

As American society has rapidly become more industrialized, more bureaucratized, and more urbanized, we have all become more dependent upon our financial, organizational, and personal relationships to each other. Today a man depends on his paycheck, his ties to large organizations, and his rating in a bureaucracy, whether it is a school, a corporation, a part of the government, or a part of the armed forces. He is more and more tied to his record in the central personnel files. We are big now, and organized, and the rough and tumble days are over. This kind of world needs mediators, administrators, managers of its economy and its government. It can't use mavericks, individualists, or rebels. Such, according to William H. Whyte, is the view of the people who run America.

Let's examine first the model as younger men see him. They are in remarkable agreement on the matter. There are dissenters, precious few that they may be, and no generalization can do justice to all the different shadings in the majority's view. On the fundamental premise of the new model executive, however, the young men who hope to be that vary little, and from company to company, region to region, you hear a litany increasingly standard. It goes something like this:

* William H. Whyte, Jr., *The Organization Man* (New York: Simon & Schuster, Inc., 1956), pp. 129–36. © 1956 by William H. Whyte, Jr. Reprinted by permission of the publishers.

Be loyal to the company and the company will be loyal to you. After all, if you do a good job for the organization, it is only good sense for the organization to be good to you, because that will be best for everybody. There are a bunch of people around here. Tell them what you think and they will respect you for it. They don't want a man to fret and stew about his work. It won't happen to me. A man who gets ulcers probably shouldn't be in business anyway.

This is more than the wishful thinking normal of youth. Wishful it may be, but it is founded on a well-articulated premise—and one that not so many years ago would have been regarded by the then young men with considerable skepticism. The premise is, simply, that the goals of the individual and the goals of the organization will work out to be one and the same. The young men have no cynicism about the "system," and very little skepticism—they don't see it as something to be bucked, but as something to be cooperated with.

This view is more optimistic than fatalistic. If you were to draft an organization chart based on some junior-executive bull sessions, the chart wouldn't look too much like the usual hierarchical structure. Instead of converging toward a narrow apex, the lines on the chart would rise parallel, eventually disappearing into a sort of mist before they reached any embarrassing turning points.

The unity they see between themselves and the Organization has deeper roots, however, than current expediency. Let's take the matter of ambition as further illustration. They do not lack ambition. They seem to, but that is only because the nature of it has changed. It has become a passive ambition. Not so many years ago it was permissible for the ambitious young man to talk of setting his cap for a specific goal—like becoming president of a corporation, building a bridge, or making a million dollars. Today it is a very rare young man who will allow himself to talk in such a way, let alone think that way. He can argue, with good grounds, that if it was unrealistic in the past it is even more so today. The life that he looks ahead to will be a life in which he is only one of hundreds of similarly able people and in which they will all be moved hither and yon and subject to so many forces outside their control—not to mention the Bomb—that only a fool would expect to hew to a set course.

But they see nothing wrong with this fluidity. They have an implicit faith that the Organization will be as interested in making use of their best qualities as they are themselves, and thus, with equanimity, they can entrust the resolution of their destiny to The Organization. No specific goal, then, is necessary to give them a sense of continuity. For the short term, perhaps—it would be nice to be head of the electronics branch. But after that, who knows? The young executive does not wish to get stuck in a particular field. The more he is shifted, the more broad-gauge will he become, and the more broad-gauge, the more successful.

But not too successful. Somewhat inconsistently, trainees hope to rise high and hope just as much not to suffer the personal load of doing so. Frequently they talk of finding a sort of plateau—a position well enough up to be interesting but not so far up as to have one's neck outstretched for others to chop at. It figures, the young man can explain. Why knock yourself out when the extra salary won't bring home much more actual pay? You can make a very good living in the middle levels—well not exactly middle, a little higher than that—and the work, furthermore, can be just as fulfilling. If the Organization is good and big, to put it another way, there will be success without tears.

For the executive of the future, trainees say, the problem of company loyalty shouldn't be a problem at all. Almost every older executive you talk to has some private qualifications about his fealty to the company; in contrast, the average young man cherishes the idea that his relationship with The Organization is to be for keeps. Some times he doesn't even concede that the point need ever come to test.

Their attitude toward another aspect of organization shows the same bias. What of the "group life," the loss of individualism? Once upon a time it was conventional for young men to view the group life of the big corporation as one of its principal disadvantages. Today, they see it as a positive boon. Working with others, they believe, will reduce the frustrations of work, and they often endow the accompanying suppression of ego with strong spiritual overtones. They will concede that there is often a good bit of wasted time in the committee way of life and that the handling of human relations involves much suffering of fools gladly. But this sort of thing, they say, is the heart of the organization man's job, not merely the disadvantages of it. "Any man who feels frustrated by these things," one young trainee with face unlined said to me, "can never be an executive."

On the matter of overwork they are particularly stern. They want to work hard, but not too hard; the good, equable life is paramount and they see no conflict between enjoying it and getting ahead. The usual top executive, they believe, works much too hard, and there are few subjects upon which they will discourse more emphatically than the folly of elders who have a single-minded devotion to work. Is it, they ask, really necessary any more? Or, for that matter, moral?

A young man's idle dream? It is a playback only mildly exaggerated of a vision of the future that is becoming stronger and stronger among personnel executives and the business-school people who intellectualize for business. And their influence should not be underrated. The personnel men are of the staff, rather than the line, but it is they who choose the trainees and administer the schools that affect trainees in their formative years with the corporations.

What personnel men have in mind as the manager of the future is more of a departure than is generally recognized. . . .

Here, in paraphrase, is the gist of it:

The rough-and-tumble days are over. Since the job is to keep things going, more than pioneering, the leader must be the professional manager, "the man who knows how to elicit participative consultation, how to motivate groups and individuals, how to enhance job satisfactions . . . how to conduct problem-solving meetings." He will be a generalist who will not think in terms of specific work but in the science of making other people work.

In the old sense of work, he does not work; he encourages others to work. He does not create; he moderates and adjusts those who do create. "Primarily he is the balance wheel on the tendency of the professional-type individual to wander into new, unexplored, and perhaps dangerous territory."

Unorthodoxy can be dangerous to The Organization. The pro-administrators sometimes conceded that the administrator could have unconventional ideas himself at times. But, they were in haste to add, he ought to be rather sober about it, and it was on the dangers rather than on the advantages of such unorthodox thinking that they dwelled.

Unorthodoxy is dangerous to The Organization. Some personnel men didn't simply omit mention of inner qualities such as "drive" and "imagination"; they went out of their way to warn against them. "Any progressive employer," said one personnel director, "would look askance at the individualist and would be reluctant to instill such thinking in the minds of trainees." Another personnel man put it in more direct terms: "Men of strong personal convictions, willing to make unorthodox decisions, are more frequently given to the characteristics of 'drive' rather than 'leadership.'" This invidious pairing of qualities once thought congenial with each other was not restricted entirely to personnel men. "We used to look primarily for brilliance," said one president. "Now that much-abused word 'character' has become very important. We don't care if you're a Phi Beta Kappa or a Tau Beta Phi. We want a well-rounded person who can handle well-rounded people."

Ideas come from the group, not from the individual. The well-rounded man is one who does not think up ideas himself but mediated other people's ideas, and so democratically that he never lets his own judgment override the decisions of the group. "The decisions should be made by the group," says a personnel director, "and agreement reached after discussion and consultation prior to action." "The leader must be attentive and receptive to the ideas of his followers," says another personnel man, "and he must adjust his ideas accordingly." . . .

8

AMERICA NEEDS MORE DISSENT*

Robert M. Hutchins

The assumptions of the foregoing article (The Well-Rounded Man) are accepted by Mr. Hutchins in the sense that he agrees that our current emphasis is on conformity. He warns, however, that America did not become great through namby-pamby conformity and agreement. In particular he stresses the need for new ideas and new institutions to match our new national situation. As individuals we must not fear dissent nor avoid becoming dissenters. Our Constitution affords legal sanction for dissent, but only tough-minded individuals can act within this permissive situation to defend unpopular truths.

We Americans, with our traditional regard for quantity, have a ready tendency to equate dissent with defeat. While we are proud of our hardy, objecting ancestors, most of us leave the premises quietly if the final returns are against us, sometimes with a faint sense of guilt at being outnumbered.

* Robert M. Hutchins, "Dissenting Opinion as a Creative Art," *Saturday Review*, August 12, 1961, pp. 12, 35–36

No such defensive role for the dissenter was envisioned for us by the Founding Fathers, nor is it evident in the history of the Supreme Court of the United States. Many of the great movements in constitutional law in the past seventy-five years were initiated by the dissenting opinions of Justices Holmes, Brandeis, Cardozo, and Black. These were opinions not to be trifled with.

Let me begin with the basic, if perhaps trite, observation that learning is a rational process. Law is an ordinance of reason, directed to the common good. The process of deciding to make or not to make a law, or the process of reaching a judicial conclusion, is to be criticized in terms of its conformity not to local or popular but to universal standards of reasonableness. If the Constitution is to teach us, and we are to learn under its instructions, the dialogue that goes on about its meaning must be about what is reasonable, right and wrong, just and unjust. The question is not what interests are at stake, not what are the mores of the community, not who has the power or who is the dominant group, but what is reasonable, right, and just.

Since, as John Dewey remarked, we have a government of lawyers, and not of men, lawyers should understand that there is or ought to be a normative jurisprudence which prescribes something more than correct procedure. The lamentable state of legal education is one of the principal obstacles to our learning through the political community.

There are others. Our situation has changed too fast for our ideas. Our ideology, by which I mean that set of ideas which has hardened into a linear series of slogans, one of which leads into the other without the intervention of thought, is far behind the facts of life. Our institutions, operated in terms of that ideology, have a character that seems sometimes primitive, sometimes unreal, sometimes fantastic, when we think of the obligations and opportunities of our country in the contemporary world. We know that tremendous changes are going on, and that still greater are impending. Of the two pillars of our society, property and work, the first has now been transformed; it has changed from visible goods into a series of claims; and the second is certain to disappear. We are going to have to live in a world without work, a world without want, a world without disease, and, if we are to live at all, in a world without war. With the gross national product hovering around an all-time high, one-third of the productive capacity of our industries lies idle. What are we going to do with our goods? What are we going to do with ourselves? We now have to learn more, and learn it faster, than any other people in history. The time to revive and reconstruct the political community is at hand.

It seems likely that this age will be one either of innovation or of extinction. Without innovation the human race may not be extinguished, though the technical means of achieving this result are now available. What will be extinguished, in the absence of innovation, is the free society, the political community. Only if we can tear ourselves loose from our prejudices, from our ideology, from slogans, only if we can take a fresh look at the world and exercise the same kind of intelligence, character, and inventiveness that the Founding Fathers showed can we hope to revive, reconstruct, and preserve the political community.

Take four successive days in the recent work schedule of the Center for the Study of Democratic Institutions. On the first day our staff economist demonstrated that the market was not working and could not work. He then demonstrated with equal clarity that economic planning, the only visible alternative to the market, was not working either. He said it would be necessary to develop new economic ideas and new economic institutions to meet the problems of a totally new world.

On the second day a Canadian expert reported to us on his experiences with commercial and noncommercial broadcasting in Canada and England, and on his observations elsewhere. He declared that no form of public, semi-public, or quasi-public control of broadcasting had been able to resist the advertising agencies anywhere and said that if the agencies were to be resisted —a move which he thought indispensable to the health, morality, and sanity of the world—new ideas would have to appear and new methods would have to be invented.

On the third day a professor from the Australian National University, beginning with a conviction that the United Kingdom would join the European Common Market, and going on to trace the effect of this action on the British Commonwealth, came to the conclusion that we were rapidly moving onto some form of world political organization, and speculated that if such an organization was to be in any sense free and democratic, new political forms would have to be developed. Something is going to replace the nation states. But what?

On the fourth day a student of the American character recalled to us de Tocqueville's remark that the individual is a defaulted citizen, that democracy produces individualism, and that individualism first saps the virtues of public life, then ends in pure selfishness. De Tocqueville said that democracy, by way of individualism, throws every man "back forever upon himself alone and threatens in the end to confine him entirely within the solitude of his own heart." The citizens of the United States, de Tocqueville thought, would escape this fate because our Constitution required us to learn together to seek the common good. We would be forced, he said, by the necessity of cooperating in the management of our free institutions, and by our desire to exercise our political rights, into the habit of attending to the interests of the public.

The student of the American character, a professor from Berkeley, California, pointed out that de Tocqueville's expectations had not been fulfilled, that the people of the United States are in fact defaulted citizens, with an indifference and even a hostility to government, politics, and law that would have astounded de Tocqueville—and the Founding Fathers. Instead of being a citizen, he contended, the American individual is a consumer, an object of propaganda, and a statistical unit. The conclusion of the professor from Berkeley was that the political community had been wrecked on the rocks of our ideology, by such slogans as "free enterprise" and "that government is best which governs least," and was now extinct. In view of the condition of our education, our mass media, and our political parties, and in view of the absence of any massive new effort to reconstruct our attitudes and our institutions, the professor believed that the outlook for democracy, for the free society, and for the political community was hopeless.

All the studies that the Center has been carrying on come out at the same place: we are entering a totally new world, and we are not very well prepared for it.

The demands of this new world, like the demands of the political community, are first of all intellectual. They are demands that we think, and learn. We face them ill-prepared. Our educational system is not unfairly characterized by reference to the course in Family Living in a high school in upstate New York. The last unit of this course is called, "How to be Livable, Lovable, and Datable." The education of adults, which might be the answer to the question of what we shall do with ourselves, is in a deplorable state. Thirty-million Americans, for example, are without any library service whatever. We have triumphantly invented, perfected, and distributed to the humblest cottage throughout the land one of the greatest technical marvels in history, television, and have used it for what? To bring Coney Island into every home. It is as though movable type had been devoted exclusively since Gutenberg's time to the publication of comic books. "Wasteland" is too good a name for it.

When it comes to learning through the political community, the object is to learn how to be a responsible citizen, enjoying liberty under law. The freedom of the individual must be protected, but in addition the citizen must grow in responsibility if our country is to become conscious of itself as a part of Humanity and to think Humanity in order to organize it. Individual freedom and liberty under law are not incompatible, and they are both indispensable.

Law is a great teacher. It does not represent that minimum of morality necessary to hold the community together. It stands rather for such moral truth as the community has discovered that can and should be supported by the authority of the community. . . . The principles of world law are the principles of thinking Humanity in order to organize it. Of necessity they must be principles of universal validity. I think they will be found to be the principles of reason, right, and justice.

We must revive and reconstruct the political community in the United States because the task before us is nothing less than the organization of the world political community. The proposition to which the Declaration of Independence and Abraham Lincoln dedicated us now extends to the whole world. Once more Americans, on a new scale, have the duty of forming a more perfect union, which will involve establishing justice, promoting the general welfare, and securing the blessings of liberty to ourselves and to all the peoples of the earth.

9

THE NEW GENERATION—COOL AND CASUAL*

Philip E. Jacob

Americans assume, rightly or no, that leaders of the next generation are being educated in our colleges. What are college students thinking? What values do they hold? What attitudes do they adopt? The extract which follows is drawn from a famous study of student values in American colleges.

A dominant characteristic of students in the current generation is that they are *gloriously contented* both in regard to their present day-to-day activity and their outlook for the future. Few of them are worried—about their health, their prospective careers, their family relations, the state of national or international society or the likelihood of their enjoying secure and happy lives. They are supremely confident that their destinies lie within their own control rather than in the grip of external circumstances.

The great majority of students appear unabashedly *self-centered*. They aspire for material gratifications for themselves and their families. They intend to look out for themselves first and expect others to do likewise.

But this is not the individualistic self-centeredness of the pioneer. American students fully accept the conventions of the contemporary business society as the context within which they will realize their personal desires. They cheerfully expect to conform to the economic status quo and to receive ample rewards for dutiful and productive effort. They anticipate no die-hard struggle for survival of the fittest as each seeks to gratify his own desires, but rather an abundance for all as each one teams up with his fellow self-seekers in appointed places on the American assembly-line.

Social harmony with an *easy tolerance of diversity* pervades the student environment. Conformists themselves, the American students see little need to insist that each and every person be and behave just like themselves. They are for the most part (with some allowance for sectional difference) ready to live in a mobile society, without racial, ethnic or income barriers. But they do not intend to crusade for nondiscrimination, merely to accept it as it comes, a necessary convention in a homogenized culture.

The traditional *moral virtues are valued* by almost all students. They respect sincerity, honesty, loyalty, as proper standards of conduct for decent people. But they are not inclined to censor those who choose to depart from these canons. Indeed they consider laxity a prevalent phenomenon,

---

* Philip E. Jacob, *Changing Values in College* (New York: Harper and Row, Publishers, 1957), pp. 1–5.

even more prevalent than the facts seem to warrant. Nor do they feel personally bound to unbending consistency in observing the code, especially when a lapse is socially sanctioned. For instance, standards are generally low in regard to academic honesty, systematic cheating being a common practice rather than the exception at many major institutions.

Students normally express a *need for religion* as a part of their lives and make time on most weekends for an hour in church. But there is a "ghostly quality" about the beliefs and practices of many of them, to quote a sensitive observer. Their religion does not carry over to guide and govern important decisions in the secular world. Students expect these to be socially determined. God has little to do with the behavior of men in society, if widespread student judgment be accepted. His place is in church and perhaps in the home, not in business or club or community. He is worshipped, dutifully and with propriety, but the campus is not permeated by a live sense of His presence.

American students are likewise *dutifully responsive towards government.* They expect to obey its laws, pay its taxes, serve in its armed forces—without complaint but without enthusiasm. They will discharge the obligations demanded of them though they will not voluntarily contribute to the public welfare. Nor do they particularly desire an influential voice in public policy. Except for the ritual of voting, they are content to abdicate the citizen's role in the political process and to leave to others the effective power of governmental decision. They are politically irresponsible, and often politically illiterate as well.

This disposition is reflected in *strangely contradictory attitudes towards international affairs.* Students predict another major war within a dozen years yet international problems are the least of the concerns to which they expect to give much personal attention during their immediate future. The optimism with which they view their prospects for a good long life belies the seriousness of their gloomy prophecy. They readily propose some form of supranational government as a means of preventing war, but a very large number display only a limited knowledge of and confidence in the United Nations as an instrument of cooperative international action.

Turning to their immediate preoccupation, the pursuit of an education, students by and large *set great stock by college* in general and their own college in particular. The intensity of their devotion varies quite a little bit with the institution and sometimes with the nature of the students' educational goals. And the real point of the devotion is not the same for all. Only a minority seem to value their college education primarily in terms of its intellectual contribution, or its nurturing of personal character and the capacity for responsible human relationships. Vocational preparation, and skill and experience in social "adjustment" head the rewards which students crave from their higher education. . . .

Against the background of earlier generations, these values of today's students look different. The undergirding of the Puritan heritage on which the major value assumptions of American society have rested is inconspicuous, if it is present at all. Perhaps these students are the forerunners of a major cultural and ethical revolution, the unconscious ushers of an essentially secular (though nominally religious), self-oriented (though group-conforming) society. . . .

The values of the college graduate

do differ in some respects from the rest of the society. He is more concerned with status, achievement and prestige. Proportionately more college graduates distrust "welfare economics" and "strong" government than in the country at large. Paradoxically they tend to be somewhat more tolerant and less repressive of "radical" ideas and unconventional people, also less prejudiced towards minority groups and alien cultures. They share few of the cold-war suspicions of the subversiveness of college faculties, nor do they support the popular stereotype of the colleges' godlessness. Religiously, they may be less superstitious or other-worldly than their fellow countrymen. The college man or woman thus tends to be more self-important—more conservative—more tolerant—and less fearful of evil forces in this world and outside than those who have not been "higher-educated." . . .

10

YOUNG PEOPLE HAVE A NEW MORALITY*

Millicent McIntosh

Not every investigator has filed a negative report on today's young people. They may be different, say some reporters, but they are not necessarily worse than their elders. In fact, the following report finds them to be a superior product—more honest, more moral, more concerned with justice, more dedicated to beauty.

Two world wars, a world-wide depression, and the advancement of science, especially of psychology and psychoanlysis, have knocked away the framework of the world in which I was brought up during the first quarter-century. The younger generation today is not confident, as we were, that God is in His heaven and we can know and must do His will, that sex should be confined to marriage and that man's first duty, as an agent for progress toward the establishment of the Kingdom of God, is to his fellow man.

These comfortable precepts, which enabled us to pass our youth in a climate of secure values, social, political, and religious, have been replaced not by a decline in morality but by what I prefer to call a "new morality": a new approach to religion, to sex behavior, and to the obligations of an individual to those around him. This "new morality" has created a stronger and broader sense of right and wrong than we had in my own day.

Young men and women today have an immense sense of justice. This underlies much of their social philosophy. It makes them practically concerned with problems of integration, and active on a mature level in organizations and conferences to discuss the problems of their country. It is shown

---

* Millicent McIntosh, "What Is Happening to Our Morality?" from a symposium on youth in *The New York Times Magazine*, June 10, 1962, pp. 12, 34. Copyright by The New York Times Company. Reprinted by permission.

also in their excitement about the Peace Corps and in their wide participation in projects like Crossroads Africa. It is true that the problems of today are of such magnitude that many may at times feel a sense of despair and be tempted to shrug their shoulders and turn aside. But essentially there is an impressive shift here from the morality of the social worker to that of the social builder.

No word of mine is necessary to indicate that the new approach to sex among the young represents a revolutionary change. Although much of the younger generation's behavior today does not appeal to me aesthetically or personally, I believe that their sex ethics, founded on knowledge instead of ignorance, are often definitely moral. They are seeking for the clearest possible understanding of each other as a preliminary to marriage. . . .

Many adults are ignorant of the genuine preoccupation of the younger generation with the arts. They write them off as a "TV" generation, or as one eager to acquire material possessions. These critics forget that they are passionate builders of hi-fi phonographs and collectors of classical records; that they write and buy the latest poetry; that they fill the off-Broadway shows and haunt the openings of new painters. Their search for beauty seems in many ways far more cultivated and active than that of their elders, who collapse into reading the latest best-seller. . . .

. . . The new understanding of religion is clearly an individual one. It may be founded on disillusionment and on a realization of man's weakness and conflict, but . . . today's youth find much in common with the Existentialists, who recognize the fallibilities of human nature but sustain a conviction of the moral nature of man's struggle to realize himself. In place of a well-meaning but rather smug optimism, they have a humility in the face of the mystery and conflict of life, and a determination to meet their problems with honesty and realism.

11

WHAT'S POLITICS TO YOU?*

Edward J. Heubel, William Monat, and Henry C. Bush

What is politics? It is competition among groups for certain things they want and against things they don't want. It largely determines the kind of America we live in. It largely determines who gets what. In theory it means government by the people, yet in practice it usually means government by minorities skilled enough and concerned enough to push their *particular ideas and protect* their *particular interests.*

Never before have political speeches fallen on deafer ears. Consider a few examples and opinions. It was 1956. A national election was near. A party leader, speaking to a college audience, held up an "Ike" button. Loud cheers.

"Who wants Ike for President?" he asked. More applause, and most hands went up. "Who wants Whittier for Governor?" Again enthusiastic cheers, with most hands up. "Who'll work for them in this campaign?" Cheers and laughter, but no hands.

The failure to respond, however, was not quite total. After the meeting one boy came up to the party leader and asked "How much do you pay an hour?"[1]

The apathy isn't only at our level. Take a sounding in 1960. Again, a national election was nearing. One observer summed it up this way:

. . . the men in power do not think politically either. For instance, this year we have had the usual spectacle of politicians going about the country looking for nominators for the Presidency, presumably (why else?) because they have important new programs to offer. But as soon as it becomes clear that the county leaders of the party do not want them, they retire from the race and rally to elect whomever. Since this is what political responsibility means to a politician, why should the electorate respect politics? . . .[2]

The awareness at professional levels that politics today isn't public discussion is easy to see. A few men speak from their hearts and talk about what they mean, but more and more political speeches are ghostwritten by public relations professionals, canned stuff, each as like the speech or pronunciamento or policy statement immediately before or after it as adjacent cans on a shelf in a supermarket.

. . . what must be the effect on a boy when he comes to realize that the public

---

* Edward J. Heubel, William Monat, and Henry C. Bush, "Why Major in Political Science?" Pamphlet, revised by Henry C. Bush (Detroit, Wayne State University, n.d.)

[1] Ralph K. Huitt, "Learning Politics at the Campus Roots," *The New York Times Magazine,* April 20, 1958, p. 42

[2] Paul Goodman, *Growing Up Absurd* (New York: Random House, 1960) pp. 107–08.

spokesman up there is not even speaking his own words, but repeating, like a performer, something written for him by a staff from Madison Avenue?[3]

Such is political dialogue today. What's politics to you? Not much.

Yet the issues are big. Many aren't even familiar ones; they're new. The chief candidates for office don't argue about the great depression anymore, or public power, or freedom from government. They argue about new things—public water supply, air pollution, the tariff against battery-fed chickens shipped to Europe, Vietnam, desegregation of labor unions, bus transport, how not to teach science, and how many billions to reach the moon. But the issues aren't remote. They are arguing about *you*. Are you going to be able to water the lawn without a police ticket? Will you have lung cancer in 20 years from the big city smog? Are all those shiny new German and Japanese things crowding your dad's company's markets? Will the stuff you are learning in the courses you are now taking be obsolete when you enter the market with your brand-new but maybe useless M.B.A. or M.Sc.? Are they going to desegregate your neighborhood? This is you, me, us. Politics, like earning a living, is your problem whether you are in engineering, business, teaching, or any other field seemingly remote from government. *It is always affecting you.* What can you do about something which is affecting you all the time? What must you do? You get with it and master it because it's with you. You get with it because you are somebody and to continue to be somebody you must get with it.

The problem these decades of almost full employment is not so much getting a job or keeping a job or living comfortably middleclass on your job but, in David Riesman's and Nathan Glazer's words, that

> . . . one is supposed to have an opinion, to cope with the world as well as with one's job and immediate surroundings. . . . Having . . . won respectability in paycheck and consumption style . . . you will find this achievement menaced by a political and more broadly cultural outlook tending to lower barriers . . . between this nation and other nations, between groups in this nation . . . between housing projects . . . and suburbs . . . [you will] want an interpretation of the world. . . .

You will have the feeling of being lost and overwhelmed by the giant government bureaucracies, each a maze of channels, procedures, and private ways "in." There will be giant national issues for which proponents demand your consent or assume it, giant condemnations of vague evils by publicists, editors, legislators, and others, and giant international issues involving friends and foes whose names and places on the globe you barely know—Nasser and others in the Middle East, the Chinese in the Far East, who knows who in Central and South Africa, and the Russians everywhere. These will seem somehow to threaten you personally. Such is our common future. It is how to understand the political trends and possibilities of action in our time. It is *how to live responsibly*. Perspective in this is the only sensible solution. If you know political techniques you can recognize the possibilities of action. If you understand the trends in American and world politics you can appraise policies and actions instead of being confused, fearful, and eager to find a scapegoat. If you know where to lean your and your friends' small political weight you can shove a course of action into motion, or keep it in motion—slightly of

[3] Goodman, p. 107–08.

the big issues, swiftly of the small ones. *And it is easy.* We don't mean that President Johnson's or Senator Douglas' or Governor Brown's jobs are easy. At the top policy levels it's a hard frustrating task, and it is harder because of the omnipresent question "is anybody listening out there?" Good men get discouraged. (President Kennedy, talking to college students who had spent the summer working in government offices in Washington, said "Sometimes I wish I only had a summer job here myself.") But it is easy to get into the act, whether it is corporation or government or academic or neighborhood politics. All it takes is a few men with ideas, and effort. An academic colleague recently gave an example:

You know, we were picking a Personnel and Promotions Committee. They serve for three years. These people have power! If they don't like you you stay an Assistant Professor an extra three years. If they're a bunch of incompetents they hire more incompetents and the outfit goes downhill, standards run down to meanness, and pretty soon you aren't working much because you're busy in-fighting.

There were 35 of us involved; it's a large department. We had a meeting scheduled, to vote to pick this committee in two days. I talked it over with two others I knew—knew where they stood and knew they stood where I wanted the department to stand. We worked out five men we thought would do a decent job, and we divided up the thirty-some and talked up our slate to them privately, answered questions, told them where we stood and why we stood for these five. It couldn't have taken me more than ten hours' time.

The election came around. Our boys were nominated. So were others, including some who could have made this job hell for years. Ours won. We had done a little thinking and a little talking and arguing and we had the goods. It was easy.

It was interesting how easy it was. We didn't sell them anything phony. We had a point of view and a proposal—a slate of five good men. Nobody else had worked at it. It was easy.

The field is wide open.

II

Democracy or Direction: Theory and Practice

Democracy—Government by the Worst, or Government in the Interests of Most?

Traditional theory of democracy assumes that men are intelligent, that they know their own interests, that they can keep an eye on government and know what it is doing, and that they have enough sense to give way when the other fellow's interests are more reasonable.

Consider these traditional assumptions about all of us in terms of our everyday experience. Consider, for example, those prime movers of our economy, the ads on TV and radio. Is there much appeal to our intelligence in them? Listen in on conversations in a bus or while waiting in the cashier's line in a supermarket and how often do you hear something like this?

"Was you to the dance last night out at the Royal?"
"I was there, was you?"
"Yeah, I was there, I never seen you though."
"Well I never seen you neither."
"That's funny, I was there."
"Well, I never seen you."

"Where was you at? I never seen you."
"Well, it's funny we never seen each other."*

Did you ever see father add up the check stubs and then kick the cat? Did you ever hear two people discuss something and see that the further they got into their discussion the louder they shouted and the angrier each became and the further they got from agreement?

Traditional theory of democracy also holds that citizens' elected representatives meet in bodies called legislatures where men discuss alternatives, debate issues, persuade each other, and then agree on the most reasonable course of action. Every year some 3,000,000 Americans visit Washington, D.C. Most of them visit the principal monuments to American democracy—the Lincoln Monument, the Jefferson Memorial, etc. A large percentage of them visit Congress and expect, as they look down from the visitors' gallery, to see our legislators listening to debate and making up their minds on difficult issues. The visitors are usually disappointed to find an almost empty chamber, a mere handful of Senators or Representatives, some of them obviously not listening.

Our point is that *in practice* democracy does not work the way our traditional lore says it does because *in practice* we citizens are not what traditional democratic theory assumes us to be. Most of us are sometimes rational, sometimes irrational, often selfish, and quite likely to confuse justice with our own point of view or our own demands. Our population of 180,000,000 consists in great part of persons much too concerned with their immediate personal interests (guys chasing dolls, dolls chasing guys, men concerned about the details of their work at the office, mothers concerned almost exclusively about their children) to keep an eye on government. Moreover government is too big and complicated. Consider, for example, that in the Department of State alone over 2,000,000 documents, each representing some decision or action, go out over the Secretary of State's signature each year. How many of them do you have an informed opinion about? What, for example, is your opinion of our policy respecting Pakistan right now? The answer is that most of us cannot keep up with things even if we wanted to and even if we had time to.

The "rules of the game" which do describe the practice of democracy are these. Democratic theory assumes certain things about humans. It assumes that we citizens want to be different. Individualism is the essence of it. The individual is the end product of democratic government. If you assume that individuals differ and want to differ and will continue to differ then of course *you avoid trying to get agreement on fundamentals of ideology and religion.* You assume we are civilized enough not to have to. Democracy also assumes we are not too bigoted to learn, and so *it builds opposition into the system.* It establishes rules for competing for power, rules which specify that only talking and writing are legitimate means. Violence is taboo. The losers in any political contest live to argue, run for office, and possibly win another year. The losers in any public argument live to argue their point of view another time on another issue. Democracy assumes that men (or at least enough men so that there will be some such men among all groups) can conceive it possible that they might be wrong about things, and if they can't do that they can at least realize that even if they

---

* Richard Bissel, 7½ *Cents* (Boston: Little, Brown & Co., 1953), p. 4.

are right and the others are wrong they've got to live with the others, haven't they?—and can, grudgingly or generously, bend their point of view and compromise, and so, slowly, change. To insure that this minimum tolerance will operate, the democratic system in America frustrates and checks the political power of any preponderant majority at any moment in time by a complex system of wide distribution of power called checks and balances.

Within these "rules of the game," it is a system in which most of us get into the act only at periodic elections and express only a general approval or disapproval of how things have been going lately. It is a system in which small, vigilant, vocal, skillful, and usually selfish minorities are aways in the act, minorities which help shape government policy and help bend government action most of the time between elections and between big decisions. It is *government by competing minorities.*

In the first part of this chapter we shall examine and discuss these assumptions.

Government by One Minority— Error and Exploitation and Sometimes Terror? or Efficiency and Direction?

One way to judge whether democracy works well or badly is to compare it to nondemocratic political systems in which, as the leaders and advocates put it, somebody is able to run things without a lot of gabble-gabble and back-talk and delay and compromise. We will look into several types: into the regime in control of the Communist prototype, the U.S.S.R.; into a temporarily deceased type, Fascism (into its prototype, National Socialist Germany, 1935–45), and into a kind very widespread these decades—the one-party, strongly led type based on a mix of theory (part Marxist, part Western world, part home-cooked), usually anticapitalist, always Socialist or pseudo-Socialist, action-oriented (they say), the type usual in countries recently emerged from the fire of revolution and busily on the road to somewhere (industrialization? The Higher Life? "Socialist Man"?).

To us, born and raised free, *any* kind of nondemocratic regime is almost incomprehensible. More than that, when we look, however momentarily, into any system such as Castro's Cuba or Duvalier's Haiti (or Sukarno's Indonesia, or Ho-Chi-Minh's North Vietnam or Nasser's Egypt or Sekou Touré's Guinea, etc., etc.) we react as if we had seen something obscene. We call them all dictatorships and dismiss them as temporary aberrations. They go against our grain. They make us squirm. "How can people . . . ?" we ask ourselves.

Remember those assumptions of democracy! Conceive it possible that we might be wrong. Or at least that we've got to live with other systems. Nondemocratic (to us, antidemocratic) governments outnumber democratic ones in the world about five to one. Democracy as we (and the French, British, Swedes, Uruguayans, and a few others) practice it—as a permanent habit—is a rare type. Some practice it but now and then toss it out and try antidemocratic methods, then toss those out. The highly civilized nations, Germany and Japan, recently did this. Some are democratic in one locale but not in others (e.g., the British

Empire in all its ramifications). We have our own large areas where the democratic writ sometimes does not run. Democracy is normative and imperfect in operation and it takes effort, motion, action, to constantly reaffirm it and reestablish it.

Leaders in nondemocratic countries usually claim to speak for the average citizen. But how can the head men in such regimes know what needs to be done? They never listen to anybody. Is such a system progressive and efficient, or does it merely make its citizens move, work, march—like an army, disciplined, obeying orders? But marching where? Down blind alleys? Besides, who believes an army is really disciplined, really efficient, really obeys, except sometimes in actual battle? Ever been in an army? Any army (the Chinese army, the United States army, Coxey's army). Command is *not* an efficient means of leadership; democratic persuasion can be.

But in one sense, many if not most, dictatorships rest on persuasion. To Indonesians Bung Karno (brother Sukarno) is them, is Indonesia, their leader, their ego ideal, their hero—all in one. There is no doubt that in North (Communist, antidemocratic) Vietnam "Uncle Ho" Chi Minh is loved and admired. There are people who admire Castro, inconceivable to us though this is!

> Without doubt, the tremendous welcome that greeted Dr. Fidel Castro in Moscow [on May Day, 1963] was spontaneous. To the thousands of predominantly young Russians who thronged into Red Square last Sunday the Cuban leader is a romantic reminder of the heroic phase of their own revolution. He . . . personifies for the Russians the hope of the ultimate victory of communism . . . The symbolic significance . . . should not be underestimated. . . .

Thus reports the good grey solid sane democratic anticommunist pro-Western London *Economist* (May 4, 1963).

These one-man Great Leader types sometimes say things which make a great deal of sense. Their proposals are concrete and direct. ("Philosophy does not interest us. We have enough concrete tasks," said Sekou Touré, in a press conference recently.) On the other hand, our own democratic politicians say vague, meaningless things a good deal of the time. Pick any speech on TV or radio by any American Senator or British Member of Parliament and see if you can find any kernel of meaning in it. It says yes, no, maybe, under certain circumstances, if . . . It has to be this way, except in crisis, because the democratic audience is many audiences, diverse, ornery, and free to buy it or not buy it. The democratic politician must, a large part of the time, use the microphone to mean (almost magically!) many different things to many different men. The Great Leader can decide. He can command.

But this power is, as we have argued, seldom used efficiently and history suggests that those instances where power is used to the full effect can produce terrible, direct and devastating consequences. It is the threat that we may personally be faced with such unequivocal, unchecked decision-making in all its terror that reconciles us to "muddling through" with democratic procedures. History seems to bear out the proposition of Winston Churchill, who suggested democracy was a bad system of government that was merely less bad than all the others that had been tried.

1

DISSECTION OF THE MASS MAN*

Jose Ortega y Gasset

The arguments of Jose Ortega y Gasset (of America and of the whole of the Western democratic world) are that the rise of the common man in politics has everywhere meant a decline in standards. The common man is a creature of appetites, no more. He is convinced he is perfect. He listens to almost no one. He is like a spoiled child. He is using politics and mass democracy for his own advantages, particularly for his own economic advantages, but he contributes nothing to the further growth and development of democratic politics and government. He recognizes no standards other than his own whims and desires. The more he comes into political power and is wooed and solicited for his biases and whims (called public opinion) the more civilization weakens.

There is one fact which, whether for good or ill, is of utmost importance in the public life of Europe at the present moment. This fact is the accession of the masses to complete social power. . . .

Perhaps the best line of approach to this historical phenomenon may be found by turning our attention to a visual experience, stressing one aspect of our epoch which is plain to our very eyes. This fact is quite simple to enunciate, though not so to analyze. I shall call it the fact of agglomeration, of "plentitude." Towns are full of people, houses full of tenants, hotels full of guests, trains full of travelers, cafés full of customers, parks full of promenaders, consulting-rooms of famous doctors full of patients, theatres full of spectators, and beaches full of bathers. What previously was, in general, no problem, now begins to be an everyday one, namely, to find room. . . .

What about it? Is this not the ideal state of things? . . .

The concept of the multitude is quantitative and visual. Without changing its nature, let us translate it into terms of sociology. We then meet with the nation of the "social mass." Society is always a dynamic unity of two component factors: minorities and masses. The minorities are individuals or groups of individuals which are specially qualified. The mass is the assemblage of persons not especially qualified. By masses, then, is not to be understood, solely or mainly, "the working masses." The mass is the average man. In this way what was mere quantity—the multitude—is converted into a qualitative determination: it becomes the common social quality, man as undifferentiated from other men, but as repeating in himself a generic type. . . .

The mass is all that which sets no value on itself—good or ill—based on specific grounds, but which feels itself

---

* Jose Ortega y Gasset, *The Revolt of the Masses* (New York: W. W. Norton & Company, Inc., 1932). Pp. 11–15, 17–18, 55, 60–65. Copyright renewed 1960.

"just like everybody," and nevertheless is not concerned about it; is, in fact, quite happy to feel itself as one with everybody else. . . .

For there is no doubt that the most radical division that it is possible to make of humanity is that which splits it into two classes of creatures: those who make great demands on themselves, piling up difficulties and duties; and those who demand nothing special of themselves, but for whom to live is to be every moment what they already are, without imposing on themselves any effort towards perfection; mere buoys that float on the waves. . . .

The old democracy was tempered by a generous dose of liberalism and of enthusiasm for law. . . . Today we are witnessing the triumphs of a hyperdemocracy in which the mass acts directly, outside the law, imposing its aspirations and its desires by means of material pressure. It is a false interpretation of the new situation to say that the mass has grown tired of politics and handed over the exercise of it to specialized persons. . . . Now, on the other hand, the mass believes that it has the right to impose and to give force of law to notions born in the café. I doubt whether there have been other periods of history in which the multitude has come to govern more directly than in our own. That is why I speak of hyperdemocracy. . . .

The characteristic of the hour is that the commonplace mind, knowing itself to be commonplace, has the assurance to proclaim the rights of the commonplace and to impose them wherever it will. . . .

Public authority is in the hands of a representative of the masses. These are so powerful that they have wiped out all opposition. They are in possession of power in such an unassailable manner that it would be difficult to find in history examples of a Government so all-powerful as these. And yet public authority—the Government—exists from hand to mouth, it does not offer itself as a frank solution for the future, it represents no clear announcement of the future, it does not stand out as the beginning of something whose development or evolution is conceivable. In short, it lives without any vital program, any plan of existence. It does not know where it is going, because, strictly speaking, it has no fixed road, no predetermined trajectory before it. When such a public authority attempts to justify itself it makes no reference at all to the future. On the contrary, it shuts itself up in the present, and says with perfect sincerity: "I am an abnormal form of Government imposed by circumstances." Hence its activities are reduced to dodging the difficulties of the hour; not solving them, but escaping from them for the time being, employing any methods whatsoever, even at the cost of accumulating thereby still greater difficulties for the hour which follows. Such has public power always been when exercised directly by the masses: omnipotent and ephemeral. The mass-man is he whose life lacks any purpose, and who simply goes drifting along. Consequently, though his possibilities and his powers be enormous, he constructs nothing. And it is this type of man who decides in our time. . . .

In the schools, which were such a source of pride to the last century, it has been impossible to do more than instruct the masses in the technique of modern life; it has been found impossible to educate them. They have been given tools for an intenser form of existence, but no feeling for their great historic duties; they have been hurriedly inoculated with the pride and power of modern instruments, but not with their spirit. Hence they will have nothing to do with their spirit, and the new generations are getting ready to take over command of the world as if the world were a paradise without trace of former footsteps, without traditional and highly complex problems. . . .

What appearance did life present to that multitudinous man who in ever-increasing abundance the nineteenth century kept producing? To start with, an appearance of universal material ease. Never had the average man been able to solve his economic problem with greater facility. . . .

To this ease and security of economic conditions are to be added the physical ones, comfort and public order. Life runs on smooth rails, and there is no likelihood of anything violent or dangerous breaking in on it. . . . That is to say, in all its primary and decisive aspects, life presented itself to the new man as exempt from restrictions. . . .

But still more evident is the contrast of situations, if we pass from the material to the civil and moral. The average man, from the second half of the nineteenth century on, finds no social barriers raised against him. . . . There are no civil privileges. The ordinary man learns that all men are equal before the law. . . .

Three principles have made possible this new world: liberal democracy, scientific experiment, and industrialism. . . . The world which surrounds the new man from his birth does not compel him to limit himself in any fashion, it sets up no veto in opposition to him; on the contrary, it incites his appetite, which in principle can increase indefinitely. . . . Even today, in spite of some signs which are making a tiny breach in that sturdy faith, even today, there are few men who doubt that motorcars will in five years' time be more comfortable and cheaper than today. They believe in this as they believe that the sun will rise in the morning. The metaphor is an exact one. For, in fact, the common man, finding himself in a world so excellent, technically and socially, believes that it has been produced by nature, and never thinks of the personal efforts of highly endowed individuals which the creation of this new world presupposed. Still less will he admit the notion that all these facilities still require the support of certain difficult human virtues, the least failure of which would cause the rapid disappearance of the whole magnificent edifice. . . .

This leads us to note down in our psychological chart of the mass-man of today two fundamental traits: the free expansion of his vital desires, and therefore, of his personality; and his radical ingratitude towards all that has made possible the ease of his existence. These traits together make up the well-known psychology of the spoilt child. And in fact it would entail no error to use this psychology as a "sight" through which to observe the soul of the masses of today. Heir to an ample and generous past—generous both in ideals and in activities—the new commonalty has been spoiled by the world around it. To spoil means to put no limit on caprice, to give one the impression that everything is permitted to him and that he has no obligations. The young child exposed to this regime has no experience of its own limits. By reason of the removal of all external restraint, all clashing with other things, he comes actually to believe that he is the only one that exists and gets used to not considering others, especially not considering them as superior to himself. This feeling of another's superiority could only be instilled into him by someone who, being stronger than he is, should force him to give up some desire, to restrict himself, to restrain himself. He would then have learned this fundamental discipline: "Here I end and here begins another more powerful than I am. In the world, apparently, there are two people: I myself and another superior to me." The ordinary man of past times was daily taught this elemental wisdom by the world about him, because it was a world so rudely organized, that catastrophes were frequent, and there was nothing in it certain, abundant, stable. But the new masses find themselves in the presence of a prospect full of possibilities, and furthermore, quite secure, with everything ready to their hands, independent of any previous efforts on their part, just as we find the sun in the heavens without hoisting it up on our shoulders. No human being thanks another for the air he breathes, for no one has produced the air for him; it belongs to the sum total of what "is there," of which we say "it is natural," because it never fails. And these spoiled masses are unintelligent enough to believe that the material and social organization, placed at their disposition like the air, is of the same origin, since apparently it never fails them, and is almost as perfect as the natural scheme of things.

My thesis, therefore, is this: the very perfection with which the nineteenth century gave an organization to certain orders of existence has caused the masses benefited thereby to consider it, not as an organized, but as a natural system. Thus is explained and defined the absurd state of mind revealed by these masses; they are only concerned with their own well-being, and at the same time they remain alien to the cause of that well-being. As they do not see, beyond the benefits of civilization, marvels of invention and construction which can only be maintained by great effort and foresight, they imagine that their role is limited to demanding these benefits peremptorily, as if they were natural rights. . . .

2

THERE'S NOTHING WRONG WITH THE RAW MATERIAL OF DEMOCRACY HERE*

Eric Hoffer

There's nothing wrong with the raw material of democracy according to Eric Hoffer. Aside from the (let us hope!) temporary problem of the corroding effect of unemployment, he sees no cause for concern either about American character or about contemporary trends and tastes.

How does one find out what Americans are really like? Is it by listening to the radio and watching television? By reading our newspapers, magazines and books? By talking to people and listening to their opinions? No. You cannot gauge the character and the intelligence of an American by talking with him. The American is infinitely better than his words. In other

* Eric Hoffer, from a symposium on U.S. morality, *The New York Times Magazine*, June 10, 1962, pp. 34, 36.

countries it is reasonable to assume that what people profess is likely to be more noble than what they practice. With the mass of people in America it is the other way around: their actions are more humane, sensitive and original than their professed opinions. They practice, as it were, an inverted hypocrisy.

To find out what the American is really like you must work with him. I have spent twenty years as a migratory worker and another twenty as a longshoreman on the docks of San Francisco, and I have a high opinion of my fellow Americans. There is hardly a day I have not been put to shame by their alertness to help others, their forbearance, their innate fairness and lack of malice. I have a feeling that in this country there is no cesspool underneath our social structure—no real evil. There are an innocence and a naïveté which make us seem childish and lightheaded, but also render us impervious to real corruption. . . . The threat to our moral fiber and social health comes not from "vulgarity, sensuality—indeed downright filth,"[1] or that we dance the twist and not the minuet, but from the fact that we have between five and six million unemployed and no cure in sight.[2] Chronic unemployment is likely to breed hopelessness and bitter recklessness which may shake our society to its foundations.

What ails America is not the deterioration of "our concept of beauty and decency and morality," but that millions of us are being rendered superfluous and are robbed of our sense of worth and usefulness. "The characteristics that have made America great" are our readiness and capacity to get things done. Inaction is the only poison that can corrupt and deprave us.

---

[1] The charge Hoffer is refuting (that Americans today are corrupted by "vulgarity, sensuality—indeed downright filth") was made recently by former President Eisenhower.

[2] Unemployment has since decreased somewhat.

3
AND THERE'S NOTHING WRONG WITH THE DEMOCRATIC RESPONSE*

James Reston

James Reston, too, refutes the argument that we haven't got what it takes to survive and prosper as free men. The American people, when shown what must be done, respond and do the job.

But he agrees with Gasset that "public authority—the Government—exists from hand to mouth, it does not offer . . . a frank solution, it represents no clear announcement of the future . . . its activities are reduced to dodging the difficulties of the hour. . . ."

We need, argues Reston, more linkage, less gap, between the men of ideas who can and do read the trends and problems correctly, the men in political office who have the power to lead and to act, and the public.

. . . writers have always been grumbling, mainly to each other, about the feebleness of the national will.

The main difference between today's lamentations and those of the past is that the language is milder and the pay better. Thomas Paine, roaring about America's mulish indifference in 1775, makes today's orators sound complacent. And even Ralph Waldo Emerson, who was really a pretty cheery fellow, could wail in 1847:

"Alas for America, the air is loaded with poppy, with imbecility, with dispersion and sloth. . . . Eager, solicitous, hungry, rabid, busy-bodied America: catch thy breath and correct thyself."

Thus, criticism of the American people for lack of purpose is not new. What is new is that leaders now seem to think they must follow the nation instead of leading it. What is new is that a hostile coalition of nations now has the military power to destroy the Republic. The margin of error granted to us in past wars and crises has vanished. What could be won before with partial effort, late starts, feeble alliances and mediocre administration can no longer be won in a contest with the Communists.

It is not that they are so efficient but that they are so purposeful. They are all working on the main target and we are not. Life, tyranny and the pursuit of Capitalists is the Russian way of life. They have obliterated the difference between war and peace. They are always at war, all of them, women as well as men—teachers, philosophers, scientists, engineers, lady discus throwers, airmen, and three or four million foot soldiers.

None of this need trouble us very

---

* James Reston, "Our History Suggests a Remedy," in *The National Purpose*, by J. K. Jessup, Adlai Stevenson, Archibald MacLeish, David Sarnoff, Billy Graham, John W. Gardner, Clinton Rossiter, Albert Wohlstetter, James Reston, and Walter Lippman (New York: Holt, Rinehart & Winston, Inc., 1960), pp. 110–17 and 122–23. Courtesy of *Life* magazine © 1960 by Time, Inc.

much except for *their* national purpose, which is simply to replace our system of individual freedom with their system of state control wherever they can, including regions vital to our security such as Germany, Japan and even Cuba.

I must say they have been very frank about it. They have given us timely if not fair warning. They are directing all the energies of all their people to that goal. They are not arguing about the conflict between private interests and the national interest. They have simply eliminated private interest. They have put everybody to work on "burying" capitalism, and since our national purpose, among other things, is to avoid being buried, this creates an awkward and even nasty situation.

How, then, shall we approach the problem? I was brought up on the Church of Scotland's shorter catechism, the first question of which is: "What is the chief end of man?"

Accordingly, I am all for self-direction and self-criticism. Nevertheless, I have my doubts about the imminence of any self-induced renaissance or epoch of austerity.

When I consider attacking the problem through the people, I think of Harry Ashmore's old story about the man who acquired a reputation for training mules with honeyed words and kindness. Hearing about this remarkable achievement, the Society for the Prevention of Cruelty to Animals dispatched a lady emissary to present the mule-trainer with a medal.

Upon arrival, she asked for a demonstration. The trainer obligingly trotted out a young mule, reached for a long two-by-four, and clouted the beast over the head. As the mule struggled back to his feet the good lady exclaimed in horror, "Good heavens, man, I thought you trained these animals with kindness." "I do, ma'am," he replied, "but first I got to git the critters' attention."

I don't know how just anybody gets the attention of 180 million people these days. They are engaged in the pursuit of happiness, which, incidentally, the Declaration of Independence spells with a capital "H," and to be frank about it, I suspect that public debates on the national purpose give them a pain.

It will not, I think, be wise to underestimate America's current resistance to exhortations from the preachers, professors, columnists, and editorial writers of the nation. For unless I miss my guess, the Americano, circa 1960, is in no mood to rush off on his own initiative to "emancipate the human race," or to set any new records as the greatest benefactor of all time, or engage in any of the other crusades mapped out for him in Cambridge, Mass.

He may do many of these things because he is honest enough to know that he doesn't know all the facts of this dangerous and complicated era, but he is not likely to set out to do them because of his own "reflection and reason" of the arguments of talkers or writers he seldom sees.

Accordingly we must, I think, start with the national leadership . . . this is the engine that has pulled us out of the mud before. . . .

The president of the United States is the one man who can get the attention of the American people. If he says the nation is in trouble, they will listen to him. If he addresses himself to their doubts and questions, they will hear him out. If he presents programs and legislation to do what he thinks is necessary for the safety of the Republic and explains and keeps explaining why these are essential, he may very well prevail.

All the magazine articles on the national purpose, all the reports by all the foundations on all our manifold weaknesses, all the speeches . . . all the exhortations to return to the faith of our fathers—all are nothing compared to serious programs eloquently expressed and strongly pushed by a determined president of the United States.

"His is the only national voice in affairs," wrote Woodrow Wilson. "Let him once win the admiration and confidence of the country and no other single force can withstand him, no combination of forces will easily overpower him. His position takes the imagination of the country. . . . His is the vital place of action in the system. . . ."

Of course, he has to act. He cannot ask for half-measures and run away. But once he expresses the national need, once he decides to try to remove rather than to perpetuate the illusions of the past, then his specific remedies will affect the spirit and direction of the nation.

I remember when the Marshall Plan for Europe was devised in Washington. It was perfectly obvious that the sickness of the European economy was creating a crisis of great magnitude, and the bare bones of a four-year plan, costing perhaps as much as $20,000,000,000 were worked out and approved by President Truman.

I printed a long story about it one Sunday in the New York *Times*, and by 10 o'clock that morning, the late Senator Arthur H. Vandenberg of Michigan, then Chairman of the Foreign Relations Committee, called me at home and said: "You must be out of your senses. No administration would dare to come to the Senate with a proposal like that."

Yet once the lead was taken and the need documented, Senator Vandenberg ended up as a key supporter of what almost everybody agrees was the most far-sighted piece of legislation since the war.

I do not underestimate the task. I agree with much that has been said in these essays about the slackness of our society, but I find the present mood understandable, perhaps inevitable, under the circumstances, and not without hope.

At the end of the last war, the American people made a genuine effort to clear the wreckage and understand the new situation. They went through the biggest geography and history lesson in their history, always with the false optimism that they were dealing with a temporary situation that would eventually go away.

Instead of going away, the problems became larger and more complex: after Europe, it was the Middle East; after the Middle East, the Far East; after the Far East, Africa; after Africa, outer space; and after outer space a lot of inner tensions over U-2, me too, inflation, deflation, rising cost of living, balance of payments, nuclear testing, sputniks, luniks and a lot of other things that everybody seemed to be differing about.

There was no panic about any of this. The people merely turned from what they did not understand to what they did understand. They turned inward from the world to the community and the family. In the 15 years of the atomic age, they increased the population of the nation by more than 40,000,000, which is not the action of a frightened people. . . .

A distinction has to be made, I think, between the façade of America and the other more genuine America. There is, of course, this big obvious clattering America of Hollywood and Madison Avenue and Washington, but there is also the outer, quieter America, which has either kept its religious faith or at least held on to the morality derived from religious tradition.

I do not wish to glorify the multitude. Much can be said about the dubious effects on the American character of very early marriage, easy credit, cheap booze, cheaper TV, low education standards and job security even for sloppy work. Nevertheless, there is more concern for the outside world, more interest in its problems, more generosity, and more resourcefulness in this society than in any free society I know anything about.

If it is true, as I believe, that this generation of Americans is doing less than it could, it is also true that it has done everything it was asked to do. It may be more concerned about its private interests than about the public interest, but if a man is offered a choice between a Cadillac and swift kick in the pants, we should not be surprised if he doesn't bend over.

What has it been asked to do that it has not done?

It was asked to restore the broken economy of Europe, and it helped bring that continent, within a decade, to the highest level of prosperity in history.

It was asked to accept high taxation and military conscription to police the world, and it has done so from the North Cape of Norway to Japan and Korea.

It was asked to keep a standing army of a quarter of a million men in Western Europe and it has done so for 15 years, with scarcely a murmur of protest from a single American politician.

It was asked to abandon its tradition of isolation, and it took on more responsibilities involving more risks—in Korea and elsewhere—than the British ever did at the height of their imperial power.

These are not the acts of a slack and decadent people. There is nothing in the record of free peoples to compare with it. This is not a static society. The problem is merely that the pace of history has outrun the pace of change. Ideas and policies have lagged behind events, so that by the time policies were formulated, debated and put in force, the situations they were intended to remedy had changed.

Thus, in a torrent of change, in a revolution of science, a social revolution at home and an unprecedented political revolution in Asia, Africa, and Latin America, it is scarcely surprising that there is a crisis of understanding in the nation. This is all the more true because there has been a serious weakening of the ties between the men of ideas and the men of politics in this country during the last decade.

"Our slow world," wrote Woodrow Wilson in 1890, "spends its time catching up with the ideas of its best minds. It would seem that in almost every generation men are born who embody the projected consciousness of their time and people.

"Their thought runs forward apace into the regions whither the race is advancing, but where it will not for many a weary day arrive. . . . The new thoughts of one age are the commonplaces of the next. The men who act stand nearer to the mass than the men who write; and it is in their hands that new thought gets its translation into the crude language of deeds. . . ."

It cannot be said that the men of ideas in the country have not performed in these last few years their traditional tasks. They have observed the convulsions of our time and let their minds run ahead to the logical consequences for the nation.

I cannot remember a time when there has been more purposeful thought on contemporary problems in the universities and foundations than now. Their reports and conclusions would fill a good-sized library, but the alliance between them and the White House has been feeble. . . .

What, then, can be done?

We can, at least, look at the world as it is instead of the world as we would like it to be. . . .

* * *

I believe, however, that there is still a lot of spunk and spirit in this country that can be brought by free methods into the service of the nation, provided presidential power is used to clarify where the nation stands. The first national purpose is to know who we are and what we stand for; it would be an impertinence to try to improve on the second paragraph of the Declaration of Independence as a guide to the problem.

"We hold these truths to be self-evident," it says in the first sentence. It thereupon lists, as if they were the indisputable facts of last Sunday's American League batting averages, a whole catalogue of wonderful things that are not only not "self-evident" in 1960, but are actually in violent dispute among men all over the world, including quite a few in our own country.

"All men are created equal," it says, and, of course, this is just the trouble, for you can get an argument on that one anywhere in the province of Georgia, U.S.S.R., or the state of Georgia, U.S.A.

In the minds of the Founding Fathers, the moral idea came before the political, and the latter was merely an expression of the former. This, too, was apparently the idea Matthew Arnold had in mind when he came to this country before the turn of the century and discussed our national purpose in New York.

He made two points: "We must hold fast to the austere but true doctrine," he said, "as to what really governs politics, overrides with an inexorable fatality the combinations of so-called politicians, and saves or destroys states. Having in mind things true, things elevated, things just, things pure, things amiable, things of good report: having these in mind, studying and loving these, is what saves states."

However, the old gentleman, when writing these exuberant sentences had no illusion about their being put into force by the majority. These moral concepts would prevail, he said, only as they were upheld by "the remnant" of leaders and thinkers who loved wisdom, for the majority, he insisted, was full of "prosperities, idolatries, oppression, luxury, pleasures and careless women. . . . That shall come to nought and pass away."

"The remnant" in America of those who love wisdom and have the ability to compete with any nation in the world is very large. It has greatly increased as the population of the nation has increased, but it needs to be brought to bear on the great purposes of the nation more than it is today, and this is obviously one task of presidential leadership. . . .

4

THE CRIMES OF THE STALIN ERA*

Nikita S. Khrushchev

Joseph Stalin began his rise to power in the U.S.S.R. in 1922. In 1929–33 because of his orders 10,000,000 were sentenced to forced labor. In 1936–38 great purges disorganized the Russian regime. In 1941 his errors more than any other's led to the loss, for about three years, of half of European Russia to the Germans. In 1948, another purge. In 1952 he ordered Russian officials to begin an anti-Semitic purge. In 1953 he died. In 1956 his survivors in power found it expedient to tell the world of the terror and errors of Stalinist government.

All this happened under a framework of law, with a Constitution listing "rights," and where there was a formally elected legislature. The framework of democracy was there—but no one dared use it. No minority other than the chosen minority, the Communist Party of the Soviet Union, had any access to politics. No other minority was permitted to organize, much less to speak and explain its point of view.

Stalin ceased to an ever greater degree to consider the members of the party's Central Committee and even the members of the Political Bureau. Stalin thought that now he could decide all things alone and all he needed were statisticians; he treated all others in such a way that they could only listen to and praise him.

After the criminal murder of Sergei M. Kirov, mass repressions and brutal acts of violation of socialist legality began. On the evening of December 1, 1944 on Stalin's initiative (without the approval of the Political Bureau—which was passed two days later, casually), the Secretary of the Presidium of the Central Executive Committee, Yenukidze, signed the following directive:

"1. Investigative agencies are directed to speed up the cases of those accused of the preparation or execution of acts of terror.

"2. Judicial organs are directed not to hold up the execution of death sentences pertaining to crimes of this category in order to consider the possibility of pardon, because the Presidium of the Central Executive Committee of the USSR does not consider as possible the receiving of petitions of this sort.

"3. The organs of the Commissariat of Internal Affairs are directed to execute the death sentences against criminals of the above mentioned category immediately after the passage of sentences."

* Nikita S. Khrushchev, "The Crimes of the Stalin Era," Section 2, *The New Leader*, July 16, 1956 (annotated by Boris I. Nicolaevsky), pp. 520–22, 526–31, 535–43, 548–50, and 558–9.

This directive became the basis for mass acts of abuse against socialist legality. During many of the fabricated court cases, the accused were charged with "the preparation" of terroristic acts; this deprived them of any possibility that their cases might be reexamined, even when they stated before the court that their "confessions" were secured by force, and when, in a convincing manner, they disproved the accusations against them.

It must be asserted that to this day the circumstances surrounding Kirov's murder hide many things which are inexplicable and mysterious and demand a most careful examination. There are reasons for the suspicion that the killer of Kirov, Nikolayev was assisted by someone from among the people whose duty it was to protect the person of Kirov.

A month and a half before the killing, Nikolayev was arrested on the grounds of suspicious behavior but he was released and not even searched. It is an unusually suspicious circumstance that when the Chekist assigned to protect Kirov was being brought for an interrogation, on December 2, 1934, he was killed in a car "accident" in which no other occupants of the car were harmed. After the murder of Kirov, top functionaries of the Leningrad NKVD were given very light sentences, but in 1937 they were shot. We can assume that they were shot in order to cover the traces of the organizers of Kirov's killing. (Movement in the hall.)

* * *

Using Stalin's formulation, namely, that the closer we are to socialism the more enemies we will have . . . the provocateurs who had infiltrated the state-security organs, together with conscienceless careerists, began to protect with the party name the mass terror against party cadres, cadres of the Soviet state and the ordinary Soviet citizens. It should suffice to say that the number of arrests based on charges of counterrevolutionary crimes had grown ten times between 1936 and 1937. . . .

Now, when the cases of some of these so-called "spies" and "saboteurs" were examined, it was found that all their cases were fabricated. Confessions of guilt of many arrested and charged with enemy activity were gained with the help of cruel and inhuman tortures. . . .

Comrade Eikhe was arrested on April 29, 1938 on the basis of slanderous materials, without the sanction of the Prosecutor of the USSR, which was finally received 15 months after the arrest.

Investigation of Eikhe's case was made in a manner which most brutally violated Soviet legality and was accompanied by willfulness and falsification.

Eikhe was forced under torture to sign ahead of time a protocol of his confession prepared by the investigative judges, in which he and several other eminent party workers were accused of anti-Soviet activity.

On October 1, 1939 Eikhe sent his declaration to Stalin in which he categorically denied his guilt and asked for an examination of his case. In the declaration he wrote: "There is no more bitter misery than to sit in the jail of a government for which I have always fought."

A second declaration of Eikhe has been preserved which he sent to Stalin on October 27, 1939. . . .

Eikhe wrote in his declaration:

". . . The confessions which were made part of my file are not only absurd but contain some slander toward the Central Committee of the All-Union Communist Party (Bolsheviks) and toward the Council of People's Commissars, because correct resolutions of the Central Committee of the

All-Union Communist Party (Bolsheviks) and of the Council of People's Commissars which were not made on my initiative and without my participation are presented as hostile acts of counterrevolutionary organizations made at my suggestion. . . .

"I am now alluding to the most disgraceful part of my life and to my really grave guilt against the party and against you. This is my confession of counterrevolutionary activity. . . . The case is as follows: Not being able to suffer the tortures to which I was submitted by Usakov and Nikolayev—and especially by the first one—who utilized the knowledge that my broken ribs have not properly mended and have caused me great pain, I have been forced to accuse myself and others.

"The majority of my confession has been suggested or dictated by Ushakov, and the remainder is my reconstruction of NKVD materials from Western Siberia for which I assumed all responsibility. If some part of the story which Ushakov fabricated and which I signed did not properly hang together, I was forced to sign another variation. The same thing was done to Rukhimovich, who was at first designated as a member of the reserve net and whose name later was removed without telling me anything about it; the same was also done with the leader of the reserve net, supposedly created by Bukharin in 1935. At first I wrote my name in, and then I was instructed to insert Mezhlauk. There were other similar incidents.

". . . I am asking and begging you that you again examine my case, and this not for the purpose of sparing me but in order to unmask the vile provocation which, like a snake, wound itself around many persons in a great degree due to my meanness and criminal slander. I have never betrayed you or the party. . . ."

During the examination in 1955 of the Komarov case Rozenblum revealed the following fact: When Rozenblum was arrested in 1937, he was subjected to terrible torture during which he was ordered to confess false information concerning himself and other persons. He was then brought to the office of Zakovsky, who offered him freedom on condition that he make before the court a false confession fabricated in 1937 by the NKVD concerning "Sabotage, espionage and diversion in a terroristic center in Leningrad." (Movement in the hall.) With unbelievable cynicism, Zakovsky told about the vile "mechanism" for the crafty creation of fabricated "anti-Soviet plots."

"In order to illustrate it to me," stated Rozenblum, "Zakovsky gave me several possible variants of the organization of this center and of its branches. After he detailed the organization to me, Zakovsky told me that the NKVD would prepare the case of this center, remarking that the trial would be public. Before the court were to be brought four or five members of this center: Chudov, Ugarov, Smorodin, Pozern, Shaposhnikova (Chudov's wife) and others together with two or three members from the branches of this center. . . .

". . . the case of the Leningrad center has to be built solidly, and for this reason witnesses are needed. Social origin (of course, in the past) and the party standing of the witness will play more than a small role.

"'You, yourself,' said Zakovsky, 'will not need to invent anything. The NKVD will prepare for you a ready outline for every branch of the center; You will have to study it carefully and to remember well all questions and answers which the Court might ask. This case will be ready in four-five months, or perhaps a half year. During all this time you will be preparing yourself so that you will not compromise the investigation and yourself. Your future will depend on how the trial goes and on its results. If you begin to lie and to testify falsely, blame yourself. If you manage to endure it, you will save your head and we will feed and clothe you at the Government's cost until your death.' "

This is the kind of vile things which were then practiced. . . .

* * *

The power accumulated in the hands of one person, Stalin, led to serious consequences during the Great Patriotic War [World War II].

When we look at many of our novels, films and historical "scientific studies," the role of Stalin in the Patriotic War appears to be entirely improbable. Stalin had foreseen everything. The Soviet Army, on the basis of a strategic plan prepared by Stalin long before, used the tactics of so-called "active defense," i.e., tactics which, as we know, allowed the Germans to come up to Moscow and Stalingrad. Using such tactics, the Soviet Army, supposedly thanks only to Stalin's genius, turned to the offensive and subdued the enemy. The epic victory gained through the armed might of the land of the Soviets, through our heroic people, is ascribed in this type of novel, film and "scientific study" as being completely due to the strategic genius of Stalin. . . .

What are the facts of this matter?

Before the war, our press and all our political-educational work was characterized by its bragging tone: When an enemy violates the holy Soviet soil, then for every blow of the enemy we will answer with three blows, and we will battle the enemy on his soil and we will win without much harm to ourselves. But these positive statements were not based in all areas on concrete facts, which would actually guarantee the immunity of our borders.

During the war and after the war, Stalin put forward the thesis that the tragedy which our nation experienced in the first part of the war was the result of the "unexpected" attack of the Germans against the Soviet Union. But, comrades, this is completely untrue. As soon as Hitler came to power in Germany he assigned to himself the task of liquidating Communism. The fascists were saying this openly; they did not hide their plans. . . .

Documents which have now been published show that by April 3, 1941, Churchill, through his Ambassador to the USSR, Cripps, personally warned Stalin that the Germans had begun regrouping their armed units with the intent of attacking the Soviet Union. . . .

Stalin took no heed of these warnings. What is more, Stalin ordered that no credence be given to information of this sort, in order not to provoke the initiation of military operations.

We must assert that information of this sort concerning the threat of German armed invasion of Soviet territory was coming in also from our own military and diplomatic sources; *however, because the leadership was conditioned against such information, such data was dispatched with fear and assessed with reservation.* . . .

Despite these particularly grave warnings, the necessary steps were not taken to prepare the country properly for defense and to prevent it from being caught unawares.

. . . At the outbreak of the war we did not even have sufficient numbers of rifles to arm the mobilized manpower. I recall that in those days I telephoned to Comrade Malenkov from Kiev and told him, "People have volunteered for the new Army and demand arms. You must send us arms."

Malenkov answered me, "We cannot send you arms. We are sending all our rifles to Leningrad and you have to arm yourselves." (Movement in the hall.)

Such was the armament situation.

In this connection we cannot forget, for instance, the following fact: Shortly before the invasion of the Soviet Union by the Hitlerite army, Kirponos, who was chief of the Kiev Special Military District (he was later killed at the front), wrote to Stalin that the German armies were at the Bug River, were preparing for an attack and in the very near future would probably start their offensive. In this connection, Kirponos proposed that a strong defense be organized, that 300,000 people be evacuated from the border areas and that several strong points be organized there: antitank ditches, trenches for the soldiers, etc.

Moscow answered this proposition with the assertion that this would be a provocation, that no preparatory defensive work should be undertaken at the borders, that the Germans were not to be given any pretext for the initiation of military action against us. Thus, our borders were insufficiently prepared to repel the enemy.

When the fascist armies had actually invaded Soviet territory and military operations began, Moscow issued the order that the German fire was not to be returned. Why? It was because Stalin, despite evident facts, thought that the war had not yet started, that this was only a provocative action on the part of several undisciplined sections of the German Army, and that our reaction might serve as a reason for the Germans to begin the war. . . .

As you see, everything was ignored: warnings of certain Army commanders, declarations of deserters from the enemy army, and even the open hostility of the enemy. . . .

* * *

All the more shameful was the fact that, after our great victory over the enemy which cost us so much, Stalin began to downgrade many of the commanders who contributed so much to the victory over the enemy, because Stalin excluded every possibility that services rendered at the front should be credit to anyone but himself.

Stalin was very much interested in the assessment of Comrade Zhukov as a military leader. He asked me often for my opinion of Zhukov. I told him then, "I have known Zhukov for a long time; he is a good general and a good military leader."

After the war Stalin began to tell all kinds of nonsense about Zhukov, among others the following, "You praised Zhukov, but he does not deserve it. It is said that before each operation at the front Zhukov used to behave as follows: He used to take a handful of earth, smell it and say, 'We can begin the attack,' or the opposite, 'The planned operation cannot be carried out.' " I stated at that time, "Comrade Stalin, I do not know who invented this, but it is not true." . . .

In the same vein, let us take, for instance, our historical and military films and some literary creations; they make us feel sick. Their true objective is the propagation of the theme of praising Stalin as a military genius. Let us recall the film, "The Fall of Berlin." Here only Stalin acts; he issues orders in the hall in which there are many empty chairs and only one approached him and reports something to him—that is Poskrebyshev,[1] his loyal shield-bearer. (Laughter in the hall.)

And where is the military command? Where is the Political Bureau? Where is the Government? What are they do-

---

[1] Alexander N. Poskrebyshev was long the head of Stalin's personal secretariat and the latter's trusted aide in all sorts of nefarious undertakings. He was by no means merely Stalin's "shield-bearer," but played a tremendous role behind the scenes; in particular, he was a principal instigator of the Yezhovshchina. He disappeared immediately after Stalin's death.

ing and with what are they engaged? There is nothing about them in the film. Stalin acts for everybody; he does not reckon with anyone; he asks no one for advice. Everything is shown to the nation in this false light. Why? In order to surround Stalin with glory, contrary to the facts and contrary to historical truth.

The question arises: And where are the military, on whose shoulders rested the burden of the war? They are not in the film; with Stalin in, no room was left for them. . . .

I recall the first days when the conflict between the Soviet Union and Yugoslavia began artificially to be blown up. Once, when I came from Kiev to Moscow, I was invited to visit Stalin, who, pointing to the copy of a letter lately sent to Tito, asked me, "Have you read this?"

Not waiting for my reply, he answered, "I will shake my little finger—and there will be no more Tito. He will fall."

We have dearly paid for this "shaking of the little finger." This statement reflected Stalin's mania for greatness, but he acted just that way: "I will shake my little finger—and there will be no Kossior; I will shake my little finger once more and Postyshev and Chubar will be no more; I will shake my little finger again—and Voznesensky, Kuznetsov and many others will disappear."

But this did not happen to Tito. No matter how much or how little Stalin shook, not only his little finger but everything else that he could shake, Tito did not fall. . . .

You see to what Stalin's mania for greatness led. He had completely lost consciousness of reality; he demonstrated his suspicion and haughtiness not only in relation to individuals in the USSR, but in relation to whole parties and nations. . .

Let us also recall the "affair of the doctor-plotters." (Animation in the hall.) Actually there was no "affair" outside of the declaration of the woman doctor Timashuk, who was probably influenced or ordered by someone (after all, she was an unofficial collaborator of the organs of state security) to write Stalin a letter in which she declared that doctors were applying supposedly improper methods of medical treatment.

Such a letter was sufficient for Stalin to reach an immediate conclusion that there were doctor-plotters in the Soviet Union.[2] He issued orders to arrest a group of eminent Soviet medical specialists. He personally issued advice on the conduct of the investigation and the method of interrogation of the arrested persons. He said that the academician Vinogradov should be put in chains, another one should be beaten. Present at this Congress as a delegate is the former Minister of State Security, Comrade Ignatiev. Stalin told him curtly, "If you do not obtain confessions from the doctors we will shorten you by a head." (Tumult in the hall.)

---

[2] The case of the "doctors' plot" was concocted on Stalin's orders in the winter of 1952–53 by the then Minister of State Security, S. D. Ignatiev, and his deputy, Ryumin. Several dozen of the leading doctors in Moscow were arrested, headed by the top specialists of the Kremlin hospital who treated Stalin and all the Soviet chieftains. They were officially charged with using improper medical techniques in order to murder their patients. Specifically, they were accused of having poisoned Andrei A. Zhdanov and Alexander S. Sgcherbakov and of attempting to poison Marshals Konev, Vasilevsky, Govorov, and others.

The first official announcement of the case appeared on January 13, 1953 in *Pravda* and *Izvestia*. Two of the arrested doctors, Professor M. B. Kogan and Professor Y. G. Etinger, died under torture. The stage was being set for a major trial, with the doctors and their accomplices accused of being agents of foreign intelligence (chiefly American). . . .

Stalin personally called the investigative judge, gave him instructions, advised him on which investigative methods should be used; these methods were simple—beat, beat and, once again, beat.

Shortly after the doctors were arrested, we members of the Political Bureau received protocols with the doctors' confessions of guilt. After distributing these protocols, Stalin told us, "You are blind like young kittens; what will happen without me? The country will perish because you do not know how to recognize enemies."

* * *

We felt, however, that the case of the arrested doctors was questionable. We knew some of these people personally because they had once treated us. When we examined this "case" after Stalin's death, we found it to be fabricated from beginning to end.

This ignominious "case" was set up by Stalin; he did not, however, have the time in which to bring it to an end (as he conceived that end), and for this reason the doctors are still alive. Now all have been rehabilitated; they are working in the same places they were working before; they treat top individuals, not excluding members of the Government; they have our full confidence; and they execute their duties honestly, as they did before.

In organizing the various dirty and shameful cases, a very base role was played by the rabid enemy of our party, an agent of a foreign intelligence service—Beria, who had stolen into Stalin's confidence. In what way could this provocateur gain such a position in the party and in the state, so as to become the First Deputy Chairman of the Council of Ministers of the Soviet Union and a member of the Central Committee Political Bureau? It has now been established that this villain had climbed up the government ladder over an untold number of corpses. . . .

Stalin never traveled anywhere, did not meet city and kolkhoz workers; he did not know the actual situation in the provinces.

He knew the country and agriculture only from films. And these films had dressed up and beautified the existing situation in agriculture. Many films so pictured kolkhoz life that the tables were bending from the weight of turkeys and geese. Evidently, Stalin thought that it was actually so. . . .

Stalin separated himself from the people and never went anywhere. This lasted ten years. The last time he visited a village was in January 1928, when he visited Siberia in connection with grain deliveries. How then could he have known the situation in the provinces?

And when he was once told during a discussion that our situation on the land was a difficult one and that the situation of cattle breeding and meat production was especially bad, a commission was formed which was charged with the preparation of a resolution called "Means toward further development of animal breeding in kolkhozes and sovkhozes." We worked out this project.

Of course, our proposals of that time did not contain all possibilities, but we did chart ways in which animal breeding on kolkhozes and sovkhozes would be raised. We had proposed then to raise the prices of such products in order to create material incentives for the kolkhoz, MTS (machine-tractor station) and sovkhoz workers in the development of cattle breeding. But our project was not accepted and in February 1953 was laid aside entirely.

What is more, while reviewing this project Stalin proposed that the taxes paid by the kolkhozes and by the kolkhoz workers should be raised by 40 billion rubles; according to him the peasants are well off and the kolkhoz worker would need to sell only more chickens to pay his tax in full.

Imagine what this meant. Certainly, 40 billion rubles is a sum which the kolkhoz workers did not realize for *all* the products which they sold to the Government. In 1952, for instance, the kolkhozes and the kolkhoz workers received 26,280 million rubles for all their products delivered and sold to the Government.

Did Stalin's position, then, rest on data of any sort whatever? Of course not. In such cases facts and figures did not interest him. If Stalin said anything, it meant it was so—after all, he was a "genius," and a genius does not need to count, he only needs to look and can immediately tell how it should be. When he expresses his opinion, everyone has to repeat it and to admire his wisdom. . . .

5

ANOTHER EXAMPLE OF GOVERNMENT BY *ONE* MINORITY*

The Testimony of Hermann Friedrich Graebe

Lest we think that in a totalitarian state orders are not obeyed by the little people "down the line," lest we think, wishfully, that the terror and errors imposed by Stalin were possible only by a man in high position, a man isolated from the facts, consider the following example of what systematic brutality does to people.

Before me, Homer B. Crawford, being authorized to administer oaths, personally appeared Hermann Friedrich Graebe, who, being by me duly sworn through the interpreter Elisabeth Radziejewska, made and subscribed the following statement:

I, Hermann Friedrich Graebe, declare under oath:

From September 1941 until January 1944 I was manager and engineer-in-charge of a branch office in Sdolbunow, Ukraine, of the Solingen building firm of Josef Jung. In this capacity it was my job to visit the building sites of the firm. Under contract to an Army Construction Office, the firm had orders to erect grain storage buildings on the former airport of Dubno, Ukraine.

On 5 October 1942, when I visited the building office at Dubno, my foreman Hubert Moennikes of 21 Aussenmuehlenweg, Hamburg-Haarburg, told me that in the vicinity of the site, Jews from Dubno had been shot in three large pits, each about 30 meters long and 3 meters deep. About 1500 persons had been killed daily. All of the 5000 Jews who had still been living in Dubno before the program were to be

* *Nazi Conspiracy and Aggression* (Washington, D.C.: Government Printing Office, 1946), V, 696–99.

liquidated. As the shootings had taken place in his presence he was still much upset.

Thereupon I drove to the site, accompanied by Moennikes and saw near it great mounds of earth, about 30 meters long and 2 meters high. Several trucks stood in front of the mounds. Armed Ukrainian militia drove the people off the trucks under the supervision of an SS man. The militia men acted as guards on the trucks and drove them to and from the pit. All these people had the regulation yellow patches on the front and back of their clothes, and thus could be recognized as Jews.

Moennikes and I went directly to the pits. Nobody bothered us. Now I heard rifle shots in quick succession, from behind one of the earth mounds. The people who had got off the trucks —men, women, and children of all ages—had to undress upon the order of an SS man, who carried a riding or dog whip. They had to put down their clothes in fixed places, sorted according to shoes, top clothing and underclothing. I saw a heap of shoes of about 800 to 1000 pairs, great piles of underlinen and clothing. Without screaming or weeping these people undressed, stood around in family groups, kissed each other, said farewells and waited for a sign from another SS man, who stood near the pit, also with a whip in his hand. During the fifteen minutes that I stood near the pit I heard no complaint or plea for mercy. I watched a family of about eight persons, a man and woman, both about 50 with their children of about 1, 8, and 10, and two grown-up daughters of about 20 to 24. An old woman with snow-white hair was holding the one-year-old child in her arms and singing to it, and tickling it. The child was cooing with delight. The couple were looking on with tears in their eyes. The father was holding the hand of a boy about 10 years old and speaking to him softly; the boy was fighting his tears. The father pointed toward the sky, stroked his head, and seemed to explain something to him. At that moment the SS man at the pit shouted something to his comrade. The latter counted off about 20 persons and instructed them to go behind the earth mound. Among them was the family, which I have mentioned. I well remember a girl, slim and with black hair, who, as she passed close to me, pointed to herself and said, "23." I walked around the mound, and found myself confronted by a tremendous grave. People were closely wedged together and lying on top of each other so that only their heads were visible. Nearly all had blood running over their shoulders from their heads. Some of the people shot were still moving. Some were lifting their arms and turning their heads to show that they were still alive. The pit was already ⅔ full. I estimated that it already contained about 1000 people. I looked for the man who did the shooting. He was an SS man, who sat at the edge of the narrow end of the pit, his feet dangling into the pit. He had a tommy gun on his knees and was smoking a cigarette. The people, completely naked, went down some steps which were cut in the clay wall of the pit and clambered over the heads of the people lying there, to the place to which the SS man directed them. They lay down in front of the dead or injured people; some caressed those who were still alive and spoke to them in a low voice. Then I heard a series of shots. I looked into the pit and saw that the bodies were twitching or the heads lying already motionless on top of the bodies that lay before them. Blood was running from their necks. I was surprised that I was not ordered away, but I saw that there were two or three postmen in uniform nearby. The next batch was approaching already. They went down into the pit, lined themselves up against the previous victims and were shot. When I walked back round the mound I noticed another truckload of people which had just arrived. This time it included sick and infirm people. An old, very thin woman with terribly thin legs was undressed by others who were already naked, while two people held her up. The woman appeared to be paralyzed. The naked people carried the woman around the mound. I left with Moennikes and drove in my car back to Dubno.

On the morning of the next day, when I again visited the site, I saw about 30 naked people lying near the pit—about 30 to 50 meters away from it. Some of them were still alive; they looked straight in front of them with a fixed stare and seemed to notice neither the chilliness of the morning nor the workers of my firm who stood around. A girl of about 20 spoke to me and asked me to give her clothes, and help her escape. At that moment we heard a fast car approach and I noticed that it was an SS detail. I moved away to my site. Ten minutes later we heard shots from the vicinity of the pit—then they had themselves to lie down in this to be shot in the neck.

I make the above statement at Wiesbaden, Germany, on 10th November 1945. I swear before God that this is the absolute truth.

HERMANN FRIEDRICH GRAEBE

Subscribed and sworn to before me at Wiesbaden, Germany, this 10 day of November 1945.

HOMER B. CRAWFORD, Major, AC
Investigator Examiner,
War Crimes Branch

I, Elisabeth Radziejewska, being first duly sworn, state: That I truly translated the oath administered by Major Homer B. Crawford to Hermann Friedrich Graebe and that thereupon he made and subscribed the foregoing statement in my presence.

ELISABETH RADZIEJEWSKA
Interpreter

6

THE CASE FOR CONTROL AND DIRECTION*

Mao Tse-Tung

But there is another kind of nondemocratic government in the world. There are a lot of examples—forty or fifty at any moment in time. These (which we call dictatorships), are ruled by one party led by a strong personality, a charismatic leader. We find them in many countries recently emerged *from the timeless, changeless past which economists and sociologists call* "traditional society." *Revolution leaves a society in turmoil. It is a break, a shattering break, with the institutions of the past. The Asian and African nations in which it has recently occurred are* not industrialized. *Without exception they are backward technologically and politically.*

The argument by their authoritarian leaders is that only by direct action and a good deal of compulsion can the backward nation they govern be driven and pushed toward modernization and a complete break with its backward, timeless, mindless past. In this respect, they may feel an affinity for the Chinese above all others. In the statement of the problem, Mao's views may typify those of many noncommunist leaders of such countries.

"You are dictatorial." My dear sirs, what you say is correct. That is just what we are. All the experiences of the Chinese people, accumulated in the course of many successive decades, tell us to carry out a people's democratic dictatorship. . . .

* From Mao Tse-Tung, "On the Present Situation and Our Tasks," report to the Central Committee of the Chinese Communist Party, December 25, 1947; from Report of the Second Plenary Session of the Central Committee of the Seventh Party Congress, Communist Party of China, released in Peking March 23, 1949; and from Mao Tse-Tung, "On People's Democratic Dictatorship," July 1, 1949. The English versions used are from Part IV, "Documents," in *New China: Three Views*, by Otto B. van der Sprenkel, Robert Guillain, and Michael Lindsay (New York: The John Day Company, Inc., 1951) pp. 154, 156, 165–67, 171, 174–75, 177–78, 180–81, 185–86, 190–92, 197.

"You are not benevolent." Exactly. We definitely have no benevolent policies toward the reactionaries or the reactionary deeds of such classes. Our benevolent policy does not apply to such deeds or to such persons, who are outside the ranks of the people; it applies only to the people. . . .

The job of reforming the reactionary classes can be handled only by a state having a people's . . . dictatorship. . . .

Our party is entirely different from the political parties of the bourgeoisie. They are afraid to speak of the elimination of classes, state power, and parties. We, however, openly declare that we are energetically striving to set up conditions just for the sake of eliminating these things. The Communist Party and the state power of the people's dictatorship constitute such conditions.

. . . Communists everywhere are more competent than the bourgeoisie. They understand the laws governing the existence and development of things. They understand dialectics and can see further ahead. . . .

In this our land of China, the People's Liberation Army has already reversed the counterrevolutionary course. . . . This is a turning point in history. . . . This is a great event. . . .

The victory of China's New Democratic revolution is impossible without the broadest united front. . . . But this is not all. This united front must also be firmly led by the Chinese Communist Party. Without the firm leadership of the Chinese Communist Party, no revolutionary united front can be victorious. . . .

As long as their reactionary tendencies can still influence the masses, we must expose them among the masses who are open to their influence, and strike at their political influence in order to liberate the masses from it. But political blows are one thing and economic extermination is another. . . . The existence and development of small and middle capitalist elements is not at all dangerous. The same thing applies to the new-rich peasant economy, which, after agrarian revolution, will inevitably come into existence. . . .

Many of China's conditions are identical with or similar to those of Russia before the October Revolution. Both had the same sort of feudal oppression. Economically and culturally they were similarly backward, though China was the more so. . . .

We must take our destinies into our own hands. We must rid our ranks of all flabby and incompetent thinking. . . . We are well aware of the fact that there will still be all kinds of obstacles and difficulties in the path of our advance. . . . We must be up and doing! . . .

. . . they [the business men] have monopolized the economic life of the entire country. . . . This monopoly capitalism, closely combined with foreign imperialism and the native landlord class and old type of rich peasants, becomes comprador-feudal, state-monopoly capitalism. . . . This . . . not only oppresses the workers and peasants but also oppresses the petty bourgeoisie and harms the middle bourgeoisie. . . .

. . . the Party must do its utmost to learn how to lead the urban people . . . and how to administer and build up the cities. . . . The Plenary Session called on all Party comrades to devote all their energies to learning the technique and management of industrial production; and to learning commercial banking and other work closely related to production. . . . if the Party is ignorant in production work . . . the Party . . . will fail. . . .

We must overcome all difficulties and must learn the things we do not understand. We must learn to do economic work from all who know . . . (no matter who they are). We must respect them as teachers, learning from them attentively and earnestly. We must not pretend that we know when we do not know. We must not put on bureaucratic airs. If one bores into a subject for several months, for one year or two years, perhaps three years or four years, it can eventually be mastered. . . .

The war of the People's Liberation Army is of a patriotic, just and revolutionary nature which must of necessity gain the support of the people. . . . the Communist Party seeks earnestly to unite the whole of the working class, the whole of the peasantry and the vast number of the revolutionary intelligentsia as the leading and foundation forces of this dictatorship. . . .

On the basis of the experience of

these twenty-eight years, we have reached the same conclusions that Sun Yat-sen, in his will, mentioned gaining from "the experience of forty years." That is, "we must awaken the masses of the people and unite ourselves in a common struggle. . . ."

Internally, the people must be awakened. . . .

Basing itself on the science of Marxism-Leninism, the Chinese Communist Party clearly assessed the international and domestic situation. . . .

The Constitution: Frame or Framework?

A depression and a world war plus the cold war produced no major changes in the written American Constitution. Even the changes of interpretation, custom and convention that have occurred have been shifts in relative power rather than differences in the total structure. The American Constitution, through the centuries, has proved exceedingly resilient and tough. Classifying the Bill of Rights as one group of changes and the Civil Rights Amendments as another, there have been perhaps a half dozen amendments or groups of amendments in the entire history of the nation.

Considering the magnitude of some of the crises that have produced no major change, it seems fair to assume that the Constitution will continue to be the basis for American government for the foreseeable future. For this reason, many of the grandiose schemes for wholesale change in our system seem unrealistic. There is no reason to believe that the American people have or will suddenly develop a genuine desire for parliamentary government or regionalism or, indeed, a new constitution.

The Constitution: Symbol of What?

The present document seems, in short, destined to be around for quite a while longer. It has served and will continue to be a symbol and means for national unity. Some writers even say Americans have made Constitution worship a national religion.

But the document also is an instrument and framework for carrying out the operations of government. As such, it creates and maintains three basic conditions. The first is *geographic* division of powers. This is evident not only in the greater weight in proportion to population that the small states have, but also in the freedom to follow local policy that they continue to maintain. In short, geography as well as numbers is given voice by the Constitution.

Secondly, the Constitution defines *functional* distribution of powers. What each branch of the national government and what each level of government can do is set out in a form, no doubt flexible but still confining. Some find in this overlapping arrangement both confusion and over-restriction; to others this is the only realistic way to check autocratic power and a way of defending American liberty.

The third pattern of distribution is *political* distribution over *time*. The majority in any one era is checked by what has gone before. The Constitution changes only slowly and over time, and only when there is widespread consensus in favor of change. Again, this is a source of controversy. Some see this as the dead hand of the past controlling the present, others view it as the congealed wisdom of many generations operating to make a unity.

We will consider the Constitution itself as both symbol and instrument, and the place it plays in keeping our government on an even keel, according to some, or firmly anchored to a past that is gone forever, according to others. We will consider a particular aspect of this basic scheme of government, namely the federal system, and attempt to evaluate the place played by the states and the federal government today, as well as present points of view as to what place they should in fact play.

The Constitution: Symbol or Instrument?

The British writer, Walter Bagehot, in a famous passage suggested that a government must have two types of agencies—efficient instruments for carrying out actions and decorative branches of government for satisfying deep-felt human needs and emotions. In the British system, of course, this decorative or symbolic function is satisfied by the royal family. The furor aroused by criticism of that family shows that there are real emotional ties between the monarchy and the people.

In the American system most of this symbolism has centered around the Constitution and the Court. By providing a decorative element, a tie with the past, and a set of mysteries, the Constitution enriches American life with a focus for unity.

But if the Constitution is a symbol, the question remains: what does it symbolize? There have been many interpretations; most, but by no means all, favorable.

And the Constitution is not just a symbol but is an operating instrument as well. As such, it is not just the written Constitution that counts but also the customs, patterns, and conventions that have grown around it. So, for example, the Vice President succeeds on the death of the President and becomes President, although the Constitution does not make clear whether this was to have been the case or whether he would merely become Acting President. It is, in other words, the Constitution in operation that is the working Constitution.

As an instrument the Constitution is a source of political power, and is fought over because the wording of the Constitution is a form of strength or weakness for a particular group or program. The Constitution also provides a framework of operation which may accidentally or by purpose determine outcomes. It is also a method of governmental operations which either induces the solution of practical problems or hinders them. We will deal with basic operations of the American Constitutional system as a symbol of basic values and as an instrument in dealing with the problems of government.

1

AMERICAN SOCIETY*

Robin M. Williams, Jr.

How can the Constitution be a symbol of unity? If it is to have a definite symbolic content wouldn't that divide the country much as political parties or specific measures would? The following reading by Robin Williams attempts to show that different groups can read into the Constitution entirely different interpretations. To him it is the ambiguities of the Constitution that are its strength.

The powers of the government of the United States are set by the somewhat elastic but definitely constricting bounds of a written constitution. Around that document has gradually accumulated a tremendous number of interpretations and commentaries, of court decisions, of beliefs and myths. The Constitution enjoys a veneration that makes it a substantial barrier against sudden or far-reaching changes in the structure of the states. There is a "psychology of constitutionalism," a widespread conviction that the Constitution is sufficient to cover all emergencies, that deviations from its provisions are unnecessary and dangerous, that a breach of the Constitution would bring down the whole structure of ordered and lawful government.

When it was written, the Constitution was a drastic innovation, not only in its content but in its basic idea that the form of government could be pur-

---

* Robin M. Williams, Jr., *American Society* (New York: Alfred A. Knopf, Inc., 1951), pp. 224–25. © 1951 by Alfred A. Knopf, Inc. Reprinted by permission.

posively determined. It was radical in the root sense of that word. Yet, in a similar root sense, it has had conservative consequences. During the period of consolidation of authority and partial return to prerevolutionary conditions that always follows the instituting of a new state, the Constitution was one of the few symbols of national scope available to the loose federation of weak and disunited provinces. Furthermore, it has been a rallying point for conserving (maintaining) the political and civil liberties of individuals. But it has been conservative in a more conventional sense, also, for it was actually adopted in a period of what was close to counterrevolution, and a major force in its drafting and adoption was the desire to insure internal stability and the protection of property and trade. (The classical reference is Charles A. Beard: *An Economic Interpretation of the Constitution of the United States*, New York: 1913.) Undoubtedly the Constitution can be interpreted to conform to the interests of the more prosperous and propertied groups, and a stable legal order and venerated symbol of that order is advantageous to those interests.

This dual conservatism partly explains how it is that the Constitution can be defended with equal fervor by individuals whose motivations and interests are in most respects sharply opposed. The document has become almost a symbolic "sponge" that can absorb the allegiances of persons having amazingly diverse interests, values, ideas, political philosophies. Although the process by which this absorption occurs is not well understood (and is a research problem of first interest), its existence is probably of real importance to social stability. As with many other symbols of government, the very indefiniteness of the popularly imputed meanings facilitates a sense of order and integration not derivable from the specific applications of political doctrine. . . .

2

NINE MEN*

Fred Rodell

The ambiguities that Mr. Williams finds so desirable seem to Mr. Rodell to be a source of problems. The vagueness of the Constitution, says this Professor at Yale Law School, means that the judges are in the saddle. It is they who interpret the Constitution. The Constitution, then, symbolizes rule by the judiciary, which in turn means rule by the appointments of presidents elected years before.

. . . The old saw, beloved of history textbooks and political speeches, that "ours is a government of laws, not of men," is an insult and an undemocratic canard. Laws are words, nothing more. Laws do not write or enforce or interpret themselves. Even constitutions are no more than words except as

* Fred Rodell, *Nine Men* (New York: Random House, 1955), pp. 6–9. © 1955 by Fred Rodell. Reprinted by permission of the publishers.

men give them flesh and muscle and meaning in action; then the flesh and muscle are molded and the meaning in action is directed by men. The words of the Soviet constitution are in many ways more democratic than those of ours—as are the words of the constitutions of several Latin-American countries now run by dictators. And the cold truth about "laws, not men" was never better put than by one of the Founding Fathers, John Mercer of Maryland, who said what all of them were wise enough to know as they hammered out the U.S. Constitution back in 1787: "It is a great mistake to suppose that the paper we are to propose will govern the United States. It is the men whom it will bring into the government and interest in maintaining it."

Among those men, and most powerful of all of them for the past century and a half, are the Justices of the U.S. Supreme Court. They may say—and often do—that it is not *they* who make the decisions, lay down the rules, give orders to every other governing official in the land; they may say they do nothing but "interpret" the laws, including the Constitution; they may talk at times as though they neither had nor need human minds, as though they might almost as well be a nine-headed calculating machine, intricately adjusted to the words of the Constitution and of lesser laws, and ready to give automatic answers to any attorneys who drop their briefs in the proper slot and push the button. But even nonlawyers have come to find a trifle naïve and unconvincing the old fantasy that our government, especially its judicial branch, is mechanically controlled by laws, not by men. If it were, how explain split Supreme Court decisions (5–4, 6–3, 7–2, even 8–1); how explain dissenting opinions that too often make more sense than the majority "opinions of the Court"; how explain the "overruling" of past decisions—a term which means that the same question, decided one way before, is now decided exactly the opposite way? There was more truth than lawyerly discretion in the comment of Charles Evans Hughes, before he became Chief Justice of the United States: "We are under a Constitution, but the Constitution is what the judges say it is." The judges who say what the Constitution is have ranged throughout our history from the wise to the stupid, from the broad and brilliant to the narrow-minded and uninformed. No more than election to Congress or the Presidency ensures the ability of the man who is elected, does appointment to the Supreme Court ensure an able judge. For every Marshall, for every Holmes—who comes along sadly seldom, as does a Jefferson or a Lincoln—there will be scores of merely competent or middling or quite inept justices, who can often outweigh by numbers alone, if not by depth of insight or clarity of vision, their more capable colleagues. It is a telling and disturbing fact that no Supreme Court justice in the past half-century, save only Hughes, has achieved a generally acknowledged greatness except in dissent.

When a lame-duck senator is named to the Court to pay off a party's political debt to him, or a querulous attorney-general is kicked upstairs to the Court, or a lawyer-politician attains the Court because the president, by happenstance, knows and likes him personally, he does not become, by the process of donning a black gown and a solemn mien, a different man. He retains the same mind, the same personality, the same political perspectives and prejudices—plus the same ability or inability to govern wisely. But he has now been entrusted with tremendous governmental power, untrammeleled by anyone except his own colleagues, who may be as unable—or as able—as he. Warren G. Harding is not widely regarded as one of our first-rate presidents, but most people assume that his influence on national policy ended when death cut short his term of office. What is too easily forgotten is that the four mediocre or worse-than-mediocre justices whom he appointed dominated the Court and, through it, the country for years after his death. It has been said that the good a president does is oft interred with his bones but his choice of Supreme Court justices lives after him. It has also been said that "the Supreme Court follows the election returns"—although Mr. Dooley might have added "of ten or twelve years before."

* * *

3

READING THE CONSTITUTION ANEW*

Richard Hofstadter

What kind of men were these Founding Fathers who for many are symbolized by the Constitution? What did they intend by that document? Until the turn of the century they were uncritically admired in what one writer has called "the star-spangled manner." Under the impetus of the Progressive movement historians reevaluated this. The works of Charles Beard provided a shocking interpretation. He saw the Constitution as the product of an upper class trying to preserve property. This Economic Interpretation of the Constitution *was, until recently, the dominant approach to that period. Current work has thrown this into real question. The following book review of one of the most serious challenges to the Beard interpretation by one of the very leading American historians evaluates both Beard and the new theories.*

Every major turn in events seems to bring with it a turn in historical consciousness. . . . Such recent assessments of the American past as those made by Daniel Boorstin and Louis Hartz rest upon conceptions very different from those inherited by this generation from such of their forebears as Charles A. Beard or Frederick Jackson Turner. . . .

Beard had emphasized the social conflicts that gave rise to the Constitution and the political controversy that it caused. As he saw it, the Constitution was desired and created by a relatively small group of men who had a special interest in "personalty"—that is, not in land, but in property invested in commerce, shipping, manufacturing, and, above all, public securities. The framers of the Constitution, alarmed at the democratic tendencies of the state legislatures and at the feebleness of the Articles of Confederation, drafted a stronger instrument of central government. . . . The new government, far from being an extension of democracy, was an effort to check the power of majorities by men whose

* Richard Hofstadter, "Reading the Constitution Anew," *Commentary*, XXII, September 1956, 270–74.

political theory, as expressed in their deliberations, was antidemocratic. The presentation of the Constitution to the several states for ratification aroused a bitter conflict, which Beard traced to distinct social groupings. Although the document seemed to challenge the interests of agrarians generally, who constituted a majority of the population, and of debtors in particular, the proponents of the Constitution were able to win its acceptance because they were an aggressive elite, educated, concentrated in strategic places, keenly aware of their own interests; and because their agrarian opponents were scattered through the countryside, slow to move, ignorant of political affairs, or disfranchised by their inability to satisfy the property qualifications for voting.

In his *Charles Beard and the Constitution*, Professor Brown, a student of Colonial history who has written an important book on *Middle Class Democracy and the Revolution in Massachusetts, 1691–1780*, dogs Beard chapter, page by page, and paragraph by paragraph through his classic work, challenging practically every significant assessment of the evidence. No review can do justice to the bulk of even the important criticisms Brown makes. I hope it is not unjust to select two differences that he seems to consider of particular importance. The first of these is over the relative role of real and personal property among the interests that made the Constitution. Brown has little trouble in showing that the preponderance of real property among the propertied interests of America in 1787–88 was so heavy (even among the very men designated by Beard as the important "personalty holders") as to give us grave cause indeed to doubt the validity of Beard's strong emphasis on personalty. . . .

Brown's second major criticism, however, raises fundamental questions about the interpretation of American political experience. He asks once again how democratic, or undemocratic, the society was which adopted the new Constitution in 1788. Where Beard emphasized the disfranchisement of adult males through the suffrage qualifications, Brown's own study of Massachusetts has done much to prove the wide availability of the right to vote in that province in Colonial times; and other recent studies dealing with other states tend to bear out his thesis. Brown properly points out that some of the efforts to minimize the breadth of the suffrage have rested upon the elementary fallacy of comparing the number of eligible voters, or even the number of actual voters in a given election, with the *total* population instead of with the whole number of *adult males*. Using the suffrage as his primary test of democracy, he argues that the Constitution must be understood not as the product of a class society with acute internal conflicts between the elite and the mass, but rather of a "democratic middle-class society." . . .

The whole effect of Beard's book is to suggest that a great many . . . opposed it bitterly, but that "the people," being disfranchised and outmaneuvered by "the interests," went down to defeat. . . . Although Beard believed that this was in large part because they were disfranchised by property qualifications, he conceded in one very revealing passage that "far more were disfranchised through apathy and lack of understanding of the significance of politics," and in another, gave away a great part of his case with the sweeping admission that "the wide distribution of property created an extensive electorate." The difference for our view of the period between disfranchisement by property qualifications and "disfranchisement" through apathy or ignorance is an enormous one. . . . Brown puts it well when he says: "One of the master keys to an understanding of the Constitution is not how many men could not vote, but why so many having the vote did not use it. . . . When we stop talking about the 'mass of men' who *could not* vote on the Constitution and start talking about the 'mass of men' who *could* vote but did not bother to do so, then, and only then, will we understand the Constitution and its adoption. . . . The Constitution was adopted with a great show of indifference. . . ."

. . . The historiography of the future will be much closer to the argument of Brown's book than to Beard's. . . .

4

THE TWO CONSTITUTIONS*

Harold Stannard

What some see as a mere restraint others see as a rigid barrier. So some writers have suggested that the American system suffers from too many and too divergent rigid rules. One, for example, often criticized is the separation of presidential and congressional elections, resulting in hostile parties sometimes controlling the two political branches. Some of this criticism can be glimpsed in this picture by a British writer of the place of time in the American Constitution.

In America, on the other hand, there is no King; in his place there is the Constitution; and while the King never dies, the Constitution, being in itself a mere form of words, constantly needs to have the breath of life put into it. This process serves the same purpose and operates with the same motive of insuring the rule of law as the maintenance of custom (or more strictly convention) in England, and has thus taken over the English name. But the attendant circumstances are utterly diverse. The King who never dies has vanished, leaving a constitutional void to be filled, and the constitutional convention which fills it is one that is called into existence on a specific date for a specific job, and every detail of its progress can be chronologically indicated. The convention that gave the United States its Constitution began its work at Philadelphia on May 25th, 1787, reached its first vital decision at the end of that month, came to its crisis when June was passing into July, revised and considerably altered its decisions throughout August, and dissolved on September 17th. The ticking of the clock can be heard right through its proceedings and it can still be heard throughout the processes of the American Constitution. A member of the House of Representatives is elected for two years, a president for four, and a senator for six. The dates of their elections are fixed by the Constitution, and all the elaborate mechanism of constitutional amendment had to be put in operation a few years ago

* Harold Stannard, *The Two Constitutions* (Princeton, N.J.: D. Van Nostrand Co., Inc., 1949), pp. 19–21. © 1949, by the D. Van Nostrand Co., Inc.

to enable the interval between a President's election and his assumption of office to be shortened by some weeks.

All American politics are governed by the calendar and American life appears to regulate itself by the constitutional clock. Thus, the history of the world was substantially affected by the fact that 1916 was a presidential year and 1941 was not, and arrangements which, unless foreign policy remains common ground between parties, will put the United States out of action internationally for about one year in every four have still to be correlated with the march of events. In British politics the calendar does not count. In the last two and a half centuries Parliament has fixed the term of its life first at three years, then at seven, and then at five, and in no case has the term meant very much. The life of a Parliament can always be prolonged by its own legislation or shortened by dissolution. In the British Constitution time does not exist, because the Crown is immortal; in the American Constitution time dominates everything in place of the evicted Crown. The consequent difference, both in the structure and in the working of the institutions of the two countries, is enormous. . . .

* * *

5

CONSERVATISM BY AMENDMENT*

Clement E. Vose

The notion that the American system is too confining is an old one. But in recent years, alarmed at some of the political and constitutional developments of the last quarter century, conservatives have argued for more rather than less restrictions on governmental power. Professor Vose summarizes these proposals below. As he points out, conservatism through change is a paradoxical situation brought about by the onrush of events.

. . . Conservatives have responded to the national government's growth in power by producing a group of eight amendments designed to put a stop to it. This is a new departure. In the early part of this century it was the progressive reformer who was in the forefront of the effort to amend the Constitution. . . .

Now it is the political right that wants constitutional reform by amendment. So far it has scored only one success—the ratification, in 1951, of the 22nd Amendment, limiting the President to two terms in office. The remaining amendments being urged would (1) reform the system of electing the President; (2) set the number of Supreme Court justices at nine and provide for their retirement at 75; (3) prevent, without congressional approval, presidential seizure of private property in an emergency; (4) control the power of the President to make

---

* Clement E. Vose, "Conservatism by Amendment," *The Yale Review*, XLVI, Winter 1957, 176–78, 182, 185, 190.

executive agreements and limit the effect of national treaties on the states; (5) ease the procedure of amending the Constitution provided by Article V; (6) restrict the authority of Congress to levy taxes beyond 25 per cent of income; (7) limit the power of Congress to spend. . . .

To understand these procedures is to understand in large part the whole movement for new amendments to the Constitution. Since recent changes in the American constitutional system have been brought about by acts of Congress, by presidential action, by decision of the Supreme Court, those who wish to reverse these developments have to find some way to bypass these branches of the national government if their work is to be undone. Unless the nature of the President's electoral support is changed, these groups doubt their ability to elect or control a Chief Executive, and they have lost control of the Supreme Court. Accordingly, it is their design to make amendments to the formal, written Constitution because the established procedures permit this without any possible interference from President or Court.

The American Bar Association has been closely involved in the movement for constitutional reform. At one time, years ago, the association "owned" the Constitution, and now it hopes to regain control. Yet it is a big, heterogeneous organization with a broad spectrum of political shades within it. Dominated by small-town lawyers, the association's complicated committee system has been exploited to a high degree by proponents of the amendments. . . .

The movement for amendments sometimes appears to be a phenomenon of lawyers talking to each other.

These conflicts over federalism and the separation of powers should not be resolved without serious consideration by the entire American public. After all, the expansions in national power and the growth of the presidency took place under the constant influence of popular opinion. The constitutional system has evolved in its present form not through carelessness or neglect, not by conspiracy or hidden political sleight of hand, but through the wishes of a dominant majority. Changes in the constitutional order of things may be needed but we will not make satisfactory adjustments unless they are agreeable to most of the people of the country. Whether these can now be made through the infrequently used method of formal amendment is a doubtful proposition.

6

"OPPOSITION SLOWS AMENDMENT PUSH"*

Anthony Lewis

The principles suggested by Vose are still operative. The following recent news item suggests the potential of the amending process, which is itself susceptible of amendment.

The campaign for three "states' rights" amendments to the Constitution is running into stiffening opposition.

Politicians, newspapers, good-government groups, labor unions and civil rights organizations are beginning to speak out against the proposals. As a result, the rapid progress they made in the early months of 1963 has slowed almost to a stop.

However, conservative forces are still pressing hard for the proposals. Critical tests are coming up soon in Ohio and New Jersey.

The proposed amendments are being pushed by a committee of state legislators and officials. The backers are using the device, never before invoked, of petitioning Congress to call a constitutional convention on the proposals. Two-thirds of the state legislatures, 34, would have to ask Congress to call the convention.

One amendment would remove all constitutional restrictions on how the states apportion their legislatures, and bar federal courts from dealing with the problem. The effect would be to wipe out the Supreme Court's apportionment decision of 1962, which opened legislative districts to the scrutiny of Federal courts.

The second amendment would permit the state legislatures themselves to amend the Constitution in the future, without consideration in any national forum. Amendments must now be approved either by Congress or by a national convention.

The third amendment would set up a "Court of the Union" to review decisions of the Supreme Court. It would be made up of the chief justices of the 50 states.

A dozen state legislatures have approved the apportionment amendment, eleven the proposal on the amending process and three the suggested Court of the Union.

All this progress has been made since just last January. For most of this period the campaign for the amendments went on in virtual silence, with no publicity and frequently no debate in the legislatures voting for the proposals.

PUBLICITY STARTED

National publicity about the campaign began last month. This has apparently been responsible for arousing various forces that could be expected to oppose the amendments once they knew about them.

Newspapers and other communica-

* *The New York Times,* May 19, 1963, pp. 1, 81. Copyright by The New York Times Company. Reprinted by permission.

tions media began to note the swift progress of the amendments. Chief Justice Earl Warren commented, in a speech, on the lack of attention they had been getting.

Then, last week, President Kennedy spoke critically of the proposed amendments at his news conference. He said he believed that the efforts to pass them would "come to nothing, and I will be glad when they do."

Other critical comments were made by such groups as the American Civil Liberties Union, the American Jewish Committee and American Jewish Congress, the Liberal party in New York and others concerned with civil liberties. Branches of the League of Women Voters began taking an interest.

The National Association for the Advancement of Colored People and other civil rights organizations also started to protest. They said the apportionment proposal could be used to rig legislatures against Negroes—a politically powerful argument in northern urban states.

* * *

In addition to the other forces now working against the amendments, there have been signs of arousal in the legal community. Some bar groups are studying the proposals, and law professors are speaking against them.

7

UNWRITTEN RULES OF AMERICAN POLITICS*

John Fischer

John Fischer, editor of Harper's, *points up the difficulties of changing the Constitution in his discussion of the unwritten rules of American politics. The American Constitutional system represents a legal distribution of powers built on a diversified series of power groups. The result, as Fischer points out, is all too often inaction in the face of crisis, and the lack of anyone who can speak for the nation as a whole. Thus change, while always tantalizingly possible, is almost always out of political reach.*

. . . Surprisingly little has been written about the rules of American politics during our generation . . . The most useful discussion of this tradition which I have come across is the work of John C. Calhoun, published nearly a century ago. . . .

Calhoun summed up his political thought in what he called the Doctrine of the Concurrent Majority. He saw the United States as a nation of tremendous and frightening diversity—a collection of many different climates, races, cultures, religions, and economic patterns. He saw the constant tension among all these special interests, and he realized that the central problem of American politics was to find some way of holding these conflicting groups together.

It could not be done by force; no one

* John Fischer, "Unwritten Rules of American Politics," *Harper's Magazine,* November 1948, pp. 29–31. © 1955 by Harper & Row, Publishers, Incorporated. Reprinted from *Harper's Magazine* by permission of the author.

group was strong enough to impose its will on all the others. The goal could be achieved only by compromise—and no real compromise could be possible if any threat of coercion lurked behind the door. Therefore, Calhoun reasoned, every vital decision in American life would have to be adopted by a "concurrent majority"—by which he meant, in effect, a unanimous agreement of all interested parties. No decision which affected the interests of the slaveholders, he argued, should be taken without their consent; and by implication he would have given a similar veto to every other special interest, whether it be labor, management, the Catholic church, old-age pensioners, the silver miners, or the corn growers of the Middle West. . . .

. . . government by concurrent majority can exist only when no one power is strong enough to dominate completely, *and then only when all of the contending interest groups recognize and abide by certain rules of the game.*

These rules are the fundamental bond of unity in American political life. . . .

It is a rule which operates unofficially and entirely outside the Constitution—but it has given us a method by which all the official and constitutional organs of government can be made to work. It also provides a means of selecting leaders on all levels of our political life, for hammering out policies, and for organizing and managing the conquest of political power. . . .

The weaknesses of the American political system are obvious. . . . It is enough to note that most of the criticism has been aimed at two major flaws.

First, it is apparent that the doctrine of the concurrent majority is a negative one—a principle of inaction. A strong government, capable of rapid and decisive action, is difficult to achieve under a system which forbids it to do anything until virtually everybody acquiesces. In times of crisis, a dangerously long period of debate and compromise usually is necessary before any administration can carry out the drastic measures needed. The depression of the early Thirties, the crisis in foreign policy which ended only with Pearl Harbor, the crisis of the Marshall program all illustrate this recurring problem.

This same characteristic of our system gives undue weight to the small but well-organized pressure group—especially when it is fighting *against* something. . . .

An even more serious flaw in our scheme of politics is the difficulty in finding anybody to speak for the country as a whole. Calhoun would have argued that the national interest is merely the sum of all the various special interests, and therefore needs no spokesmen of its own—but in this case he clearly was wrong.

In practice, we tend to settle sectional and class conflicts at the expense of the nation as a whole—with results painful to all of us. . . .

IV

The Federal System: Instrument of Liberty or Inefficiency?

The federal system is certainly one of the distinguishing characteristics of American government. The existence within the same territory of two sets of governments, both at least theoretically deriving their powers separately creates problems and puzzles observers. When Khrushchev visited the United States, he was irritated by remarks of state and local officials, being convinced that they really were under the control of Washington. The federal system was really quite inexplicable to him, even though the Soviet Union is nominally a federal republic.

The independence of the states in many aspects of their activities has been held as a bulwark to freedom. It has been described as the product of a people that want "unity without uniformity." They see it as a protection against any tyranny which could not control the diverse states. They find these separate governments "laboratories for experimentation" and chambers for new programs.

But there are clearly costs as well. The boundaries, sizes, and populations vary tremendously. The existence of 51 different legal systems means that American government is highly legalized. Businesses must deal with elaborate sets of laws. Individuals often are penalized by the existence of different systems of laws while those who make a study of the complexities can often use them to personal advantage at the expense of the community.

Because of the rapid growth of national economy and dissatisfaction with state government, observers for a long time have been predicting the demise of the states. But, events belie these predictions. The states are as strong and as active as ever, growing in functions and in expenditures. The federal system seems to take on new patterns and meets new crises, but the American public appears to be very satisfied with the system as a whole.

States' Rights: Principle or Pretext?

From the time of Jefferson, the issue of states' rights has been a key slogan in American politics. Many claims have been made for federalism and continue to be made.

The slogan of states' rights has two aspects. On the one hand, it may be a claim of divisions of power and abstract issues. Maintenance of the federal system is a desire of American public opinion, particularly in the name of freedom or diversity.

The claim that federalism fosters freedom has some very responsible backing. Roscoe Pound has observed that no government of continental size has been governed except as a federal system or as an autocracy. The American suspicion of power is a source of the support that states' rights can evoke. From Madison to Calhoun to modern writers, the argument is advanced that too much centralism is a threat to human liberty. While Nelson Rockefeller presents the traditional American viewpoint, the late Professor Neumann of Columbia University examines the historical record and suggests that the evidence for the identification if freedom with federalism is shakier than others argue.

States' rights though is often used as an argument in the course of debate to strengthen a particular issue. While the argument is in terms of abstract states' rights, the real purpose is to advance a particular cause. History seems to suggest that any party long out of power begins to stress states' rights, while the dominant party increasingly finds virtues in greater Federal activity. The classical example is Jefferson's purchase of Louisiana, but the reversal in our times of the positions of the Democratic and Republican parties is also suggestive.

Federal Aid to the States: Help or Hindrance?

This century has seen a shift of power to the national government. This has been a relative matter; all units of government have grown so far as the expenditures and personnel are concerned. But, the federal government's have grown faster than the states', and the states' have grown more rapidly than the local governmental units. Today money is received from the national government and dispersed to local units.

Some see these programs as weakening state governments. The states, they argue, have lost their power of independent choice. They follow along in the trail of federal grants and aid. Others see these programs not only as socially desirable but as fostering better state government. They recognize the problems of state government—regarded as the weakest link in our current American governmental structure—but find the fault to lie in their own internal problems —notably their failure to reapportion and to develop strong leadership in the governor's office and in the legislature. The shift of powers to the federal government then is seen as the result of state weakness rather than the cause.

Nation, State, Cities: Partners or Rivals?

Grants-in-aid are only part of a bigger picture. The essential point is the relationship between the two (or three) levels of government. How do they get along in our system? What should be an ideal relationship? Does the existence of the states create rivalries and conflicts that perplex the citizen?

In recent years, there has been an increasing tendency for the national government to deal directly with the cities and eliminate the "middle man" states. Is this a healthy development or an increasing emasculation of the federal system?

Some have hailed interpenetration of the various levels of government as a brand new development. Others find it simply an application of principles and practices that have been in existence since the nineteenth century. Depending on your point of view, the sharing of functions in American federalism can be seen as a new "cooperative federalism" or as simply an application of the basic principles of the Constitution.

1

FREEDOM AND FEDERALISM*

Nelson Rockefeller

Nelson Rockefeller, while a serious candidate for presidential nomination, took time out to develop a series of lectures on the future of federalism. In this extract, he eloquently states the basis for identifying liberty and dispersion of power.

In the ominous spring of 1939, a bright and sunny May 3rd was a day marked by Adolf Hitler with another bellicose speech to the Reichstag calling for a showdown on Poland. On the same day, the League of Nations opened its "peace pavilion" at the World's Fair in New York City. And also on this same day, which seems so remote from the present instant, there was published a vigorous critique of

* Nelson Aldrich Rockefeller, *The Future of Federalism* (Cambridge, Mass.: Harvard University Press, 1962), pp. 1–9. Copyright, 1962, by The President and Fellows of Harvard College.

American political life by a visitor from abroad, famed in intellectual and academic circles, who had just delivered a series of lectures on the American presidency. The visitor was Harold J. Laski. And the obituary he wrote upon an historic American political doctrine bore the title: "The Obsolescence of Federalism."

How did Professor Laski conclude that the age of federalism was languishing near death?

He did concede that "federalism is the appropriate governmental technique for an expanding capitalism." But, he declaimed, a "contracting capitalism cannot afford the luxury of federalism." Leaping from this premise, he insisted that the failure of the federal idea was unmistakably plain not only in the United States but also elsewhere in the world—in Canada, Australia, Germany. And he explained this universal failure in these words: "Whether we take the conditions of labor, the level of taxation, the standards of education, or the supply of amenities like housing and recreation, it has become clear that the true source of decision is no longer at the circumference, but at the center, of the state. For 48 separate units to seek to compete with the integrated power of giant capitalism is to invite defeat in almost every element of social life where approximate uniformity of condition is the test of the good life."

The two decades since have dealt a harsh retort to Professor Laski's pronouncement on federalism in the United States. It has been proven wrong in economic, social, and political terms. . . .

Private enterprise has become more vigorous, more creative. . . . The grim prognosis of 30 years ago has also been proven wrong in strictly political terms. For federalism—its ideas and its practice—has continued to show itself the adaptable and creative form of self-government that the Founding Fathers of this nation conceived it to be. Decisions vital to national well-being have increasingly been made at the "circumference"—the states—as well as at the national "center," of political power.

These lectures are dedicated to the conviction that these basic political, social, and economic facts of life—and the lessons they carry for us—are crucial to the whole fate of freedom and of free men everywhere in this mid-twentieth century.

I do not use the word "freedom" casually. For nothing less than the historic concept of the free individual's worth and dignity, defined and attested by the whole Judeo-Christian tradition, is at stake in our world. . . .

THE FEDERAL IDEA

The federal idea: what does this mean?

Let me first make it clear that I do not speak of the federal idea as merely a mechanical or technical or abstract formula for government operations. I refer to the federal idea broadly as a concept of government by which a sovereign people, for their greater progress and protection, yield a portion of their sovereignty to a political system that has more than one center of sovereign power, energy, and creativity. No one of these centers or levels has the power to destroy another. Under the Constitution, for example, there are two principal centers of government power—state and federal. As a practical matter, local government, by delegation of state authority under the principle of "home rule," is a third such key center of power. The federal idea, then, is above all an idea of a shared sovereignty at all times responsive to the needs and will of the people in whom sovereignty ultimately resides.

Our federal idea is complex and subtle. It involves a balance of strengths. It puts into play a sharing of powers not only among different levels of government but—on each level—a separation of powers between the legislative, executive, and judicial branches of government. And it clearly signifies more than mere governmental structure. It demands faith in—and an environment for—the free play of individual initiative, private enterprise, social institutions, political organizations, and voluntary associations—all operating within a framework of laws and principles affirming the dignity and freedom of man.

A federal system, then, seeks stability without rigidity, security without inertia. It encourages innovation and inventiveness—governed by principle, and guided by purpose. It assures responsiveness more thoughtful than mere reflex—and liberty that does not lapse toward anarchy. In short, it seeks to hold the delicately precarious balance between freedom and order upon which depend decisively the liberty, peace, and prosperity of the individual. . . .

By providing several sources of political strength and creativity, a federal system invites inventive leadership—on all levels—to work toward genuine solutions to the problems of a diverse and complex society. These problems—whether they concern civil rights or urban development, industrialization or automation, natural resources or transportation—never arise at the same instant and in the same way throughout a great nation. A federal system, however, allows these problems to be met at the time and in the area where they first arise. If local solutions are not forthcoming, it is still possible to bring to bear the influence, the power, and the leadership of either the state or the national government.

2

FEDERALISM AND FREEDOM: A CRITIQUE*

Franz L. Neumann

Not all writers find the argument conclusive. Franz Neumann examines the record of history and finds the case not proven. Freedom's link to federalism is vague, but the costs of federalism are clear.

The theoretical argument for federalism revolves around the potential of political power for evil. Federalism is seen as one of the devices to curb the evil use of power by dividing power among a number of competing power-units.

In its most radical form, this sentiment appears in the various anarchist schemes. It has been popular in the anarcho-syndicalist theories and prac-

---

* Franz L. Neumann, "Federalism and Freedom: A Critique," in *Federalism Mature and Emergent*, ed. Arthur W. MacMahon. (New York: Doubleday & Company, Inc., 1955), pp. 45–49, 53–54. © by the Trustees of Columbia University in the City of New York. Reprinted by permission.

tices of the Latin-speaking countries and with the IWW of the United States.

It is Lord Acton's statement on the corruptive effect of political power which appears to have today the greatest influence: Power tends to corrupt and absolute power corrupts absolutely. Great men are almost always bad men.[1] And Montesquieu[2] said this even more clearly. According to him[3] power could be checked only by power—a statement that few would be willing to quarrel with. Not ideologies and beliefs but only a counterpower can check power. In this he applies Cartesian principles and stands in the tradition of Spinoza who saw no way of limiting the state's absoluteness (which was logical consequence of his assumptions and of his geometric method) except by a counterpower.

The Montesquieu generalization is, of course, designed to give his doctrine of the separation of powers an adequate theoretical base. But as little as the theory of separate powers follows from his sociological observation, as little does that of the preferability of the federal state. Bentham[4] rejected the separation of powers not only as incompatible with democracy but also because it could not really maximize freedom if the three organs of government were controlled by the same social group. A quite similar argument can be raised against federalism as a guarantee for liberty. Those who assert that the federal state through the diffusion of *constitutional* powers actually diffuses *political* power often overlook the fact that the real cause for the existence of liberty is the pluralist structure of society and the multiparty (or two-party) system.[5] Federalism is not identical with social pluralism; and neither the two-party nor the multiparty system is the product of the federal state or the condition for its functioning.

Whether the federal state does indeed increase freedom[6] cannot be abstractly determined. We have some evidence that the federal state as such (that is, regardless of the form of government) has not fulfilled this role. The German Imperial Constitution certainly created a federal state but there is little doubt that politically it had a dual purpose: to be a dynastic alliance against the forces of liberalism and democracy,[7] and to secure the hegemony of Prussia.[8]

Perhaps more striking are the respective roles of federalism and centralism in the coming to power of National Socialism. Some believe, indeed, that the centralization under the Weimar Republic is wholly or at least partly responsible for the rise of National Socialism. But there is no evidence for this statement—nor indeed for the opposite one. It is certain that Bavaria, with the strongest states' rights tradition, gave shelter to the National Socialist movement and it is equally certain that the federal character of the

---

[1] Quotations taken from G. Himmelfarb, *Lord Acton, A Study in Conscience and Politics* (Chicago: University of Chicago Press, 1952), p. 161.

[2] My edition of the *Spirit of the Laws* (New York: Hafner Library of Classics, 1949), XI, 4.

[3] See my Introduction, *ibid.*, pp. lvii–lviii.

[4] Bowring, ed., IX, 41ff.; and Elie Halevy, *The Growth of Philosophical Radicalism* trans. Mary Morris (New York: The Macmillan Company, 1928), pp. 258–59.

[5] See my Montesquieu Introduction, pp. lvii and lxiv.

[6] Cf. Carl J. Friedrich, *Constitutional Government and Democracy* (Boston: Ginn & Company, 1946), pp. 216–17.

[7] Rudolf Schlesinger, *Federalism in Central and Eastern Europe* (New York: Oxford University Press, Inc., 1945), p. 71.

[8] K. C. Wheare, *Federal Government* (New York: Oxford University Press, Inc., 1947), p. 15.

Weimar Republic did not, after Hitler's appointment, delay the process of synchronization (*Gleichschaltung*) of the various state governments. Nor is there any definable relation between democratic conviction and federalist (or unitary) sympathies. The National Socialists were both centralists and reactionary, as were the Nationalists. Democrats and Social Democrats were antifederalists and committed to the preservation of political freedom. The Catholic center was not wholeheartedly committed to any position, and the Communists were, in theory, for the unitary state but did not hesitate, during the revolution of 1918, to advocate the secession of Brunswick which they believed they had in their pocket.

The evidence is certainly too slight to be of great value in determining whether the federal system is preferable to the unitary state as an instrument to preserve or enhance civil liberties. Nor is it likely that convincing evidence can be obtained, since other factors—the plurality of the social structure, the functioning of a truly competitive party system, the strength of a favorable tradition, the intellectual level of the population, the attitude of the courts—do far more easily permit the formation of a counterpower against forces hostile to civil liberties than does the federal structure of the government.

If federalism, as such, has nothing in it that automatically guarantees the preservation of political freedom, American federalism may have features that have hindered the solution of pressing economic problems.[9] The impact of the American federal system, of the division of powers, on the condition of this country in the Thirties was not reassuring.

George C. S. Benson, in his book *The New Centralization*,[10] tried to show how federalism worked in the setting of the Great Depression.

First, he found federalism as an "obstruction of social legislation." The states hesitated to enact this legislation not only for fear of placing their manufacturers at a competitive disadvantage with manufacturers of states that did not regulate wages and hours and provide benefits, but also for fear of driving larger industries into these latter states.[11]

Secondly, there was great disparity among the states' financial resources. Not only were most states incapable of financing serious efforts at reform, but "Complete decentralization—complete local responsibility for governmental services—may then result in a 'spread' between the standards of different districts which would shock even the uncritical believer in a national 'American' standard."[12]

Thirdly, Benson found little evidence that the states were really the "experimental laboratories" they were pictured to be.[13]

Fourthly, the ability of the states to put programs into action in an efficient way was seriously questioned.

Lastly, the nature of the economic system is such that its workings were and are obviously not confined to the territory of any given city or state. "As our great business concerns grow more specialized and conduct larger scale operations in an age of complicated machinery, government cannot be ex-

[9] For a discussion of this situation in Australia, see A. P. Canaway, *The Failure of Federalism in Australia*, London, Oxford University Press, 1930.

[10] New York, Farrar and Rinehart, 1941. On this problem see, in addition, Harold Laski, "The Obsolescence of Federalism," *The New Republic*, Vol. 98 (May 3, 1939), pp. 367–69.

[11] Benson, *op. cit.*, pp. 23–24.

[12] *Ibid.*, p. 30.

[13] *Ibid.*, p. 38.

pected to remain simple and pastoral."[14]

In sum, as Professor Key has written, "A characteristic of the federal system seems to be that entrenched interests in the long run can better protect themselves in dealing with state legislatures than with Congress or with federal administrators."[15]

[14] *Ibid.*, p. 40.

[15] V. O. Key, Jr., *Politics, Parties, and Pressure Groups*, 3rd ed. (New York: Thomas Y. Crowell Company, 1952), p. 102.

3

THE SOVEREIGN STATES*

James Jackson Kilpatrick

States' rights has also in recent years been asserted by critics of the Supreme Court decisions with regard to measures of internal security and segregation, in particular. This has led in turn to calls for changes in the Court, on the one hand, or resistance, on the other. A leading exponent until 1958 of massive resistance as a program for averting integration, James Jackson Kilpatrick is a Southern editor who is regarded as being closely informed and consulted on current Virginian policy. He here calls for interposition—the final extension of states' rights.

The decision in the school segregation cases was not the first major usurpation of power by the Supreme Court in the postwar period. It was merely the most flagrant. It is keenly important to understand that the trend put newly in motion under Vinson's court continues, at increasing speed, under Warren's administration. If states outside the South are to comprehend the peril before them, they would do well to look beyond the frontal fight of Brown vs. Board of Education to the flanking decisions in which state powers also are being steadily destroyed.

Half a dozen such mileposts will suffice to mark the way. They involve drillers for oil off California and the Gulf; a small trucker in Pennsylvania; a railwayman named Hanson; a Communist, Steve Nelson; a professor of German, Harry Slochower; a thief named Griffin. Their cases are all a part of the ending and beginning. . . .

These cases (and countless others could be cited) define a trend: The deification of the federal government, and the steady stultification of the states. They point to a problem, a great and difficult constitutional problem. It certainly is not a new one. It existed in Jefferson's day, and in Calhoun's, and for that matter, in Teddy Roosevelt's also. It is to preserve unto the states, for good or ill, that which is the proper function of the federal government. Yet to an ominous degree, the problem now is far more acute than it has ever been before. When Jefferson and Cal-

* James Jackson Kilpatrick, *The Sovereign States* (Chicago: Henry Regnery Company, 1957), pp. 286–87, 304–5

houn were protesting most furiously, enormous areas of public administration remained to the states; even at the turn of the century, states' rights still held some meaning. Now, month by passing month, the states steadily are being stripped of the last of their sovereign powers—not by their own wish, as expressed through constitutional amendment—but by judicial usurpation. Those who had conceived the Constitution itself to be the supreme law of the land are now told, imperiously, that today's opinions of the Court, however palpably in violation of the Constitution these mandates may be, are supreme above all things. We are told to bow and fawn before a judicial oligarchy which has asserted unto itself powers as arrogant as those of any tyrant: "This is compassionate," says the Court, "*therefore* it is constitutional." This, in the Court's view, is socially desirable; therefore the Court will make it the law. And to resist, as in Clinton, is to travel in handcuffs to Knoxville, there to face prosecution for contempt.

The end of this process is the corruption of a constitutional Union, by judicial fiat, into a consolidated government in which the states are mere political dependencies. The end is a centralization of all meaningful powers in the hands of federal authority. And so long as the constructions placed by the Court upon the Constitution are agreeable to one-third of the House of Representatives, plus one, timely remedy cannot even be found in constitutional amendment.

The remedy lies—it must lie—in drastic resistance by the states, *as states*, to federal encroachment. "If those who voluntarily created the system cannot be trusted to preserve," asked Calhoun, "who can?" The checking and controlling influence of the people, exerted as of old, through their states, can indeed preserve the constitutional structure. The right to interpose the will of the sovereign people, in order that the evils of encroachment may be arrested, once more can be exerted toward the preservation of a Union and the dignity of states.

A long time ago, a great Virginian had this to say: "So far as our (federal) government is concerned, I venture to predict that it will become absolute and irresponsible, precisely in proportion as the rights of the states shall cease to be respected and their authority to interpose for the correction of federal abuses shall be denied and overthrown."

Abel Parker Upshur's prediction of 1840 has been grimly fulfilled. The American people have lost sight of the old concept that the states, as such, form the balance wheel—in Upshur's term, "The only effectual check upon federal encroachments." We have lived to see the truth of his prophecy, that the danger to constitutional separation of powers is "not that the states will interpose too often, but that they will rather submit to federal usurpations, than incur the risk of embarrassing the government, by any attempts to check and control it."

The states have submitted too long to federal usurpations. At their grave peril, they can submit no longer. Through every device of interposition they can bring to bear—political, legislative, judicial—once more they must invoke their sovereign powers to insist that federal encroachments be restrained. . . .

4

THERE IS NO STATE POINT OF VIEW*

Edward W. Weidner

States' rights, however, is not just an argument for state power. At its roots the argument stems from the claims and programs of groups seeking to advance some cause. As such, states' rights may be a valid argument or simply a mask for some privileged group.

It is a thesis of the present discussion that in the federal system in the United States there are relatively few direct clashes or compromises between state and national governments on large issues of national domestic policy. . . . The disagreements and conflicts that do arise and that may be encouraged by federalism's structural features are not basically clashes between much smaller groups of people, and the opposing groups are located within a single governmental level as often as not. . . .

While differences on public policy or values are to be expected in a country containing as many heterogeneous elements as are to be found in the United States, it does not necessarily follow that officials in the several states will take one policy position and those of the national government another. Indeed, . . . it would seem surprising if this were the case, given the diversity of conditions in the several states and the fact that the union is made up of all states. "States' rights" is only one of numerous values held by state officials, and it is relatively unimportant to many of them. The prime thing that the states have in common is their existence; it is possible that if an issue were presented that threatened the very existence of the states, their political officials might be brought together. In actual fact, a major issue of this kind has not been presented. Consequently, usually national government officials can find many of their state counterparts who support national policy objectives and many others who oppose. And among the states, differences in values are the rule. . . .

The states have been unable to follow a single course even in such comparatively noncontroversial areas as are covered by the so-called uniform state laws. If minimum standards are desired for the nation as a whole in a particular policy area such as health or welfare, it is the central government that must act to assure these ends. To leave the matter exclusively to the states means that there will be a variation in standards from very low to quite high. To set up a system of joint national-state participation means that standards and practices will vary much more than in a system of central action alone. It also means that some disagreement and conflict are inevitable because officials in various states will not all see eye-to-eye with those of the

* Edward W. Weidner, "Decision-Making in a Federal System," *Federalism Mature and Emergent*, ed. Arthur W. MacMahon. (New York: Doubleday & Company, Inc., 1955), pp. 363, 365–69, 376–77.

national government in terms of the objectives of the program.

This is not to blame the states in any way for their actions. Rather it is to recognize that public policy is in large part the result of the values that men hold and that these values vary from individual to individual and group to group. It would be unexpected and surprising if the several states followed identical or even similar courses of action on important public issues. The normal expectancy is that they will differ in greater or lesser degree among themselves in regard to policies they enact and in regard to the policies of the national government. . . .

The values that individuals hold are so diverse that there is no definable "state" point of view in intergovernmental relations as a whole. Even if the 48 governors were considered to be spokesmen for their entire states, there does not emerge a single state approach to intergovernmental relations. Occasionally all the governors will agree on a minor point or two but they have never agreed that a specific general reallocation of activities should take place between national and state governments. This is understandable since some of them are Democrats, some Republicans; some are liberals, others conservatives; some have national political ambitions, others do not; some come from poor states, others from well-to-do areas. These are only a few of the variables that affect the approach governors take on national-state relations. Much of the publicity arising from recent political events, Governors' Conferences, and the Council of State Governments tends to give the impression that all governors demand that certain functions and tax resources of the national government be turned over to the states. The impression is erroneous. It is true that the governors probably defend states' rights as vigorously as any other group of public officials; they tend to stress expediency values relative to state government. In part this is a function of their role as chief executive and chief party leader. Nevertheless, such a set of values may be subordinate to many other considerations, and consequently consensus is not easily forthcoming. . . .

Disagreement or conflict in national-state relations is limited. It is not a matter that normally determines election results or on which there is a clear public opinion. General issues of national-state relations have concerned only a small minority of individuals and groups in recent decades, usually a group of public officials at each level and a few interest groups outside the framework of government. When an important new substantive policy for the national government is under consideration, national-state wide relations may take on a broader significance, as was the case in welfare and labor policy during the Thirties. As a whole, however, interest groups and public opinion have not found states' rights an attractive theme unless by the defense of states' rights they could defend some programmatic value. . . .

Administrative and legislative officials alike are of the opinion that the main clash of values occurs within a unit of government rather than between units. This is true even in regard to the issues arising from intergovernmental programs. . . . This is not to deny that there are some who defend states' rights or local self-government through a genuine concern for decentralism and not on the basis of expediency. . . . However, situations where the programmatic values of professional administrators are overridden by their expediency values are not frequent. . . .

5
HOW TO KEEP OUR LIBERTY*

Raymond Moley

Advocates of states' rights have diagnosed their problem as in part constitutional and in part financial. They deplore Supreme Court decisions and actions by President and Congress forwarding national power. But they especially argue that it is the present system of taxation which gives the federal government the lion's share of the tax dollar that ultimately makes it powerful. This has resulted in such proposals as the one to limit the income tax. Here is a sample argument by a leading columnist and political science professor, who was one of the first architects of the New Deal—the original head of Roosevelt's "Brain Trust"—and is currently a leading spokesman for conservative ideas.

THE FEDERAL INVASION OF THE STATES—ROBBING PETER

The American Constitution was designed to preserve personal liberty by several means. Very important among these was the assurance of state sovereignty and, with it, local government. The ascendancy of the federal government is the deadly enemy not only of the states but of the citizens of the states. For socialism must seek its final objective on a national level.

To attain domination, the federal leviathan must first seize the sources of state and local revenue—revenue that is the life blood of government. The extent of this seizure has already been most alarming.

The Hoover Commission's task force on federal-state relations points out that in 1890 the Federal government spent 36.2 per cent of all governmental outlays in the nation. In 1946, it spent 85.2 per cent. In 1890 local units spent 55.6 per cent. The state governments in 1946 spent 7.6 per cent.

The adoption of the federal income tax marked the beginning of a rapid rise of federal authority and the decline of state and local importance. Before the federal income tax was adopted, the federal government derived nearly all its revenue from customs, liquor, and tobacco taxes. The income tax immediately assumed major importance, but during World War I the federal government seized several other sources of revenue, including various admissions taxes, stamp taxes, and manufacturers' excise taxes. Later it added motor fuel, gifts, and estates to its taxable sources. Other sources have been seized as they have been found, always with small regard for the prior possession of states and localities.

This money is not made in Washington. It comes from the states. The sources from which states have drawn their own revenue have been taken by the federal suction pump. Almost every

* Raymond Moley, *How to Keep Our Liberty* (New York: Alfred A. Knopf, Inc., 1952), pp. 109–13. © 1952 by Raymond Moley. Reprinted by permission of the publishers.

productive source of taxation, except the property tax, has been lost to most of the states.

The result is utter confusion and overlapping of taxes. The same sources may be taxed several times, and taxpayers themselves have only the faintest notion of what they pay, what they pay for, and whom they are paying.

A large part of the collections of the federal government comes from such overlapping taxes. And the proportion of the federal "bite" from these sources is steadily getting larger. In 1934 its share of the taxes from these sources was 63 per cent. In 1946, it was 91 per cent.

Since all governments—federal, state, and local—follow the Donnybrook slogan, "Hit the heads you see!" obvious sources are hit hard, and more difficult but fair sources are neglected.

Since the greatest growth of federal power has taken place in the two wars and in the depression, it is easy to predict that in the great crisis created by the threat of communism this absorption of local sources of revenue will continue at an increasing rate. States are at a great disadvantage in this competition. The federal income tax is all-powerful. Moreover, an individual state has the handicap of trying to avoid driving individuals and businesses to other states that have more favorable taxes.

TO PAY PAUL

The grave danger of all this is that the state and local governments, which are close to the vital needs of the people and are under close observation by them, will become less competent to perform their proper functions. These protective divisions of our nation will wither for lack of nourishment.

Along with this progressive seizure of state and local sources of revenue, and on the overworked theory that under modern economic conditions the problems of government override state boundaries, the federal government has stolen from the states many of their traditional powers and functions. Assistance to the aged and unfortunate, highway building, the regulation of business and labor, the control of elections and primaries, the enforcement of criminal law, and many other activities of the states have been partially taken over by federal authority.

Under a constant enlargement of federal jurisdiction made possible by a more and more "liberal" interpretation of the Constitution by the Supreme Court, almost every aspect of competition and private business and labor is now subject to federal law. Consequently, state legislation in many of those fields has become meaningless. Regulation has loosed upon the states a horde of federal bureaucrats who have little sympathy for local customs, preferences, and protections, and who are responsible only to Washington. This condition has grown much worse during the war and in the subsequent cold war.

Great federal enterprises for defense and related purposes have grown up, with payrolls so large that local communities have become increasingly dependent upon them. This has seriously impaired local independence.

Federal power has grown immensely through grants-in-aid to the states. Through such grants the federal government now influences or controls 75 per cent of state activities. Under the pretext of successive crises—the depression, the war, and the cold war—the size and variety of these grants have grown at a tremendous rate. Fifty years ago, only $3,000,000 was paid out of federal funds to the states. By 1912, grants had risen to $4,255,000. From then on, the march began in earnest, in part because the federal income tax with its unlimited power over incomes became operative, and in part because of the great requirements of World War I. . . . Under President Truman's administration, these grants have risen until in 1950 the sum was nearly $2,234,700,000. This is the most graphic way of describing the deterioration of a great constitutional system.

There has also been a parallel and consistent decline of local self-government through the increase of state grants to cities, counties, and other small units of government. In five years, state grants to localities have increased by a third.

A special evil in the development of federal power under President Roosevelt was the habit of by-passing the states in extending aid to cities and other local units of government. In the administration of relief under Harry Hopkins, this was a calculated political objective. The federal machine thus made a close alliance with city machines through the granting of relief money, to the political advantage of both.

Where money goes the bureaucrat follows. Money means power. And power begets control.

This trend, if continued, will ultimately erase local self-government and reduce the states to the status of mere agents or provinces of the federal government. The balance system created by the Constitution will be gone, and national socialism will have eliminated its most formidable barrier.

6

RESOLUTION OF THE 85TH GENERAL ASSEMBLY OF THE STATE OF INDIANA*

Moley's analysis was accepted by the 85th General Assembly of the State of Indiana. That state has long had a vigorous conservative wing of the Republican party. Under the leadership of that group, it adopted the following resolution which reflects some of the classic arguments of state sovereignty.

Indiana needs no guardian and intends to have none. We Hoosiers—like the people of our sister states—were fooled for quite a spell with the magician's trick that a dollar taxed out of our pockets and sent to Washington will be bigger when it comes back to us. We have taken a good look at said dollar. We find that it lost weight in its journey to Washington and back. The political brokerage of the bureaucrats has been deducted. We have decided that there is no wealth to tax that is not already within the boundaries of the 48 states.

So we Propose henceforward to tax ourselves and take care of ourselves. We are fed up with subsidies, doles and paternalism. We are no one's stepchild. We have grown up. We serve

* House Concurrent Resolution No. 2. Reprinted from *The Freeman*, November, 1958, p. 33.

notice that we will resist Washington, D.C. adopting us.

Be it Resolved by the House of Representatives of The General Assembly of the State of Indiana, The Senate concurring: That we respectfully petition and urge Indiana's Congressmen and Senators to vote to fetch our county court house and city halls back from Pennsylvania Avenue. We want government to come home. *Resolved, further,* that we call upon the legislatures of our *sister states* and on *good citizens everywhere* who believe in the basic principles of Lincoln and Jefferson to join with us, and we with them to restore the American Republic and our 48 states to the foundations built by our fathers.

7

"WHAT'S REALLY WRONG WITH STATE GOVERNMENTS?"*

Richard L. Neuberger

Is the present weakness of state government to be accounted for by the grant-in-aid system or by their own failures? The following discussion by the late United States Senator from Oregon, a former state legislator as well, is typical of many who believe that the states, by and large, have been inefficient and inadequate to the problems of the twentieth century. This, they see as the cause of federal expansion.

. . . the loudest devotees of states' rights often act more anxious than anyone else to get on the federal payroll. . . . This is demonstrated by the fact that nearly a third of the present Senate consists of erstwhile governors. The old, gingerbread state executive mansions have been only halfway-houses on the road to Washington for these 28 men, who blithely deserted state duties to serve the federal colossus. And they number in their ranks . . . lusty verbal champions of state supremacy . . . On many dramatic occasions the governor was invested with the power of life and death. Monarch of all he surveyed, the governor could command a vast horde of state employees, few of them fettered by civil service. Furthermore, he was constantly titillated by knowledge of governors of the recent past who had gone all the way, such as Woodrow Wilson of New Jersey, Calvin Coolidge of Massachusetts, and Franklin D. Roosevelt of New York.

But state government has not been up to the triple challenge of the great depression, global war, and rocketing inflation. The problems created by these events have been far beyond its scope. Anchored though the federal government may be by tradition and checks and balances, it has the agility of a ballet troupe contrasted with the 48 states.

---

* Richard L. Neuberger, *Adventures in Politics* (New York: Oxford University Press, Inc., 1954), pp. 4–7; 11–16; 26. Copyright by Maurine Neuberger. Reprinted by permission.

A lawyer who aspires to be Attorney General of Idaho must, if he is resolutely honest, gear himself to a salary of $5000 a year. . . . While a United States Senator from Oregon is allowed $39,540 annually to hire an office staff, the Governor of Oregon must handle infinitely more administrative responsibilities with a payroll of $28,296. Utah's governor has ruled a state of 700,000 people for a wage of $7500, which is less than that paid to innumerable functionaries in federal bureaus. And the pay for state legislators makes even these salaries seem of movie-star proportions by comparison. Few states compensate their lawmakers enough to pay for bacon and beans and blankets while bivouacked at the state capitol, to say nothing of keeping the home-fires going. . . .

Why have the states lost so much of their sovereignty? Why do many able men contradict their own speeches by rushing pell-mell to Washington, D.C. at the first political opportunity and then rarely returning to state government after defeat at the polls?

With a few exceptions—New York being one—state government is attempting to operate with stone-age tools. Legislators who write state laws and state executives who enforce them are, for the most part, part-time officials. They can give their responsibility to the state only a lick and a promise. Other sources provide their basic incomes. Where the treasure is, there is the heart—and the vote. These men are not free to make the public interest their exclusive concern. They must cater to special interests or they don't eat. . . .

I would list five fundamental reasons for the decline of state government in the United States, a deterioration which has accelerated in recent years. These are the reasons:

1. The part-time status and negligible salaries of state legislators and most state district attorneys.
2. The failure to reapportion legislatures so they will represent a state's population as it exists today, not as it did in the frontier past.
3. Detailed and cluttered state constitutions that lace state governments in a rigid strait jacket.
4. The one-party political domination which prevails in nearly half the states.
5. The fact that state elections are held simultaneously with presidential elections and congressional elections.

The last point may seem innocuous, and yet it tells why the bulk of the basic problems confronting state government seldom get through to the electorate.

Nearly everywhere in the country candidates for governor and the state legislature run as Republicans or Democrats. But people judge the two parties preponderantly on such questions as the Korean War or federal price controls or an ability to cope with the menace of Russian communism. Occasionally some burning state issues break through the federal curtain, but they must generate great heat to do so. Who can ignore the fact that the only Democrat to be elected governor of California in modern times was successful at the height of FDR's national glory? On the other hand, Republicans achieved their most decisive recent victories in Washington state legislative elections during 1946 and 1952, when the Democratic party was not necessarily at low ebb in the state of Washington but when it was faring badly in the country as a whole. . . .

I have a mustached friend in the parliament of one of Canada's prairie provinces. He at first refused to believe my comment that state and national elections were held customarily on the same day in the United States. "Why," he exclaimed, "that's bound to put the result in the state almost completely at the mercy of the national trend! We wouldn't think of scrambling up our provincial and federal elections. They don't have any relation to each other." . . .

On a national basis the one-party states tend to cancel out each other, which explains why the rule of neither Democrats nor Republicans in Washington, D.C., ever has remotely approached the political tyranny which is the normal condition of things in many states. It also explains why the states have been so backward in responding to public opinion. Does a majority party heed popular rumblings when its hegemony is almost as secure as if held by whip and fire? The Republicans with whom I serve in the Oregon legislature are as arrogant as maharajas, and I have no doubt that my fellow Democrats in Raleigh, the state capitol of North Carolina, are every bit as smug and superior. . . .

Thus we find that state government is determined by two strangely contrasting sets of factors: in half the states the election of the legislature and governor is dictated almost entirely by national tendencies that are remote from state affairs; and in the other half of the states, there almost might as well be no election at all, for regardless of corruption or reaction or extravagance with the taxpayers' money, the same dominant party within the state just keeps rolling along.

A person unfamiliar with state constitutions would not believe what he was reading if he had thrust upon him the basic charters that govern many of the 48 states.

To begin with, most of these constitutions are incredibly long. Although the Constitution of the United States contains but 7500 words, the constitution of the state of Oklahoma totals 34,000 words, that of Louisiana 63,000 words, and that of California a massive 72,000 words. By attaining the length of a detective novel, a constitution inevitably will include many needless and absurd inhibitions on state government. . . .

Most of the circumstances which have put state government on the toboggan slide can be rectified through a wholesale overhauling of state constitutions. . . .

Constitution revision can provide the states with twentieth-century tools. It will not, of course persuade men and women in the one-party states to let the hated opposition have a try. That is a matter for education and for future generations.

8
THE MISTAKES OF THE ULTRA-CONSERVATIVE STATES' RIGHTERS*

Wayne Morse

One of the first acts of the Eisenhower Administration in 1952 was to establish a Commission on Intergovernmental Relations to make the first over-all evaluation of American federalism ever officially attempted. It was expected that drastic curtailment of federal power would be recommended by the Commission. Instead, the Kestnbaum Report, as it came to be called, made very moderate recommendations for strengthening the states, and found the system now operating healthy and efficient. At least one member of the Commission thought this rather friendly report still not strong enough in endorsing the ultimate responsibility of the federal government for general welfare. Senator Morse, known for his strong statements, emphatically rejects any states' rights argument built on hostility to the national government.

The ultra-conservative point of view fails to give due emphasis to the general welfare clause of the Constitution. It fails to recognize that the impelling motivation of our constitutional forefathers was to form a political society of free men and women for the purpose of promoting the general welfare of all, through a system of representative government in which the people by way of checks and balances would remain the masters of governmental affairs.

The ultra-conservative tends to overlook the dynamics of the constitutional doctrines written into our basic law. He overlooks the flexibility and adjustability of those doctrines to changing social, economic, and political conditions from decade to decade. He tends to interpret the Constitution as a system of static rules to be applied by a dead, rather than a living, hand of the law. The ultra-conservative would take us back to a laissez-faire economy which, if actually put into practice, would undermine the economic freedom of choice for individual citizens, upon the basis of which system the very perpetuation of enlightened capitalism depends. He prates about the need for a hands-off policy on the part of the federal government, or for that matter the state governments too, in economic affairs. He recommends an unfettered operation, as far as government is concerned of the economic jungle law of supply and demand, even though experience shows the resulting exploitation of the economic weak whenever the doctrines of laissez-faire and supply and demand come to domi-

* Separate statement by Senator Morse regarding the Commission Report, in *Report to the President*, Commission on Intergovernmental Relations (Washington, D.C.: Government Printing Office, 1955), pp. 277–79.

nate our national economy. He would have the federal government relinquish more and more of its sovereign rights and duties in the field of interstate commerce, natural resources, monopoly control, taxation, civil rights, and yes, in almost every field in which the enforcement of federal jurisdiction is essential to promoting and protecting the general welfare of the people of the nation as a whole.

We cannot escape the fact that the general welfare of our people as a whole cannot be dissected according to state lines. If the constitutional liberal is right in his contention that the promotion of the general welfare of our people is the keystone of our constitutional system, then that fact dictates that the several states and the federal government should approach issues involving national interests on a coordinated and cooperative basis. However, that does not mean that coordination and cooperation is a one-way street, calling upon the federal government to delegate more and more of its federal sovereignty to the states. To the contrary, the constitutional liberal contends that the general welfare of our people will not be promoted unless the sovereign rights of the federal government are applied and administered uniformly across the nation as a whole.

One of the great dangers in the growing demand on the part of ultraconservative pressure groups for a delegation of more and more federal jurisdiction to the states, as in the case of labor legislation, for example, is growing legal, economic, social and political inequality within the United States. This unfortunate trend violates a basic guarantee of the equality of justice, to which guarantee our constitutional fathers were dedicated.

It is my deep conviction that the American people, as the masters of their federal government through the application of our constitutional system of checks and balances, have no cause in fact to fear their federal government. To the contrary, the promotion of their general welfare is dependent in no small measure upon the federal government, through their elected representatives exercising—through constitutional legislation—the jurisdictional sovereignty of the federal government. . . .

9

THE QUESTION OF THE STATES*

Daniel P. Moynihan

Are state governments really declining? A good deal of evidence points to their continued vitality. A former state official, now with the federal government, argues that they have expanded and will expand for both practical and ideological reasons. The impetus has been federal aid.

* * *

Increasingly, those who view government as a positive force have turned elsewhere. The state capitals have on the whole been left to special interests, and to conservatives who find much there to reinforce their inclination to discount how much people know or care about public affairs—for the attention of the public has turned elsewhere as well.

This lack of public attention is enough to break the heart of anyone who does accomplish something at the state level. As an example, one of the most significant advances made in the field of public welfare since the New Deal has been the establishment of disability benefits systems in four states, Rhode Island, New York, Wisconsin and California. Disability benefits are sickness insurance: any worker covered (generally, those covered by unemployment insurance) who becomes sick or injured *off the job* receives a weekly payment equal to about what he would receive if unemployed. Thus in California a stenographer who breaks her leg skiing, or a farm laborer who falls ill, can receive up to $70 a week for as long as six months.

It is idle to suppose that any such program would pass the Congress *de novo*. Yet there may be a long-term prospect for a national disability benefits program because four important states have tried it out on their own, and have shown that it is workable. This is a splendid instance of the states experimenting with new ideas: yet it has hardly added to the reputation of state government, nor, I suspect, to the political reputations of those who brought it about.

* * *

. . . Something like a revival of state government is possible, even likely. There are a number of reasons for thinking this. For one thing, there has got to be. This was put as directly as may be by President Eisenhower's Commission on Intergovernment Relations (the Kestnbaum Report) which declared that "the success of our federal system . . . depends in large measure upon the performance of the states." As there is not the least likelihood that we will change our federal

* DANIEL P. MOYNIHAN is Executive Assistant to the Secretary of Labor. Formerly he was Acting Secretary to Governor Averell Harriman of New York. Reprinted by permission from *The Commonweal*, October 12, 1962, pp. 65–68.

system, the performance of the states gets very close to determining the success of American government in a range of matters universally acknowledged to be of the first consequence.

The political economics behind this generalization are really quite simple. Following a venerable but limited practice, the most important developments occurred a generation ago when so much New Deal social legislation provided that the states would administer the new programs. Unemployment insurance is a good example. The arrangement worked. Since then it has become a standard pattern for new federal programs, to the point that today one-quarter of the revenue of the states comes as grants-in-aid from the federal government.

The increase of federal aid to governments has been accompanied by an even greater increase in the expenditures of the states themselves. Governor Rockefeller is quite correct in stating that "the striking fact in our domestic political experience since World War II has not been the growth of federal government—but the far more rapid expansion of state and local government, to meet growing social needs." In the decade of the 1950's state expenditures increased at six times the rate of federal nondefense spending. Since 1957, state and local government has been the only sector of the economy in which the rate of employment growth has increased.

In the 1930's when the big New Deal grant-in-aid programs were begun, the distinction between policy and administration was more popular among political scientists than it is today. Many persons in Washington at the time no doubt felt the states would leave little mark on the programs they were to administer. But has this been the case? Certainly not in the wide range of grant-in-aid programs involving questions of racial integration, to cite a fundamental issue on which different states hold widely divergent views. If it is difficult to cite other differences of similar degree, this is principally because of the tendency of state government professionals, e.g., highway engineers, to adopt uniform national standards on their own. But it is not necessarily the case. Any day now some state could turn up with a transportation genius, such as Robert Moses was forty years ago, and the resulting use of federal highway funds could startle the nation.

This is not to say that the influence of the states has grown at the expense of the federal government or of local governments. The over-all impact of government has grown, and so also that of the three basic components. In turn these have got quite mixed up themselves, producing an effect that Morton Grodzin has called "Marble Cake Federalism" in contrast to the neat three-tiered arrangement of the past (or at least the textbooks of the past). It follows that the over-all effectiveness of American government is increasingly dependent on the effectiveness of all its elements.

In a somewhat different sense from saying there must be a revival of state government, it is possible also to declare that there ought to be. The quality of life in America is too much influenced by state government to permit the present neglect to continue much longer. For a great range of government activities the nuance of excellence is added, or lost, at the state level. Nearly a million students are now enrolled in state universities. Some are at Berkeley, others are—elsewhere. Each year a million persons enter state mental hospitals. Some fall into the healing hands of Paul Hoch in New York, others end up sitting on iron beds staring at the bars on the windows.

. . . Foreign affairs are the preoccupation of the federal government, particularly the executive branch, and are equally the preoccupation of the strong ideological movements of our period. . . .

For the most part this preoccupation simply reflects the changed reality that foreign affairs do come first. But there can also be sensed a certain disenchantment with social reform among those who have heretofore been its strongest advocates. (Thus Maurice F. Neufeld has described the turning away of the "generous-minded segments of the middle-classes . . . from unions in prosperity to the destitute peoples of the world.") All this would seem to result in diminishing pressure for social innovation at the federal level. . . .

This prospect happens also to come at a moment when the persisting financial difficulties of state governments seem to be easing. For some time the overwhelming share of state funds has gone to three areas: education, highways, and mental health. The combined drain on revenue has produced one crisis after another since 1945, with the tempo, if anything, increasing. This itself has been a prime source of instability. A Buffalo factory foreman recently remarked to Samuel Lubell: "I change governors every four years hoping that sometime I'll get one who will cut our taxes." Now, however, the federal government has begun pouring funds into state highway coffers. Federal aid to education is already considerable, and certain to grow. The pharmacological revolution in psychiatry has brought about a six-year continuing decline in the population of mental hospitals. For the larger states, at all events, these developments ought to provide a sufficient level of "discretionary" funds with which to resume (or assume) their role as innovators and experimenters within the federal system.

* * *

Because so much power and authority already rest with the states—is laying there in most cases, waiting for someone to use it—the future of state government is especially dependent on the type of political leaders and career employees that it can attract. What the states lack most is people. What they need, above all, is vocation.

* * *

Let it also be noted that there is money to be made in state government. Some of the legislative posts pay fantastic, albeit occasionally clandestine, salaries and civil service pay is getting better all the time. Already New York and California have established what are surely the highest government salary scales in the free world. In Albany, for example, the Secretary to the Governor makes more than a cabinet officer in Washington.

* * *

Perhaps another source of interest, surely a matter to be noted, is that the state governments are still places where a man can hope to see the results of his own work. The Department of Defense now has one million, two hundred thousand civilian employees. Is it not time for a closer look at the possibilities of Tallahassee, Boise, Montpelier, Dover, Frankfort, Santa Fe, Cheyenne . . . ?

10

WASHINGTON AND THE CITIES: AN INTRODUCTION*

Roscoe C. Martin

Roscoe Martin, a life long observer of the political process, is engaged in extensive study of the growing relations between the cities and the federal government. This provocative interpretation of a new federalism is the result.

"The time has come in the United States for those interested in the progress of our institutions to consider the relations existing between the national and the municipal authorities." Thus wrote William Anderson in an article published in the *National Municipal Review* 36 years ago. Suiting action to affirmation, Professor Anderson proceeded to review some of the principal areas of relations between the national government and the cities. He found a wide variety of federal activities with important effects for urban residents, but of direct federal concern for the cities *as cities* he discovered almost none. . . .

In the last three decades the "more direct and organic relationship" summoned by Mr. Anderson has come into being, and moreover promises to achieve an important place in the practice of American federalism. . . . The increasing participation by the cities in the practice of federalism is in the process of introducing a new element into American government, so that in the course of time the federal system will have three active partners instead of the time-honored two.[1]

* * *

FEDERAL-CITY RELATIONS: AN INTRODUCTION

In one important sense there have always been active relations between the federal government and the cities, for the national government from the beginning has performed functions of importance to city dwellers. For the most part these functions have not been designed to benefit the cities as such, but rather have been aimed at national objectives with the cities and their people as incidental beneficiaries. Thus, for example, the early post roads, built to facilitate the transmission of

* Roscoe C. Martin, "Washington and the cities," *The Federal Government and the Cities* (Washington, D.C.: George Washington University, School of Government, Business, and Cultural Affairs, 1961), pp. 1–2, 8–10, 13–15.

[1] The word "city" is not employed here in any restrictive sense. The "new new federalism" concept has a place for the urbanized county which has taken on a broad range of municipal functions. That there will be more such in the future is hardly to be doubted.

mail, at the same time enabled Bostonians to travel to New York and Philadelphians to Washington. Thus again the national interest in navigation vastly benefited the cities, though not conceived primarily for that purpose. . . .

Moreover, the cities have benefited greatly from modifications in federal programs made in response to changing needs. Over the course of somewhat more than a century America has changed from an agrarian/rural to an industrial/urban society. Public programs, state and local as well as federal, have changed correspondingly, with the urban center tending to become more and more the focus of governmental action. For the federal government, this has meant relatively less emphasis on farm problems and relatively more on urban problems. The establishment of the Departments of Commerce and Labor is symbolic of this shift in emphasis. Among the newer agencies created in response to stimuli largely urban are the Federal Communications Commission and the Securities and Exchange Commission. The programs of both are nationwide in scope, but they center on the cities, since that is where both communications and securities activities converge.

* * *

A second category of federal-city relations inheres in a number of programs which, though federal in inspiration and (in substantial part) support, come down to the cities through the state as intermediary. Included here are those areas in which the national government stimulates the states to action and makes grants-in-aid of the resulting programs. By far the largest of these are the public assistance and the highway programs, for which in 1958 the states received some three-and-a-quarter billions of dollars in federal aid, more than three-fourths of all federal grant-in-aid payments to the states in that year. Some small grants are made by the federal government direct to the cities in these fields, but they are minuscule in comparison with the sums which go to, or through, the states.

* * *

A third major category comprises federal-city relations which are direct in nature. The most important of these arise from federal grants-in-aid to the cities. The Urbanism Committee of the National Resources Committee traced with care the rise of the system of direct grants, noting that, though not unknown before 1930, it took firm root in the soil provided by the depression.[2] The federal government, in an effort to maximize the impact of its relief and public works programs and to minimize the time required for their implementation, dealt with the cities direct, and vast sums in federal monies were poured into municipal works from 1933 forward.

Urban programs multiplied and prospered with the growth of federal support, and most observers soon agreed that a new and profitable and mutually satisfactory relationship between the national government and the cities had come into being. It did not appear likely that the device of federal grants-in-aid to the cities, though widely employed first as a means of combating the depression, would be relinquished with the return of prosperity. That device proved, indeed, with the passing of the years to have become firmly es-

[2] Urbanism Committee of the National Resources Committee, *Urban Government* (Washington, D.C.: Government Printing Office, 1939). Part II of this volume is titled "Federal Relations to Urban Governments." It comprises a detailed examination of that subject as of January 1939.

tablished in American federal practice.[3]

Finally, what may be said provisionally of the consequences of federal-city relations for the federal system? There can be no doubt that the new federal-aid programs have had significant effects on the cities, but what import have they had for the relations between the cities and the higher levels of government? What has happened to the capacity of the city for meaningful interlevel cooperation? And what have been the effects on the states?

* * *

If the states have been damaged either in capacity to govern or in ability to cooperate by the developments of the last three decades, that fact remains to be demonstrated. As regards grants-in-aid in general, the evidence available suggests that the states have been strengthened rather than weakened; in particular, their programs undoubtedly are richer and more varied than they would have been without federal assistance. The adverse effects of the grant system on state organization appear to have been negligible. The Commission on Intergovernmental Relations arranged for a series of surveys of the effects of grants-in-aid on state and local government. A general analysis of 25 such reports concludes that

A reading of the state chapters suggests that the over-all impact of federal grants has had relatively little adverse effect in a majority of the states studied. In other words, the political complaints on this score have been exaggerated.[4]

Concerning federal-city relations as such, the role of the states, as a general proposition, is what they wish it to be. All direct-aid programs recognize the traditional sovereignty of the state over the city, and all concede the right of the state to participate in local programs to the extent it desires. That the states (with a few exceptions) have not entered actively into the fields of airport development, urban renewal, and public housing is attributable to the nature of those programs rather than to federal-city pre-emption. They represent areas in which the state simply has evinced little interest: in which, normally, it has foregone administrative organization or activity, in which it has seen fit to spend relatively small amounts of money. . . .

The cities, on the other hand, have been influenced markedly by federal support. Urban problems previously minimized or ignored have received recognition in a series of vigorous new programs looking to their melioration. These problems might not have been addressed yet but for federal encouragement and assistance. Coincidentally, other local functional areas have been stimulated by the example of the federal-city programs.

In terms of extra-mural relations, the cities have not been freed of state control; it has, however, been considerably relaxed. This very likely is more a consequence of normal trends than of federal intervention. The cities remain legally the creatures of the states, but they have gained a good deal more

---

[3] Commission on Intergovernmental Relations, *Twenty-Five Federal Grants-In-Aid Programs* (Washington, D.C.: Government Printing Office, June 1955). Among the programs summarized here are several of those which bring the federal government and the cities into direct relations.

[4] Commission on Intergovernmental Relations, *A Survey Report on the Impact of Federal Grants-In-Aid on the Structure and Functions of State and Local Governments* (Washington, D.C.: Government Printing Office, June 1955), p. 18.

operating room than they enjoyed earlier. . . . Their contacts with federal authorities have given them both cause and opportunity to break out of their provincial shells. Their national organizations have lifted their eyes to wider horizons. They now sense that they are dealing not with purely local issues, but with phenomena which are but urban manifestations of national problems. The cities, too, have become members of the American society.

In 1886, John W. Burgess commented to this effect:

> The two natural elements in our system are now the Community and the Nation. The former is the point of real local self-government; and the latter that of general self-government; and in the adjustments of the future these are the forces which will carry with them the determining power.[5]

Professor Burgess' write-off of the states represented a harsh judgment, though it is interesting that his view finds support in the fears voiced by Leonard White more than sixty-five years later. But we do not have to agree with either Burgess or White to conclude that a new force has asserted itself in our federal system. . . .

[5] John W. Burgess, "The American Commonwealth: Changes in Its Relationship to the Nation," *Political Science Quarterly,* I, No. 1 (March 1886), 34.

11

MINORITY VIEWS ON S. 1633*

During his administration, President Kennedy suggested legislation creating a Department of Urban Affairs and Housing, a proposal which became politically controversial and explosive. The following excerpts from the minority views of the Senate Committee dealing with the bill question not only the proposal, but the whole nature of relationships between the nation and the cities.

The introduction of legislation to create a Department of Urban Affairs and Housing carries this Nation toward the dangerous policies of political spending which hits hard at self-reliance. There has been a growing tendency to begin programs which aggressively make larger and larger segments of our population dependent on the federal system, solely on the theory that local government cannot handle these special problems.

* * *

Every pressure group in the nation, looking for federal funds, wants to have its representative crowding to the President's Cabinet table, not to advise and guide him on the problems of government, but to push for special favors for special interests.

The eventual demolition of power and authority of lesser levels of government such as city, county, or state, can be seen in the blueprints and the plans

* Committee on Government Operations, United States Senate, Report No. 879, 87th Cong., 1st Sess. September 6, 1961 (Washington, D.C.: Government Printing Office, 1961), pp. 24–25, 27–28, 30.

for a department of government which will take over the handling of problems which are, in a large part, entirely local responsibilities. A line of communication will be set up directly from the city mayor's office to the center of the federal government. County commissioners, state legislatures, governors will be ignored since they will be asked to contribute nothing.

It should not be necessary to stress the value of keeping local controls over local problems, but, with the increased tendency to diminish the authority of governors, state legislatures, and other levels of local government, such warnings must be sounded whenever the opportunity arises.

The Advisory Commission on Intergovernmental Relations, in a letter to the chairman of the Government Operations Committee, warned—

> * * * the Commission believes that activities of the Federal Government with respect to urban problems should be conducted in such a way as to give free rein and encouragement to the initiative of the States in exercising leadership with respect to the solution of problems involving their political subdivisions.

The representative of the National Association of County Officials said in his testimony—

> * * * such a Department may well empower large metropolitan cities to deal directly with the Federal Government, bypassing not only the States, but local communities as well. Those of us at the local government level have grave concern the proposed Department * * * might strengthen the hand of the metropolitan core city to the extent that it would be in a position to dominate, because of its close association with the Federal Government, other local municipalities who operate contiguously to or within the periphery of the core city's metropolitan area.

Enactment of this legislation will not encourage the initiative of states or of cities, but will violate the principles of the federal system, usurp authority vested in state governments, crumble the walls of self-determination, demolish local leadership, and build ever higher the stronghold of central government.

The people who live in the cities of this nation, themselves, should be warned that the espousal of such a cause will eventually demean their own stature in a political sense. If Washington pays the bill, Washington will direct the action. It has been ever thus. We are, more and more, moving toward a directed economy in this country. The theory of those who support more federal intervention is that Washington knows best, works best, pays best, and all lesser segments of government must change, they must reshape their concepts of self-determination, and accept the blueprint of the planners.

More than hopscotching over the state and county governments, this new department can eventually nullify local city government.

A department of government, which will carry out the functions envisioned by the supporters of the plan, will be the most powerful cabinet post, and it will be the most expensive. There is a steady stream of pious protestations in government that we need to cut down the deficit and the public debt, but we will, in one sweeping gesture, create a goliath which will drain our treasury and which will keep a watchful, police eye on every urban community and its citizens, planning, spending, directing until citizens will not call city hall when streets need repair, or a water main needs replacing, but will notify their congressman to contact the cabinet member handling such problems, seeking repairs and services.

More than losing control over local city government, these citizens of urban areas may find corrupt administrations in certain city governments perpetuated. The attention of Congress should be called to the many scandals currently being aired,which involve the city governments of some of our largest cities, where, as one columnist expressed it, "there is a municipal system that is shoddy, incredibly inefficient, and complacently corrupt." Congress should consider carefully before making federal funds available for the corrupt administrators to dispense for their own political gain.

* * *

The assumption by proponents of this legislation is that the majority of our people, because they live in urban areas, have no Cabinet-level representation. The fact is that they are served in a variety of ways by every department of government, including the Department of Agriculture.

The concept of a Department of Urban Affairs applies the principle of creating a department to assist people because of their location and not because of functions which need to be performed in their behalf. In other words, this would be the only department whose services would be denied some people merely on a geographic basis. It does not, as other departments do, have "something in it for everyone."

* * *

Supporters of the bill admit that nearly 70 per cent of our population and nearly 80 per cent of our productive capacity are in urban areas. Further, the areas of needed slum clearance, blight, and other big city problems are in our most populous, and wealthiest states and cities.

Statements before the committee suggested that cities had not yet utilized their own resources to solve their problems and it was pointed out that many cities had failed to continue to use existing programs when information was circulated that a Department of Urban Affairs was to be created.

* * *

There have been charges made that cities have been "sitting on their hands," allowing problems to accumulate, or to remain unattended, in order to make a more impressive showing of need.

Surely this subject matter needs more study and consideration than it has thus far received. It is therefore our view that this measure should be rejected.

Respectfully submitted.

JOHN L. McCLELLAN
KARL E. MUNDT
CARL T. CURTIS
SAM J. ERVIN

12

"THEY WANT TO GET AWAY FROM IT ALL"*

Robert Redinfield

The existence of fifty-one relatively independent governments in the same territory mean much more than fifty-one times as many sources of friction and creates boundary problems which may result in a stalemate.

What is the attraction that the little three-county state of Delaware (Pop. 318,000) holds for so many of America's corporations? . . . The answer lies neither in size nor in quaintness.

Corporations, like any other creatures, make their homes, if they can, where they are well treated and feel comfortable. . . . The climate, as represented by the corporation laws of Delaware and of three or four other of the [fifty] states, is particularly salubrious to corporations of broad, interstate character. It is no wonder that of some 1,100 corporations listed on the New York Stock Exchange, 350 have their corporate domiciles in Delaware.

The figure probably would be even greater were it not for the costs of shifting a corporation's home. In one notable case, the Southern Pacific Company, which gets no closer to Kentucky, or Delaware either, than Shreveport, La., spent $1,500,000 in 1947 moving its corporate home from Spring Station, a tiny village in Kentucky's blue grass country, to Wilmington. . . .

Delaware also collects taxes . . . but is considerably more lenient. . . . The minimum tax is $5.50 . . . Delaware does not limit its benevolence to the matter of taxes. The state's courts seem to have a predilection in favor of management as against insurgent forces. Whether this stems from the juridicial structure or from the circumstance that Delaware is dominated by a family with large corporate interests (duPont) is beside the point. An indidividual stockholder who tried to carry on a crusade against entrenched management seems to get somewhat less help from the Delaware courts than from those in other states. . . .

---

* Robert E. Redinfield, *The New York Times,* April 21, 1957. Copyright by The New York Times Company. Reprinted by permission.

13
THE FEDERAL SYSTEM*

Morton Grodzins

This provocative reinterpretation of our federal past by Morton Grodzins suggests that there has been rather more continuity in the American system than is usually assumed. It also points to an optimistic prediction of the future of American federalism.

THE SHARING OF FUNCTIONS

The American form of government is often, but erroneously, symbolized by a three-layer cake. A far more accurate image is the rainbow or marble cake, characterized by an inseparable mingling of differently colored ingredients, the colors appearing in vertical and diagonal strands and unexpected whirls. As colors are mixed in the marble cake, so functions are mixed in the American federal system. Consider the health officer, styled "sanitarian," of a rural county in a border state. He embodies the whole idea of the marble cake of government.

The sanitarian is appointed by the state under merit standards established by the federal government. His base salary comes jointly from state and federal funds, the county provides him with an office and office amenities and pays a portion of his expenses, and the largest city in the county also contributes to his salary and office by virtue of his appointment as a city plumbing inspector. It is impossible from moment to moment to tell under which governmental hat the sanitarian operates. His work of inspecting the purity of food is carried out under federal standards; but he is enforcing state laws when inspecting commodities that have not been in interstate commerce; and somewhat perversely he also acts under state authority when inspecting milk coming into the county from producing areas across the state border. He is a federal officer when impounding impure drugs shipped from a neighboring state; a federal-state officer when distributing typhoid immunization serum; a state officer when enforcing standards of industrial hygiene; a state-local officer when inspecting the city's water supply; and (to complete the circle) a local officer when insisting that the city butchers adopt more hygienic methods of handling their garbage. But he cannot and does not think of himself as acting in these separate capacities. All business in the county that concerns public health and sanitation he considers his business. Paid largely from federal funds, he does not find it strange to attend meetings of the city council to give expert advice on matters ranging from rotten apples to rabies control. He is even deputized as a member of both the city and county police forces.

---

* President's Committee on National Goals, *Goals for Americans* (Englewood Cliffs, N.J.: Prentice-Hall, Inc., 1960), pp. 265–66, 268–69, 271–78, 280–81.

The sanitarian is an extreme case, but he accurately represents an important aspect of the whole range of governmental activities in the United States. Functions are not neatly parceled out among the many governments. They are shared functions. It is difficult to find any governmental activity which does not involve all three of the so-called "levels" of the federal system. In the most local of local functions—law enforcement or education, for example—the federal and state governments play important roles. In what, a priori, may be considered the purest central government activities—the conduct of foreign affairs, for example—the state and local governments have considerable responsibilities, directly and indirectly.

* * *

A POINT OF HISTORY

The American federal system has never been a system of separated governmental activities. There has never been a time when it was possible to put neat labels on discrete "federal," "state," and "local" functions. Even before the Constitution, a statute of 1785, reinforced by the Northwest Ordinance of 1787, gave grants-in-land to the states for public schools. Thus the national government was a prime force in making possible what is now taken to be the most local function of all, primary and secondary education. More important, the nation, before it was fully organized, established by this action a first principle of American federalism: the national government would use its superior resources to initiate and support national programs, principally administered by the states and localities.

The essential unity of state and federal financial systems was again recognized in the earliest constitutional days with the assumption by the federal government of the Revolutionary War debts of the states. Other points of federal-state collaboration during the Federalist period concerned the militia, law enforcement, court practices, the administration of elections, public health measures, pilot laws, and many other matters.

The nineteenth century is widely believed to have been the pre-eminent period of duality in the American system. Lord Bryce at the end of the century described (in *The American Commonwealth*) the federal and state governments as "distinct and separate in their action." The system, he said, was "like a great factory wherein two sets of machinery are at work, their revolving wheels apparently intermixed, their bands crossing one another, yet each set doing its own work without touching or hampering the other." Great works may contain gross errors. Bryce was wrong. The nineteenth century, like the early days of the republic, was a period principally characterized by intergovernmental collaboration.

* * *

A long, extensive, and continuous experience is therefore the foundation of the present system of shared functions characteristic of the American federal system, what we have called the marble cake of government. It is a misjudgment of our history and our present situation to believe that a neat separation of governmental functions could take place without drastic alterations in our society and system of government.

* * *

The constitutional restraints on the expansion of national authority are less important and less direct today than they were in 1879 or in 1936. But to say that they are less important is not to say that they are unimportant.

The nation's politics reflect these decentralizing causes and add some of their own. The political parties of the United States are unique. They seldom perform the function that parties traditionally perform in other countries, the function of gathering together diverse strands of power and welding them into one. Except during the period of nominating and electing a president and for the essential but nonsubstantive business of organizing the houses of Congress, the American parties rarely coalesce power at all. Characteristically they do the reverse, serving as a canopy under which special and local interests are represented with little regard for anything that can be called a party program. National leaders are elected on a party ticket, but in Congress they must seek crossparty support if their leadership is to be effective. It is a rare president during rare periods who can produce legislation without facing the defection of substantial numbers of his own party. (Wilson could do this in the first session of the 63rd Congress; but Franklin D. Roosevelt could not, even during the famous hundred days of 1933.) Presidents whose parties form the majority of the congressional houses must still count heavily on support from the other party.

The parties provide the pivot on which the entire governmental system swings. Party operations, first of all, produce in legislation the basic division of functions between the federal government, on the one hand, and state and local governments, on the other. The Supreme Court's permissiveness with respect to the expansion of national powers has not in fact produced any considerable extension of exclusive federal functions. The body of federal law in all fields has remained, in the words of Henry M. Hart, Jr. and Herbert Wechsler, "interstitial in its nature," limited in objective and resting upon the principal body of legal relationships defined by state law. It is difficult to find any area of federal legislation that is not significantly affected by state law.

In areas of new or enlarged federal activity, legislation characteristically provides important roles for state and local governments. This is as true of Democratic as of Republican administrations and true even of functions for which arguments of efficiency would product exclusive federal responsibility. Thus the unemployment compensation program of the New Deal and the airport program of President Truman's administration both provided important responsibilities for state governments. In both cases attempts to eliminate state participation were defeated by a crossparty coalition of pro-state votes and influence. A large fraction of the Senate is usually made up of ex-governors, and the membership of both houses is composed of men who know that their reelection depends less upon national leaders or national party organization than upon support from their home constituencies. State and local officials are key members of these constituencies, often central figures in selecting candidates and in turning out the vote. Under such circumstances, national legislation taking state and local views heavily into account is inevitable.

Second, the undisciplined parties affect the character of the federal system as a result of senatorial and congressional interference in federal administrative programs on behalf of local interests. Many aspects of the legislative involvement in administrative affairs are formalized. The Legislative Reorganization Act of 1946, to take only one example, provided that each of the standing committees "shall exercise continuous watchfulness" over administration of laws within its jurisdiction. But the formal system of controls, extensive as it is, does not compare in importance with the informal and extralegal network of relationships in producing continuous legislative involvement in administrative affairs.

Senators and congressmen spend a major fraction of their time representing problems of their constituents before administrative agencies. An even larger fraction of congressional staff time is devoted to the same task. The total magnitude of such "case work" operations is great. In one five-month period of 1943 the Office of Price Administration received a weekly average of 842 letters from members of Congress. If phone calls and personal contacts are added, each member of Congress on the average presented the OPA with a problem involving one of his constituents twice a day in each five-day work week. Data for less vulnerable agencies during less intensive periods are also impressive. In 1958, to take only one example, the Department of Agriculture estimated (and underestimated) that it received an average of 159 congressional letters per working day. Special congressional liaison staffs have been created to service this mass of business, though all higher officials meet it in one form or another. The Air Force in 1958 had, under the command of a major general, 137 people (55 officers and 82 civilians) working in its liaison office.

The widespread, consistent, and in many ways unpredictable character of legislative interference in administrative affairs has many consequences for the tone and character of American administrative behavior. From the perspective of this paper, the important consequence is the comprehensive, day-to-day, even hour-by-hour, impact of local views on national programs. No point of substance or procedure is immune from congressional scrutiny. A substantial portion of the entire weight of this impact is on behalf of the state and local governments. It is a weight that can alter procedures for screening immigration applications, diverting the course of a national highway, changing the tone of an international negotiation, and amending a social security law to accommodate local practices or fulfill local desires.

The party system compels administrators to take a political role. This is a third way in which the parties function to decentralize the American system. The administrator must play politics for the same reason that the politician is able to play in administration: the parties are without program and without discipline.

In response to the unprotected position in which the party situation places him, the administrator is forced to seek support where he can find it. One ever-present task is to nurse the Congress of the United States, that crucial constituency which ultimately controls his agency's budget and program. From the administrator's view, a sympathetic consideration of congressional requests (if not downright submission to them) is the surest way to build the political support without which the administrative job could not continue. Even the completely task-oriented administrator must be sensitive to the need for congressional support and to the relationship between case work requests, on one side, and budgetary and legislative support, on the other. "You do a good job handling the personal problems and requests of a Congressman," a White House officer said, "and you have an easier time convincing him to back your program." Thus there is an important link between the nursing of congressional requests, requests that largely concern local matters, and the most comprehensive national programs. The administrator must accommodate to the former as a price of gaining support for the latter.

One result of administrative politics is that the administrative agency may become the captive of the nation-wide interest group it serves or presumably regulates. In such cases no government may come out with effective authority: the winners are the interest groups themselves. But in a very large number of cases, states and localities also win influence. The politics of administration is a process of making peace with legislators who for the most part consider themselves the guardians of local interests. The political role of administrators therefore contributes to the power of states and localities in national programs.

Finally, the way the party system operates gives American politics their over-all distinctive tone. The lack of party discipline produces an openness in the system that allows individuals, groups, and institutions (including state and local governments) to attempt to influence national policy at every step of the legislative-administrative process. This is the "multiple-crack" attribute of the American government. "Crack" has two meanings. It means not only many fissures or access points; it also means, less statically, opportunities for wallops or smacks at government.

If the parties were more disciplined, the result would not be a cessation of the process by which individuals and groups impinge themselves upon the central government. But the present state of the parties clearly allows for a far greater operation of the multiple crack than would be possible under the conditions of centralized party control. American interest groups exploit literally uncountable access points in the legislative-administrative process. If legislative lobbying, from committee stages to the conference committee, does not produce results, a cabinet secretary is called. His immediate associates are petitioned. Bureau chiefs and their aides are hit. Field officers are put under pressure. Campaigns are instituted by which friends of the agency apply a secondary influence on behalf of the interested party. A conference with the President may be urged.

To these multiple points for bringing influence must be added the multiple voices of the influences. Consider, for example, those in a small town who wish to have a federal action taken. The easy merging of public and private interest at the local level means that the influence attempt is made in the name of the whole community, thus removing it from political partisanship. The Rotary Club as well as the City Council, the Chamber of Commerce and the mayor, eminent citizens and political bosses—all are readily enlisted. If a conference in a senator's office will expedite matters, someone on the local scene can be found to make such a conference possible and effective. If technical information is needed, technicians will supply it. State or national professional organizations of local officials, individual congressmen and senators, and not infrequently whole state delegations will make the local cause their own. Federal field officers, who service localities, often assume local views. So may elected and appointed state officers. Friendships are exploited, and political mortgages called due. Under these circumstances, national policies are molded by local action.

In summary, then, the party system

functions to devolve power. The American parties, unlike any other, are highly responsive when directives move from the bottom to the top, highly unresponsive from top to bottom. Congressmen and senators can rarely ignore concerted demands from their home constituencies; but no party leader can expect the same kind of response from those below, whether he be a President asking for congressional support or a congressman seeking aid from local or state leaders.

* * *

In a governmental system of genuinely shared responsibilities, disagreements inevitably occur. Opinions clash over proximate ends, particular ways of doing things become the subject of public debate, innovations are contested. These are not basic defects in the system. Rather, they are the system's energy-reflecting life blood. There can be no permanent "solutions" short of changing the system itself by elevating one partner to absolute supremacy. What can be done is to attempt to produce conditions in which conflict will not fester but be turned to constructive solutions of particular problems.

A long list of specific points of difficulty in the federal system can be easily identified. No adequate congressional or administrative mechanism exists to review the patchwork of grants in terms of national needs. There is no procedure by which to judge, for example, whether the national government is justified in spending so much more for highways than for education. The working force in some states is inadequate for the effective performance of some nation-wide programs, while honest and not-so-honest graft frustrates efficiency in others. Some federal aid programs distort state budgets, and some are so closely supervised as to impede state action in meeting local needs. Grants are given for programs too narrowly defined, and over-all programs at the state level consequently suffer. Administrative, accounting and auditing difficulties are the consequence of the multiplicity of grant programs. City officials complain that the states are intrusive fifth wheels in housing, urban redevelopment, and airport building programs.

* * *

The geography of state boundaries, as well as many aspects of state internal organization, are the products of history and cannot be justified on any grounds of rational efficiency. Who, today, would create major governmental subdivisions the size of Maryland, Delaware, New Jersey, or Rhode Island? Who would write into Oklahoma's fundamental law an absolute state debt limit of $500,000? Who would design (to cite only the most extreme cases) Georgia's and Florida's gross underrepresentation of urban areas in both houses of the legislature?

A complete catalogue of state political and administrative horrors would fill a sizeable volume. Yet exhortations to erase them have roughly the same effect as similar exhortations to erase sin. Some of the worst inanities—for example, the boundaries of the states, themselves—are fixed in the national constitution and defy alteration for all foreseeable time. Others, such as urban underrepresentation in state legislatures, serve the overrepresented groups, including some urban ones, and the effective political organization of the deprived groups must precede reform.

Despite deficiencies of politics and organizations that are unchangeable or slowly changing, it is an error to look at the states as static anachronisms. Some of them—New York, Minnesota, and California, to take three examples spanning the country—have administrative organizations that compare favorably in many ways with the national establishment. Many more in recent years have moved rapidly towards integrated administrative departments, state-wide budgeting, and central leadership. The others have models-in-existence to follow, and active professional organizations (led by the Council of State Governments) promoting their development. Slow as this change may be, the states move in the direction of greater internal effectiveness.

The pace toward more effective performance at the state level is likely to increase. Urban leaders, who generally feel themselves disadvantaged in state affairs, and suburban and rural spokesmen, who are most concerned about national centralization, have a common interest in this task. The urban dwellers want greater equality in state affairs, including a more equitable share of state financial aid; nonurban dwellers are concerned that city dissatisfactions should not be met by exclusive federal, or federal-local, programs. Antagonistic, rather than amiable, cooperation may be the consequence. But it is a cooperation that can be turned to politically effective measures for a desirable upgrading of state institutions.

If one looks closely, there is scant evidence for the fear of the federal octopus, the fear that expansion of central programs and influence threatens to reduce the states and localities to compliant administrative arms of the central government. In fact, state and local governments are touching a larger proportion of the people in more ways than ever before; and they are spending a higher fraction of the total national product than ever before. Federal programs have increased, rather than diminished, the importance of the governors; stimulated professionalism in state agencies; increased citizen interest and participation in government; and, generally, enlarged and made more effective the scope of state action.[1] It may no longer be true in any significant sense that the states and localities are "closer" than the federal government to the people. It is true that the smaller governments remain active and powerful members of the federal system.

* * *

The American federal system exhibits many evidences of the dispersion of power not only because of formal federalism but more importantly because our politics reflect and reinforce the nation's diversities-within-unity. Those who value the virtues of decentralization, which writ large are virtues of freedom, need not scruple at recognizing the defects of those virtues. The defects are principally the danger that parochial and private interests may not coincide with, or give way to, the nation's interest. The necessary cure for these defects is effective national leadership.

The centrifugal force of domestic politics needs to be balanced by the centripetal force of strong presidential leadership. Simultaneous strength at center and periphery exhibits the American system at its best, if also at its noisiest. The interests of both find effective spokesmen. States and localities (and private interest groups) do not lose their influence opportunities, but national policy becomes more than the simple consequence of successful, momentary concentrations of nonnational

[1] See the valuable report, *The Impact of Federal Grants-in-Aid on the Structure and Functions of State and Local Governments,* submitted to the Commission on Intergovernmental Relations by the Governmental Affairs Institute (Washington, D.C.: Government Printing Office, 1955).

pressures: it is guided by national leaders.[2]

[2] Messrs. Perkins and Redford state:

Professor Grodzins has made a significant contribution. The federal system has contributed to a "mild chaos" both administratively and financially. He accurately assesses the several quite futile attempts to disentangle the administrative and fiscal relationships of the states and the national government.

At this juncture, however, it should be remembered that the present system of shared responsibility confuses rather than fixes responsibility. Ascertainable responsibility for policy, administrative performance, and financing is an essential feature of effective self-government. The possibility of achieving it needs to be explored.

A reduction of the sharing of power would to some degree cause greater centralization of responsibility in the federal government. It would not necessarily result in loss of appropriate administrative decentralization and the loss of influence by the ordinary citizen over the activities of government. This is illustrated by what Mr. Grodzins himself says concerning the influence of the localized party structure on administration of centralized national functions.

The chaos of party processes itself impairs leadership for national functions and national aims. Mr. Grodzins' conclusion that the costs of this chaos are tolerable may be drawn too easily. Whether the centrifugal pulls of party decentralization are so strong as to seriously threaten national leadership and responsibility in our government deserves careful assessment.

Decentralization is an essential goal of American policy. So also are responsibility and leadership. Public concern needs to manifest itself about both of these goals.

V

Public Opinion and Interest Groups: Who Speaks for Me?

Few concepts in democracy are more widely held and more fluently expressed than the belief in the validity of public opinion. The American literary tradition is full of lyrical references to "The sovereignty of the people" and our everyday language contains such aphorisms as "You can't fool all of the people all of the time," or "Know the truth and the truth shall make you free."

In the middle of the nineteenth century, Abraham Lincoln said, "Public sentiment is everything," and a few years later James Bryce referred to our political system as "Government by popular opinion." This idealistic appraisal of public opinion was rudely shattered after World War I by the opinion theorists who, using the tools and findings of some of the new social sciences, tended to discount or to deglamorize the earlier exaltations. New concepts of mass and individual psychology, many emphasizing the irrational and emotional basis of opinion, refuted or at least modified some of the previous assumptions.

In the 1920's Walter Lippmann published *Public Opinion* and *The Phantom Public*. Both of these books reappraised the nature of public opinion and the role of the average man in the process of self-government. In the 1950's there were alarming concerns that the passive persuasiveness of mass media and the "engineering of consent" would do serious damage to the integrity and critical power of public opinion. Today there is still great solicitude regarding the impact of mass media and the danger of manipulation by public opinion experts. However, there may well be a trend toward more confidence in public opinion or, at least, a greater feeling of the importance of public opinion. As V. O. Key, Jr. points out, "Unless mass views have some place in the shaping of public policy, all the talk about democracy is nonsense."

From a consideration of public opinion it is just one short step to a discussion of interest groups. Public opinion, like all forms of social interaction, has a group basis. Groups meet. They have opinions. They take public positions. Their views are expressed frequently with great skill and great effectiveness. In many ways public opinion is simply a common denominator of group opinion.

The following chapter discusses the role of public opinion and the function of interest groups in representative government. The material is presented in the framework of two issues—"Public Opinion—The Voice of the People or the Echo of the Makers of Opinion?" and "Are Interest Groups Incompatible With Representative Government?"

The Voice of the People or the Echo of the Makers of Opinion?

Do the people have the same opportunity to be heard as they had a century ago? Is public opinion becoming merchandized and manipulated? How powerful is the public relations industry? Some students of contemporary trends see great danger in the combination of electronic communication and "the engineering of consent." Other writers take a more relaxed view of the present scene. These individuals point out that there are protections built into the system. For example, there are many publics and subpublics and we know the things that sway one public will alienate another. We also know there is a difference between the "attentive" public and the public at large and that public opinion may be silent as well as active. The latent public, however, serves as a check upon irresponsible and unrestrained leadership. Finally, there is a system of interaction between democratic leadership and the mass and in this interaction public opinion rules an area within which permissive governmental discussion and action may occur.

Stanley Kelley, Jr. discusses the role of the public relations man and his influence in certain campaigns in American politics. The selection following Kelley's brings to bear the thoughts of V. O. Key, Jr. who analyzes public opinion in terms of its composition and the limits of its operation.

Are Interest Groups Incompatible with Representative Government?

Interest groups have been described all the way from "one of the perils of our times" to an "irresponsible monster which will destroy representative government." There is no doubt that the excessive influence of certain groups with great financial resources and access to powerful mass media present a threat to the whole concept of democratic government. However, unrestrained condemnation of interest group activity is a dead-end street. It solves nothing. Not only are groups here to stay but in a complex society such as ours interest group activity is necessary if government is to be a dynamic institution. Without interest groups government cannot solve the continuing problems of contemporary life. As David B. Truman points out, "The process of government cannot be adequately understood apart from the groups . . . which are operative at any point in time."

It is instructive to note that while groups do represent great power, their membership is multiple and overlapping. Out of this multiple, overlapping membership comes the conflict of loyalties and aspirations. This conflict is a check in itself against the exercise of total power or even dominant power by any one group. There is also a balancing in the interplay of intergroup activity and the role of unorganized and potential interest groups. All of these serve to protect the democratic process.

In this problem the late Senator Styles Bridges discusses the dilemma which occurs when interest groups ignore the public interest. David B. Truman present a different point of view in suggesting that organized groups are a necessary part of the political process and that the first step toward an approach to dealing with interest groups is to understand their complexity and function.

1

P. R. MAN: POLITICAL MASTERMIND?*

Stanley Kelley, Jr.

Today the public relations expert plays an important role in the strategy and campaign planning of both major political parties. What effect will the continued and, perhaps, extended use of professional public relations have upon our system of free elections? Will the voter simply become a pawn in the hands of the party with the greatest resources, or is there a saturation point beyond which public relations techniques lose their effectiveness? In the following selection, Mr. Kelley discusses the role of professional public relations in the 1952 presidential election.

Despite the fact that mass communication techniques have been undergoing rapid change and development for over half a century, the extent to which they have modified American campaigning is too little recognized. The typical nineteenth-century campaign combined public stumping and private talks with local bosses. Local organizations were the national parties' real point of contact with the voter.

Now, the mass media have given

* Stanley Kelley, Jr., "P.R. Man: Political Mastermind," *The New York Times Magazine*, September 2, 1956, pp. 10, 54–56.

new dimensions to campaigning. They are fast. They allow the campaigner to talk to a truly national audience and to focus its attention on particular events, personalities and issues. They have greatly increased the cost of campaigning, but they have enormously reduced the *unit* cost of reaching voters. They allow political parties to put their cases before a vast group of mass media consumers that local organizations have never been able to interest in politics. By 1952, Presidential candidate Eisenhower's professional advisers were telling him that in one half-hour television show he could reach more voters than he could in three years of whistle-stopping at his then current rate.

Just as the big city boss symbolized the political techniques of the nineteenth century, so the public relations man is a characteristic figure in today's campaign. In his brand of politics, propaganda has become the central concern. For the boss, the principal aim was to build a bloc of votes that would stick by him regardless of the candidates and regardless of the issues. In contrast, the public relations man fights his battles in the mind of the voter; he specializes in building attitudes and standardizing opinions on controversial issues. Says one of them, "We use campaign funds, not to dispense favors, but to mold public sentiment. . . ." This kind of politics has a logic of its own and calls for study of political "markets," alternative ways of framing appeals, and methods of distributing ideas.

It also requires meticulous planning. Neat brochures, one paragraph to a page, for all kinds of projects, are a sort of trademark of public relations men in politics. The 1952 Republican campaign strategy was laid out in advance in a long blueprint that outlined organization, basic appeals, types of speeches, literature, advertising, television and radio programs, the relative weight to be given to the various media, the kinds, places and times of campaign trips and rallies, and the areas in which efforts were to be concentrated.

Advertising and public relations men may sometimes serve as little more than campaign technicians, but it is not unusual for them to have a seat at the strategy table. In California, it is normal practice for major candidates to put the management of their campaigns in the hands of any one of about half a dozen independent political public relations firms. Payment is on a fee basis. In other parts of the country, it is more usual for the public relations man to be the political committee's permanent employe.

What determines the public relations man's political style? Partly it is his judgment of what kind of slogans and candidates the market will bear. The public relations man's conception of his market differs little from that of ordinary political analysis. He, too, is interested in all the groupings of society, whether based on age, sex, income, occupation or some other factor. Though he prides himself on knowing the psychology of the "little man" much more intimately than the client he serves, he checks his feel for the issues with the help of polling and market research organizations. . . .

In part, also, the way the public relations expert approaches issues is determined by certain characteristics of mass communication. He is acutely aware that radio and television dials turn easily. He knows that the lead sentences of a newspaper story are those that have the largest readership. He expects to be listened to, but not to be listened to for very long. As a result, he telescopes his arguments into themes and slogans. For the p. r. man, a phrase like "that mess in Washington" may truly cover a multitude of sins. Losing something in balanced discussion, he hopes to gain in emotional impact.

For somewhat similar motives he makes a liberal use of gimmicks. Tricks and novelties—barrage balloons, singing jingles, pretty girls—are essentially a way of attracting the attention of a public that is distracted by thousands of competing appeals. In the modern forum getting attention is the hard first step in selling opinions.

Gimmicks can border on the fantastic. In a Los Angeles mayoralty recall campaign, a prize was offered to the person who most nearly estimated the number of votes by which Mayor Fletcher Bowron would be recalled, thus making the award of the prize contingent on the Mayor's defeat.

The p. r. man is devoted to the strategy of attack. To attack is to choose one's battleground; to defend is to accept the issues as they have been pictured by others. In 1952, constant attack was an essential feature of Republican plans, for Republican strategists hoped to arouse apathetic citizens who had failed to vote in previous elections and win them for Eisenhower.

Getting from a defensive to an offensive posture, however, sometimes calls for considerable ingenuity. On one occasion in San Francisco, a p. r. firm was managing former Mayor Lapham's campaign against a recall. In the absence of an opposing candidate, the issue seemed to be, "Has Lapham done a good job?" This made the Mayor's campaign an essentially defensive operation.

The p. r. men met the situation by inventing an enemy—"The Faceless Man." All over San Francisco, billboards pictured a sinister, cigar smoking, faceless politician and asked, "Who's Behind the Recall?" Leading members of the recall movement were accused of fronting for "a faceless man, a nameless candidate for Mayor." By the end of the campaign, which Lapham won handily, these recall leaders were spending a good deal of their time denying the existence of the California p. r. team's powerful fiction.

. . . Wendell Willkie, a year before the 1940 convention, was a man of stature and ability, but a political unknown. By the time the convention met, he was a candidate. In between were the newspaper and magazine stories, carefully planted by p. r. men, that had fired the public imagination with Willkie's underdog fight against party regulars.

P. r. men may serve candidates as "build-up boys" or, more modestly, simply as coaches. Vice President Nixon's 1952 defense of his political fund has been a subject of great controversy ever since. Friends have emphasized its spontaneity; enemies, its "soap opera" calculation. Both versions have a substantial degree of truth. There is little doubt that Nixon prepared his own speech and that he delivered it only from notes. But there was also a background of careful preparation.

Delivery of the speech was held up to allow public excitement to mount. Wording of the speech was carefully gone over with Nixon's public relations adviser and his television consultant. . . .

Nixon and his managers were early in appreciating the subtle changes of style that are required if a new medium is to be used effectively. . . .

The method chosen to reach a group of voters will depend in part on the nature of the group. In Maryland's 1950 senatorial campaign, a Chicago p. r. man retained by Republican candidate John M. Butler wanted to get his message before first generation Catholic immigrants. He felt that Butler's pro-McCarthy appeals had a good chance of winning votes in this group of normally Democratic voters—if he could get his story before them. One tactic he tried was to work through a popular bakery supply man who asked local bakers to put in a good word for candidate Butler with their customers. First generation immigrants, he reasoned, had not deserted the bread of the old countries for the cellophane-wrapped product available at the supermarket. He could reach them at the bakery.

Sometimes calculation will proceed in the opposite direction: The p. r. man discovers a ready-made audience and then seeks some way to influence it politically. In an interoffice memorandum, one advertising executive noted that people returning by automobile from Saturday night baseball games form a semi-captive audience. Usually, these people turn on their car radios, tune to a program of popular music, and then sit back and listen. Why not, proposed the memorandum, make the agency's client, the Governor of an Eastern state, a disk jockey? He could play his favorite records, mixing music with a few chatty political remarks.

Discovering the most economical way to distribute propaganda requires an intimate knowledge of listening, viewing and reading habits and of popular behavior patterns in general. Television may be the most powerful communication medium yet invented, but on a sunny Sunday afternoon, radio may be a better bet. To pass on matters of this kind, the p. r. man has to be a kind of practicing sociologist. Even before a number of academic social scientists discovered "opinion leaders"—those people from whom their associates habitually seek authoritative opinions—p. r. men systematically fed them direct mail in campaigns. Probably the opinion leader is flattered by such special attention. In any case, he is in a position to put a general propaganda line before his special public with the force of his own prestige behind it. Other kinds of observation can also be turned to political advantage. One p. r. man put campaign literature into beauty parlors and barber shops. His theory: patrons of these establishments read obsessively.

To what extent do all the calculations of the p. r. man end by winning votes? One of the more ironic facts about the deference candidates give to the p. r. man's opinions is that the latter can rarely show the extent to which he caused the voter's decision. The voter's environment is filled with words and images. He casts his ballot. The relation between these two phenomena is rarely clear. . . .

Still, there is evidence, if not proof, of the value of p. r. skill and knowledge. Good p. r. advice, for instance, may mean the difference between talking to TV sets that are tuned in or turned off. In the 1952 Presidential campaign, the theories that governed Republican and Democratic television time buying were in sharp contrast. The Democrats scheduled regular half-hour spots from 10:30 to 11 P.M. on Tuesdays and Thursdays. The Republicans, acting on professional advice, placed their programs in periods usually taken by the most successful commercial shows, hoping to capture a part of their viewers. Nielsen ratings showed Eisenhower's speeches drew consistently larger audiences than Stevenson's, except in the one case where Stevenson, too, fell heir to a popular feature's time period. Examples like this, bolstered by data from clipping services, public opinion polls and audience rating agencies, help the p. r. man convince his clients that he has a real product to sell.

And however inconclusive such evidence may appear to the skeptical, it is altogether likely that the public relations man will continue to play an increasingly important role in campaigns. With the decline of political clubs and old-fashioned machines in all parts of the country, the mass media have now emerged as the most important single road to political power. The public relations man who took early note of this fact is beginning to reap the rewards.

2

PUBLIC OPINION AND DEMOCRATIC POLICIES*

V. O. Key, Jr.

Public opinion is frequently pictured as a monolithic force which, like the atmosphere, covers and colors everything. V. O. Key, Jr. offers a corrective to this approach by showing how complex the phenomenon of public opinion really is.

Analytically it is useful to conceive of the structure of a democratic order as consisting of the political activists and the mass of people. Yet this differentiation becomes deceptive unless it is kept in mind that the democratic activists consist of people arranged along a spectrum of political participation and involvement, ranging from those in the highest post of official leadership to the amateurs who become sufficiently interested to try to round up a few votes for their favorite in the presidential campaign. In the preceding discussion we sought to isolate some of the characteristics of both activists and mass that appear to be compatible with, if not essential for, the operation of a democratic order, thus setting up a static picture of two broad political strata. It is in the dynamics of the system, the interactions between these strata, that the import of public opinion in democratic orders becomes manifest. Between the activists and the mass there exists a system of communication and interplay so complex as to defy simple description; yet identification of a few major features of that system may aid in our construction of a general conception of democratic processes.

OPINION DIKES

In the interactions between democratic leadership echelons and the mass of people some insight comes from the conception of public opinion as a system of dikes which channel public action or which fix a range of discretion within which government may act or within which debate at official levels may proceed. This conception avoids the error of personifying "public opin-

* V. O. Key, Jr., *Public Opinion and American Democracy* (New York: Alfred A. Knopf, Inc., 1961), pp. 551–55.

ion" as an entity that exercises initiative and in some way functions as an operating organism to translate its purposes into governmental action.

In one of their aspects the dikes of opinion have a substantive nature in that they define areas within which day-to-day debate about the course of specific action may occur. Some types of legislative proposals, given the content of general opinion, can scarcely expect to attract serious attention. They depart too far from the general understandings of what is proper. A scheme for public ownership of the automobile industry, for example, would probably be regarded as so far outside the area of legitimate public action that not even the industry would become greatly concerned. On the other hand, other types of questions arise within areas of what we have called permissive consensus. A widespread, if not a unanimous, sentiment prevails that supports action toward some general objective, such as the care of the ill or the mitigation of the economic hazards of the individual. Probably quite commonly mass opinion of a permissive character tends to develop in advance of governmental action in many areas of domestic policy. That opinion grows out of public discussion against the background of the modal aspirations and values of people generally. As it takes shape, the time becomes ripe for action that will be generally acceptable or may even arouse popular acclaim for its authors.

The qualities of this substantive opinion doubtless differ widely from issue to issue and from person to person. On some issues opinion may be oriented favorably toward broadly defined objectives; on others, perhaps extremely few, opinion may become focused on sharply defined proposals. On any issue the more alert and informed persons may have fairly well-formed opinions about sharply defined issues; others may have broad preferences—for example, something ought to be done for the farmers but not too much.

Opinion dikes may bear on the manner as well as on the substance of action. And it may be that in a democratic order those opinions that control or guide the mode of action may be of special importance as substantive action moves into areas where it encounters formidable opposition. Action taken in a seemingly fair and equitable manner may be acceptable, but arbitrary action to the same effect may be regarded as intolerable. The procedural content of American public opinion has been little explored. The division of opinion and the spontaneous comment on the proposition that government employees accused of communism ought to be fired even though the charge is not proved suggest that notions of fair play may be widely held within the population. Doubtless other procedural notions have wide popular acceptance that could be demonstrated by survey methods.

The idea of public opinion as forming a system of dikes which channel action yields a different conception of the place of public opinion than does the notion of a government by public opinion as one in which by some mysterious means a referendum occurs on every major issue. In the former conception the articulation between government and opinion is relatively loose. Parallelism between action and opinion tends not to be precise in matters of detail; it prevails rather with respect to broad purpose. And in the correlation of purpose and action time lags may occur between the crystallization of a sense of mass purpose and its fulfillment in public action. Yet in the long run majority purpose and public action tend to be brought into harmony.

MODIFICATIONS OF THE OPINION CONTEXT

The content of mass opinion changes through time; it is perhaps in such alterations that the power of mass opinion is made manifest. Though changes in opinion content occur continuously, at some moments combinations of events, imaginative leadership, and action induce relatively rapid and marked changes in popular preferences and expectations. These episodes may bring new opinion orientations, which in turn become rather rigid elements of the pattern of popular attitudes.

The movement of opinions and the expectations that accompanied the fulfillment of the program of the New Deal illustrate well the process of change and its consequences for governmental action. A spirited leadership with programs of action deviating markedly from past practice won approval and generated a new set of popular expectations about governmental action. The "power" of public opinion manifested itself in a negative way. Those candidates and leaders tainted with the suspicion that they wanted to turn the clock back had hard sledding for years. Until they could make a show of acceptance of changes they could not capture control of the government. Thus, through elections opinion ratified past reforms by its rejection of those who appeared to be at odds with the new balance of public sentiment.

Similarly, in the area of foreign policy World War II brought with it a reorientation of the context of public opinion, which became more supportive of involvement in international politics. Probably the body of popular opinion in this area has a less solid base and a less constricting effect upon public action than does opinion on domestic welfare policy. The radically changed position of the United States in world affairs creates new problems not only for a government that rests on public opinion, but also for those who seek to inform and to lead that opinion. The conduct of domestic debates over foreign policy carries hazards for external policy. On the other hand, repression of debate results in a failure to inform the people of incompetence in the conduct of foreign affairs.[1]

Mass opinions, aspirations, and expectations change as the political system moves through time. It is in this moving situation that the power of mass opinion makes itself manifest in its interactions with democratic leadership—chiefly in its rejection of leadership factions whose outlook lags notably behind or strikes out markedly ahead of the moving average of opinion. Those who wish to turn the clock back, to reverse decisions already rooted in popular acceptance, gradually learn their lesson as they meet rebuff after rebuff. Those too far ahead of opinion, though they may contribute to the forces impelling alteration of the opinion context, likewise find themselves

[1] The dilemma which the circumstances of a garrison state creates for democracies leads some American scholars to advocate fundamental reconstruction of the structure of government. The fixed term of the president makes it impossible for a bumbling administration to be thrown out of power until the date for the next presidential election rolls around. The limitations on debate and discussion imposed by the necessities of external unity and by diplomatic secrecy make it difficult adequately to inform the electorate. The remedy urged by some scholars is some variant of the cabinet system by which Congress, a body better informed than the electorate, could cast out an incompetent administration.

rejected. Deviants from dominant opinion, though, play a critical role in the preservation of the vitality of a democratic order as they urge alterations and modifications better to achieve the aspirations of men. Hence the fundamental significance of freedom of speech and agitation. Those activists closest to the core of power may hesitate to assume the risks of political entrepreneurship, but others, with less to lose, may by their efforts gradually make the endeavor that is not "practical politics" today feasible tomorrow.

OPINION CONTEXT AND GOVERNMENTAL DISCRETION

This discussion of the anchorage of leadership to public opinion should not be taken to mean that wide ranges of discretion do not exist within which a creative role may be played by popular leadership. Glum political philosophers meditate in their melancholy fashion about how the pursuit of the good of the Republic is frustrated as the mass pulls superior men down to its own mean and grasping material level. The long-run good of the polity, the argument goes, must be neglected as leadership is compelled to cater to the greed and to the ignorance of the masses. Measures that obviously promote the greater public good cannot be undertaken because of mass opposition and misunderstanding.

That at times mass opinion may handicap desirable action cannot be denied. Yet as one puzzles over the nature of interactions between government and mass opinion and ponders such empirical data as can be assembled on the matter, he can arrive only at the conclusion that a wide range of discretion exists for whatever wisdom leadershp echelons can muster in the public service. The generality of public preferences, the low intensity of the opinions of many people, the low level of political animosities of substantial sectors of the public, the tortuousness of the process of translation of disapproval of specific policies into electoral reprisal, and many other factors point to the existence of a wide latitude for the exercise of creative leadership. While the winning of consent for innovation may require skill in popular exposition and in political technique, those political leaders who shirk the task of popular education are misfits who do not understand the responsibilities of their jobs. And those leaders who act as if they thought the people to be fools responsive only to the meanest appeals deserve only scorn.

3

A SENATOR OBJECTS TO PRESSURE*

Styles Bridges

Frequently lobbying is regarded as an abstract, even an esoteric process, far removed from the life of the average citizen. In the following selection, the late Senator Styles Bridges of New Hampshire personalizes the activity and demonstrates how undue pressure is the bane of every conscientious legislator.

Do you want your government run by pressure groups?

I ask because there is danger that our democratic processes will be thwarted unless something is done—by you, the voter—to put the pressure of public opinion on the pressure groups that infest the halls of Congress.

Now, you will agree that lobbying is wicked when it goes beyond the legitimate expression of opinion as to public issues; when it seeks to sway members of Congress in the selfish interests of a particular faction.

You will acknowledge that elected representatives of the people should have freedom to vote according to their convictions.

You will concede that any senator or representative who yields to the urging of "legislative agents" without considering the interests of the people ought to be drummed out of office.

But have you ever signed a petition without reading it closely—a petition "demanding" that your representative vote as the sponsors of the petition would have him vote?

Have you ever fired a telegram at your representative—a telegram sent simply because someone asked you to send it and you want to be obliging?

Have you ever clipped a "coupon" from a newspaper and sent it in with your signature affixed to the plea of some organization—a plea that your representative vote for a specific measure; a plea made without regard to your representative's convictions?

If you have done any of these things, or any one of the dozen other things that fall into the same category, then you too have been guilty of lobbying.

"But," you say, "I have a perfect right to express my opinion." Of course you have. I have no quarrel with the citizen who sincerely voices his own views. But, from my ten years of experience in the Senate, I believe that before you voice them to congressmen there are certain things you should know.

The first thing you should know is that it is not possible to buy the vote of any member of Congress. That form of approach is crude and outmoded. The worst it could get you would be a term in prison. The "best" it could get you would be bodily ejection from the office of the representative.

Secondly, it is idle to make threats of political retaliation if your congress-

* Styles Bridges, "I Don't Like Pressure Groups," *Pageant*, September 1946, pp. 17–20.

man doesn't vote they way you want him to vote. Such threats just don't impress a senator or a congressman anymore.

He knows that he has to stand on his record as a whole. He knows that decisions may cost him his job if he misgauges public opinion too many times. But he knows that few letter-writers or telegram-senders have any real influence over any vote beyond those of their friends.

And it is no good trying to influence a senator or congressman through his family. By the time any man gets to Congress, the members of his family are pretty wise politically. What you'll get as a reward for such an approach probably will be a word of warning from Mrs. Blank to Senator Blank.

Neither is it advisable to try to influence a senator or congressman through a friend. When Edwin W. Pauley was nominated to be Under Secretary of the Navy, I was against confirmation. I said so.

One day I got a telephone call from New Mexico. It was from a man who said that he was an acquaintance of a friend of a friend my family. He told me at length, and at considerable cost in long-distance tolls, that I was making a great mistake in opposing Pauley.

What did I reply? Well, I told him that how I voted was my business; that I did not appreciate his attempt to influence me, and that I would take pleasure in informing the family friend of his action and of my disapproval.

Form letters or form telegrams are also poor means of influencing members of Congress. Most members are hard-working men. Few have time to read all their mail. They have to delegate the task to secretaries. And their secretaries, being politically wise, are adept at sorting out the honest, sincere mail from the propaganda junk that comes in bunches. Furthermore, putting "personal" on a letter means nothing. A substantial amount of our mail has "personal" on it. Nevertheless, it goes to the secretaries.

"But," you ask, "what can I do to acquaint my congressman with my views?"

First, if you write, make your letter clear and brief. Argue your case. You'll find your representative willing to consider your arguments on their merits. Obviously, if enough of his constituents take the same side on an issue, he will be bound to give their views serious consideration.

But remember this: while a senator is sworn in as a senator from his state, when he takes office he becomes a Senator of the United States. His first obligation is to decide whether legislation is in the national interest. His second is to see if the national interest can be reconciled with the interests of his state or a section of his state. Often he will have to vote against something that his state wants very much, because he is convinced that it would not be in the best interest of the nation. . . .

Similarly, some individuals, indignant when others try to use pressure on men in public office, are not above using a little pressure of their own when they themselves have something at stake.

Let me tell you a story about one senator. A middle-aged couple visited his office. They told him, with details, that their son, 21, was in the navy at Norfolk. They complained that he had fallen in love with a girl and intended to marry her three days hence. They said they had checked up on her; had found out she was "nothing but a little tramp." They begged the senator to "do something" to stop the marriage. The senator telephoned the commandant. Fortunately, he found out that he didn't have to do anything; that the boy was being shipped out next day.

He turned from the telephone and so informed the parents. What was his reward? Why, the mother burst into tears (the same mother who had asked him to "do anything" to break up the marriage). "You have sent my boy to his death," she said.

Let me tell you a story about myself. A father and his son visited my office early in the war. The father said the boy's mother was in a highly nervous condition. He demanded that I intercede with the local draft board to keep the boy out of the army. He promised me political support if I complied and threatened me with political vengeance if I didn't. I finally had to order them both out of my office, with the parting shot that my own son was overseas and was taking his chances just as all Americans should take them.

Those are comparatively harmless types of lobbying, but there have been more vicious types. Perhaps the most vicious was the form of "persuasion" attempted by an organization calling itself the Mothers of America in the days when they were opposing the draft, passage of the Lend-Lease Act and repeal of the Neutrality Act.

They actually waylaid senators after the draft vote and spat on them. I know because I was one of the senators. They even went so far as to knock down the late Senator Carter Glass in front of his office. After the Lend-Lease bill's passage, they hung crepe on the doors of senators who had voted for it.

Now what can we do about all this? I think lobbyists and the pressure groups they represent should be required to register. They should be required to state: (a) who is paying them; (b) how much; (c) what legislation they are trying to advocate or defeat.

Then Congress would be able to throw a searchlight on the activities of such groups. If some group is spending a million dollars to back or defeat a bill, the public is entitled to know it—and know why.[1]

---

[1] In 1946, Congress passed the Federal Regulations of Lobbying Act requiring every person hired to influence bills in Congress to register and disclose the amount of money paid to him and the identity of his employer. The Courts, however, have narrowly construed the registration provision and in the first four years of operation only 500 individuals and organizations registered.

4

INTEREST GROUPS AND REPRESENTATIVE DEMOCRACY*

David B. Truman

In many quarters the very mention of "interest groups" or "pressure groups" stirs unrestrained irritation, righteous indignation or even uncritical anger. Obviously none of these reactions is very helpful. More useful, perhaps, is David B. Truman's suggestion that the best initial response is to become better informed on the role of interest groups in the governmental process.

Within limits organized interest groups, gravitating toward responsive points of decision, may play one segment of the [governmental] structure against another as circumstances and strategic considerations permit. The total pattern of government over a period of time thus presents a protean complex of crisscrossing relationships that change in strength and direction with alterations in the power and standing of interests, organized and unorganized.

There are two elements in this conception of the political process in the United States that are of crucial significance and that require special emphasis. These are, first, the notion of multiple or overlapping membership and, second, the function of unorganized interests, or potential interest groups.

The idea of overlapping membership stems from the conception of a group as a standardized pattern of interactions rather than as a collection of human units. Although the former may appear to be a rather misty abstraction, it is actually far closer to complex reality than the latter notion. The view of a group as an aggregation of individuals abstracts from the observable fact that in any society, and especially a complex one, no single group affiliation accounts for all of the attitudes or interests of any individual except a fanatic or a compulsive neurotic. No tolerably normal person is totally absorbed in any group in which he participates. The diversity of an individual's activities and his attendant interests involve him in a variety of actual and potential groups. Moreover, the fact that the genetic experiences of no two individuals are identical and the consequent fact that the spectra of their attitudes are in varying degrees dissimilar means that the members of a single group will perceive the group's claims in terms of a diversity of frames of reference. Such heterogeneity may be of little significance until such time as these multiple memberships conflict. Then the cohesion and influence of the affected group depend upon the incorporation or accommodation of the conflicting loyal-

---

* David B. Truman, *The Governmental Process* (New York: Alfred A. Knopf, Inc., 1951), pp. 506–12.

ties of any significant segment of the group, an accommodation that may result in altering the original claims. Thus the leaders of a Parent-Teacher Association must take some account of the fact that their proposals must be acceptable to members who also belong to the local taxpayers' league, to the local chamber of commerce, and to the Catholic church.

The notion of overlapping membership bears directly upon the problems allegedly created by the appearance of a multiplicity of interest groups. Yet the fact of such overlapping is frequently overlooked or neglected in discussions of the political role of groups. James Madison, whose brilliant analysis in the tenth essay in *The Federalist* we have frequently quoted, relied primarily upon diversity of groups and difficulty of communication to protect the new government from the tyranny of a factious majority. He barely touched on the notion of multiple membership when he observed, almost parenthetically: "Besides other impediments, it may be remarked that, where there is a consciousness of unjust or dishonorable purposes, communication is always checked by distrust in proportion to the number whose concurrence is necessary." John C. Calhoun's idea of the concurrent majority, developed in his posthumously published work, *A Disquisition on Government* (1851), assumed the unified, monolithic character of the groups whose liberties he was so anxious to protect. When his present-day followers unearth his doctrines, moreover, they usually make the same assumption, although implicitly.[1] Others, seeking a satisfactory means of accounting for the continued existence of the political system, sometimes assume that it is the nonparticipant citizens, aroused to unwonted activity, who act as a kind of counterbalance to the solid masses that constitute organized interest groups.[2] Although this phenomenon may occur in times of crisis, reliance upon it reckons insufficiently with the established observation that citizens who are nonparticipant in one aspect of the governmental process, such as voting, rarely show much concern for any phase of political activity. Multiple membership is more important as a restraint upon the activities of organized groups than the rarely aroused protests of chronic nonparticipants.

Organized interest groups are never solid and monolithic, though the consequences of their overlapping memberships may be handled with sufficient skill to give the organizations a maximum of cohesion. It is the competing claims of other groups *within* a given interest group that threaten its cohesion and force it to reconcile its claims with those of other groups active on the political scene. The claims within the American Medical Association of specialists and teaching doctors who support group practice, compulsory health insurance, and preventive medicine offer an illustration. The presence within the American Legion of public-housing enthusiasts and labor unionists as well as private homebuilders and labor opponents provides another example. Potential conflicts within the Farm Bureau between farmers who must buy supplementary feed and those who produce excess feed grains for the market, between soybean growers and dairymen, even between traditional Republicans and loyal Democrats, create serious political problems for the interest group. Instances of the way in which such cleavages impose

[1] Cf. John Fischer: "Unwritten Rules of American Politics," *Harper's Magazine* (November 1948), pp. 27–36.

[2] Cf. Herring: *The Politics of Democracy*, p. 32.

restraints upon an organized group's activities are infinitely numerous, almost as numerous as cases of multiple membership. Given the problems of cohesion and internal group politics that result from overlapping membership, the emergence of a multiplicity of interest groups in itself contains no dangers for the political system, especially since such overlapping affects not only private but also governmental "members" of the organized group.

But multiple membership in organized groups is not sufficiently extensive to obviate the possibility of irreconcilable conflict. There is little overlapping in the memberships of the National Association of Manufacturers and the United Steelworkers of America, or of the American Farm Bureau Federation and the United Automobile Workers. Overlapping membership among relatively cohesive organized interest groups provides an insufficient basis upon which to account for the relative stability of an operating political system. That system is a fact. An adequate conception of the group process must reckon with it. To paraphrase the famous words of John Marshall, we must never forget that it is a going polity we are explaining.

We cannot account for an established American political system without the second crucial element in our conception of the political process, the concept of the unorganized interest, or potential interest group. Despite the tremendous number of interest groups existing in the United States, not all interests are organized. If we recall the definition of an interest as a shared attitude, it becomes obvious that continuing interaction resulting in claims upon other groups does not take place on the basis of all such attitudes. One of the commonest interest group forms, the association, emerges out of severe or prolonged disturbances in the expected relationships of individuals in similar institutionalized groups. An association continues to function as long as it succeeds in ordering these disturbed relationships, as a labor union orders the relationships between management and workers. Not all such expected relationships are simultaneously or in a given short period sufficiently disturbed to produce organization. Therefore only a portion of the interests or attitudes involved in such expectations are represented by organized groups. Similarly, many organized groups—families, businesses, or churches, for example—do not operate continuously as interest groups or as political interest groups.

Any mutual interest, however, any shared attitude, is a potential group. A disturbance in established relationships and expectations anywhere in the society may produce new patterns of interaction aimed at restricting or eliminating the disturbance. Sometimes it may be this possibility of organization that alone gives the potential group a minimum of influence in the political process. Thus Key notes that the Delta planters in Mississippi "must speak for their Negroes in such programs as health and education," although the latter are virtually unorganized and are denied the means of active political participation.[3] It is in this sense that Bentley speaks of a difference in degree between the politics of despotism and that of other "forms" of government. He notes that there is "a process of representation in despotisms which is inevitable in all democracies, and which may be distinguished by quantities and by elaboration of technique, but not in any deeper 'qualitative' way." He speaks of the despot as "representative of his own class, and to a smaller, but none the less real, extent

[3] Key: *Southern Politics*, pp. 235 *et passim*.

of the ruled class as well."[4] Obstacles to the development of organized groups from potential ones may be presented by inertia or by the activities of opposed groups, but the possibility that severe disturbances will be created if these submerged, potential interests should organize necessitates some recognition of the existence of these interests and gives them at least a minimum of influence.

More important for present purposes than the potential groups representing separate minority elements are those interests or expectations that are so widely held in the society and are so reflected in the behavior of almost all citizens that they are, so to speak, taken for granted. Such "majority" interests are significant not only because they may become the basis for organized interest groups but also because the "membership" of such potential groups overlaps extensively the memberships of the various organized interest groups.[5] The resolution of conflicts between the claims of such unorganized interests and those of organized interest groups must grant recognition to the former not only because affected individuals may feel strongly attached to them but even more certainly because these interests are widely shared and are a part of many established patterns of behavior the disturbance of which would be difficult and painful. They are likely to be highly valued.

These widely held but unorganized interests are what we have previously called the "rules of the game." Others have described these attitudes in such terms as "systems of belief," as a "general ideological consensus," and as "a broad body of attitudes and understandings regarding the nature and limits of authority."[6] Each of these interests (attitudes) may be wide or narrow, general or detailed. For the mass of the population they may be loose and ambiguous, though more precise and articulated at the leadership level. In any case the "rules of the game" are interests the serious disturbance of which will result in organized interaction and the assertion of fairly explicit claims for conformity. In the American system the "rules" would include the value generally attached to the dignity of the individual human being, loosely expressed in terms of "fair dealing" or more explicitly verbalized in formulations such as the Bill of Rights. . . .

---

[4] Bentley: *The Process of Government*, pp. 314–15. Copyright 1908 by and used with the permission of Arthur F. Bentley.

[5] See the suggestive discussion of this general subject in Robert Bierstedt, "The Sociology of Majorities," *American Sociological Review*, No. 6 (December, 1948), 700–710.

[6] Kluckhohn, *Mirror of Man*, pp. 248 *et passim;* Sebastian de Grazia, *The Political Community: A Study of Anomie* (Chicago: University of Chicago Press, 1948), pp. ix, 80, *et passsim;* Almond, *The American People and Foreign Policy*, p. 158; Charles E. Merriam, *Systematic Politics* (Chicago: University of Chicago Press, 1945), p. 213.

VI

Political Parties and Political Philosophies

Both the critics and the supporters of the American party system strongly believe that political parties are essential to a modern democracy. The two groups divide over whether the two major parties should be stronger, should develop more party discipline, and should adopt distinguishing principles and distinctive tenets. Those who advocate stronger political parties emphasize what they consider to be the consequences of the "flabbiness of party structure." They insist that the end result of the two-party (Professor Burns suggests we have actually four parties) system is deadlock, stalemate, and drift.

Other students of American government hail the alleged weaknesses of our parties as the true genius of the American system. They say the nonideological character of American parties has kept the country together by preventing class from dividing against class and section against section. Because both major parties contain diverse groups supporting all kinds of causes, the parties themselves must conciliate and compromise and tone down the divisive issues. The result is unity and general tranquility.

Within each political party there are liberal and conservative groups which make themselves heard on every national issue. In this section we propose to examine political parties in the first problem, "Do American Political Parties Mean Anything?" Then we turn to a discussion of conservatism and liberalism in the section, "Which Direction Are We Turning—Right, Left, Neither?"

Do American Political Parties Mean Anything?

It is generally assumed that the function of political parties is to focus public attention on governmental problems, to debate issues, and to translate the will of the people into action. The manner in which American political parties achieve these objectives is a matter of dispute. A number of political scientists, some journalists, and many foreign observers feel that the American party system is too weak to provide the necessary responsibility in government. These critics believe that parties frustrate the will of the people and make collective leadership impossible. As a result, they contend, power is dangerously personalized in the Presidency and the Executive's office has impossible burdens thrust upon it.

On the other hand, an equally impressive number of scholars and political writers insist that the American party system is good in its present form—in fact, it is very good. For one thing, the system has worked, it is favored by the American people, and in times of crisis it has provided strong leadership. In addition, proponents of the present system argue that only flexible and resilient parties can accommodate the conflicting interest groups in our society. Since the parties are loose associations, the struggle for power between opposing groups can take place within the party. In the resulting compromise both the party and the nation gain in unity and integration.

The first section points up the divergent viewpoints on what political parties should do. It also discusses the dilemma of each party and the role the parties are now playing. The topic ends on the question of the future of both parties.

Which Way America—Left, Right, Neither?

There is a fairly widespread assumption that political parties in America have no discernible differences but that the terms "conservative" and "liberal" are solid words with fixed dictionary meanings. This may be true to some extent in the abstract. However, it is confusing and sometimes utterly misleading to apply the conservative and liberal label to individuals and groups on the contemporary political scene. Here one finds a range of views, a complexity of loyalties, and a whole spectrum of personal convictions.

In his book, *Conservatism in America: The Thankless Persuasion,* Clinton Rossiter classifies American conservatives into three main groups—ultra-conservatives, middling conservatives, and liberal conservatives. He dramatizes the difficulties of definition by distinguishing between "conservative" (a generic heading for those who believe in a philosophy based upon order and tradition) and "Conservative" (a precise term for those who hold a philosphy reaching back to Edmund Burke). Nor is the problem of the conservatives a singular one. Liberals face the same dilemma in attempting to encompass the views of all who march under their banner. In fact, liberalism has been referred to as a "wild deuce" that can fit in any hand.

All of this makes categorical statements hazardous. As an alternative to definitive explanations, we present the views of two distinguished United States senators, one a noted conservative; the other an eloquent liberal. Senator Barry Goldwater of Arizona states his views in "The Conscience of a Conservative" and Senator Eugene McCarthy of Minnesota sets forth his convictions in "The Conscience of a Liberal." To add to the picture, a noted scholar, Daniel Bell, comments on the radical right and the politically dispossessed.

1

SHOULD PARTIES MEAN SOMETHING?*

Richard L. Strout

There are those who believe that the two major political parties fail to provide the American people with real choices on important issues. In the following selection, Washington writer, Richard L. Strout, calls for a more meaningful party realignment which would encourage both parties to take stands on issues and to debate important questions.

It was a cool spring evening in May 1950, and the notables in formal attire went into the Statler Hotel in Washington to enjoy a merry gag that the bright minds of the Gridiron Club had cooked up. There were to be rival political speakers to wind up the dinner, and the representative of the Truman Fair Deal Democrats was to be ultra-conservative, Senator Harry S. Byrd of Virginia, while for the supposedly conservative Republicans the speaker was liberal Wayne Morse of Oregon, who had yet to break from his party.

The situation neatly dramatized how little party labels mean in America. This meaninglessness has continued so long as to be accepted. Indeed now it is rationalized and a whole school of thought has grown up on the philosophy that if American party labels meant anything the nation would founder. Spokesmen of this belief generally ignore several penalties the United States pays for having its curious, unparalleled amorphous party system.

First, let me look at three current rationalist of the parties—shouldn't-mean-anything philosophy.

The able Alfred Friendly, reviewing Sidney Hyman's new book *The American President*[1] (Harper's) in the *Washington Post,* praises Hyman's "dissection of the folly of replacing what have often been called the Tweedledum Republican Party and Tweedledee Democratic Party with parties of 'pure' liberals and conservatives." Mr. Friendly observes, "The idea is, mercifully, heard less often now than at other times in our history."

Another new book is the paper-

---

* Richard L. Strout, "Should Parties Mean Something?," *The New Republic,* April 12, 1954, pp. 8–10.

1 Sidney Hyman, *The American President* (New York: Harper & Row, Publishers, 1954).

bound *The United States Political System* by David Cushman Coyle[2] (a Signet Key book). This is a really excellent little book, for all its aberration on the subject I have under discussion. Since these excellent gentlemen, Friendly, Hyman and Coyle are so often right in what they say (though unaccountably dead wrong on this issue), I have no hesitation in commending their works. But "once it is admitted," says Mr. Coyle, "that the American two-party system requires both parties to adopt practically all the principles and programs that any large bloc of voters may demand" then—says Mr. Coyle—"the resemblance to Tweedledum and Tweedledee is seen to be sensible and necessary." The text leaves in some question whether the sensible Mr. Coyle accepts this initial postulate or harbors mental reservations. At any rate he seems to accept it, though he adds immediately that it is "not surprising that American voters often feel that the Democratic and Republican platforms are practically alike, and that the parties merely have different candidates."

The third and final sample of this approach came in the October 1950, *Atlantic Monthly*, under the significant title, "Why Have A Labor Party?" The eminent Herbert Agar notes and deplores the fact that, "Many Americans have grown impatient with their illogical parties." Why shouldn't they be illogical, he asks? "Parties based on ideas and principles may be suitable for a little country like England," Mr. Agar says, "but would not be suitable here." He recalls that the Founding Fathers were afraid of parties and that while parties have, it is true, been created, their danger has been reduced by the fact that they are largely shifting coalitions of sectional and local groups. Lack of logic and absence of unifying principles is all for the best, he argues. Once when a party finally did take a position on "principle" see what happened: there was a Civil War. Mr. Agar also supports the Senate filibuster, if I understand him, on the same basis that he supports Tweedledum parties: "The filibuster is an undemocratic veto. . . . Nevertheless, like the amorphous party system . . . it has played a vital role in preserving our federal compromise."

This rationalization of make-believe parties is a symptom of the age. Everywhere there is escapism. The mood brings to politics what is already visible in the arts. In music the avant garde gives us symphonies full of discords and cacophonies which nobody enjoys but the musical elite and tomcats. In poetry there is a whole school of sophisticated and unintelligible writers some of whom omit capital letters and punctuation. In prose there are obscurantists like Joyce and Gertrude Stein. In drama and philosophy there are the Dadaists and Surrealists, pasting pennies on oil paintings or delivering stage lines dressed in diving helmets. You and I wonder about these things but are told it is for the best. Why shouldn't the same advanced mood enter politics? We already have Tweedledum parties that couldn't be improved upon from the foregoing rules so let us rejoice they are here, say they are necessary, and insist that the introduction of something logical, realistic and sensible would crack the Republic. None of the good fellows cited above would, or could, add the next argument, that party reform is probably "un-American" and "subversive," but I am sure somebody can be found who will take that line.

And yet the apologists for illogical

---

[2] David Cushman Coyle, *The United States Political System* (New York: The New American Library, 1954).

parties ignore the price we pay for them. Mean-nothing parties may reduce political heat, but they also dampen political interest. The turn-out at American elections is mortifyingly small. Nobody can seem to understand why. All the exhortations of all the civic groups in America can't raise the percentage of those who vote at Presidential elections much above 55 per cent, it seems, or 33 per cent at mid-term elections. And the dear people try so hard. Isn't it because American voters are increasingly cynical about parties that lump Byrd and Humphrey together, and Bricker and Ives?

Another thought rises. Why do supporters of illogical parties want to get voters to the polls anyway? Isn't the safeguard of this volatile, hysterical America the fact that it has meaningless political parties? Then isn't it a good thing on the whole to keep the untrustworthy people from participating in government on election day?

Yet many people are deeply worried at American apathy. In 1948, 47 million of voting age didn't vote. In 1952 it was better—only 37 million stayed home. This ratio of 55 per cent compares to 70 to 90 per cent in lands where parties have coherence.

When parties decline in meaning there is a tendency toward leader-worship. The voter gropes for a label better than "In" or "Out." Where he can't find a principle he grabs a personality. Political scientists ask if this couldn't lead toward demagoguery, and in Presidential elections, executive aggrandizement and even personal government?

Americans have curiously stable institutions. Few nations are so tenacious of ancient practices. Congressional procedure is an attic of hoopskirts and powdered wigs. Is a nation so durable in its loyalties likely to break away from the traditional two-party system? I think we are wedded to it for keeps, with occasional honorable third parties giving the old ones a transfusion of new ideas. The two-party system will continue, whether the rival politicians are divided over patronage or over principles. The theory that America would fly apart if its political parties introduced order, meaning and judicious discipline is refuted by the experience of Britain, Scandinavia, Canada and all the rest where it is done. In Canada's 1953 general election 70 per cent of the voters voted. How little faith Americans have in their own countrymen who fear they can't be trusted with realities. Personally I believe America's genius for self-government surpasses the vaunted British; Britain would collapse under our antique practices in a week.

In 1950 a distinguished committee of the American Political Science Association, in a unanimous report, concluded that American political parties are "now probably the most archaic institutions in the United States." The committee, headed by Professor E. E. Schattschneider of Connecticut Wesleyan, observed in its document "Toward A More Responsible Two-Party System," that "the alternatives between the parties are defined so badly that it is often difficult to determine what the election has decided even in the broadest terms." Although every communication and transportation agency is shrinking America, the party structure "is still substantially what it was before the Civil War." Party rivalry itself, they confidently predict, will gradually bring modernization, with the reward going to the first party which acts.

Here are their main criticisms of present party structure:

There is no continuing agency to interpret the party "platform" after its slap-dash invention every four years.

There is no authoritative agency to decide party policies on issues springing up between four-year intervals.

State and federal branches of the

same party often have diametrically opposite views of crucial issues.

Even House and Senate groups of the same party differ on what their party stands for and nobody can discipline them.

There is little machinery for members of the party to express the continuing desire to party leaders who formulate party platforms and party positions.

So runs the indictment.

The apologists for the Tweedledum system may charge that I am unfairly over-simplifying their views. But I assert that is just what the Tweedledum boys do to their opponents.

Typical is the tendentious heading of Herbert Agar's article in which he defends the status quo. The title is "Why Have a Labor Party?" The implication is, of course, that if you disagree with Agar you want a "Labor Party," or that, in any event, that is what you will get.

But this is nonsense. You can go in the direction of reform without falling off the precipice of having a Labor party (assuming that having a Labor party is falling off the precipice). Not falling off precipices is what Anglo-Saxon democracy has been doing for a couple of centuries. Canada, incidentally, has no Labor party. A historical accident has made the South Democratic, but even the Solid South is tending to break up a bit. The United States could, and should, have two political parties more consistently and coherently approximating the liberal and conservative approaches in America, with discipline enough so that the voter would know what he was voting for and—if his side won—what he was getting.

As for the Congressman, he could have the fun of telling a selfish pressure group to go to blazes if he carried the insurance of a reasonably disciplined party supporting specific principles. It is hard for me to think of anything more democratically stimulating than giving the nation real parties.

2

THE FUNCTION OF THE TWO MAJOR PARTIES*

Herbert Agar

While some political scientists deplore the lack of principles and distinctive tenets in American political parties, Herbert Agar finds the absence of these characteristics a "sign of health and vigor."

During Grover Cleveland's first term in the White House, James Bryce published his remarkable book *The American Commonwealth*. Surveying the party system from the English point of view, and with quiet surprise, he made the classic statement of the difference between the Republicans and the Democrats.

What are their principles [he wrote], their distinctive tenets, their tendencies?

* Herbert Agar, *The Price of Union* (Boston: Houghton Mifflin Company, 1950), pp. 688–91.

Which of them is for free trade, for civil-service reform, for a spirited foreign policy . . . for changes in the currency, for any other of the twenty issues which one hears discussed in the country as seriously involving its welfare? This is what a European is always asking of the intelligent Republicans and intelligent Democrats. He is always asking because he never gets an answer. The replies leave him in deeper perplexity. After some months the truth begins to dawn on him. Neither party has anything definite to say on these issues; neither party has any principles, any distinctive tenets. Both have traditions. Both claim to have tendencies. Both have certainly war cries, organizations, interests, enlisted in their support. But those interests are in the main the interests of getting or keeping the patronage of the government. Tenets and policies, points of political doctrine and points of political practice, have all but vanished. They have not been thrown away but have been stripped away by Time and the progress of events, fulfilling some policies, blotting out others. All has been lost, except office or the hope of it.

This is a true description of the parties as they were, and as they still are; but Bryce's explanation of how they came to be that way is misleading. He assumes that if the American parties were healthy they would resemble the parties of Great Britain. They would have "principles" and "tenets," and would thus be forced to take sides on all "the twenty issues that one hears discussed." And he assumes that "Time and the progress of events" have deprived the parties of their principles, leaving them with nothing but "office or the hope of it." But this is too short a view; Lord Bryce was confused by the brief history of the Republican party, which possessed principles in 1856 and none in 1886. He thought this was a sign of failure and decay; but in fact it was a sign of health: 1856 had been the exception and the danger; 1886 was the reassuring norm.

The purpose—the important and healthy purpose—of an American party is to be exactly what Lord Bryce describes, and by implication deplores. The party is intended to be an organization for "getting or keeping the patronage of government." Instead of seeking "principles," or "distinctive tenets," which can only divide a federal union, the party is intended to seek bargains between the regions, the classes, and the other interest groups. It is intended to bring men and women of all beliefs, occupations, sections, racial backgrounds, into a combination for the pursuit of power. The combination is too various to possess firm convictions. The members may have nothing in common except a desire for office. Unless driven by a forceful president they tend to do as little as possible. They tend to provide some small favor for each noisy group, and to call that a policy. They tend to ignore any issue that rouses deep passion. And by so doing they strengthen the Union.

The decisive American experience—the warning against politics based on principles—took place between 1850 and 1860. A subtle and healing compromise had been effected in 1850; yet year by year, whether through fate or through human folly, it slowly disintegrated. The best men watched in anguish but could not halt the ruin. In the name of principles and distinctive tenets the Whig party was ground to bits. A new party was born which met Lord Bryce's requirements. The Republicans knew exactly where they stood on the major issue and would not give an inch. Finally, the same "principles" broke the Democratic party, and the Union of 1789 perished.

The lesson which America learned was useful: in a large federal nation, when a problem is passionately felt, and is discussed in terms of morals, each party may divide within itself, against itself. And if the parties divide, the nation may divide; for the parties, with their enjoyable pursuit of power, are a unifying influence. Wise men, therefore, may seek to dodge such problems as long as possible. And the easiest way to dodge them is for both parties to take both sides. This is normal American practice, whether the issue turns section against section, like "cheap money"; or town against country, like Prohibition; or class against class like the use of injunctions in labor disputes. It is a sign of health when the Democrats choose a "sound-money" candidate for the presidency and a "cheap-money" platform, as they did in 1868, or when they choose a "wet" Eastern candidate for the presidency and a "dry" Western candidate for the vice-presidency, as they did in 1924. It is a sign of health when the Republicans choose a "sound-money" platform but cheerfully repudiate it throughout the "cheap-money" states, as they did in 1868.

A federal nation is safe so long as the parties are undogmatic and contain members with many contradictory views. But when the people begin to divide according to reason, with all the voters in one party who believe one way, the federal structure is strained. We saw this in 1896, during the last great fight for "free silver." To be sure, there remained some "gold Democrats" and some "silver Republicans" in 1896; yet the campaign produced the sharpest alignment on principle since the Civil War. And the fierce sectional passions racked the nation. Luckily, the silver issue soon settled itself, and removed itself from politics, so the parties could relapse into their saving illogicality.

The faults of such irrational parties are obvious. Brains and energy are lavished, not on the search for truth, but on the search for bargains, for concessions which will soothe well-organized minorities, for excuses to justify delay and denial. Unofficially, and in spite of any constitution, successful federal politics will tend to follow Calhoun's rule of concurrent majorities. Every interest which is strong enough to make trouble must usually be satisfied before anything can be done. This means great caution in attempting new policies, so that a whole ungainly continent may keep in step. Obstruction, evasion, well-nigh intolerable slowness —these are the costs of America's federal union. And the endless bartering of minor favors which we saw at its silliest in President Arthur's Congress is also part of the price. And so is the absence of a clear purpose whenever the President is weak or self-effacing, since the sum of sectional and class interests is not equal to the national interest, and the exchange of favors between blocs or pressure groups does not make a policy.

Yet no matter how high one puts the price of federal union, it is small compared to the price which other continents have paid for disunion, and for the little national states in which parties of principle can live (or more often die) for their clearly defined causes. And the price is small compared to what America paid for her own years of disunion. The United States, of course, may some day attain such uniformity (or have it thrust upon her) that she will abandon her federal structure; but until that happens she will be governed by concurrent majorities, by vetoes and filibusters, by parties which take both sides of every dangerous question, which are held together by the amusements and rewards of office-seeking, and which can only win an election by bringing many incompatible groups to accept a token triumph in the name of unity, instead of demanding their full "rights" at the cost of a fight.

The world today might do worse than study the curious methods by which such assuagements are effected.

3

THE FOUR PARTY SYSTEM*

James MacGregor Burns

In a brilliant study of American political parties, The Deadlock of Democracy, *James MacGregor Burns argues that we have a four-party political structure rather than a two-party system. He also contends the consequence of this is stalemate and deadlock and the loss of control of our parties.*

We can conclude that the pattern of national politics is essentially a four-party pattern. The Democratic and Republican parties are each divided into congressional and presidential structures, with all the elements that comprise the American type of party.

The division of Democrats and Republicans into two parties each is of course the immediate cause of the national four-party pattern. The four parties would not last long, however, if they lacked strong attitudinal bases in the electorate. They might not continue, for example, if people divided only over economic issues, for such a situation, combined with the tendency of politicians toward combinations, would normally produce two groupings, presumably of those who got smaller slices of the economic loaf against those who got bigger. At least two factors operate against such a simple two-way division in America.

One is the obvious fact that people divide over issues other than economic ones and—a crucial point—that the economic divisions are not congruent with the others. By "other issues" I mean those that have been variously called "moral" or "style" issues but that I will call "way-of-life" issues—that is, issues that pose choices about a nation's whole culture and way of life and that cannot be calculated in terms of immediate and tangible economic return for specific groups of people. Taxes, wages, social security, farm prices, tariffs, public housing are examples of economic issues: while civil liberties, women's rights, disarmament, immigration, corruption in government, defense strategy, racial tolerance and integration, government, and religion are examples of way-of-life issues. The presumed motivational appeal of the former, Berelson, Lazarsfeld, and McPhee suggest, is self-interest of a relatively direct and tangible kind, while that of the latter is self-expression and self-gratification of a more subjective, symbolic, and projective kind. Issues do not fall neatly into the two categories. An expansion of civil rights, such as job opportunity, or of immigration of certain types of workers, or of certain types of defense activities, could mean economic benefits or deprivations for various groups as well as psychic benefits or deprivations for a wider

* James MacGregor Burns, *The Deadlock of Democracy* (Englewood Cliffs, N.J.: Prentice-Hall, Inc., 1963), pp. 257–64.

public. But the difference between the two seems sharp enough to affect the shape of our party structure.

Data on the noncongruence of economic and way-of-life issues are limited but highly suggestive. Polls indicate that there has been in recent years little if any relationship between persons' relative positions on domestic and foreign issues. "An interventionist position in foreign affairs was as likely to be taken by a domestic conservative as by a domestic liberal" in 1956, report Campbell and associates, "and the relative isolationist was as likely to favor social welfare activities in Washington as he was to oppose them." By cross-tabulating distributions of responses in 1952 to an "international involvement" question and a "social welfare activity" question, Key finds four combinations of opinion: isolationist-liberal, internationalist-liberal, isolationist-conservative, internationalist-conservative (with the last the smallest of the four in numbers).

Evidence on the noncongruence of economic and domestic way-of-life issues is even more limited but still suggestive. Much of it stems from historians' observations. The political parties have usually had their "conscience" and "cotton" wings. Under Theodore Roosevelt the Republican party numbered hosts of high-income business and professional men who looked on their party mainly as a weapon to attack the moral and social evils of the day. The Democratic party in Bryan's and Wilson's days and also more recently has numbered not only hosts of economic reformers but also workers and farmers who took a hostile or stunted view of civil liberties, women's rights, civil rights, civic betterment, and other way-of-life problems.

A second root cause of the four-party pattern is the disarticulation of the national and state party systems, stemming from the workings of federalism in a sectional society combined with some of our special political arrangements. The impact of national politics on state and local politics in our sectional nation has been noted in these pages—the creation of one-party states and districts. Balance and competition at the national level, especially in presidential contests, helped produce local noncompetition and imbalance, most notably in the South and rural North. These one-party areas tended to be ignored by presidential candidates, who concentrated on the swing areas, and hence the one-party areas became less important to the presidential parties, but they received extra representation in Congress because of the seniority system, and hence became the buttress of the congressional parties.

This double cleavage, institutional and attitudinal, between the presidential parties and the congressional parties is largely responsible for the conflicting positions that a President, whether Democratic or Republican, and a Congress, whether Democratic or Republican controlled, take on the crucial affairs of state.

Willmore Kendall has pointed to the curious fact that the Executive "is able, with good show of reason, to put itself forward on any particular issue as the spokesman for . . . lofty and enlightened principle. . . . The Executive tends, that is to say, to have the nation's ministers and publicists with it on 'peace,' the nation's professors and moralizers with it on desegregation, the nation's economists with it on fiscal policy and redistribution, the nation's political scientists with it on political reform and civil rights, etc. . . . The Executive is for world government, for the outlawry of war, for unselfishness in our relations with the outside world, for the brotherhood of man, for majority-rule, for progress, for generosity toward the weak and lowly, for freedom of thought and speech, for equality, for the spreading of the benefits of modern civilization to 'underdeveloped' lands, for science and the 'scientific outlook,' for civil rights. . . ." Congress, according to Professor Kendall, stresses other values: small group discussion in the community, deference to highly prestiged and presumably wiser citizens, and an antiquixotic concern for the "realities, problems, the potential benefits and potential costs (and for whom?)" of presidential proposals.

Why this gap between President and Congress over way-of-life issues? Why, in Professor Kendall's own terms, do the two presidential parties win a much larger share of the "moralizers" and reformers and utopians than do the two congressional parties? Possibly—and here I can only speculate, for we do not have adequate data—because the most persisting major conflicts in American politics have been over economic issues; hence the national parties have offered the most meaningful alternatives in the realm of economic policy; so that if divisions of the voters over economic and way-of-life issues are not congruent, as we have reason to think they are not, millions of voters more concerned with way-of-life issues than economic ones have had to operate in a party limbo. They are simply not aroused by the state and local contests, including congressional contests, that turn on the old bread-and-butter issues; they have not been geared into the local two-party alignment over the years because they have had no meaningful alternatives presented to them on the issues that mean most to them: corruption, human rights, social reform, and the rest. Hence the voices of the mugwumps have often been ignored in the obscure politics of the local, often noncompetitive struggle. But the presidential contest does reach and arouse such independents because their collective voice nationally is loud, and because in the sharply competitive presidential race the two candidates must move beyond the traditional economic issues and find way-of-life issues that may reach the uncommitted.

The consequence of the four-party system is that American political leaders, in order to govern, must manage multiparty coalitions just as heads of coalition parliamentary regimes in Europe have traditionally done—as the French did, for example, before De Gaulle. But the task of governing in a sense is harder in the United States, for the leaders' job is not simply to pick up enough parliamentary votes to form a cabinet, or even just to pass a bill. They must bring together the right combination of presidential party and congressional party strength to accomplish a great variety of tasks day after day and year after year. And the leaders' job is further complicated by the fact that continuous, effective government policy-making is impossible without a strong working alliance between at least some combination of presidential and congressional parties. For the presidential side and the congressional side each wields power not only in its own "constitutional" orbit but in the opposite side's orbit as well.

The extent to which the congressional and presidential parties share the same powers and hence can block each other is extraordinary. The President has a broad range of legislative power besides his veto: he can issue executive orders that have the force of law; he can draw up with other nations executive agreements that are as controlling under international law as treaties ratified by the Senate; he can make war "by the push of a button" and let Congress ratify it later, if at all. But Congress inserts itself into the executive process too. The Senate can refuse to confirm appointments—even one lone Senator can induce the whole upper body to withhold approval through the device of "senatorial courtesy." The standing committees closely affect administrative arrangements through their control of policy, and the appropriations committees and subcommittees have a profound impact through their control of funds. The more "independent" an agency or commission may be of the President, the more dependent it may be on a committee or faction of Congress. The relation, of course, changes over time. After the Civil War Congress tried to control the administration through such means as the Tenure of Office Act; the act is long since gone but not some of the motivation behind it. Today the Army Chief of Engineers has legislative authority to plan public works and report to Congress without clearing with the President.

In less obvious fields too, the two-party coalitions, the congressional and the presidential, maintain countervailing institutional apparatus. The President can publicize an issue and influence public opinion by appointing a "blue-ribbon" presidential commission controlled by the President's men, and he and his lieutenants can set into action other varieties of administration inquiries, probes, and explorations. Congress at the same time has its standing committees, including the Un-American Activities Committee, which can investigate at the drop of a hat, and it can set up special committees to conduct grand investigations.

The President can call Congress back into special session after it adjourns, but the houses can recess instead of adjourn and thus retain more control of their own operations. If the President can act on many matters through executive orders not subject to congressional veto, Congress can legislate, at least to a modest extent, through Concurrent Resolutions, which are not subject to presidential veto. Congress can limit White House legislative power by setting statutory expiration dates in the original act, as Ernest Griffith has noted, "as a device to circumvent a possible presidential veto of some future measure designed to change a particular policy to which it has given reluctant or experimental agreement." On the other hand, Congress has had to delegate to the President an immense amount of policy-making power. The bureaucracy of the executive department has grown enormously—but so has that of Congress. The General Accounting Office, which has a theoretically executive duty, supplies information on administrative lapses to congressional watchdogs.

An executive impetus and a legislative tendency confront each other at every junction. The executive impetus is to combine legislative and administrative power, to coordinate functions, to exert control from the top. Whether it is Elihu Root, Theodore Roosevelt's Secretary of War, trying (unsuccessfully) to nationalize the state guard, or Hoover and Truman trying to centralize administration, or Kennedy trying to reorganize the executive branch, the instinct of the executive is to integrate government for the sake of better control. The legislative instinct is pluralistic. Congress and the state legislatures, under the control of the legislative parties, seek to fragmentize the executive by means of individual or committee influence over administrative units, or control of specific budgetary items, or through hobbling the executive's power to reorganize. State legislatures have in some instances kept whole sections of the executive branch out from the governor's control, and have resisted efforts to shorten the long ballot, which gives state officials electoral strength independent of the governor.

This bewildering array of countervailing and overlapping powers compels American political leaders to piece together a new patchwork of party fragments, factional chieftains, congressional votes, constitutional usage, and bureaucratic officials in order to put through each major new program. Presidential party leaders do this through endless persuading, pressuring, manipulating, and bargaining. Congressional party leaders use the same methods to balk or modify administration proposals, and their task is all the easier because of the many points at which action can be slowed or stopped in the narrow, twisting, and crowded legislative channels. Since each set of parties, congressional or presidential, is a coalition itself, action depends on the alignment of coalition with coalition.

Not that the presidential and congressional party coalitions are of the same type. The former, to use Dahl's apt expression, is an "executive-centered coalition." The President has means of direction and discipline unmatched by the congressional parties or by the presidential party out of power. He has a public position, a command of the media, a control over personnel, and a direct electoral link with the people that enable him to maintain and exploit a somewhat hierarchical system in the presidential party. The congressional party is led by a coalition of parties, allied through their common attitudes and mutual dependence, and with an internal party system marked more by bargaining than by hierarchy. The essential operational process differs: the congressional reliance on committees, with their tendency to protect an existing consensus over the status quo, contrasts with the executive emphasis on single-leader activism. The out-of-power presidential party, to use Dahl's terminology, is a network of "independent sovereignties with sphere of influence." But even this network, inchoate though it is, has the attributes of party—ideology, program, leadership, machinery, and existing or potential electoral support.

Any one of the four parties can—and does—coalesce with any one of the others. We take for granted the coalition of the Democratic presidential and congressional parties, and of the two Republican parties—though often we should not. The durable alliance of the congressional parties has long been publicized by liberals as the "unholy alliance of Old Guard Republicans and Dixie Democrats" in Congress. Less obvious is another alliance, holy or unholy, between presidential Democrats and presidential Republicans. These parties occasionally combine in Congress, as Republicans from urban and suburban districts support the proposals of Democratic Presidents. But the main focus of the presidential party alliance is in the foreign policy and fiscal agencies. Roosevelt's enlistment of Stimson and Knox in his Cabinet in 1940, Truman's appointment of a host of Republicans to foreign-policy and foreign-aid agencies, Eisenhower's choice of Texas Democrat Robert Anderson as Secretary of the Treasury, and Kennedy's retention of Douglas Dillon and other Republicans from the Eisenhower Administration and his selection of an internationalist Republican, McGeorge Bundy, as an assistant, reflect a wide community of interest between the two parties. The alliance is consecrated in the name of "bipartisanship in foreign policy," or the hoary slogan "Party politics stops at the water's edge." What mainly stops at the water's edge is not party politics in general but congressional party politics in particular. The real "unholy alliance" to a good congressional Republican is the historic coalition between the internationalists in both parties. And the internationalist newspapers that approve so highly of foreign-policy bipartisanship today were never so enthusiastic about it in the 1920's and the early 1930's, when it represented a coalition of isolationists.

No political system is neutral—certainly not the congressional and presidential. Power is inseparable from structure. It is not by chance that liberal and internationalist presidents in this century have been "strong" presidents, and that men like Taft and Harding are relegated to the ranks of the weak. The stronger the exertion of presidential power, the more liberal and internationalist it will be because of the make-up and dynamics of the presidential party. The stronger the exertion of congressional power, the more conservative and isolationist will be our national policy because of the structure of the congressional forces. The man who is all for liberalism and internationalism "as long as the President's power is not increased" (as for example in the trade agreements act) is a man who has not grasped the relation of ends and means, of power and structure. The man who favors cutting down the powers of Congress because it is "slow and inefficient" is cutting down conservative influence, whether he wants to or not. The structure of coalition politics is inevitably the structure of "who gets what, when and how" in American national politics. As the Madisonian system in being, it is also the structure of slowdown and stalemate in American government.

4

AMERICAN POLITICAL PARTIES*

Stephen K. Bailey

A close student of American political parties, Professor Stephen K. Bailey suggests reasons why our political parties should be strengthened. He also analyzes some of the social changes which are currently taking place in American society and ventures an opinion on how these changes are affecting our party system.

One reason why it is safe to suggest that the national party system must be strengthened in order to bring sustained power in our government is that the safeguards of the Constitution will continue to discourage any force that becomes so unified as to threaten our freedom. The American people hold firm to the sanctity of the Constitution. It is inconceivable that they would countenance a wholesale revision of the Constitution in the foreseeable future. No model of a new or improved party system that rests on substantial constitutional change is realistic.

In suggesting new directions for our

* Stephen K. Bailey, *The Condition of Our National Parties* (New York: The Fund for the Republic, 1959), pp. 12–13, 17–21.

national party system, therefore, the British parliamentary model is ruled out. But it is not ruled out simply because its wholesale adoption here is unthinkable. It is ruled out because it has shortcomings which do not warrant emulation. The relative independence of the legislature in the American system of government is, within limits, a powerful asset. At its best, it assures continuing social criticism and review of the bureaucracy without which big government might easily become lethargic and unresponsive or officious and dangerous.

What we are after is a national two-party system that will continue to have room for diversity and compromise but will nevertheless bring about more coherent and responsible programming by the executive and legislative branches and more coherent and responsible criticism of policy and administration. We are after a system that will make parties compete vigorously to find the right answers; that will organize political power at the national level so that it is adequate to carry out those answers; and that will make this power ultimately accountable to popular majorities.

This neither presumes nor suggests ideological or highly disciplined parties, although it does presume differences in the ideological propensities of each party and also presumes that party members who vote consistently against their own party's majority will not be favored with positions of party power inside or outside the Congress.

Various changes in state primary laws, in methods of choosing national convention delegates and national committee members, and in grass-roots political organization could have a profound influence on national party behavior. But, in my opinion, changes of this sort will come about rapidly only if prior attention is given to the following political reforms (some of which are already under way):

One: To create mass-based, long-range, and (in part) tax-supported national party financing—not only to underwrite and extend present functions but to increase national committee services and financial aid to congressional campaign committees and to individual candidates running in primary as well as general elections;

Two: To expand two-party competition into all congressional districts and states;

Three: To create, by formal action of the two national conventions, permanent advisory councils and staffs to both national committees;

Four: To provide social and office facilities for each national party along the Mall, between the White House and Capitol Hill, to serve as symbolic and practical links between the executive and legislative branches of government, as well as between the party and its membership across the country;

Five: To provide, by constitutional amendment, for the simultaneous election every four years of the President, the House of Representatives, and half the members of the United States Senate—all Senators to serve for eight years;

Six: To establish or strengthen party policy committees in the House and Senate to guide congressional business; hold reasonably frequent party caucuses; nominate members for committee assignments, who would then be elected in the caucuses; and receive, hold joint hearings, and report on all general presidential messages;

Seven: To find a mathematical formula for computing congressional seniority which will give added weight to those legislators who come from competitive two-party districts and states;

Eight: To repeal the 22nd Amendment;

Nine: To develop machinery for keeping an active roster of talented people for the important executive posts in the national government.

. . . The national parties have become what they are because of these historical conflicts which they have had to settle, hide, or gloss over. In some cases they have been the master brokers between rich and poor, country and city, butter and oleo, capital and labor, Italian and Irish, new and old. At other times, they have hidden certain conflicts in order to satisfy powerful economic interests which have stood to gain by exploiting conflict locally and disguising it nationally. Each party has been caught in the dilemma, on the one hand, of trying to forge an image of harmony in the interests of the majority in order to win the Presidency, and, on the other hand, of being unable to eradicate the very different kind of image which generations of conservative log-rolls and bipartisan "innerclubism" in the Congress have created in the public eye.

But what happens when the conditions of conflict change? For they are changing, and rapidly, in the United States.

THE SOCIAL CHANGES

Take the struggle between the old and the new. We used to be able to tell the difference between old and new settlers by their accent, or dress, or occupational level. But we are fuller of hundred per cent Americans every day and are rapidly reaching the time when nationality politics will be as anachronistic as the trolley car. Samuel Lubell has set the beginning of the end of this traditional conflict in the late Thirties, with the coming of age of those whose parents and grandparents had arrived in the great immigration surge at the turn of this century. With the acceptance of the stranger as a person has come acceptance of his ways and his beliefs. A Jew is Governor of Connecticut; a Catholic is almost certain to be on the national ticket of at least one of our two national parties in 1960.[1] Matters which once split us and made us fearful are now absorbed almost without question as our population becomes increasingly homogenized.

Or take sectional and class conflict. The heart has been cut out of sectionalism by vast changes in technology and communications which have dispersed industry and revolutionized agriculture. Where are the one-crop "Cotton Ed" Smiths of a few years back? The fact is that there are precious few one-crop areas left in America. And even where there are, as in some of the great agricultural regions of the Great Plains, technology is bringing a revolution of another kind. In the last five years almost four million people have left the farm. The forecast for reapportionment of congressional seats after the 1960 census suggests a dramatic decrease in rural representation in the United States Congress, and this trend will continue as the rise in population throws more and more people into metropolitan areas.

The movement in urban politics tends to be toward class rather than regional politics. But even class politics has changed. It is no longer a kind of rabble vs. gentry rivalry. Rather, among other things, it is national industry against highly bureaucratized and well-paid national labor. Senator Barry Goldwater of Arizona is not a regional figure. In the congressional elections of 1958, national giants contended in that sparsely populated desert state, and for national stakes.

---

[1] John F. Kennedy destroyed the prevailing political myth that a Catholic could not be elected President of the United States by winning that highest elective office in 1960.

What bothers the auto worker in Detroit bothers the auto worker in Los Angeles. What worries the businessman in Chicago worries his competitor in Boston. With transcontinental jet planes, the political or labor or industrial leader whose home is in San Francisco is almost more accessible to his counterpart in New York than is a train traveler from Boston; and, in any case, distance has been obliterated by electricity, electronics, and the direct-dial telephone.

And what is happening to the Negro issue? It, too, is becoming nationalized. Today there are more Negroes in New York than in New Orleans; more in Detroit than in Birmingham, Alabama; more in Pittsburgh than in Little Rock; more in Los Angeles than in Richmond; more in Chicago than in Atlanta. The Negroes' locustlike migration to northern metropolitan centers may have brought new problems to city governments, but it has aroused a critical competition between the two major parties in the North and West to capture the Negro vote. In heavily populated, evenly divided states, a bloc shift of a few votes can mean thirty or forty electoral college votes for a presidential candidate.

Perhaps more than any one other factor, the northern migration of the Negro is working tremendous transformations in our political life. The South no longer can exercise a veto in either presidential convention. Some diehards may walk out in 1960, but the result will only be that they will risk losing what waning power they have in the Congress. For, in more than sixty congressional districts in the North and West, the Negro holds the political balance of power if he decides to bloc-vote; and in the South his political power is likely to increase steadily despite the present tensions.

As for the clash of personal political ambitions in the United States, they are being completely submerged by the international and domestic concerns of the American public. War and peace, inflation and depression, are both personal and universal issues; tariffs, taxes, foreign aid, military spending, federal reserve policies, and hosts of other national policies affect local economic activities across the land. Politicians who wish to become statesmen must be able to talk intelligently about issues that concern people in *all* constituencies. The extraordinary social and economic changes now going on are absorbing and transcending the old conflicts of personal ambitions.

THE PARTY CHANGES

The shifts in the nature of the conflicts are reflected in the changes that are already taking place in our party system:

(1) The number of one-party states and one-party congressional districts is dramatically declining.

In less than twenty years, the number of one-party delegations in Congress (in which the two Senators and all members of the House from a single state are of one party) has dropped more than 50 per cent—from twenty-four in 1942 to eleven in 1958.

The number of Southern congressional districts which had contested elections increased from forty-eight to sixty in the brief period from 1952 to 1956. In the same period of time, the total Republican vote in the South for members of the House rose from 1,872,000 in 1952 to 2,371,000 in 1956.[2]

---

[2] The Republican Nixon-Lodge ticket polled around a half million more votes in the South than Eisenhower-Nixon received in 1956. It is said that in 1960 there were 4.6 Republican votes cast in the South for every 5 Democratic votes. See O. Douglas Weeks, "The Presidential Election of 1960–Texas and the South," *Public Affairs Comment*, University of Texas, VII. No. 1 (January 1961), 1.

(2) The permanent staffs of the national party committees and the variety of committee functions have grown greatly during the past decade. Until World War II both national committees were served by skeletal staffs, except for the few months before national presidential elections. Today both of them maintain year-round staffs of between seventy-five and a hundred people. In election years this number doubles or triples. The annual budget of each committee amounts to almost a million dollars—a figure which skyrockets during election years.

(3) Both national committees are doing everything within their power to spread their financial base. The evolution has been from fat-cats and expensive fund-raising banquets to mass appeals and direct-mail solicitation.

(4) Almost unnoticed, a revolution has occurred in the "nationalization" of off-year senatorial and congressional campaigns. As recently as 1938, the press and the public criticized President Roosevelt for campaigning in an off-year election. But in 1954, when both the President and the titular leader of the Democrats actively campaigned in their parties' congressional elections, both the newspapers and the voters seemed to accept the fact that it was perfectly all right for the executive wings of the parties to interest themselves actively in the outcome of the legislative contests. In 1958, both national committees sent out representatives to help develop party strength in various regions and to give services to local campaigns. The campaign committees on Capitol Hill also provided services to these campaigns as a matter of course and, in spite of occasional frictions, worked in closer cooperation with the national committees than in any previous off-year election in history.

(5) Since 1937, the presidents have met regularly with party leaders in the Congress on matters of legislative priority and strategy. This has elevated the prestige and power of these men, particularly on matters of foreign policy and national defense. The passage of the Legislative Reorganization Act of 1946 further recognized the need for party leadership in the Congress, and succeeded to some degree in institutionalizing the leadership function in the Senate which established party policy committees with paid staffs.

(6) The creation of the Democratic Advisory Council and the recent appearance of an embryonic Republican counterpart show a new concern in both parties for clarifying the party image. There is little doubt that, eventually, pronouncements of these "executive wings" of the parties will be more effective than similar attempts by congressional leaders or individual party spokesmen excepting the president.

THE CONCLUSION

This far from exhaustive list of the responses of our political system to nationalizing forces represents only the beginnings of adaptation and adjustment. Our basic political institutions, and their relationships to each other and to the public, are in a state of flux. If we want a political system designed to give full play to America's political energies and to hold them within bounds set by a popular majority, we are obligated to modify the system still further.

The reforms outlined in these pages will not obviate America's continuing need for personal force and political virtuosity in the office of the presidency and in top positions in the Congress Nor will these or any other party reforms dispel the terrifying military, diplomatic, and social problems of our age. But they will help the parties toward stronger leadership in a more responsible framework than has been traditional. To paraphrase Emerson, they can help us to perceive the terror of life and to man ourselves to face it. In this apocalyptic age, can we ask for greater service from our political parties? We must not ask for less.

5

THE CONSCIENCE OF A CONSERVATIVE*

Barry Goldwater

The most interesting phenomenon in recent American politics has been the rise of a very articulate conservative movement, and the most noted of the political conservative spokesmen is Senator Barry Goldwater of Arizona. In the following paragraphs the Senator sets forth his beliefs on the meaning of conservatism and the steps that should be taken to translate these beliefs into action.

I have been much concerned that so many people today with conservative instincts feel compelled to apologize for them. Or if not to apologize directly, to qualify their commitment in a way that amounts to breast-beating. "Republican candidates," Vice-President Nixon has said, "should be economic conservatives, but conservatives with a heart." President Eisenhower announced during his first term, "I am conservative when it comes to economic problems but liberal when it comes to human problems." Still other Republican leaders have insisted on calling themselves "progressive" conservatives.[1] These formulations are tantamount to an admission that conservatism is a narrow, mechanistic economic theory that may work very well as a bookkeeper's guide, but cannot be relied upon as a comprehensive political philosophy.

The same judgment, though in the form of an attack rather than an admission, is advanced by the radical camp. "We liberals," they say, "are interested in people. Our concern is with human beings, while you conservatives are preoccupied with the preservation of economic privilege and status." Take them a step further, and the liberals will turn the accusations into a class argument: it is the little people that concern us, not the "malefactors of great wealth."

Such statements, from friend and foe alike, do great injustice to the conservative point of view. Conservatism is not an economic theory, though it has economic implications. The shoe is precisely on the other foot: it is socialism that subordinates all other considerations to man's material well-being. It is conservatism that puts material things in their proper place—that has a structured view of the human being and of human society, in which economics plays only a subsidiary role.

The root difference between the con-

* Barry Goldwater, *The Conscience of a Conservative* (Shepherdsville, Kentucky: Victor Publishing Company, 1960), pp. 9–14.

[1] This is a strange label indeed: it implies that "ordinary" conservatism is opposed to progress. Have we forgotten that America made its greatest progress when conservative principles were honored and preserved?

servatives and the liberals of today is that conservatives take account of the whole man, while the liberals tend to look only at the material side of man's nature. The conservative believes that man is, in part, an economic, an animal creature; but that he is also a spiritual creature with spiritual needs and spiritual desires. What is more, these needs and desires reflect the superior side of man's nature, and thus take precedence over his economic wants. Conservatism therefore looks upon the enhancement of man's spiritual nature as the primary concern of political philosophy. Liberals, on the other hand—in the name of a concern for "human beings"—regard the satisfaction of economic wants as the dominant mission of society. They are, moreover, in a hurry. So that their characteristic approach is to harness the society's political and economic forces into a collective effort to compel "progress." In this approach, I believe they fight against nature.

Surely the first obligation of a political thinker is to understand the nature of man. The conservative does not claim special powers of perception on this point, but he does claim a familiarity with the accumulated wisdom and experience of history, and he is not too proud to learn from the great minds of the past.

The first thing he has learned about man is that each member of the species is a unique creature. Man's most sacred possession is his individual soul—which has an immortal side, but also a mortal one. The mortal side establishes his absolute differentness from every other human being. Only a philosophy that takes into account the essential differences between men, and, accordingly, makes provision for developing the different potentialities of each man can claim to be in accord with nature. We have heard much in our time about "the common man." It is a concept that pays little attention to the history of a nation that grew great through the initiative and ambition of uncommon men. The conservative knows that to regard man as part of an undifferentiated mass is to consign him to ultimate slavery.

Secondly, the conservative has learned that the economic and spiritual aspects of man's nature are inextricably intertwined. He cannot be economically free, or even economically efficient, if he is enslaved politically; conversely, man's political freedom is illusory if he is dependent for his economic needs on the State.

The conservative realizes, thirdly, that man's development, in both its spiritual and material aspects, is not something that can be directed by outside forces. Every man, for his individual good and for the good of his society, is responsible for his own development. The choices that govern his life are choices that he must make: they cannot be made by any other human being, or by a collectivity of human beings. If the conservative is less anxious than his liberal brethren to increase social security "benefits," it is because he is more anxious than his liberal brethren that people be free throughout their lives to spend their earnings when and as they see fit.

So it is that conservatism, throughout history, has regarded man neither as a potential pawn of other men, nor as a part of a general collectivity in which the sacredness and the separate identity of individual human beings are ignored. Throughout history, true conservatism has been at war equally with autocrats and with "democratic" Jacobins. The true conservative was sympathetic with the plight of the hapless peasant under the tyranny of the French monarchy. And he was equally revolted at the attempt to solve that problem by a mob tyranny that paraded under the banner of egalitarianism. The conscience of the conservative is pricked by anyone who would debase the dignity of the individual human being. Today, therefore, he is at odds with dictators who rule by terror, and equally with those gentler collectivists who ask our permission to play God with the human race.

With this view of the nature of man, it is understandable that the conservative looks upon politics as the art of achieving the maximum amount of freedom for individuals that is consistent with the maintenance of social order. The conservative is the first to understand that the practice of freedom requires the establishment of order: it is impossible for one man to be free if another is able to deny him the exercise of his freedom. But the conservative also recognizes that the political power on which order is based is a self-aggrandizing force; that its appetite grows with eating. He knows that the utmost vigilance and care are required to keep political power within its proper bounds.

In our day, order is pretty well taken care of. The delicate balance that ideally exists between freedom and order has long since tipped against freedom practically everywhere on earth. In some countries, freedom is altogether down and order holds absolute sway. In our country the trend is less far advanced, but it is well along and gathering momentum every day. Thus, for the American conservative, there is no difficulty in identifying the day's overriding political challenge: it is to preserve and extend freedom. As he surveys the various attitudes and institutions and laws that currently prevail in America, many questions will occur to him, but the conservative's first concern will always be: Are we maximizing freedom? I suggest we examine some of the critical issues facing us today with this question in mind.

6

THE CONSCIENCE OF A LIBERAL*

Eugene J. McCarthy

Senator McCarthy examines the term "liberalism" and points out what it is and what it is not. He shows some of the strengths and some of the pitfalls into which liberals are prone to fall, but most of all Senator McCarthy explains what it means to be a liberal at this point in the twentieth century.

Politics in the United States is nondoctrinaire and nonideological. Two terms, however, applied to politics seem to have doctrinal or ideological content for those who use them. These are the words "liberal" and "conservative." In states which do not have party designation for legislators—like my own state, Minnesota—it is a practice to hold organizing caucuses of

* Eugene J. McCarthy, *Frontiers in American Democracy* (New York: World Publishing Company, 1960), pp. 63–70.

"liberals" and of "conservatives." Americans for Democratic Action, a "liberal" organization, regularly calls for the purification of the Democratic party by the elimination of the "conservative" members. The Conservative Citizens Committee, in companionship with a new organization called simply the New Party, is trying to purge the Republican party of its "liberal" tendencies.

The clarification of the terms liberal and conservative, at least as they are applied to politics, is made more difficult because many explanations and definitions of liberals and liberalism have been offered by conservatives, and on the other hand, many explanations and definitions of conservatives and of conservatism have been offered by liberals.

In line with this practice William F. Buckley, Jr., admitted conservative and editor of the *National Review*, makes his case against the liberals by saying that "there is an enormous area in which the liberal does not know how to think. More specifically," says Buckley, "he is illogical, he is inconsistent, and he cannot assess evidence."

Liberals on the other hand are inclined to be less direct and harsh, but rather given to more subtle or sophisticated explanations of their conservative opponents. Witness Arthur Schlesinger, Jr.'s analysis of the new conservatism as having strong interior tendencies toward schizophrenia.[1] He asserts that it is out of touch with reality. There are less sophisticated liberals, I admit, who are satisfied to call conservatives "medieval" or "Neanderthal."

Life would certainly be made much easier for liberals if it were possible to define carefully the word "liberalism" and limit its use according to this restricted definition. Until such a definition can be worked out, it would be helpful if the word "liberal" were used only as a modifier. If this were general agreement, no one would be merely a liberal, or a "pseudo-liberal" in the terminology of J. Edgar Hoover. Anyone to whom the word was applied would have to be a liberal something. In politics he would not be merely a liberal, but a liberal Republican, a liberal Democrat, or a liberal Vegetarian, or a liberal something else. There no longer would be religious liberals, but liberal Methodists, liberal Presbyterians, liberal Catholics, and so on. The word "intellectual" and the word "liberal" would no longer be considered synonymous. There would henceforth be liberal intellectuals and illiberal intellectuals, and when *Time* magazine's phrenological distinctions were applied, liberal eggheads and illiberal eggheads—or turnip-heads, if you prefer.

The truth is that American liberalism is not a twentieth-century manifestation of nineteenth-century liberalism. It is not even a development from that earlier liberalism.

Liberalism in the United States is not a system of philosophy, or a religion, or a school of political, economic, or social thought. It is not a way of life, as some of its proponents claim and as some of its opponents charge. It is not a "demanding faith" as Americans for Democratic Action say; nor is it on the contrary an "undemanding faith" as Professor William Leuchtenburg of Harvard University critically described it; nor is it without faith, or at least without a home for "faith," as Frederich K. Wilhelmsen of Santa Clara University wrote in *Commonweal.*

I believe it fair to say that American liberalism is no more materialistic in its

[1] "The New Conservatism: Politics of Nostalgia," *The Reporter,* June 16, 1955, p. 11.

metaphysics than is American conservatism. It is no more rationalistic in its psychology than is American conservatism. It cannot be described as more utilitarian, more positivistic, or relativistic in its ethics and in its value judgments than can conservatism. Nor can it be described as more opportunistic or Machiavellian in its politics.

To the extent that the liberal movement in the United States in this century can be given historical position and positive content, it must be identified and associated with the New Deal of the first two Roosevelt administrations. The New Deal involved political and economic changes which were the results of a response to urgent practical demands, rather than a fulfillment or an advancement of an ideology or a doctrinaire theory of political, economic, or social organization.

The total program provided for the pooling of social risks, as in the case of the social security program, and the pooling of economic risks, as in the case of the Federal Deposit Insurance program. It included such projects as the Tennessee Valley Authority and the hydroelectric developments in the Far West. In each case, the decision to include the specific program or project was based on practical considerations—the development and distribution of power, for example, or the related problems of navigation and flood control, rather than to an ideological demand for social ownership or collectivization. At the same time that the above-mentioned programs were advanced, or projects begun, along with others providing for greater control by government over such things as the investment market and the wages and hours of workingmen, efforts were made to protect the small independent business and the independent family-size farm.

As the general economic well-being of the people of the United States improved, the positive content of the liberal movement narrowed and popular support fell away. When there is a call for volunteers to make and carry the bricks of domestic economic reform, the liberal response is strong. The Marshall Plan and Point IV programs too—foreign-aid programs closely akin in spirit to our domestic programs—were strongly endorsed by liberal groups.

In short, if American liberalism has one mark it is its economic emphasis. Yet few if any liberal thinkers really believe the "belly" communist argument, or believe that communism can be overcome by dropping Montgomery Ward catalogues from airplanes flying over communist countries.

The lack of ideological unity among American liberals, beyond agreement on economic programs and civil rights, explains in part their attachment to individual leaders manifest in their enthusiasm for President Roosevelt, their short-lived courtship of General Eisenhower in the Eisenhower-and/or-Douglas campaign of 1948, and since then their enthusiastic support of Adlai Stevenson. The attachment to one person eliminates or at least moderates the division, reduces the uncertainties and conflicts, and provides in the person a unity of cause.

If the bond among American liberals today is not one of ideas or even of program, how can we distinguish them? The common trait, I believe, is one of method or manner of approach to human problems. It is this manner of approach that distinguishes the liberal from the illiberal and establishes the characteristics of modern liberalism and the modern liberal.

The liberal is ideally and characteristically an optimist, not blindly so as one who fails to understand or to comprehend the reality of the times, but rather as one who, with full awareness of the difficulties of a situation and with full awareness also of the potentiality for failure of man and his institutions, remains hopefully confident that improvement and progress can be accomplished. This does not mean that he believes that things are necessarily getting better and better, nor does it require any belief in the inevitability of progress.

The ideal liberal is normally progressive, willing both to advocate and to accept change—really a safe general position since no individual person or human institution can ever claim perfection. But he need not always advocate something wholly new; he can support elements of the status quo, or he may even advocate a return to conditions known in the past. He does not necessarily believe in change for the sake of change or, as some critics of liberals insist, in historical determinism and the inevitability of collectivization.

The liberal is normally tolerant of the opinions and actions of others, yet he exercises this tolerance without abjectly denying the certainty of his own position, without conceding that another's position may be right, without agreeing to disagree, and certainly without accepting that one man's opinion is as good as that of another. The basis for his tolerance must be a genuine humility arising from the awareness of the limitations of the human person and from a sense of the dignity of every man.

There are, of course, dangers in the liberal approach. Optimism can become self-delusion, change an obsession. Because the future is not the past, the liberal may be led, as Vincent McNabb points out, to think that it must be something entirely different from the past. He may therefore neglect or take lightly the lesson of history and underestimate the value of custom and of tradition. He may accept that there must be an absolute break between past and present, and again between present and future. His tolerance gone too far may lead him to accept unsound positions of religious indifferentism, of intellectual pluralism, and of subjective morality. However, such excesses are not inherent in liberalism.

In his concern for freedom, the liberal is in danger of forgetting the obligations and restraints that are the price of freedom and of discounting the importance of institutions and their function in the perfecting of individual persons.

The liberal of today cannot be satisfied in the belief that his approach to human problems is the better one, but must clarify his ideas as to the nature of man and the meaning and goal of human existence. The liberal of today must do more than "feel free." He must concern himself not only with claiming freedom, but with understanding it, since time has worked significant changes in the meaning of this word.

The liberal who speaks much of freedom must stop to consider its meaning. He should recall that the free man of the Greek philosophers is the man who has achieved freedom, who has overcome ignorance and acquired a measure of self-mastery. In this classical philosophical tradition, the concept of freedom is applied principally to the state of being, rather than to the conditions under which man lives and works in order to attain that state. In our time the emphasis has been upon the condition of the striving, rather than upon the status which might be reached. The meaning which we give to the term "freedom," either in the static sense or as it relates to the condition of man's living and seeking for fulfillment, depends basically upon our concept of the nature of man and the purpose of his existence.

It is not enough to want freedom for its own sake. Freedom is not baseless or relative, but desired and pursued to make man more responsible, more in control of his life and his time. Thus freedom from want makes a man more surely free to choose poverty if he wishes. Freedom from oppression or domination leaves a man more truly free to choose the object of his allegiance, or to whom he will give obedience.

The complexity of modern problems, the quickened pace of historical change, the involvement with people of other races and cultures—all call for a liberal response. American liberalism as a force bearing on American politics can be a positive force for good only if it clarifies its positive content and becomes something more than the liberalism of the immediate past. Optimism, generosity, tolerance, and even humility, good and necessary as they are, are of little use unless there can be some agreement as to what is good.

American liberals today are faced with the pluralistic society they once only dreamed and talked about. There is no longer a dominant group in our American culture, although it will take time for the popular mind to cast off the image of the American prototype, to whose loyalties and mores all other groups conformed and were American in so far as they conformed. The liberal's task is to secure this individualistic society with his tolerance and generosity and at the same time in the words of Woodrow Wilson, "to make sure of the things which unite."

7

OUR RADICAL RIGHT—THE DISPOSSESSED*

Daniel Bell

A phenomenon of the 1960's has been the rise throughout the country of various radical right groups—the John Birch Society, Christian Crusade, White Citizen Councils, and others. Although they may differ in detail, on many points these disparate groups are united. Most political, social, military, and economic trends are viewed with alarm. They also exhibit something of a nostalgia for an earlier age. What groups are a fertile recruiting ground for the radical right? Why do these people feel dispossessed? Is this rebellion a transitory movement, or does it have deep roots?

Most of the political changes that have transformed American life, the changes that have aroused such notable right-wing rancor today, originated in legislative measures passed thirty years ago and before—the income tax, social security, welfare measures, and the like. In many instances, the changes have been irrevocably built into the structure of American society.

* Daniel Bell, "The Dispossessed—1962," *Columbia University Forum* (Fall, 1962), pp. 4–12.

Why then have the consequences of these changes become manifest only at this very late date? And what is the nature of the right-wing rancor? . . .

Over the years since 1932, then, there has been a steady erosion of conservative influence. The expansion of the executive agencies of government in the past three decades, drawing key personnel largely from the major universities, has given the middle and (later) top echelons of government a predominantly liberal coloration; and this is one of the factors that accounts for the tension between the Executive and the Congress which has been so marked in the last decade and a half. More slowly, the personnel of the lifetime federal judiciary began to change through appointments by Democratic presidents.

The right-wing Republicans hoped that the election of Dwight Eisenhower would reverse this massive trend. But it did not—perhaps could not. Eisenhower's Labor Secretary courted the unions; social security benefits increased; during the 1957–59 recession, unemployment benefits were extended; and to reverse the economic slowdown, the government, in good Keynesian style, ran a $12,000,000,000 budgetary deficit. Only Congress, reflecting the disproportionate power of the small-town areas and the established seniority system, has remained, practically speaking, under conservative control. For the Radical Right, then, eight years of "moderation" proved as frustrating as twenty years of New Dealism.

To this extent, the meaning of the Kennedy victory for the members of the Radical Right was the gnawing realization that as a social group they were becoming dispossessed of their power in American society. But more than a generational change has taken place. Until thirty years ago, the source of "visible" political and social power in American life was predominantly the small-town leaders: lawyers, real estate dealers, bankers, merchants, and small manufacturers. Their political hegemony in the states was virtually complete; nationally, the values of the society reflected the influence of the business community.

The first challenges to this dominance came from the ethnic groups in the large urban centers and from the trade union movement. Only after considerable friction were these challenges absorbed; power became more diffused. But the newer threat does not arise from any direct political competition, as was true in the case of the urban political machines. It arises from the fact that the complex problems of contemporary economic and political and military management require a technical expertise which is far beyond the understanding of the dispossessed groups for whom the "simple virtues" and the "traditional moralities" were the only guides that were felt to be necessary to the formulation of public policy. It arises from the fact that social change now has to be directed and planned. For the ramifications of many major changes—whether it be space exploration, counterforce military strategy, urban renewal, or medicare—are widespread and produce a whole series of secondary effects whose consequences have to be anticipated lest chaos result. (The passage of medicare, for example, would require a widespread hospital-building program and a stepped-up recruitment of nurses to meet the shortages that would certainly ensue.) As a corollary to these general conditions, it is a new "technocratic" elite—scientists, mathematicians, economists, sociologists, with their new techniques of decision-making: input-output matrices, systems analysis, linear programming—that now becomes essential, if not to the wielding of power, then to the formulations and analyses on which political judgments have to be made. It is these complexities and the rise of the new skill groups which pose the real threat of dispossession to those who once held power by virtue of their wealth or property or gerrymandered political control.

THE SMALL-TOWN MIND

In identifying "the dispossessed" it would be misleading to apply economic labels. It is not economic interest alone that elicits their anxieties. A small businessman may have made considerable amounts of money in the last decade (in part, because he has wider scope in masking profits than a large corporation), and yet . . . strongly resent the regulations in Washington, the high income tax, or, more to the point, the erosion of his own political status. Indeed, to the extent that any such economic location is possible, one can say that the social group most threatened by the structural changes in society is the "old" middle class: the independent physician, farm owner, small-town lawyer, real estate promoter, home builder, automobile dealer, small businessman, and the like. But the common denominator of such groups is the life-style and value of Protestant Fundamentalism—the nativist nationalism, the good-and-evil moralism through which they see the world. Theirs are the values of the dominant thought of the nineteenth century; and they have been defending these values—in what is now a rear-guard action—for the last forty years.

The present upsurge of American nativism on the Radical Right is most directly paralleled, in fact, in the virulent assaults on teachers' loyalty which were levied in the 1920's by fundamentalist churchmen in the name of God and by patriotic organizations like the American Legion in the name of country. Such conflicts—most vividly the Scopes trial and the bellicose efforts of Mayor "Big Bill" Thompson in Chicago to expunge favorable references to Great Britain from the school textbooks—were between "fundamentalists" and "modernists," between "patriots" and 'internationalists." These skirmishes in the 1920's were the first defensive reactions of the nativist and the old middle-class elements to the entry into society of formerly "disenfranchised" elements, particularly the children of immigrants and members of minority ethnic groups—an entry made through the only major route open to them, the urban political machines. In short, theirs was a reaction to the rise of a mass society. . . .

The social ideas of fundamentalism are quite familiar—a return to the "simple" virtues of individual initiative and self-reliance. In political terms, this means a dismantling of much of the social security program, the elimination of the income tax, the reduction of the role of the federal government in economic life, and the return to the state and local governments of the major responsibilities for welfare, labor, and similar legislation. Now from any realistic political view, the dismantling of social security, income tax, etc., is quite hopeless, as elections since 1936 have proved. But what gives the fundamentalist Right its political momentum today is its effort to hitch these attacks on "collectivism" to a high-powered anticommunist crusade, which identifies *any* extension of government power as communism. What in effect it seeks to do is identify the welfare state with socialism and equate liberalism with communism. In this respect, it represents a crude but powerful effort to resist *all* social change, to use the emotions generated by foreign policy conflicts to confuse domestic issues.

Until now, much of the political strength of the small-town right wing has stemmed from its ability to block the reapportionment of seats in the state legislatures and to gerrymander seats for Congress; the result is a heavily disproportionate representation of the small towns and rural areas in both assemblies. In the U.S. House of Representatives, for example, 260 of the 437 seats—or almost 60 per cent of all the seats—are in districts dominated by small towns and rural areas. In thirteen states, fewer than a third of the voters—and these are primarily in small towns—can elect a majority of the state legislators; in forty-four states, less than 40 per cent can elect a majority. The Supreme Court decision of April, 1962, ordering a redistricting of seats in the Tennessee legislature (which had blocked all reapportionment since 1901) may be the most important political act of the decade. Certainly it will break the hold of the small town on many state legislatures and reduce its influence in Congress—but how soon remains to be seen.

THE MANAGERIAL DISPOSSESSED

To list the managerial executive class as among "the dispossessed" seems strange, especially in the light of the argument that a revolution which is undermining property as the basis of power is enfranchising a new class of technical personnel, among whom are the business executives. Yet the managerial class has been under immense strain all through this period, a strain arising, in part, from the discrepancy between their large power and prestige within a particular enterprise and their lesser power and esteem in the nation as a whole.

The modern corporation, even though it holds its legitimation from the institution of private property, is vastly different from the family firm which it has succeeded. The family firm of old was securely rooted in the legal and moral tradition of private property. The enterprise "belonged" to the owner, and was sanctioned, depending on one's theological tastes, by God or by Natural Right. The modern manager clearly lacks the inherited family justifications: increasingly he is recruited from the amorphous middle class. He receives a salary, bonus, options, expense accounts, and "perks" (perquisites, like the use of company planes [and] memberships in country clubs), but his power is transitory and he cannot pass on his position; the manager needs an ideology. In no other capitalist order but the American—not in England, or Germany, or France—has this drive for ideology been so compulsive. . . .

Already in 1960, the efforts of a number of corporations, led by General Electric, to go "directly" into politics by sending out vast amounts of propaganda to their employees and to the public, by encouraging right-to-work referendums in the states—indicated the mood of political dispossession in many corporations. Since then, a significant number of corporations have been contributing financially to the seminars of the Radical Right evangelists. The National Education Program, at Harding College in Arkansas, which prepares films on communism and materials on free enterprise, has been used extensively by General Electric, U.S. Steel, Olin Mathieson Chemical, Monsanto Chemical, Swift & Co., and others. Boeing Aviation and the Richfield Oil Co. has sponsored many of the anticommunism seminars on the West Coast. The Jones and Laughlin Steel Company has a widespread propaganda program for its employees. One of the most politically active companies is the Allen Bradley Co. of Milwaukee, which makes machine tools and electrical equipment. The Allen Bradley Co. advertises in the John Birch Society magazine and reprinted the testimony before the House Un-American Activities Committee on Fred Schwarz, a reprint which Schwarz claims had "wider distribution than any other government document in the history of the United States, with the possible exception of the Bill of Rights, the Declaration of Independence, and the Constitution." Ironically, the Allen Bradley Co., which continually extols the virtue of free enterprise, was one of the electrical companies convicted of collusive bidding and illegal price-rigging.

Despite the failure of the corporations to affect significantly the 1960 elections—their failure on the right-to-work issue being one key indicator—it is likely that the Kennedy-Blough imbroglio of 1962 will provide an even greater impetus for corporations to finance right-wing political activity in the coming years.

THE MILITARY DISPOSSESSED

The irony for the American military establishment is that at a time when the military in the new states overseas has emerged as one of the ruling forces of those states (often because it is the one organized group in an amorphous society), and while at this time in United States history the amount of money spent for military purposes (roughly 50 per cent of the federal budget) is the highest in peacetime history, the U.S. military is subject to grave challenges in its very own bailiwick. The problems of national security, like those of the national economy, have become so staggeringly complex that they can no longer be settled simply by military common sense or past experience. . . .

In the last decade, most of the thinking on strategic problems, political and economic has been done in the universities or in government-financed but autonomous bodies like the RAND Corporation. A new profession, that of the "military intellectual" has emerged, and men like Kahn, Wohlstetter, Brodie, Hitch, Kissinger, Bowie, Schelling "move freely through the corridors of the Pentagon and the State Department," as the TLS writer observed, "rather as the Jesuits through the courts of Madrid and Vienna three centuries ago."

In structural terms, the military establishment may be one of the tripods of a "power elite," but in sociological fact the military officers feel dispossessed because they often lack the necessary technical skills or knowledge to answer the new problems confronting them. Since the end of World War II, the miltary has been involved in a number of battles to defend its elite position, beginning in 1945 with the young physicists and nuclear scientists, down to the present action against the "technipols" (the military's derisive term for technicians and political theorists) whom Secretary McNamara has brought into the Department of Defense. For in present-day decision-making the nature of strategy involves a kind of analysis for which experience alone is insufficient. Consider the complex problem of choosing a "weapons system": the long lead time that is necessary in planning and testing—let alone producing—such weapons compels an analyst to construct mathematical models as almost the only means of making rational choices. The recent controversy over the desirability of the RS-70 bomber is a case in point. The systems analysts in the office of the Secretary of Defense, led by

Charles Hitch, an economist from RAND who has become the comptroller in the Pentagon, decided on the basis of computer analysis that the manned RS-70 bomber would be outmoded by the time it could come into full production, and that it would be wiser to concentrate on missiles. . . .

The traditional services, and their chiefs, have reacted to all this with dismay. As a recent article in *Fortune* put it:

> It was at this point that the military professionals began to exhibit real alarm. McNamara did not ignore them; they had their say, as usual, in defense of their service budgets. But his drive, his intense preoccupation with figures and facts, left the Chiefs and their staffs with the feeling that the computers were taking over.

And the *Fortune* article, reflecting the dismay of the service Chiefs, was also a veiled attack on McNamara's penchant for "quantification," for his failure to respect "the uncomputable that had made Curtis Le May (the head of the big bomber command) the world's finest operational airman," for his "inexperience" in military strategy and for his reliance on the technipols, "the inner group of lay experts who were dispersed through State, the White House, and Defense." The import of the article was clear: the traditional military professionals were being dispossessed. . . .

One can already see, in the behavior of retired officers, the rancor of an old guard that finds its knowledge outdated, its authority disputed or ignored, and that is beginning to argue, bitterly, that if only its advice had been followed, America would not be on the defensive. A surprising number of high-ranking officers on active duty, as well as high-ranking retired officers, have become active in extreme Right organizations. A few—Major General Walker is an example—may feel that all intellectuals are involved in a "plot" against the nation. No doubt most of the military men will be forced—a number have already plunged—into the more complex and bureaucratic game of recruiting particular groups of scientists for their own purposes (in part through the power of the purse) or attempting to make alliances. In the long run, the military profession may itself become transformed through new modes of training, and a new social type may arise.

THE SOUTHERN DISPOSSESSED

In his primer on "one-upmanship," Stephen Potter observed that one could destroy any political generalization by asking, "but what about the South?" The American South contains many of "the dispossessed," and partakes of the Radical Right, but, to be sure, the reasons for this evolution may be of a somewhat different order.

For many decades, there has not been one South but two Souths, that of myth and that of reality, and the fact is that for the past hundred years the South has lived more by its myth than its reality. . . .

At the heart of the myth is this idea of a community, of an organic way of life, which is morally superior to the deracinated, vulgarized, tinseled North. Mr. Davidson's words merely reiterate the note struck by George Fitzhugh, in his *Sociology for the South* (1854), when he attacked the North for instituting an industrial wage slavery which was worse than the direct master-slave relationship in the South. ("There can never be among slaves a class so degraded as is found about the wharves and suburbs of cities.") The pastoral society of the South ("quiet and contented . . . has suffered so little from crime or extreme poverty") was contrasted with the brutish system of industrial laissez-faire (which only promoted selfishness [and] indifference to community and to liberty itself).

But any "traditional" view of the Southern past usually ignores, in the most extraordinary way, not only the direct economic exploitation of the Negro slave, but the *unrestrained* way in which the Negro could be dehumanized—unrestrained as Stanley Elkins has pointed out in his book *Slavery*, because of the lack of any moral agency, such as existed in Catholic countries, which could impose a set of limits through a conception of the Negro as a human soul.

All this has left its mark. One rarely finds in other former slave-holding societies the fear of color and especially the sense of guilt (deriving in considerable measure from unconscious sexual fantasies and fears) over the treatment of the Negro as subhuman, a buffoon, or a child that one finds in the American South. To say of the post-Civil War South, as Mr. Davidson does, that its difficulty lies in having lived with Negroes as "technical citizens, endowed with their citizenship without Southern consent," is a nicety that begs the question whether the South is indeed a part of the larger American polity and its moral code (or only a "defeated union"), and to ignore altogether the exploitative economic and social nature of the "organic community."

If a huge portion—in some areas the majority—of a population has to be exempted from the Southern "community," so, too, must one subtract the large stratum of "poor whites." For a society that, in myth at least, describes itself as reproducing the "constitutional order of the early Republic," the existence of Southern populism, with its raw appeals to violence, with its rant and swagger, with its contempt for culture, must be most embarrassing. It is much too easy—and simply false—to ascribe Southern populism to "northern theories of egalitarianism." Tom Watson, Tom Heflin, Gene Talmadge, Cole Blease, James K. Vardaman, Theodore Bilbo, Huey Long, John Rankin, and Orville Faubus (Snopeses that they may be)—are as indigenous to the South as John C. Calhoun, George Fitzhugh, Thomas R. Dew, or any other genteel intellectual and political figures. . . .

THE REVOLT AGAINST MODERNITY

In the broadest sense, the attitude of the Right in the United States is a revolt against modernity and the requirements of planned social change in the society. (By "planned social change" I mean the attempt to be aware of the ramified consequences of any social action and to plan accordingly; a modern corporation could not exist without planning its future; neither can a society.) Often, as in the jibe of Senator Goldwater against the "whiz kids in the Pentagon" or the heavy-handed attack by former President Eisenhower against the "theorists" in government, these attitudes are part of an anti-intellectualism which is a defensive posture against the complexities of modern problems. But more is at stake for the Right. There is a deeper threat which they correctly perceive—the threat of displacement.

The new nature of decision-making, its increasing technicality, forces a displacement of the older elites. Within a business enterprise, the newer techniques of operations research and linear programming almost amount to the "automation" of middle management and its displacement by mathematicians and engineers, working either within the firm or as consultants. In the economy, the businessman finds himself subject to price, wage, and investment criteria laid down by the economists in government. In the polity, the old military elites find themselves challenged in the determination of strategy by scientists, who have the technical knowledge on nuclear capability—missile development and the like—or by the "military intellectuals" whose conceptions of weapon systems and political warfare seek to guide military allocations.

In the broadest sense, the spread of education, of research, of administration and government creates a new constituency, the technical and professional intelligentsia. While these are not bound by the common ethos that would constitute them a new class, nor even a cohesive social group, they are the products of a new system of recruitment for power (just as property and inhertiance represented the old system) and those who are the products of the old system understandably feel a vague and apprehensive disquiet —the disquiet of the dispossessed.

VII

Civil Liberties: The Bill of Rights

"All declare for liberty," former Justice Reed once suggested, "and proceed to disagree among themselves as to its true meaning." Americans assume that the legacy of the Constitution not only assures freedom but solves all problems with regard to their interpretation as well. But each day presents new problems in the field of human freedom. Reconciling liberty and authority, freedom and order, and the rights of the individual with the needs of the community is a continuous and demanding task.

History helps in understanding some of our civil liberties problems, but no amount of historical knowledge will completely solve such questions as how to treat our giant new mass media—movies, radio, television. Traditional notions of freedom of the press have to be adjusted to deal with these new resources. National defense and national security in the modern world present problems different at the very least in size and scope from the situations of 1789.

In this chapter we shall try to approach some of the basic questions in civil liberties. This is an area with many ramifications and where events change rapidly, and only highlights can be discussed. The rapid pace of developments in this area means the treatment and even the terms used in discussing civil liberties are not as standardized as those used in some of the other areas of American government. We will discuss the issues under three major headings.

First we will consider political rights and the rights of expression and association. These rights are, in a very real sense, basic to the democratic system. But not everything done in the name of these freedoms can be allowed. "The most stringent protection of civil liberties," wrote Justice Holmes, "could not protect a man in falsely shouting 'Fire!' in a crowded theatre." But what divides what is to be protected from that which should be regulated? Drawing the line in practice has been one of the most difficult problems of our times—and the issues of communism and subversion have made the public, philosophers and judges think hard and long, and yet end up in sharp disagreement.

A second category—almost equally debated—concerns the rights of the individual in his individuality—his right to privacy, to individual opinions, procedural rights in criminal trials, and religious freedom. In a society that pushes people together into giant cities and involves us with each other to an increasing degree, the problem gets greater year by year. Just because conformity is the easy way to get along in an organizational society the need for individual rights is so great. But not every claim can be recognized.

Finally, there is the problem of the treatment of individuals and groups by the government—the problem of equal protection of the laws. This question of equality under the law also blends into the problem of equality through the law and the responsibility by government for the maintenance of equality. The debate in the country since the 1954 Supreme Court decision on segregation is only the most dramatic aspect of this controversial area.

In short, American democracy has to face the problem of maintaining its freedom in a cold war situation hostile to liberty. At the same time, we must face the problem of adjusting liberty to modern conditions and of creating and establishing new rights where changing conditions and the conscience of the community demands them.

How Free Can We Be and Still Be Safe?

The heart of a democratic political system is the right of criticism of the rulers and of meaningful analysis of their policies. The right to change rulers not only implies but requires the right to weigh their merits and demerits. The First Amendment freedoms of free speech, press, assembly, and petition are also first in the sense that they must prepare the way for free government.

But important as these rights are, they don't make up the totality of man's existence. We demand other privileges as well. For example, we would all like freedom from being falsely maligned and insulted by other citizens—and this, of course, means that there would be some limit upon their rights of expression.

Political freedom also implies some sort of political organization, and this is recognized in the Bill of Rights in the freedoms of petition and assembly. Again it would seem there must be some limits; assembly will not be permitted at the busiest corner in town during rush hour, and assembly will not be permitted for the purpose of lynching, robbery or general mayhem.

It is easy enough to explain the extremes—that which we think should obviously be allowed or forbidden. It is much harder to find a principle that separates the doubtful cases in the middle. This next section presents some points of view on this problem, particularly in the light of a recent and perplexing complication—the problem of freedom in the face of a group that would subvert democratic processes for the benefit of a foreign power. The communists make a problem, unsolved for centuries, even more vexing today.

The Right to Be Let Alone Versus the Need to Organize Society

In his novel, *1984*, George Orwell paints a terrible picture of life in a society where almost every move is spied upon and controlled by the government. Readers have found this more blood-curdling and terrifying a story than many a thriller. Instinctively we all feel that there is some corner of our world that is our own and should be untouched by other human hands.

Our first series of discussions concerns the dramatic questions of the rights of citizens in a democratic process as against other paramount considerations—the needs of national security; the second will be concerned with a number of smaller problems of individualism versus social order. In one sense they are not as vital, yet in another sense they touch us in our daily lives in a more intimate and personal sense.

Not all of the dangers to individualism come from the government: private groups and even individuals present problems here too. A key issue in recent years has been the claims of censorship, advanced in the name of crime prevention and discouragement of pornography. Recurrently communities fight the battle of how much freedom of the newsstand is to be allowed. Films, books, libraries have their problems of censorship too.

Another issue that has plagued society through history and over which wars have been fought is the problem of separation of church and state. American society has emphasized the essentially secular nature of the government and has left religion largely to operate in its own sphere. But, the talk of a "wall of separation" between church and state is partly belied by our insistence on religious ceremonies in connection with government on the one hand, and governmental support at least indirectly on the other. We exempt churches from taxation, and we have chaplains in the army. In recent years, the line of separation has become fuzzy in the area of education. On the one hand, claims have been pressed for aid to parochial schools on the grounds that it is discriminatory not to help children in religious schools to get an education through public funds. At the same time, argument is advanced as to whether religious education should be allowed in the schools at all. The Supreme Court has taken the position that a state may not hold religious instruction on school grounds, but may release children to go to a religious instruction on school time. But, what of ceremonial prayers, required by school authorities? A number of such questions have caused court rulings and public controversy.

Negroes and Whites: The Challenge of Equal Protection of the Laws

It may not be literally true that "one-half of the Constitution is to be found in the Commerce Clause and the other half in the Fourteenth Amendment." Still, a good deal of constitutional litigation and questions of power have centered around these two provisions. In recent years, in particular, the Fourteenth Amendment has come into its own.

Among the provisions of that post-Civil War-Reconstruction amendment is the prohibition that "nor shall any State . . . deny to any person within its jurisdiction the equal protection of the laws." As with some other parts of the Fourteenth Amendment, the language is not self-explanatory. In 1896 the Supreme Court, in the well-known case of *Plessy v. Ferguson,* held that laws requiring Negroes to board separate cars of a railroad train did not violate this provision so long as the accommodations were "equal but separate." The majority opinion held that there was no implication of inferiority in such segregation, although Justice John Marshall Harlan of Kentucky questioned this argument, insisting that the Constitution was "colorblind," and that the "thin disguise of separate accommodations will fool no one nor atone for the wrong this day done."

The reasoning of the majority in *Plessy v. Ferguson* was dominant in the upholding of most segregation laws in the early part of the century. However, in 1923 zoning laws requiring Negroes to live in separate sections of towns were declared unconstitutional. Beginning in 1937 a series of cases undermined the principle of "separate but equal" in the field of graduate education. Finally, in 1954, the Supreme Court ruled that "in the field of education 'separate but equal' has no place." In later decisions the Court extended the doctrine to public recreation, when operated by a governmental authority.

Enforcing the Supreme Court decision has created controversy. The justices anticipated this in the pattern of their decision. They waited a year for their decision in principle to be accepted, heard argument on the question of the enforcement pattern, and then announced in a separate opinion their plan for desegregation. Under it the local school authorities are to formulate plans "with all deliberate speed" under the authority of the Federal District Courts.

In practice there has been compliance in the border states, defiance in the Deep South hard core, and efforts at nominal compliance with minimum consequences of desegregation in states like North Carolina and Virginia.

In the meantime, the country has been debating the questions posed by the decision. Should nine men, wise as they may be, impose a pattern of social behavior upon a considerable segment of our society? Does the majority of the nation have the right to insist upon compliance? Does a regional majority have the right to establish a pattern of separation and pariahhood for a segment of its population? Can one evade or defy a major legal decision reiterated by the courts without a threat to the whole fabric of law and order?

1
FREE SPEECH AND FREE GOVERNMENT*

Alexander Meiklejohn

Probably the strongest defense of free speech is that made by a little book of about 100 pages by one of the most respected of American philosophers and educators, and a man known for maintaining the courage of his convictions where personal sacrifice was involved. Professor Meiklejohn maintains that all speech in the public domain, without exception, is to be allowed and actions alone proscribed. This he sees not as an individual right, a privilege owed by the community to a citizen, but rather as a social right. When we allow an idea to be expressed we are benefiting ourselves and not the expresser. In recent years Justice Black has openly come about to a similar form of "absolute" free speech, arguing even that libel laws are unconstitutional.

. . . What do we mean when we say that "Congress shall make no law . . . abridging the freedom of speech . . .?" . . . Are we, for example, required by the First Amendment to give men freedom to advocate the abolition of the First Amendment? Are we bound to grant freedom of speech to those who, if they had the power, would refuse it to us? The First Amendment, taken literally, seems to answer, "Yes," to those questions. It seems to say that no speech, however dangerous, may, for that reason, be suppressed. But the Federal Bureau of Investigation, the un-American Activities Committee, the Department of Justice, the President, are, at the same time, answering "No" to the same question. Which answer is right? What is the valid American doctrine concerning the freedom of speech? . . .

. . . Here . . . the town meeting suggests an answer. That meeting is called to discuss and, on the basis of such discussion, to decide matters of public policy. For example: Shall there be a school? Where shall it be located? Who shall teach? What shall be taught? The community has agreed that such questions as these shall be freely discussed and that, when the discussion is ended, decision upon them will be made by vote of the citizens. Now, in that method of political self-government, the point of ultimate interest is not the words of the speakers, but the minds of the hearers. The final aim of the meeting is the voting of wise decisions. The voters, therefore, must be made as wise as possible. The welfare of the community requires that those who decide issues shall understand them. They must know what they are voting about. . . .

The First Amendment, then, is not the guardian of unregulated talkativeness. It does not require that, on every occasion, every citizen shall take part

* Alexander Meiklejohn, *Free Speech and Its Relation to Self-Government* (New York: Harper and Row, Publishers, 1948), pp. vi–xii, 24–27, 49–50. © 1948 by Harper and Row, Publishers.

in public debate. Nor can it even give assurance that everyone shall have opportunity to do so. If, for example, at a town meeting, twenty like-minded citizens have become a "party," and if one of them has read to the meeting an argument which they have all approved, it would be ludicrously out of order for each of the others to insist on reading it again. No competent moderator would tolerate that wasting of the time available for free discussion. What is essential is not that everyone shall speak, but that everything worth saying shall be said. To this end, for example, it may be arranged that each of the known conflicting points of view shall have, and shall be limited to, an assigned share of the time available. But however it be arranged, the vital point, as stated negatively, is that no suggestion of policy shall be denied a hearing because it is on one side of the issue rather than another. . . . When men govern themselves, it is they—and no one else—who must pass judgment upon unwisdom and unfairness and danger. And that means that unwise ideas must have a hearing as well as wise ones, unfair as well as fair, dangerous as well as safe, un-American as well as American. Just so far as, at any point, the citizens who are to decide an issue are denied acquaintance with information or opinion or doubt or disbelief or criticism which is relevant to that issue, just so far the result must be ill-considered, ill-balanced planning for the general good. *It is that mutilation of the thinking process of the community against which the First Amendment to the Constitution is directed.* . . .

If, then, on any occasion in the United States it is allowable to say that the Constitution is a good document it is equally allowable, in that situation, to say that the Constitution is a bad document. If a public building may be used in which to say, in time of war, that the war is justified, then the same building may be used in which to say that it is not justified. If it be publicly argued that conscription for armed service is moral and necessary, it may likewise be publicly argued that it is immoral and unnecessary. If it may be said that American political institutions are superior to those of England or Russia or Germany, it may, with equal freedom, be said that those of England or Russia or Germany are superior to ours. These conflicting views may be expressed, must be expressed, not because they are valid, but because they are relevant. If they are responsibly entertained by anyone, we, the voters, need to hear them. When a question of policy is "before the house," free men choose to meet it not with their eyes shut, but with their eyes open. To be afraid of ideas, any idea, is to be unfit for self-government. . . .

. . . Holmes' . . . formula tells us that whenever the expression of a minority opinion involves clear and present danger to the public safety it may be denied the protection of the First Amendment. And that means that whenever crucial and dangerous issues have come upon the nation, free and unhindered discussion of them must stop. . . . Under that ruling, dissenting judges might, in "dangerous" situations, be forbidden to record their dissents. Minority citizens might, in like situations, be required to hold their peace. No one, of course, believes that this is what Mr. Holmes or the court intended to say. But it is what, in plain words, they did say. The "clear and present danger" opinion stands on the record of the court as a peculiarly inept and unsuccessful attempt to formulate an exception to the principle of the freedom of speech. . . .

2

HERESY, YES: CONSPIRACY, NO*

Sidney Hook

Here we have a statement by a leading anti-Communist philosopher, himself a great admirer of civil liberties who condemns what he regards as soft-headed thinking among many defenders of these liberties. He distinguishes between freedom in the realm of ideas and the menace of the conspiratorial element in Communism.

The failure to recognize the distinction between heresy and conspiracy is fatal to a liberal civilization, for the inescapable consequence of their identification is either self-destruction, when heresies are punished as conspiracies, or destruction at the hands of their enemies, when conspiracies are tolerated as heresies.

A heresy is a set of unpopular ideas or opinions on matters of grave concern to the community. The right to profess publicly a heresy of any character, on any theme, is an essential element of a liberal society. The liberal stands ready to defend the honest heretic no matter what his views against any attempt to curb him. It is enough that the heretic pays the price of unpopularity which he cannot avoid. In some respects each of us is a heretic, but a liberal society can impose no official orthodoxies of *belief*, disagreement with which entails loss of liberty or life.

A conspiracy, as distinct from a heresy, is a secret or underground movement which seeks to attain its ends not by normal political or educational processes but by playing outside the rules of the game. Because it undermines the conditions which are required in order that doctrines may freely compete for acceptance, because where successful it ruthlessly destroys all heretics and dissenters, a conspiracy cannot be tolerated *without* self-stultification in a liberal society.

A heresy does not shrink from publicity. It welcomes it. Not so a conspiracy. The signs of a conspiracy are secrecy, anonymity, the use of false names and labels, and the calculated lie. It does not offer its wares openly but by systematic infiltration into all organizations of cultural life, it seeks to capture strategic posts to carry out a policy alien to the purposes of the organization. There is political conspiracy, which is the concern of the state; but there may also be a conspiracy against a labor union, a cultural or professional association, or an educational institution which is not primarily the concern of the state but of its own members. In general, whoever subverts the rules of a democratic organization and seeks to win by chicanery what cannot be fairly won in the process of free discussion is a conspirator.

* Sidney Hook, *Heresy, Yes: Conspiracy, No* (New York: The John Day Company, Inc., 1953), pp. 21–22, 25–26, 30, 32.

Communist *ideas* are heresies, and liberals need have no fear of them where they are freely and openly expressed. They should be studied and evaluated in the light of all the relevant evidence. No one should be punished because he holds them. The Communist *movement*, however, is something quite different from a mere heresy, for wherever it exists it operates along the lines laid down by Lenin as guides to Communists of all countries, and perfected in great detail since then. . . .

. . . Liberals in the twentieth century are confronted by a situation quite unfamiliar to their forbears. For they must contend not with fearless heretics, indigenous elements of the community who, like the abolitionists and revolutionists of old, scorn concealment, and who make no bones about their hostility to the principles of liberalism. They find themselves in the unique historical predicament of having to deal with native elements who, by secrecy and stratagem, serve the interests of a foreign power which believes itself entitled to speak for all mankind, and whose victory spells the end of all liberal civilization and with it the right to heresy. . . .

The problems which underground conspiracy creates for a liberal society are of tremendous magnitude. They cannot be dismissed by a quotation from Jefferson. . . .

. . . "Association" by way of membership in the Communist party is not innocent or coincidental but is *a form of active cooperation and collaboration* in carrying out the purposes of a conspiratorial organization. The Communist party sees to it that all members are instructed about the purposes as soon as they join. Continued membership is possible only in virtue of a series of continued *acts* of obedience to instructions. Those who dub the active cooperation required of all members of the Communist party "guilt by association" coyly suggest by that phrase the innocuous association of chance or occasional encounters with Communists in social gatherings. They simply ignore the fact that all members of the Communist party must "associate" by active cooperation with its purposes or be expelled. . . .

David Lilienthal, a realistic not a ritualistic liberal, has warned us against the "Scare-the-dopes!" method of discussing nuclear energy. There is also a "Scare-the-dopes!" method of discussion of the problem of communistic conspiracy. It is used by those who employ the term "communist" with scandalous looseness as a synonym for any economic or political heresy, and who shout conspiracy where there is only heresy. It is also used by those who do not tell us how to meet the real dangers of Communist conspiracy but shout "Hysteria!," "Fascism!," or "Police State!" when the first faltering efforts are made to cope with dangers hitherto unprecedented in the history of American democracy. . . .

3

SEDUCTION OF THE INNOCENT*

Fredric Wertham

A prominent psychiatrist who has specialized in treating juvenile delinquents concluded that comic books were the source of crime. This is an extract from his book urging governmental action to reduce violence in children's literature. His argument suggests a number of questions, which should be borne in mind. Should individuals profit from the freedom of the press at the expense of readers of publications? Who should decide whether material is dangerous or not? Is the road of censorship a simple one or does embarking on one bit of censorship encourage more?

* * *

All comic books with their words and expletives in balloons are bad for reading, but not every comic book is bad for children's minds and emotions. The trouble is that the "good" comic books are snowed under by those which glorify violence, crime and sadism. . . .

Slowly, and at first reluctantly, I have come to the conclusion that . . . chronic stimulation, temptation and seduction by comic books, both their content and their alluring advertisements of knives and guns, are contributing factors to many children's maladjustment.

No one had any idea of the enormous number of such books. The industry had not given out any figures, nor had a magazine or newspaper published any. When I made public the result of my own estimates and computations, namely that there were (then) some 60 million comic books a month, my statement was met with absolute incredulity. Some people thought that it was a misprint, and that 60 million must be a *yearly* figure. But shortly afterwards authoritative magazines and newspapers (such as *Business Week*) repeated my figure as an authentic one. . . .

Some time ago I saw a Western movie in which the villain shoots the sheriff straight in the face. It was a children's matinee and at that point the children first laughed and then loudly applauded. This was not the so-called natural cruelty of children that adults like to speak about. This particular type of response was inculcated in these children by the most persistent conditioning in habits of hate ever given to children in the world's history.

There is at present in all the media, especially as they affect children, a pattern of violence, brutality, sadism, blood lust, shrewdness, callous disregard for human life and an ever-renewed search for subhuman victims, criminal, racial, national, feminine, political, terrestrial, supernatural and interplanetary. Brutality is the keynote. It is self-understood that such a pattern

---

* Fredric Wertham, *Seduction of the Innocent* (New York: Holt, Rinehart & Winston, Inc., 1953), pp. 2, 10–11, 360–61, 388, 390.

in a mass medium does not come from nothing. There must be clues in real life as to why violence is in the air.

* * *

Granted that this cult of violence originates somewhere in our social life, there is a dynamic reciprocal relationship between the audience and the creators of mass entertainment. The same influences come to bear on both producers and audience. Gradually, through constant reiteration, brutality is accepted and the producers can say that this is what the children (and adults) wanted in the first place. . . . The audience, on the other hand, feels that this is what it is supposed to like, in order to be virile and up-to-date. So there is a vicious circle. . . . The aberration becomes the norm and the norm creates the aberration.

What all media need at present is a rollback of sadism. What they do to children is that they make them confuse violence with strength, sadism with sex, low necklines with femininity, racial prejudice with patriotism and crime with heroism.

If one studies this phenomenon carefully, one will see that in this orchestra of violence the comic-book industry has set the tone and the rhythm. For a while, before 1945, it seemed that the crime-comic-book industry had a monopoly on the brutalization of children. Now it has some competition from television and the other media. So children may get the idea that violence is natural from any or all of the media, as well as from other children exposed to these media too. . . . A boy once described a movie where the hero strangled the girl. "Why did he have to strangle her?" I asked. The answer was "Well, there has to be some adventure in the world." The story is told of the two little boys who had gone to see a romantic movie. "It was boring," said one. "Not to me," said the other. "I didn't mind. Whenever they kissed I closed my eyes and pretended he was choking her." . . .

Scholars will be interested in this new version of Shakespeare's *Hamlet:*

THE DEATH SCENE (Hamlet speaking):

> . . . Alas! I have been poisoned
> And now I, too, go
> To join my deceased father!
> I, too–I–AGGGRRRAA! . . .

Set the children free! Give them a chance! Let them develop according to what is best in them. Don't inculcate in them your ugly passions when they have hardly learned to read. Don't teach them all the violence, the shrewdness, the hardness of your own life. Don't spoil the spontaneity of their dreams. Don't lead them halfway to delinquency and when they get there clap them into your reformatories. Don't stimulate their minds with sex and perversity and label the children abnormal when they react. Don't continue to desecrate death, graves and coffins with your horror stories and degrade sex with sordid rituals of hitting, hanging, torturing. Don't sow in their young minds the sadistic details of destruction.

* * *

4

INDIVIDUAL FREEDOM AND GOVERNMENTAL RESTRAINTS*

Walter Gellhorn

Almost in direct reply, a noted teacher of law finds little effect from reading on behavior. Again some questions not covered by these two readings seem worth thinking about: Who should decide which of these two arguments is the better? Assuming Mr. Wertham and J. Edgar Hoover are correct about the effects of reading, should the government take action? In some neighborhoods parents have formed organizations and have threatened to boycott storekeepers handling comic books they thought in bad taste. Is this a better way of handling the problem? Or perhaps might it have some dangers too?

The view that reading is readily translated into behavior is shared by many reputable persons. Mr. J. Edgar Hoover, as an example, has been quoted as contending that "the increase in the number of sex crimes is due precisely to sex literature madly presented in certain magazines. Filthy literature is the great moral wrecker. It is creating criminals faster than jails can be built." And Dr. Fredric Wertham, a psychiatrist of high standing, has waged a virtual crusade against comic books because his clinical observation has convinced him that the comics have sexually stimulated and emotionally brutalized many children. . . .

We start with the proposition that an interest in pornography is seemingly not the molder of a man's personality but the reflection of it. Indeed, certain psychological experiments suggest that one who finds pornographic elements in allegedly obscene books is very likely to discover them also in apparently innocuous books, through a process of self-selection and emphasis that the reader himself brings to the words. This same process of self-selection—this tendency to read and see what accords with pre-existing interests—probably controls the effects of reading as well as the determination of what will be read. The fact that "sex maniacs" may read pornography does not mean that they became what they are because of their reading, but that their reading became what it is because of them. Their personality, according to modern scientific findings that confirm a proposition stated long ago by the Jesuit fathers, was probably basically formed before they ever learned to read.

So far as disclosed by the most exhaustive study of juvenile delinquency yet made in America, reading seems to be of small moment in shaping antisocial tendencies. Sheldon and Eleanor

* Walter Gellhorn, *Individual Freedom and Governmental Restraints* (Baton Rouge: Louisiana State University Press, 1956), pp. 60–65.

Glueck searchingly inquired into numerous cases to identify the influences that produced delinquency. Reading (if it was influential at all) was of such slight significance that it was altogether omitted from their statement of "factors with probable causal significance." . . .

The question remains, however, whether fiction will frequently provide what Dr. Wertham calls the "added impetus" to antisocial impulses, serving as a trigger mechanism to set off an explosion that otherwise might not have occurred.

Nobody is in a position, on the basis of what is now known about human beings, to deny this possibility. But . . . the *probability* is that fictional reading (even comic book reading) about sexual conduct or about violence and brutality has small behavioral consequence as compared with the more realistic impressions derived from reading newspapers—or even from seeing motion pictures or television that purport to mirror reality. . . .

Unless all children are to be wrapped in cotton batting and utterly removed from the world, we cannot hope to immunize every one of them against contact with something that might conceivably energize his savage side. G. K. Chesterton once noted a complaint that a child had been induced to kill his father with a carving knife, through having seen a similar episode in a motion picture. "This may possibly have occurred," Chesterton conceded, "though if it did, anybody of common sense would prefer to have details about that particular child, rather than about that particular picture. But what is supposed to be the practical moral of it, in any case? Is it that the young should never see a story with a knife in it? . . . It would be more practical that a child should never see a real carving knife, and still more practical that he should never see a real father. . . . If the cinema exhibited nothing but views of country vicarages or vegetarian restaurants, the ugly fancy is as likely to be stimulated by these things as by anything else." Experts in abnormal psychology agree with Chesterton. . . .

5

STATE-SPONSORED PRAYER*

Leo Pfeffer

A leading spokesman for those who advocate "absolute" separation of church and state has been Leo Pfeffer. Here, the distinguished authority on the law of church and state and active attorney in many of the cases discusses the meaning of separation. He repudiates the argument that the government may aid religion so long as it does not discriminate within or among religions.

Said Representative George W. Andrews of Alabama: "They put the Negroes in the schools, and now they've driven God out." Representative Andrews' grievance against the Supreme Court is more valid in respect to the decision that put the Negroes in than to the one that drove God out. The school segregation decision of 1954 expressly overruled a long-standing precedent of the Supreme Court, one going back at least to 1896. The decision outlawing the public school recitation of the New York Regents' prayer overruled no precedent, but was completely consistent with and indeed required by all the decisions in the area of the relationship of church and state handed down by the Supreme Court in the past 15 years. . . .

In 1947, in the *Everson* school bus decision, the Court defined the meaning of the establishment clause of the First Amendment in the following words:

"The 'establishment of religion' clause of the First Amendment means at least this: Neither a state nor the federal government can set up a church. Neither can pass laws which aid one religion, aid all religions, or prefer one religion over another. . . . No tax in any amount, large or small, can be levied to support any religious activities or institutions, whatever they may be called, or whatever form they may adopt to teach or practice religion. In the words of Jefferson, the clause against establishment of religion by law was intended to erect 'a wall of separation between church and state.' "

If anything can be said to be settled in constitutional law, it is that the First Amendment's no establishment clause means what this paragraph says it means. Of the nine justices who constituted the Court in 1947 when this paragraph was written, only two, Black and Douglas, participated in the Regents' prayer decision. Yet every person who sat on the Court since it was written has in one case or another indicated his approval of the principles set forth in this interpretation of the First Amendment.

What the Court said in the *Everson* case was that the amendment imposes

* "State-Sponsored Prayer," *The Commonweal*, July 27, 1962, pp. 417–19. Mr. Pfeffer's article appeared as part of a discussion of the issue and does not represent the position of the journal.

upon the federal and state governments in the United States a mandate of neutrality not only as among competing faiths, but between religion and nonreligion. It may use its instrumentalities neither to aid religion nor to injure it. In short, government in the United States is secular and its powers may be employed only to further secular ends. The Preamble to the Constitution sets forth the purposes for which the new republic on the Western hemisphere was established, and all the purposes listed are secular. . . .

In its effectuation of its secular purposes, governmental action may, as an incidental by-product, benefit religion —indeed, one would assume that this would generally be so—and that fact, the Court has consistently held, does not restrict government in the manner in which it carries out those purposes. Thus, as in the *Everson* case, a state may effectuate the secular purpose of protecting children from the hazards of traffic by paying for their transportation to schools, parochial as well as public. This is constitutional even though an incidental by-product is relieving the parochial schools of a substantial part of their budgetary obligations. (Those who disagree with the *Everson* decision do not quarrel with the underlying principle. They contend that the purpose of school bus legislation is not to protect children but to help finance what has become a necessary part of the school budget.)

So, too, a state in operating its secular school system may adjust its schedule to meet the needs of its students, including their religious needs. Also, in furthering the secular purpose of assuring to every person at least one day's rest in seven, the state may require businesses to close down on Sundays even though the Christian religion, or that part of it which observes Sunday as the Sabbath, may obtain an incidental benefit. (Here, again, those who disagree with the majority decisions in the New York released-time case and the Sunday Law cases quarrel not with the principle but with the application.)

Where, however, the state's purpose is exclusively or primarily religious rather than secular, its violation of the First Amendment is clear and hardly disputable. Therefore, the Court held in the *McCollum* case, a state may not introduce religious instruction into the public school, for it is thereby employing a state instrumentality to further a religious purpose. For the same reason, the Court unanimously held last year, a state may not require applicants for public office to take an oath that they believe in the existence of God.

When, therefore, the Regents' prayer case came before the Court, even Representative Andrews should have realized that a decision outlawing state-sponsored prayer recitation was inevitable, unless the Court overruled all the decisions since the *Everson* case and abrogated the principles set forth in that case. For there could hardly be any question that the purpose of the Regents, who are state officials, was exclusively religious. To leave no doubt about their intentions, the Regents, in formulating the prayer in 1951 and calling for its daily recitation in the public schools, issued a "policy statement" in which it said that thereby each of the children "will be properly prepared to follow the faith of his or her father, as he or she receives the same at mother's knee or father's side and as such faith is expounded and strengthened by his or her religious leaders."

What this policy statement lacks in elegance of style it makes up in innocent clarity of expression. Nor did John F. Brosnan, a member of the

Board of Regents, conceal his motivation when he charged . . . that the only criticism of the proposal "came from those who do not believe in God." . . .

This easy identification of opposition to government-sponsored religion with opposition to religion was echoed and re-echoed in the stridency of the reaction to the Court's decision outlawing the Regents' program. . . .

State-sanctioned prayer has a long and ignoble history, from the early days of persecuted Christianity in Rome to the twentieth century in Russia when the Jews were compelled to recite in synagogue every Sabbath a prayer for the welfare of the Tsarist government that instigated and encouraged terrible pogroms against them. It was not so long ago that England experienced an event which illustrated vividly that state sponsorship of prayer is not beneficial but harmful to religion and conscience. In 1927 the Church of England wished to revise the Anglican Prayer Book. Since it is the established church, it could not do so without approval by Parliament. In that year and again in the following year, it petitioned Parliament to permit the change but in each year the proposal was rejected by the House of Commons because it was felt that the proposed revisions manifested too much Roman Catholic influence. The result is that for the past 35 years Anglicans have been praying in a manner which does not fully accord with their conscience only because the government possesses the power to formulate prayer.

The lesson of history is clear. It supports fully the statement in the Court's opinion in the Regents' prayer case that the First Amendment "rested on the belief that a union of government and religion tends to destroy government and degrade religion," that "whenever government had allied itself with one particular form of religion, the inevitable result had been that it had incurred the hatred, disrespect and even contempt of those who held contrary beliefs," and that "many people had lost their respect for any religion that had relied upon the support of government to spread its faith."

It was for that reason that the deeply religious fathers of our Constitution wrote a Preamble which carefully refrained from listing among the purposes of government any power or obligation to promote religious ends and deliberately kept out of the Constitution itself not only any prayer or invocation to God but even any mention of God at all. The decision of the Supreme Court in outlawing public school recitation of prayer is consistent not only with its own prior decisions but with the intent of the founders of our republic and with the cause of religious liberty.

6

"ABSOLUTE IS IN THE DARK"*

Erwin N. Griswold

A quite different point of view is developed by Dean Erwin Griswold of the Harvard Law School. He sees the question of separation of church and state as much more flexible and the political tradition of America as favoring some sort of religious tone in our daily life. He questions the approach suggested by Pfeffer as one of absolutism —perhaps growing out of Justice Black's views—that is both inflexible and dangerous. Minorities as well as majorities must be tolerant, he argues, and religion in schools can play a positive role in the development of pluralism in American society.

* * *

I venture the thought, quite seriously, that it was unfortunate that the question involved in the *Engel* case was ever thought of as a matter for judicial decision, that it was unfortunate that the Court decided the case, one way or the other, and that this unhappy situation resulted solely from the absolutist position which the Court has taken and intimated in such matters, thus inviting such litigation in its extreme form.

What do I mean by this? I have in mind at least two separate lines of thought. One is the fact that we have a tradition, a spiritual and cultural tradition, of which we ought not to be deprived by judges carrying into effect the logical implications of absolutist notions not expressed in the Constitution itself, and surely never contemplated by those who put the constitutional provisions into effect. The other is that there are some matters which are essentially local in nature, important matters, but nonetheless matters to be worked out by the people themselves in their own communities, when no basic rights of others are impaired. It was said long ago that every question in this country tends to become a legal question. But is that wise? Is it inevitable? Are there not questions of detail, questions of give and take, questions at the fringe, which are better left to nonjudicial determination?

First, as to the long tradition. Is it not clear as a matter of historical fact that this was a Christian nation? . . . It is perfectly true, and highly salutary, that the First Amendment forbade Congress to pass any law "respecting an establishment of religion or prohibiting the free exercise thereof." These are great provisions, of great sweep and basic importance. But to say that they require that all trace of religion be kept out of any sort of public activity is sheer invention. Our history is full of these traces; chaplains in Congress and in the armed forces; chapels in prisons; "In God We Trust" on our money;

* Erwin N. Griswold, "Absolute Is in the Dark—A Discussion of the Approach of the Supreme Court to Constitutional Questions," 8 *Utah L. Rev.* 167 (1963).

to mention only a few. God is referred to in our national anthem, and in "America," and many others of what may be called our national songs. Must all of these things be rigorously extirpated in order to satisfy a constitutional absolutism? What about Sunday? What about Christmas? Must we deny our whole heritage, our culture, the things of spirit and soul which have sustained us in the past and helped to bind us together in times of good and bad?

Does our deep-seated tolerance of all religions—or, to the same extent, of no religion—require that we give up all religious observance in public activities? Why should it? It certainly never occurred to the Founders that it would. It is hardly likely that it was entirely accidental that these questions did not even come before the Court in the first hundred and fifty years of our constitutional history. . . . Now let me turn to the other point—that there are some matters which should be settled on the local level, in each community, and should not become great Supreme Court cases. . . . The prayer involved in the *Engel* case was not compulsory. As the Supreme Court itself recited, no pupil was compelled "to join in the prayer over his or his parents' objection."[1] This, to me, is crucial. If any student was compelled to join against his conviction, this would present a serious and justiciable question, akin to that presented in the flag salute case.[2] . . .

No pupil is compelled to participate. Must all refrain because one does not wish to join? This would suggest that no school can have a Pledge of Allegiance to the flag if any student does not wish to join. I heartily agree with the decision in the Barnette case[3] that no student can be compelled to join in a flag salute against his religious scruples. But it is a far cry from that decision to say that no school district can have a flag salute for those who want to participate if there is any student who does not wish to join. This is a country of religious toleration. That is a great consequence of our history embodied in the First Amendment. But does religious toleration mean religious sterility? . . . Does the fact that we have officially adopted toleration as our standard mean that we must give up our history and our tradition? The Moslem who comes here may worship as he pleases, and may hold public office without discrimination. That is as it should be. But why should it follow that he can require others to give up their Christian tradition merely because he is a tolerated and welcomed member of the community?

Though we have a considerable common cultural heritage, there have always been minority groups in our country. This, I am sure, has been healthy and educational for all concerned. We have surely gained from having a less homogeneous population. Of course, the rights of all, especially those of minorities, must be protected and preserved. But does that require that the majority, where there is such a majority, must give up its cultural heritage and tradition? Why?

Let us consider the Jewish child, or the Catholic child, or the nonbeliever, or the Congregationalist, or the Quaker. He, either alone, or with a few or many others of his views, attends a public school, whose school district, by local action, has prescribed the Regents' prayer. When the prayer is re-

---

[1] *Engel v. Vitale,* 370 U.S. 421, 423 (1962).

[2] *West Virginia Board of Education v. Barnette,* 319 U.S. 624 (1943).

[3] *West Virginia Board of Education v. Barnette,* 319 U.S. 624 (1943).

cited, if this child or his parents feel that he cannot participate, he may stand or sit, in respectful attention, while the other children take part in the ceremony. Or he may leave the room. It is said that this is bad, because it sets him apart from other children. It is even said that there is an element of compulsion in this—what the Supreme Court has called an "indirect coercive pressure upon religious minorities to conform."[4] But is this the way it should be looked at? The child of a nonconforming or a minority group is, to be sure, different in his beliefs. That is what it means to be a member of a minority. Is it not desirable, and educational, for him to learn and observe this, in the atmosphere of the school—not so much that he is different, as that other children are different from him? And is it not desirable that, at the same time, he experiences and learns the fact that his difference is tolerated and accepted? No compulsion is put upon him. He need not participate. But he, too, has the opportunity to be tolerant. He allows the majority of the group to follow their own tradition, perhaps coming to understand and to respect what they feel is significant to them.

Is this not a useful and valuable and educational and, indeed, a spiritual experience for the children of what I have called the majority group? They experience the values of their own culture; but they also see that there are others who do not accept those values, and that they are wholly tolerated in their nonacceptance. Learning tolerance for other persons, no matter how different, and respect for their beliefs, may be an important part of American education, and wholly consistent with the First Amendment.[5] . . .

---

[4] *Engel v. Vitale,* 370 U.S. 421, 431 (1962).

[5] "Acquainting the student with religious pluralism is part of democratic public education's duty to introduce future citizens to pluralism of all types: economic, political, ethnic, racial and others. Schooling should enable the student to face the actualities of free society. If instead it gives him only silly, sentimental notions concerning the unity of all Americans he will be an incompetent citizen." R. M. Healey, *Jefferson on Religion in Public Education* (New Haven, Conn.: Yale University Press, 1962), p. 270.

7
THE DOCTRINE OF "SEPARATE BUT EQUAL" HAS NO PLACE*

Chief Justice Earl Warren, on May 17, 1954, for a unanimous Court, announced the decision in Brown v. Board of Education. *His statement that the doctrine of "separate but equal" would no longer be upheld in the field of education has inaugurated "a generation of litigation." This momentous and far-reaching decision was deliberately written in a less legalistic style than usual, in an effort to explain to a wider audience the reasons for the ruling.*

APPEAL FROM THE UNITED STATES DISTRICT COURT FOR THE DISTRICT OF KANSAS.

Mr. Chief Justice Warren delivered the opinion of the Court:

These cases come to us from the States of Kansas, South Carolina, Virginia, and Delaware. They are premised on different facts and different local conditions, but a common legal question justifies their consideration together in this consolidated opinion.

* * *

The plaintiffs contend that segregated public schools are not "equal" and cannot be made "equal," and that hence they are deprived of the equal protection of the laws. Because of the obvious importance of the question presented, the Court took jurisdiction. Argument was heard in the 1952 Term, and reargument was heard this Term. . . .

Reargument was largely devoted to the circumstances surrounding the adoption of the Fourteenth Amendment in 1868. It covered exhaustively consideration of the Amendment in Congress, ratification by the states, then existing practices in racial segregation, and the views of proponents and opponents of the Amendment. This discussion and our own investigation convince us that, although these sources cast some light, it is not enough to resolve the problem with which we are faced. At best, they are inconclusive. The most avid proponents of the post-War Amendments undoubtedly intended them to remove all legal distinctions among "all persons born or naturalized in the United States." Their opponents, just as certainly were antagonistic to both the letter and the spirit of the Amendments and wished them to have the most limited effect. What others in Congress and the state legislatures had in mind cannot be determined with any degree of certainty.

An additional reason for the inconclusive nature of the Amendment's history, with respect to segregated schools, is the status of public education at that time. In the South, the movement toward free common schools, supported by general taxation, had not yet taken hold. . . . As a consequence, it is not surprising that there should be so little

* *Brown v. Board of Education of Topeka,* 347 U.S. 483 (1954).

in the history of the Fourteenth Amendment relating to its intended effect on public education.

In the first cases in this Court construing the Fourteenth Amendment, decided shortly after its adoption, the Court interpreted it as proscribing all state-imposed discriminations against the Negro race. The doctrine of "separate but equal" did not make its appearance in this Court until 1896 in the case of *Plessy v. Ferguson, supra,* involving not education but transportation. American courts have since labored with the doctrine for over half a century. In this Court, there have been six cases involving the "separate but equal" doctrine in the field of public education. . . . In none of [the four recent] cases was it necessary to re-examine the doctrine to grant relief to the Negro plaintiff. And in *Sweatt v. Painter, supra,* the Court expressly reserved decision on the question whether *Plessy v. Ferguson* should be held inapplicable to public education.

In approaching this problem, we cannot turn the clock back to 1868 when the Amendment was adopted, or even to 1896 when *Plessy v. Ferguson* was written. We must consider public education in the light of its full development and its present place in American life throughout the Nation. Only in this way can it be determined if segregation in public schools deprives these plaintiffs of the equal protection of the laws.

Today, education is perhaps the most important function of state and local governments. Compulsory school attendance laws and the great expenditures for education both demonstrate our recognition of the importance of education to our democratic society. It is required in the performance of our most basic public responsibilities, even service in the armed forces. It is the very foundation of good citizenship. Today it is a principal instrument in awakening the child to cultural values, in preparing him for later professional training, and in helping him to adjust normally to his environment. In these days, it is doubtful that any child may reasonably be expected to succeed in life if he is denied the opportunity of an education. Such an opportunity, where the state has undertaken to provide it, is a right which must be made available to all on equal terms.

We come then to the question presented: Does segregation of children in public schools solely on the basis of race, even though the physical facilities and other "tangible" factors may be equal, deprive the children of the minority group of equal educational opportunities? We believe that it does.

In *Sweatt v. Painter, supra,* in finding that a segregated law school for Negroes could not provide them equal educational opportunities, this Court relied in large part on "those qualities which are incapable of objective measurement but which make for greatness in a law school." In *McLaurin v. Oklahoma State Regents, supra,* the Court, in requiring that a Negro admitted to a white graduate school be treated like all other students, again resorted to intangible considerations: ". . . his ability to study, to engage in discussions and exchange views with other students, and, in general, to learn his profession." Such considerations apply with added force to children in grade and high schools. . . . The effect of this separation on their educational opportunities was well stated by a finding in the Kansas case by a court which nevertheless felt compelled to rule against the Negro plaintiffs:

"Segregation of white and colored children in public schools has a detrimental effect upon the colored children. The impact is greater when it has the sanction of the law; for the policy of separating the races is usually interpreted as denoting the inferiority of the Negro group. . . . Segregation with the sanction of law, therefore, has a tendency to retard the education and mental development of Negro children and to deprive them of some of the benefits they would receive in a racially integrated school system."

Whatever may have been the extent of psychological knowledge at the time of *Plessy v. Ferguson*, this finding is amply supported by modern authority. Any language in *Plessy v. Ferguson* contrary to this finding is rejected.

We conclude that in the field of public education the doctrine of "separate but equal" has no place. Separate educational facilities are inherently unequal. Therefore, we hold that the plaintiffs and others similarly situated for whom the actions have been brought are, by reason of the segregation complained of, deprived of the equal protection of the laws guaranteed by the Fourteenth Amendment. . . .

Because these are class actions, because of the wide applicability of this decision, and because of the great variety of local conditions, the formulation of decrees in these cases presents problems of considerable complexity. . . . We have now announced that such segregation is a denial of the equal protection of the laws. In order that we may have the full assistance of the parties in formulating decrees, the cases will be restored to the docket, and the parties are requested to present further argument on Questions 4 and 5 previously propounded by the Court for the reargument this Term. The Attorney General of the United States is again invited to participate. The Attorneys General of the States requiring or permitting segregation in public education will also be permitted to appear. . . .

8

"LETTER FROM BIRMINGHAM CITY JAIL"*

Martin Luther King, Jr.

The most prominent Negro leader has in recent years been Martin Luther King, Jr. A clergyman and an advocate of nonviolent resistance, he has come to the fore of the Negro community through leadership, first of CORE and now the Southern Christian Leadership Conference. His sponsoring of Negro demonstrations in order to achieve objectives provoked a letter from eight white clergymen in Birmingham in April 1963. They argued that "however technically peaceful" the demonstrations, they were extreme in operation and dangerous in their potentiality. The standing and responsibility of the clergymen provoked from Dr. King what was perhaps the fullest statement of his position.

APRIL 16, 1963

MY DEAR FELLOW CLERGYMEN,

While confined here in the Birmingham City Jail, I came across your recent statement calling our present activities "unwise and untimely." Seldom, if ever, do I pause to answer criticism of my work and ideas. . . . But since I feel that you are men of genuine good will and your criticisms are sincerely set forth, I would like to answer your statement in what I hope will be patient and reasonable terms.

I think I should give the reason for my being in Birmingham, since you have been influenced by the argument of "outsiders coming in." I have the honor of serving as president of the Southern Christian Leadership Conference, an organization operating in every Southern state with headquarters in Atlanta, Georgia. . . .

Moreover, I am cognizant of the interrelatedness of all communities and states. I cannot sit idly by in Atlanta and not be concerned about what happens in Birmingham. Injustice anywhere is a threat to justice everywhere. We are caught in an inescapable network of mutuality tied in a single garment of destiny. . . . Never again can we afford to live with the narrow, provincial "outside agitator" idea. Anyone who lives inside the United States can never be considered an outsider anywhere in this country.

You deplore the demonstrations that are presently taking place in Birmingham. But I am sorry that your statement did not express a similar concern for the conditions that brought the demonstrations into being. I am sure that each of you would want to go beyond the superficial social analyst who looks merely at effects, and does not grapple with underlying causes. I would not hesitate to say that it is unfortunate that so-called demonstrations are taking place in Birmingham at this time, but I would say in more emphatic terms that it is even more unfortunate that the white power structure of this

* Martin Luther King, Jr., "Letter from Birmingham City Jail," *The New Leader*, June 24, 1963, pp. 3–11.

city left the Negro community with no other alternative.

In any nonviolent campaign there are four basic steps: 1) collection of the facts to determine whether injustices are alive; 2) negotiation; 3) self-purification; and 4) direct action. We have gone through all of these steps in Birmingham. There can be no gainsaying of the fact that racial injustice engulfs this community. Birmingham is probably the most thoroughly segregated city in the United States. Its ugly record of police brutality is known in every section of this country. Its unjust treatment of Negroes in the courts is a notorious reality. There have been more unsolved bombings of Negro homes and churches in Birmingham than any city in this nation. These are the hard, brutal, and unbelievable facts. On the basis of these conditions Negro leaders sought to negotiate with the city fathers. But the political leaders consistently refused to engage in good faith negotiation. . . .

You may well ask, "Why direct action? Why sit-ins, marches, etc.? Isn't negotiation a better path?" You are exactly right in your call for negotiation. Indeed, this is the purpose of direct action. Nonviolent direct action seeks to create such a crisis and establish such creative tension that a community that has constantly refused to negotiate is forced to confront the issue. It seeks so to dramatize the issue that it can no longer be ignored.

I just referred to the creation of tension as a part of the work of the nonviolent resister. This may sound rather shocking. But I must confess that I am not afraid of the word "tension." I have earnestly worked and preached against violent tension, but there is a type of constructive nonviolent tension that is necessary for growth. Just as Socrates felt that it was necessary to create a tension in the mind so that individuals could rise from the bondage of myths and half-truths to the unfettered realm of creative analysis and objective appraisal, we must see the need of having nonviolent gadflies to create the kind of tension in society that will help men rise from the dark depths of prejudice and racism to the majestic heights of understanding and brotherhood. So the purpose of the direct action is to create a situation so crisis-packed that it will inevitably open the door to negotiation. We, therefore, concur with you in your call for negotiation. Too long has our beloved Southland been bogged down in the tragic attempt to live in monologue rather than dialogue.

One of the basic points in your statement is that our acts are untimely. . . . We know through painful experience that freedom is never voluntarily given by the oppressor; it must be demanded by the oppressed. Frankly I have never yet engaged in a direct action movement that was "well timed," according to the timetable of those who have not suffered unduly from the disease of segregation. For years now I have heard the word "Wait!" It rings in the ear of every Negro with a piercing familiarity. This "wait" has almost always meant "never." It has been a tranquilizing Thalidomide, relieving the emotional stress for a moment, only to give birth to an ill-formed infant of frustration. We have waited for more than 340 years for our constitutional and God-given rights. The nations of Asia and Africa are moving with jet-like speed toward the goal of political independence, and we still creep at horse and buggy pace toward the gaining of a cup of coffee at a lunch counter.

I guess it is easy for those who have never felt the stinging darts of segregation to say wait. But when you have seen vicious mobs lynch your mothers and fathers at will and drown your sisters and brothers at whim; when you have seen hate-filled policemen curse, kick, brutalize, and even kill your black brothers and sisters with impunity; when you see the vast majority of your 20-million Negro brothers smothering in an air-tight cage of poverty in the midst of an affluent society; when you suddenly find your tongue twisted and your speech stammering as you seek to explain to your six-year-old daughter why she can't go to the public amusement park that has just been advertised on television . . . and see the depressing clouds of inferiority begin to form in her little mental sky . . . when you take a cross-country drive and find it necessary to sleep night after night in the uncomfortable corners of your automobile because no motel will accept you; when you are humiliated day in and day out by nagging signs reading "white" men and "colored"; when your first name becomes "nigger" and your middle name becomes "boy" (however old you are) and your last name becomes "John," and when your wife and mother are never given the respected title "Mrs."; when you are harried by day and haunted by night by the fact that you are a Negro, living constantly at tip-toe stance never quite knowing what to expect next, and plagued with inner fears and outer resentments; when you are forever fighting a degenerating sense of "nobodiness"—then you will understand why we find it difficult to wait. . . .

You express a great deal of anxiety over our willingness to break laws. This is certainly a legitimate concern. Since we so diligently urge people to obey the Supreme Court's decision of 1954 outlawing segregation in the public schools, it is rather strange and paradoxical to find us consciously breaking laws. One may well ask, "How can you advocate breaking some laws and obeying others?" The answer is found in the fact that there are two types of laws: There are *just* laws and there are *unjust* laws. One has not only a legal but a moral responsibility to obey just laws. Conversely, one has a moral responsibility to disobey unjust laws. I would agree with Saint Augustine that "An unjust law is no law at all."

Now what is the difference between the two? How does one determine when a law is just or unjust? A just law is a man-made code that squares with the moral law or the law of God. An unjust law is a mode that is out of harmony with the moral law. . . .

I hope you can see the distinction I am trying to point out. In no sense do I advocate evading or defying the law as the rabid segregationist would do. This would lead to anarchy. One who breaks an unjust law must do it *openly, lovingly* (not hatefully as the white mothers did in New Orleans when they were seen on television screaming "nigger, nigger, nigger") and with a willingness to accept the penalty. I submit that an individual who breaks a law that conscience tells him is unjust, and willingly accepts the penalty by staying in jail to arouse the conscience of the community over its injustice, is in reality expressing the very highest respect for law. . . .

You spoke of our activity in Birmingham as extreme. At first I was rather disappointed that fellow clergymen would see my nonviolent efforts as those of the extremist. . . . I stand in the middle of two opposing forces in the Negro community. One is a force of complacency made up of Negroes who, as a result of long years of oppression, have been so completely drained of self-respect and a sense of "somebodiness" that they have adjusted to segregation, and of a few Negroes in the middle class who, because of a degree of academic and economic security, and because at points they profit by segregation, have unconsciously become insensitive to the problems of the masses. The other force is one of bitterness and hatred and comes perilously close to advocating violence. It is expressed in the various black nationalist groups that are springing up over the nation, the largest and best known being Elijah Muhammad's Muslim movement. This movement is nourished by the contemporary frustration over the continued existence of racial discrimination. It is made up of people who have lost faith in America, who have absolutely repudiated Christianity, and who have concluded that the white man is an incurable "devil."

I have tried to stand between these two forces saying that we need not follow the "do-nothingism" of the complacent or the hatred and despair of the black nationalist. There is the more excellent way of love and nonviolent protest. I'm grateful to God that, through the Negro church, the dimension of nonviolence entered our struggle. If this philosophy had not emerged I am convinced that by now many streets of the South would be flowing with floods of blood. And I am further convinced that if our white brothers dismiss us . . . and refuse to support our nonviolent efforts, millions of Negroes, out of frustration and despair, will seek solace and security in black nationalist ideologies, a development that will lead inevitably to a frightening racial nightmare. . . .

I must close now. But before closing I am impelled to mention one other point in your statement that troubled me profoundly. You warmly commended the Birmingham police force for keeping "order" and "preventing violence." I don't believe you would have so warmly commended the police force if you had seen its angry, violent dogs literally biting six unarmed, nonviolent Negroes. . . .

I wish you had commended the Negro sit-inners and demonstrators of Birmingham for their sublime courage, their willingness to suffer, and their amazing discipline in the midst of the most inhuman provocation. One day the South will recognize its real heroes. . . . One day the South will know that when these disinherited children of God sat down at lunch counters they were in reality standing up for the best in the American dream and the most sacred values in our Judeo-Christian heritage, and thus carrying our whole nation back to great wells of democracy which were dug deep by the founding fathers in the formulation of the Constitution and the Declaration of Independence. . . .

If I have said anything in this letter that is an overstatement of the truth and is indicative of an unreasonable impatience, I beg you to forgive me. If I have said anything in this letter that is an understatement of the truth and is indicative of my having a patience that makes me patient with anything less than brotherhood, I beg God to forgive me. . . .

Let us all hope that the dark clouds of racial prejudice will soon pass away and the deep fog of misunderstanding will be lifted from our fear-drenched communities and in some not too distant tomorrow the radiant stars of love and brotherhood will shine over our great nation with all of their scintillating beauty.

Yours for the cause of
Peace and Brotherhood
M. L. KING, JR.

9

CIVIL RIGHTS MUST NOT DESTROY LIBERTY*

William F. Buckley, Jr.

How far should the national government go in this implementation of the Supreme Court's decision? An editor of the National Review, *a leading organ of American conservatism, here argues that the course suggested by* Brown v. Board of Education *will lead to the destruction of liberty for the white and Negro community alike. The advantages of integration are problematic, Buckley suggests; but the costs of federal power are clear and decisive.*

. . . Let us take the word of the predominating school of social scientists and stipulate that segregation is the cause of personality disturbances. And—mark this—not only against the Negro, but also against the white. The argument is not new; it has often been used against corporal punishment. It is not only the victim who is damaged, psychiatrists report, but also the executioner, in whom sadistic impulses are dangerously encouraged. No one who has contemplated a man brandishing a fiery cross and preaching hatred needs help from social science to know that the race problem has debasing effects on black and white alike.

Assume all this to be true. Assume, also, that the legal and political power is wholly at the disposal of the society to effect its point of view in the South. Assume, in other words, that *Brown v. Board of Education* and the supporting decisions of the Supreme Court deconstitutionalized segregated public schooling beyond the point of argument. Then assume that the raw power necessary to enforce that decision is available to the present administration, and that the will of the nation is such as to insure that Congress will supply power where power is lacking. Should the federal government then proceed?

The list of sanctions available to the government is endless. The economic power of the federal government has in our time reached the point where it cannot be denied; cannot, in fact, be defied. If Congress can seriously entertain the question whether to spend money to aid public schooling in any state whose public schools are segregated, why can't Congress debate the question whether it is prepared to spend money for road-building in a segregated state? Or for unemployment? Or for farmers' subsidies? Already the Attorney General has hinted he is considering (for purely punitive reasons) recommending to his old friend the Commander-in-Chief the removal of our large military installations from segregated areas.

In a word, the federal government is in a position to visit intolerable economic sanctions against the defiant state. Not to mention the government's arsenal of legal weapons. Why cannot

---

* William F. Buckley, Jr., "Civil Rights Must Not Destroy Liberty," *The Saturday Review*, November 11, 1961, pp. 21–22.

the Congress (assuming always a purposive mood on the subject of segregation) pass laws increasing the penalties for those held guilty of contempt of court in a certain category of cases? And why can't the courts rule—as Professor Auerbach of the University of Wisconsin has recommended—that any state which, having fought to the end of the legal road, sets out to close down its public schools rather than integrate them, be forbidden to do so on the grounds that such action, under such circumstances, becomes not the free exercise of the state's power, but an act of defiance of a federal court? By such reasoning the federal government could take over the operation of the schools. . . .

What would be accomplished by turning the legislative, judicial, and executive resources of this country over to a crash program of integration? Let us suppose the program were so successful as to make South Carolina like New York City. This spring a distinguished New York Negro told the audience of the television program "Open End" that he did not know three white people in all of New York with whom he felt genuinely comfortable, such is the prevalence of prejudice even in this cosmopolitan center. Louis Lomax may be more sensitive, and hence more bitter, than the average New York Negro, and so unrepresentative of the state of Negro serenity in the North; but then, too, Dr. Martin Luther King is more sensitive, and so more bitter, than the average Southern Negro, and hence unqualified as a litmus of the Southern Negro's discontent. . . .

The deep disturbances isolated by the social scientists are not, I think, of the kind that are removed by integrating the waiting rooms and the schools. It has even been revealed (*Villanova Law Review*, Fall 1960) that the very tests cited by the Supreme Court in *Brown* as evidence that Southern Negro children were suffering personality damage, when administered in the North yielded not merely similar results, but results that seemed to indicate a greater psychic disturbance in integrated Northern Negroes than in segregated Southern Negroes! I believe that the forms of segregation, which so much engross us at the moment and which alone are within the reach of the law to alter, are of tertiary importance, and of transitory nature; and under the circumstances the question arises even more urgently: *Should* we resort to convulsive measures that do violence to the traditions of our system in order to remove the forms of segregation in the South? If the results were predictably and unambiguously successful, the case might be made persuasively. If a clean stroke through the tissue of American mores could reach through to the cancer, forever to extirpate it, then one might say, in due gravity: let us operate. But when the results are thus ambiguous? Use the federal power to slash through the warp and woof of society in pursuit of a social ideal which was never realized even under the clement circumstances of a Chicago or a New York or a Philadelphia?

I say no. A conservative is seldom disposed to use the federal government as the sword of social justice, for the sword is generally two-edged ("The government can only do something for the people in proportion as it can do something to the people," Jefferson said). If it is doubtful just what enduring benefits the Southern Negro would receive from the intervention of government on the scale needed to, say, integrate the schools in South Carolina, it is less doubtful what the consequences of interposition would be to the ideal of local government and the sense of community, ideals which I am not ready to abandon, not even to kill Jim Crow.

What, meanwhile, are the Negroes actually losing that they would not lose if the government took over in the South? One thing alone, I think, and that is the institutional face of segregation. That is important; but it is in the last analysis only a form. What matters is the substance of segregation. The kind of familiarity that might lessen racial consciousness is outside the power of the government to effect. I would even argue that it is outside the power of the government to accelerate. . . .

It is true that the separation of the races on account of color is nonrational, then circumstance will in due course break down segregation. When it becomes self-evident that biological, intellectual, cultural, and psychic similarities among the races render social separation capricious and atavistic, then the myths will begin to fade, as they have done in respect of the Irish, the Italian, the Jew; then integration will come—the right kind of integration. But meanwhile there *are* differences between the races which surely will not be denied by an organization explicitly devoted to the advancement of colored people. The Negro community must advance, and is advancing. The Reverend William Sloane Coffin of Yale University, returning from his whirl with the Freedom Riders, rejected the request of Mr. Robert Kennedy that the Riders withdraw to let the situation cool off with the words: "The Negroes have been waiting for ninety years." Mr. Coffin spoke nonsense, and showed scant respect for the productive labors, material and spiritual, of three generations of Negroes. A sociologist at Brooklyn College only a few weeks before had observed that never in the history of nations has a racial minority advanced so fast as the Negroes have done in America. How far will they go on to advance? To the point where social separation will vanish?

I do not know, but I hope that circumstance will usher in that day, and that when the Negroes have finally realized their long dream of attaining to the status of the white man, the white man will still be free; and that depends, in part, on the moderation of those whose inclination it is to build a superstate that will give them Instant Integration.

VIII

Congress and Representation

Since representative government has such a high place in our value system, it is rather curious that Congress should have such a poor public image. The droll story and the humorous anecdote frequently satirize the national legislature while the Senators Phogbounds and Claghorns in the mass media tend to stereotype the average congressman.

Part of the problem stems from a failure to understand the critical function of Congress in compromising controversial issues and achieving a degree of consensus among disparate interest groups. At the same time the substantial committee work in Congress is seldom seen. Instead the public eye falls upon a listless, half-empty chamber ignoring a prepared speech by an equally disinterested colleague or a newspaper headline describing the circus-like performance of a reckless investigating committee.

Congress has its shortcomings—inertia and delay, conservatism, and a tendency, at times, to intervene in the province of the Executive. The system, nevertheless, does work and it works despite a congressman's lack of systematic information, his overburdening committee duties, and the endless demands of constituents who regard a congressman as something of a cross between a Capitol guide and a glorified bell boy. In a nation where 70 per cent of the people do not know the name of their senator or congressman, it is highly probable that the national legislators do a better job than most apathetic citizens realize, or perhaps, deserve.

The following section explores two major issues relating to Congress as a political institution. The first of these, "How effective is Congress?," deals with the question of whether the machinery of Congress is adequate to cope with the problems of the twentieth century. The second problem, "How Many Votes Should One Man Have?," relates to representation and its political consequences.

How Effective Is Congress?

Because of the dominance of local spokesmen in Congress, the seniority basis for selection of committee chairmen (favoring one-party regions), and the absence of a relevancy rule for debate in the Senate, the prevailing point of view in Congress is conservative. It is claimed that in passing on progressive legislation Congress is more likely to say "no" rather than "yes" and that Congress favors the producing concerns (agriculture and oil) rather than those of the consumer (urban factory workers). In short, the critics of Congress insist that the national legislature tends to support the status quo rather than to promote the social and economic needs of a complex society.

Congress, of course, has its defenders as well as its critics. There as those who say that all that is needed are a few procedural changes. There are others, like political scientist and former Congressman T. V. Smith, who contend the function of Congress is to deliberate and adjudicate. They argue that the individuals who want to reform the mechanics of Congress mistake the real problem which is moral rather than technical. Further, if Congress did not compromise and bargain and negotiate, it would not be Congress. The very "wrongs" which some critics cite are regarded as blessings in other quarters.

How Many Votes Should One Man Have?

The Founding Fathers never intended that Congress should be a completely representative body. Out of deference to the interests of small states, the Constitution guaranteed each state equal suffrage in the Senate. Geography rather than population thus became the basis of representation in the upper house. The men who wrote the Constitution, however, did intend that the House of Representatives be what the named implied—the representative branch of the national legislature.

Today the rural-dominated state legislatures draw the boundary lines for congressional districts (gerrymander) in such a way that virtually every urban and suburban area fails to get its share of congressional power. For many years there appeared to be no redress in the courts. However in 1962, the Supreme Court held in *Baker v. Carr* that federal judges may hear complaints and provide relief, in some cases, to voters who have been discriminated against in the formation of state legislative districts.

Many supporters of greater urban representation have contended that rural dominance in the state legislatures and in Congress is a roadblock to progressive, liberal legislation. Is this supposition correct? What would be the political consequences of a more equitable system of representation? In this problem, a statement of the prevailing opinion at a conference of scholars and writers sponsored by the Twentieth Century Fund on legislative apportionment makes a strong case for population as the basis of representation in state legislatures. In the second selection, Andrew Hacker's article, "Reapportionment: Who Will Benefit?" broadly examines the whole issue of representation and suggests that the consequence of *Baker v. Carr* may be disappointing.

1

WHAT'S THE MATTER WITH CONGRESS?*

Howard E. Schuman

As a legislative assistant to Senator Paul H. Douglas, Mr. Schuman has had first hand opportunity to observe both houses of Congress. He concludes that Congress is dominated by conservative and sectional forces. In the following article, Mr. Schuman examines the institutions and practices which permit conservative interests to operate against the public welfare.

. . . And while Congress is inherently limited in its functions, it is being prevented today from doing what it *can* do by needless and senseless obstructions. Conservative and sectional forces have set up roadblocks which are making it nearly impossible to move forward with progressive legislation. In this period of presidential abdication, those who want to go forward must of necessity turn their attention to how some of these barriers can be removed. If there is to be even some modest measure of protection for the public welfare, congressional institutions themselves must be reexamined and revised.

As anyone who has observed Congress knows, proponents of change must wheel their pet projects through and around a formidable series of obstacles before the projects become law, while those who oppose change may impose a veto at any one of many way-stations along the legislative route. The system of checks and balances—of which George Norris said in a cynical mood that "the politicians have the checks, and the special interests the balances"—is meant to protect the status quo. The most obvious of these "checks" is the equal representation of each state, thus allowing the eight largest states with almost half the population to have only one-sixth the senators or a number equal to that of the eight smallest states with less than 3 per cent of the population. There is no way, short of a constitutional amendment, to change this fact.

But some facts about Congress are not immutable. And these facts include the gerrymandering of congressional districts by state legislatures, the seniority system, the absence of party caucuses, the nature of the committee

* Howard E. Schuman, "What's the Matter with Congress?" *The New Republic*, April 1, 1957, pp. 14–16.

system, the exercise of power by the "inner circle" . . . a system which punishes party loyalty and rewards irregularity—and the intricately designed rules, including the filibuster, which protect the interests of a regional minority.

The problem of underrepresentation of liberal sentiment in the Congress differs only in degree from the same underrepresentation in the states themselves. Because the state legislatures draw the boundary lines for congressional districts, even seats in the House of Representatives are so gerrymandered that rural and conservative districts have an advantage of about 60 House seats. These 60 seats can make the difference between bold congressional action and the irresolution bordering on chaos that we have today.

The remedy lies in proper enforcement of constitutional provisions and legislation requiring states to set up contiguous and equally populated districts. A determined group in Congress could and should force this issue at every opportunity.

The seniority system is another artificial device enabling a conservative coalition to dominate Congress. In the Senate not a single major chairmanship is held by a Northern liberal from any one of the eight states where almost half our population lives. But the Deep South has eight chairmen and the border states two. Four others are held by senators from states which rank 36th, 37th, 39th and 42nd in population. Only one of the 15 chairmen is from even a moderately large Northern state. This is with the Democratic party in charge.

The Republican picture is a little better. Eight ranking Republican members of Senate committees are from the Mississippi Valley where right-wing Republicans dominate policy. States ranking 44th, and 45th and 48th in population have three others. Only four ranking members are from any one of the eight states which make up half the population.

The seniority system favors either the very small, the one-party Southern, or the right-wing trans-Mississippi Republican states. Urban (which is to say, usually liberal) forces are deliberately counted out. This is a wholly artificial situation, required neither by the Constitution nor the written rules of the Senate.

The consequences of this system are disastrous for liberal senators. If they behave, accept the system and do not upset party unity—a euphemism, in the case of Democrats, for doing nothing to offend the South—they will be fed a few political crumbs. If they fight a bold and lonely battle, the seniority system by some mysterious process becomes less than sacred when applied to them. A Harry Byrd is rewarded with the chairmanship of the Finance Committee after bolting to Eisenhower in 1952, but the request for a key committee post by the party's 1956 vice-presidential nominee is shunted aside. For the conservative, seniority is a perpetual free ride. For the liberal it is a dizzy merry-go-round of futilty. It penalizes, in particular, the large, two-party states where a senator's tenure is insecure. With the Republicans in power, Congress is dominated by their right-wing—the Knowlands, the Bridges and the Brickers. The country soon decides that it wants a change—a vote for a Republican is said to be a vote for McCarthy. Then there are new elections. Liberal Democrats replace Republican senators in the large swing states.

Congress is then organized by the Democrats. Did I say the Democrats? I mean the Southerners, who are *not* from swing states. Liberal pledges and Democratic party platforms are left behind as "campaign oratory." At the *next* election a vote for a Democrat becomes a vote for Eastland! Liberals of both parties are spurned by the voters; they are knocked off the escalator of seniority while their conservative brethren rise higher. This cycle could be called a political *La Ronde*.

A modest remedy would be to have rotating committee chairmen for which there is ample precedent in Congressional joint committees. Appointments and chairmanships based on seniority would be kept, but a chairman could serve for only one Congress. By this procedure we would preserve automatic selection, while avoiding much personal in-fighting and jockeying for place and position. We would also diminish the power and influence of a single chairman or a single sectional interest.

Another major congressional weakness is that except for casual meetings at the beginning of a session, party caucuses are rarely held, they are never binding, and when held are seldom devoted to policy discussions.

One example of the results will suffice. At the moment the leaders of both House and Senate are from Texas. The basic economic interests of Texas are gas and oil. No political figure from Texas could survive if he fought the principal interests of his state. It is too much to expect even the bravest Texas politician to slash his own wrists by voting for federal regulation of natural gas.

Yet the Democratic party, if it is to be true to the traditions it espouses nationally, must oppose the outrageous privileges demanded by the oil companies. What, after all, is the difference between one party—the Republican—which lets big business in by the front door, and another party—the Democratic—which lets it sneak in the back door?

A majority of the Democrats in the party and in the Congress opposed the off-shore oil "give-away" and removing the regulations on natural gas. But the voters may have understandably been confused. For Democratic (Texas) leadership, loyal to what it conceived to be the interest of Texas, did use the machinery of the Democratic party to promote legislation opposed by a clear majority in the party.

In the House the Speaker has great influence over appointments to the tax-writing Ways and Means Committee. That committee protects the 27.5 per cent depletion bonanza for the big oil companies. When the Democrats are in power it functions as the party's committee on committees. In turn a majority sympathetic to the oil and gas industries is appointed to the House Interstate and Foreign Commerce Committee where gas legislation is sent. Further, when the gas regulatory bill was last before the House and Senate, the leadership used its great powers—the scheduling of bills, future committee appointments, the numerous legislative employees who round up the votes—to advance this legislation that was opposed by the majority of Democrats.

The result was that while the Democrats in 1956 had a farm issue in the Midwest (or thought they did) and a public power issue in the Far West (which they did), they had no effective campaign issues in the big cities and the East.

Related to this problem is the nature of the committee system. In the British House of Commons the House establishes policy while the committees iron out the wrinkles. In Congress, the committees, for the most part, determine policy and their parent bodies carry them out. As one enlightened senator has pointed out, action on the Senate floor is like a Greek tragedy. Real action takes place off-stage and precedes both speeches and votes.

The committees themselves are unrepresentative of the Congress. The Senate Finance Committee is unadulterated ultra-conservatism. The Interior Committee seldom has members from other than Western states. Rural Congressmen flock to the Agriculture committees. Sectional and class axes grind in unison.

Brave indeed is the senator or representative who rises on the floor to knock out a "pork-barrel" appropriation, to fight a special interest subsidy, or to argue against a policy which a committee has established. I have seen both the chairman and members of committees take personal offense at a noncommittee member who has the temerity to challenge a committee's action on the floor. And I have seen the leadership angered when a member fought for a plank in the Democratic platform to which the leadership was opposed. In these situations other chairmen rush to the rescue of their embattled leader, and those members who get along by going along are shoved into the breach to stop the attack.

Even when the Senate or House successfully overrides a committee action, the victory is often lost in conference for it is the committee chairmen who determine the members of conference committees.

These defects could be overcome, at least in part by regular party meetings. Although rigid party obedience is undesirable, party meetings could determine general policies and programs for which at least the committees and the leadership would be committed to work.

There is, finally, the "filibuster" rule in the Senate. Some like *New York Times* correspondent William S. White in his book on the Senate, *The Citadel,* have argued that unlimited debate is needed to protect minority rights and prevent a ruthless temporary majority from acting too fast. If our states had unitary systems; if urban groups were fairly represented in their legislatures; if seats in the House of Representatives were not gerrymandered; if the Senate were based on population; if there were no system of checks and balances; if the seniority system did not exist; and if committees and their chairmen were more representative; then a good case might be made for unlimited debate. But in existing circumstances fears of a ruthless temporary majority are wholly unfounded. The real problem is the opposite—the power of permanent, regional minorities.

These are some of the things that are the matter with Congress, preventing its assuming its proper responsibilities. Can they be corrected? If we take comfort and guidance from the past the answer is "yes." There was a time not so long ago when the Democratic party in the Senate reflected the views of the party in the country. The result was one of our great periods of reform. The story is told by Claude Bowers in his *Life of John W. Kern.*

When the Senate was organized in March 1913, Senator John Kern of Indiana, who had been in the Senate for only two years, was chosen chairman of the Democratic caucus, the steering committee, and as floor leader. Kern, who had been Bryan's running mate in 1908, appointed five new members to the nine-man Democratic steering committee. They, in turn, set aside the seniority system without compunction. Said the *Literary Digest:*

> . . . the reorganization of the Senate has been accomplished in a way paralleling the overturn of Cannonism in the house by practical abolition of the seniority rule in making up committees.

In turn, the committee rules were reformed. Chairmen were deprived of their arbitrary control. A majority of a committee could call meetings at any time and consider any pending bill. Appointments to subcommittees and conference committees could be determined by a simple majority of the majority members. As Bowers summed up:

> Thus the election of Senator Kern to the leadership of the majority at the beginning of the first Wilson administration, with all that followed . . . marked a revolutionary change in the United States Senate, broke down the fetish of the seniority rule, smashed superannuated precedents and traditions, made difficult if not impossible the domination of the body by a small coterie of men entrenched in powerful chairmanships, and did more toward the democratization of the Senate than had been done in half a century.

In recent weeks we have seen a spate of articles complaining of the absence of new ideas for liberals to champion. I rise to offer a suggestion. Could not a campaign for congressional reform stir men to act? Some may argue that there is little "political mileage" or political sex appeal in the reform of little-known procedures, or the modification of intricately designed rules and practices of Congress. But what political sex appeal did there seem to be in changing the rules of the House to provide that the Rules Committee should be elected by the House membership rather than appointed by the Speaker? Yet this *was* the issue by which George Norris clipped the wings of Speaker Cannon. What political mileage was there in changing the date of convening Congress from March 4th to January 3rd? Yet, this became the popular "Lame Duck" amendment. In January 1957, Senate liberals did catch the country's eye—if only for a moment—when they dramatized the intricacies and evils of Rule 22 and the filibuster.

The reform of the seniority system, the revival of party caucuses, the proper distribution of House seats, the subordination of congressional committees to general party policies, the overthrow of the filibuster could, I am persuaded, not only be made exciting objectives, but these reforms would lead to a restoration of congressional responsibility. In the absence of presidential leadership such a restoration becomes a national necessity.

2

THE CONGRESS AND MAJORITY RULE*

Stephen K. Bailey

Majority rule is frequently frustrated by congressional action. Why should this be so? In the following selection, Stephen K. Bailey analyzes the rules and procedures which often cause the will of the majority to become rule by the minority. Professor Bailey suggests changing this policy to reaffirm the slogan "majority rule and minority rights."

. . . Healthy, first-term presidents, guided by the long perspectives of able civil servants, tend to be instruments of majority rule. Congress, on the other hand, wobbles between outright minority rule (what Woodrow Wilson once called rule by a "disintegrate ministry"), and rule by Majority Leader and Speaker. But Majority Leader rule is not necessarily equivalent to majority rule. The Speaker is not necessarily the true majority's spokesman. Perhaps this is unfair. Perhaps the proper statement is that both Houses of Congress are presently ruled by distinguished leaders of disintegrate and timid majorities. But why are the majorities timid and disintegrate? Why are they not organized and courageous? Why has America not known firm and responsible majority rule in the Congress since 1915? The 100 days of the New Deal must be ruled out. This was not rational majority rule; this was congressional (and bipartisan) default in a time of panic. In the years of danger which lie ahead, we cannot count on having this kind of "crisis consensus."

By majority rule in Congress I mean rule in the interests of a majority of American citizens by a sufficient majority of the winning party in each House. Today, congressional rule in the interest of a majority of American citizens is effectively strangled. The noose is not the Constitution. The noose is made up of strands of congressional rules and procedures designed to rope off from majority control two citadels of power: white supremacy and big-farm, big-business influence over public policy.

Underlying the inordinate influence of the South and of economic privilege in the Congress is a collection of carefully cultivated myths. These myths have probably captivated or unnerved a sufficient number of Northern and Western congressmen effectively to have immobilized last November's majority on key issues of congressional organization and procedure.

The myth of seniority. The old-timers claim that no other system of selecting committee chairmen is automatic. If chairmen were to be selected by party caucus—by *ad hominem* judgments—Congress, it is reasoned (?), would be squeezed to death in infinite log-rolls.

* Stephen K. Bailey, "Congress and Majority Rule," *The New Republic*, January 5, 1959, pp. 7–8.

This, of course, is one of the sillier rationalizations of this or any other century. But let us accept it. Let us assume that we wish to keep the seniority principle because it provides a method for automatic succession. But why should the majority's imagination be immobilized? There is a simple solution. At the beginning of every Congress, each member could tote up the number of general (as distinct from primary) elections he has won against at least a 20-per cent oppositon vote. For these general election victories he would receive *double* credit for purposes of seniority. Seniority would still provide automatic election; but power would gravitate into the hands of those who come from two-party districts in which partisan competition tends to search out the majority's interest.

A second myth is that, except on race issues, Southern Democrats are really National Democrats. Some bad political science has bolstered this myth with statistics. It takes the *Congressional Quarterly* to remind us that in this last session of Congress the Southerners bolted the National Democratic Party on 84 key roll calls. The issues: Housing, unemployment benefits, federal aid to education, slum clearance, taxes and a host of other matters that bother the majority of American citizens.

Perhaps the most important job before the Democratic National Committee is to create a truly national Democratic party in the South. In some areas, this may necessitate a brand-new grass-roots organization. In others it means strengthening and registering existing National Democrats—Negro and white. For if National Democrats could organize the Congress, the power of the Eastlands and the Byrds could easily be contained.

There is a third myth. This one goes in and out of focus like a slide in an old kodachrome projector. It is that centralized control of each House of the Congress is dangerous to the freedom of individual members. This myth plays up to two human vanities: (1) the desire not to be subordinated; (2) the desire to avoid responsibility so as to avoid making enemies. The myth is a cruel one because the average senator and congressman *is* subordinated. Congressional behavior is not anarchic; it simply operates on the assumption that compromise will normally fall to the advantage of powerfully-entrenched minority interests. This subordination of the individual members to an economic conservatism and a social reaction which is heedless of majority interests is at the crux of what ails the Congress. But the answer is not to end subordination; the answer is to achieve a responsible majority rule. Unfortunately, many liberals in Congress think the answer to existing minority rule *is* anarchy. They dislike the Rules Committee not only because it is conservative, but because it *rules*. With this in mind, liberals are busily working out devices to cut the power of the Rules Committee. But what is wrong with the Rules Committee is not that it rules, but that it rules irresponsibly, and for minority interests.

The ultimate cure is not to make it easier for temporary coalitions of congressmen to break the power of the Rules Committee. Nor is the answer to strengthen the Rules Committee as an instrument of bipartisan coalitions in the Congress. The only answer that squares with majority rule and political responsibility is to make the Rules Committee an instrument of the majority party. This means the abolition of the Rules Committee in its present form, and its reconstitution as a majority policy committee under the chairmanship of the Speaker. Policy committee members would, of course, be chosen by caucus.

If this is the direction of political

morality and responsible majority rule, House liberals should understand in advance that easier discharge petitions and 21- or 14-day rule—necessary as they may be in the short run—are in the long run potential *enemies* of responsible government. The legislative agenda *must* be narrowed. Traffic *must* be controlled. What the liberals should want is to *capture* power—not to dissipate, hamstring or by-pass it.

The final myth that immobilizes everyone is that America survives because its parties are meaningless. Any attempt to strengthen party responsibility, it is argued, will immediately divide the Congress and the nation into warring factions. We will no longer be "so fundamentally at one that we can safely afford to bicker." We get along now because we fuzz up responsibility and save everybody's political face. But this is nonsense. There is little chance of monolithic, tightly-disciplined parties developing—either inside or outside of the Congress. We still have separation of powers, staggered elections, federalism. The task of democratically-selected leaders and leadership committees in each House is to lead, not order; to provide a responsible focus of leadership on major issues; to act as a sympathetic bridge with the Executive and with the majority leadership in the other House on matters of national survival and the general welfare.

Let us develop the myth that legislators have a right to be ornery; but that when the orneriness has had its day, legislative machinery will be so constructed that compromises will fall in the direction of the interests of the *majority* of American citizens. Let us reaffirm the slogan: majority rule and minority rights. . . .

3

TO MOVE CONGRESS OUT OF ITS RUTS*

Hubert H. Humphrey

Congress probably gets more undeserved criticism than any other branch of the national government. It has a bad press and a poor public image. Yet when allowance is made for misrepresentation and exaggeration, most Americans would still agree that the national legislature is not as effective as it should be. In the following paragraphs, Senator Humphrey offers his suggestions for improving Congress and increasing the confidence and respect of the people in the work of the world's foremost legislative body.

Most members of Congress are dedicated and conscientious legislators and public servants, aware of the power they hold over the dollars and destiny of the American people and so many others throughout the world. If they are given extra time—or rather freed from unnecessarily time-consuming duties—they will spend most of it tackling

---

* Hubert H. Humphrey, "To Move Congress Out of Its Ruts," *The New York Times Magazine*, April 7, 1963, pp. 130–31. Copyright by The New York Times Company. Reprinted by permission.

the huge task of informing themselves.

Several steps can be taken to give them that extra time. These are not the final answers to the time problem of members of Congress, but they would help.

First, more joint meetings of congressional committees. A legislative question involving disarmament and arms control, for example, normally requires consideration by the Foreign Relations and Armed Services Committees of the Senate and the House and the Joint Committee on Atomic Energy. Joint meetings would save the time of members serving on more than one of these committees.

Second, more standing joint committees including members of both the House and the Senate. Such committees would save time, particularly toward the end of each congressional session, by paving the way to speedier conference agreements between the Senate and the House on controversial issues.

Third, more efficient scheduling of the work days of Congress. Certain days could be scheduled specifically for floor debate and action by the full House or Senate. Other days could be restricted exclusively for hearings and action by the congressional committees.

In the early months of the session, the full House or Senate would meet only a few days each week. As committees completed their action in the later months of the session, the Senate and House would meet more often. This pattern would save time for members, and end the absurd necessity of members literally running from committee room to Senate or House chamber when issues in which they are involved are up for action at different places at the same time.

Fourth, modification of the "Morning Hour" in the Senate, in which members read miscellaneous speeches of marginal or undated importance and insert various articles into the *Congressional Record*. Instead, members would be permitted to send their "morning hour" speeches and articles to the clerk for insertion in the *Record*, without taking their own time and the time of other senators to read them word-for-word.

Fifth, a requirement in the Senate that members restrict their remarks to the issue formally listed as the business of the Senate. In a debate over agricultural programs, for example, a senator would not be able to spend an hour discussing a totally unrelated subject. This "Rule of Germaneness" now applies only to debate in the House of Representatives.

Sixth, a summer recess of Congress of at least three weeks. This would take time away from legislative duties, but ultimately, I am convinced, would save time. The immediate value would be the opportunity for members of Congress to spend some time with families and constituents in a period (June or July) when schools are closed and citizens are not tied at home because of weather.

The indirect value would be the change of pace and rest such a recess would give to each member. He would return for the final busy weeks of the session refreshed for more efficient performance of his legislative duties. Congressmen are human beings; they get tired and their nerves can become frayed from long months of pressure and hard work. A summer recess would probably reduce the inevitable tensions and bickering so common in the final weeks of congressional sessions.

Seventh, modification and adoption of the British "Question Period," in which administration leaders would report on and answer questions of general importance before the full Senate and House. This would save time, help to keep members of Congress better informed on administration programs and policy and sustain the necessary frequent contact between the Executive and Legislative branches of government.

This final suggestion—and some of the others—would have a valuable side-effect; it would save the time of high administration leaders who have their own crucial problems of too many duties for too few hours.

It is not unusual for the Secretary of State and the Secretary of Defense and other Cabinet officers to give basically the same testimony and answer basically the same questions for several different congressional committees. The Secretary of State, for example, might be called early in the session to outline the foreign aid program—including military aid—to the Senate Committee on Foreign Relations. He will then repeat the same testimony to the Senate Armed Services Committee, and again to the House Armed Services Committee.

The result, I believe, is an excessive demand on the time of these officials. Secretary of State Dean Rusk made 54 personal appearances before congressional committees during the 87th Congress—29 in 1961 and 25 in 1962. Secretary of Defense Robert McNamara spent a total of 203 hours before congressional committees during the 87th Congress—88.75 in 1961 and 114.25 in 1962.

Standing Joint Committees, more joint meetings of committees and a "Question Period" for the full House or Senate would save the time of congressmen and these high officials—and serve to inform all members of Congress more thoroughly.

Another congressional defect which tends to waste time—and to cause confusion and occasional conflict between members—rests with the line-up of Senate and House committees. New problems and programs created by a world transformed by nuclear power and the space age are being handled by a congressional committee system which has changed little in 50 years.

There were two weeks of confusion following introduction of my bill in 1961 to establish a United States Arms Control and Disarmament Agency. This measure was first assigned to the Foreign Relations Committee, then switched to the Government Operations Committee, then back to the Foreign Relations Committee. At one point, it almost went to the Armed Services Committee. (The bill finally remained with Foreign Relations, was approved and signed into law.)

The Communications Satellite Act bounced from committee to committee before it was finally processed and sent to the floor last year. At one time or another, this bill involved the Interstate and Foreign Commerce Committee, the Foreign Relations Committee, the Government Operations Committee, the Space and Astronautics Committee and, of course, the Appropriations Committee.

Is a more up-to-date committee line-up, responsive to modern problems and modern opportunities, needed? I believe it is, and that a thorough review of the present committee and subcommittee line-ups and jurisdictions is necessary.

That review would be one of the prime responsibilities of a "Joint Committee on the Organization of Congress," which would be established by a resolution sponsored by Senator Joseph S. Clark (D., Pa.) and 31 other senators representing both parties. A companion measure in the House agrees that this committee of seven senators and seven representatives should conduct a complete review—the first since 1946—of Congress and produce recommendations for its improvement.

I expect this "Joint Committee on the Organization of Congress" to be established. Its work will be one of the most significant efforts of the 88th Congress. And its task will be difficult, because there is little popular interest or direct political advantage in the tedious effort for procedural reform within Congress.

But the American people want good government, and sense that the legislative branch has not been performing its functions with the order and effectiveness the nation deserves. The waning weeks of the 87th Congress included fights over such petty issues as what room the Appropriations Conference Committee should meet in, and long delays over minor details of legislation.

Displays of bickering and pettiness tend to obscure the real record of achievement written by recent Congresses and to diminish the respect and confidence of the people in their own representative government. Perhaps the greatest need in Congress today is not so much for studies, procedural changes and committee modernization. It may rather be a more thoroughly responsive attitude by members of Congress, who need to realize that the rules and traditions of Capitol Hill are not sacred, and that the national interest and public service are more important than individual or committee powers and prerogatives.

4

CUSTODIAN OF THE TENDER CONSCIENCES*

T. V. Smith

T. V. Smith taught politics and practiced it. As a professor at the University of Chicago and later at Syracuse University he taught and wrote about the political process. As a practical politician, he served in the Chicago City Council, the Illinois Legislature, and the House of Representatives. In the following selection politician-scholar Smith argues that Congress is already doing a good job.

What needs reforming, if the criticism of Congress is to be stopped, is not reformable in a democratic society. Only a totalitarian society can enable one set of convictions to have its way. What "good" people want reformed is already good, is very good. It is this that they ask, and for the lack of which they blame Congress: to cease having differences of conviction over matters that seem to citizens most important, or if we must have major differences and must argue about them, then to settle the arguments "right" and not, as Congress does, make them worse by some hodgepodge compromise. That's what people want; that's what they, finding lacking, criticize Congress for. That's what Congress is not doing, because it does not know how. That's what Congress is not going to do, for no-

* T. V. Smith, "Custodians of the Tender Consciences," *The Saturday Review*, December 14, 1946, pp. 12–13.

body knows how, least of all the critics of Congress. That's what cannot be done without deserting democracy. If there is something that "should be done" which cannot be done collectively, then what should be done instead is for the critics of Congress to be brought to understand what democracy is, to understand how good a job Congress is already doing of it, and to quit applying private standards to public bodies if citizens are to remain both democratic and happy. It is a disservice to democracy to raise hope that by the reform of machinery citizens can get what they can get only by reforming themselves individually.

"For most of the things that properly can be called evils . . . ," says Justice Holmes, "the main remedy is for us to grow more civilized."

The crucial crossroads of Congress is, I repeat, moral, not technical. The business of this body is to turn inevitable conflicts of provincial interests and narrow consciences into compromises that create new standards of justice. So long as good men insist upon standards of justice antiquated by the very conflicts that call their reassertion forth, so long must Congress, as much by stalling as by legislating, be midwife to the ethically novel always straining at the birth. There is no other known way to keep conscience on the grow.

Someone has well said that there is no pain like the pain of a new idea; and we may add, as the proper sign to be hung at the main crossroads: "especially if the new idea be either a moral or a religous one." To budge the consciences of earnest men from rifts in the cake of custom created by honest conflict, leaving an anodyne to ease consciences too tender to bear up under their own self-built guilt—this is the glory and the doom of Congress. The better it fulfills this, its moral vocation, the more noisily will it be criticized by those who admit themselves to be better than congressmen, but the more gallantly will it be thanked in wise retrospect by the children of those selfsame critics. (There is much more profundity than cynicism in the wisecrack that the statesman is the dead politician.) In this game of disciplining honest men into accepting the utter minimum that is possible collectively, they also serve, often serve heroically, who only sit and stall.

Citizens, citizens, why do you ever kick against the collective goads of your own individual growth?

5

ONE MAN—ONE VOTE*

Upon what factors should representation in a democracy be based—population, geographic areas, economic groups? The following statement is a consensus of a conference of scholars and writers sponsored by the Twentieth Century Fund to consider the problem of legislative apportionment.[1]

. . . The purpose of legislative representation in a democratic system of government is just that—to represent. The legislature acts on behalf of the voters. The proper goal of the system of apportionment must, therefore, be to provide effective representation for the body politic.

The history of democratic institutions points compellingly in the direction of population as the only legitimate basis of representation today.

The first parliamentary institutions reflected their feudal origins. Social, economic and political power were in the hands of a few families. Communications and transportation were primitive. Government itself had only a marginal effect on most men's lives. In those circumstances it was natural that parliaments should represent not people but great estates, titles, wealth, geographic strongholds. But as feudal concepts of privilege ended and social and economic leveling took place, political responsibility spread also.

Under generally accepted democratic theory, that responsibility falls upon every citizen. At the same time, in an increasingly complex industrialized society, government becomes vastly more important and impinges more heavily on men's lives. It is no longer tolerable for a House of Lords to exercise real legislative power over a people with no voice in it. As transportation and communications are revolutionized, the logic of separate representation for geographic stronghold disappears. The cry of "one man, one vote" heard today in the emerging new lands of Asia and Africa is no more than a reflection of democratic philosophy learned from the West.

In the year 1962 no basis of representation other than population[2] is defensible if candidly stated and examined for what it is. There is talk, for example of "area representation." But acres do not vote; nor do trees. When a sparsely settled area is given as many representatives as one much more populous, it simply means that the people in the sparse area have more representation. No matter how stated, it is people who choose the representatives.

And now any forthright statement

* From a pamphlet prepared for The Twentieth Century Fund. Reprinted in "The Mirror of Public Opinion," *St. Louis Post-Dispatch*, September 23, 1962, p. 2C.

[1] Alfred de Grazia, Professor of Government, New York University, attended the conference but did not wish to have his name associated with the statement and offered a general dissent.

[2] The conferees discussed defining population for apportionment purposes as residents or, alternatively, as actual voters. No position was taken on the question, it being considered one suitable for further research and state experimentation.

of a nonpopulation theory of representation must rest on one or two propositions: Either there must be an implication that the residents of sparsely populated areas are more virtuous than other Americans and hence deserve more representation in legislatures, or else a contention that they have special needs which can only be met by giving them greater representation than that afforded others.

Belief in rural virtue does exist, but that is not likely to be advanced seriously as a reason for nonpopulation apportionments. Not many legislators would stand up and argue openly that their constituents are so much more honest and intelligent than others that each should have two or three or ten votes. In any case, it is impermissible in a mature democracy to start comparing the merits of different population groups for purposes of weighting their votes.

The principal reliance, then, of those who advanced something other than population as a basis for representation must be on the argument that certain classes of citizens have special problems that justify giving them more than proportionate power in the legislature. This contention is indeed made in behalf of the rural areas which are now so generally overrepresented in state legislatures; it is often said that the rural population is a minority with special needs that would be neglected in a legislature faithfully representing the state's population as a whole. But surely the problems of cities and suburbs, and their need for government aid, have been as great as those of rural areas in recent decades; yet no one has been heard to argue that city and suburban voters should therefore have been given disproportionate weight in legislatures. As for the argument that rural citizens are a minority needing special protection, would anyone contend that in the states still predominantly rural—North Dakota, for example, or Mississippi—the urban minorities should be given extra legislative seats?

Our constitutional system protects minorities by other means than giving them majority control of legislatures (as rural minorities now have in many states); and the claim that such legislative control is needed by the rural minority leads to some absurd results. In Maryland rural counties containing less than 15 per cent of the state's population elect a majority of the members of the state senate. This apportionment has been defended against legal attack on the ground that the rural counties must have such control for protection of their minority rights. But of course it is not and logically cannot be true.

Regionalism remains a factor within states, but regional interests can be recognized without distortion of voting power. It is desirable to consider regional characteristics when drawing up districts for a state legislature, but it is neither necessary nor proper to give any one regional population group greater voting power than some other group. It is good for dairy farmers in New York, for example, to have a voice in the legislature through one or more members from dairy areas; it does not follow that the votes of dairy farmers should carry greater weight than those of businessmen or union members.

The central fact is that any basis of representation other than population gives one citizen's vote greater value than another's. There is no justification in our democratic heritage, in logic or in the practical requirements of government for choosing such a course.

6

REAPPORTIONMENT: WHO WILL BENEFIT?*

Andrew Hacker

A great deal of criticism is directed against the unrepresentative character of our legislatures. Just what would happen if all legislative districts were equalized in population? In the following article, Professor Andrew Hacker examines some of the consequences of reapportionment.

Legislatures in this country have remained citadels of conservatism despite an upsurge of liberal sentiment in both the executive and judicial arms of the government. It is often said that our lawmaking bodies do not represent today's America, but society as it existed several decades ago. Last spring's Supreme Court ruling in *Baker v. Carr*, placing apportionment of legislative districts within the jurisdiction of the courts, raised the hope that state legislatures will at last be ushered into the mid-twentieth century.

The decision was certainly long overdue, for states have, generally, failed to reapportion their legislative districts despite migrations from the countryside to the city and thence out to the suburbs. For example, Indiana's most recent reapportionment was in 1921 and Mississippi's in 1914. Alabama, Connecticut, Oklahoma and Tennessee had not redrawn their constituency maps since the first decade of the century. And at least one house in Delaware, Maryland, South Carolina and Vermont was based on districts created before 1900.

Every state, to a degree, has been guilty on this score. The inequities stretched from New Hampshire's lower house where one district had 1,000 times as many residents as another, to California's upper house where the vote of a farmer in Alpine County was worth 400 times that of an aircraft worker in Los Angeles.

Nor was disproportionate representation due solely to outdated districts. State constitutions persisted in giving at least one representative to each county regardless of population. Thus in Iowa's lower house each of the 99 counties in the state was awarded one legislator and the nine largest counties were given an additional representative. The result was that Ringgold County, with 7,910 people, had one representative and Polk County (Des Moines), with 266,315 had two. And this arrangement was confirmed in a 1961 statute.

Greatest attention has been given to the so-called anachronisms in the general economic outlook of legislatures. This emphasis is proper, as the most important responsibilities of the state legislatures are in the area of taxes, public debt, education, industry and public services. Only in the South does a noneconomic issue tend to predominate.

---

* From an article in *Challenge*, Vol. XI, No. 5, February 1963, pp. 4–7. Published by the Institute of Economic Affairs, New York University.

It is often said that economic thinking in the states is unsophisticated and reflects the rural domination of the legislatures. Their economic ideology is said to be provincial and founded on an outdated view of the facts. Undue emphasis is placed on economy, and as a result needed services are not provided.

Consequently, funds for education, welfare and mental health are only grudgingly appropriated, and never in sufficient amounts. The legislatures, moreover, are antiurban, antiunion and often fail to understand how the modern economy works. They subscribe to the belief that only small towns and farms are true strongholds of individualism. Hence they show little sympathy for either cities or labor unions, both of which allegedly treat men as masses. It has yet to be demonstrated that the states are capable of dealing with industrial unemployment; and while they seek to attract industry, they are mistrustful of large corporations once branch plants are established.

The decision in *Baker v. Carr* has stirred expectations that profound changes will occur in both the personnel and policies emerging from state capitals. Less than six months after the Supreme Court spoke, Paul T. David and Ralph Eisenberg of the University of Virginia reported that half the states of the Union were involved in redistricting litigation, and courts in 14 states had invalidated old systems of apportionment. Quite obviously the ruling in *Baker v. Carr* was acknowledged as the law of the land and was being implemented with all deliberate speed. The best example of obedience is to be found in Mississippi. Even while Gov. Ross Barnett was defying the federal judiciary's order to desegregate the University of Mississippi, he had summoned a special session of the legislature to draw up a redistricting plan.

It is clear that urban residents and liberals have been working for reapportionment. They feel that the states are behind the times, especially in the economic area, and that only an enhanced urban influence will bring new scope and vigor into the legislative process. Already forecasts are being made that cities will soon receive a fair share of tax revenues which will enable them to cope with problems such as housing and transportation. Many anticipate that state agencies will be given resources to become more active in medical care, unemployment insurance and kindred fields. In short, as provincial legislators become a minority, the states will once again become vital units of government eager to experiment and assume responsibility for fulfilling the needs of the times.

These prophecies may have a liberal ring. But a great many executives of large corporations have also reevaluated their judgment of legislatures dominated by rural interests. An increasing number of executives have discovered that the small business bias of the legislatures can harm large companies.

When Indiana enacted a "right-to-work" bill several years ago, labor unions were not its only opponents. Critics included such corporate giants as Radio Corporation of America, Seagram Distillers and the Allison Division of General Motors, although their dissent was not publicized. These corporations have learned to live with unions, and they regard the "loyal employee" who is supposed to be protected by "right-to-work" laws as fictional.

A number of businessmen, despite their conservatism, sense that they will benefit from reapportionment. They see more state aid for industry, a possible expansion of branch banking and a chance for more tax-exempt borrowing. Undeniably, real though unexpressed tension exists betwen small, locally owned businesses and large nationwide firms.

The trouble with these predictions regarding the consequences of redistricting is that they disregard certain hard political realities. Most of those who hope for a shift in economic legislation lack understanding of either the legislatures themselves or the voters who select them. Certainly there will be changes. But the pace will be very slow, indeed. It is also apparent that rural representation will diminish and districts will become more equal in population. However, the new power alignment in the legislatures must be scrutinized carefully.

To begin with, there is no reason to either fear or forecast the advent of arithmetical democracy. The Supreme Court's opinion in *Baker v. Carr* was couched in general terms. It simply stated that "gross disproportion of representation" violated the "equal protection of the laws" clause of the Fourteenth Amendment. The Court did not rule that both chambers of the state legislature had to be based on population. Indeed, the status of the state senates remains unclear. But it seems that the senate will be allowed to remain the bulwark of rural power and hence will be able to veto legislation approved by the other house. Nor did the Court assert that even one house had to exemplify the principle of one man, one vote. Extreme discrimination against voters of some areas would obviously have to be eliminated; but *Baker v. Carr* implied that discrimination had to be diminished rather than removed altogether.

Cities and suburbs will gain representatives, but not as many as they feel they ought to have. And their disappointment will be aggregated by the persistence of gerrymandering, with district lines being redrawn to benefit the dominant party. City dwellers, in particular, will find that their votes will be dissipated by the concentration of like-minded citizens in a few constituencies.

If the legislators seem to have placed a premium on limiting the functions of the state governments, this may not entirely be due to ideological considerations. The state legislative process is geared for the simpler needs of an earlier day. In most states the lawmaking bodies convene only once every two years, and in some cases the sessions last only 90 days. The legislators are part-time politicians who bestow upon themselves only token salaries. In several instances they receive from $10 to $20 a day while the legislature is in session.

Minutiae of all sorts clutter the agenda, and the solons spend their time debating the proper labeling of eggs and whether beauty parlor attendants should have high school diplomas. There is also a high rate of turnover among members, meaning that few gain either experience or expertise in government. The disorganized army of novices falls easy prey to the swarm of lobbyists who descend on the state capitals. The governor and the legislative majority are frequently of different parties, which often produces stalemates. In addition, the public simply is not interested in state legislative politics. The average voter is burdened with so many concerns, both personal and national, that he cannot check on the performance of those representing him in the state legislature.

The legislatures themselves have the

power to solve some of these problems, but not others. While provincial lawmakers may prefer an arrangement that leads to enactment of few laws, there is no guarantee that a change in the composition of the legislature will lead to serious reform. For the key dilemma is the role of the states in an age when national institutions overshadow local units. Reapportionment may help elect representatives who seek a more active role for their state governments, but they will have to work in a setting designed for a more quiescent age.

It is hard, perhaps impossible, to relate the economic thinking and the political behavior of the American people. For example, it may be said that John F. Kennedy, by being elected, received a mandate to go ahead with a liberal program. On the other hand, a majority of Americans voted for conservative congressmen who are unenthusiastic about the Kennedy administration's proposals for developing welfare and other public services. This casts some doubt on the assumption of reapportionment proponents that there is a "liberal majority" being denied its fair share of legislative power.

If the policies of state legislatures seem impervious to urban needs, this is not necessarily because provincial lawmakers have imposed their will on their urban cousins. Professor David Derge of Indiana University, after studying the Illinois legislature's record over a 10-year period, concluded that Chicago's greatest enemies were not the backwoodsmen from the rural areas. "The city's bitterest opponents in the legislature," wrote Prof. Derge, "are political enemies from within its own walls and those camped in the adjoining suburban areas." George D. Young of the University of Missouri reached much the same conclusion about his state. "The difficulty in passing city legislation does not come from rural members," he said, "but from members of the city's own delegation."

There are several, often overlooked, reasons for this. The first is that the central cities in most states are actually losing population. Those who remain behind are often poor and politically indifferent. Registration is low in the low-income wards and voter turnout is spotty, especially during the off-year elections and in the balloting for lesser offices. The "bloc vote" of the cities is all too often exaggerated, as is the power of the urban machines. Furthermore, the party organizations in the cities are nonideological in orientation, more concerned with putting a man in office than with what he does once he gets there. Consequently, most urban representatives in the state legislatures can hardly be called "liberal" in any meaningful sense.

Labor unions, which might be expected to support redistricting measures, are not particularly strong in most cities. Their strongest efforts are made during national elections for presidential and congressional candidates who are often more sympathetic to labor's aims. All in all, many of the legislators representing cities, if not conservative in outlook, lack interest or imagination to strike out in new directions.

Just as important as the decline of the central city is the growth of the metropolitan middle class. Managerial, sales, professional and other white-collar citizens now comprise over half of the nation's population. Living on the fringes of the cities and in the suburbs, they are temperamentally conservative and elect representatives reflecting this outlook. The number of middle-class wards in a city, usually some distance from the center, should not be minimized nor should the voting power of the people who live there. The provincial economics of rural legislators are not completely uncongenial to many of their urban colleagues.

In fact, reapportionment would increase the representation of suburban areas, for they have suffered the most discrimination. Redistricting might increase commuters' influence, diminish the power of the countryside, and still perpetuate the old political and economic thinking. This is why Senator Barry Goldwater, an articulate conservative, is not worried over the eventuality of reapportionment. "I know there are those that say the conservatives' political strength will be reduced if the cities gain more representation in the legislation," he said, "But I don't agree with that. I don't think it will make any change. There are proportionately just as many conservatives in the metropolitan as in the rural areas."

The Senator's hunch may be generally correct. Since the *Baker v. Carr* decision, I have been doing research on the apportionment of congressional districts. My investigation, sponsored by the Brookings Institution, shows that, on the whole, the House of Representatives is fairly equitably apportioned. While there are instances of a few grossly overpopulated and underpopulated districts, Congress' record is far better than that of any of the states. Indeed, the cities receive their fair share of representation and have no real cause for complaint. In all there were about 15 too many rural seats, and these were gained primarily at the expense of suburban areas.

Several key proposals President Kennedy submitted to the 87th Congress were defeated in the House of Representatives. They included the Educational Aid Bill (HR 8890), the plan to create a Department of Urban Affairs (HR 530) and the Food and Agriculture Bill (HR 11222). But suppose that each congressman had a "weighted" vote proportionate to the size of his district. For instance, a congressman representing an abnormally large constituency might be given a vote "worth," say, 2.15. At the same time, the vote of a colleague from an underpopulated district might be worth, say, .69.

The result shows that the conservative vote was underrepresented in every instance. On the urban affairs proposal, the side supporting the administration received 11 more votes than it would have had the balloting been based on district populations. The administration received a bonus of 36 votes in the balloting on the education bill and 29 extra votes for its farm bill. Therefore, it is not the liberals who suffer from whatever malapportionment may exist in Congress. Indeed, if current inequities were corrected, the administration and its liberal friends might expect a loss in influence.

We conclude that legislative reapportionment will not bring any sweeping changes. The most glaring inequalities in electoral influence will be corrected, and this will produce legislatures which more closely mirror public sentiment. In the final analysis, however, the American people seem to prefer legislators who are conservative in their political and economic thinking and who will be slow to embrace programs that depart greatly from existing arrangements. If there is to be a change, it will not be the product of reapportionment, but the result of a basic change in the public's outlook.

IX

The Presidency–The Hardest Job in the World?

The American Presidency is a product of growth as much as creation. The office was "made" not only by the framers at the Constitutional Convention but by virtually every strong president who has occupied the White House. Today the Presidency is described as "the nerve center of the nation," "our main contribution to democratic government," and "the great glue factory that binds the party and the nation."

The dramatic increase in presidential power and responsibility has spotlighted certain institutional and operational problems. The office places enormous burdens upon one man. Unlike the British monarch who merely reigns and the British Prime Minister and his cabinet who rule, the American president must both "reign and rule." Furthermore the president has no strong party system to help him steer a program through an independent and sometimes hostile legislature. It is not at all curious that a number of scholars urge reform and regeneration of the office. On the other hand, equally strong and more numerous voices caution, "Leave Your Presidency Alone."

This chapter deals with two problems: (1) the nature of the Presidency and its strengths and weaknesses as a political institution; and (2) the character and limits of presidential power.

Is the Office Equal to the Job?

The problems of the Presidency are manifold. Woodrow Wilson who knew the office during a stress period in American history warned, "Men of ordinary physique and discretion cannot be presidents and live, if the strain be not somehow relieved. We shall be obliged always to be picking our chief magistrates from among wise and prudent athletes—a small class."

The sprawling Executive Office still defies complete presidential direction and control. There is a wide gap between the president's responsibility and his authority to administer. At times the breech between president and Congress seems to grow larger rather than smaller. There is no strong party or cabinet system to give the president needed help. In short, it appears as though intolerable burdens were placed upon one man.

At least this is the theme of Herman Finer's acute diagnosis of the shortcomings of the Presidency as a political institution. His views, however, are not shared by Richard Neustadt who contends that the office is dependent upon the competency of the president and his skillful use of power. Clinton Rossiter, while not unaware of certain defects, finds the Presidency in a state of "sturdy health" and urges only minor readjustments rather than root and branch reforms.

Presidential Leadership: The Coming Caesars or the Requirements of the Twentieth Century?

Every commentator has observed the significant changes that have taken place in the office of the Chief Executive through the years. These changes have come about as the result of domestic and world crises, technological developments, growing urbanization, and the increasing complexity of our society.

To some the changes which have taken place in the Presidency have been logical and necessary. However, the steady growth of presidential power and influence has not met with universal approval and acceptance. There are those who believe that the concentration of power in the office of the President is a threat to our basic freedoms. They decry "One Man Rule" and "Presidential Government." These individuals favor a limited Presidency.

The two viewpoints on presidential power frequently clash over the proper role of the president. Should the president be a "lobbyist for the people" or should he play a restrained and limited role? What happens when the president doesn't lead? Finally, can the president lead us too far?

1

PRESIDENT JOHNSON'S FIRST ADDRESS BEFORE THE JOINT SESSION OF CONGRESS

Following is the text of Lyndon B. Johnson's first formal address as President of the United States, delivered to a Joint Session of Congress, November 27, 1963.

Mr. Speaker, Mr. President, members of the House, members of the Senate, my fellow Americans:

All I have I would have given gladly not to be standing here today.

The greatest leader of our time has been struck down by the foulest deed of our time. Today John Fitzgerald Kennedy lives on in the immortal words and works that he left behind. He lives on in the mind and memories of mankind. He lives on in the hearts of his countrymen.

No words are sad enough to express our sense of loss. No words are strong enough to express our determination to continue the forward thrust of America that he began.

The dream of conquering the vastness of space—the dream of partnership across the Atlantic and across the Pacific as well—the dream of a Peace Corps in less developed nations—the dream of education for all of our children—the dream of jobs for all who seek them and need them—the dream of care for our elderly—the dream of an all-out attack on mental illness—and, above all, the dream of equal rights for all Americans whatever their race or color.

These and other American dreams have been vitalized by his drive and by his dedication. And now the ideas and the ideals which he so nobly represented must and will be translated into effective action.

Under John Kennedy's leadership this nation has demonstrated that it has the courage to seek peace, and it has the fortitude to risk war. We have proved that we are a good and reliable friend to those who seek peace and freedom. We have shown that we can also be a formidable foe to those who reject the path of peace and those who seek to impose upon us or our allies the yoke of tyranny.

This nation will keep its commitments from South Vietnam to West Berlin. We will be unceasing in the search for peace; resourceful in our pursuit of areas of agreement even with those with whom we differ; and generous and loyal to those who join with us in common cause.

In this age when there can be no losers in peace and no victors in war we must recognize the obligation to match national strength with national restraint. We must be prepared at one and the same time for both the confrontation of power and the limitation of power. We must be ready to defend the national interest and to negotiate the common interest.

This is the path that we shall continue to pursue. Those who test our courage will find it honorable. We will demonstrate anew that the strong can be just in the use of strength, and the just can be strong in the defense of justice. And let all know we will extend no special privilege and impose no persecution.

We will carry on the fight against poverty and misery and disease and ignorance in other lands and in our own.

We will serve all the nation, not one section or one sector or one group—but all Americans.

These are the United States—a united people with a united purpose. Our American unity does not depend upon unanimity. We have differences but now, as in the past, we can derive from those differences strength, not weakness; wisdom, not despair. Both as a people and a Government we can unite upon a program—a program which is wise and just, enlightened and constructive.

For 32 years, Capitol Hill has been my home. I have shared many moments of pride with you—pride in the ability of the Congress of the United States to act, to meet any crisis, to distill from our differences strong programs of national action.

An assassin's bullet has thrust upon me the awesome burden of the Presidency. I am here today to say I need your help. I cannot bear this burden alone. I need the help of all Americans in all America.

This nation has experienced a profound shock and in this critical moment it is our duty, yours and mine, as the Government of the United States to do away with uncertainty and doubt and delays and to show that we are capable of decisive action—that from the brutal loss of our leader we will derive not weakness but strength—that we can and will act, and act now.

From this chamber of representative government let all the world know, and none misunderstand, that I rededicate this Government to the unswerving support of the United Nations—to the honorable and determined execution of our commitments to our allies—to the maintenance of military strength second to none—to the defense of the strength and the stability of the dollar—to the expansion of our foreign trade—to the reinforcement of our programs of mutual assistance and cooperation in Asia and Africa—and to our Alliance for Progress in this hemisphere.

On the twentieth day of January in nineteen hundred and sixty-one, John F. Kennedy told his countrymen that our national work would not be finished "in the first 1,000 days, not in the life of this Administration, nor even perhaps in our lifetime on this planet."

"But," he said, "let us begin."

Today in this moment of new resolve, I would say to all my fellow Americans, let us continue.

This is our challenge: not to hesitate, not to pause, not to turn about and linger over this evil moment, but to continue on our course so that we may fulfill the destiny that history has set for us.

Our most immediate tasks are here on this Hill:

First, no memorial oration or eulogy could more eloquently honor President Kennedy's memory than the earliest possible passage of the civil rights bill for which he fought so long.

We have talked long enough in this country about equal rights. We have talked for a hundred years or more.

It is time now to write the next chapter, and to write it in the books of law.

I urge you again, as I did in nineteen hundred and fifty-seven and again in nineteen hundred and sixty, to enact a civil rights law so that we can move forward to eliminate from this nation every trace of discrimination and oppression that is based upon race or color. There could be no greater source of strength to this nation, both at home and abroad.

And, second, no act of ours could more fittingly continue the work of President Kennedy than the early passage of the tax bill for which he fought all this long year. This is a bill designed to increase our national income and Federal revenues, and to provide insurance against recession. That bill, if passed without delay, means more security for those now working, more jobs for those now without them, and more incentive for our economy.

In short, this is no time for delay. It is a time for action—strong, forward-looking action on the pending education bills to help bring the light of learning to every home and hamlet in America; strong, forward-looking action on the pending foreign aid bill, making clear that we are not forfeiting our responsibilities to this hemisphere or to the world, nor erasing Executive flexibility in the conduct of our foreign affairs; and strong, prompt and forward-looking action on the remaining appropriation bills.

In this new spirit of action the Congress can expect the full cooperation and support of the Executive branch, and in particular I pledge that the expenditures of your Government will be administered with the utmost thrift and frugality.

I will insist that the Government get a dollar's value for a dollar spent. The Government will set an example of prudence and economy. This does not mean that we will not meet our unfilled needs or that we will not honor our commitments. We will do both.

As one who has long served in both houses of the Congress, I firmly believe in the independence and the integrity of the legislative branch. And I promise you that I shall always respect this. It is deep in the marrow of my bones.

With equal firmness, I believe in the capacity and I believe in the ability of the Congress, despite the divisions of opinions which characterize our nation, to act—to act wisely, to act vigorously, to act speedily when the need arises.

The need is here. The need is now. I ask your help. We meet in grief, but let us also meet in renewed dedication and renewed vigor. Let us meet in action, in tolerance and in mutual understanding.

John Kennedy's death commands what his life conveyed—that America must move forward.

The time has come for Americans of all races and creeds and political beliefs to understand and to respect one another. So, let us put an end to the teaching and the preaching of hate and evil and violence. Let us turn away from the fanatics, from the far left and the far right, from the apostles of bitterness and bigotry, from those defiant of law, and those who pour venom into our nation's bloodstream.

I profoundly hope that the tragedy and the torment of these terrible days will bind us together in new fellowship, making us one people in our hour of sorrow.

So let us here highly resolve that John Fitzgerald Kennedy did not live—or die—in vain. And on this Thanksgiving Eve, as we gather together to ask the Lord's blessing and give him our thanks, let us unite in those familiar and cherished words:

> America, America,
> God shed His grace on thee,
> And crown thy good
> With brotherhood,
> From sea to shining sea.

2

THE BURDEN OF THE PRESIDENCY*

Herman Finer

The ceremonial functions of the Presidency alone present an impossible load for one man. In addition every major domestic problem and every foreign crisis finds its way to the Chief Executive's desk. Periodically, there are suggestions for relieving the president of some of his burdens. Professor Finer goes behind the usual criticism and puts his finger on the root causes of the president's problems.

I have argued, and I believe that I have established, that certain features of the authority, structure, and operation of the Presidency give cause for serious civic concern. Our sober criteria are the nation's economic, social, and cultural needs, the needs and aspirations of many representative groups and thoughtful men and women, the reliable protection of the nation's interests and honor abroad, and the assurance of the nation's survival as a power for moral good.

1. In our time, the qualities demanded in the presidential office, with no foreseeable easing of responsibilities, are those of a genius; and how rarely a genius is found!

2. The president is required by oath to bear too heavy a burden. The weight of office is impossible; the intellectual demands are unfulfillable; the charge on the conscience is too exacting for one man alone.

3. The selection and election of the president is a gamble on folly, genius, and all the stations between.

4. The president's responsibility is demagogic rather than democratic, for he is not subjected to the continuous scrutiny and influence of a body intermediate between him and the masses which can exercise a discriminating surveillance from a foundation of independent power. American government is a government by quadriennial plebiscite.

5. The president and his cabinet are not selected by a process of intense and close competition before a discriminating forum. Once elected, there is no concerted opposition to offer alternative constructive policies expressed with responsible vigor. The Presidency becomes "a privileged sanctuary," in part because the president is a symbol of the nation, however inept a Chief Executive he may be.

6. The speeches and reported actions attributed to the president are too frequently public deception. So demanding is the presidential office that even a relatively unsophisticated voter must realize, at least from time to time, that "someone must be doing it for him behind the scenes." The president becomes a "ghost," supported by ghostwriters, thinkers, and deciders. If it is rejoined that the

---

* Herman Finer, *The Presidency: Crisis and Regeneration* (Chicago: The University of Chicago Press, 1960), pp. 300–303. Reprinted by permission of The University of Chicago Press.

"ghosts" have a mighty effect on the United States, I heartily agree. It remains a deception in which it becomes almost impossible to "talk sense," but this augurs badly for the future of the Republic.

7. It has become difficult to provide adequately for the succession to the president in case of disability or death. If the electorate keeps its eyes on the president at the head of the ticket, the vice-president becomes nothing but a vote-catching makeweight, and the nation courts trouble, already reaped on several occasions.

8. The president has a fixed term and for at least four years can damage the interests of the nation with impunity and, in the international hostilities of today, damage them irrevocably. He can be ejected only by impeachment. But impeachment is of little help when the president is likely to be a fool, an ignoramus, listless, or irresponsive to the changing mood and needs of the nation. It is presidential incompetence, not criminality, that urges an appropriate instrument of correction.

9. The prohibition of more than two terms takes away from the American people and from the burden and discretion of the political parties the continuance by successive re-elections of a man who proves to be competent. It subtracts from his power, and it reduces his responsiveness to his tasks. If the knowledge that his second and last term is about to end makes a president feel strong in his own right, having nothing to gain or lose by concern for either the electorate or Congress, and causes him, as he would say, "to do only what is right," such high-handed behavior cannot be condoned by any view of the democratic principle.

10. The separate elections for the Presidency, the Senate, and the House of Representatives fractures the nation's vision and will, destroys cogency of thought, and pits legislature and executive branch against each other.

11. The lack of a collective executive, a responsible body in which the members share in all national policies as well as the major policies of separate departments, robs the American nation of an organ of ordered, continuous, and cogent thought and persisting will. A one-man executive has not the brains, the vision, the patience, or the mental and physical capabilities to draw intellectual and spiritual nourishment from a multitude of sources.

Drastic changes are needed in the Presidency, far more drastic than the provisions for auxiliary institutions enable the office to have. As much thought should be expended on the regeneration of the Presidency as on the creation of a modern weapons system or progress in the direction and structure of the nation's economy.

Many scholars have been disturbed by the inadequacy of the Presidency to discharge the responsibilities with which the office is charged today and have made various proposals to regenerate the political leadership of the nation. It is convenient, however, to relegate an account of the more important proposals to an appendix, although two comments on these proposals deserve to be made here.

First, the criticism of existent practices made by their authors tally with my own, and, indeed, some are more severe.

Second, and more important, their recommendations do not go far enough. They propose—to summarize with extreme brevity—these various courses:

Congressional-presidential leadership should be linked by simultaneous elections of both houses at the time of the presidential election and for the same term. Linkage could be further developed by having cabinet members participate in congressional debate and answer questions in Congress.

Presidential leadership could be strengthened by joint council of legislative leaders and the president, promising cooperation and a clearer definition of the business of both branches.

Institutionalization, already embarked on, should be further developed and improved wherever it is found to sag and to be ungeared to policy-decision and command.

To provide responsible, concentrated, and harmonious advice and will, to get more cogency of thoughts and a firmer execution of decisions, it is deemed important to have president and his immediate colleagues nominated and elected on the same ticket.

Finally, recognition is given to the value of a coherent and continuously organized opposition around the defeated candidate or an alternate nominee of the party.

All of these recommendations have merit, but I believe that their intentions cannot be fulfilled by the measures so far proposed. I am persuaded that tinkering in ineffectual and may do harm. A thoroughgoing reform is indispensable.

3

THE PRESIDENCY IS POWER AND SKILL*

Richard E. Neustadt

During the Kennedy administration it was jokingly said that every bright young man in Washington had "a copy of Richard E. Neustadt's Presidential Power *on his bookshelf and an autographed picture of the President on his bureau." More seriously, it was said that many individuals, including the president himself, were impressed with Professor Neustadt's analysis of presidential power.*

. . . Governmental power, in reality not form, is influence of an effective sort on the behavior of men actually involved in making public policy and carrying it out. Effective influence for the man in the White House stems from three related sources: first are the bargaining advantages inherent in his job with which to persuade other men that what he wants of them is what their own responsibilities require them to do. Second are the expectations of those other men regarding his ability and will to use the various advantages they think he has. Third are those men's estimates of how his public views him and of how their publics may view them if they do what he wants. In short, his power is the product of his vantage points in government, together with his reputation in the Washington community and his prestige outside.

A president, himself, affects the flow of power from these sources, though whether they flow freely or run dry he never will decide alone. He makes his

* Richard E. Neustadt, *Presidential Power* (New York: John Wiley & Sons, Inc., 1960), pp. 179–85.

personal impact by the things he says and does. Accordingly, his choices of what he should say and do, and how and when, are his means to conserve and tap the sources of his power. Alternatively, choices are the means by which he dissipates this power. The outcome, case by case, will often turn on whether he perceives his risk in power terms and takes account of what he sees before he makes his choice. A president is so uniquely situated and his power so bound up with the uniqueness of his place, that he can count on no one else to be perceptive for him. Yet he can scarcely see and weigh his power stakes himself unless he is alerted by significant details and deals with his decisions in good time. Useful information, timely choices may not reach him; he must do the reaching. To do so is to help himself enhance his personal influence. This is the sort of help he needs the most. But he will neither feel that need nor fill it if his image of his office keeps him faced away from power.

It is natural that Franklin Roosevelt, hungry for the Presidency's power as his birthright, should exemplify the man who helps himself. It is ironic that a Truman, who felt no such hunger and laid claim to no such birthright, still created from his background, and his heroes, and his reading, an image of the office that impelled him toward self-help. It is an equal irony that Eisenhower, hailed by commentators and by voters (and by many intellectuals) as quite uniquely qualified for power in the Presidency, was turned away from self-help by his very qualifications. Only an extraordinary politician could have managed to exploit the opportunities for influence created by the presence of a hero in the White House. But had Eisenhower been a man of politics he never would have come there as the hero that he was. And being what he was, he looked upon his presence there through the eyes of an *anti*-politician. There can be little doubt that he exchanged his hero's welcome for much less than its full value in the currency of power. But how could Eisenhower have done otherwise? His image of himself in office dictated the terms of that exchange.

One never can be sure that when a man becomes the President of the United States his sense of power and of purpose and his own source of self-confidence will show him how to help himself enhance his personal influence. But there is every reason to believe that he will be shown nothing of the sort if he has made the White House his first venture into politics. The Presidency is no place for amateurs.

* * *

To make the most of power for himself a president must know what it is made of. This book has treated power in the sense of personal influence and influence in the sense of effectiveness *prospectively*, looking toward tomorrow from today. That look conveys the essence of the task before a man who seeks to maximize his power. If he wants it for the future, he must guard it in the present. He mounts guard, as best *he* can, when he appraises the effects of present action on the sources of his influence. In making that appraisal he has no one to depend on but himself; his power and its sources are a sphere of expertise reserved to him. But the issues that present themselves for action day by day rarely show his personal risks upon their surface. His expertise must first help him to see beneath the surface if it is to help him weigh what may be there. The president as expert does himself a double service. Without the expertise he cannot do it.

The Presidency, to repeat, is not a place for amateurs. That sort of expertise can hardly be acquired without deep experience in political office. The Presidency is a place for men of politics. But by no means is it a place for every politician.

There is no reason to suppose that politicians, on the average, have the wherewithal to help themselves build *presidential* power. The men of politics who specialize in organization work and party office scarcely qualify at all; governmental office is the relevant experience. For present purposes we can regard as politicians only those who build careers in public office. Yet expertise in presidential power does not follow automatically from such experience. No post in government at any level necessarily equips a man to recognize the Presidency's peculiar sources of influence. Those sources have as many parts as a president has constituencies, foreign and domestic; the posts that furnish insights into one part often obscure others. Besides, past officeholding is no guarantee that any man brings with him to the White House the degree and kind of feeling for direction that can help him once he gets there. Former Commerce Secretary Hoover had a sense of purpose so precise as to be stultifying. Former Senator Harding seems to have had none at all. And mere experience, however relevant, is no assurance that a president will find the confidence he needs just when he needs it most. Such confidence requires that his image of himself in office justify an unremitting search for personal power. But it requires, also, that his image of himself allow for failures and frustration in the search. F.D.R. is said to have remarked that Lincoln "was a sad man because he couldn't get it all at once. And nobody can."[1] If a president is to assist himself through the vicissitudes of four long years or eight, his source of confidence must make him capable of bearing Lincoln's sadness with good grace. The power-seeker whose self-confidence requires quick returns and sure success might make a mess of everything including his own power. Grace calls for humor and perspective. Political experience does not assure those qualities. Indeed, it may diminish them in the degree it brings a taste for power. The officeholder who combines them with an insight into presidential influence and hunger for it is no average politician.

Expertise in presidential power seems to be the province not of politicians as a class but of extraordinary politicians. What sets such men apart? Mr. Justice Holmes once characterized Franklin Roosevelt as a "second-rate intellect but a first-rate temperament." Perhaps this is a necessary combination. The politics of well-established government has rarely been attractive to and rarely has dealt kindly with the men whom intellectuals regard as first-rate intellects. Temperament, at any rate, is the great separator. Experience will leave its mark on expertise; so will a man's ambitions for himself and his constituents. But something like that "first-rate" temperament is what turns know-how and desire to his personal account. The necessary confidence is nourished by that temperament. It is a human resource not discovered every day among American politicians.

If expertness in maximizing power for himself served purposes no larger than the man's own pride or pleasure, there would be no reason for the rest of us to care whether he were powerful or not. More precisely, there would be no reason except sentiment and partisanship. But a president's success in that endeavor serves objectives far beyond

[1] Arthur M. Schlesinger, Jr., *The Age of Roosevelt*, Vol. 2: *The Coming of The New Deal* (Boston, Mass.: Houghton Mifflin Company, 1959), p. 529.

his own and far beyond his party's. For reasons I will come to in a moment, an expert search for presidential influence contributes to the energy of government and to the viability of public policy. Government is energized by a productive tension among its working parts. Policy is kept alive by a sustained transformation of intent into result. Energetic government and viable public policy are at a premium as we begin the seventh decade of the twentieth century. Expertise in presidential power adds to both. A President's constituents, regardless of their party (or their country for that matter), have a great stake in his search for personal influence.

In the American political system, the president sits in a unique seat and works within a unique frame of reference. The things he personally has to do are no respecters of the lines between "civil" and "military," or "foreign" and "domestic," or "legislative" and "executive," or "administrative" and "political." At his desk—and there alone—distinctions of these sorts lose their last shred of meaning. The expectations centered in his person converge upon no other individual; nobody else feels pressure from all five of *his* constituencies; no one else takes pressure in the consciousness that *he* has been elected "by the Nation." Besides, nobody but the president lives day by day with *his* responsibility in an atomic age amidst cold war. And he alone can claim unquestionable right to everybody's information on the mysteries of that age and that war. His place and frame of reference are unique. By the same token, though, his power is mercurial. Since no one shares his place, nobody is committed to uphold what he may do there. The consequences are described by every illustration in this book.

The things a president must think about if he would build his influence are not unlike those bearing on the viability of public policy. The correspondence may be inexact, but it is close. The man who thinks about the one can hardly help contributing to the other. A president who senses what his influence is made of and who means to guard his future will approach his present actions with an eye to the reactions of constituents in Washington and out. The very breadth and sweep of his constituencies and of their calls upon him, along with the uncertainty of their response, will make him keen to see and weigh what Arthur Schlesinger has called "the balance of administrative power."[2] This is a balance of political, managerial, psychological, and personal feasibilities. And because the president's own frame of reference is at once so all-encompassing and so political, what he sees as a balance for himself is likely to be close to what is viable in terms of public policy. Viability requires three ingredients. First is a purpose that moves with the grain of history, a direction consonant with coming needs. Second is an operation that proves manageable to the men who must administer it, acceptable to those who must support it, tolerable to those who must put up with it, in Washington and out. Timing can be crucial for support and acquiescence; proper timing is the third ingredient. The president who sees his power stakes sees something very much like the ingredients that make for viability in policy.

Presidential expertise thus serves effective policy. Deciding what is viable has grown more critical and more complex with almost every turn of world events (and of home politics) since

---

[2] Richard E. Neustadt, *Presidential Power: The Politics of Leadership* (New York: John Wiley & Sons, Inc., 1960), p. 158.

World War II. Substantive considerations have become so specialized that experts in one sphere lose touch with expertise in any other. Substantive appraisals have become so tricky that the specialists in every sphere dispute among themselves. In consequence the viability of policy may be the only ground on which a substantive decision can be reached. When that ground is itself inordinately complicated by the tendency of policies to interlock, and overlap, and to leap national boundaries, it becomes a sphere of expertise as specialized as others. In the sphere of viability our system can supply no better expert than a president intent on husbanding his influence—provided that he understands what influence is made of.

The more determinedly a president seeks power, the more he will be likely to bring vigor to his clerkship. As he does so he contributes to the energy of government. In Congress and the agencies and in the national parties, energy is generated by support or opposition. But first there must be something to support or to oppose. Most Washingtonians look to the White House for it. There often is no other place to look. The need of others for a president's initiatives creates dependence on him. Their dependence becomes his advantage. Yet he can only capture the advantage as he meets the need. An energetic clerk will energize all government; the man intent on influence will be that sort of clerk. (So may a man intent on history, provided that he has the heroes of a Harry Truman. But one cannot expect that many men will know their history as well as he, and those who know it may choose other heroes.)

The contributions that a president can make to government are indispensable. Assuming that he knows what power is and wants it, those contributions cannot help but be forthcoming in some measure as by-products of his search for personal influence. In a relative but real sense one can say of a president what Eisenhower's first Secretary of Defense once said of General Motors: what is good for the country is good for the president, and vice versa. There is no guarantee, of course, that every president will keep an eye on what is "good" for him; his sense of power and of purpose and the source of his self-confidence may turn his head away. If so, his "contributions" could be lethargy not energy, or policy that moves against, not with, the grain of history. The way he sees his influence and seeks it will affect the rest of us, no matter what becomes of him.

4

LEAVE YOUR PRESIDENCY ALONE*

Clinton Rossiter

As a governmental institution, Clinton Rossiter finds the American Presidency to be not without fault. In fact, he urges several reforms and corrections. In the main, however, he concludes that the office may be tinkered with for minor adjustments but that it should not be radically changed. As it now stands, the Presidency is "one of our chief bulwarks against decline and chaos."

. . . I detect a deep note of satisfaction, although hardly of complacency, with the American Presidency as it stands today. A steady theme seems to have run all through this final review of its weaknesses and problems, a theme entitled (with apologies to the genius of Thurber) "Leave Your Presidency Alone!" This feeling of satisfaction springs, I am frank to admit, from a political outlook more concerned with the world as it is than as it is said to have been by reactionaries and is promised to be by radicals. Since this outlook is now shared by a staggering majority of Americans, I feel that I am expressing something more than a personal opinion. If we accept the facts of life in the 1960's, as we must, and if we shun the false counsels of perfection, as we do, then we are bound to conclude that we are richly blessed with a choice instrument of constitutional democracy. Judged in the light of memory and desire, the Presidency is in a state of sturdy health, and that is why we should not give way easily to despair over the defects men of too much zeal or too litle courage claim to discover in it. Some of these are not defects at all; some are chronic in our system of government; some could be cured only by opening the way to others far more malign.

This does not mean that we should stand pat with the Presidency. Rather, we should confine ourselves to small readjustments—I have noted a dozen or more that might be worth a try—and leave the usual avenues open to prescriptive change. We should abolish the electoral college but leave the electoral system to pursue its illogical but hitherto effective way. We should plan carefully for mobilization in the event of war but take care that the inherent emergency power of the president—the power used by Lincoln to blockade the South, by Wilson to arm the merchantmen, and by Roosevelt to bring off the Destroyer Deal—be left intact and untrammeled. We should experiment with a joint executive-legislative council and the item veto but be on our guard against the urge to alter radically the pattern of competitive coexistence between Congress and President. We should give the president all the aides he can use but beware the deceptively simple solution of a second and even

* Clinton Rossiter, *The American Presidency*, rev. ed. (New York: Harcourt, Brace & World, Inc., 1960), pp. 258–61.

third vice-president for executive purposes. And we should tinker modestly with the president's machinery but wake from the false dream of perfect harmony in high places, especially in the highest place of all. For if the Presidency could speak, it would say with Whitman:

> Do I contradict myself?
> Very well then I contradict myself.
> (I am large, I contain multitudes.)

"Leave Your Presidency Alone": that is the message of this chapter, and I trust I have made clear . . . why I transmit it so confidently. To put the final case for the American Presidency as forcefully as possible, let me point once again to its essential qualities:

It strikes a felicitous balance between power and limitations. In a world in which power is the price of freedom, the Presidency, as Professor Merriam and his colleagues wrote in 1937, "stands across the path of those who mistakenly assert that democracy must fail because it can neither decide promptly nor act vigorously." In a world in which power has been abused on a tragic scale, it presents a heartening lesson in the uses of constitutionalism. To repeat the moral of an earlier chapter, the power of the Presidency moves as a mighty host only with the grain of liberty and morality. The quest of constitutional government is for the right balance of authority and restraint, and Americans may take some pride in the balance they have built into the Presidency.

It provides a steady focus of leadership: of administration, Congress, and people. In a constitutional system compounded of diversity and antagonism, the Presidency looms up as the countervailing force of unity and harmony. In a society ridden by centrifugal forces, it is, as Sidney Hyman has written, the "common reference point for social effort." The relentless progress of this continental republic has made the Presidency our one truly national political institution. There are those who would reserve this role to Congress, but as the least aggressive of our presidents, Calvin Coolidge, once testified, "It is because in their hours of timidity the Congress becomes subservient to the importunities of organized minorities that the president comes more and more to stand as the champion of the rights of the whole country." The more Congress becomes, in Burke's phrase, "a confused and scuffling bustle of local agency," the more the Presidency must become a clear beacon of national purpose.

It is a priceless symbol of our continuity and destiny as a people. Few nations have solved so simply and yet grandly the problem of finding and maintaining an office of state that embodies their majesty and reflects their character. Only the Constitution overshadows the Presidency as an object of popular reverence, and the Constitution does not walk about smiling and shaking hands. "The simple fact is," a distinguished, disgruntled Briton wrote at the end of the "Royal Soap Opera" of 1955, "that the United States Presidency today is a far more dignified institution than the British monarchy." In all honesty and tact we must quickly demur, but we can be well satisfied with our "republican king."

5

THE COMING CAESARS*

Amaury de Riencourt

We frequently hear that presidential power is the menacing threat to our free system of government. The threat is accompanied by emotional and sometimes hysterical pronouncements. In the following article, however, the French political writer, Amaury de Riencourt, states the problem lucidly and dispassionately.

New concentrations of power during the past fifty years of world wars, revolutions, and crises, have made this threat of Caesarism increasingly evident. Political power in the Western world has become increasingly concentrated in the United States of America, and in the office of the president within America. The power and prestige of the president have grown with the growth of America and of democracy within America, with the multiplication of economic, political, and military emergencies, with the necessity of ruling what is virtually becoming an American empire—the universal state of a Western civilization at bay.

Caesarism is therefore the logical outcome of a double current very much in evidence today: the growth of a world empire that cannot be ruled by republican institutions, and the gradual extension of mass democracy, which ends in the destruction of freedom and in the concentration of supreme power in the hands of one man. This is the ominous prospect facing the Western world in the second half of the twentieth century. But just as Caesarism could arise only in Classical Rome and not in Greece, it will, if left free to develop unchecked, arise in modern America and not in Europe. It is in Washington and not in London, Paris, or Berlin that the Caesars of the future will arise. It will not be the result of conspiracy, revolution, or personal ambition. It will be the end result of an instinctive evolution in which we are all taking part like somnambulists.

The evidence is all around us today, but to see it in its full magnitude we must step back into history and look at the present from a distance. We shall then have a clear perspective of the road on which we have been traveling for centuries—and a glimpse of the road that lies ahead. We shall then notice that, instead of forever inclining toward the republican left, we are in fact swinging toward the autocratic right and that it is our leftist leaders who, whenever they are in power, are unwittingly taking us in this direction. In fact, they have quite unconsciously been driving us around in a century-wide circle, back to the point from which our ancestors started when they revolted in the name of liberty against the tyranny of absolute monarchs.

Familiarity breeds contempt, dulls

---

* Amaury de Riencourt, *The Coming Caesars* (New York: Coward-McCann, Inc., 1957), pp. 5–8, 328–31.

perception and understanding. What is familiar has to become unfamiliar and strange before we can truly grasp its full meaning. We must see in the President of the United States not merely the Chief Executive of one of the Western democracies, but one always endowed with power of truly Caesarian magnitude. Today, one man is directly in command, either as peacetime President or wartime Commander-in-Chief, of more than half the globe's economic and technical power. Along the militarized borders of the Western world he is in full control, as Augustus and the Roman emperors after him were in full control of the *limes*. As an autonomous executive who is constitutionally free from parliamentary interference, he is all at once Chief of State and head of government in control of all cabinet appointments as well as Commander in Chief of the most powerful armed forces in the world. He is the only statesman in the Western world who can make major decisions alone in an emergency. He is in control of a *de facto* empire into which the scattered fragments of the dissolving British Commonwealth are gradually being merged. Everywhere, on the European continent, in the Western Hemisphere, and in the Far East, he can make the weight of his incalculable power felt with immediate and crushing speed.

Yet, all this is nothing but the reflection of an underlying reality. The prime element in this situation is neither political nor strategic—it is essentially psychological. It is the growing "father complex" that is increasingly evident in America, the willingness to follow in any emergency, economic or military, the leadership of one man. It is the growing distrust of parliaments, congresses, and all other representative assemblies, the growing impatience of Western public opinion at their irresponsibility, lack of foresight, sluggishness, indecisiveness. This distrust and impatience is evident in America as in Europe. Further, it is the impulsive emotionalism of American public opinion, which swings widely from apathetic isolationism to dynamic internationalism, lacks continuity in its global views, stumbles from one emergency into another, and mistakes temporary lulls for the long-expected millennium. Such was Rome's public opinion in the first century B.C. Each new crisis calls for a strong man and there are always strong men present who are willing to shoulder responsibilities shirked by timid legislatures.

When, at the beginning of 1955, for instance, President Eisenhower went to Congress and requested emergency powers to deal with Formosa's offshore islands, how many congressmen recoiled in fear and pointed out to him that he already had those powers, implying in effect that they wanted no part of this terrifying responsibility? Even with the utmost good will, a president who sincerely attempts to build up the sense of responsibility of the legislature cannot halt a secular trend. And this development suits public opinion perfectly well. The public wants to personalize issues and responsibilities and instinctively looks down upon the collective anonymity of assemblies. Those who doubt that today an American president might be elected for life should remember that no constitutional amendment, such as was voted after World War II, can stand in the way of public opinion if it truly wishes to elect a Caesar for life. In fact, the amendment limiting presidential terms of office is itself proof that many in America saw in Franklin Roosevelt the first pre-Caesarian who was, as it turned out, virtually elected for life. . . .

The United States Congress has repeatedly expressed its fear, especially since the New Deal and World War II, that the Constitution and the separation of powers is being steadily undermined—and so it is. Under present conditions, democratic equality ends inevitably in Caesarism. No system of checks and balances can hold out against this profound evolution, a psychological alteration that by-passes specific institutions. The thirst for equality and distrust of any form of hierarchy have even weakened Congress itself through its seniority rule. Dislike for aristocratic distinctions eventually ends by eliminating that most indispensable of all elites—the aristocracy of talent. This is the elite that in Britain, substituting for the former aristocracy of birth and wealth, makes the parliamentary system workable. Since most of the work of the United States Congress is done in committees, there is little occasion for great debates on the floor of either House or Senate comparable with the dramatic debates of European parliaments. The need of Americans to personalize and dramatize all issues can be satisfied only by concentrating attention on the president—thereby giving him increasing power. Because he can now communicate over the head of Congress with the nation, he can always dominate legislative proceedings. He can dramatize, Congress cannot—or if it does, as in the case of Senator Joseph McCarthy, it is largely because of presidential failure or unwillingness to use the immense potentialities vested in the White House.

Long ago, James Bryce discounted the usual fears of Americans and Europeans who thought that some ambitious president might attempt to seize absolute power through a brutal *coup d'etat*. But he added this warning: "If there be any danger, it would seem to lie in another direction. The larger a community becomes, the less does it seem to respect an assembly, the more it is attracted by an individual man."[1] The reason for this is plain: the larger the masses, the more they display *feminine* traits by emphasizing emotional reactions rather than rational judgment. They instinctively tend to look for masculine leadership as a compensation—the leadership they can find in a strong man but never in an assembly, which is after all only a reproduction in miniature of their own faults and weaknesses. Instinct always prevails in the end. The great predominance of women in contemporary America can only bolster this trend.

Alongside this internal evolution, another trend asserts itself unmistakably: the development of imperial expansion, military might, and foreign commitments continues to increase the power of the American Executive. This trend was still concealed a century ago when Alexis de Tocqueville wrote:

> "The President of the United States, it is true, is the Commander-in-Chief of the army, but the army is composed of only six thousand men; he commands the fleet, but the fleet reckons but few sail; he conducts the foreign relations of the Union, but the United States is a nation without neighbors. Separated from the rest of the world by the ocean, and too weak as yet to aim at the domination of the seas, it has no enemies and its interests rarely come into contact with those of any other nations on the globe."[2]

Now, compare this picture with the present: armies of millions of men, the most powerful fleets in the world, commitments all over the globe, and vast nuclear power.

The president's role as Commander-in-Chief has now become preponderant in an age of world-wide wars and tensions. His role as director of American

[1] James Bryce, *The American Commonwealth,* i, p. 68.

[2] A. de Tocqueville, *Democracy in America,* i, p. 126.

foreign policy has grown correspondingly. He can take many steps that are beyond recall or repair. He can start a war according to his own judgment. Single-handed, he can influence decisively the political situation in scores of foreign nations. President Truman sent American troops into the Korean fray without waiting for congressional approval, in spite of Senator Taft's vehement protests. But there can be no collective initiative, no collective action, and no collective responsibility.

President Truman's formula "the buck stops here" sums up the immense responsibility of the one man who heads the American government. His cabinet is entirely his own tool because he alone decides on policy and is not bound to consult its members as a prime minister in a parliamentary regime. New emergencies after World War II led to the creation of the National Security Council in 1947, a body independent of both the cabinet and Congress. And to what extent can Congress control the actual working of the Atomic Energy Commission? The president's already considerable veto power has been reinforced by the new possibility of applying it to single items of the appropriation bills. The veto becomes more sensitive and discriminating. From being largely negative, the president's legislative power becomes increasingly positive, fulfilling Henry Clay's dire prophecy:

"Really and in practice, the veto power drew after it the power of initiating laws, and in its effects must ultimately amount to conferring on the executive the entire legislative power of the government. With the power to initiate and the power to consummate legislation, to give vitality and vigor to every law, or to strike it dead at his pleasure, the President must ultimately become the ruler of the nation."

His power has been increasingly emphasized in the annual legislative program submitted in the "State of the Union" message, and, if he controls his party, through his overriding influence in pushing it through.

In truth, no mental effort is required to understand that the President of the United States is the most powerful single human being in the world today. Future crises will inevitably transform him into a full-fledged Caesar, if we do not beware. Today he wears ten hats —as Head of State, Chief Executive, Minister of Foreign Affair, Chief Legislator, Head of Party, Tribune of the People, Ultimate Arbitrator of Social Justice, Guardian of Economic Prosperity, and World Leader of Western Civilization. Slowly and unobtrusively, these hats are becoming crowns and this pyramid of hats is slowly metamorphosing itself into a tiara, the tiara of one man's world imperium.

Wars are the main harbingers of Caesarism. The Punic and Macedonian wars proved to Rome that great undertakings in an increasingly equalitarian society can be the responsibility of one man only, never of a democratic assembly. In grave emergencies, leadership can never be collective, and we are now living in an age of permanent emergency. Presidential power in America has grown as American power and expansion have grown, one developing within the other. This fact has not remained unnoticed in America since the passing of Franklin Roosevelt and a great deal of the postwar developments in American politics can be written down as congressional reaction against the power of the White House.

Although by no means a weak President, Harry Truman did not have the authority of his predecessor and Congress raised its head once more. And when the Republicans came back to power in 1952, a deliberate effort was made by President Eisenhower to restore to Congress that dignity and prestige which had been so damaged during the New Deal and World War II. A similar reaction took place in Rome when Sulla attempted to undo some of the worst features of Marius' New Deal and eliminate all possibility of another such concentration of supreme power in the hands of one man.

After World War II, the American Congress voted a constitutional amendment forbidding future presidents more than two terms of office. But the precedent has been set and in America historical precedents have an overwhelming influence. Such belated moves can no more halt the trend toward Caesarism than those of Sulla limiting all offices to a one-year tenure, specifying that no one can ever be, as Marius had been, both Commander-in-Chief and supreme magistrate, and handing back military authority to the Roman Senate.

6

THE NEED FOR LEADERSHIP*

James MacGregor Burns

Rather than viewing strong presidential leadership as a threat to democratic institutions, Professor Burns sees such leadership as the salvation of our free society. Responsible, effective leadership would reorganize the party system and substitute a resolute national purpose in the place of drift and deadlock.

The presidential leader must, in short, be more than a skillful manipulator or brilliant interpreter. He must be a constructive innovator, who can reshape to some degree the constellation of political forces in which he operates. To reach the acme of leadership he must achieve a creative union of intellectual comprehension, strategic planning, and tactical skill, to a degree perhaps not paralleled since Jefferson.

Is such leadership possible in America? What would it require for a President of the United States?

Such leadership would require so strong a commitment to his program that the president would be willing to break with old traditions and take political risks, if these were necessary to realize the goals of his administration. This would mean for a Republican president that he be willing, at least for the short run, to jeopardize support among highly conservative Republicans and in the more rural areas of the North; it would mean, for a Democratic president, that he risk losing the electoral backing of conservative Southerners—to such an extent that he might have to write them off and undertake the herculean task of building a new basis of Democratic support in the South, and one that would pay off politically only in the long run. Such presidential leadership would also mean extensive intervention in Congress. Not

* James MacGregor Burns, *The Deadlock of Democracy* (Englewood Cliffs, N.J.: Prentice-Hall, Inc., 1963), pp. 338–40.

only would the minority devices of the congressional parties be swept away, but the president would have to throw himself into the legislative battle to fashion party machinery for the more effective debating and handling of legislation. Hence he would have to ignore the absurd "rule" (usually ignored in practice) that the president does not interfere in the legislative department. He must interfere, and openly so.

This intervention need not be the negative, abortive, and even vengeful action that it so often has been in the past. The president's job is to strengthen the presidential party machinery in Congress, not simply to circumvent or undermine the present machinery. Similarly, in the House and Senate elections he should intervene to help presidential party candidates for Congress, not simply to oppose the men who disagree with him. The trouble with Roosevelt's purge was not the objective, but the hasty, improvised, and negative way in which it was carried out. If he had strengthened the presidential party in selected states and districts, had recruited the ablest candidates, had seen that they had ample help on finance, registration, publicity, and other campaign needs—if, in short, he had worked through a local, indigenous unit of the presidential party instead of coming in from the outside, he might have come nearer to his goal of a more unified and liberal party. What congressmen in competitive districts need from the president is less to be coaxed, bribed, or threatened—they need *help*.

Nothing fails like failure, or is so educational. The purge was a failure; what is needed is a purge in reverse. The great task of the presidential party is to forge a new majority, just as the Jeffersonians and Jacksonians did, organized down to the wards and precincts, towns and villages, and effective in Congress as well as in the executive branch. Whether this task will be accomplished by the presidential Democrats under John F. Kennedy, or by the presidential Republicans under someone like Rockefeller, is one of the tantalizing questions of the future. Tantalizing—and epochal, for the presidential party that first gains control of its congressional party will dominate the politics of the center left or center right for decades to come.

It may be that Kennedy will be the first president to grasp the great possibilities open to a creative party leader. "Legislative leadership is not possible without party leadership," he said early in the year that he was elected to the Presidency. "No president, it seems to me, can escape politics. He has not only been chosen by the nation—he has been chosen by his party. And if he insists that he is 'president of all the people' and should therefore offend none of them—if he blurs the issues and differences between the two parties—if he neglects the party machinery and avoids his party's leadership—then he has not only weakened the political party as an instrument of the democratic process—he has dealt a death blow to the democratic process itself."

The cure for democracy, people used to say, is more democracy. A half century of hard experience has shown this cliché to be a dangerous half-truth. The cure for democracy is leadership—responsible, committed, effective, and exuberant leadership. The man and the party who take the lead in modernizing our political system, in establishing a majority party able to govern and a minority party able to oppose, will have helped put an end to the dangerous cycle of drift and deadlock in our national affairs. They will have enabled Americans to regain control of their national politics and to define and assert their national purpose.

7

KENNEDY MOVES ON STEEL: A CASE STUDY*

Wallace Carroll

To catch a glimpse of big government in action there is no substitute for on-the-spot personal experience. The closest thing to this personal experience is the detailed reporting of an actual case.

The following account centers around the dramatic events of four days—April 10, 11, 12, 13, 1962. The dramatis personae *includes a United States President, outstanding Senators and Representatives, members of the Cabinet, leaders of administrative agencies, some of the nation's highest paid corporation executives, newspapermen, and the average citizen. It involves such far-reaching questions as the relationship between government and the economy, national economic growth, the establishment of prices in a concentrated industry, and the role of public opinion in national policy.*

It was peaceful at the White House on the afternoon of Tuesday, April 10—so peaceful that the President of the United States thought he might have time for a nap or a little relaxed reading.

Just to be sure, he called his personal secretary, Mrs. Evelyn Lincoln, and asked what the rest of the day would bring.

"You have Mr. Blough at a quarter to six," said Mrs. Lincoln.

"Mr. Blough?" exclaimed the President.

"Yes," said Mrs. Lincoln.

There must be a mistake, thought the President. The steel negotiations had been wound up the previous week.

"Get me Kenny O'Donnell," he said.

There had been no mistake—at least not on the part of Kenneth P. O'Donnell, the President's appointment secretary.

Whether Mr. Blough—Roger M. Blough, chairman of the board of United States Steel Corporation—had made a mistake was a different question.

For when Mr. Blough walked into the President's office two hours later with the news that his company had raised the price of steel, he set off 72 hours of activity such as he and his colleagues could not have expected.

During those 72 hours, four antitrust investigations of the steel industry were conceived, a bill to roll back the price increases was seriously considered, legislation to impose price and wage controls on the steel industry was discussed, agents of the Federal Bureau of Investigation questioned newspaper men by the dawn's early light, and the Defense Department—biggest buyer in the nation—began to divert purchases away from U.S. Steel.

Also in those 72 hours—and this was

* *The New York Times,* April 23, 1962, pp. 1, 25.

far more significant—the administration maintained its right to look over the shoulders of capital and labor when they came to the bargaining table and its insistence that any agreement they reached would have to respect the national interest.

And in those 72 hours, new content and meaning were poured into that magnificent abstraction, "the Presidency," for the historically minded to argue about as long as men remained interested in the affairs of this republic.

A full and entirely accurate account of those 72 hours may never be written. The characters were many. They moved so fast that no one will be able to retrace all of what they did.

Understandably, industry participants —facing official investigation now— would not talk much. Nor were government participants willing to tell all.

Nevertheless, a team of *New York Times* reporters undertook to piece the tale together while memories were fresh. Here is what they learned:

Early on that afternoon of April 10, Roger Blough had met with his colleagues of U.S. Steel's executive committee in the board room on the twentieth floor at 71 Broadway, New York. Three of the 12 members were absent, but Leslie B. Worthington, president of the company, and Robert C. Tyson, chairman of the finance committee, were there.

For several months these men had been giving out hints, largely overlooked in Washington, that the company would have to raise prices to meet increasing costs.

The Kennedy administration had striven last fall to prevent a steel price increase, and there had been no increase. It had pressed again for a modest wage contract this year, and a modest contract had been signed a few days earlier. The administration expected no price increase now.

The company's executive committee reviewed the situation. The sales department had concurred in a recommendation to increase prices by 3½ per cent—about $6 on top of the going average of $170 a ton.

Mr. Blough had taken soundings within the company on the public relations aspects. Everyone realized that the move would not win any popularity prize, but the committee voted unanimously to go ahead.

With the decision made, Mr. Blough took a plane to Washington. Word was telephoned to the White House that he wanted to see the President and had something "important" to say about steel.

A few minutes after 5:45 the President received him in his oval office, motioned him to a seat on a sofa to his right and made himself comfortable in his rocking chair.

With little preliminary, Mr. Blough handed the President a four-page mimeographed press release that was about to be sent to newspaper offices in Pittsburgh and New York.

The President read:

"Pittsburgh, Pa., April 10—For the first time in nearly four years, United States Steel today announced an increase in the general level of its steel prices."

Mr. Kennedy raced through the announcement. Then he summoned Arthur J. Goldberg, the Secretary of Labor. Minutes later Mr. Goldberg reached the President's office from the Labor Department four blocks away.

Grimly, the President gave the paper to Mr. Goldberg and said it had been distributed to the press. Mr. Goldberg skimmed over it and asked Mr. Blough what was the point of the meeting, since the price decision had been made.

Mr. Blough replied that he thought he should personally inform the President as a matter of courtesy. Mr. Goldberg retorted it was hardly a courtesy to announce a decision and confront the President with an accomplished fact.

In the half-hour discussion that followed, President Kennedy seems to have kept his temper. But Mr. Goldberg lectured Mr. Blough with some heat. The price increase, the Secretary said, would jeopardize the government's entire economic policy. It would damage the interests of U.S. Steel itself. It would undercut responsible collective bargaining. Finally, he said, the decision could be viewed only as a double-cross of the President because the company had given no hint of its intentions while the administration was urging the United Steelworkers of America to moderate its wage demands.

Mr. Blough, a high school teacher turned lawyer and company executive, defended himself and the company in a quiet voice.

When he had gone, Mr. Kennedy called for the three members of his Council of Economic Advisers. Dr. Walter W. Heller, the chairman, a lean and scholarly looking man, came running from his office across the street. Dr. Kermit Gordon followed in three minutes. James Tobin, the third member, hurried back to his office later in the evening.

Into the President's office came Theodore C. Sorensen, the White House special counsel, Mr. O'Donnell and Andrew T. Hatcher, acting press secretary in the absence of Pierre Salinger, who was on vacation.

Now the President, who usually keeps his temper under rein, let go. He felt he had been double-crossed—deliberately. The office of the President had been affronted. The national interest had been flouted.

Bitterly, he recalled that:

"My father always told me that all businessmen were sons-of-bitches but I never believed it till now!"

It was clear that the administration would fight. No one knew exactly what could be done, but from that moment the awesome power of the federal government began to move.

To understand the massive reaction of the Kennedy administration, a word of background is necessary.

Nothing in the range of domestic economic policy had brought forth a greater effort by the administration than the restraint it sought to impose on steel prices and wages.

Starting last May the administration worked on the industry, publicly and privately, not to raise its prices when wages went up in the fall. And when the price line held, the administration turned its efforts to getting an early and "noninflationary" wage contract this year.

Above all, the administration constantly tried to impress on both sides that the national interest was riding on their decisions. A price increase or an inflationary wage settlement, it argued, would set off a new wage-price spiral that would stunt economic growth, keep unemployment high, cut into export sales, weaken the dollar and further aggravate the outflow of gold.

On Friday and Saturday, April 6 and 7, the major steel companies had signed the new contract. President Kennedy had hailed it as "noninflationary." Privately, some steel leaders agreed with him.

Thus the President confidently expected that the companies would not increase prices. And the standard had been set, he hoped, for other industries and unions.

This was the background against which the group in the President's office went to work.

By about 8 P.M. some decisions had been reached.

President Kennedy would deliver the first counterattack at his news conference scheduled for 3:30 the following afternoon.

Messrs. Goldberg, Heller and Sorensen would gather material for the President's statement. Other material of a statistical nature would be prepared in a longer-range effort to prove the price increase was unjustified. While the discussion was going on, the President called his brother, Robert F. Kennedy, the Attorney General; Secretary of Defense Robert S. McNamara, and Secretary of the Treasury Douglas Dillon, who had just arrived in Hobe Sound, Fla., for a short vacation.

At his home on Hillbrook Lane, Senator Estes Kefauver of Tennessee, chairman of the Senate antitrust subcommittee, was getting ready to go out for the evening. The phone rang. It was the President. Would Senator Kefauver publicly register "dismay" at the price increase and consider an investigation?

The Senator certainly would. He promised an investigation. So did the Justice Department.

In the President's office, meanwhile, there had been some talk of what could be done to keep other steel companies from raising prices. Most of the discussion centered on the economic rebuttal of the case made by U.S. Steel.

Mr. Goldberg and Dr. Heller decided to pool resources. Mr. Goldberg called Hymen L. Lewis, chief of the Office of Labor Economics of the Bureau of Labor Statistics and asked him to assemble a crew.

Mr. Lewis reached three members of the bureau—Peter Henle, special assistant to the Commissioner of Labor Statistics; Arnold E. Chase, chief of the Division of Prices and Cost of Living, and Leon Greenberg, chief of the Productivity Division.

He told them what was wanted and asked them to go to Dr. Heller's office in the old State Department Building.

Dr. Heller who had been working on the problem in his office, hurried off after a few minutes to the German Ambassador's residence on Foxhall Road.

The Ambassador was giving a dinner, a black tie affair, in honor of Professor Walter Hallstein, president of the European Common Market. The guests were well into the meal when Dr. Heller arrived, looking, as one of the guests remarked, like Banquo's ghost in a tuxedo.

Back at the White House the President had also changed to black tie. The members of Congress and their wives were coming to his annual reception at 9:45. Ruefully, the President recalled that the news of the Cuban disaster had arrived during his reception in 1961.

"I'll never hold another congressional reception," he remarked. But as he and Mrs. Kennedy received the leaders of Congress and their wives, he easily relaxed into small talk.

What did the men think, he asked, of the break with tradition by making this a black tie, instead of a white tie, affair? Republicans and Democrats unanimously favored the change. Many of the younger members of Congress, they pointed out, did not have a white tie and all that went with it.

With the party spread through three rooms, no one could tell how many times Mr. Kennedy slipped out to talk about steel. He stayed until 12:08 A.M. Then he retired.

By that time, the White House staff, the Council of Economic Advisers and the Departments of Labor, Justice, Defense, Commerce and the Treasury were all at work on the counterattack.

WEDNESDAY

Midnight had struck when Walter Heller, still in black tie, returned to his office from the German Embassy. With him, also in black tie, came another dinner guest, George W. Ball, Under Secretary of State.

At about 2:45 A.M. the four men from the Bureau of Labor Statistics left the session. Their assignment from then on was to bring up to date a fact book on steel put out by the Eisenhower administration two years ago.

The idea was to turn it into a kind of "white paper" that would show that the price increase was unjustified.

Toward 4 o'clock Dr. Heller and Dr. Tobin went home for two or three hours' sleep. Dr. Gordon lay down on the couch in his office for a couple of hours.

As the normal working day began, President Kennedy held a breakfast meeting at the White House with Vice President Johnson; Secretary of State Dean Rusk (who played no part in the steel crisis); Secretary Goldberg; Mr. Sorensen; Myer Feldman, Mr. Sorensen's deputy, Dr. Heller and Andrew Hatcher. The meeting lasted an hour and forty-five minutes.

Mr. Goldberg and Mr. Heller reported on the night's work. Mr. Sorensen was assigned to draft the President's statement on steel for the news conference. Goldberg gave him a two-page report from the Bureau of Labor Statistics headed:

"Change in Unit Employment Costs in the Steel Industry 1958 to 1961."

It said in part:

"While employment costs per hour of all wage and salaried employes in the basic iron and steel industry rose from 1958 to 1961, there was an equivalent increase in output per man-hour.

"As a result, employment costs per unit of steel output in 1961 was essentially the same as in 1958."

The latter sentence was quoted that afternoon in the President's statement.

During the morning the President had called Secretary Dillon in Florida and discussed with him the Treasury's work on tax write-offs that would encourage investment in more modern plant and machinery. The two decided that the course would not be altered.

The President also telephoned Secretary of Commerce Luther H. Hodges, who was about to testify before a House maritime subcommittee. After giving his testimony Secretary Hodges spent most of the day on the phone to businessmen around the country.

In Wall Street that morning U.S. Steel shares opened at 70¾, up 2¾ from the day before. But on Capitol Hill the company's stock was down.

Senator Mike Mansfield, the Democratic majority leader, called the price increase "unjustified." Speaker John W. McCormack said the company's action was "shocking," "arrogant," "irresponsible." Senator Hubert H. Humphrey, the Democratic whip spoke of "an affront to the President."

Senator Albert Gore of Tennessee suggested a law that would empower the courts to prohibit price increases in basic industries such as steel until there had been a "cooling-off period."

Representative Emanuel Celler of Brooklyn, chairman of the House antitrust subcommittee scheduled a broad investigation of the steel industry. So did Senator Kefauver.

The pressures on U.S. Steel were beginning to mount. But now some of the other titans of the industry began to fall in line behind Big Steel.

As the President came out of the White House shortly before noon to go to the airport where he was to welcome the Shah of Iran, he was shown a news bulletin, Bethlehem Steel, second in size only to U.S. Steel, had just announced a price increase.

Others followed in short order—Republic, Jones and Laughlin, Youngstown and Wheeling, Kaiser and Colorado Fuel and Iron said they were "studying" the situation.

When he faced the newsmen and television cameras at 3:30, President Kennedy spoke with cold fury. The price increase, he said, was a "wholly unjustifiable and irresponsible defiance of the public interest." The steel men had shown "utter contempt" for their fellow citizens.

He spoke approvingly of the proposed investigations. But what did he hope to accomplish that might still save the administration's broad economic program?

In his conference statement the President had seemed to hold out no hope that the price increases could be rolled back. If the increases held what imminent comfort could there be in possible antitrust decrees that would take three years to come from the courts?

Actually the possibility of making U.S. Steel retract the increase had been considered early in the consultation.

Doctors Heller and Gordon, and possibly some of the other economists, had argued that the principal thrust of the administration's efforts should be to convince one or two significant producers to hold out. In a market such as steel, they said, the high-priced sellers would have to come down if the others did not go up.

This suggested a line of strategy that probably proved decisive.

As one member of the Big Twelve after another raised prices, only Armco, Inland, Kaiser, CF&I and McLouth were holding the line. These five holdouts represented 14 per cent of total industry capacity or 17 per cent of the capacity of the Big Twelve.

Everything pointed to Inland as the key to the situation.

Inland Steel Corp., with headquarters in Chicago, is a highly efficient producer. It could make a profit at lower prices than those of some of the bigger companies. And any company that sold in the Midwest, such as United States Steel, would feel Inland's price competition.

Moreover there was a tradition of public service at Inland. Clarence B. Randall, a former chairman of the board, had served both the Eisenhower and Kennedy administrations (but he played no part in this crisis).

Joseph Leopold Block, Inland's present chairman, who was in Japan at the moment, had been a member of President Kennedy's Labor Management advisory committee.

At 7:45 that Wednesday morning, Phillip D. Block Jr., vice chairman of Inland, was called to the telephone in his apartment at 1540 North Lake Shore Drive in Chicago.

"Hello P.D.," said Edward Gudeman, Under Secretary of Commerce, a former schoolmate and friend of Block's, calling from Washington.

"What do you think of this price increase of U.S. Steel's?"

Mr. Block said he had been surprised.

"I didn't ask P.D. what Inland might do," said Mr. Gudeman several days later. "I didn't want them to feel that the administration was putting them on the spot. I just wanted him to know how we felt and to ask his consideration."

"Inland executives said they had not been coaxed or threatened by any of the officials who called them.

The approach, which appears to have developed rather spontaneously in many of the calls that were made to businessmen, was to ask their opinion, state the government's viewpoint, and leave it at that.

But there were also calls with a more pointed aim—to steel users, asking them to call their steel friends and perhaps even issue public statements.

Another call to Inland was made by Henry H. Fowler, Under Secretary of the Treasury and Acting Secretary in Mr. Dillon's absence.

After Mr. Kennedy's afternoon news conference Mr. Fowler called John F. Smith Jr., Inland's president. Like other Treasury officials who telephoned other businessmen, Mr. Fowler talked about the effect of a steel price increase on imports and exports and the further pressure it would place on the balance of payments.

A third call went to Inland that day. It was from Secretary Goldberg to Leigh B. Block, vice president for purchasing.

Both Inland and government officials insist that there was no call from the White House or from any government office to Joseph Block in Japan.

Though no concrete assurance was asked or volunteered, in these conversations, the administration gathered assurance that Inland would hold the line for at least another day or two.

Next came Armco, sixth largest in the nation. Walter Heller had a line into that company. So did others. Calls were made. And through these channels the administration learned that Armco was holding off for the time being, but there would be no public announcement one way or the other.

Meanwhile Mr. Gudeman had called a friend in upper reaches of the Kaiser company. Secretary McNamara had called a number of friends, one of them at Allegheny-Ludlum, a large manufacturer of stainless.

How many calls were made by President Kennedy himself cannot be told. But some time during all the activity he talked to Edgar Kaiser, chairman of Kaiser Steel, in California.

According to one official who was deeply involved in all this effort, the over-all objective was to line up companies representing 18 per cent of the nation's capacity. If this could be done, according to friendly sources in the steel industry, these companies with their lower prices soon would be doing 25 per cent of the business. Then Big Steel would have to yield.

Parallel with this "divide-and conquer" maneuver, the effort moved forward on the antitrust line.

During the morning someone had spotted in the newspapers a statement attributed to Edmund F. Martin, president of Bethlehem Steel. Speaking to reporters on Tuesday after a stockholders' meeting in Wilmington, Del., Mr. Martin was quoted as having said:

"There shouldn't be any price rise. We shouldn't do anything to increase our costs if we are to survive. We have more competition both domestically and from foreign firms."

If Martin had opposed a price rise on Tuesday, before U.S. Steel announced its increase, and if Bethlehem raised its prices on Wednesday after that announcement, his statement might prove useful in antitrust proceedings. It could be used to support a government argument that U.S. Steel, because of its bigness, exercised an undue influence over other steel producers.

About 6 o'clock Wednesday evening, according to officials of the Justice Department, Attorney General Kennedy ordered the FBI to find out exactly what Mr. Martin had said.

At about this same time, Paul Rand Dixon, chairman of the Federal Trade Commission, told reporters that his agency had begun an informal investigation to determine whether the steel companies had violated a consent decree of June 15, 1951.

That decree bound the industry to refrain from collusive price fixing or maintaining identical delivered prices. It provided penalties running up to $5,000 a day.

Meanwhile more calls were going out from Washington.

The Democratic National Committee called many of the Democratic governors and asked them to do two things:

First, to make statements supporting

the President and, second, to ask steel producers in their states to hold the price line.

Among those called were David L. Lawrence of Pennsylvania, Richard J. Hughes of New Jersey and Edmund G. Brown of California. But the National Committee said nothing in its own name. The smell of "politics" was not to be allowed to contaminate the administration's efforts.

Another call was made by Robert V. Roosa, an Under Secretary of the Treasury, to Henry Alexander, chairman of the Morgan Guaranty Trust Company in New York. Morgan is represented on U.S. Steel's board of directors and is widely considered one of the most powerful influences within the company.

Thus by nightfall on Wednesday—24 hours after Blough's call on the President—the administration was pressing forward on four lines of action:

First, the rallying of public opinion behind the President and against the companies.

Second, divide-and-conquer operation within the steel industry.

Third, antitrust pressure from the Justice Department, the Federal Trade Commission, the Senate and the House.

Fourth, the mobilization of friendly forces within the business world to put additional pressure on the companies.

That night at the White House the Kennedys gave a state dinner for the visiting Shah and his Empress.

In a toast to his guests, President Kennedy, a man seemingly without a care in the world, observed that he and the Shah shared a common "burden." Each of them had made a visit to Paris and each of them might as well have stayed at home, for the Parisians had eyes only for their wives.

When the guests had gone, the President put in a call to Tucson, Arizona. It came through at 12:15 A.M.

Archibald Cox, the Solicitor General, had left by plane on Wednesday afternoon for Tucson, where he was to make two speeches to the Arizona Bar.

On arriving at his hotel that night, he received a message to call the President. When he called he was asked what suggestions did he have for rolling back steel prices?

Mr. Cox had been chairman of the Wage Stabilization Board during the Korean War and had worked with young Senator Kennedy on statements about steel prices and strikes of the past.

After the call, Mr. Cox stayed up all night, thinking and making notes, mostly about legislation.

THURSDAY

At 3 A.M. Lee Linder, a reporter in the Philadelphia Bureau of the Associated Press, was awakened by a phone call. It was the FBI. At first Mr. Linder thought he was being fooled. Then he determined that the call was genuine. The agents asked him a question or two and then told him:

"We are coming right out to see you."

Mr. Linder had been at the stockholders' meeting of Bethlehem Steel in Wilmington on Tuesday and had quoted Mr. Martin about the undesirability of a price increase. Bethlehem Steel later called the quotation incorrect.

The agents were checking on that quotation. Mr. Linder said later that he had given them the same report he had written for the Associated Press.

At 6:30 A.M. James L. Parks Jr. of the Wilmington Evening Journal arrived at his office. Two FBI agents were waiting for him. He had talked to Martin after the meeting, together with

Mr. Linder and John Lawrence of the Wall Street Journal. Later in the day the federal agents interviewed Lawrence.

This descent of the FBI on the newsmen was the most criticized incident in the 72 frenzied hours.

Republicans, who had kept an embarrassed silence up to this point, pounced on the FBI episode. Representative William E. Miller of upstate New York, chairman of the Republican National Committee, compared it to the "knock on the door" techniques of Hitler's Gestapo.

In Chicago, as the day progressed, Philip Block and two other high officials of Inland reached a decision: prices would not be raised. They called Joseph Block in Kyoto. He concurred and they agreed to call a directors' meeting to ratify their decision the next morning.

No announcement was to be made until the morning and no one in Washington was told.

Back in Washington, the President was holding an early meeting in the Cabinet room at the White House. Present were: Attorney General Kennedy; Secretaries McNamara, Goldberg, Hodges; Under Secretary of the Treasury Fowler; Mr. Dixon, Chairman of the Federal Trade Commission; Dr. Heller and Mr. Sorensen.

Roger Blough was scheduled to hold a televised news conference in New York at 3:30 that afternoon. The White House meeting decided that the administration should put in a speedy rebuttal to his case for U.S. Steel.

Secretary Hodges had long-scheduled engagements that day in Philadelphia and New York. It was decided that he would hold a news conference in New York at 5 P.M. and try to rebut Mr. Blough point by point.

Meanwhile two of the most secret initiatives of the entire 72 hours had been set in motion.

The first involved a newspaperman —Charles L. Bartlett, the Washington correspondent of the Chattanooga *Times*. All Mr. Bartlett would say later was:

"I helped two friends get in touch with each other again."

One friend was President Kennedy —Mr. Bartlett and his wife are members of the Kennedy social set. The other friend was an officer of U.S. Steel. His identity has not been definitely established, but Mr. Bartlett knows Mr. Blough.

What came of this effort to reopen "diplomatic relations" is not known, although at least one cabinet member thought it was useful. What came of the second secret initiative, however, can be reported.

At noon or earlier on Thursday President Kennedy phoned Clark Clifford, a Washington lawyer who had first come to national prominence as counsel for President Truman.

Secretary Goldberg, said the President, knew the officers of U.S. Steel very well and could, of course, talk to them on behalf of the administration. But Mr. Goldberg, he went on, was known to the steel men mainly as an adversary. Would Mr. Clifford, familiar as he was with the outlook of corporation executives through his law work, join Mr. Goldberg in speaking to United States Steel?

Mr. Clifford agreed, flew to New York and met Mr. Blough.

He presented himself as a friend of the disputants, but he made clear that he was in 100 per cent agreement with the President. His purpose, he said, was to see if a tragic mistake could be rectified. The mistake he left no doubt, was on the company's side—What Mr.

Blough said in reply could not be learned. But he indicated at the end that he would welcome further talks and he hoped Mr. Clifford would participate in them. Mr. Clifford returned to Washington the same day.

Secretary Hodges, meanwhile, arrived at the University Club in New York about 3:40, ten minutes after Mr. Blough had begun his news conference.

The Blough news conference was held in the ground floor auditorium at 71 Broadway.

"Let me say respectfully," Blough began, "that we have no wish to add acrimony or misunderstanding."

On several occasions, he said he had made it clear that U.S. Steel was in a cost-price torque that could not be tolerated forever, that a company without profits is a company that cannot modernize, and that the price increase would add "almost negligibly" to the cost of other products—$10.64 for the steel in a standard automobile, 3 cents for a toaster.

One question and answer in the 58-minute session caught the ears of people in Washington: Could U.S. Steel hold its new price if Armco and Inland stood pat?

"It would definitely affect us," conceded Mr. Blough. "I don't know how long we could maintain our position."

A half-hour after Blough finished, Hodges held a press conference in rebuttal in the Empire State Building.

But words that probably hit Big Steel the hardest came that day from two Pennsylvania Republicans—Representatives William W. Scranton, the party's candidate for governor, and James E. VanZandt, the candidate for senator.

"The increase at this time," they wired Mr. Blough, "is wrong—wrong for Pennsylvania, wrong for America, wrong for the Free World. The increase surely will set off another round of inflation. It will hurt people most who can least afford to be hurt."

Meanwhile, Justice Department agents appeared at the headquarters of U.S. Steel, Bethlehem, Jones and Laughlin and other companies and served subpoenas for documents bearing on the price increase and other matters.

And at 7 P.M. Attorney General Kennedy announced that the Justice Department had ordered a grand jury investigation of the increase.

By that time, President and Mrs. Kennedy were getting ready for another state dinner with the Shah and Empress—this time at the Iranian Embassy.

FRIDAY

The first big news of the day came from Kyoto, Japan. Joseph Block, Inland's chairman, had told a reporter for the *Chicago Daily News:*

"We do not feel that an advance in steel prices at this time would be in the national interest."

That news heartened the administration but it did not stop planning or operations. Nor did Inland's official announcement, from Chicago at 10:08 A.M., Washington time, that it would hold the price line.

At 10:15 Solicitor General Cox met in Mr. Sorensen's office with representatives of the Treasury, Commerce and Labor Departments, Budget Bureau and Council of Economic Advisors.

The discussion was on emergency wage-price legislation of three broad kinds:

First, ad hoc legislation limited to the current steel situation; second, permanent legislation imposing some mechanism on wages and prices in the steel industry alone, and third, permanent legislation for steel and other basic industries, setting up "fact-finding" procedures.

At 11:45 Senator McNamara said at his news conference that the Defense Department had ordered defense contractors to shift steel purchases to companies that had not raised prices. Later in the day the department awarded to the Lukens Steel Company, which had not raised prices, a contract for more than $5,000,000 worth of a special armorplate for Polaris missile submarines.

At 12:15 President Kennedy and most of the Thursday group met again in the Cabinet room. It was estimated at that time that the price line was being held on 16 per cent of the nation's steel capacity.

Inland had announced. Armco had decided to hold but not announce. Kaiser's announcement came in while the meeting was on. This might be enough to force the bigger companies down again, but the sentiment of the meeting was that the retreat would not come soon.

Accordingly, preparations continued for a long struggle. Lists of directors of the companies that were holding the line were distributed, and each man present was asked to call men he knew.

Notably absent from this meeting was Secretary Goldberg. He was on his way to New York with Mr. Clifford in a Military Air Transport plane.

A secret rendezvous had been arranged with Mr. Blough and some of the other leaders of U.S. Steel at the Carlyle Hotel.

At this meeting as in Mr. Clifford's talk with Mr. Blough on the previous day, no demands or threats or promises came from the government side.

The discussion seems to have been a general one about what lay ahead. The outlook said Mr. Clifford, was "abysmal."

United States Steel, he continued, had failed to weigh the consequences of its action. If it held this position, its interest and those of the industry would inevitably be damaged, and the nation as a whole would suffer.

While the talk was going on, Mr. Blough was called to the phone. Then Mr. Goldberg was called. Each received the same message. Bethlehem Steel had rescinded the price increase—the news had come through at 3:20 P.M.

President Kennedy heard the news while flying to Norfolk for a weekend with the fleet. It was unexpected.

The administration had made no special effort with Bethlehem. To this day, officials in Washington are uncertain what did it.

Among other things, Bethlehem's officials were struck by the Inland and Kaiser announcement that morning, Inland posed direct competiton to Bethlehem's sales in the Midwest—the largest steel market—and Kaiser posed it on the West Coast.

Further, special questions were raised by the Pentagon's order to defense industries to shift their steel buying to mills that did not raise prices. What did this mean for Bethlehem's vast operations as a ship builder?

Whatever the compelling factors were, Bethlehem's decision brought the end of the battle clearly into sight. The competitive situation was such that U.S. Steel's executive committee was not called into session to reverse its action of the previous Tuesday. The company's officers acted on their own.

The big capitulation came at 5:28. Mrs. Barbara Gamarekian, a secretary in the White House press office, was checking the Associated Press news ticker. And there was the announcement—U.S. Steel had pulled back the price increase.

Mrs. Gamarekian tore it off and ran into the office of Mr. Sorensen, who was on the phone to the acting press secretary, Mr. Hatcher, in Norfolk.

"Well," Mr. Sorensen was saying, "I guess there isn't anything new."

Mrs. Gamarekian put the news bulletin under his eye.

"Wait a minute!" shouted Mr. Sorensen.

Mr. Hatcher gave the news to the President as he came off the nuclear submarine, Thomas A. Edison, in Norfolk.

It was just 72 hours since Roger Blough had dropped in on Mr. Kennedy.

X

The Supreme Court: Supreme in What?

The United States Supreme Court puzzles not only foreigners but Americans as well. Its combination of powers and functions is one source of confusion, the limits of its power another. In one sense the Court can do so much, yet in another sense it can do very little. And a clear picture of this situation is difficult even for lawyers to understand, because, as we shall see, the Court is a legal institution but not merely a legal body.

The Court can only hear cases—that is, issues must come before them in the form of arguments between two individuals or groups of individuals where one party genuinely claims something from the other. The something at issue may be, but doesn't have to be, monetarily valuable; one of the parties may want to imprison the other or interfere with what is claimed as the other one's freedom of religion, for example. (This limits what the Court can do right there, for it can't create cases from whole cloth.)

Controversies may reach the Supreme Court on appeal from decisions of lower federal courts and (through these courts) from federal administrative decisions. The second great stream of cases comes directly from the highest state court having jurisdiction (not necessarily the state supreme court) in cases where a right is claimed under the federal Constitution or a federal law or a treaty of the United States. This, of course, means that most state cases cannot be appealed to the Supreme Court; only a very small number involve a federal right. It also means that very often the Supreme Court does not review the whole case involved but only that part of the controversy dealing with the federal right. There are a few cases that start right in the Supreme Court, cases involving ambassadors and suits between states, but these are comparatively unimportant most of the time.

The important thing to remember in these cases that come up on appeal is that the Court can pretty well decide whether it wants to hear a case. Over three-quarters of the cases yearly come up by grant of the writ of *certiorari,* which is just a Latin way of saying the Court wants to hear the case and is ordering the lower court to send up the record. The judges must rule on a number of other cases, usually about fifteen per cent of their total, where, for example, a state court rules a federal law unconstitutional or upholds its own law against a claim that it violates the federal Constitution. This is to keep the laws in the various states uniform, as much as possible. Even in these cases, however, the Court may reach a decision after a fairly cursory examination of the issue, and so keep a large measure of control over its docket.

What makes the United States Supreme Court the most important court in the world? It is the fact that: (1) it has all of the powers that most high courts have to overrule the lower courts of the same judicial system; (2) it has many powers of review over federal administrative agencies; (3) it has power to interpret the words of Congress subject, of course, to "correction" of this interpretation by Congress; (4) it has the power to interpret the Constitution subject only to correction by the very difficult method of amendment; (5) it has the power exercised successfully at least since 1803 and *Marbury v. Madison* to declare congressional and presidential actions out of bounds as having violated the Constitution; (6) it can declare state laws unconstitutional as violating rather vague provisions (particularly of the due process and equal protection clauses of the Fourteenth Amendment and the interstate commerce clause, which the Court in the absence of any words at all has held since the great steamship case of *Gibbons v. Ogden* to be a limit on what states can do).

It is those last two powers that make the difference. Here the Court not only tries cases; in the course of hearing cases it can put on trial the very laws passed by the legislature or the acts of the Executive and the administration on the national level and all parts of the state governments. That means that within certain limits it is a censor of the actions of all other branches of government, and in many cases has the last say (short of amendment of the Constitution). Major laws and programs, then, in the United States may and have been brought to a standstill as a result of lawsuits involving a corner chicken dealer or drugstore owner. Important issues may hinge on a legal technicality. The judge is caught between worrying about the technicalities and seeing the greater issues behind them. The power to discard laws as unconstitutional presents problems different in very real and obvious ways from a traffic court case or a divorce or a suit in an automobile collision.

There are some who claim that this power makes the Court the real ruler of America—one critic spoke of the United States as an example of "government by the judiciary." Others see in the Court a defense of free government. Some would like the Court to be tightly bound by the rules of the past; others call for a Court with statesmanlike vision to fashion the Constitution to the future.

In order to help you understand and choose from these positions this chapter will focus on several questions. We will first take a quick look at the operations of the Court and attempt to get a vision of the Court's place in our governmental system—to see what kind of institution we have here and to see how it is conceived of by different writers. Our second problem will be one of recruitment—where do the judges come from and where should they come from? What is the experience that qualifies them for their position of power? Our third problem is also a question of sources, but of the sources of the law. Is the law a "fixed" discoverable thing like the laws of physics used to be thought of or is it the last guess of the fifth member of the Court or the prejudices of the majority of the Court? Finally, what is the place of the Court with regard to making policy? Can it lead the country and should it try to? Running throughout these problems there is an underlying issue which virtually all of the readings inevitably try to answer—how do you reconcile the power of these nine men with majority rule and democracy?

What Manner of Institution?

What does the Court do? This simple question has many different answers depending on how you want to view it. We will first look at what the Court does in the simplest way—the day-to-day routines of the Court. Then in a broader view we will consider its role in our political system. Finally, we will consider several different views of its basic meaning. By first understanding the operations of the Court and of its position in the system we can approach this deeper question. Does the Court represent the finest in American thought, a gyroscope keeping the system on an even keel, doing things no other institution can do? Or does it represent a strange and un-American oligarchy, more powerful than the men in the Kremlin?

Where Do the Judges and the Law Come From?

How should judges of the Supreme Court be selected? One former president has described his way of choosing:

> When I was president I always tried to have the cabinet and advisors around me interested in a whole cross section of the country's economy and political thought, and I think the highest court in the land should be so constituted that every viewpoint is expressed in the opinions of the court.*

Other presidents have followed much the same pattern. One thing they have been consistent in is choosing the vast majority from their own party. In this century, according to the American Bar Association, every president has chosen well over eighty per cent of all federal judges from his own political party.

Does this of itself suggest that the Supreme Court is a political body?

* Harry S. Truman to Samuel Krislov, May 20, 1954.

Is it perhaps wrong to choose judges to represent parts of the country, points of view, or political affiliation? In recent years there has been a cry for more judicial experience on the part of appointees to the Court. Some have suggested promotion from the lower courts with previous experience being a prerequisite. Still others call for a more radical approach—perhaps the replacement of our present system of appointment by the president and ratification by the Senate.

Apparently these criticisms bore some fruit, for President Eisenhower made four consecutive appointments from the lower federal judiciary and state courts. President Kennedy however did not continue these policies, perhaps in response to discussions such as the strong speech by Justice Frankfurter reprinted below. He has however continued the Eisenhower policy of "clearing" appointments to the bench with the American Bar Association, though making some appointments disapproved by them.

Do these represent desirable developments? Will it perhaps lead to an aristocracy of the robe and "government by lawyers and not men?" Or does it not go far enough in insuring a wall of separation between politics and the Court? Finally there are those who say it is a step in exactly the wrong direction—that what we should have is more, not less, political control of so political a branch of the government.

What Can the Court Do?

The ultimate test of a political institution is its ability to satisfy the people on whose behalf it acts. The Supreme Court is no exception to this rule. The Court must serve some useful function or go under. Another test of institutions is accountability; unchecked power is a source of danger both to the community and to the wielders of it. What is the function the Court serves? As we shall see, there are jobs in our system it alone does and which, some argue, it alone can do.

There are also definite limitations on the power of the Supreme Court. Some of these exist in law, others in fact. There is the power that other branches of the government wield over the Court. There is also the simple fact that public acceptance is necessary to enforce decisions of the Court. As the desegregation controversy reflects so well, the arsenal of weapons of the judicial system is not unlimited in the face of popular hostility. This, in turn, raises questions: How far can the Court go in defying public opinion? When should it attempt to do so and when should it not?

Yet another problem exists in the field of civil liberties. Can the Court lead in requiring freedom of speech and other political freedoms? In so doing will it serve democracy or perhaps weaken it by diluting majority rule and the responsibility of the community? The Supreme Court does not have tight self-defined limits to guide it in defining its total position in our government. For that reason the judges often disagree among themselves on this question. Ex-Justice Frankfurter and the late Learned Hand (who has been called the greatest judge never to serve on the Supreme Court) would argue that the Court should interfere almost never at all with laws of Congress. Black and Douglas represent a group that argues that where basic freedoms are concerned the Court should be less tolerant of majority rule. Because these freedoms are the heart of the political process of a democracy and are necessary to maintain political parties and the whole system of responsible scrutiny of policies, the judges argue that these are in a "preferred position." This argument has spilled over into popular discussion; it is one of the major problems now facing the Court and which will continue to face it in the years to come.

Again, some people ask whether the Court should attempt to deal with problems of far-reaching social importance, like the segregation question. Do such problems lend themselves to legal solution? Is democracy served by nine men deciding such problems?

1

HOW THE SUPREME COURT REACHES DECISIONS*

Anthony Lewis

The following is a detailed step-by-step breakdown of Supreme Court routine as described by The New York Times' *Supreme Court reporter.* The Times *has a great tradition in careful coverage of the Court, which has usually been poorly covered by the press because of the intricacies of the legal process. Mr. Lewis was given legal training as preparation for his reportorial role.*

The first step in any case is for the Court to decide whether it will decide. Congress has given the justices almost complete discretion to say what cases they will hear and the volume of business requires stringent exercise of that discretion.

To help get through the approximately 1,500 petitions filed each term, most of the justices have their law clerks prepare a short memorandum on each case. But the justices make the decision, and their grounds will of course vary. A class of cases which seems vitally important to one member of the Court may appear to another one entirely unworthy of Supreme Court review. The issue of what cases to take has provoked bitter public argument among the justices.

The Court's formal choice of cases to be heard is made in a weekly conference which is the heart of the processes of decision in the Court. The conference meets each Friday at 11 o'clock during or preceding the weeks the Court is in session. It usually runs on until evening and may go over to Saturday. By tradition each justice shakes hands around the table as he enters the room. (That is thirty-six handshakes altogether.) By another tradition, designed to assure secrecy, no one but the nine is ever allowed in the room during the conference. When clerks bring messages, the junior justice goes to the door to get them.

The late Justice Robert H. Jackson

* Anthony Lewis, "How the Supreme Court Reaches Decisions," *The New York Times Magazine,* December 1, 1957, pp. 51–54.

noted in 1954 that conference time would allow on the average only five minutes of discussion per item. He wrote: "All that saves the Court from being hopelessly bogged down is that many of the items are so frivolous on mere inspection that no one finds them worthy of discussion and they are disposed of by unanimous consent."

The Chief Justice has a special responsibility for making the conference work, for disposing of its heavy case load. He announces each case on the list in turn and then leads the discussion. On a "frivolous" petition for review he may do no more than remark that he will put it with the rejects unless someone objects. Or he may indicate other reasons for not taking the case. Justice Frankfurter in a 1955 talk to Illinois lawyers gave an example of what a Chief Justice may say:

"This is a very interesting and important question . . . , but we can't do any better than Judge Julian Mack (late judge of the United States Court of Appeals) did with it below. He really knows more about this field of law than the rest of us. I suggest we deny this petition for *certiorari*."

It takes the votes of four justices to grant a petiton for *certiorari*, the formal device usually used to bring a case up for review. Those cases which the Court does agree to hear are put on the calendar. The clerk of the Court picks a date for oral argument, usually several months after the decision to hear the case and sometimes now—because of a clogged calendar—more than a year.

Before oral argument begins, both sides submit printed briefs giving their versions of the facts in detail and their legal positions. A printed record is also prepared. This includes all, or significant portions, of the transcript made in the trial of the lawsuit, exhibits and previous judicial opinions in the case. This record may run to thousands of pages.

* * *

The critical moment in the process of decision is in all likelihood the oral argument of a case. And here the ways of decision—often, indeed, the minds of the justices—are open to public view. For anyone who wants to understand the workings of the Court, the printed text of an opinion is a poor substitute for listening to argument.

The Court hears argument two weeks out of each month during the October–June term. It sits Monday through Thursday from 12 to 4:30, with a half-hour out for lunch. Each side is usually limited to an hour, in some simpler cases to a half hour.

In the marble-pillared courtroom the justices look down at the speaker's stand from their raised seats. The lawyer for the party which lost in the lower courts begins: "Mr. Chief Justice, may it please the Court . . ." Speaking preferably without a prepared text, he states the facts briefly, then moves on to his legal positions. The other side has its turn; then there is a brief rebuttal.

Before he gets very far, the lawyer is likely to be interrupted by questions from one or more of the justices: Will he clarify such-and-such a fact? Does the case he just cited really stand for what he said? Will he agree that the Court cannot find for him unless . . .?

The Court sees itself not "a dozing audience for the reading of soliloquies," Justice Frankfurter has said, "but as a questioning body, utilizing oral argument as a means for exposing the difficulties of a case with a view to meeting them." The questions show the attorney the doubts he must put at rest if he is to carry the Court.

They may forecast the decision of the Court.

The conference discussion of cases just argued begins with the Chief Justice. The senior associate, now Justice Black, speaks next, and so on down the line of seniority. Voting follows, but in reverse order—from the junior justice up.

As presiding officer, the Chief Justice shapes the character of the conference by deciding, for example, how long to let debate continue before calling for a vote.

Immediately after the conference, and the resulting vote, the job of writing opinions in the decided cases is divided among the justices. The Chief Justice assigns the majority opinion if he is in the majority; if not, the senior associate in the majority makes the assignment. The writer of the dissent, if any, is selected the same way. And, of course, any justice may write a concurring or dissenting opinion on his own. Thomas Jefferson thought every member of the Court ought to publish his views on every case—to be sure they weren't just blindly following John Marshall.

Assigning opinions is an art all its own, and an important one. To prevent fragmentation of the Court, for example, it may be wise to pick as the writer the justice who takes the middle view in a case. Hughes was said to pick "liberal" justices to write opinions in "conservative" decisions, and vice versa, so as to hold the Court as near as possible to a centrist position. Assigning the opinion to a member of the majority who holds an extreme view of the case may make other justices break away and write concurring opinions, giving their own reasons for the results. . . .

Underlying the opinion-writing process is the great problem of producing a collective judgment from the labors of individuals. It goes without saying that the result in a Supreme Court case may be less important than the reasons for it. And it may not be easy to agree on the reasons.

As opinions are drafted, copies are circulated among the other members of the Court. The copies come back with comments. Further drafts follow. One justice's price for adherence may be enough to send another into dissent. The writer may have to squelch some of his own views to carry the Court.

In contrast to the caution of the writer for the majority, the dissenter frequently indulges in exaggeration, painting the majority's view blacker than it really is. Majority opinions are revised to answer draft dissents which have been circulated. A notorious example of this was the Dred Scott case; the statements in Chief Justice Taney's majority opinion which most infuriated the North were added in answer to the furious dissent by a minority of the Court.

The drafting and redrafting of opinions may take months. Some Monday the last corrections will have been made in the Court's basement print shop. Shortly after noon one of the justices will begin reading, pneumatic tubes will carry copies of the opinion to the press room, and the process of decision in another case will be ended.

2

POWERFUL, IRRESPONSIBLE, AND HUMAN*

Fred Rodell

Not all people see the Court in the admiring way Mr. Lewis seems to. Oldline Democrats and Progressives like Robert LaFollette and even Teddy Roosevelt were suspicious of the Court. These and others thought the power of the judges was a denial of majority rule. This point of view still persists, and has much logic behind it. Justice Frankfurter, for example, has accepted this argument and builds his defense for limits on judicial review on this assumption. Another prominent example—more critical of the Court than Frankfurter—is Fred Rodell, a professor at Yale Law School and, incidentally, a close friend of Justice William Douglas. Whether any of the justices, including Douglas, would agree with the rather strong statements that follow seems doubtful.

At the top levels of the three branches of the civilian government of the United States sit the Congress, the President plus his Cabinet, and the Supreme Court. Of these three—in this unmilitary, unclerical nation—only one wears a uniform. Only one carries on its most important business in utter secret behind locked doors—and indeed never reports, even after death, what really went on there. Only one, its members holding office for life if they choose, is completely irresponsible to anyone or anything but themselves and their own consciences. Only one depends for much of its immense influence on its prestige as a semi-sacred institution and preserves that prestige with the trappings and show of superficial dignity rather than earning it, year after working year, by the dignity and wisdom of what it is and does. Under our otherwise democratic form of government, only one top ruling group uses ceremony and secrecy, robes and ritual, as instruments of its *official* policy, as wellsprings of its power.

The nine men who are the Supreme Court of the United States are at once the most powerful and the most irresponsible of all the men in the world who govern other men. Not even the bosses of the Kremlin, each held back by fear of losing his head should he ever offend his fellows, wield such loose and long-ranging and accountable-to-no-one power as do the nine or five-out-of-nine justices who can give orders to any other governing official in the United States—from the members of a village school board who would force their young charges to salute the flag, to a president who would take over the steel industry to keep production going—and can make those orders stick. Ours may be, for puffing purposes, a "government of checks and balances," but there is no check

* Fred Rodell, *Nine Men: A Political History of the Supreme Court from 1790 to 1955* (New York: Random House, 1955), pp. 3–6.

at all on what the Supreme Court does—save only three that are as pretty in theory as they are pointless in practice. (These are the Senate's power to reject a newly named justice, used only once this century, and in the past usually unwisely; the power to impeach a justice, only once tried and never carried through; the power of the people to reverse a Supreme Court decision by amending the Constitution, as they have done just three times in our whole history.) The nine justices sit secure and stand supreme over Congress, president, governors, state legislatures, commissions, administrators, lesser judges, mayors, city councils, and dog-catchers—with none to say them nay.

Lest these words sound like arrant overstatement, here are what three of the most thoughtful men who ever held high national office said about the Supreme Court's flat and final power of government. Thomas Jefferson, who was president when the Court first fully used this power, exploded, prophetically but futilely: "Our Constitution . . . intending to establish three departments, coordinate and independent, that they might check and balance one another . . . has given, according to this opinion, to one of them alone the right to prescribe rules for the government of the others, and to that one, too, which is unelected by and independent of the nation. . . . The Constitution, on this hypothesis, is a mere thing of wax in the hands of the judiciary which they may twist and shape into any form they please." Jefferson was talking of the Court's then brand-newly wielded power to override Congress and the president. More than a century later, Justice Holmes, revealingly in dissent, berated his brethren for freely using their judicial power to upset *state* laws: "As the decisions now stand I see hardly any limit but the sky to the invalidating of those rights ['*the constitutional rights of the states*'] if they happen to strike a majority of this Court as for any reason undesirable. I cannot believe that the [Fourteenth] Amendment was intended to give us carte blanche to embody our economic or moral beliefs in its prohibitions." And a few years after, Justice Stone, he too in dissent, exclaimed: "The only check upon our own exercise of power is our own sense of self-restraint."

In Stone's same angry protest against the Court's six-to-three veto of the first Agricultural Adjustment Act—a protest that helped spark Franklin Roosevelt's "Court-packing" plan and later led FDR to reward its author with the Chief Justiceship—he also said: "Courts are not the only agency of government that must be assumed to have capacity to govern." This statement, while true on its face, is essentially and subtly—though of course not deliberately—misleading. No "agency of government" governs; no "court" governs; only the men who run the agency of government or the court or the Supreme Court do the governing. The power is theirs because the decisions are theirs; decisions are not made by abstractions like agencies or courts. Justice Stone, who knew what he meant, might a little better have said: "Five or six of the nine men who make up this Court are not the only men in our government who must be assumed to have the capacity to govern." And he might have added: "Nor are they necessarily the wisest in their judgments; I work with them and have reason to know."

3

ARE JUDGES POLITICIANS?*

Charles A. Beard

What do the presidents look for in selecting a candidate? Are there politics involved in the selection? The following discussion by Charles A. Beard in his The Republic *puts these questions in historical perspective. Professor Beard, always a realist, had little use for the myth that most judges were chosen for legal ability alone without knowledge of any efforts on their behalf. He also puts into perspective the sense in which justices of the Court can be said to be partisan.*

Dr. Smyth: What about Judge Ranyin's statement that Supreme Court justices are above partisanship? I presume he meant that they ought to be above partisanship, for he has been vociferous in contending that President Franklin D. Roosevelt's judges are just New Deal judges. Perhaps he thinks that until the New Deal all justices were above partisanship. If so, that is a question of historical fact which a study of history can answer.

Beard: If partisanship is taken in the narrow sense to mean that judges of the Supreme Court have perverted the Constitution and the law to serve some low interests of party managers, I think it would be true to historical facts to maintain that the Supreme Court has been remarkably free from partisanship. There have been a few cases in which traces of political jobbery have appeared, but they are so few that they may be discarded and the Supreme Court acquitted of partisanship in this sense.

But in the larger sense of grand public policies espoused by political parties, the Supreme Court has not been above and indifferent to the great conflicting interests of parties. On the contrary, the justices on that bench have reflected those interests in the momentous cases of American history—such as the Dred Scott case of 1857, the Legal Tender cases of 1872, the income tax case of 1895, the Insular cases after the Spanish war, and some of the New Deal cases. This is not to say that the justices of the Court in such cases always divide according to their party labels. They do not. Nor indeed do hot partisans in general divide sharply over such issues. There are Republicans sympathetic to the New Deal, and there are Democrats who have fought it from the beginning.

Mrs. Smyth: I should think that one test would be whether, in selecting Supreme Court justices, presidents have been indifferent to party considerations and chosen freely or equally from both parties. If it is just a matter of getting a competent lawyer who knows the

* Charles A. Beard, *The Republic* (New York: The Viking Press, Inc., 1943), pp. 229–34. Copyright 1943 by Charles A. Beard. Reprinted by permission of the publishers.

Constitution, then presidents might choose men outside their party about as often as they do men inside. For instance President Roosevelt appointed Harlan Stone Chief Justice after the resignation of Mr. Hughes, and Mr. Stone is a Republican. How many such cases of such nonpartisanship have there been in our history?

Beard: Not many. I recall only two offhand. Let us look at the roll: . . .

President Taft elevated Edward D. White, of Louisiana, a Democrat, to the place of Chief Justice. White was a good, sound, conservative like Taft, but a party Democrat, no Bryan Democrat.

The next Chief Justice was William H. Taft, nominated by President Harding. As to their party politics, no comment is necessary.

After Taft's resignation, President Hoover selected Charles E. Hughes. No comment on party politics is needed here.

With the elevation of Justice Harlan Stone to the Chief Justiceship by President Roosevelt came the second break. . . .

Dr. Smyth: But all of President Roosevelt's other appointees to the Court were good, sound New-Deal Democrats—Black, Reed, Murphy, Douglas, Frankfurter, Jackson, Byrnes, and Rutledge. Stone had often been favorable to the New Deal in his opinions. . . . Give me that list of Chief Justices. I want to show it to Judge Ranyin and ask him whether he still thinks that the Supreme Court is above partisanship. As a doctor of medicine I do not know a thing about jurisprudence, but I need only common sense to see through a hole in a millstone.

Beard: Here is the list and also a list of all the other Supreme Court justices since the creation of the Court under President Washington, with annotations relative to their politics and their appointments. Look it over.

Dr. Smyth, dryly, after running through the list: This very string of facts indicates to me that there has been a lot of partisanship in the narrow sense of the term.

Beard: In some appointments, perhaps so, but my rule still holds good, namely, that even partisan judges have seldom, if ever, sunk to the level of petty politics, although they have often sustained or struck at actions involving grand national politics. It is right here that they have displayed their power, for good or ill. Yet I would warn you that the work of the Court is not all on dramatic cases. What it does by decisions and opinions relative to routine matters, in the aggregate may well outweigh in terms of national interest and welfare its actions in highly controversial cases. . . .

Mrs. Smyth: Innocently no doubt, I have always thought of that membership as an honor which went to great lawyers, with no seeking or political maneuvering on their part.

Beard: There are of course a number of cases in which the honor has apparently gone to men who have not sought it or perhaps even permitted their friends to seek it for them. . . .

For many of the . . . justices the records are ample and convincing. They permit us to say that ambitious men, usually though not always active politicians, have zealously sought membership on the Court and employed great ingenuity in their own behalf. William Howard Taft's early ambition was to be a justice of the Supreme Court. After the election of Harding in 1920, as Pringle shows in his *Life and Times of William Howard Taft,* Mr. Taft made a point of visiting Harding, enlisted the interest of Harry Daugherty in his behalf, and, with great trepidation of spirit, pulled wires to secure the Chief Justiceship. His labors were successful, thanks partly to

Daugherty's sympathetic cooperation. And no man in the United States was more concerned than Taft with getting the right kind of justices for the Court—that is, good, sound conservatives who held his own views respecting the powers and functions of the Court.... Presidents have recognized the fact that the Supreme Court is a center of great power and have tried to select justices in general sympathy with their policies. This rule applies to Republicans and Democrats alike.

And why not? The Supreme Court is not a group of disembodied spirits operating in a vacuum on logical premises that express or affect none of the powerful interests over which party conflicts rage. In a refined but none the less real way, its members express these conflicts of interest. It would be preposterous for a president who believes that his policies are sound and constitutional to nominate judges who hold opposite views—judges who would declare his policies unconstitutional. Presidents are sometimes disappointed in details but in the general run they get what they expect.

Dr. Smyth: I remember hearing that Theodore Roosevelt was disappointed—yes, angry—because Justice Holmes did not decide some cases to suit him.

Beard: That is true. But one of the reasons Theodore Roosevelt assigned for nominating Holmes was the progressive views on labor and social legislation Holmes had expounded as judge in Massachusetts. These views Holmes continued to expound as a justice of the Supreme Court throughout his entire career in that tribunal. . . .

Dr. Smyth: But justices of the Supreme Court abstain from politics after they are appointed, however active they have been previously?

Beard: Though in general they abstain from active participation in party politics, here again there have been exceptions. A number of justices during the past hundred years have actively, if quietly, carried on underground campaigns to get the nomination for the presidency. I know of no evidence that Justice Charles E. Hughes worked to get the Republican nomination in 1916; still he got it and resigned from the Court to run for president. Many justices while in service on the bench have maintained intimate relations with their party brother in the White House, and have advised him in law, tactics, and strategy. There is some popular resentment at this, but the practice has been common to the latest hour.

Mrs. Smyth: At least they do not make political speeches for their party brother in the White House.

Beard: Campaign speeches, no. At all events I never heard of any case under that head, although justices have occasionally been accused of injecting campaign speeches into their opinions, sometimes with an eye to their own political prospects. Yet justices of the Supreme Court have gone around making speeches in support of presidential policies. Speaking more politely, we should perhaps call them addresses. They are usually delivered on ceremonial occasions, such as the Fourth of July, or at commencements when justices receive honorary degrees from colleges and universities. . . .

4

ELECT SUPREME COURT JUSTICES?*

David Lawrence

If the Supreme Court is political shouldn't it be subject to political controls? This is the position taken in the following article by David Lawrence, who is a political columnist, publisher of U.S. News and World Report, *and one of the leading and most vocal critics of the Court's desegregation decision. The suggestion he makes, however, is one that has been discussed several times in our history, and, he argues, has precedent and logic behind it.*

Now that the Supreme Court has transformed itself into what is being termed "another legislative body," a movement has started to bring about the election of the high court justices by the people. It would require a constitutional amendment.

The idea, of course, is not novel. This happens to be the custom in the several states with few exceptions. Thirty-six states elect their highest court judges at the polls, four states elect their top judges by vote of the state legislatures, and only eight states follow the federal custom of appointment by the Executive with the consent of the Legislature.

Since the Supreme Court of the United States has set itself up as having the right to tell Congress how to run its committees and the executive departments that they must retain employees they don't like, the question of how the Supreme Court, itself, shall be held accountable for its acts has arisen. This has happened several times before in American history.

The late President Franklin D. Roosevelt thought the answer to an arbitrary or capricious court was to increase the number of justices so he could appoint those who would decide cases as he thought they should be decided. This scheme was called "court-packing." It required legislation and was frowned on by Congress in 1937. Former President Theodore Roosevelt, as a candidate for the presidency in 1912, urged that there be a system of "recall of judicial decision" so the people, by referendum, could affirm or reverse decisions, especially in state courts.

Today the Supreme Court of the United States has rendered so many conflicting and confusing decisions that many lawyers throughout the country are perplexed and bewildered. The issue was succinctly stated by a member of the Supreme Court itself, the late Justice Robert H. Jackson, who, in the course of an opinion in 1953, wrote:

"Rightly or wrongly, the belief is widely held by the practicing profession that this court no longer respects impersonal rules of law, but is guided in these matters by personal impres-

---

* David Lawrence, "Elect Supreme Court Justices?" *Washington Evening Star,* June 20, 1957.

sions which from time to time may be shared by a majority of justices. Whatever has been intended, this court also has generated an impression . . . that regard for precedents and authorities is obsolete, that words no longer mean what they have always meant to the profession, that the law knows no fixed principles."

For the last 20 years many of the professors of law in the university law schools, particularly in the East, have raised a whole generation of so-called "liberals" who believe the Supreme Court should make "policy" and that to adhere to historic principles is out of keeping with the spirit of the times. This is the type of thinking which has bred throughout the country a feeling that the court pays more attention to sociology or political science or ideological considerations nowadays than it does to fundamental interpretation of the Constitution and to the enduring principles of jurisprudence.

If, therefore, the Supreme Court is to make "policies," to whom should it be responsible? It now places itself above both the Congress and the Executive, which are themselves accountable to the people. The justices, however, are accountable to no one but themselves. Such an autocracy was never envisioned by the Founding Fathers when they authorized life tenure for justices. The several states have wisely written into their constitutions that judges must go before the people —sometimes after six-year and sometimes after twelve- or fourteen-year terms. But there is a check by the people.

Criticism of the Supreme Court is mounting. Unfortunately, it is a criticism that attributes political or ideological motives to the justices. Many Republicans and Democrats, moreover, are blaming President Eisenhower for the peculiar attitude Chief Justice Warren has taken since being on the high court. "Why was Warren ever appointed?" is asked repeatedly in political circles. He was known as a middle-of-the-roader for many years. Eisenhower, however, is reported to be as much surprised as the general public that Warren has become enamored of the Douglas-Black philosophy and consistently follows the radical line without the slightest show of independence.

Justice Black wrote extensively on the rights of congressional investigating committees when he was a United States Senator, and so did Justice Frankfurter before he came to the court. They both thought investigating committees shouldn't be restricted in gathering information and in browbeating recalcitrant witnesses. They wrote approvingly of the harassment of the businessmen of those days. But when the harassment now turns to persons who have had "past associations" with Communists and who conceal their connections, both Justices Frankfurter and Black seem to become champions of the very individual rights which they once urged should be denied as businessmen sought to exercise them against the witch-hunting and fishing expeditions of congressional committees.

So, since it is all so obviously political, there are many persons here in Congress who are coming reluctantly to the conclusion that election of judges for fixed terms, with the right to run for re-election, is the only way out of the political dilemma which the present court has created by its "legislative" decisions.

5

THE SUPREME COURT IN THE MIRROR OF JUSTICES*

Felix Frankfurter

What of the argument that judges should have previous judicial experience? Here is one argument that the "correlation between prior judicial experience . . . and fitness . . . for the Supreme Court is zero." The argument comes from a rather authoritative source. Felix Frankfurter is, of course, a prominent figure in Supreme Court history, but he was also an authority on the judicial system before his appointment. As Professor of Law at Harvard, the author of many leading works on the Court, and friend of Brandeis and Holmes, his judgment is of especial interest.

What is the teaching of history on this? Of the seventy-five justices, twenty-eight had not a day's prior judicial service. Seven more had sat on some bench from a few months to not more than two years. Nine sat six years or less. Several bills have in recent years proposed "judicial service" of not less than five years in a lower federal court or as a member of the highest court of a state; some bills would require ten years of such service. A five-year requirement would have ruled out at least thirty-five of seventy-five judges (in fact more, because several of the justices who had had judicial experience did not sit on a federal bench or on the highest court of a state), and the ten-year requirement would have barred certainly forty-five of our seventy-five justices.

Who were these justices who came on the Supreme Court without any "judicial service," without even the judicial experience of an Iredell, who at the age of twenty-six sat on the Superior Court of his state, North Carolina, only long enough—six months—to resign. They begin with . . . James Wilson and include Bushrod Washington, Marshall, Story, Taney, Curtis, Campbell, Miller, Chase, Bradley, Waite, Fuller, Moody, Hughes, Brandeis, Stone, and Roberts. Of the twelve Chief Justices within our period, five had not had any judicial experience at the time of their appointment as Chief Justice and two more had had none when they first came on the Court.

Assessment of distinction in the realm of the mind and spirit cannot exclude subjective factors. . . . [But] it would indeed be a surprising judgment that would exclude Marshall, William Johnson, Story, Taney, Miller, Field, Bradley, White, Holmes, Hughes, Brandeis, and Cardozo in the roster of distinction among our seventy-five. I myself would add Curtis, Campbell, Matthews and Moody. (Some might prefer Harlan I or Brewer or Brown.) Of the twelve, five had had judicial

* Felix Frankfurter, "The Supreme Court in the Mirror of Justices," *Vital Speeches,* May 1, 1957, pp. 432–33, 435–36.

experience and seven none, before coming on the Court, and of the others only Matthews can be counted a judge, for a brief period, before he came to Washington. Of the sixteen justices whom I deem preeminent, only six came to the Court with previous judicial experience, however limited. It would require discernment more than daring, it would demand complete indifference to the elusive and intractable factors in tracking down causes, in short, it would be foolish, to attribute acknowledged greatness in the Court's history either to the fact that a justice had had judicial experience or that he had been without it.

Apart from meaning that a man had sat on some court for some time, judicial service tells nothing that is relevant about the qualifications for the functions exercised by the Supreme Court. . . . "judicial experience" does not convey anything that is definite and fixed. To an uncritical mind it carries emanations of relevance in that it implies . . . that a man has not the qualifications for sitting on a higher court unless he has had the experience of having sat on a lower court, just as a man presumably cannot run a mile in less than four minutes unless he had already run it in six.

Need I say that judicial experience is not like that at all? For someone to have been a judge on some court for some time, having some kind of business resulting in some kind of experience, may have some abstract relation to the Supreme Court conceived of as an abstract judicial tribunal. It has no significant relation whatever as such to the kinds of litigation that come before the Supreme Court, to the types of issues they raise, to qualities that these actualities require for wise decision.

To begin with, one must consider the differences in the staple business of different courts and the different experiences to which different judicial business gives rise, and the bearing of different experiences so generated on the demands of the business of the Supreme Court. Thus, there is a vital difference so far as substantive training is concerned between the experience gained on state courts and on the lower federal courts. . . .

After having spent twenty years on the Supreme Judicial Court of Massachusetts, part of it as its Chief Justice, in the course of which he wrote more than a thousand opinions on every conceivable subject, Mr. Justice Holmes found himself not at all at home on coming to the Supreme Court. . . . Nor did Cardozo, after eighteen years on the New York Court of Appeals, five of them as Chief Judge, in the course of which he gained the acclaim of the whole common-law world, find that his transplantation from Albany to Washington was a natural step in judicial progression. On more than one occasion he complained to friends (sometimes as bitterly as that gentle soul could) that he should not have been taken from judicial labors with which he was familiar and which were congenial to him, to types of controversies to which his past experience bore little relation and to which, though these were the main concern of the Supreme Court, he was not especially drawn. . . .

What of the lower [federal] courts as a training ground for the Supreme Bench? The fact is that not one so trained emerged over a century and a half among the few towering figures of the Court. Oblivion has overtaken almost all of them. . . .

It is essentially accurate to say that the Court's preoccupation is with the application of rather fundamental aspirations and what Judge Learned Hand calls "moods," embodied in provisions like the Due Process Clauses, which were designed not to be precise and positive directions for rules of action. The judicial process in applying them involves a judgment on the processes of government. The Court sits in judgment, that is, on the views of the direct representatives of the people in meeting the needs of society, the views of presidents and governors, and by their construction of the will of legislatures the Court breathes life, feeble or strong, into the inert pages of the Constitution and the statute books. . . .

I have now come to the end of my story with its self-evident moral. Since the functions of the Supreme Court are what they are and demand the intellectual and moral qualities that they do, inevitably touching interests not less than those of the Nation, does it require an explicit statement that in choosing men for this task, no artificial or irrelevant consideration should restrict choice?

The search should be made among those men, inevitably very few at any time, who give the best promise of satisfying the intrinsic needs of the Court, no matter where they may be found, no matter in what professional way they have manifested the needed qualities.

One is entitled to say without qualification that the correlation between prior judicial experience and fitness for the functions of the Supreme Court is zero.

6

"JUDGES, LAWYERS, AND LIARS"*

Jonathan Swift

Law and lawyers have always been unpopular; "woe unto you lawyers," the Bible scolds. The law is sometimes regarded as a mask for injustice and a mumbo-jumbo designed to fool the uninitiated. This point of view is expressed in the following excerpt from Jonathan Swift's great satire, Gulliver's Travels. *To what extent Swift believed what he was writing is hard to say; but this point of view expressed over two centuries ago is one that people—sometimes unthinkingly—accept even today.*

Judges are persons appointed to decide all controversies of property, as well as for the trial of criminals, and picked out from the most dexterous lawyers, who are grown old or lazy, and having been biased all their lives against truth and equity, are under such a fatal necessity of favoring fraud, perjury and oppression, that I have known several of them refuse a large bribe from the side where justice lay, rather than injure the faculty, by doing anything unbecoming their nature or their office.

It is a maxim among lawyers, that whatever hath been done before may legally be done again: and therefore they take special care to record all the decisions formerly made against common justice and the general reason of mankind. These, under the name of precedents, they produce as authorities,

* Jonathan Swift, *Gulliver's Travels.*

to justify the most iniquitous opinions; and the judges never fail of directing accordingly. In pleading they studiously avoid entering into the merits of the cause, but are loud, violent and tedious in dwelling upon all circumstances which are not to the purpose.

It is likewise to be observed, that this society hath a peculiar chant and jargon of their own, that no other mortal can understand, and wherein all their laws are written, which they take special care to multiply; whereby they have wholly confounded the very essence of truth and falsehood.

7

LAYMEN ARE EVERY BIT AS HARD-BOILED AND PRECEDENT-MINDED*

Lloyd Garrison

In a more modern statement Lloyd Garrison, formerly Dean of the University of Wisconsin Law School, and a former federal administrative official as well, disagrees with the Swift idea. Laymen, too, like precedents and rules, he argues. They are ways of dealing quickly with difficult decisions.

I have received the distinct impression that laymen in a judicial position are quite as eager as lawyers in pursuing, and quite as contentious in dissecting, the available precedents; and that precedents are thus magnified not because of any notion of the social desirability of certainty but because they are a godsend to men harassed by the necessity of making up their minds in close cases and of justifying their decisions when made. I have concluded also that lay judges are fully as hard-boiled as ordinary judges in cleaving to the result, however harsh, which precedent or the letter of the contract dictates, and are equally loath to commit themselves upon moot or hypothetical questions.

. . . It is curious to note how seriously lay members treat the precedents and with what skill they are able to urge that this case should be distinguished or that analogy applied. It is interesting also to note that the "equities," save in the relatively rare "grievance" cases, of discipline or refusal to promote, are not, in theory at least, considered. All the members agree that the question in every case (save the ones just mentioned) is what the contract means, and this question must be answered as a cold-blooded matter of construction, however inequitable the outcome. That a referee, or a division without a referee, should reach a manifestly unfair result in a particular case by strict application of the rules and precedents is considered far better than to do equity by glossing over or reading exceptions into the rules or by disregarding clear precedents.

---

* Lloyd Garrison, "The National Railroad Adjustment Board," *Yale Law Journal*, Vol. XLVI, 1937, pp. 567, 583–84.

8

WE MUST GO BACK IN ORDER TO GO FORWARD*

John T. Flynn

Here we have a sample of the position most of our writers have suggested is out of fashion—namely that the law and the Constitution have a definite meaning which the judges should enforce. Where they don't do so they are clearly violating the Constitution, and should be called to account. Mr. Flynn is a critic of the New Deal and of decisions of the Supreme Court since 1937. He suggests a simple remedy for the decisions he regards as erroneous, a suggestion which itself should raise some questions about the meaning and nature of law. (Not everyone, of course, would agree with Mr. Flynn's historical statements, but they represent a definite point of view.)

The Supreme Court is empowered, under the Constitution, to "interpret" the meaning of the Constitution where questions of judicial differences appear. It had, according to its time-honored practice, interpreted the Constitution to mean what its framers wanted it to mean, and declared Roosevelt's first-term acts unconstitutional—in the most important case by unanimous decision. . . .

Once a Supreme Court subservient to the president and the new collectivist revolution was installed, the job was easy. It was simply necessary for the Supreme Court to give new and utterly different meanings to *four words* in the Constitution—meanings those words had never had in the preceding 148 years. The four words are comprised in the terms "general welfare" and "interstate commerce."

The term "general welfare" was clearly understood for a century and a half. I have listed the specific powers conferred upon Congress. Congress was empowered to collect taxes, etc., "to provide for the common defense and *general welfare of the United States.*" That did not mean that Congress could tax for any project which might seem good to Congress to "promote the general welfare." It did not refer to general welfare in the sense the word "welfare" is now used—as a system of handouts to the indigent, etc. . . .

The Courts never wavered, throughout our history, in their clear understanding of the term "commerce" and of "interstate commerce." It meant trade; and it included transportation as an inevitable function of trade. They understood precisely what the Constitution meant and why the terms were used. . . . In 1871 an attempt was made to show that commerce included manufacture. Justice Field rejected that theory and held that interstate

* John T. Flynn, *The Decline of the American Republic: And How to Rebuild It* (New York: Devin-Adair Co., 1955), pp. 99, 101, 105–107, 165–66.

commerce in a commodity begins "*whenever a commodity has begun to move as an article of trade from one state to another.*"

Of course, the subject became troublesome when large corporations began to spread their activities over many states, and when the growing evil of corporate monopoly began to make itself felt. Communities and smaller interests clamored for action by the federal government against the growing power of the trusts, and for every abuse there was a band of organized reformers calling for action against their own pet abuse. They all overlooked the fact that while there was the problem of curbing predatory or antisocial man on one side, there was also the continuing great adventure, attempted in America, of keeping in leash the abuses of too-powerful antisocial government.

But the Courts always, to their credit, kept foremost in mind the meaning of the Constitution and in decision after decision on questions involving "interstate commerce" kept to the true meaning of the clause. . . .

. . . *We must go back in order to go forward. We must return to the great highway of the American Republic.*

Obviously the nation faced a tremendous reconstruction job on our mutiliated Constitution and on our sadly battered Republic.

The first, the most challenging enterprise is to return the federal Constitution to its historic limits as construed by the Supreme Court for 145 years. No proof is necessary of the bold design of President Roosevelt, guided by the audacious crew of socialist and communist revolutionaries who surrounded him. That design was to alter the Constitution by judicial interpretation. The amendment of the Constitution can be legally effected by only one method—and that is set out in the instrument itself. Unable to carry out this revolutionary alteration of the government by lawful methods, Roosevelt turned to an outrageous assault upon the judges of the Supreme Court for the purpose of driving them off the bench and replacing them with compliant political judges—some of them social revolutionists—who could be depended on to torture the words of the Constitution into such meanings as would literally alter the whole shape and nature of our federal system. This assault was made possible by the lawless mind of the President, the boldness of the conspirators who surrounded him, and the disturbed and troubled state of the public mind under the influence of the depression.

The escape from the consequences of this great crime against our society is perhaps the most difficult of all the problems that confront us. The infamy which characterizes this adventure, however, justifies a bold counterstroke to correct it. But it is a stroke that can be carried out within the clear meaning of the Constitution. I urge a constitutional amendment, and suggest the following wording:

The decisions of the Supreme Court between 1937 and the date of the final adoption of this amendment, rendered by a Court designedly packed to alter by interpretation the clear meanings of the Constitution, are hereby declared to have no force and effect as precedents in judicial or other proceedings in determining the meaning of the words, sections and provisions of the Constitution of the United States.

9

LITIGATION AS A FORM OF PRESSURE GROUP ACTIVITY*

Clement E. Vose

In recent years political scientists have been studying another source of law, namely the operations of pressure groups on the Court. A pioneer in the study of this type of pressure group activity, Clement Vose has found that such groups commonly appear on both sides of many important cases. The following is a summary of some of his findings in a recent article. It is Mr. Vose's contention that these groups are inevitable and useful if properly controlled.

. . . It is the thesis of this article that organizations—identifiable by letterhead—often link broad interest in society to individual parties of interest in Supreme Court cases.

The important place of judicial review in the American system of government and the attention demanded by litigation dealing with large issues of public law have drawn organizations into many important court cases. In Supreme Court cases, organizations have participated openly by filing briefs as "friend of the court." They have also played a less noticed role either by aiding individuals in whose name "test cases" have been brought or by providing assistance to government attorneys defending a statute in which the organization has an interest. Particular attention is drawn to the activities of the American Liberty League, the National Consumers' League, and the National Association for the Advancement of Colored People. The practices of these and other organizations have led to controls designed to assure the integrity of the judicial process. It is contended that controls must be applied with caution lest there be interference with freedom of association and with the concomitant rights of access to the courts. . . .

There is a logical relationship of organizational interest in litigation and the importance of courts in forming public policy. Although courts act only in cases between parties with concrete interests at stake, organizations concerned with the impact of the outcome may become quite active participants. Organizations may do this by sponsoring a "test case" brought in the name of a private party, they may aid the government attorney in a case, or they may file a brief as an *amicus curiae* ("friend of the Court"). Considering the importance of the issues resolved by American courts, the entrance of organizations into cases in these ways seems in order. Indeed the essential right of organizations to pursue litigation would appear to follow from the generous attitude of American society

* Clement E. Vose, "Litigation as a Form of Pressure Group Activity," *Annals of the American Academy of Political and Social Science*, Vol. 319, September 1958, pp. 20, 21, 31.

toward the freedom of individuals to form associations for the purpose of achieving common goals. Of course, traditional judicial procedures should be followed and the attorneys for organizations, as well as for individuals, must address their arguments to reason. If these standards of conduct are followed there is no incompatibility between the activity of organizations in litigation and the integrity or independence of the judiciary.

10

YESTERDAY'S CONSTITUTION OR TODAY'S?*

Charles P. Curtis

This discussion by four leading authorities, some of whom we have read previously, pinpoints some of the different points of view about the responsibilities of the Court. Charles Curtis, a Boston attorney and author, argues that the judge should interpret the Constitution in the light of today's public opinion. The other authorities are disturbed by this argument, and suggest other sources for judicial standards. Their examples sum up some of the problems in this area.

To whom is the Constitution addressed? To whom are we speaking? Barring the egregious Dred Scott case, up to 1868 all the acts of Congress which the Supreme Court held unconstitutional related to the organization of the courts. The Constitution was speaking directly to the Court. Since then, the Court has been concerned with other parts of the Constitution which are addressed to other agencies of our government. Here the Court has been exercising a secondary judgment, on a meaning which has already been given to the Constitution by someone who had likewise sworn to support it and who therefore had also a right to construe it.

To be sure, the Court has its own opinion as to what the constitutional words mean, but when they are addressed to someone else, the Court uses its own meaning only for the purpose of comparing it with the meaning already given it by that other. The Court is only a critic who compares a picture for its likeness to the object.

This is one reason why only present current meanings are pertinent. We cannot have our government run as if it were stuck in the end of the eighteenth century, when we are in the middle of the twentieth. It is idle to think that we shall become either better or wiser than we are, or have nobler aspirations than our best, just because our forefathers hoped we would or even intended we should. "What's past is prologue, what to come in yours and my discharge."

This . . . is also the reason why the Court respects what the Congress, or the governmental agency, or the official, thought the proper meaning to be. As much deference is due as is deserved, and it is due as a matter of fact,

* Charles P. Curtis, "The Role of the Constitutional Text," *Supreme Court and Supreme Law*, ed. Edmond Cahn (Bloomington, Ind.: Indiana University Press, 1954), pp. 67–68, 72–75.

not as a presumption of law. The deference depends on the dignity, the local or expert knowledge, and the known wisdom of the official, agency, or legislative authority whose meaning has been brought before the Court for judgment. This makes it all the more inappropriate, even offensive, to judge their meanings by any but current standards.

It is plain, therefore, that any theory of the Court's interpretation of the Constitution must be the same theory on which the other government agencies act, consciously or unconsciously, when they interpret the Constitution for their purposes. The Court cannot fairly compare its own interpretation with theirs unless they are both made to the same pattern and based on the same principles. . . . It must be current, because the interpretations on which the Court is passing judgment are now and immediate. It must be practical, because these official interpretations concern our lives, and meaning and life are intertwined if not inextricable. At the same time and for the same reason, there is no possibility of its being easy to operate. Life is not simple nor do we really want it to be.

John P. Frank: I suspect that the audience like me finds Mr. Curtis an extraordinarily stimulating man. If he were as persuasive on the subject as he is stimulating, I would have nothing to say.

Solely, therefore, for definitional purposes, I would like to direct his attention to three concrete questions and ask him how, in his view of the proper approach to the matter, he would decide those questions or how he approaches them.

In order to test his technique, I will ask him to accept my assumptions as to what the law is or as to what the documents will show. First, take the cruel and unusual punishment clause in the Constitution. It is clear that the punishment of whipping was used almost universally in the eighteenth century and it was a common practice when that clause was adopted. However, at the present time only two states have whipping and only one has it for general purposes.

I would like to know whether in his view the practice of whipping should be held unconstitutional on the ground it may not have been a cruel and unusual punishment in the eighteenth century but it is now.

Curtis: Indeed, yes.

Frank: Let me give you all three because it is a comparison that I want to get. Secondly, let us suppose that we have on the face of the First Amendment an ambiguity which I think is clearly there, and that is: Does the protection of freedom of speech mean to allow for those exceptions which existed in English common law or doesn't it?

This is a disputable point. Let us assume that by no amount of analysis of the words of the First Amendment will we know for sure what was intended (if we care what was intended) in respect of the English common law exceptions. But we do have a complete, detailed, contemporary writing of Madison which shows without any doubt at all that the Amendment was intended not to allow for the English common law exceptions. Do we look to what Madison had to say and to what extent are we bound by it?

Finally, in connection with the impairment of contracts clause, let us suppose that a particular enactment of mortgage moratorium is offered and we know for sure that this is the kind of mortgage moratorium the Founding Fathers meant to preclude by the adoption of the contracts clause. Using Mr. Curtis' techniques, will he tell us what attention, if any, he will pay to the intent and practice of the eighteenth century with regard to each?

Curtis: I think the first one is a very neat example of why I should discard original intention entirely. It is cruel as of the present, and it is unusual. There is no basis for restriction to what was unusual at that time. I should certainly hold whipping unconstitutional, looking for guidance to the present meaning of the word "unusual."

Take your second one, freedom of speech. I should ignore any restrictions put on it by the common law or the practices of the eighteenth century and look rather to what We believe now—I am using "We," as the Constitution does, with a capital W—and I should expect the Supreme Court to pick out the best views and try to give us their version of modern freedom of speech.

Answering your third question, I should ignore the contemporary practice. I would ignore any common law or eighteenth-century notions with respect to mortgage moratoriums.

Edmond Cahn: You would not feel a duty to consult what Madison said on the subject?

Curtis: I should be exceedingly interested in reading it in exactly the same way that I should be interested to read his biography or any other relevant history; but I was asked whether that bound the Supreme Court. To that I say no. . . .

Willard Hurst: I think some of this discussion is unduly abstract because it seems to ignore the fact that when you are talking about constitutional law, you are talking about the balance of power in the community and that the question of how you find meaning boils down concretely here to who finds the meaning.

I say that because I suspect in concrete cases Mr. Curtis and I would not find ourselves far apart, but I think a large part of the difference in formulation boils down to the fact that he is a greater friend of the Court than I am.

It seems to me that his approach is a way of practically reading Article V out of the federal Constitution. The men who wrote the Constitution, after all, included that Article as being as important a part as anything else. They provided a defined, regular procedure for changing or adapting it.

Many times what we are talking about here boils down to the question: Do you want your community policy choices to be made by judges, by legislators, by presidents, or by the electorate? And I stick to my basic distinction that you are dealing with language that sets up a standard. We have set up a way of doing business, which means we are willing to delegate adaptations and adjustments in certain realms to those who hold official power when the adjustment happens to become necessary. Nevertheless, a very basic principle of our constitutionalism is a distrust of official power. Hence I am not anxious to see the category of standards expanded.

We may not like everything to which the men of 1787 commit us. Of course, the world has changed. Nobody wants to run a twentieth-century society according to the eighteenth century. The real issue is who makes the policy choices in the twentieth century: judges or the combination of legislature and electorate that makes constitutional amendments. If you are dealing in an area (like the due process clause) which involves the matter of standards, there we have, for better or worse, committed our fortunes to the current holders of official power at the time the problem arises. So be it! If we are dealing with a question which is not in the realm of standards, we have a different way of dealing with it. Personally I am satisfied with the difference.

11

A TENANT AT SUFFERANCE*

Charles P. Curtis

Charles Curtis calls the Court "tenant at sufferance"—one that must remember that the other branches of government can limit its power. President Roosevelt's famous "Court-packing" plan is one example of a method by which the Court can be brought to heel; in 1958 Senator Jenner and Senator Butler introduced bills that would have limited the Court's jurisdiction over matters involving state powers and internal security. These weapons are always there, and the Court cannot forget it.

. . . The first fact to be recognized is that the Court exercises the doctrine at the sufferance of Congress. To begin with, the very jurisdiction of the Court in all important cases is subject to "Such exceptions and under such regulations as the Congress shall make." That is the language of the Constitution, Article III. To be sure, its original jurisdiction as a court of first instance cannot be taken away from it, but that covers only cases affecting ambassadors, ministers, consuls, and between the states themselves. None of them bring suit very often and when they do it is more important to them than to us. If that were all the business the Court had, the place would be an honorable sinecure for tired lawyers and others, and nobody but themselves would want to write a book about it. It is the Court's appellate jurisdiction that counts, and that is held and exercised at the pleasure of Congress. Congress can even take away the Court's jurisdiction in a case already pending before it. Once Congress did just that, and the Court unanimously agreed that Congress had power to do it.

That was the McCardle case in 1869. McCardle was a Mississippi editor who was arrested and held for trial before a military commission under one of the Reconstruction Acts. After McCardle's case had been argued, Congress apprehended the Court might interfere in a matter of personal liberty. So Congress repealed the section which gave McCardle a right to appeal to the Court. Johnson, stouthearted fellow, vetoed the repeal right in the middle of his impeachment trial but Congress passed it over his veto. And the Court acquiesced. With dry dignity—the grapes were sour—Chief Justice Chase, for a unanimous court, said, "Judicial duty is not less fitly performed by declining ungranted jurisdiction than in exercising firmly that which the Constitution and the laws confer." The Court, he said, was "not at liberty to inquire into the motives of the Legislature." B. R. Curtis, the ex-justice, who had dissented in the Dred Scott case, remarked, "Congress, with the acquies-

* Charles P. Curtis, *Lions Under the Throne* (Boston, Mass.: Houghton Mifflin Company, 1954), pp. 35–38. Reprinted by permission of the publishers.

cence of the country, has subdued the Supreme Court, as well as the President."

Congress sets the times when the Court is to sit. Once, long ago now, in Marshall's time, the Seventh Congress forced the Court to adjourn for over a year. Senator Bayard asked, "May it not lead to the virtual abolition of the Court?" Yet Marshall acquiesced. "The office still remains," he said, "to receive and exercise any new judicial powers which the Legislature may confer."

Congress has complete power over the enforcement of the Court's judgments. The president might use the army to prevent their enforcement, just as he can use the army to enforce the law. . . . If the use of the army against embattled deputy marshals is too fanciful, the power of Congress to cut off appropriations is not. It could do to the Court what it has done to any other department of the government.

Congress has complete authority under the Constitution to fix the number of justices. It has changed the members more than once. Even the American Bar Association admitted that Roosevelt's proposal to Congress in 1937 to increase the Court to fifteen would be constitutional. They denounced it, and the bar cried out, four to one, that it would be "constitutionally immoral." Immoral or not, you will agree, as they did, that it was within the constitutional power of Congress to do it.

Bryce called this "a joint in the court's armour." The Fathers of the Constitution, he said, studied nothing more than to secure the complete independence of the judiciary. The president was not permitted to remove the judges, nor Congress to diminish their salaries. One thing only was either forgotten or deemed undesirable, because highly inconvenient, to determine—the number of judges in the Supreme Court. Here, he said, was a weak point, a joint in the court's armor through which a weapon might some day penetrate. . . .

Bryce asks what prevents such immoral assaults on the fundamental law. Not the mechanism of government, he answers himself, for all its checks have been evaded. Not the conscience of the legislature and the president, for heated combatants seldom shrink from justifying the means by the end. Nothing but the fear of the people, whose broad good sense and attachment to the great principles of the Constitution may generally be relied on to condemn such a perversion of its forms. Yet if excitement has risen high over the country, a majority of the people may acquiesce; and then it matters little whether what is really a revolution be accomplished by openly violating or by merely distorting the forms of law. To the people we come sooner or later, said Bryce, and it is upon their wisdom and self-restraint that the stability of the most cunningly devised scheme of government will in the last resort depend. . . .

12

THE DIMENSIONS OF COURT POWER*

John P. Frank

Under what circumstances does the Court have the most say and under what circumstances the least? Obviously, there are differences depending upon the issues, the times, and the parties involved. Here a former law clerk to Justice Black attempts to evaluate the dimensions of Court power.

In this vast, unruly, undisciplined country of ours, the fact that as few as five men in distant Washington may say that something is to be done does not always automatically mean that it will be done. It is one thing to order, and another to be obeyed. When is the Supreme Court most and when least effective?

The Supreme Court's most obvious effect is on the actual case being decided. When in the case of the West Coast Communists in 1957 the Supreme Court said that certain of the cases should be dismissed, that was the end of the matter, and the cases were dismissed. If in a controversy over money the Court directs payments, generally speaking, the amount will be paid. When at the time of the post-World War II coal strike the Court held that John L. Lewis had to pay a fine of ten thousand dollars, he paid.

The Court is not invariably effective even in the particular or concrete case. Sometimes the situation has changed so drastically that the decision has no effect, as when the Court decided a case about a criminal who had been drowned in an escape attempt while the decision was pending. No one had bothered to inform the Court of this. If a lower court is determined to frustrate the Supreme Court and takes the bit in its teeth, on occasion it may successfully do so; and occasionally when the order of the Court is not effectively carried out, the matter may be abandoned because of either lack of funds or declining interest. A few years ago the Supreme Court of Nebraska decided against a prisoner on a particular ground. The Supreme Court of the United States reversed that decision. Thereupon the Supreme Court of Nebraska took the matter up again and redecided the case against the petitioner on some other ground that, for technical reasons, was beyond the Supreme Court's reach. This is not a unique example. Nonetheless, day in and day out, it may be expected that most of the time the Court will have its way in the particular case.

To illustrate the general effectiveness of the Court: when it declares an act of Congress unconstitutional, that ends it. The lower courts thereafter will not enforce the statute in other cases. Again, if the Supreme Court

---

* John P. Frank, *Marble Palace: The Supreme Court in American Life* (New York: Alfred A. Knopf, Inc., 1958), pp. 20–22, 24–25, 27–29, 35–37, 40–41.

uses its rule-making power to make general rules for the conduct of cases, there will be an effort on the part of all the lower courts to obey such rules. . . . Also, when well-publicized general principles of law are announced by the Supreme Court, the lower courts commonly attempt to apply them. A good current example is the ruling of the Supreme Court on the duty of the government to produce reports made to the government by its own eyewitnesses. The widespread publicity given to the decision resulted in the general application of the rule all over the country.

But this acceptance and enforcement of Supreme Court general principles by the other courts of the country is far from universal. There is an imperfect bridge between the 100 to 200 opinions filed by the Supreme Court and the 160,000 new cases filed in the lower federal courts in a year.

The illustrations just given in which the Supreme Court has been undoubtedly effective are cases in which it has enunciated well-publicized, broad, general principles. If the principles are less broadly stated or less well publicized, there is the solid practical possibility that the lower-court judges may never know that they exist. The trial and appellate judges of the country by no means carry the teachings of the 350 or more volumes of the United States Supreme Court Reports in their heads, nor do they commonly stand anxiously at the mailbox to receive the new wisdom ground out weekly. If a principle is not called to its attention by counsel, the lower court may not know that it exists.

Particularly when the Supreme Court sets off on some new course or opens up some new subject, it may take reversal after reversal to get the word about the country. A few years ago the Court enunciated certain principles on the respective powers of the state versus the national government in the field of labor relations. How those principles should be applied to concrete cases was not wholly clear. In 1957, the high courts of Idaho, Ohio, Utah, and California were each reversed for not following the earlier decisions. Now they know. But sometimes the matter never gets back to the Supreme Court. Remember that something under two per cent of all the cases started in the federal system ever gets to the federal appellate courts, and only a small fraction of those goes the rest of the way to the Supreme Court. As a result of the mammoth size of the country, Supreme Court decisions on lesser points may be ignored. . . .

Perhaps the greatest single failure of the Supreme Court is in relation to the patent system. In the running war between the Patent Office and the Supreme Court, there are zealots for each side. In turning to it now it is necessary to put aside altogether the question of whether one *likes* the Supreme Court approach or the Patent Office approach. The sole question here is whether the Supreme Court is able to make the Patent Office respond to its mandates.

* * *

The problem arises in determining what is patentable and what is not. Real, honest-to-God inventions should have patents; this is what the system is meant to encourage. On the other hand, mere imitative gimmicks or copies of other men's work should not have patents, because each patent operates as a tax on the public that pays the royalties, and this the public should pay only when it gets a fair return. If someone believes that the Patent Office has made a mistake and that it has given a patent for something which is not really an invention at all, then the courts and eventually the Supreme Court must decide whether the patent is good.

There is your war. The Court's standard of invention, or of what it considers patentable, is infinitely higher than the standard of the Patent Office. For example, the Court invalidated a patent on a three-sided wooden frame used by cashiers in supermarkets to pull groceries forward in order to ring them up. That the gadget is useful, no one doubts. That it is an invention in the sense that the telegraph and the combustion engine and the radio are inventions, no one believes. . . .

For the last forty years the Supreme Court has regularly invalidated far more patents than it has upheld, and from 1936 to 1940 it held thirteen patents invalid and none valid. . . .

To sum it up, in the war between the Patent Office and the Supreme Court, the Supreme Court has lost. Almost incessantly for a hundred years the Court has attempted to raise the standard of invention. Yet it is more than probable that in the year 1958 ten thousand new patents will be issued which, to paraphrase Justice Jackson, would be invalid if the Supreme Court could get its hands on them.

The Court has been more successful in maintaining a free flow of interstate commerce. The United States of America is one of the largest free-trade areas in the world. There are practical impediments on this free flow of commerce; for example, the freight rates may be rigged to favor one section as against another. However, at least some possible extra charges are knocked off because this is one big country instead of [fifty] little ones.

* * *

The segregation cases are a measure of the effectiveness of a Court in a highly turbulent situation. The decision followed from twenty to thirty years of national examination of the country's greatest internal problem. Large sections of the country were morally vibrant to the issue, and an overwhelming majority of Americans felt a sense of wrong about segregation. The Supreme Court's decision put the Court at the head of a moral force, and by the same token added its weight to the increase of that force, so that in the so-called fringe areas, such as the District of Columbia, Kentucky, and parts of Kansas and Missouri, segregation stopped. A little farther to the south, in Tennessee and Arkansas, segregation began to crumble. This by itself is a great deal. The hard core remains, to date, thoroughly stirred up but not as yet practically affected by the ruling from Washington.

To sum up: The Court normally can decide the case before it, and that conclusively. Exceptional situations exist, but they are rare. When the Court lays down broad general principles, clear and decisive, as when it declares a law unconstitutional, its mandate is widely effective. When the decision, though more minute, governs a cooperative agency of government, it is also likely to be effective.

But when the Court moves into an area of highly qualified decisions in which cases depend on fine details, then the effectiveness of the Court is largely dependent upon the responsiveness and cooperation of the lower courts, agencies, or legislative bodies that must apply the Court's general principles. The Court has power, and great power, but it is no puppet-master pulling the strings of American life.

13

THE COURTS CANNOT SAVE DEMOCRACY*

Robert Jackson

The position that judicial review dilutes democratic responsibility and encourages a "let the judges take care of it" attitude among the public was advanced long ago by J. B. Thayer of Harvard Law School. In a posthumously published work, the late Justice Jackson here argues for judicial restraint to encourage a sense of responsibility on the part of the majority.

That the Supreme Court, in some instances, can interpose judicial authority between political forces and those whose liberty they would override is a great distinction from those governments abroad which have been subverted by dictatorship. But I have tried to point out that while our judiciary is an effective instrument for applying to the case of an individual the just laws enacted by representatives of a freedom-respecting society, it has grave jurisdictional, procedural, and political shortcomings. These counsel against leaving the protection of liberty wholly to the judiciary, while heedlessly allowing the elected branches of the government to be constituted without regard to their members' attitudes toward liberty.

Let us take the factor of delay. Since the Court may pronounce a judgment of unconstitutionality only in deciding a case or controversy, obviously it cannot take the initiative in checking what the justices may know to be constitutional violations. It has no self-starting capacity and must await the action of some litigant so aggrieved as to have a justiciable case. Also, its pronouncement must await the decision in the lower courts. Often it is years after a statute is put on the books and begins to take effect before a decision on a constitutional question can be heard by the Supreme Court. The Smith Act of 1940 was held constitutional for the first time in 1951, and the Alien Registration Act, also of 1940, was passed on in 1952. The run of constitutional litigation, like that of all litigations, is slow and costly.

Such delays often mean that the damage is done before the remedy for invasion of civil liberties is available. For example: In 1951 the Court cast serious doubt upon the legality of the Attorney General's list of subversive organizations promulgated in 1947. But the list had long been widely circulated and accepted, and despite the Court's views it has never ceased to be used in the press, in the executive department, by and before congressional committees, and even in courts to prejudice individuals in their liberty, position, and good name. . . .

---

* Robert Jackson, *The Supreme Court in the American System of Government* (Cambridge, Mass.: Harvard University Press, 1955), pp. 24–25, 59, 80–82. © 1955 by William Eldred Jackson and G. Bowdoin Craighill, Jr., Executors. Reprinted by permission of the publishers.

Then, too, many of the most vital acts of government cannot be challenged at all by the case and controversy route, because the questions are political or involve the spending power, foreign affairs, or the war power. The Supreme Court is a tribunal of limited jurisdiction, narrow processes, and small capacity for handling mass litigation; it has no force to coerce obedience, and is subject to being stripped of jurisdiction or smothered with additional justices any time such a disposition exists and is supported strongly enough by public opinion. I think the Court can never quite escape consciousness of its own infirmities, a psychology which may explain its apparent yielding to expediency, especially during war time. . . .

If an organized society wants the kind of justice that an independent, professional judicial establishment is qualified to administer, our judiciary is certainly a most effective instrument for applying law and justice to individual cases and for cultivating public attitudes which rely upon law and seek justice. But I know of no modern instance in which any judiciary has saved a whole people from the great currents of intolerance, passion, usurpation, and tyranny which have threatened liberty and free institutions. The Dred Scott decision did not settle the question of the power to end slavery, and I very much doubt that had Mr. Justice McLean not dissented in that case it would have done any more to avoid war. No court, whatever its powers, could have saved Louis XVI or Marie Antoinette. None could have avoided the French Revolution, none could have stopped its excesses, and none could have prevented its culmination in the dictatorship of Napoleon. In Germany a courageous court refused to convict those whom the Nazi government sought to make the scapegoats for the Reichstag fire, clandestinely set by the Nazis themselves, and other courts decreed both the Nazi and Communist parties to be illegal under German law. Those judgments fell on deaf ears and became dead letters because the political forces at the time were against them.

It is not idle speculation to inquire which comes first, either in time or importance, an independent and enlightened judiciary or a free and tolerant society. Must we first maintain a system of free political government to assure a free judiciary or can we rely on an aggressive, activist judiciary to guarantee free government? While each undoubtedly is a support for the other, and the two are frequently found together, it is my belief that the attitude of a society and of its organized political forces, rather than its legal machinery, is the controlling force in the character of free institutions.

I am a fairly consistent reader of British newspapers. I have been repeatedly impressed with the speed and certainty with which the slightest invasion of British individual freedom or minority rights by officials of the government is picked up in Parliament, not merely by the opposition but by the party in power, and made the subject of persistent questioning, criticism, and sometimes rebuke. There is no waiting on the theory that the judges will take care of it. In this country, on the contrary, we rarely have a political issue made of any kind of invasion of civil liberty. On the contrary, district attorneys who have been rebuked by the courts are frequently promoted by the public. The attitude seems to be, leave it to the judges. Years after the event takes place, the judges make their pronouncement, often in the form of letting some admittedly guilty person go, and that ends the matter. In Great Britain, to observe civil liberties is good politics and to transgress the rights of the individual or the minority is bad politics. In the United States, I cannot say that this is so. Whether the political conscience is relieved because the responsibility here is made largely a legal one, I cannot say, but of this I am sure: any court which undertakes by its legal processes to enforce civil liberties needs the support of an enlightened and vigorous public opinion which will be intelligent and discriminating as to what cases really are civil liberties cases and what questions really are involved in those cases. I do not think the American public is enlightened on this subject.

14

CAN THE SUPREME COURT DEFEND CIVIL LIBERTIES?*

Edmond Cahn

Edmond Cahn is one of the leading authorities on American law. His work is regarded as among the most brilliant and profound writings on the American legal scene. He is also a firm defender of the "preferred freedoms" wing of the Court.

In recent years, innumerable speeches and articles, not to mention Justice Robert H. Jackson's posthumous book, have been devoted to contending that the Supreme Court can do little or nothing. Most of this literature sounds like the querulous excuses of a hypochondriac. Back in 1935 and 1936, the court drank some raw wine and woke up with a bad headache in 1937. You would think the hangover would have ended by now, but such is not the case. On the contrary, the memories of the 1930s still haunt many of the justices. They keep wringing their hands over the court's impotence, while they tell us that unlike Congress, it must sit and wait for cases to come before it, that unlike Congress it cannot launch its own investigations, and that it must depend on other branches of the government to define its appellate jurisdiction and enforce its decrees. Justice Jackson said that no court decree could have stopped the downfall of the French monarchy or the onslaught of the French Revolution, as though he believed that our conditions were similar to those of Paris in 1789 and as though our Secretary of Agriculture had looked unsympathetically at some starving employees of General Motors and said "Let them eat cake."

Of course, the Supreme Court must function like a court; it cannot perform the operations of a legislature. Of course, like all governmental institutions, there are limits to its powers. But Congress and the President do

* Edmond Cahn, "Can the Supreme Court Defend Civil Liberties?" Pamphlet No. 9, Sidney Hillman Foundation, n.d., pp. 7–8, 15–18.

not refuse to perform their duties just because they cannot also act like a court. We know and the court knows it *can* act forcefully and courageously when it wills to. It has done so on many occasions, for example, in the steel seizure case and very recently in the school segregation cases.

FOUR WAYS TO SAY NO

A hypochondriac can gradually convince himself that day by day he is able to do less and less. Then, if he is a really imaginative hypochondriac, he will find a complicated variety of ways to say "No, I can't." There are at least four technical ways for the Supreme Court to say "no" without appearing to do so. (1) It can say the party who is trying to present the question to it has no standing to sue. In other words, the question may be an important question, but the party who poses it is not the right party. (2) The court can say the proceeding is not a true "case or controversy" and is, therefore, not within its power under the Constitution. (3) It can say the question in the case is a "political question," which means that the executive or legislative or perhaps the electorate must find the answer, not the courts. (4) In the majority of instances, the Supreme Court can simply refuse to take the case at all, without publishing any explanation. Most of the Supreme Court's appellate jurisdiction is taken or refused at the justices' option by granting or denying a writ of *certiorari*. . . .

THE CLASH ON THE SUPREME COURT

On the present Supreme Court, there is comparatively little disagreement about the constitutionality of federal economic and social legislation; that is no longer the problem. But when a case involves freedom of personal and political expression, that is to say, a right under the First Amendment, then philosophy clashes against philosophy. The majoritarian justices acknowledge that the First Amendment is couched in absolute and categorical terms, forbidding *any* abridgement of free expression, whether reasonable or unreasonable. Nevertheless, majoritarian justices take a neutral, laissez-faire attitude toward laws abridging free expression if they can find some "reasonable" ground for the legislation.

The libertarians emphasize the absolute language of the First Amendment, which says that Congress shall make "no law" abridging these freedoms. They say that there are three basic reasons why this language is so very absolute: (1) Some of the rights of free expression, such as worshipping God and forming one's private opinions, cannot become the proper business or concern of any government; (2) without active exchange of information and ideas, a society stagnates and ultimately loses its freedom; and (3) representative government needs the criticism of a free press and free debate so that the people may be able to make informed decisions. This is the libertarian philosophy.

In one important field of constitutional law, the Supreme Court's majoritarians do follow the principles of the libertarians. I refer, of course, to the rights of Negroes to equal protection of the laws. We have made such magnificent, though—Heaven knows—belated, strides toward racial equality in the past generation because on this front the *whole* court has adopted a libertarian view. As libertarian justices see it, this record shows that the court need not surrender fundamental American ideals, or follow a laissez-faire policy, or exhibit an abject humility when it comes to deal with the enemies of freedom. If, in the teeth of prejudice and passion, the court can uphold equal protection of the laws, why is not the Jeffersonian philosophy likewise applicable when First Amendment liberties are attacked, or when security procedures violate elementary standards of fairness?

THE U.S. AND ENGLAND

There is another string to the majoritarian bow. They like to point to the superiority of the English system, under which Parliament is supreme and the courts possess no right of constitutional review. The majoritarians claim that Americans rely too much on the Supreme Court to protect their liberties, and thus become lazy and flaccid. In England, we are told, they order these things better. Since Englishmen cannot turn to the courts to invalidate an act of Parliament, the newspapers speak up more actively and the House of Commons is peculiarly sensitive to any infringement of liberty or miscarriage of justice. Thus, it is claimed, the English system reposes genuine trust in the people. . . .

HALF A LOAF

The difficulty with the majoritarians is that they are trying to graft an incomplete slice of the English system on ours. They don't say, "Let us change to a parliamentary government, headed by a prime minister who will be subject, along with the other heads of departments, to regular scrutiny at a 'question hour.'" They don't say that, if the legislature censures a minister's action, the whole government will resign. Thus the majoritarians are proposing to take away one of our major protections—the Supreme Court's intervention—without putting anything in its stead. After a century and a half of relying on the Supreme Court as one, though of course not the only, means of defense, why should we acquiesce in its abandoning the function unless we are provided with some equivalent shield for our rights?

Finally, which philosophy puts more trust in the people? The majoritarians claim it is theirs, because they follow a policy of laissez-faire toward the people's elected representatives, and refuse to accord a preferred position to First Amendment freedoms. Here I think is the very nucleus of their error. When a problem arises under the First Amendment, it may appear on the surface as though the majoritarians favor deferring to the people and the libertarians favor defying the people.

On deeper analysis, we discover precisely the contrary. For what happens when a majoritarian court yields to legislative excitement in a First Amendment case? The restrictive law or administrative order becomes effective and reduces the people's access to information and opinion. What happens when a libertarian view prevails and such a law is struck down? Then the channels of information and persuasion are kept open, and the people remain free to examine, evaluate, and decide for themselves. Real confidence in the people will give them credit for capacity to reject Communist propaganda and Communist advocacy. If the mass of Americans were so myopic that they could not be trusted to see the conspicuous folly and falsity of Communist advocacy, the republic would indeed be in a hopeless state. It is the libertarians who have a genuine and robust faith in the people and in the republic. . . .

15

THE HIGH COURT'S ROLE IN POLICY*

The news clipping here reprinted summarizes a study by Robert Dahl of Yale University attempting to assess the political conditions under which the Court may flourish. The point of view here is an interesting supplement to the idea that a political conflict determines the question of Court influence.

Washington, Sept. 30—Two questions that have arisen in the minds of many Americans, particularly in the South, about the Supreme Court these past few years are:

1. Can the court really make new national policy, and make it stick even if it is widely disapproved?

2. What can a disapproving citizenry do to reverse or modify new policies set by the court? And with what chance of success?

Question number 1 has been studied of late by an expert, and his findings have been published in the Journal of Public Law, issued by the Emory University Law School in Atlanta.

In this study, Dr. Robert A. Dahl, a Yale University Professor of Political Science, analyzed what had happened in the seventy-eight cases in which the high tribunal, in its history up to 1957, had struck down as unconstitutional eight-seven (sic) provisions of federal law.

There were instances in which the court was changing policy fixed by Congress and, in nearly every case, approved by the President.

DECISIONS MODIFIED

No fewer than twenty-six times Congress passed new legislation that had the effect of reversing the court. In other instances the situation itself changed, and the new court policy was unimportant. Or, several times, the court modified its own earlier decisions.

This led Dr. Dahl to the conclusion that the policy views of the court never remain for long out of line with the policy views of the lawmaking majority. And he noted that to have a strong lawmaking majority, Congress and the White House must be controlled by the same party.

He found that, on rare occasion, the court could "delay the application" of policy up to twenty-five years. But, he said, it is most likely to be successful when faced with a "weak" lawmaking majority. And, he added, "by itself the court is about powerless to effect the course of national policy."

Dr. Dahl said he felt the court had got by so far with its school segregation decision of 1954 because of an unusual situation in political leadership. He said, in effect, that advocates of school integration while "not strong enough to get what they wanted enacted by Congress, still were and are powerful enough to prevent any suc-

---

* "High Court's Role in Policy Studied: Bench and Congress Never Split Permanently on an Issue, Survey Finds," *The New York Times*, October 5, 1958.

cessful attack on the legislative powers of the court."

This leads to the second question: What can be done?

If Dr. Dahl is right about pro-integration strength, present attempts to limit the appellate jurisdiction of the court are doomed to failure.

In certain limited areas—such as spelling out that Congress must specify that a new federal law is to supersede state laws on the same subject before the High Court can rule that Congress intended to do so—Congress may well curb the court.

History shows that presidents over a period of years have exerted powerful influence over the court. This is due, obviously, to their power of nomination (which usually amounts to appointments) of new High Court justices.

XI

The Politics of Agriculture

Throughout most of our history the farmer stood as a symbol of rugged individualism—a free agent who neither asked nor received aid from government. In our tradition he is the pioneer, the trail-blazer, the man who tamed a continent and made it flourish. With his family (a close economic unit) he was, in the American myth, self-sufficient and far removed from the crass commercialism of urban life.

Upon close examination, however, this symbolic picture dissolves into a maze of complicated issues. In recent decades, for example, agriculture has become a chronic invalid within the national economy. Farm population has steadily declined. Land concentration continues apace, to the extent that it is sometimes alleged that the family farm is disappearing. Mechanization and research have produced an embarrassing surplus of many farm products. In the midst of this plenty, farm income has fallen and the farmer receives a smaller share of the consumer's dollar.

Today the so-called "farm problem" is deeply enmeshed in our domestic and foreign policy. Both Democrats and Republicans woo the farm vote with carefully drafted farm planks. In congressional halls there is much debate over such issues as "parity," "soil bank," "acreage allotments," "cost-sharing programs," and "surplus commodities." The relationship between modern agriculture and government is a close if uneasy alliance. Farm problems, therefore, are in part political problems.

In this chapter we shall examine certain basic issues involved in the politics of agriculture. First, we will explore the roots of agricultural discontent —the changing economy and the revolution in production which have created many of the political problems.

Second, we will examine current farm policy in the United States and the criticism of that policy. In this section falls the debate over such issues as parity, the soil bank, restrictions on production, and conservation of our soil and water resources.

Finally, we will explore new policies being urged in government circles and by the spokesmen for agriculture—such policies as "cross compliance," relocation and rehabilitation of "surplus" farmers, and a "two-price" system.

What Are the Roots of Agricultural Discontent?

Many farm problems can be traced to a revolution in production that has swept over rural America during the past thirty years. In these three decades farm efficiency has risen tremendously, almost completely destroying the time-honored relationship that existed between men, draft animals, machines, and capital investment. This revolution (whose basic components are the new chemicals, improved animal breeding, hybrid seeds, and a multitude of complex, efficient machines) has made it possible to cut the farm share of the labor force to 8 per cent (productivity per farm worker has doubled since 1930); it has dethroned the horse as the major source of farm power; it has eliminated one-third of all farmers while boosting total output; it has radically altered the capital requirements of agriculture, so that the average farm worker now requires a capital investment of between $14,000–$60,000. Most ironically, too, the farmer, in the midst of this abundance, has seen his net income fall in the face of continuous national inflation.

The fury of the farm revolution has not abated. Some evidence exists that it has not yet reached its peak. Is the family farm to be replaced by corporate enterprise? Such an organization as the United States Wheat Corporation of Harding, Montana, for example, that annually harvests 95,000 acres of wheat (150 square miles)? Or Adams Bros. and Company of Iowa that harvests 6500 acres of corn?

Should Americans welcome without question the shifts in agriculture that the last three decades have wrought? Would a sweeping reduction in the number of farmers and still greater efficiency solve the farm problem? Or would it result in more unmanageable surpluses? Is farming a "way of life" or should it be judged solely in economic terms? Or is it the root stock of most solid American virtues? These questions and others are unanswered as the United States approaches her second centennial of the Declaration of Independence.

What Direction Should a New Farm Policy Take?

Many Americans have the uneasy feeling that present farm policies are a palliative, rather than a cure. Have present policies solved the problem of land concentration and the disappearance of the small farmer? Some would answer that the process has been speeded up. Have surpluses been reduced by the Soil Bank and acreage allotments? The answer is debatable. Do commodities stored by the government protect the free market price, or do they hang like a great depressant over it? Has the concept of parity actually given farmers equality of status in the free market? Critics point to current farm prices as their answer.

Obviously, it is much easier to criticize current policies than to propose alternatives. Suppose that government were to withdraw entirely from the farm scene. Most observers believe that half of all present farmers could be "busted" in five years by the free operation of natural economic laws. Should government policy be chiefly geared toward an orderly transfer of these less able farmers into our industrial society—perhaps with training programs and re-employment aid? Can anyone justify the preservation of the inefficient, high-unit-cost farmers? Is the Jeffersonian ideal outmoded in the modern world?

Consider another issue. Currently we have an economy of abundance—we are buried in an avalanche of unwanted food and fibre. Yet on the world scene perhaps two-thirds of all people are chronically ill-clothed and ill-nourished. Do we have at our disposal a foreign policy "ace" which we do not play effectively? What of the two-price system, under which farmers would sell most goods in a protected, high-price, domestic market and government would sell the surplus abroad at competitive world prices?

Furthermore, what of our own population? Is the current abundance only temporary? Since 1900 our population has increased by 120,000,000—from 75 to 195 million. Probably by 1975 we shall have 30 million more people. At what point, if any, will the race between human fertility and technology be won by the former? Is it possible that our chief aim today should be the storing of soil fertility in acres that are temporarily idle?

Other questions might be posed. But at this point, after examining the following articles, the student has reached the present frontiers of our social inventiveness. The dimensions of the "farm problem" should now be clear. "Easy" solutions are not to be found. But in one sense the problem has unique qualities. Throughout all of recorded history, man has struggled with scarcity and hunger. Only in twentieth-century America has the issue become surpluses and abundance. Compared to the earlier problem, our present difficulty is modest and not a true crisis in the older sense.

1

FEWER FARMS, FEWER FARMERS*

The basic source of many farm problems is an overabundance of products resulting from the technological revolution that has swept over rural America in the last decades. From the research laboratories have come such products as hybrid corn that tripled production. Fertilizer use has quadrupled in twenty years: the use of chemicals has increased by twelvefold. But the great revolution has been the development and adoption of machines as a substitute for horse and man power.

Changes in the structure of agriculture in the United States have continued at an accelerated rate in recent years. In some cases these changes began a century or more ago.

In 1959 there were only 3.7 million farms in the nation, 23 per cent less than in 1954 and the smallest number for any census year since 1870. The proportion of the nation's labor force engaged in agriculture has declined in each decade since 1820, dropping from 72 per cent of the total in that year to about 8 per cent in 1959.

The declining use of labor in agriculture has been achieved through technological changes which have occurred at varying rates throughout the history of the nation and have been very rapid in recent years.

The number of farms in the nation declined from 4.8 million in 1954 to 3.7 million in 1959. Although 232 thousand of the 1.1 million drop can be attributed to a change in definition of a farm, even under the old definition the number was down 18 per cent, a greater decline than had occurred in any previous five-year period recorded by the census.

The number of farms in the nation rose from 1.4 million to 5.7 million during the last half of the nineteenth century and reached a plateau in excess of 6 million in the early 1900's. The total held near this level until the 1930's, when a "back-to-the-farm" movement in the early depression years pushed the total up to a peak of 6.8 million in 1935. A decline has occurred during each interim census period since that time, with a greater rate of decline in the Fifties than in earlier years. By 1959 the total was about one-half the level of a quarter of a century earlier.

The average size of farms in the United States almost doubled between 1935 and 1959, increasing from 155 to 302 acres. Size of farms has trended upward since 1880, but the rate of increase has accelerated in recent years. During the entire 55 years from 1880 to 1935 the average size of farm increased 16 per cent, while the rate of increase was about 12 per cent for each five-year period from 1935 through 1954 and 25 per cent in the period 1954 to 1959.

While the number of farm workers

---

* Condensed from "Changes in the Structure of Agriculture," *Monthly Review*, Federal Reserve Bank of St. Louis (Sept. 1961), pp. 6–11.

declined 42 per cent from 1935 to 1959, the total civilian labor force increased 31 per cent. In 1935 almost 20 per cent of the labor force was engaged in agriculture. In 1959 about 8 per cent was similarly employed.

In addition to the substantial decline in the number of farm workers, relatively more farmers work off their farms than formerly. While some of this employment is work on other farms, it is believed that the greater part is nonfarm work. More than 30 per cent of all farm operators worked off their farms 100 days or more in 1959. In comparison, 28 per cent worked off their farms a similar number of days in 1954 and only 23 per cent in 1949.

Technological change has come into play on a wider scale and with a greater impact on the industry. The trend toward mechanization has continued at an increasing rate as more labor-saving devices and larger equipment and power units have been introduced. This is a major force working toward fewer farm workers and larger farms. In 1959 one worker, in addition to performing more off-farm work, farmed an average of 192 acres compared to an average of 104 acres per worker in 1935.

This ability to farm more acres has been a force working toward larger farms. Full owners have obtained additional acres either by purchasing or renting. Greater output per acre and per animal unit have also been factors tending to reduce the number of farm workers. Approximately the same amount of labor is required for basic operations in the fields with livestock on mechanized farms regardless of the level of output per unit. Thus, when production per acre or per animal rises, output per worker increases proportionately.

In recent years crop output per acre has been pushed up substantially. Total crop production per acre averaged 63 per cent higher in the three years 1958–1960 than in the decade of the Thirties. Better seed, increased fertilization, better disease and insect control, and irrigation have been major yield-increasing factors. With the increased yields and government crop control programs, marginal acres have been removed from crop production, further increasing average output per acre and per man.

2

AGRIBUSINESS IN THE MACHINE AGE*

Earl L. Butz

Frequently the upheaval in American agriculture is viewed in nostalgic terms that mourn the disappearance of old family homesteads, harvest suppers, and shady lanes. The following article rejects this approach and celebrates the fact that "agriculture is changing from a way of living to a way of making a living." To underscore this change, the author uses a coined word "agribusiness."

Agriculture is now in the middle of its third great revolution. Agricultural engineers have had a big part in all three revolutions.

The first revolution came in the middle of the nineteenth century, when we began to substitute animal energy for human energy. The invention of the reaper is the best-known event associated with it. This and other developments called for considerable retooling in agriculture. They increased output per worker on farms and started us on the path of feeding our growing nation with a constantly shrinking proportion of our total population in the field. Agriculture began to take on some characteristics of a commercial enterprise, although sometimes the change was almost imperceptible.

The second great revolution began in the 1920's, with the substitution of mechanical energy for animal energy. It likewise increased the commercialization of agriculture, shifted a number of production functions off the farm, increased output per worker substantially, and resulted in a further reduction in the proportion of our total working population on farms.

The third revolution is the undergirding of agricultural production and marketing with vast amounts of science, technology, and business management. This revolution is transferring still additional production and marketing functions off the farm and continues to underscore the importance of specialization at all levels of the agribusiness complex.

Agricultural historians a generation hence may characterize the decade of the 1950's as the decade of the scientific breakthrough. In this decade we experienced an unprecedented number of discoveries, which have changed all [facets of] agriculture. . . .

The decade of the 1960's opens with the march of agricultural science in full stride. Agriculture is changing from a way of living to a way of making a living. It is changing from a business of arts and crafts to a business undergirded with large amounts of science and technology.

It is *wrong* to think of agriculture as a declining industry.

* Extracted from Earl L. Butz, "Agribusiness In The Machine Age," *Power To Produce, The Yearbook of Agriculture, 1960* (Washington, D.C.: United States Government Printing Office, 1961), pp. 380, 381, 382, 383.

American agriculture is an expanding industry in every important respect except one—the number of people required to run our farms. Our agricultural plant each year uses more capital, more science and technology, more managerial capacity, more purchased production inputs, more specialized marketing facilities, and more research than the year before.

We do not think of air transportation as a declining industry just because a pilot in a jet airliner can now take 100 passengers from coast to coast in half a day, compared with 20 passengers in a day and a half two decades ago. This, like agriculture, is a strong and growing industry.

Although a smaller share of our total population is engaged directly in farming, the agricultural industry is big, broad, and basic. Of 68 million persons employed in America in 1960, about 26 million worked somewhere in agriculture—8 million worked on farms, 7 million produced goods and services purchased by farmers, and 11 million processed and distributed farm products. Hence, almost two-fifths of all our employed people are engaged in work related to agriculture.

The declining trend in farm population is itself a sign of a strong agriculture. Brainpower has replaced horsepower as the essential ingredient on our farms. The total United States agricultural output increased by two-thirds in the past two decades, while the number of farmworkers declined some 3 million. This means that production per worker on our farms has doubled in the past 20 years. This remarkable increase in production efficiency can be matched by no other major sector of the American economy.

Progress of this kind can be continued only if we have capable and well-informed men on our farms. We will need fewer farmers in the future, but they must be better. They will be operating on a fast track, and the race will go to the swift. . . .

Today's farm production is a synthesis of several scientific disciplines.

The earning capacity of the average farmer used to be limited primarily by his physical strength and the amount of work he could do. He substituted some animal muscle for human muscle, but not a great deal. He substituted very little mechanical energy for muscle power. Agriculture was primarily a means of converting muscle energy into farm produce.

Human energy is much less important in today's farm operation. Energy can be purchased so much more cheaply than it can be provided by man. Today's farm operator is a combination manager-applicator of the life sciences, the physical sciences, and the social sciences. The research undergirding modern agriculture ranges all the way from physics to physiology, from biology to business. It is just as complex and just as far on the periphery of knowledge as is the research done in the laboratories of the nuclear scientist, for example.

The first claim of any society upon its total production resources is to get enough food to keep the population alive and well. This is true in primitive societies, in semi-developed societies, and in highly developed societies. We do this so efficiently in this country that almost nine-tenths of our population is available to produce the wide variety of goods and services that make up the American standard of living.

3

THE VANISHING FAMILY FARM*

Eric Sevareid

What the technological revolution in farming means in terms of disappearing farmers is reported here as it affects one neighborhood. Converted to statistics, it means that farm population has declined *by 15,000,000 since 1930—while the total population has* increased *by 75,000,000. The revolution described here is still in progress. At what point farm population will eventually stabilize is an open question.*

Beneath the surface of policy quarrels over stopgap measures, a profound change is coming over agricultural life in the country. It may be progress, it may just be inevitable, but it does have its tragic aspects, and it is happening with remarkable rapidity. An American way of life as old as our deepest traditions is passing away. The source spring of much of our moral outlook, our conceptions of individualism, our politics, our folklore is drying up. The small family-sized farm and farm-family life are vanishing, as fast as the Indian villages vanished a century ago. And America is never going to be quite the same.

Almost everywhere one sees this unstoppable tide of change. Three family farms adjoin the small weekend property this reporter maintains in the foothills of the Virginia Blue Ridge. One, of some three hundred acres, has just been inherited by an ex-G.I. farmer with a large family. He will try to sell, and then rent a much larger farm in order to make ends meet. The next farm, about a hundred acres, is still run by the 75-year-old man who has lived there all his life. He still works dawn to dusk, owns nothing approaching a luxury; sons in the city support him.

The third farm, about a hundred and thirty acres, is also operated by an intensely hard-working dirt farmer and his efficient wife; they have no phone, no car, and all expenses are pared to a spartan minimum. His gross cash income last year was four hundred dollars.

Generations of children grew up on these three farms, but the end has come. No small farmers will buy these places when their owners die out, for no profit is possible. They will all end up, eventually, as part of great properties owned by corporations or by city businessmen who can make farming pay on a very large scale or who will run them for tax deduction purposes.

Now this is not the best farming land in the country, but the same thing is happening in the best soil regions. You get an idea from a year-long study just published by the Farmers' Union Grain Terminal Association in Saint Paul. They studied 4300 fam-

* Eric Sevareid, from a CBS news broadcast.

ily-run farms in good farming country —Wisconsin, Minnesota, the Dakotas, and Montana.

Here are some of their findings: Net income before taxes in 1954 was $2500 —that means $50 a week. To net this much required, from the family, about 5000 working hours in the year, more than twice the standard for most city workers. If you figured a 5 per cent return on investment, then it would come out to $450 for the whole year, earned by labor alone. While home construction booms around every great city, very few new farm homes have been built in 35 years.

In these five farm states, in a five-year period, 38,000 farm homes have disappeared. That means one family in thirteen gave up the life they had tried to live. This rate of failure seems to be on the increase.

In that region, as in back-country Virginia, the story is the same: The independent farmer and his family are leaving the land; the home is vanishing and the business office is taking over.

4

POVERTY ON THE LAND*

John Stanley

Rural America is a study in economic contrasts and extremes—from shiny Cadillacs and sleek cattle to corn bread, grits and subsistence farming. The following description is an accurate portrait of impoverished rural America—the 30 per cent of farmers who produce only 3 per cent of agricultural sales. For this group such issues as parity payments and the soil bank are remote. Unless they have part-time jobs, these people are almost completely outside our present money economy.

The shower of snow mutes the ragged outlines of a farm that embarrasses the hopeful, willing country in New York and Kentucky and Maine and the rest of the states. The snow is both a promise of suffering and its alleviation; at least there will be water now after the long summer that has dried up the shallow spring up the hill; but with snow will come the cold wind that cuts its way through the thin boards. The family will huddle around the kitchen range, and the children will whine and the parents will scold—it will be a situation that is beyond homework and no one will want to go to the wintry cold bedrooms. Everyone will be longing for rest; there will be the dry fatigue that always comes from a constant diet of thin food, unsatisfying clothes and a steadily deteriorating situation.

Every decade millions leave this sort of thing and move into town. They are as worn out as the land they leave behind them. They realize that they are not receiving their share of what this

* John Stanley, "Poverty on the Land," *The Commonweal*, November 18, 1955, pp 161–63.

country has to offer. They feel like an out-group, they're not as smooth and shiny as everyone else, and everything else, is getting to be. It takes cash to get into the national rhythm and shape, and the place to do this is in town. So, at a certain point in the complex pattern of endurance and desire, and urged by the sharp pricking of abrupt personal dissatisfaction, the farmer decides to go and share the things the city can provide, even though this may, will, mean the loss of an increasingly dubious "independence," fresh air and the shredded remnants of an inherited tradition.

* * *

Picture this: a frame house of skimpy proportions, two stories high with a shaky, narrow porch along one side, built of second-hand lumber and covered with tar shingles pressed to look like yellow brick. It's on a dirt road pocked with ruts and stones—dust in August, a slough in March and a mad toboggan-slide in December; two cars cannot pass. It's more than a mile to the nearest paved road, and three miles more to the nearest general store and post office and school. The view is magnificent: a thousand feet below and miles away is a winding river lined with rich black farms where the land is as carefully utilized as it is in France. In the distance there are lavender hills, and in the winter moonlight, blue snow and black trees. Inside the kitchen door hangs the only light bulb in the whole house. Last year there was electricity for the first time in the area but there was only enough credit to wire the one room. You go to the "bathroom" and up to bed by candlelight, which makes for an atmosphere not of romance but of melancholy, and the mother of small children is ever on the alert for disaster. There is neither radio nor telephone. In the summertime the cooking is done on a kerosene stove that smokes and stinks if it is not carefully tended and expertly used; in the winter there is a kitchen range. If cash and credit are relatively adequate there is the luxury of coal, usually bought by the hundred-weight, which is more expensive than by the ton. And when things get really difficult the derelict barn gives a few more boards, and these are sawed up by hand.

The poor, both rural and urban, are forced to live constantly in extravagant debt: they must buy cheap shoes that wear out quickly, cheap foods that do not keep the body in top form, cheap tools that break and are inefficient, second-hand, broken down, wasteful cars that bad roads soon tear up completely. The result is exhaustion that permits no rest, no growth, and little joy at the bright vistas in the fertile valleys below. There is only weary dragging on from day to day, almost a guilt-sense of failure at such poverty in the midst of the nation's storied progress recorded in much expensive color in the shiny magazines each week.

Here there is no fieldstone pumphouse with cedar shingles snugly housing a plump tank of cold and sweet artesian water; there is only the shallow spring that drolls the water through for half the year; when the trickle stops, water must be fetched in buckets down the road, starting in the summertime when all the fields in the valley below are being worked by men who cannot spend their time carting water in a bucket; they're out producing. Here the fields are full of wild flowers, with only patches cultivated for the sake of quaint, small fruit that makes one say, "Well, it's not worth it, cheaper to buy it in town."

At one time this land was cleared of trees and made to yield some fruit, support some families. Up the road there is still the heaped-up wreckage of a one-room schoolhouse that served a score of families until sometime between 1918 and 1939. Now the trees are growing black, along with untidy brambles and black-eyed Susans, thistles and grape vines that run wild. Little foxes scoot across the road, and the dog barks on the leash. The children stand in the mud near the postbox in their thin clothes waiting for the school bus moving carefully in the November weather. They do not come home again until it is almost dark.

There is no hot water in the house except for what can be heated on the stove in a bucket so, except in warm weather, there are mostly sponge baths in the kitchen. There is an outhouse, frigid in winter and alive with flies and stench and foraging rats in the summer, a sweatbox under the slow-moving sun. In winter the house is a cave of draughts because everything is fitted poorly.

Discouragement and fatigue and loss of vision line the face of rural poverty. It is difficult to see beyond the muddy dooryard in the grey morning, and the mood lasts all day. No one comes and no one goes. A longing sets in for a little escape from the water-stained walls and unmended furniture, the cracked saucer and the wrinkled housedress. The supreme objective becomes the capture of a moment of spice, covered with spangles and filled with bubbles; a juke-box, a movie, a glass of lemon and lime or a comic book for the children, a permanent wave—which are wasteful as the thrifty and virtuous know. And there is always alcohol.

It is quite something to pass through a West Virginia town that looks like a movie set for a Wild West film circa 1903. There are only timber houses and covered wooden sidewalks, and a big raw sign that yells *whiskey*. There seems to be a lot of fierce-looking dark-eyed young men squatting on their haunches in the open in the middle of a weekday morning. Their eyes seem to follow strangers, and they roll cigarettes and seem silent. The report is that they don't do much of anything, many of them; they hunt and fish and from time to time cut down a tree and sell it; they make their own liquor and sell some of it. They are the men one wrote letters for in the army. They have a culture so different from the bulk of their middle-class compatriots that "foreigner" is not a completely illegitimate term to use on them.

Rural poverty is lived in isolation, in the imprisonment of broken fences and unpruned fruit trees that bear small, hard, wormy fruit. Rural poverty is as various as the terrain of the country. It is the lot, in God's mysterious justice, of millions of human beings, including the "single-men-in-barracks" types, the dark-skinned pickers in the "factories-in-the-fields," and the blue-eyed "crackers," some of whom have their huts dug into the sides of the red hills planted with stunted corn, and whose principal passion is a transference of all their resentment and frustration to a hatred of the Negro—a fellow prisoner. The rural poor are weighted down with chains of poor health and lassitude and ignorance. Their final humiliation is their removal—in one light it looks like a deliverance—from their wasted properties, rented or mortgaged, to the great institution of the industrial slum or housing project. Thomas Jefferson died a long time ago.

5

THE COUNTRY SLICKERS TAKE US AGAIN*

John Fischer

Government agricultural policy has changed very little in the past twenty years, despite shifts in party strength. Hinged on the dual concept of restricted production and parity, it has survived the Depression "Thirties," the War "Forties" and the Boom "Fifties." Are we ready for a New Look in farm policy? What has been the result of present policies? How do they affect farmers? Consumers? Who benefits? Who loses?

Our pampered tyrant, the American farmer, is about to get his boots licked again by both political parties.

Before next November's election Democrats and Republicans alike will be groveling all over the barnyard as they court the country vote—but the Democratic antics will be the most embarrassing. Nearly all Democratic politicians are now convinced that the farmers offer the largest single block of detachable votes—and many seem willing to use almost any tool of demagoguery which promises to pry it loose from the Republican grasp.

So when Congress opens up for business next month, the Democrats will set up a pious, baritone moan about the wretched plight of American agriculture. They will pass a farm-relief bill, loaded till its axles creak with rigid price supports, loans, "conservation" payments, and other shabbily-disguised subsidies. Then they will pray for the president to veto it. Quite possibly he will have the courage and honesty to do just that—and Democratic congressmen will then be sure that they have the farm vote in a gunny sack.

This cynicism is probably justified. The record of recent elections indicates that the farmer is generally eager to sell his vote to the highest bidder, and that city people are too indifferent (or benumbed) to resent this legalized corruption, even when the bribe is lifted right out of their own pockets. But don't blame the politicians for this record. They didn't make it. We did—all of us.

Our only excuse is that for twenty years—from 1920 until 1940—the farmers *were* in pretty bad shape. During these decades, city people got in the habit of giving them handouts, and haven't yet discovered that times have changed. The farmer not only got in the habit of accepting his dole; he came to believe that it belonged to him permanently, as a matter of right. When any hog keeps his jowls in the trough long enough, he gets to thinking he owns the trough.

Just how rugged is the farmer's plight today?

You should have such a plight.

When Harrison Salisbury of *The*

---

* John Fischer, "The Country Slickers Take Us Again," *Harper's Magazine*, December 1955.

New York Times traveled through the Middle West last summer, he reported that "The ordinary Iowa farmer . . . has a minimum of two new cars and they are usually brand-new Buicks or Oldsmobiles or Cadillacs." These Iowa swine-growers and steer-fatteners are of course better off than many of their brethren in other states. Still, the average farm family, taken the country over, has assets totaling about $22,000.

It is true that the slice of the national income which goes to agriculture has shrunk in the last four years —that is what the moaning is all about —but the farm population has dwindled too. As a result the individual farmer isn't much worse off— only about 5 per cent—than he was at the peak of his scandalous wartime prosperity.

Everybody knows that it is the taxpayer who keeps the farmer (or rather, a favored group of them) living in clover and Cadillacs; but even the taxpayer seldom realizes how much it is costing him. The Treasury spent nearly $3 billion during the last fiscal year to support farm prices—but that was just the beginning. The scheme is rigged to nick the taxpayer twice; once when he pays to take surplus crops off the market, thus propping up prices; and again when he has to pay these artificial prices at the grocery store.

If you complain, the farmer—or rather the highly skilled lobbyists who front for him in Washington—have a plausible answer:

"Why shouldn't I get a subsidy, when nearly everybody else does? Look at the airlines, the steamship companies, the manufacturers with their tariffs—all getting fat at the taxpayer's expense. That has become the American Way of Life."

But there is a catch to this argument. The other subsidized industries are producing something that we need, or at least can use. The farmers are being subsidized to produce millions of tons of things—cotton, wheat, rice, butter, and so on—which we don't need, can't possibly use, and can't even give away.

The government has "invested" $7 billion to hide these useless crops away in dead storage. Wheat, for example, almost a billion bushels of it, is now overflowing from every grain elevator in the country . . . stored in old Liberty ships tied up as floating warehouses . . . heaped in long yellow mounds on the bare ground all through the Southwest. Nobody wants it, because wheat is in mountainous surplus the world over. Yet Washington is encouraging the farmers to plant still more, and promising to take it off their hands at a guaranteed high price.

Who gets the money?

Not the needy farmers. There *are* some of them—about one and a half million families whose acreage produces less than $1000 a year. If the federal bounty went to them, maybe it could be justified as sheer charity. In fact, relatively little of this river of greenbacks ever trickles in their direction. The big subsidies go to the big farmers.

Such as the Delta Pine & Land Co. of Scott, Mississippi. It has $1,292,472 worth of cotton "under loan" to the government. ("Loan" is part of the elaborate semantics used by the farm lobbyists to conceal the real nature of these subsidies. "Pawn" would be more accurate, since the government is going to keep the cotton and the farmer the money. Nobody ever pretends that these "loans" will ever be paid off.)

The Chandler Co. of Saragosa, Texas, is into the treasury for $814,000 worth of cotton. Senator Homer E. Capehart, farmer, of Indiana is on the records for a $21,742 wheat loan. Adams Brothers & Co. of Odebolt,

Iowa, got $179,127. The Louisiana Irrigation & Mill Co. of Crowley, Louisiana, turned its surplus rice over to the taxpayer for $486,727.

The list runs on for page after alarming page. What it shows is that the big helpings of government gravy are going to about two million farmers—many of them corporations—who grow 85 per cent of the total farm output. They operate a little more than a third of the farms. Yet they form the most powerful vested interest in the American economy. Since they dug into their positions of special privilege during Democratic administrations, Mr. Truman does not sound entirely convincing when he describes the Eisenhower regime as "a special privilege government."

In fact, Secretary of Agriculture Ezra Taft Benson has made a few gingerly efforts to bring a little sense back into our farm economy. Whereupon Democratic congressmen—and some Republicans—promptly denounced him as a callous-hearted ogre. They pounced with even more indecent glee on one of his understrappers, Assistant Secretary Earl L. Butz, who was indiscreet enough to blurt out the truth.

"Too many people are trying to stay in agriculture," Butz said.

That is the hub of the whole story—and politicians of both parties have been avoiding it for years. At least 40 million of our 350 million acres of crop land ought to be taken out of production. At least one million out of our 5½ million farm families ought to be nudged gradually off the land, and helped to find some useful occupation.

One respected economist—Ross D. Robertson of the St. Louis Federal Reserve Bank—goes much further. He suggests that "it is not inconceivable that 5 per cent of the work force could produce all the farm products which the United States and a part of the rest of the world would take at profitable prices." If he is right, we could get along with less than half of the people we are now supporting in agriculture.

The explanation is that during the past twenty years farming has undergone a more sweeping technological revolution than anything industry has yet seen. New machinery, new fertilizers, new varieties of hybrid seed, new pest killers, new techniques have caused an astronomical rise in output, per man and per acre. Elementary common sense, then, would suggest that the unneeded people ought to be shifted into other jobs and the unneeded acres into better uses—notably timber and grass.

Our present farm policy, of course, works in precisely the opposite direction. It tends to freeze both manpower and resources into their obsolete and wasteful patterns. Moreover, the nostrum favored by most Democratic congressmen—higher and even less flexible farm supports—would merely freeze these patterns higher still.

Why is it that any word of common sense about farm problems is such political dynamite? Fundamentally, because our whole political structure, on every level, is stacked in favor of the farmer. North Dakota with its 680,000 people (mostly farmers) elects just as many senators as New York with its 12 million (mostly city folks). Many a rural congressman represents only one-half or one-fourth as many voters as his colleagues from city districts. In like fashion, nearly every state legislature is rigged to give an outrageously oversized representation to the country districts. (The political boundaries were drawn years ago, before the cities grew up; they can be changed only by legislative action; and the cornfed statesmen don't like to vote themselves out.)

A grand-scale reshuffling of districts, both for Congress and the legislatures, seems to be the only long-range remedy. That will require something akin to an insurrection by the long-swindled city voters—followed by years of patient logrolling and political maneuver. We can make a start next November, however, by throwing eggs at every candidate who poses as The Farmer's Friend. That will help get rid of one surplus, and a lot of political hypocrisy at the same time.

By way of footnote, it might be well to add that the writer of these churlish lines is not merely an exasperated city taxpayer. He is that, all right. But he also comes from a farming family, grew up in farming communities, did a certain amount of farm work himself, owns an interest in farm property, and benefits from farm subsidies which he has done nothing to deserve. This is worth mentioning only because it suggests that there may be other people with a financial stake in our present ridiculous farming system—perhaps more than anybody suspects—who are ready for a change in the direction of sanity.

6

THE NATIONAL GOVERNMENT MUST PROVIDE AGRICULTURAL LEADERSHIP*

John F. Kennedy

The most significant departure of the Kennedy administration from earlier agricultural policies was in the field of production controls. Earlier controls had been on the basis of acres planted; the Kennedy administration emphasized limits on units produced (bushels, gallons). In several nationwide votes, farmers rejected the Kennedy program in favor of fewer restrictions. The article which follows outlines the main facets of the Kennedy policies in agriculture.

Proper management of our resources of food and fiber is a key factor in the economic future of the nation. Both fiscal necessity and economic common sense require us to go beyond the gains of the last two years. Our capacity to produce still outruns the growth of both domestic and foreign demand for food and fiber. Our abundance must still be harnessed in such a way as to bring supply and demand more nearly into balance. And the benefits of our agricultural progress still need to be translated into improved income to farm families, lower prices to consumers for food and fiber, expanded exports, and reduced expenditures for price support programs.

Nevertheless, the past two years have seen substantial improvement in farm income, a substantial decrease in government holdings of agricultural products, and a substantial reduction in costs to the taxpayer for carrying farm surpluses, without increasing the consumers' burden.

* A condensation of the agricultural message delivered to the Congress, January 31, 1963.

These successes have been made possible by a series of congressional and executive actions undertaken in the last two years. The principles underlying these actions are further pursued in the recommendations contained in this message.

FARMER'S BACKING SOUGHT

The success of those principles also calls for an affirmative vote in the forthcoming wheat referendum, to be held under permanent legislation enacted by Congress last year. If two-thirds of the wheat producers vote this spring to approve the bushel marketing program authorized by that law, the present income of our wheat farms will be protected and the overhanging surpluses of wheat will be further reduced.[1] Failure to approve the wheat program will leave the wheat farmer without either supply management or effective price supports—at the mercy of unlimited production and unprotected prices. I do not believe that anyone who clearly understands the choice would prefer a return to the depression conditions that preceded the initiation of price supports a generation ago. New legislation for wheat is neither necessary nor feasible this year.

Exports of farm commodities reached a record $5.1 billion in the fiscal year 1962. Dollar markets abroad for the products of our farms expanded to a total of $3.5 billion, and thus constitute a significant factor in our balance of payments. . . .

COTTON

The time has come for us to fashion a sound and enduring national policy for cotton, to enable it to make its maximum contribution to our nation's growth at a minimum of governmental expense. At present, the domestic support level is 31.88 cents a pound. An 8½ cent export subsidy enables domestic cotton to compete with foreign cotton selling at 24 cents or less. This imposes a substantial handicap upon the domestic mill which must buy American cotton at the support price level, while competing with foreign mills which buy it at the subsidized level.

This handicap could, of course, be overcome by either eliminating the export subsidy or by reducing the support level. But elimination of the subsidy would also eliminate American cotton from the world markets and give impetus to expanding foreign production. The effect such a move would have upon the American cotton farmer, our balance of payments, and our economy prevents this from being an acceptable line of action.

Allowing domestic cotton prices to fall low enough to compete with foreign cotton is similarly unacceptable, for the average American farmer cannot, as yet, produce cotton profitably at world prices.

I urge that the Congress give early consideration to cotton legislation that will make this important fiber more competitive and help it recapture its markets. . . .

Research to reduce the cost of producing cotton in the United States will also strengthen the industry. For example, elimination of the boll weevil damage in the cotton crop could reduce production costs by 5 cents a pound in infested areas. Such research will pay for itself many times over. I am therefore asking that a special effort be made to make certain that the research resources available to the federal government are focused on this problem. The Office of Science and Technology will review the program and make recommendations. If actual

[1] Over half of wheat farmers voted against the administration proposal in May 1963.

cotton production costs fail, cotton price supports can be reduced under the stimulus of continuing research and the application of modern technology.

DAIRYING

Now dairy legislation is urgently required for the benefit of both the farmer and the taxpayer. Last year I recommended to the Congress the passage of legislation to reduce the severe drain of budgetary expenditures for the dairy price support program and at the same time increase the income of dairy farmers. Failure to pass this legislation, I pointed out, would result in government costs of over $440 million a year for supporting the price of dairy products. No legislation was enacted—with the result that costs have recently been running at a rate in excess of $500 million a year, and the income of the dairy farmer has fallen by over $100 million a year. There is little prospect of any improvement in dairy farmers' income or substantial reduction in government costs unless new legislation is enacted.

It is imperative therefore that the Congress apply the same successful principles of voluntary supply management to the dairy industry, and enact a program under which only producers who cooperate by reducing their marketings would receive through market prices and payments, a return on their marketings substantially greater than the noncooperators who choose not to join the program. Such a program would not only improve the income of cooperating farmers but also reduce government costs. . . .

EXPANDED UTILIZATION OF OUR FARM ABUNDANCE

Domestic food distribution—food stamps. More food in greater variety is now available to the needy than ever before in our history. The number of persons on public assistance receiving food under direct distribution programs rose to a peak of 7,400,000 in 1962. More than 2 billion pounds of food, valued at nearly $365 million, were distributed to needy persons, school lunch programs and charitable institutions in every state in the nation.

In addition, the (food stamp) pilot operation launched in 1961, with funds available under Section 32 of Public Law 320, 74th Congress, to enable the needy to purchase additional food through regular commercial channels by the use of food stamps has proved eminently successful. In view of its widespread and enthusiastic acceptance and its beneficial results, I recommend that enabling legislation be enacted to permit the progressive expansion of the food stamp program to all areas of the nation where conditions warrant its establishment.

Food and fiber for needy people abroad—food for peace. An increasingly important tool of American foreign policy—and of particular significance to our mutual assistance and development effort, including the Alliance for Progress—is the Food for Peace program. It is now being expanded to assume a larger share of the cost of mutual assistance. We make a grave mistake if we regard Food for Peace as merely a program for disposal of surplus commodities instead of an opportunity to utilize our agricultural capacity to encourage the economic development of new and developing nations. In the past year Food for Peace exports of wheat and flour alone filled an average of three 10,000 ton cargoes moving overseas daily. We are reaching more needy overseas than ever before —92 million people a day, including 35 million school children and 2 million preschool children. During the past six months we have undertaken to supply food as part payment for wages to 2.4 million people working on self-help projects for economic development in seven countries. I am recommending in the 1964 budget $1.9 billion for a continuation of the Food for Peace program.

RURAL AREA DEVELOPMENT AND RURAL ELECTRIFICATION

Housing. The quality of housing in rural areas has not kept pace with housing in cities. A million and a half homes on farms and in our small towns are in such a dilapidated condition they endanger the health and safety of the families living in them. Another two million rural homes need major repairs. The current housing loan program of the Farmers Home Administration has made a good start toward helping rural families, who cannot otherwise obtain credit, to improve their housing. But it falls far short of what should and could be done. The need is greatest among families in the lower income levels who have neither the resources nor the credit to make any major repairs or improvements. To remedy this situation, I recommend that federally insured loans be provided for rural housing. This will broaden the opportunity of more rural families to improve their housing, and at the same time, through the substitution of private for public credit, will reduce the demands upon the federal budget.

Training. One-third of our farm families earn only a subsistence income. Because they earn so little, they are unable to finance adequate educational and vocational training of family members; and this leads progressively to the concentration of still more poverty in rural areas. Vocational and other educational training should be made available to rural citizens who are unable to finance this training through other means. Such assistance is essential if large numbers of rural people, particularly youth and young adults, are to acquire the kinds of skills that will enable them to take advantage of new and better opportunities in an expanding economy. The alternative for many of them is a lifetime of poverty; the alternative for the whole nation is a continued waste of human resources. . . .

Land use adjustment. It is also necessary to make provision for the lands upon which conservation reserve (soil bank) contracts will expire in the next few years. Some of these lands would revert to crop production; this must not happen if we are to prevent our various crop programs from being undermined. The existing $10 million limitations on authorized appropriations for land use adjustment under section 101 of the Food and Agricultural Act of 1962 should be raised to permit such conservation reserve lands to be treated, where appropriate, as part of and expanded land use adjustment program. The cost will be substantially lower than it is over existing contracts.

Electricity. Rural electrification and rural telephone loans have made enormous contributions to the well-being and economic development of rural America. Over five million rural customers—approximately 20 million men, women and children—receive central station electric service through over 1000 local cooperatives financed by the rural electrification administration. Under the rural telephone loan program, local telephone companies and cooperatives have borrowed funds to finance modern dial telephone service for approximately two million rural subscribers. The credit record of R. E. A. borrowers is excellent; foreclosures have amounted to less than one one-thousandth of one per cent; delinquencies on repayment schedules are equally small. . . .

7

TOWARD A REALISTIC FARM PROGRAM*

Committee for Economic Development

Much of the commentary on farm programs is offered by groups that are directly involved, such as the various farm organizations and the Department of Agriculture. The following analysis is condensed from a publication of the Committee for Economic Development, a group composed of leading businessmen and scholars.

The objective of a realistic agricultural program, that is, a program that tends in fact to assist the farmer to gain a better livelihood, to give public outlays a definite, practical goal, and to serve the national objectives of economic growth, high employment, economic use of resources and over-all Free World strength, must be to create conditions in which the commercial farmer can live with free markets without undue risk.

The approach to this objective lies in three simultaneous lines of attack: one directed at reducing presently existing surplus stocks of farm products; one at bringing resources devoted to agriculture into balance with demand, at prices that yield reasonable returns; and the third at bringing farm prices to the levels at which output can be sold without government support. No one of these lines of action is independent of the others if we are to solve the farm problem without imposing unfair hardships on farmers. . . . The task immediately ahead is to pave the way to a return to freer prices by working down stocks in substantial over-supply. The adjustment problem, while of concern to all farmers and to citizens generally, involves in the main only a limited number of crops, but important ones.

REDUCING SURPLUSES

The task of moving surplus stocks out of government storage into consumption, both at home and abroad, is not an easy one for it must be done so that interferences with normal market outlets are held to a minimum.

Donations of farm surpluses to meet unfilled needs at home or abroad, where purchasing power is lacking, are laudably motivated. However, these disposal efforts—especially the barter program—can infringe upon commercial markets. Such transactions are of no net help so far as our surpluses are concerned because they merely take the place of what would otherwise be commercial sales of our crop product. Moreover, unless very carefully carried out, they may be self-defeating, because where such disposal efforts cut across agricultural trade lines they provoke retaliatory, restrictive measures by other countries that produce the same commodities for export. Thus, our efforts to dispose of our surpluses

* Committee for Economic Development, *Toward a Realistic Farm Program* (New York: 1958), pp. 24, 25, 26, 27, 28, 32, 34, 35, 36, 39, 40, 41, 42, 43.

through donations abroad can limit our commercial markets and sow ill will among our friends and allies.

Sale of surpluses for foreign currencies is subject to similar difficulties. It is argued that we can make good use of these currencies in meeting some of our outlays in the country where we sell our agricultural goods. What evidently is often overlooked is that such use does not add to the sum total of trade, because if dollars rather than farm surpluses were used as payment, the other country would decide for itself what it would buy in our markets with those dollars.

The recent emphasis given to surplus disposal by export has stimulated interest in various two-price systems. These schemes seek to maintain a higher price domestically than in the world market, or otherwise to shield our unrealistic agricultural prices from competitive world prices. Thus, they allow farmers to keep on producing at high rates at government-supported prices while excesses over consumption at the support price are disposed of under special arrangements at lower prices.

It does not seem to be generally understood that any sale abroad at lower prices than those maintained at home constitutes dumping. We have laws designed to prevent such dumping in our country. Most other nations also have means of counteracting such operations whenever they want to.

It is a very basic objection to the two-price system that it discriminates against the American consumer, who is asked to pay high prices for products we sell cheaply abroad, while we continue to ask the American consumer to pay, in taxes, to support prices that discriminate against him.

For these and other reasons, two-price arrangements will not solve our surplus dilemma. They are simply another form of seeking to postpone the inevitable reduction of output, and return to market prices.

PRICE SUPPORTS

It would be difficult to imagine more convincing evidence than we have already offered that the present system of trying to help farmers through price and income supports is futile, in fact harmful to the farmer, since his income position—in a prosperous, growing economy—has been worsening steadily.

It is plain that further use of price and income supports as they are now used can only encourage further production of surpluses; increasing, and increasingly pointless, tax outlays; a growing misallocation of needed resources of people and materials, and ever stronger pressures for disposal of surpluses in ways that conflict with other national objectives and policies.

Any program, therefore, sincerely intended to assist the farmer must include provisions for getting away from the price-income support system.

The farmer's permanent well-being, and that of the public and of the nation, can only be served by a farm program that allows the farmer to share in national prosperity and growth, and to retain freedom to make his own economic decisions, under the influence of the forces of supply and demand. The farmer must be able to live, prosperously, with market prices, otherwise his position in the economy is insecure.

Price supports, and allied measures seeking to help the farmer by supporting his income, should be *gradually* withdrawn. A five-year withdrawal period seems reasonable, but having a definite schedule and time goal is more important than the number of years allotted to the task.

During this transition, or withdrawal period, we should empty our government warehouses of their surplus holdings. Whether the government should hold any stocks of farm goods at all depends on considerations of national security not related to our farm programs.

AN EFFECTIVE LAND RETIREMENT PROGRAM

Our Land Retirement objective must be to take enough land out of production to achieve the desired elimination of surpluses in the short run, and the desired balance of output and demand over the long run.

Preferable, the lowest income farms should be retired because that would assist the largest number of people with insufficient farm income to move to better opportunities in other industries.

However, since these farmers produce little, farms with better income will also have to be retired in significant amounts, temporarily, to cut production while existing surpluses are used up.

The program should be voluntary in both directions—no farmer should be forced to come in, but, on the other hand, the government should not be forced to include any farmer's land, if its retirement does not serve the public interest.

Two additional points should be made:

We have made repeated references to the human factor in a program of resource reduction. People are involved, not just land. A survey taken for the Department of Agriculture indicates that, among farmers who put whole farms into the conservation reserve, the known availability of a job in town is one of the most frequently cited reasons. Farm people who have better earning potentials in other lines should be offered special training opportunities, as part of the resources adjustment program.

There is no danger that we would thus be contributing to the disappearance of the family farm. We have already noted that the family farm is successfully holding its own. Offering farmers now trying to make a living from the poorest soil a chance to establish themselves in other callings is actually a method of strengthening the family farm as an institution, for it would retire the weakest and most vulnerable units.

LOW INCOME FARMERS

It is useless to try and solve the problems of the low-income farm group by means of price supports. The group does not produce enough to be assisted much by price rises, no matter how extreme. Fifty-six per cent of all farms sell less than $2,500 of products a year.

Most of these farmers are in the South, although there are appreciable numbers in the cut-over areas of the Great Lakes states and the Northwest, and a sprinkling in many other areas. These are farm families who generally have too little land and too few other productive resources to earn more than a subsistence level of living, if that, solely out of farming. Outside the relatively modest Rural Development Program sponsored by the Department of Agriculture, this problem is not being attacked. It really should not be viewed, primarily, as a farm problem. It is a social problem calling for entirely different approaches than the income problem of commercial farmers.

Solutions depend on a determination

of how many in this group, with proper training and adequate resources of land and equipment, could achieve a satisfactory income. We do not have this basic information.

An analysis of those now in the low-income agricultural group who are better fitted to attain a satisfactory standard of living in some other vocation is also needed. After determining those who might shift from agriculture, means must be found for bringing their attention to the job opportunities available through federal and state employment services. In many cases, these will be outside the individual state of residence. In some cases, financial assistance may be advisable to cover transportation and immediate cash requirements for those having job opportunities available at a distance from their own locality.

CONCLUSION

We have outlined in this statement a program, or collection of interlocking programs, that we believe will be of real benefit to the farmer, to the public at large, and to the nation as a whole.

Our program means getting resources —people and land—out of agriculture and freeing farm prices. The higher average farm incomes resulting from dividing farm income among fewer operators will make many farm towns more prosperous. But the flow of people out of agriculture will decrease the trade of other rural towns. This is part of the relocation necessary to a solution of our agricultural problems. It cannot be avoided, but it can be mitigated by the same means—information and training—we have suggested for assisting low-income farmers into better livelihoods. We think public agricultural policy would include this type of assistance.

For the producers of farm equipment and supplies, such as fertilizers, a successful farm program will mean bigger markets, because a successful program means more farms in the prosperous category, and more farms of larger average size.

Prosperous, larger farms will be efficiently operated farms, making optimum use of fertilizers and of productive equipment. The farms that will be taken permanently out of production are not the farms using significant amounts of either. Except in the short run, our program requires more emphasis upon the redirection of *people* from agriculture to better opportunities elsewhere than it does upon retirement of land.

The specific benefits we look for are:

Genuine and lasting improvements in the economic position of farmers, by bringing demand and production into balance at market prices profitable to the farmer, with supplemental programs to assist farmers who cannot make a good living on the farm into industries where they can broaden their economic horizon.

Public release from the expense of farm income and price support policies that have demonstrably failed, and in fact worsen the very problems they are intended to solve, with the substitution of outlays that, in our opinion, will solve the farmer's basic difficulties and will thus have a forseeable end.

A needed reallocation of the nation's human and material resources, so that we can make quicker progress in our efforts to raise our standard of living, while providing for our national security.

8

LET'S END GOVERNMENT CONTROLS*

Charles B. Shuman

One of the most vocal critics of the Kennedy farm programs has been the American Farm Bureau Federation. The Federation is generally regarded as the conservative voice of upper income farmers, and it is frequently at odds with the National Farmers Union and the National Grange. What follows is a plan for less government activity in farm affairs and a return to free market conditions.

The time for decision and action has come. This is the year, 1963, that we, the people of the United States, must make our choice and implement our decision by firm action. For too long we have followed the path of least resistance—we have postponed the tough decision on such important matters as international relations, government spending, centralization of power at the federal level and farm control and price policies. These are critical days in the life of our nation and further delay or a wrong decision in any one of these areas could result in the deterioration of our leadership of the free world or, perhaps, in the loss of freedom for our people.

WHO WILL RUN THE FARMS OF AMERICA?

Who will run the farms of America? Will it be farmers or political bureaucrats? This is the year for action to change the direction of government farm policy. The stage is set, the issues are clear, the alternatives are well defined—and most farmers have made their decisions. The battle over national agricultural policy has been intense and protracted but the vast majority of farm families are today united as never before in the determination to reduce the role of government in the management of farm businesses. After 30 years of fruitless and costly experiments, farmers generally accept the fact that there will never be a "workable" government program to control production and fix prices of agricultural commodities. However, encouraging as it is to see the signs that farmers are prepared to reject government intervention (turkey and wheat referendums, November elections), the sobering fact is that no clear path lies ahead. Our situation in agriculture brings to mind the old adage, "He who would ride a tiger should first make plans for dismounting." The challenge farmers face is how to dismount the farm program "tiger" without getting wounded. It will not be easy. A $7 billion surplus hangs over our heads. Many thousands of farms are frozen into patterns of producing unneeded crops, markets have

---

* Extracted from the address delivered by Charles B. Shuman, President, American Farm Bureau Federation, before that group's annual convention, Atlanta, Georgia, December 10, 1962.

been destroyed or captured by substitutes, consumers and taxpayers are at the end of their patience, and a vast bureaucracy of tens of thousands of political payrollers is around our neck. The utmost in skill, patience and determination will be required as we attempt to build a bridge from this morass into which we have floundered to the firm and tested grounds of the competitive market.

Those who have no faith in the free competitive market will continue to advocate political supply management or compensatory payment schemes similar to the "entering wedge" payments included in the compromise farm bill of 1962. The government interventionists who control the United States Department of Agriculture seem to be determined to either rule or ruin American agriculture. Many millions of bushels of feed grains were dumped on the market during the past year by the Secretary [of Agriculture] with the sole purpose of depressing prices. The supply managers in the department have no faith in the ability of farm families to manage their own farms, as is evidenced by their continuing efforts to transfer decision making from the family farms of America to the Department of Agriculture.

If the campaign to control and manage all farm production, marketing and pricing should succeed, it will mean the end of the family farm and all of the institutions devoted to helping farmers develop greater management and marketing skills. There would be little need for vocational training in high school and college, the agricultural extension service would become useless puppets. All that would be required of farmers would be discipline —the ability to follow orders from Washington.

The family farm has demonstrated its superiority over all other forms of agricultural operation. It will survive and prosper if farmers have the opportunity to shift resources to meet changing demands. The threat of supply management control programs to the family farm with its allocation of quotas and marketing permits cannot be overemphasized.

In contrast to the arguments for a government-managed agriculture, President Kennedy recently made the following statement regarding the competitive enterprise system:

"It is well to remind ourselves from time to time of the benefits we derive from the maintenance of a free market system. The system rests on freedom of consumer choice, the profit motive, and vigorous competition for the buyer's dollar . . .

"Our system tends automatically to produce the kinds of goods that consumers want, in the relative quantities in which people want them . . . The system tends automatically to minimize waste. If one producer is making a product inefficiently, another will see an opportunity for profit by making the product at a lower cost . . . The system encourages innovation and technological change. High profits are the reward of the innovator, but competition will soon adopt the new techniques, thus forcing the innovator to push ahead.

"The free market is the decentralized regulator of our economic system. The free market is not only a more efficient decision-maker than even the wisest central planning body, but, even more important, the free market keeps economic power widely dispersed. It is thus a vital underpinning of our democratic system . . . Unnecessary government regulation undermines the efficiency of the market . . .

"I regard the preservation and

strengthening of the free market as a cardinal objective of this or any administration's policies."

As far as can be discerned at the present time, this excellent statement by the President has not been accepted by the Secretary of Agriculture and his staff in the department.

In recent weeks the Secretary has indicated that the supply-management approach calls for government ownership of large quantities of farm products as a defense reserve. He has also proposed that supply-management be extended to the rest of the free world through international commodity agreements.

Faced with the failure of his feed grain program to materially reduce surpluses, Secretary of Agriculture Freeman now proposes to conceal the problem by declaring that the United States needs a reserve level of 45 million tons of feed grains. Such a proposal would mislead the public into a false sense of security and tend to depress farm prices because it would be a constant threat to the market.

In the event of nuclear war, there would be the threat of contamination of feed grains stored in government bins. If these stocks did escape contamination there would be the problem of moving them back to the farms for feeding livestock and dairy cattle.

There is no justification for the government of the United States to own or store any farm commodities. The place to carry a reserve against war or other emergency is in our productive soil, our livestock population and the normal channels of trade. . . .

Farmers cannot afford to settle for existing markets; we can and must build new ones. Therefore, as farmers turn once again to the market place and endeavor to supply consumer rather than political demands, they apparently cannot expect much assistance from the administration.

There are some fundamental things to be done to provide the proper national economic climate for a prosperous agriculture.

First, through an aroused citizenry we must regain some fiscal sanity in our national government. We cannot long continue down the road to bankruptcy by increased government spending, deficit financing and unbalanced budgets.

Second, we must greatly reduce government intervention not only in agriculture, but in all segments of our economy.

Third, we must eliminate all monopolies and price-fixing powers in government, business, and labor and agriculture.

Fourth, we must expand markets for farm products—both at home and abroad.

Fifth, we must use farmers' organized bargaining power to make the market price system function better.

Farmers themselves, through their Farm Bureau organization, must give increasing attention to building better markets at home and abroad and improving the operation of the market price system. While not spectacular, the progress of the Farm Bureau Trade Development Corporation and the American Agricultural Marketing Association is very encouraging. The Marketing Association was organized to help coordinate activities of state and regional marketing-bargaining associations and to improve farmers' bargaining power. The Trade Development Corporation, with offices in Rotterdam, Netherlands, was organized to acquaint foreign buyers with the products American agriculture has to offer and to inform American agricultural producers of the needs of the European market. We have had sufficient experience with both of these operations to warrant the continued expansion of their activities. We also have had sufficient experience to know that government programs to control agricultural production and fix prices are not compatible with farmers' efforts to bargain for better terms of sale; neither are government-subsidized export programs helpful in building dollar markets for farm products. When the government is in the market, farmers and their organizations are automatically ruled out. The year 1963 should be one of all-out effort to increase the scope and effectiveness of our market-bargaining activities in Farm Bureau. Success in these activities might help build the bridge from the unsuccessful political supply-management schemes to the use of the market price as an arbiter of production and consumption. With the coming of economic integration, specialization and production to meet contractual specifications of processors and handlers, the organization of farmers to negotiate with these representatives of consumers is a necessity. The only questions to be answered are how soon and by whom will farmers be organized for more effective marketing and bargaining? Will the organization be by business groups, union labor, the government or by farmers themselves through their own organization, Farm Bureau?

Just as it is appropriate to ask the question, "Who will run the farms of America?," it is equally important to ask, "Who shall speak for farmers?" The Secretary of Agriculture has tried to convince the Congress that he speaks for farmers. On several occasions, county and state A[gricultural] S[tabilization] C[onservation] committees have claimed that they speak for farmers. Some commodity organizations, financed by market check-offs, would like to represent producers. National associations of limestone crushers and rural electric cooperative corporations have claimed that they know what farmers want. During 1963, we in Farm Bureau can challenge this babble of voices by giving every farmer in the United States the opportunity to decide who speaks for him. If this choice can be presented to all farmers, their answer will be apparent in a sizable increase in Farm Bureau membership during the coming year. This would be one of the most effective means of implementing our policies and convincing the Congress of the United States that the time has come for action.

9

THE FARM PROBLEM AND INSTITUTIONAL CHANGE*

Peter Dorner

Americans are prone to examine each national problem in isolation, ignoring the interrelatedness of political, economic, and social change. Professor Dorner demonstrates that the farm problem is actually part of a greater problem in which our entire society is caught up—the search for new means of sharing the national wealth that is increasingly produced by machines. His analysis is a healthy antidote to those political medicine men who promise a one-shot, sure cure for the farm problem.

Each year Congress struggles with a seemingly insoluble dilemma known as the "farm problem," a controversial public issue since the 1920s. Since then, numerous solutions have been proposed and many farm programs enacted. But the problem persists.

Fundamentally, the problem is one of economic reorganization. There are too many farmers on too many farms that are too small for profitable operation with modern machine technology. With shrinking profit margins per unit of output (declining prices and rising costs), income per farmer can be increased only by expanding the volume of sales. Productivity per farm worker is increased in large measure by investments in modern equipment. The productive potential of the equipment, in turn, is realized—and the farmer's income improved—by enlarging the farm. In recent years almost one-half of all land sales have been for farm-enlargement purposes. Consequently, the number of farms declined over 30 per cent in the 1950s.

Significantly, this reorganization of agriculture is more or less limited by the rate at which farmers are retiring. Once established, a farm family finds it increasingly difficult to leave the farm. With present high unemployment rates, opportunities for a farmer unskilled in industrial work are not very great. Given these conditions, we cannot expect a short-term solution. An industry consisting of more than three million firms, where mergers depend largely on family retirements, cannot be reorganized in a few short years; the process may take another generation or more.

Agriculture is involved in a technological revolution that is still gaining momentum. For example, in 1820, each farm worker could produce enough food for himself and four others. This figure was doubled by 1920; it was again doubled between 1920 and 1950. By 1961, each farm worker produced enough for himself and 26 others. It appears that the next doubling, there-

---

* Condensed from Peter Dorner, "Farmers: The Real Surplus," *The Nation*, February 9, 1963, pp. 115–17, 125.

fore, will be achieved in a mere 15 years.

Present economic organization in farming is inconsistent with this new technology, and until this situation is remedied, effective production control will be difficult to achieve. It is only reasonable, therefore, to expect that farm surpluses will continue for many years. Production control is difficult for two reasons:

1. The enormous thrust of new machine technology, which can be employed efficiently only as output is expanded. This technology is developed outside the farm sector (farm-supply corporations and public experiment stations) and is available to all farmers. Some farmers can enlarge their farms and utilize the new technology effectively. But even those tied to small acreage are under great pressure to adopt the new techniques in an attempt to maintain their relative income position.
2. The great range of technological and farm-size conditions existing within any type of farming area. Over two-thirds of all commercial farms in this country have gross sales of less than $10,000 per year. Most of these are too small for economical operation with modern machine methods. Such farmers will find it difficult to accept major cutbacks in production, since they are striving for (and, in some cases, near to achieving) a size of unit which gives them a good income. And enlargement, as pointed out above, is possible only as some farmers retire and make land available for expansion.

Farm-support programs directed at raising prices to offset the losses resulting from effective production control are misdirected. The farm problem is not fundamentally a price problem; it is one of economic reorganization. Where reorganization is attained, the present price level, or even a lower one, may be quite satisfactory. Effective production control will also become feasible as reorganization becomes more widespread. Thus the degree of compulsion—and, consequently, of effectiveness—acceptable in a program of production-control becomes a function of the progress in economic reorganization. On this basis, we should expect wider acceptance of an effective control program for wheat, where reorganization has progressed very rapidly, than for dairy farming, where the new technologies have yet to make their full impact.

Present policy shifts part of the cost of farm-support programs to the consumer through higher prices at the store; another part is shifted to the United States Treasury to be paid from taxes. This is a reasonable arrangement, quite consistent without basic principle of progressive taxation. Shifting the entire cost to consumers via the grocery bill would be regressive—a disproportionate share being borne by the lower-income groups. By shifting a significant part of the cost onto the general taxpaying public, the progressive principle operates—payment in accordance with ability to pay.

Actually, present preoccupation with reducing the government cost of farm programs is misdirected effort—although, of course, it would be welcomed if all government expenditures could be reduced. Paying taxes is an onerous task. But this is not the issue. The real question is whether government price support programs, when added to the consumer's grocery bill, have resulted in a disproportionate increase in the price of farm products.

During the last decade, the consumer price index increased from 100 (1947–49) to 126.5 in 1960. Farm prices actually declined, and the cost of food per person, including government costs, rose only half as fast as the general consumer price level—this, to repeat, in spite of increased quantities and much improved quality of food purchased. Food, priced at the farm, has been the only major deflationary influence throughout the decade. Store prices have indeed gone up, but these price increases are not to be associated with the unprocessed farm products, but with the marketing services added between farmer and consumer.

The basic bottleneck in "solving" the farm problem is the rate of adjustment and reorganization in agriculture. Can this process be speeded up?

If unemployment were reduced and more city jobs opened up, more farmers might make their farms available for the enlargement of those remaining. Modification in farm-credit arrangements, with some system of shared ownership as in industry, would make it possible for farmers to acquire land thus made available. There are still too many small farms being transferred as operating units which should be combined with existing farms. New credit arrangements could be devised which would favor the buyer who needed the land for enlarging his unit and discriminate against the buyer who is interested in becoming established on a unit that is now or soon will be too small for effective operation.

It has been suggested that the government pay individuals and families on small farms to move out of agriculture. This is a theoretical possibility, and a move in the right direction, but it is not a practical alternative. A politician is reluctant to vote for funds to be used for moving people out of his district.

The above measures are directed primarily at reorganization within agriculture. But there are accompanying problems. First and foremost is the education of rural youth. Most of the young people now on farms will have to seek jobs in the cities. Unskilled labor will become increasingly superfluous in our age of mechanization and automation. These young people must be assured of a high-quality education. Likewise, those who remain to run the large farms of the future will need a better education than many of our rural schools presently provide. With declining population, increased financial aid to rural communities may be necessary to provide the better schooling.

A fundamental question must now be posed: Why deplete the population in small rural communities and add to the crowded conditions in the cities? How do we rationalize this with present unemployment rates at unacceptably high levels? Since subsidies from public funds are necessary in either case, isn't it better to subsidize people on farms rather than to uproot them and then have to subsidize them in the city?

These questions help to clarify the underlying problem. The fact is that the farm problem is only a small part of a much larger difficulty. The larger task is one of devising procedures of income distribution consistent with a productive system increasingly dominated by machine techniques.

In spite of the apparent illogic, there is no real alternative to urbanization. In the first place, the movement to the cities has been proceeding rapidly, not by any coercion, but through the voluntary choices of individuals. Problems associated with reversing these trends would be much more difficult of solution and would require even more drastic social and institutional change than those required for adjusting to present trends. But, more important, I believe that when we deal with the complex problem of institutional change, we cannot move very far beyond our present experience. The urban-industrial sector is the growing sector of our society. The problem of unemployment will likely increase and require some new arrangements even in the absence of pressures added by farmers moving to the cities. Institutional modifications must and will come at the point of greatest pressure—in the cities. Since the farm problem is only a small part of this larger problem, we cannot hope to solve it by holding people on the farm. Paradoxical though it may seem, a solution to the farm problem is dependent on institutional change in the city.

Institutional change is always peripheral and marginal. We proceed by small steps and never get far ahead of our traditional ways of doing things. Rather than moving from our present rural experience, it is certainly a smaller, more acceptable step to move from our present urban-industrial experience in meeting the problems posed by a society of abundance. Here we have unemployment compensation that can be extended, a minimum wage that can be increased, work time that can be shortened, adult educational facilities that can be expanded, etc. Farm people cannot live, or solve their problems, in isolation and apart from this main stream of American life. They must in some way become attached to those institutional arrangements whose modification and evolution hold promise for meeting the challenge of our age. This challenge is basically one of legitimatizing new means for sharing the national wealth, which is increasingly produced by machines rather than by human labor.

The implications of this view of our farm dilemma may be difficult to accept. We have been told that the farm problem can be solved, that surpluses can be controlled, that farm incomes can be improved, that government costs can be reduced, that the family farm can be preserved—and that consumers can still have an abundance of cheap food. All this, if only the "right" farm policy were adopted! But these are inconsistent and unrealistic objectives.

A deep-rooted custom in American life, growing out of our frontier experience, is to solve problems rather than learning to live with them. But, like the cold war, the farm problem must be lived with. There is no solution in the short run. Positive action is needed in the area of institutional modification which will permit evolution of a new system consistent with an age of abundance rather than with an age of scarcity.

10

FARMERS MUST ADJUST TO CHANGING TIMES*

Jerome K. Pasto

Solutions to farm problems are in part dependent upon the viewpoint of the problem-solver. The following analysis is that of a farm economist. Rather naturally, it stresses efficiency, productivity and income per farmer. Critics of this approach describe it as shortsighted and lacking social consciousness. Defenders declare that their viewpoint is realistic, rather than romantic.

Fast-moving farm trends since World War II mean that our nation's farmers, especially the small ones, face difficult decisions.

Let's take a look at what has been happening. We live in a changing world. It has always been so.

This change should not be opposed, for progress cannot come without it. But changes mean a problem in adjustment. New ways of living and working often destroy values we hold dear. In agriculture, work horses, husking bees, and home-coming days are fast disappearing. The "art of farming" largely has given way to the "science of farming." Most of this occurred during the last century, but since World War II scientific developments are coming at a rate faster than at any time in the past. This means that adjustments must come fast, too.

We naturally tend to resist change. But as individuals we cannot block for long the new developments that affect us. The forward march of science is part of our way of life and so powerful that if any person or business opposes it, certain—though perhaps slow—death is the result. Nor should we want to oppose it. Those of us with a desire to learn, and who can adjust to new conditions, will find that science can help us to attain higher and higher levels of living.

The combination of science and capital investment has been coupled with enormous economic growth. Since 1940 the output per man-hour of farm labor has about doubled. Consequently, fewer man-hours are employed in farming. Productivity is greater because of the tremendous surge in farming know-how and the ever-increasing substitution of capital for labor in the form of machinery, fertilizer, insecticides, hybrid seed, etc. The investment per farm worker in the United States averages $16,000. In the Corn Belt it is almost $60,000. In the nation generally, and especially in the East, there has been an over-all decline in land and labor devoted to farming. Between 1950 and 1954, for example, the number of farms in the

* Jerome K. Pasto, "Farmers Must Adjust to Changing Times," *Pennsylvania Farm Economics*, September 1, 1957 (A publication of Cooperative Extension Service, University Park, Pa.).

Middle Atlantic States of New York, New Jersey, and Pennsylvania declined by 13 per cent. The workers on farms in the United States have declined steadily since 1910.

ADJUSTMENT DIFFICULT

Our nation's farmers find themselves in different situations with respect to the kind of adjustments they can make and the alternatives which are available. This is so because of the wide variation in this country in the kind of soils, topography, and growing season. Furthermore, potential changes may be restricted by lack of capital, lack of nonfarm opportunities, or mere unwillingness of the operator to make a change.

We live in an age of growth through mergers. Recently steel mills, auto and appliance manufacturers, banks, and a host of other enterprises have been in the "merging" act. The need to grow also has struck businesses closely related to agriculture. The number of grocery stores declined by 20 per cent from 1948 to 1954, and the dollar sales per store increased 76 per cent. Today there are about 2500 fewer egg hatcheries than in 1948, but the average capacity has increased by at least 14,000 eggs.

Businesses merge or expand because of savings that arise from bigger operation, such as broader sources of raw materials, expanded markets, more efficient labor utilization, and pooling of management skills. They seek the size of operation which will yield them the highest return on their investment, and for their labor. Since farmers are businessmen, they are expanding for the same reasons.

Some folks are alarmed by the growing size of our farms, up 27 acres in the United States from 1950 to 1954, for fear that the "family farm" is doomed. Others view this trend as a sign of progress, no different from the trend in other businesses. They point out that this is the logical outcome of more farming knowledge and more skill in management. They add that the adoption of new production practices and use of machinery that make it possible for a farmer and his family to accomplish more is a tribute to the ingenuity and resourcefulness of America's farmers. Our commercial family farms are not doomed—they are growing, and we should not obstruct their growth.

Farmers who have enough acreage of relatively level, fertile soil can increase their productivity and size of business by applying the farming knowledge that already exists. Furthermore, if they have the kind of farm that can make use of new farm technology and thus increase income, it will be possible to buy more land. Many farmers are doing this. In the Northeast dairy region 13 per cent of the farmland purchases were for farm enlargement. The percentage varies by regions, depending to some extent on how much the farm business can be mechanized.

To stay in farming and expect a reasonable income, full-time farmers of today will need to keep their businesses growing if they expect to remain "full-timers."

WHAT ABOUT FARMING PART-TIME?

If there is no chance to expand the farm business and increase income, then perhaps the only way to earn a satisfactory income is to combine farm work with city work. In 1956 nearly 40 per cent of United States farm workers worked off the farm at least part of the time. About one-third of the net income to farm people comes from nonfarm sources.

What about this farm-city combination? In many parts of this country operators of small farms are fortunate in that industrial plants are near at hand. This means that often they can remain on their farm, and yet commute to work. Certain crop and livestock enterprises will not interfere greatly with full or part–time work off the farm, and the grocery basket can be supplemented by produce from the farm.

QUIT FARMING?

The most radical adjustment some farmers face is to quit farming. If the farm is small, or if it is handicapped by unproductive soils, poor topography or location, then it is just about impossible to maintain a profitable business in competition with other farmers who are better situated. But if a move off the farm is the answer, what skills does the farmer have that are usable in nonfarm work? Frequently, the skills a farmer has developed in operating and repairing farm machinery, or in construction and maintenance of building can be applied to nonfarm jobs. A shift to full-time nonfarm work, however, often means migration from the community, since a job may not be available in the immediate neighborhood. Studies show that about half of Pennsylvania's farm youth migrate from the rural area before they are 21. But many older persons also migrate. Most of these folks improve their income. At the same time they release some land for the farmer who needs to expand to more efficient size.

ADEQUATE FARMS

Despite the decline in land and labor devoted to agricultural production, a basic problem is that there still are too many resources, especially human resources, devoted to farming. The voluntary shift off the farm has not kept pace with rising farm productivity. The result is that there are too many small, poorly equipped, low-income farms. A big increase in prices of farm products would help some of these farmers—but only a little because they have so little to sell. Some will remain on these inadequate farms, however, because to them farming is a "way of life"—but it should be recognized that the price of this privilege may be a meager existence when it comes to income. Their problem often is a social rather than an economic one.

Persons other than farmers should be interested in the changes now taking place in farming. Bigger family farms mean greater efficiency and this helps insure our supply of food for the future; part-time farms with adequate incomes improve the market for machinery, insecticides and many other production items; farmers on submarginal land who move into nonfarm work generally improve their incomes and contribute more to society than if they remain on inadequate farms.

Our concern should not be how to stop the decline in the number of farms, or how to throttle the increase in the size of the farms that remain. Rather, we should be concerned with how good a job we can do on those farms that have the resources adequately to support farm families.

XII

Big Business and Politics

One hallmark of modern American culture is the enormous size of our major corporations. Within the past century we have moved from a simple rural society characterized by family homesteads toward an intricate industrial society characterized by giant businesses. These industrial and financial giants are a major feature on the American economic, social, and political landscape. In terms of capital the billion dollar corporation is no longer unique in the United States. A single corporation may employ 300,000 people; its products may range from refrigerators to jet planes; its markets and sources of supply may embrace the entire free world.

This shift in economic organization has raised questions regarding our traditional belief in competition, free enterprise and private property. Have developments of the past century made obsolete the idea of a self-governing economy? Are we today paying lip service to outmoded philosophies? What role should government play in the regulation, encouragement, and over-all direction of economic life?

A second question bears directly on the relationship between big business and government. In terms of politics, Jeffersonian democracy made no provision for the corporation. Since the 1890's Americans have wrestled with the problem of bigness without reaching agreement. Are big business and monopoly two sides of the same coin? Should legislation be enacted to curb bigness and favor little business? Is active, vigorous competition our goal, and is such competition stifled by bigness? Or should we deliberately encourage industrial giants, thus reaping the benefits of mass production and distribution?

Another issue centers around business and the political process. Should big business play a positive political role, thus serving as a check against big labor? Should it use money as a counterweight to the voting strength of labor? Or are its leaders part of a power elite that rules America, without accountability at the ballot box? Is the corporation a threat to American democracy, or is it at least a partial answer to the American dream of abundance for all? What connection, if any, exists between political and economic power? In one sense, at least, we have widespread dispersal of political power and concentrated blocs of economic power. How can this diversity of power be reconciled?

Government in Economic Life: Captain or Referee?

Until recently most Americans agreed that government should be a sort of economic referee who stood on the sidelines and blew the whistle when personal fouls were committed by players on the floor. Many economists today reject this concept and would agree that government in modern society must be a team captain, who organizes his players (business, labor, farmers, consumers) into a winning combination called prosperity. If any adversity such as depression threatens, it is the responsibility of government to overcome this threat to the team by calling the proper plays.

Rather obviously, government cannot be both a captain and referee in the same game. Supporters of the captain role declare that only government can meet the major threats to our economy. Only government is powerful enough to prevent inflation; only government can check a downward economic spiral. Both cold and hot wars require a firm hand on the economic tiller, rather than any self-balancing effect secured through the counterpressure of major economic groups.

Supporters of the referee role for government emphasize different aspects of the problem. They believe that political and economic freedom are closely linked. If economic freedom is limited by the state, political freedom will most certainly be curbed. Free speech, freedom of assembly and free enterprise are part of a single package, following this reasoning. Any temporary advantage gained by using government as the captain will soon be forfeited by total domination of the players' lives. The relative merit of the captain and referee roles for government is the central issue explored in this section.

Big Business and Government: Logical Partners or Natural Enemies?

The relationship between business and government is a matter of much concern to Americans. At one extreme are those who argue that the country should be governed by those who own it—that since businessmen have a great financial stake in the country they have the greatest concern that government policies do not thwart that interest—or, more positively, that government must become an active agent to preserve national prosperity. In one form, at least, this policy is reduced to the simple formula—"What's good for United States Steel is good for the United States." Expressed in another way, a comparison between business and government operations is made, with the conclusion that "we need more business in government."

At the other extreme in this debate are those who view with alarm the role played by business leaders in political affairs. To buttress their argument these spokesmen advance evidence of political control through campaign contributions, the staffing of regulatory agencies, and the attempt of corporation leaders to speak for their stockholders and employees. At a more basic level, C. Wright Mills has described a ruling class in the United States composed of business, military and political leaders, many of whom are subject to no democratic controls.

Within the foregoing framework, questions of policy are debated. Do we need more business in government? Do we already have too much? Should rigid restrictions be placed on business campaign contributions and other avenues of influence? Should unions be similarly restricted? Or should both groups be encouraged to compete for voter favor? Finally, how can we dispose of the concern (expressed in the following pages by former President Eisenhower) that we face a constant danger from the dual alliance between business and the military establishment.

1

WHAT DO YOU MEAN, FREE ENTERPRISE?*

Nathan Robertson

Our economic system is frequently described by the phrase "free enterprise." Implicit in this title are characteristics that are readily identified: private property, economic individualism and an absence of government control. This traditional picture is challenged by Mr. Robertson, who believes that it is a sort of American mythology, divorced from the real world about us. Do we really operate a free enterprise system in the United States? Or is it, as Robertson suggests, a safe enterprise system?

The United States today is in a condition comparable to that of a man suffering from schizophrenia. A few innocent fancies are safe enough in quiet times, but in a crisis, either the patient gives up his delusions, or society commits him to the firm hold of others. Our national phantasy, hateful in these edgy times, is our belief that

---

* Nathan Robertson, "What Do You Mean, Free Enterprise?" *Harper's Magazine*, November 1948.

we are living in a free-enterprise system. Since reality is quite the reverse, we are in no condition to make rational decisions. It is time to get wise to ourselves.

It is true that we have a free-enterprise system in the sense that if a man has enough money he can go into any work or any business he chooses. In most respects he can run his business to suit himself. He may make money or go under, depending upon the circumstances and his own ability. He can get out of one occupation or business and go into another whenever he can afford to.

But these are only the surface signs. Fundamentally, a free-enterprise system, as spelled out by Adam Smith, the great classical economist, is one in which there is a minimum of government or monopoly interference—in which the natural laws of supply and demand rule. In that kind of system an individual entrepreneur takes all the risks and, as a reward for bearing those risks, is entitled to all that the law of supply and demand will permit him to win.

America once had close to—although never completely—a free-enterprise system of that kind. Of course, from almost the beginning, this country had tariffs which interfered with the laws of supply and demand; subsidies to the railroads and the Western pioneers which fell considerably short of Adam Smith's ideal; prohibitions against some businesses regarded as immoral, such as the slave trade; and government competition, such as the postal system in communications.

But except for a few interferences of this kind, the laws of supply and demand were in control, and we had something rather similar to a free-enterprise system. There was little government interference or monopoly. A man could go into any business he chose, pay any wages for which he could get men to work, charge any price he could get, and make as much money as the laws of supply and demand would permit. He could even throw away the nation's basic natural resources in the most profligate manner if he chose to do so in his grab for riches and power. He could make millions—or go bankrupt.

Today we have something quite different. The individual entrepreneur still faces the risk of competition within his own segment of the economy—if he happens to be in an area of business where competition still exists, such as farming or retailing. But in many segments of our industry, competition has been drastically restricted so that the laws of supply and demand no longer operate as they are supposed to. Many of our big manufacturing industries have price-fixing schemes of one kind or another. The steel, cement, and other heavy industries, until very recently, have had the basing-point system for controlling competition, and it is not yet clear to what extent the practice has been abandoned since it was outlawed by the Supreme Court. Price-fixing has extended clear down through the retail trades under the Miller-Tydings Act, which permits manufacturers to fix the price at which their products can be retailed to the public. Patents have been used as the basis for widespread price-fixing.

Even beyond all this, American industry has become so big, with such huge industrial units, that only those with many millions of dollars to risk can enter into many fields of enterprise. This large scale, of course, limits competition. It takes huge aggregations of capital to enter most of the big industries like steel, automobile, machinery, or electrical equipment manufacturing—and even publishing. At least $10,000,000 is needed to launch a metropolitan newspaper today, and even then the chances of making a profit are slim, as Marshall Field can testify.

But a more important factor in changing our economic system is government. Today a businessman, whether he is a manufacturer or retailer or farmer, no longer faces the biggest risk of all in a free-enterprise system—the risk of uncontrolled ups-and-downs of the economy. No one believes that we have completely eliminated the business cycle, but we have today so vast a network of government supports that many economists believe we will never again have anything like the crash of 1929. Some of these economists contend that this is the reason that we escaped the postwar depression, which was expected to throw 8,000,000 men out of work after hostilities ceased.

So today, instead of having a nearly-free-enterprise system in this country—as we used to have and as most people still seem to think we have—we are operating under something quite different. It is a drastically revised system—revised by monopoly and by government supports. Partly because we still have not recognized just how different our new system is, no one has yet named it—but it might be called the "safe-enterprise system."

This "safe-enterprise system" is almost as different from the one that Adam Smith talked about or the system we once had as the economy of Nazi Germany or of Soviet Russia. But it is just as American and goes along with democracy and liberty as naturally as the original. In fact, our democracy today is probably more complete than it ever was in the past. We still have free speech and free worship. We still can protest and vote "no" if we want, and more of us have the right to vote "no" than ever before. But we no longer have the freedom to pay workers five or ten dollars a week for a 60-hour week, or to put millions of people into the breadlines.

The schizophrenic part about all of this is that we still talk and plan as though we had a system of the old kind. Proposals are rejected in Congress day after day because they will interfere with the "free-enterprise system." People tend to confuse the "free-enterprise system" with basic Americanism and put it on the same pedestal as "liberty" or "democracy."

What makes this particularly strange is that we did not even begin to call our system a "free-enterprise system," or to use that phrase as almost synonymous with capitalism, until about ten or fifteen years ago. We had occasionally referred to it earlier as a system of "free competitive enterprise." But the more simple phrase, with the competitive idea eliminated, was popularized by the business interests of this country about ten years ago, when they were fighting off some of the New Deal reforms. One of the bright young men then working for the National Association of Manufacturers is credited with promoting the new phrase.

The slogan had great value in fighting such innovations as the wage-hour law and the Wagner labor act. The businessmen were afraid that we were going to abolish the "free-enterprise system" which permitted them to pay their workers for whatever they could get them to work for individually, and perhaps to regulate how much profit they could make. Actually we did abolish the first of these "rights"—but we never tampered with their profits, except to a limited extent during the war. So far, the changes in the "free-enterprise system" have not hurt business. In fact, profitwise, business is going better today than ever before in history—with profits reaching more than $18,000,000,000 after taxes last year, or more than double what they were in the boom year of 1929.

Business pushed the phrase in speeches, advertisements, and propaganda. Politicians accepted it and won applause with it. Everything indicated that the American people wanted a free-enterprise system, except that by the time the phrase took hold we had moved on to another system without most people realizing it—although they had repeatedly approved the measures which brought the change about.

All the phrase did was to confuse America at a time when it could scarcely afford to be confused. It is important for the people of this country to get over their confusion—their schizophrenia—if they are to run the new system intelligently. Business men need to recognize the nature of the new system in order to adopt workable price policies, labor needs to recognize it to develop sound bargaining programs, and the public needs to recognize it to decide the issues of the day rationally. To decide some of the questions we now face without recognizing where we are or where we are going is like a ship captain trying to chart a course before he knows where he is or what port he wants to reach.

* * *

The federal government alone is now pumping into the economic system about $40,000,000,000 annually[1]—most of which will have to continue unless we drastically modify the services our government provides, the military force, benefits to veterans, and foreign aid. This figure, which equals our total national income of only 16 years ago, is for a period when we have been enjoying boom prosperity. State and local government expenditures swell the total beyond $50,000,000,000 a year.

Come a depression, the federal government's spending would go far beyond these figures, since it is legally obliged to cushion farm prices, pay unemployment benefits, and make good its guarantees. Furthermore, under the principle of government established by Hoover and Roosevelt in the past depression—that neither business nor people shall be permitted to go under *en masse*—the government would have an obligation to pour billions of dollars into financial and industrial enterprises and into relief of individual need. That it will do so is conceded.

What this all amounts to, in short, is not a free-enterprise system, but a comparatively safe-enterprise system under which our economic health is founded on government credit and government credit is used not only to battle depression but to avoid it. Even in good times the government will act to save an industry—as it did recently for the air-transport companies.

There is still risk in business, particularly in those areas where competition prevails. Many small businesses fail every day. Government does not guarantee a profit to every business man, or even to every farmer. An entrepreneur's rewards still depend considerably on his ability and his luck. But the risks in business today are far more limited than they were in the days when we really had the "free enterprise system" we talk so much. . . .

This is a fact with vast implications —for every businessman, for every worker, and for every citizen. Certainly every politician must recognize and face up to the new system.

And the American people must admit that the safe-enterprise system under which they live requires certain

[1] The sum had risen to about $100,000,000,000 by 1964.

adjustments. Does this system, for example, warrant such unlimited business profits as in the past, when business men risked all to win all? If business does not make the necessary adjustments in price and profit policies we must decide whether or not a large segment of industry has achieved the relative security of a public utility—a position where limited risks warrant legislation limiting profits. We will have to face up, also, to a permanent budget of $40,000,000,000 or more a year and pay the taxes that such a system of government services and supports require.[2] In good years we will have to pay in taxes considerably more than that, so that the government will be sound enough to meet the extraordinary expenses it faces in bad times.

The old free-enterprise system exists only in our nostalgic imagination, and we have spent more than enough energy defending it. If we want to retain custody of our economic fate, the first step is to admit the facts.

[2] Revised upward to $100,000,000,000 in 1964.

2

GOVERNMENT THREATENS OUR LIBERTY*

Raymond Moley

The place of government in our economic life is constantly disputed. Does government intervention automatically subtract from our liberty? Or may liberty be extended by government intervention? Mr. Moley views recent government policy with great misgivings. In the following passages he spells out his concern in some detail.

There is no such thing as certainty in a free economy or, in fact, in any economy that the world has known. It cannot be assumed in economic life that every owner of capital will seek the safest investment. Such an assumption denies not only the lessons of experience, but the plain facts of human nature. The spirit of risk, adventure, and gambling is forever on the prowl. The ages have taught men that mortal intelligence cannot calculate, weigh, and balance all the factors that affect the course of events and hence that mortal eyes cannot peer with certainty into the future. Men have also learned that some of them possess more of foresight and of daring than others and that rewards come from the exercise of these qualities. Hence, there is competitive struggle in which quick decisions, risk-taking, losses, and gains prevail. All that this contest demands is freedom of choice.

In the infinite varieties of human nature and temperament, some will possess more daring and imagination than others. A few, perhaps a small minority, will be moved to risk money, time, and energy by the ven-

* Raymond Moley, *How To Keep Our Liberty* (New York: Alfred A. Knopf, Inc., 1952), pp. 167–69, 172–75, 177–80. © 1957 by The Regents of the University of Michigan. Reprinted by permission of the publishers.

ture that promises not the smallest possible loss but the greatest possible gain. Among this minority are the greatest failures and the greatest successes. But generally when one fails another profits by that failure. And the net is progress, production, and the making of wealth.

Investments are made in the face of known uncertainties in the market place. No one deliberately chooses a bad investment. What makes an investment bad is the appearance of factors that were not or could not be anticipated.

Statists have prated for years about how "idle dollars make idle hands" and derive from this generalization the theory that government must forcibly seize—or "channel," as they put it—"idle" capital and invest or spend it through the government.

There could be no greater fallacy. For there is no "idle" capital except the dollars hidden in the mattress or in the ground. There are degrees of "safety" in investments, and there are many people to whom temperament or responsibilities dictate caution. But their capital is entrusted to others, and the very laws of survival demand that it eventually be set to work. And this capital affects economic life; it affects the volume of production, prices, and profits.

The newer the enterprise, the greater are the risks of investment in it. Here is where the venturesome man enters the picture.

The more complex and the more productive of wealth our economy becomes, the greater must be the investment in dollars per wage earner. It has been reliably estimated that the average investment necessary per wage earner is $10,000 a year. That means that $6,000,000,000 of new risk-capital is needed in the United States every year. But statism reduces, discourages, and destroys essential risk-capital. The incomes of those who have traditionally supplied it have been the prime objects of expropriation by taxation. The average income of people in that group after taxes has been reduced approximately 75 per cent in twenty years. And since what they now have left after taxes barely meets and in many cases is less than their cost of living, their margin for new investment has practically vanished. Moreover, since many are now paying their living expenses out of capital, their old investments are shrinking, too.

A wry reaction to this by many people is that they cannot feel sorry for those well-to-do people who must live on smaller incomes. That reaction is, of course, heightened by the political incitement of class feeling over the past few years. But nobody needs to feel sorry for the people who now have large incomes. They will live and live well. What has been accomplished by leveling them is the destruction of what they hitherto contributed to those economic ventures which make national wealth, and create new business and more jobs. The statist has missed his victim and injured the very people he professes to help.

Since tax resources are inadequate to support a welfare economy, the next resource of the politicians who support it must be the deadly harvest of inflation.

There is no escape so long as the trend toward the welfare state continues. The final chaos and ruin of inflation would be bound to come. Values would be meaningless in terms of money. There would be a flight from money to things. Government credit would collapse when no one would buy bonds. Financial institutions could not survive the fall in value of their securities. The past would be pillaged by the ruin of savings. The future would be buried in debt and confronted with the almost insuperable task of reconstructing a financial and industrial system.

THE MORAL CLIMATE OF STATISM

At least four of the initial assumptions of statism lead to stark materialism, domestic tensions, envy, and hatred. These assumptions are:

That the basic purpose of the state is to supply the individual with more of the material means of life;

That the political power is attained by the promise of these benefits;

That political power is further assured by creating envy and hatred among social groups—in short, class feeling;

And that since the national government is to be the source of benefits, the loyalty of the individual must be to that source, rather than to his immediate neighbors and local institutions.

The foregoing assumptions of statism have in recent years become more and more evident in our public life.

The literal application of the assumption that the state exists only for material ends is obvious in the speeches and propaganda of politicians now in power and of statist political-action organizations. The traditional spiritual values are mentioned only in the form of more or less irrelevant catchwords, mainly as material for perorations and slogans.

Reckless promises are made by politicians, with all the politicians' callous assurance that if their promises cannot be fulfilled the blame can be cast on the stubborn opposition, and that the same promises can be renewed from time to time.

Since the beginning of the great expansion of state power and indiscriminate benefits, the fissures of class and group prejudice have been widened. Unpopular minorities have been pilloried for purposes quite similar to those for which dictatorships abroad have reviled religious and racial groups. After the great depression, the businessman was used as a target for demagogues, just as was the Jew in Nazi Germany and the kulak in Soviet Russia.

With the source of benefits reserved to Washington, there has been a weakening in loyalties to the neighborhood, to fellow workmen and employees, and to local government.

There has been ample evidence in the past four or five years that as the size and power of the federal political machine have grown, shady practices have appeared in high places. Corruption will appear wherever money accumulates and responsibility is difficult to place. These evils and their revelation have their corroding effect far down the line in the private lives of citizens. An immature college boy who is approached by a gambler with a proposition to throw a basketball game might well be moved to evil by the reflection that the newspapers every day tell about offices sold for cash and bad government loans arranged through influence.

It must be underscored that these changes in the moral climate are due in the main to the materialistic postulates of statism. For even if the material objectives of statism can be obtained, the plenty that might miraculously result would be the beginning, not the end, of the good life.

But the greatest blow to morality is the self-evident fact that the promised plenty is not attainable under socialism. Thus, the appeal is not only created for ends that are not the best objectives of life, but its pretensions are themselves fraudulent.

THE TWILIGHT OF LIBERTY

From time to time I have referred to the losses of personal liberty through the progressive adoption of statist policies. In this chapter of reckoning, despite some repetition, a number of those losses should be summed up.

The farmer has paid for his benefits by successive surrenders of freedom. First, he accepted restrictions on his acreage. Then, as he exercised his remaining freedom to intensify the efficiency of his production, "marketing quotas" were established—a further denial of freedom, for which he received a cash return. . . .

The worker's freedom has been restricted by the government's alliance with its leaders. His income has grown, but his liberty has diminished. His ambition to excel other workers finds impediments in union discipline, featherbedding, and make-work practices. His livelihood becomes dependent on good standing in the union because his leaders hold over him the threat of the loss of his seniority, pension rights, and other benefits. The penalty for recalcitrance is expulsion from the protective custody of the union. . . .

The businessman hardly needs to be reminded of the growing limitations on his freedom. The shrinkage of risk capital through taxation is met by inducements to become the debtor of a government bureau. Government lending agencies often dictate in matters of business judgment. Masses of regulatory laws, many of which have outlived their purposes, impose the yoke of bureaucrats on businesses. Companies are told that they must or must not expand. Political decisions arbitrarily favor some businesses at the expense of others.

The citizen's right to keep or dispose of his savings has been greatly impaired by taxes and the inflationary spending of the welfare state. Stockholders, too, large and small, have received less and less of the proceeds of the businesses in which they have invested.

In the final end of statism everyone would work for one authority. There would be no other means of earning a livelihood. And the inflexible rules of civil service would prevail.

Under such conditions, a choice between political parties, if there were more than one party, would be merely a question of degree and of personalities. If a nation once accepts statism as a way of life, the drab choice, if there remains a choice, is between one or another set of masters. But when a political regime gets its hands on the administrative devices of an all-powerful government, it will use those means to keep itself in office.

President Roosevelt said in his Annual Message to Congress in 1936: "Our resplendent economic autocracy . . . realize that . . . we have built up new instruments of public power. In the hands of a people's government this power is wholesome and proper. But in the hands of the political puppets of an economic autocracy such power would provide shackles for the liberties of the people."

Those "instruments" are much more numerous and more powerful now. They are in other hands. They are in the hands of a "resplendent" political machine.

It is hard to see, despite the protests of such socialists as Clement Attlee, how the ultimate of socialism can be but one party and, in that party, one master.

Free speech might theoretically remain. But the power and vitality of expression would slowly ebb in a society without wide freedom of choice. Public debate might prevail, but it would be without bite or purpose.

In Britain, where government has a strong hand in the administration of the Church of England, there were evidences under the Attlee government that strongly socialistic ministers of the Gospel were assigned to strongly Conservative parishes. Thus, along with the Lord's word there was scattered among the faithful overtones of the great doctrine of "fair shares."

Finally, under growing government, the invasions of privacy multiply. Hosts of inspectors and others are at large, checking the citizen's whereabouts, peering at his business records for one reason or another, and flooding him with government directives and propaganda. These invasions of liberty are inevitable. The terms of statist philosophy demand them.

The moral and spiritual implications of a paternal state under the external forms of free institutions were vividly described by Alexis de Tocqueville in his comments on American institutions in the 1830's. This is his prophecy, which may yet be fulfilled:

I think, then, that the species of oppression by which democratic nations are menaced is unlike anything that ever before existed in the world; our contemporaries will find no prototype of it in their memories. I seek in vain for an expression that will accurately convey the whole idea I have formed of it; the old words despotism and tyranny are inappropriate; the thing itself is new, and since I cannot name, I must attempt to define it.

I seek to trace the novel features under which despotism may appear in the world. The first thing that strikes the observation is an innumerable multitude of men, all equal and alike, incessantly endeavoring to procure the petty and paltry pleasures with which they glut their lives. Each of them, living apart, is as a stranger to the fate of all the rest; his children and his private friends constitute to him the whole of mankind. As for the rest of his fellow citizens, he is close to them, but he does not see them; he touches them, but he does not feel them; he exists only in himself and for himself alone; and if his kindred still remain to him, he may be said at any rate to have lost his country.

Above this race of men stands an immense and tutelary power, which takes upon itself alone to secure their gratifications and to watch over their fate. That power is absolute, minute, regular, provident, and mild. It would be like the authority of a parent if, like that authority, its object was to prepare men for manhood; but it seeks, on the contrary, to keep them in perpetual childhood: it is well content that the people should rejoice, provided they think of nothing but rejoicing. For their happiness such a government willingly labors, but it chooses to be the sole agent and the only arbiter of that happiness; it provides for their security, foresees and supplies their necessities, facilitates their pleasures, manages their principal concerns, directs their industry, regulates the descent of property, and subdivides their inheritances: what remains, but to spare them all the care of thinking and all the trouble of living? . . .

After having thus successively taken each member of the community in its powerful grasp and fashioned him at will, the supreme power then extends its arm over the whole community. It covers the surface of society with a network of small complicated rules, minute and uniform, through which the more original minds and the most energetic characters cannot penetrate, to rise above the crowd. The will of man is not shattered, but softened, bent, and guided; men are seldom forced by it to act, but they are constantly restrained from acting. Such a power does not destroy, but it prevents existence; it does not tyrannize, but it compresses, enervates, extinguishes, and stupefies a people, till each nation is reduced to nothing better than a flock of timid and industrious animals, of which the government is the shepherd.

3

ECONOMIC POWER IN AMERICAN SOCIETY*

A. A. Berle, Jr.

The degree of economic concentration in modern America is summarized below. The information presented here will serve as a point of departure in our exploration of government policy as it applies to the giant corporations. Does the giant business represent a threat to which government should react? Or is it an achievement worthy of national self-congratulation? Do the government activities described here represent the beginning of a national policy? Or are they examples of uncoordinated action?

Today approximately 50 per cent of American manufacturing—that is everything other than financial and transportation—is held by about 150 corporations, reckoned, at least, by asset values. If finance and transportation are included, the total increases. If a rather larger group is taken, the statistics would probably show that about two-thirds of the economically productive assets of the United States, excluding agriculture, are owned by a group of not more than 500 corporations. This is actual asset ownership. (Some further statistical analysis is called for if financial corporations be included, for these, of course, double up. One of the largest and most plainly oligarchically controlled corporations in the United States, the Metropolitan Life Insurance Company, duplicates assets because it holds securities of other corporations.) But in terms of power, without regard to asset positions, not only do 500 corporations control two-thirds of the nonfarm economy but within each of that 500 a still smaller group has the ultimate decision-making power. This is, I think, the highest concentration of economic power in recorded history. Since the United States carries on not quite half of the manufacturing production of the entire world today, these 500 groupings—each with its own little dominating pyramid within it—represent a concentration of power over economics which makes the medieval feudal system look like a Sunday school party. In sheer economic power this has gone far beyond anything we have yet seen.

We can talk about the various alleged legal controls which somehow

* A. A. Berle, Jr., *Economic Power and the Free Society* (New York: The Fund for the Republic, 1957), pp. 14–16, 18–20.

or other, when the chips are down, neither control nor even seek to control. We can point out the fear of "monopoly" and "restraint of trade" and say that from time to time this fear has checked the process. True, our law has prevented any one of these power groups from becoming a monopoly, but it has not seriously prevented the concentration of power as power, though it has prevented certain ultimate results. The question is then: Why has concentrated economic power in America not got completely out of hand? Many of these corporations have budgets and some of them have payrolls, which, with their customers, affect a greater number of people than most of the ninety-odd sovereign countries of the world. American Telephone and Telegraph, for example, based on combined population and wealth, would be somewhere around the thirteenth state of the union in terms of budget, and certainly larger than many of the countries of South America. Some of these corporations are units which can be thought of only in somewhat the way we heretofore thought of nations.

Whether we like it or not, this is what has happened. As noted, it is not the product of evil-minded men. I believe that we must try to work with the system. The dangers are obvious. But history cannot usually be reversed. Until the engineers and economic forces give us a way by which a man can manufacture an automobile in his back yard we will continue to have organizations the size of General Motors or Ford—as long as people want Chevrolets or Fords. We will have railroads the length of the Union Pacific as long as people want to go across the continent by railroad. In other words, until a combination, a technique and organization can be invented permitting *individuals* to do the job, we are bound to try to make the best we can out of the situation. To my mind most of the results are rather surprisingly good.

This does not mean, however, that I am not afraid. I am. I believe it is the *content* of these systems rather than their *form* that matters. Their power can enslave us beyond present belief, or perhaps set us free beyond present imagination. The choice lies with the men who operate the pyramids, and with the men affected who can demand what they really want. Our Anglo-Saxon democratic liberties, after all, were beaten out, not against the framework of the personal possessory property regime, but against the background of two of the most brutal despotisms in Western history. Both the Angevin dynasty in Normandy and the Tudor dynasty in England were rank despotisms. The content of our democratic liberties from Magna Carta down was dumped in by extraneous moral processes. Our institutionalized liberties present the case of an institution conscripted into utility, rather than something that emerged full-armed from the head of Jove. It was probably better that way; the democracy of the Greeks did not work so very well.

We have to accept this power situation as, let us call it, a neutral mechanism subject to the control of the body politic as long as we keep it subject to that control. That control, I believe, will be essentially intellectual and philosophical, capable of being translated into legal rules when necessity arises. . . .

Roughly two-thirds of American industry and much of American finance is now controlled by a formal or informal federal industrial plan. Here are two illustrations at each end of the cycle.

The oil industry claims to be the most nonsocialist, free-wheeling, private business that ever was. But the fact is that after many vicissitudes it sought control by, and is controlled by, various Acts of Congress. After orderly discussion certain laws were passed. Under these laws, first, the Bureau of Mines of the Department of Interior estimates the probable consumption month by month of gasoline and the chief oil products. Second, an interstate treaty exists among the oil-producing states, ratified by the Congress. Third, a Congressional Act makes it illegal to transport oil in interstate commerce which has been produced in excess of a state allowable. This legislation might break down if it were not for the fact that because there is a relatively concentrated system in the oil industry the refineries will not buy "noncertified" oil anyway. As a result, the big companies do not violate the Act; the little ones cannot; and the result is a planned oil economy by which supply is equated to demand and the oil industry from well to refinery to gas station is more or less geared to meet it.

Here is a disorderly example: Aluminum was manufactured by a monopoly which was ordered to be split up under an antitrust decree. By a combination of administrative orders entirely without administrative rationale but all working toward the same end the federal government used the aluminum plants it had itself created during World War II in order to set up two competitors to Alcoa. It likewise required Alcoa to sell its Aluminium of Canada shares. This was not enough by itself, so the government for a period of years handled its defense orders in such a way that the new companies had adequate assurance of a market until they could get properly under way. The policy still is to make certain that the new companies, which can stay in business only by being assured a reasonable market, will get the extent of market they need. There was a stockpiling arrangement at one time, followed later by the release of part of the stockpiled aluminum. In a wholly disorderly way which only the American system could ever conceive, there arose the equivalent of a *de facto* planned economy in aluminum. At the moment this industry now sails away, freewheeling. But there is not the slightest doubt that if conditions required transition back into a planned economy, it would happen.

These two illustrations could be multiplied. The point is merely that (a) through constitutionalization of the corporation some attention is being paid to the protection of the individual; and (b) through a slowly emerging, industry-by-industry, flexibly-planned economy, some protection of the community is coming about.

Obviously a system like this is just as good as the ideas and strength of the body politic behind it. The same system in the hands, for example, of a Latin American dictator could produce terrible oppression.

I close by returning to my first point, which related to the desperate search for a field of responsibility and accountability referent to some point of view outside the system: that is, to some modern "lords spiritual." I suggest that the real purpose of the Fund for the Republic's basic issues program is to supply exactly that.

4

GEARING DEMOCRACY TO BIGNESS*

Michael Reagan

Is the Sherman Anti-Trust Act outdated, its approach a holdover from the classical economic thought of the nineteenth century? Should we discard all attempts to control bigness in business? Or should we develop new yardsticks and new controls that better fit the contemporary scene? Are big business and democracy compatible, or basically in conflict? Professor Reagan wrestles with these questions in the article which follows.

Our political system has grown in size and complexity along with the economic system, but unlike production technology and business management, government has grown haphazardly and without basic adjustment to the new forces of our times. Mass-production technology has revolutionized the economic system, while the political framework in which it is contained continues in much the same institutional and ideological patterns as prevailed a half-century ago. Despite the present concentrations of social power produced by economic giantism, we still pretend that regular, frequent elections are a sufficient structure for a viable democracy. We still pretend that economics and politics are separate; and while much ranting is heard concerning the "intrusions" of politics into the economy, little attention is paid to the impact of twentieth-century corporate industrialism upon our eighteenth-century political system. Increasingly, the democratic elements in our social system are becoming isolated, impotent segments in a world of large, hierarchically organized, institutionally unaccountable organisms.

Nowhere is the gap between economic change and political stagnation more evident than in our continued adherence to the rhetoric of antitrust. In 1890, when Senator Sherman's bill was passed, one could entertain seriously, perhaps, the thought that giantism was still new enough to be stopped. In 1957, to think that the big ones can ever be broken up sufficiently to recreate the power-diffused economy of pure competition is but a dream. The high technology, mass-production orientation of our system simply doesn't permit the number of firms and the smallness of each which a self-regulating economy presupposes. The most vigorous antitrust program imaginable could offer no more than a slight—and temporary—easing of the present centralization of economic power.

So the problem of bigness is with us to stay. Since we can't live without it—and maintain the standards of economic welfare to which we aspire—we had better find some way to take the

* Michael Reagan, "Gearing Democracy to Bigness," *The Nation*, June 8, 1957, pp. 496–98.

curse off of bigness and learn to live with it. Time spent exhorting the Department of Justice to "bust 'em up," and exhorting the public to support such a drive, is time wasted.

What is needed instead is hard thought about how we can control what Mr. Dooley called the "heejeous monsthers" to ensure that they serve our ends, not we theirs. The first step would be to devise criteria for separating those enterprises which, because of their power, require public supervision from those whose impact on economic activity is so slight as to make it safe to leave them alone. Obviously, we don't want to attempt public control of every frozen-custard stand in the land. At the other extreme, the need for some public accountability for those decisions of General Motors or U.S. Steel which may affect the livelihood of millions (their investment plans, or G. M.'s tax ultimatum to the state of Michigan, for example) should also be manifest to democrats. But where to draw the line?

The American Institute of Management has suggested that a firm be considered "too big" when its sales volume equals one per cent of gross national product. With G.N.P. at 400 billion dollars, however, this is probably too restrictive a category; it would permit many firms having a substantial impact on the economy to escape control. Another easy standard would be regulation of the billion-dollar firms (in assets or sales); but here, too, the same objection would apply.

The country's top 100 manufacturing firms, which in 1950 accounted for 33.3 per cent of the total value of manufactured products, and whose control over employment and wage patterns is commensurable with their share in production, constitute a more promising group. The top 199 of *all* corporations, whether manufacturing or not, constitutes a group whose combined impact on the economy is sufficiently great to make control over them a crucial lever over the activities of the rest. Typically, the giants are firms with self-administered (rather than market-regulated) prices and administered profits (G.M. aims at an after-tax profit of 15 to 20 per cent on invested capital, and for the past eight years has averaged over 25 per cent). They are able to finance much or all of their expansion internally, thus escaping the test of the capital market. And they are the determiners of the fate of countless suppliers and dealers. As leaders in a highly interdependent system, their failure could not be permitted by governments responsible for full employment. For this reason they represent little or no element of capitalist risk, and so a strong argument exists for the imposition of a trusteeship concept to their operations.

The trusteeship in mind here, however, is not the one, dear to the hearts of managerial spokesmen, which rests on a self-imposed ethic permitting management to remain judge in its own cause. Rather it is one which makes management accountable to the people of the United States, for whose welfare our economic institutions supposedly exist. Just what form this accountability might take, and which functions of the giants would require public participation, are questions whose answers require certain additional information, as suggested by the following queries:

1. Which base for regulation—federal chartering, public ownership, regulatory commission, or labor and public co-determination—offers the best means of channeling the power of the giants to public ends?

2. Is control over the rate and direction of investments sufficient for

purposes of economic stabilization, or is it also necessary to regulate the proportions of expenditures as between wages and stockholder dividends? (And if wage rates are a crucial factor, what accountability needs to be imposed upon unions as well as upon corporations?)

3. Even in a system which accepts bigness under administrative controls is there a useful though limited function for the antitrust approach in limiting each firm to the size at which maximum technical efficiency is attained? Can such size be determined, or is the pace of technological change too rapid to make determination feasible?

4. Once adequate control devices are available, should *combination* rather than *competition* be encouraged in lines where the product is simple and standard, such as soap, salt, sugar or matches? As things stand now, the consumer pays a heavy advertising tax to support the competition among producers of dozens of basically identical detergents. Might we not be better served by noncompetitive production in such cases, thus avoiding the tax? And think of the by-product benefits: no soap advertising, no soap operas!

5. Does bigness reach a point of diminishing returns, after which the producer or distributor gets out of touch with the people whom he claims to be serving? Can we determine what that point is for each major industry? That this may have already happened is indicated in at least two instances. One was the apparent failure of Detroit to recognize the potential demand for a light, maneuverable automobile until foreign imports had led the way. (Or did Detroit see the possibility, but simply hope it could be ignored in the interest of avoiding the extensive innovations involved?) Another is the situation of mass magazines. Originally designed for upper middle-class tastes, the periodicals whose circulations have reached four or five million may so have diluted their level of content as no longer to appeal to the original market.

6. Can a suitable institutional mechanism be devised for allocating scarce materials in such a way that the criterion of public benefit, rather than of private profit, is applied to avoid situations in which houses and schools go unbuilt while less essential items using the same materials abound?

7. How big a slice of industry needs to be included to operate a system of key-point controls? What indexes of measurement are available for determining the impact of firms or industrial groups upon the total operation of the economy?

These questions make no attempt at completeness; they are intended merely to suggest some of the areas where knowledge might give us a basis for a policy compatible with present economic realities. The biggest questions of all, of course, are those most obfuscated by ideological nonsense and public-relations propaganda; i.e., what ends, and whose, does our economic system now serve? What ends do we, the whole people, want that system to serve? As Joan Robinson put it recently, is industry "a field for adventure" in which the needs of the consumer are "an incidental by-product of the sport?" Or "do we regard meeting the needs of the nation as the prime end and purpose and think of industry as a kind of public service?"

Quite a different facet of the problem of bigness is management's inevitable orientation toward its workers as producers of goods rather than as people with aspirations of their own. It is in the discretion of the managers, exercising hierarchic authority, to decide how much the production and profit goals can be reconciled with the employee's search for personal expression and growth. But this authority is neither selected by, nor accountable to, the employees; indeed, since the separation of management from control, it is not even accountable in practice to the shareholder-owners of large corporations.

Again, the source of the problem is bigness, for as the size of an organization increases, it is necessary to increase proportionately the degree of "specialization" within the firm. Specialization produces in turn a corresponding need for coordination of the manifold specialties; and the coordinators constitute a hierarchy of command from foreman through middle management to top executive. Life for the participant at any level in such a bureaucratic structure is one of subordination to organizational compulsions.

As these units become increasingly typical of our economic organization, the political question becomes ever more pressing: how much of our lives can we spend in authoritarian relationships of command and subordination without destroying our ability to participate, in a creative sense, in political life? Can we call our society democratic when democracy—which means participation on a basis of equality in the making of decisions affecting our search for the good life—is restricted to the formal political process? In nineteenth-century America, the social structure was more equalitarian because the simpler economic system of that time did not have the range of status gradations characteristic of large organizations today. In the relative absence today of social structures which make democracy a part of our daily lives, the survival of political democracy itself may be a questionable proposition.

To make hierarchic rule compatible with democracy, those subject to controls from above must have a voice in the selection of the controllers and—this is even more essential—in setting at least the broad goals of the organization for which they labor. How to achieve this control is perhaps the Number One social and political problem of industrial democracy.

5

FOR WHOM DOES THE CORPORATION SPEAK?*

Andrew Hacker

If corporations are active in American political life, what policies should they pursue? Should they adopt a simple bread-and-butter philosophy that implies that "what's good for General Motors is good for the United States"? Or can they approach politics as disinterested observers, concerned only with the general welfare?

"Many younger businessmen who would like to participate actively in the Democratic party do not do so because they are afraid to," Governor Williams of Michigan has written in the *Harvard Business Review*. "In some areas the young man in a profession or in business is ostracized if he becomes or remains a Democrat."

It is understandable that politicians in the Democratic party feel this more deeply than their Republican counterparts. Yet it is increasingly apparent that younger employees of corporations shy away from participating in either party.

At first this avoidance may be based on the fear of jeopardizing their careers, but in time "being nonpolitical" simply becomes an aspect of their personalities. In a recent article on business men in politics, *Time*'s business editor concluded that "there is more talk than action."

Unlike their colleagues in other countries, *Time* said, "United States businessmen, whether Democrats or Republicans, have a deep-seated aversion to political activity. Even in the last presidential campaign an upsurge in political interest on the part of businessmen generally took the form of discreet, behind-the-scenes aid. Few businessmen shrink from political action in cases that directly affect their industry, e.g., for higher tariffs on imported textiles. But most executives shrink from open support of political parties for fear of offending customers, stockholders or powerful public officials."

If the executive does not participate in the party politics, it is obvious that the junior executive and the middle-management employee will stay even farther away from it.

Full-fledged participation in a party is the essential ingredient in democratic politics. It would be wrong to say merely that the middle-class corporation employee is afraid to join in; it is rather that he has neither the interest nor the inclination to identify himself with politics.

There are several dangers inherent in this renunciation of politics. First, if the emerging middle class is unable to fill the role in politics which has been

* Andrew Hacker, *Politics and the Corporation* (New York: The Fund for the Republic, 1958).

traditionally assigned to it, we will be confronted with a vacuum in political leadership.

This void will be most important at the outset at the state and local level. Certainly this has been the tragedy in the South. The moderate and law-abiding people of Little Rock and similar cities are members of the middle class, and an increasing number of them are corporation employees.

The same may be said of the North in the area of civil liberties: the middle class, while tolerant in informal social relationships, has not been notable in defending the freedom of dissident groups and individuals. Such a defense would require political participation, and the middle class has forsaken such commitment.

Second, the idea of corporate citizenship is nondemocratic. The bounties are received from a paternalistic organization which is responsive to the needs of its employees but is not accountable for what it does or for the way it does it.

The middle-class corporate employee must live with the hope and faith that he will be provided for, especially because he has no union. Faith in the beneficence of nonaccountable rulers is a shaky foundation for citizenship.

There are serious questions to answer before we can affirm that a corporation's political activities—party contributions, legislative lobbying, public relations, and community relations—are methods of representing employees and stockholders.

In what ways, for example, do the members of a corporate community benefit from the increased freedom which the corporation gains through its political participation? If we saw that the corporation is representing its members—that the interests of corporate citizens become identical with those of their corporate community—it can only be in the sense of virtual representation.

This idea was made popular by Disraeli in the nineteenth century and postulated that while large sections of the population would not participate in politics, their interests would be looked after by a benign ruling class. The corporation seems to be accepting this: it acts as it thinks best for its members' welfare, and its wisdom is accepted on faith. The corporation has certainly not set out to weaken the foundations of democratic politics, but its growth as the characteristic institution of our time is having this consequence.

6

BUSINESS MUST BECOME A POLITICAL FORCE*

Harry R. Hall

The proper role for business in American political life is debated with great heat. At one extreme are those who would erect an impregnable barrier between business and politics. Others would dismiss such a course as impractical, but would rigidly restrict the political activities of business. Still others would urge the necessity and merit of business intervention to give direction to our national life.

Several centuries before the birth of Christ an Athenian philosopher made a statement that applies today as aptly as it did in his own time. He said: "The punishment wise men suffer for indifference to public affairs is to be ruled by unwise men."

If we paraphrase that ageless and remarkable prophetic formula to meet the theme of today's discussion, we could say something like this: "The punishment businessmen suffer for traditional indifference to public affairs is to be ruled by unsympathetic men—unfriendly to their concepts—uninformed about their needs—unresponsive to their entreaties."

Traditionally, politics has been avoided by businessmen. Politics has carried an unsavory connotation. The attitude has been to let the professional politicians run politics, while the businessman runs business.

So, businessmen have become highly skilled in planning, organizing, directing, coordinating and controlling the business operations—and generally taken a fifth amendment approach to politics.

In the meantime, the so-called professional politicians have become just as adept in the business of politics. They have structured and established controls of the political machinery of the local, state and national governmental bodies with the same degree of efficiency. *But* they have not stopped there.

These elected and appointed men and women have decided that they will plan, organize, direct, coordinate and control business through the various legislative, judicial, and administrative mechanisms created for their convenience. The result is inevitable. The businessman, through his deliberate avoidance of political responsibility, finds himself hampered in his business operations by the political process that he has ignored, and ineffective in political operations that now dictate his business actions. He is taken for granted by one party and ignored by the other. While the businessman was too busy or unwilling to accept political activity as an essential business ac-

* Harry R. Hall, "The Need for Politically Sophisticated Managers," *Vital Speeches*, November 1, 1961, pp. 51–54.

tivity, certain politically sophisticated groups, hostile to the concepts of the private, competitive, capitalistic enterprise system, have been electing sheriffs, judges, city councilmen, school superintendents, state representatives, governors, congressmen, and even presidents.

These organized groups have elected large numbers of people to office committed to a political philosophy that minimizes business freedom of action, individual responsibility, and self-reliance, and maximizes governmental intervention and controls in every phase of personal and business life.

The most successful group in gaining overwhelming influence of governmental operations has been organized labor. Labor organizations and their alert leaders have not shunned politics.

While business has talked, labor has acted. While business has decried new discriminatory controls, burdensome taxes, and all encompassing government-imposed welfare programs, organized labor has told their own elected officials what is wanted. The results are a matter of record.

While businessmen have passed anonymous resolutions at their Chamber of Commerce and trade association meetings, labor has been grooming candidates, building effective precinct doorbell ringers, conducting political action education classes, and winning friends and influencing people.

While businessmen have been filling their expensive, well-edited publications with trifling trivia, meaningless minutiae, and gossipy generalities, the unions have been writing hard-hitting, punchy, emotion-stirring editorials about take-home pay, social security, minimum wage issues, automation, fringe benefits, candidates for office and other attention-arousing subjects that condition workers for practical political action in the voting booth.

Fortunately there is a new trend today. There has been a mounting interest by businessmen in practical politics.

The primary reason is that government-imposed costs of doing business have a serious impact on the success or failure of the business. If a business firm is to be successful, it must remain competitive with other firms in the same business. The ability to remain both solvent and competitive is affected by an infinite variety of local, state and government regulations. Partisan politicians exert tremendous influence on competitive conditions because they have the power to write laws and to appoint administrative officials, who in turn issue administrative decisions that dictate whether and how a firm can operate.

Government intervention into management functions has accelerated at an alarming rate. Government at some level is involved in most management decisions. Can you name any one decision that you make which does not involve government at some level?

Government is involved in taxes, tariffs, excise taxes, surtaxes, wage rates, personnel practices, ability to hire or fire employees, social security, unemployment compensation, workmen's compensation, research, financing, quality controls, sales promotion, pricing, transportation, and a multiplicity of other operations. Directives, rules, regulations, agencies, bureaus, departments and branches have octopus-like tentacles extending into every phase of business management.

Therefore, it seems reasonable to assume that a businessman has a vital stake in every phase of political life, and as such should accept the responsibility for individual participation.

Once he accepts the responsibility, the next step is to become informed—to delve into the intricacies of the political system. That is simple today.

One reason for the tremendously increased interest in practical politics by businessmen is the Action Course in Practical Politics. Such courses are being sponsored by Chambers of Commerce, trade associations, business firms, churches, women's clubs, and numerous other groups. The best accepted course was developed by the Chamber of Commerce of the United States. It was written by practical political leaders of both parties. It is designed to provide a practical working knowledge of politics so that each person can become sufficiently aware of the political structure to utilize his skills, abilities and interests in the party and in the manner of his personal choice.

To be effective, management needs to be informed on major issues that affect business and be willing to voice an opinion on the issues. Some time ago I mentioned economic illiteracy as a cause of much of our illogical legislation. Unfortunately too few businessmen have been willing to speak out publicly on how these issues affect the employer and employee alike. Business management needs to use all the multiple media available to him to inform employees, stockholders, customers, competitors, community-thought leaders, legislators and the general public on his opinions of issues that are vital to business and the public interest, regardless of how controversial the issues may be. Silence by business in the past has meant that many people have no alternatives when making a decision. When the businessman fails to speak nobody else is going to speak for him. When fallacious concepts about our economic system are espoused, they need to be answered with convincing facts by the men best qualified to give the facts.

A mass of evidence has been gathered through opinion polls and employee surveys to prove that employees want to hear management views on issues that concern their jobs, their future, their investments, their security, and their standard of living. These surveys show conclusively, for example, that a large percentage of employees have confidence in what they read in employee publications. There is a high rate of believability and a high degree of credibility by employees.

Businessmen are able to observe these issues from a vantage point. Their judgments are based on practical experience in complying with rules, regulations and policies while still trying to meet competition. The businessman serves his own best interest, as well as that of the public, when he expresses his opinion boldly, frankly and publicly. He makes a genuine contribution to the public understanding and gives the vast voting public a choice to help in its decision.

Finally, to be informed, to be enlightened, to be effective, to be politically sophisticated if you will, the businessman has to recognize politics as the well-developed science of government—and not a necessary evil conducted by shady, questionable characters. He needs to divest himself of that popular misconception that politics is a game to be played spasmodically a few months before election time, with particular emphasis in the quadrennial presidential election and with little more than checkbook effort. The fallacy of this approach is evident.

To be effective, the business manager needs to recognize politics as a deadly serious business involving strenuous work. Personal political participation cannot be automated. It cannot be delegated. It must be accepted as personal work. It is work all the time because government works all the time. Elections are won or lost by the work that is done or left undone day after day,

365 days in the year. Elections are merely manifestations of changing government personnel. The philosophy, the character, the views, the motives, the integrity, the ability, the understanding of elected or appointed officials in government decide the efficiency, the equity, and the direction of government.

Remember Plato's sage observation: "The punishment wise men suffer for indifference to public affairs is to be ruled by unwise men."

7

BUSINESS AS A SOURCE OF CAMPAIGN FUNDS*

Richard H. Rovere

One of the most comprehensive analyses of campaign funds ever prepared was compiled by the Senate Subcommittee on Privileges and Elections in 1956–1957. The committee's Report *(consisting largely of names and addresses) was the size and weight of a metropolitan telephone book.*

The Report *sheds much light on sources and expenditures of national campaign funds. Identified expenditures total $33 million with a 2:1 ratio in favor of Republicans. Some observers believe that the total sum may be four times the amount listed by the committee.*

Within the context of the present chapter, those campaign funds drawn from business sources are of particular interest. These figures are summarized in the following article. Assuming that the over-all pattern of campaign sources is accurately portrayed here, what conclusions can be drawn?

Though the subcommittee was unable to account for all contributions and expenditures, its figures unquestionably come closer to accuracy and completeness than those in any previous study, and even where they fall far short on both counts they are not necessarily misleading. The chances are that the errors and oversights are just about equally distributed along partisan lines and among the states; if due attention is paid to the caveats recommended by the subcommittee members themselves, the report is as statistically trustworthy as anything we are ever likely to have. As might be expected, the Democratic senators who signed the majority report missed no opportunity to picture the Republicans as the party of wealth and privilege and the Democrats as the party of the poor but honest. Senator Curtis made a powerful effort to show that this is not so and to prove that organized labor, in

* Richard Rovere, "Business as a Source of Campaign Funds," *The New Yorker Magazine*, February 23, 1957, pp. 111–12, 115.

contributing the time of thousands of members and funds from union treasuries, redresses the balance. His argument on manpower and time is a formidable one; it is well known to every political observer that the manpower resources of the Democrats are in most parts of the country superior to those of the Republicans. Nevertheless, though time is money, as Senator Curtis insists, so is legal tender, and it is a fact beyond dispute that the coin of the realm is mostly on the side of the Republicans. The union treasuries are reported to have yielded $941,271, most of which was turned over to the Democrats, and union officials made personal donations of $16,500. Individual members of twelve wealthy families, however, contributed $1,040,526 to the Republicans, which more than offsets the labor contributions and the large donations from union leaders. And if the labor figures are suspiciously low, as some people believe, they could be doubled and they would still be offset by the gifts of another twelve or fifteen families. The forty-seven leading underwriters of investment bonds contributed $237,800 to the Republicans and $2,000 to the Democrats. Officers of the thirty-seven largest advertising agencies gave $51,600 to the Republicans and nothing to the Democrats. Officers and directors of the American Iron & Steel Institute gave $45,100 to the Republicans; those of the American Petroleum Institute gave $171,750; those of the Association of American Railroads $3,500; those of the National Association $28,500; and those of the United States Chamber of Commerce $10,700. No officer or director of any of these organizations is reported to have contributed anything to the Democrats. All told, the officers and directors of the two hundred and twenty-five largest corporations in the country gave $1,816,000 to the Republicans and $103,000 to the Democrats.

It would be idle for anyone to deny that our party system has a class structure. It is not the most rigid class structure imaginable, but it is a clearly perceptible one. There are some people here who deplore this, but their numbers do not appear to be very considerable. The major parties have appealed to and been supported by the same groups for nearly a century, and the republic is not less democratic or less republican now than it used to be. In any event, no outpouring of laments will alter circumstances. If the wealthy find their interests better served on the whole by the Republicans, they will give the Republicans money in large amounts and votes in small amounts. If the masses feel themselves better served by the Democrats, they will give the Democrats their votes, which are numerous, and their money in small amounts. In the view of the subcommittee, the one practical thing that can be done is to bring the laws into line with reality. It is plainly ridiculous to have on the books a law limiting the expenditures of national committees to three million dollars when the Republicans are spending in excess of five million for radio and television alone, and the Democrats in excess of four million. And it is plainly ridiculous to have a law intended to hold individual contributions to five thousand dollars when the law, as the subcommittee says, is so "studded with loopholes" as to make possible numerous gifts of ten times that amount. In a thoughtful review of the subcommittee's report, the Washington *Post* suggests that whatever is done about the laws—whether they are retained with all their loopholes, or rewritten, or thrown out altogether—the most important thing is to go on providing the kind of public information found in this report.

8

CAN BUSINESS BE REGULATED?*

Richard H. Rovere

During the past half century the American people have embarked on a major attempt to control big business through government regulatory agencies. In recent years the adequacy of this program has been questioned because of widespread influence-peddling within these agencies. Is it possible to safeguard the public interest through regulatory commissions? Or do they inevitably become spokesmen for the business they are appointed to curb? How can a high standard of morality be established in these agencies? How can good men be recruited? How can they be protected from outside pressures?

In the Truman administration as well as in the Eisenhower administration, the regulatory agencies have been regarded more or less as patronage bureaus, upon which any politician from any party is free to exert all the pressure he can muster. Sherman Adams is not the only virtuous man to have been caught up in this investigation. [The late] Senator Estes Kefauver, himself a renowned investigator of corruption, offered his help to a political associate who was seeking a television license from the Federal Communications Commission. Senator Kefauver's letter to his friend is a nice gauge of atmospheric conditions. It reads in part:

> I have been waiting for a go-ahead from you. In incidental conversations, I have talked with Bob Bartley, Frieda Hennock, and Commissioner Lee (in other words, with three of the six F.C.C. commissioners) by letting them bring up the subject in some way, and I think this is the best way to be helpful.
>
> But if there is anything in the way of a more direct approach to anyone I can make or be useful to you, let me know, because it would break my heart if you didn't get the final approval.

Attempting to influence the regulatory agencies is an old bipartisan tradition, and it is not always done covertly. In the late Forties, there were open campaigns in the Senate to drive from office two commission chairmen—Leland Olds, of the Federal Power Commission, and James M. Landis, of the Civil Aeronautics Board—whose decisions had not been to the taste of the senators seeking their removal. Senator Kerr, of Oklahoma, a man with large oil and natural-gas holdings, did not rest until he had got rid of Mr. Olds, who had wanted the commission to keep a strict control over both the flow of gas into the pipelines and the price to the consumer. Somewhat earlier, Senator Brewster, of Maine, campaigned for and won the removal of Mr. Landis, who had not gone along with Brewster's plan to award all transatlantic air routes to a single carrier. This sort of thing has been going on for quite a while, and there is not much doubt

---

* Richard Rovere, "Can Business Be Regulated?" *The New Yorker Magazine*, March 1, 1958, pp. 97–103.

that one reason the subcommittee began backing away from its investigation was that it quickly realized that a good many congressional names were going to turn up.

Down through the postwar years, the regulatory commissions have more and more been staffed by men of meager distinction. For this, the Truman administration bears far heavier responsibility than the Eisenhower administration. The Republicans, after all, never thought that these agencies had any reason for existence to begin with. In being required to administer them, the Republicans' situation is roughly analogous to that of a vegetarian who finds that he has been made a trustee of a butcher shop and is expected to promote the sale and consumption of meat. They had no hand in creating the commissions; all the major ones were established by Democrats. The Interstate Commerce Commission was set up under Grover Cleveland; the Federal Trade and the Federal Power Commissions under Woodrow Wilson; and the Federal Communications Commission, the Securities and Exchange Commission, the Civil Aeronautics Board, and the Maritime Commission under Franklin Roosevelt. All exist to restrain and restrict and police private enterprises, and Republicans consider this the Devil's work, though they are forced by the terms of their trusteeship to see that it is done. It is understandable that they should fulfill their obligations as permissively as the law allows, and that they should not seek out devotees of regulation to staff the agencies, particularly when they are able to cite Democratic precedents for a casual treatment of the whole business. And this they are easily able to do. President Truman dropped Landis, a former Dean of the Harvard Law School, as chairman of the Civil Aeronautics Board and appointed a former airline official in his place, and when the airline official left, his successor was a trade-association lobbyist. Mon Wallgren, who succeeded Leland Olds as chairman of the Federal Power Commission, was a defeated Governor of Washington, and a political mediocrity with no known competence in the field—though he developed, early on, a sympathy for the gas interests that undoubtedly left Senator Kerr feeling that he had done a good day's work in getting rid of Olds. The Eisenhower administration was breaking no new ground when it made a gas-company lawyer the chairman of the Federal Power Commission and put a protectionist congressman on the Tariff Commission.

The appointment of third-raters, honest or not, and of willing tools of the industries that are subject to regulation by the commissions not only made the commissions less wise, impartial, and responsible but also made them less interesting. And this failing, too, has contributed to the present squalor. When Dean Landis, Leland Olds, William O. Douglas, Joseph Kennedy, and Jerome Frank were sitting on regulatory commissions, the work they did, the ideas they spawned, and the decisions they made seemed worthy of notice in the press. In the Thirties, the great age of the commissions, the newspapers and magazines kept the public advised of what was being said and thought and done in the offices of these men. For the past ten or twelve years, this has not been the case. Not even the largest of the news services make a serious attempt to keep the public abreast of what the commissions, with their vast powers over commerce, entertainment, transportation, and finance, are doing. Chosen from the ranks of the obscure and the politically necessitous, the commissioners—or most of them, anyway—remain in relative obscurity and are rewarded with salaries that compare most unfavorably with those of the businessmen who seek their good opinion. The fact that some of them remain conscientious and unpurchasable may well be more remarkable than the fact that some, apparently, can be got to.

Sooner or later, though, something will have to be done about the regulatory agencies. If regulation is to continue, either Congress will have to transfer the commissions' administrative functions to administrative agencies and their judicial ones to the courts—which is essentially what the two Hoover Commissions have proposed—or it will have to recreate by some means the atmosphere of the Thirties, when it was recognized that a man issuing licenses for great enterprises, establishing regulations for industries that involve the public safety, fixing prices that affect the whole economy, and weighing the rights and claims of individuals and corporations must be above suspicion in the first place and, in the second place, must be removed and protected from the people he is dealing with.

9

BIG BUSINESS, MILITARISM, AND DEMOCRACY*

Dwight D. Eisenhower

During the past decade the relationship between government and the economy has changed most drastically in the field of military expenditures. More than ten per cent of the American gross national product is now spent each year for defense purposes. A single military contract can be worth five or six billion dollars. Cancellation of a contract can mean economic disaster for an entire area. A multimillion dollar award means boom times. With so much at stake it is not surprising that an uneasy business-military power axis has arisen. President Eisenhower voices his concern over this new facet of American life in the article that follows.

I

My fellow Americans: Three days from now, after half a century in the service of our country, I shall lay down the responsibilities of office as, in traditional and solemn ceremony, the authority of the Presidency is vested in my successor.

This evening I come to you with a message of leavetaking and farewell and to share a few final thoughts with you, my countrymen.

Like every other citizen, I wish the new President and all who will labor with him Godspeed. I pray that the coming years will be blessed with peace and prosperity for all.

* Excerpts from the "Farewell to the Nation" speech delivered by President Dwight D. Eisenhower over radio and television on January 17, 1961.

II

We now stand ten years past the midpoint of a century that has witnessed four major wars among great nations. Three of these involved our own country. Despite these holocausts, America is today the strongest, the most influential, and most productive nation in the world. Understandably proud of this preeminence, we yet realize that America's leadership and prestige depend not merely upon our unmatched material progress, riches, and military strength but on how we use our power in the interests of world peace and human betterment.

III

Throughout America's adventure in free government our basic purposes have been to keep the peace, to foster progress in human achievement, and to enhance liberty, dignity, and integrity among people and among nations. To strive for less would be unworthy of a free and religious people. Any failure traceable to arrogance or our lack of comprehension or readiness to sacrifice would inflict upon us grievous hurt both at home and abroad.

Progress toward these noble goals is persistently threatened by the conflict now engulfing the world. It commands our whole attention, absorbs our very beings. We face a hostile ideology—global in scope, atheistic in character, ruthless in purpose, and insidious in method. Unhappily the danger it poses promises to be of indefinite duration. To meet it successfully there is called for not so much the emotional and transitory sacrifices of crisis but rather those which enable us to carry forward steadily, surely, and without complaint the burdens of a prolonged and complex struggle—with liberty the stake. Only thus shall we remain, despite every provocation, on our charted course toward permanent peace and human betterment.

Crises there will continue to be. In meeting them, whether foreign or domestic, great or small, there is a recurring temptation to feel that some spectacular and costly action could become the miraculous solution to all current difficulties. A huge increase in newer elements of our defense, development of unrealistic programs to cure every ill in agriculture, a dramatic expansion in basic and applied research—these and many other possibilities, each possibly promising in itself, may be suggested as the only way to the road we wish to travel.

But each proposal must be weighed in the light of a broader consideration: The need to maintain balance in and among national programs—balance between the private and the public economy, balance between cost and hoped-for advantage, balance between the clearly necessary and the comfortably desirable, balance between our essential requirements as a nation and the duties imposed by the nation upon the individual, balance between actions of the moment and the national welfare of the future. Good judgment seeks balance and progress; lack of it eventually finds imbalance and frustration.

The record of many decades stands as proof that our people and their government have, in the main, understood these truths and have responded to them well in the face of stress and threat. But threats, new in kind or degree, constantly arise. I mention two only.

IV

A vital element in keeping the peace is our military establishment. Our arms must be mighty, ready for instant action, so that no potential aggressor may be tempted to risk his own destruction.

Our military organization today bears little relation to that known by any of my predecessors in peacetime, or indeed by the fighting men of World War II or Korea.

Until the latest of our world conflicts, the United States had no armaments industry. American makers of plowshares could, with time and as required, make swords as well. But now we can no longer risk emergency improvisation of national defense; we have been compelled to create a permanent armaments industry of vast proportions. Added to this, 3½ million men and women are directly engaged in the defense establishment. We annually spend on military security more than the net income of all United States corporations.

This conjunction of an immense military establishment and a large arms industry is new in the American experience. The total influence—economic, political, even spiritual—is felt in every city, every statehouse, every office of the federal government. We recognize the imperative need for this development. Yet we must not fail to comprehend its grave implications. Our toil, resources, and livelihood are all involved; so is the very structure of our society.

In the councils of government we must guard against the acquisition of unwarranted influence, whether sought or unsought, by the military-industrial complex. The potential for the disastrous rise of misplaced power exists and will persist.

We must never let the weight of this combination endanger our liberties or democratic processes. We should take nothing for granted. Only an alert and knowledgeable citizenry can compel the proper meshing of the huge industrial and military machinery of defense with our peaceful methods and goals so that security and liberty may prosper together.

Akin to and largely responsible for the sweeping changes in our industrial-military posture has been the technological revolution during recent decades. In this revolution research has become central; it also becomes more formalized, complex, and costly. A steadily increasing share is conducted for, by, or at the direction of the federal government.

Today the solitary inventor, tinkering in his shop, has been overshadowed by task forces of scientists in laboratories and testing fields. In the same fashion the free university, historically the fountainhead of free ideas and scientific discovery, has experienced a revolution in the conduct of research. Partly because of the huge costs involved, a government contract becomes virtually a substitute for intellectual curiosity. For every old blackboard there are now hundreds of new electronic computers.

The prospect of domination of the nation's scholars by federal employment, project allocations, and the power of money is ever present and is gravely to be regarded.

Yet, in holding scientific research and discovery in respect, as we should, we must also be alert to the equal and opposite danger that public policy could itself become the captive of a scientific-technological elite.

It is the task of statemanship to mold, to balance, and to integrate these and other forces, new and old, within the principles of our democratic system—ever aiming toward the supreme goals of our free society.

XIII

Big Labor and Politics

In the past thirty years organized labor has become a major economic, social, and political force in the United States. As late as 1932 less than four million workers belonged to unions, with one-third of this total being claimed by company unions. Today, the total membership exceeds 18 million, and between one-quarter and one-third of all American workers are dues-paying members. For all practical purposes this organized segment of the working force is the voice of labor. Several major unions have members in excess of one million; union leaders wield great national power and influence; union treasuries contain millions of dollars.

The creation of this new center of power in American life poses many questions that are as yet unanswered. Within the mass production industries, unionization is virtually complete. But this giant aggregation of power produces numerous conflicts within the American system. Tensions arise between big labor and corporate management, big labor and consumers, and big labor and the general public. Since the total fabric of American society is thus affected, government is frequently called upon to resolve the issues at stake.

In this chapter we will attempt to gain a panoramic view of American workers and unions on the contemporary scene, with particular emphasis on their aspirations and the struggle for security and status. The potential for union growth will be explored also.

Beyond the foregoing issues, some of the more controversial aspects of big unions will be examined. First, we will sift the conflicting testimony regarding the effect of unions on our political life in terms of campaign contributions, organized voting at the polls, and pressure upon elected representatives.

Finally, we will examine the extent of union graft, corruption and violence and trace the proposals that have been made to curb unions and to institute reform within the house of labor.

The Labor Union: Unique American Institution or Temporary Power Bloc?

No agreement exists regarding the present status and future prospects of the American worker and his union. Optimists insist that class lines are gradually being blurred in the United States—that thanks to unions American workers are increasingly middle class in terms of their income and attitudes. Many people who subscribe to this theory believe that the remaining underprivileged groups in American society will eventually be raised to a position of equality by a combination of factors that includes the extension of union membership.

Skeptics find this picture of the future quite unrealistic. Some critics challenge the belief that unions must inevitably expand. Following this thesis, the replacement of basic production workers by white collar workers will steadily sap union strength. Other critics challenge the belief that workers are increasingly middle class in outlook. According to their analysis, factory workers in our society remain as a species of industrialized helots who have no way of escape.

Beyond the questions of class, status and union growth are the issues posed by automation. Few union spokesmen today oppose the extension of automation. Their concern is primarily directed toward bridging the transition period between the present and an automated America. Issues raised by automation include the wholesale transfer and retraining of workers; a shorter work day and week; and wage adjustments that reflect the new productivity. This problem, because of its scope, will not only involve all workers (union and nonunion) but also management and government.

This introductory section, therefore, provides something of an overview of the current American labor scene and attempts to link it to the foreseeable future. It examines in turn the trends in union leadership, the class and status concepts of the American worker, and the potential for union growth.

Unions in Politics: A Decisive Force or Overrated Bogeymen?

A power of such magnitude as the labor union cannot easily be confined to its original objective, collective bargaining. Inevitably union influence tends to spread into questions of government policy, social organization, and the political process.

The impact of unions on American political life is a topic that is hotly debated at several levels in the United States. Unions now have a total membership in excess of 18 million. With sweethearts, wives, and other relatives this potential voting group probably numbers nearly 50 million. The opponents of labor view such statistics with great misgivings. On paper, at least, an obedient labor force and their allies, marching as a unit to the polls on election day, can win every election and control the destiny of the United States. To underline their alarm, these opponents point to the fact that organized labor has made determined efforts to mobilize its membership. The CIO originally created a political arm, the Political Action Committee (PAC) and the American Federation of Labor operated Labor's League for Political Education. After merger of the AF of L and CIO these two political units were merged into the Committee on Political Education (COPE). As evidence of the financial strength of labor the critics note that in both 1952 and 1954 these labor organizations spent over $2,000,000 in political campaigns. This entire question is further complicated, however, by the fact that corporate officers contributed a far larger sum to political parties.

Much of the debate concerning labor's political role is based on disagreement as to its effectiveness. Some observers picture labor in politics as a potential Frankenstein that will destroy American democracy unless it is checked. Other observers agree as to labor's power but celebrate its strength as an extension of democracy. Still other observers belittle labor's political role as largely sound and fury, without much in the way of concrete results at the polls.

Should labor play an active role in politics? Should it endorse candidates, raise campaign funds, play an active part in the registration and mobilization of voters? Should it maintain active lobbies in Washington and the state capitols? Is such labor activity a wholesome counterweight to the influence of big business? Or should legislative checks be placed on labor's political activity? If such legislation is desirable, what form should it take?

Financial aspects of this issue are blurred, largely because of fuzzy accounting practices. What sum have unions actually spent to elect a favorite senator? Does the legal limitation that unions fight their political crusades with voluntary contributions impose any real handicap? What price tag should be placed on intangible items such as voluntary political workers, registration drives, and "educational" television programs?

More basic are questions regarding the proper sphere of union activity. Should unions serve as both the economic and political voice of their membership? Are union political activities a threat to American democracy? Or are unions good citizens, educating and stimulating their members toward responsible citizenship? Finally, should the political power of unions (assuming its existence) be greatly curbed?

Labor Faces Automation: Boon or Blight?

Automation is a "good" or "bad" word, depending largely upon the experience of the reader. To many Americans it means that man has finally conquered his environment—that he will no longer be harnessed to heavy, dull, repetitive tasks. Instead, in a society of growing leisure he will be able to practice the arts and commune with his soul while a mounting tide of goods rises around him.

This rosy picture bears no resemblance to the bleak reality of West Virginia's desolate coal towns, filled with unemployed miners who have been replaced by machines. Nor does it parallel the soaring unemployment patterns of steel, automobile and railroad towns, where automatic processes have displaced workers by the thousands.

What does automation really mean? Can the present period be compared to a highway detour, carrying the sign "the inconvenience is temporary: the improvement is permanent?" Or is automation a spreading danger? Does it carry within it self-adjusting forces that guarantee that "machines make jobs"? Perhaps, instead, any problems should be disposed of in orderly fashion through negotiation, by labor-management leaders. Or is the issue so great that only intervention by the national government can provide for the retraining, unemployment compensation, and adjustments of hours and wages that automation demands.

1

THE AMERICAN WORKER*

Edward C. Marciniak

Why do American workers celebrate Labor Day rather than May Day? Why have they rejected the "class struggle" concept? In other words, why does the American labor movement differ so markedly from its European counterpart? These fundamental questions are raised by the author, who suggests some possible answers.

In almost every industrialized nation of the world, on both sides of the Iron Curtain, the official workers' holiday is the first day of May. But in the United States May Day is celebrated only by Communists and a small remainder of nostalgic Socialists, while most American workers instead celebrate Labor Day, the first Monday in September.

This choice of a September holiday symbolizes the way in which United States workingmen and their leaders have moved from European working-class traditions and accommodated themselves to the United States political and economic system. The day itself was not selected for ideological or revolutionary objectives but for highly pragmatic benefits. In choosing Monday, for example, they made certain that a regular working day would be included in a three-day holiday weekend, and by picking September they guaranteed themselves an extra day of rest midway between two holidays which had been long established, the Fourth of July and Thanksgiving.

* Edward A. Marciniak, "The American Worker," *The Commonweal,* August 31, 1956, pp. 533–37.

While it is dangerous to generalize about workers in a nation as large and varied as the United States, it can be said that any analysis of the American economic system will be inadequate and distorted if it is predicated on the presence of a class struggle. Few factory workers in the United States show any desire to carry on a class war. The impact of movies, radio, press, and magazines, advertising, and television upon a worker's attitudes has been immeasurably greater than that of his position as a worker. The country's natural wealth and high productivity; the absence generally of proletarian conditions; public education; the continual influx into cities of new immigrants and migrant workers to take over the menial jobs—all have tended to dull the class consciousness of factory workers. It is certainly true that there are millions of low-paid workers, that working and living conditions among most migratory workers are subhuman, and that certain racial groups are deprived of equal economic opportunity. But millions of factory workers who own their own homes regard themselves as "Middle Class." In addition, the most rapidly growing group in the working population is made up of white collar workers in offices, commerce, retail establishments, government service, and the professions. By and large, the aspirations and standards of this white collar population, which almost outnumbers manual workers, are indistinguishable from those of the United States middle class.

When the American Federation of Labor was founded in 1881, it was by no means certain that the new federation would follow a course plotted by non-Marxists. The opening sentence of its constitution dedicated the AFL to the class struggle: "A struggle is going on in all of the nations of the civilized world, between the oppressors and the oppressed of all countries, a struggle between capitalist and the laborer, which grows in intensity from year to year, and will work disastrous results to the toiling millions, if they are not combined for mutual protection and benefit." This preamble remained part of the AFL constitution until 1955 when its merger with the Congress of Industrial Organizations brought forth a new declaration.

The new preamble crystallizes the metamorphosis in United States unionism in the years since 1881. Nowhere in the new AFL-CIO constitution is there any ringing call to join the class struggle. On the contrary, the preamble strikes a new tone: "At the collective bargaining table, in the community, in the exercise of rights and responsibilities of citizenship, we shall responsibly serve the interests of all American people.

"We pledge ourselves to the more effective organization of working men and women; to the securing to them of full recognition and enjoyment of the rights to which they are justly entitled; to the achievement of ever higher standards of living and working conditions; to the attainment of security for all the people; to the enjoyment of the leisure which their skills make possible; and to the strengthening and extension of our way of life and the fundamental freedoms which are the basis of our democratic society.

"We shall combat resolutely the forces which seek to undermine the democratic constitutions of our nation and to enslave the human soul. We shall strive always to win full respect for the dignity of the human individual whom our unions serve. With Divine Guidance, grateful for the fine traditions of our past, confident of meeting the challenge of the future, we proclaim this constitution."

Proud of their businesslike concern

for immediate improvement in working conditions, union officials claim, with some justification, that the continued pressure upon management for higher wages and increased benefits tended to weed out inefficient and incompetent employers. They also claim that their acceptance of mechanization and technological advancement (but with some exceptions, as in the building and entertainment fields) was, in part, responsible for higher United States productivity. Certainly, this practical bent of mind made the labor movement a real stumbling-block for the Marxist Socialists at the turn of the twentieth century and for the Communists during the great depression of the 1930's. Today, most United States unionists continue to distrust the theorist, whether he be Socialist, Communist, or capitalist. They have in the main tasted the bountiful fruits of business unionism and will accept no substitutes.

Yet the transmutation from a class-conscious, Marxist union of European inspiration to a native, hard-headed allegiance to collective bargaining as the way to produce tangible, sizable benefits for working men is by no means final. The United States labor movement has yet to reach full maturity. In the last twenty years it has undergone tremendous growth—from four to seventeen million members. Most of these new union members, it is aptly said, are organized but not unionized. Union jurisdiction has yet to be extended to the great majority (65 per cent) of United States workingmen who remain potential members. Furthermore, the nation's 190 national unions, whose membership ranges from 1,000 to 1,500,000 members, differ radically in their militancy, their involvement in political affairs, their policy toward the colored races, and their concern for the welfare of people in other countries. However, postponement of the labor movement's age of maturity is chiefly attributable to two additional factors: its unfinished struggle to root out tyrannical practices in internal union affairs and its partial success in attaining some equitable status in external union relations.

First of all, the ascendancy of business unionism saw a toleration and, in some cases, actual support of violations of human dignity within the unions themselves. The capture by hoodlums of New York City's waterfront unions was public knowledge; so was the existence of father and son control—by fraud and force—on Long Island, in Chicago, and elsewhere; so was the frank admission of a Chicago business agent that his union's insurance brokers had contributed $42,000 to sponsor a girls' baseball team which was his personal property; so was the $1,400 fine levied against each of nine midwestern pipefitters whose only crime was that they asked some pointed questions about a union real estate deal; so was the lackadaisical attitude displayed by some influential leaders toward the organization of farm and migratory workers.

Some union officers behaved and talked like corporation tycoons. "I run the union just like a business. We deal in one commodity—labor," once explained Dave Beck, president of the International Brotherhood of Teamsters, the second largest union in the United States. Others, refusing to admit in practice that a union was a democratic body, regarded the union as their private property. Some paid public relations men a fancy price to write their biographies—sprinkled with heroic adjectives and hyperbole.

In some craft unions, especially in the building trades, exclusion of Negroes is still the rule rather than the exception. Such unions have exhibited deplorable indifference to racial discrimination. In collusion with contractors and material suppliers, some building trades unions still dictate the use of certain building materials and antiquated methods. The leaders of a large factory local in one city eliminate rank and file opposition by persuading the employer to fire any rebels. And the employer, eager to keep his substandard contract with the union, is more than willing to oblige.

Such cases of tyranny under business unionism are not typical. Yet there are enough of them to make top union leaders like George Meany, Al Hayes, and Walter Reuther anxious for reform and to create a distrust of the business unionism which has given shelter to such abuses.

Secondly, business unionism has not been able to secure labor's rightful place in American public affairs. For over nine years, unions have unsuccesfully been opposing the Taft-Hartley law, which imposes severe restrictions upon unions and collective bargaining. Early union demand for absolute repeal has now been replaced by a willingness to accept substantial amendments. Seventeen states have enacted "right to work" laws further restricting union activity—over the aggressive but unavailing protest of unions. State workmen's compensation benefits—in case of occupational disease or accident —are generally geared to living standards at a near starvation level. (Most state legislatures are still dominated by a coalition of middle-class farmers and small businessmen.) Since 1953, despite the expenditure of considerable money and manpower for organizing the unorganized, the growth of union membership has reached an ominous plateau. Fifteen times as many businessmen as unionists sit in Congress. Only 84 labor leaders (out of approximately 50,000 fulltime union officials in the United States) were regarded important enough to be included in a recent edition of *Who's Who in America.*

The political and economic strength of organized labor is repeatedly exaggerated to exploit fear and confusion for private gain. Most United States newspapers, for example, regularly attempt to magnify the real power of unions—implying that such power when held by workingmen and their leaders is somehow repugnant to democracy. Objections are constantly being raised to labor's exerting any important and decisive influence on national affairs—even if that power were to be democratically determined and directed toward the common good. Disappointed that the labor movement has been only partially successful in achieving greater political status and power in state capitals and in Washington, many union leaders are losing faith in the efficacy of business unionism.

These are the reasons, then, why the historical right of business unionism to set the standards for the American labor movement is being challenged by the union philosophies of "democratic unionism" and "political unionism." "Democratic unionism" concentrates on reordering a union's internal affairs and its relations with management. It strives militantly to eradicate the notion that labor is a commodity (by such measures as the guaranteed annual wage), to realize industrial democracy (by giving workingmen ownership and voice in industry), and by recognizing the justice of each worker's claim to human dignity (by eliminating all discrimination and segregation on account of race or color and by protecting the rights of union members against any despotism by some union boss). It regards political action by unions as necessary to guarantee the presence of a government friendly to such goals; political action stems not from some doctrinaire objective but from economic and moral necessity. Democratic unionism is sparked by some of that spirit which set aflame the native radicalism of the Knights of Labor in the 1870's and the Industrial Workers of the World in the 1910's: *an injury to one is an injury to all*. That is why its supporters, like the late Philip Murray, fought attempts of Communists and reactionaries to isolate the United States from the world and instead supported the Marshall Plan for Europe, technical assistance to underdeveloped countries, freedom for colonial people, and a sturdy United Nations.

Most advocates of "political unionism" would subscribe to these stated objectives of "democratic unionism," but would part company by attaching *prime* importance to labor's role in politics. In many ways, today's political unionists are legatees of those who fought against Samuel Gompers fifty years ago. They would tend to overstress the social benefits of government action and underemphasize the potency of collective bargaining. They would regard the union primarily as a stepping stone to labor's control of political life rather than as an instrument of economic democracy. They would concentrate, through a labor party, on restoring labor to its rightful place in the political sun—in contrast to democratic unionism, which would attempt to establish that place by putting the house of labor in order, and by establishing economic democracy with the aid but not the direction of government.

These three orientations do not represent sharply distinct groupings within the labor movement. They are, rather, tendencies with distinguishable lines that are frequently blurred. The philosophy of most union leaders would be a blend of these. George Meany, the president of the recently merged AFL-CIO, began his union career as a business unionist but today typifies democratic unionism. Walter Reuther started out dedicated to political unionism, but he has steadily been moving in the direction of democratic unionism. David McDonald, president of the United Steelworkers of America, a union with more than 1,000,000 members, has until recently made his home with democratic unionism, but he is now developing many of the domestic habits of business unionism. To date the purest examples of business unionism are to be found among the union leaders in the building trades, teamsters and coal miners. In general, more presidents of national unions represent the philosophy of business unionism while the leaders of national federations tend to reflect the point of view of democratic unionism. The position of political unionism is today the weakest of the competing philosophies.

Business unionism remains dominant and feeds upon its successes at the bargaining table and its power in municipal politics. The future of political unionism lies in capitalizing on failures—the failure to bring about world peace, to halt inflation, to forestall a depression, to give labor a share in increased productivity, and to prevent the government from favoring big business.

In the long run, the fate of political unionism is dependent upon the ability of democratic unionism to improve upon the legacy left the labor movement by Samuel Gompers. The most creative thinking and planning of the problems of automation, on the content of collective bargaining, and on new approaches to union-management cooperation, come from union leaders in the orbit of democratic unionism.

The new solidarity arising out of a merged AFL-CIO will enlarge the United States labor movement's influence upon national and world affairs, as it will also accelerate the competition among the rival philosophies to win the heart and mind of the labor movement. Of the triad, it is my opinion, only democratic unionism is equal to the task of simultaneously capturing the imagination of both manual and white collar workers, championing the rights of those Americans still victimized by economic and social injustice, and serving as in inspiration to trade unionists, not only in Europe, but especially in Asia and Africa.

2

LABOR'S EBBING STRENGTH*

George Kirstein

Labor unions and their leaders are frequently pictured as the decisive force in modern America. Operating from this assumption, some writers "view with alarm." Others find this assumption a cause for celebration. The following article challenges the basic assumption and marshalls evidence to prove that labor unions are a declining force in our society.

The annual paeans for organized labor's contribution to our society will ring forth [on Labor Day] from Detroit's Cadillac Square and from the editorial pages of a thousand newspapers in the customary manner and in the volume consonant with an election year. Labor's "statesmen" will be cited; labor's political strength will be hailed. No sour notes will be struck about the fight of the railroad brotherhoods for survival, and Jimmy Hoffa's uneuphonious name will barely be mentioned. But, in truth, sour notes should be the main theme of this oratorical occasion, for labor's power and prestige have sunk to a depth unequaled since World War II.

Union membership, continuing its descending curve, has shrunk to new lows for the last 25 years; still worse, perhaps, the enlistment of new members has ground to a frustrated halt on almost all fronts. We are no longer treated even to promises of the perennial "Crusade in the South," or anywhere else for that matter. If we look at the present labor scene without benefit of the politician's rose-colored glasses or the editorial writer's once-a-year dedication to the worker's cause, what do we see?

In New York, a congressional committee is conducting hearings on charges that the International Ladies' Garment Workers' Union discriminates in various ways against its Negro and Puerto Rican members. The committee intends to investigate other "nefarious conditions," including alleged racketeering in the industry. The ILGWU, which is the main financial

* George Kirstein, "Labor's Ebbing Strength," *The Nation*, September 1, 1962.

support of the Liberal party, claims that these hearings, being conducted by a Democratic congressman who failed to win Liberal party endorsement, are "political blackmail."

But the plight of the ILGWU, serious though it may be, is insignificant when compared to the life-or-death struggle that faces the railroad brotherhoods. The hard-pressed railroads are preparing to wage the long-delayed battle to eliminate the unneeded workers and scrap the outdated work rules that have added mounting labor cost to their other tribulations in recent years. At stake in one major bloc are the jobs of some 40,000 firemen who are no longer needed now that diesel locomotion has replaced the old coal-fed engines. While legal maneuvering will delay the showdown for a couple of months more, the brotherhoods have little to celebrate.

Under normal circumstances, the one bright promise in labor's future might be the growth and expansion of the Teamsters. Automation and mechanization have not taken their toll in this industry as they have in almost all others. More and more trucks use the ever-expanding highway system, and more and more men are required to drive them. Against labor's declining trend, the Teamsters are growing in membership and wealth. But success will not be permitted to spoil Jimmy Hoffa. Indictment after indictment piles up around the head of the beleaguered Teamsters' president; he is hardly acquitted of one criminal charge before he is accused of two more. In what is generally conceded to be a personal vendetta, the Attorney General of the United States pursues Hoffa from courtroom to courtroom. It is probably only a question of time before one of the many agencies of government which are competing in their pursuit of Hoffa bring him tumbling from his uneasy perch. But with or without Hoffa, this union promises to be the single exception to a trend that is sapping labor's economic and political strength.

Curiously enough, it is at this time of obvious weakness that a strident clamor is arising for further shackles to labor's strength. *Life* magazine, in its June 29 issue, voiced this chorus in a full-page editorial appropriately titled "Let's Put Teeth into the Labor Laws." In a thousand fighting words, *Life* demanded a crackdown, and warned that in dealing with labor disputes "persuasion is not enough." Not long before *Life's* plea, the Solicitor General of the United States, Archibald Cox, had urged an audience of lawyers to consider new methods of resolving industrial disputes without strikes. One would think that our economy was being brought to a halt by a rash of stoppages. The fact is that strike idleness in the first five months of this year, although higher than in 1961, was less than in either of the last two years of President Eisenhower's administration. The cries for restrictive legislation, by no means limited to the two samples cited, are additional evidence of labor's falling prestige.

Why has labor descended from yesteryear's heroic struggle for higher wages and better working conditions to the rear-guard holding actions that characterize today's scene? The answer is that manual labor, particularly the unskilled labor of the production line, is becoming a national surplus as permanent as the wheat and other grains that glut the nation's storage bins. The great industrial unions in auto production, steel, and textiles decline in membership as the machine replaces man in the manufacturing process. This is scarcely a startling observation; we have been witnessing this union erosion for the past decade. What few observers recognize, however, is that because of it the objective of organized labor has changed from a constant improvement of wages and working conditions to the liquidation of members' jobs in an orderly way. Not wages but pensions are at issue; not hiring rates but termination pay is the subject of dispute; not vacations but lay-off procedures occupy the attention of negotiators.

John L. Lewis, one of America's greatest labor leaders, was forced, by circumstances within the coal industry, to set the pattern that other union leaders are now following. As machinery replaced men in the mines, and the union's rolls decreased each year, Lewis negotiated a welfare plan based on royalties on each ton of coal, whether it was mined by men or machines. This strategy did not save the miners' jobs, but it prevented the retreat from becoming a rout. Other labor leaders, challenged by similar developments, have adopted variations of the same policy. Harry Bridges, once the storm center of the San Francisco waterfront, capitulated to the future last year by agreeing to eliminate men on the job in return for financial consideration for those displaced by the machines. Harvey Swados described what this accommodation has meant in human terms in a detailed article in *Dissent* last fall, "West Coast Waterfront—End of an Era." As each of yesterday's militant labor leaders is molded by technological progress into a labor "statesman," the process of union decline moves on its sober course. The union becomes the accomplice, no matter how unwillingly, of the machinery-minded employer determined to reduce his work force.

The official doctrine, embraced by the Kennedy administration and echoed by the financial community, is that if somehow capital were to be invested in industrial facilities, employment would increase. According to this argument, business, through tax concessions, more sympathetic depreciation schedules and allied encouragements, should be persuaded to modernize plant and equipment. Production would then rise and employment would pick up. In my opinion, nothing could be further from the truth. Does anyone seriously believe, for example, that the steel industry—which has been operating chronically below capacity and sometimes for extended periods at only one-half optimum output—would add new plants and new employees if capital were made available? On the contrary, present plants would be modernized, mechanized, and automated so that less and less manpower would be required for the same productive capacity. Industry, if capital were more readily available, would invest it to eliminate jobs, not to create them. This would certainly improve the profit picture, but it is difficult to see how it would pump new blood into the unions. A similar situation has developed with the investment of large capital sums to renovate office buildings and apartment houses. Invariably, a major step in such improvements is to replace attendant-operated elevators by passenger-operated ones. In New York alone thousands of elevator operators have been displaced, and we will not have to live much longer to remember the "elevator boy" with the same nostalgia that now surrounds the blacksmith.

Because the United States will unquestionably be the first nation to move into the final stages of the industrial revolution, when mechanization and automation will reach their ultimate development, it is of value to ask what institutions will replace the doomed blue collar unions that initiated so many of the progressive programs of the past. To review briefly—the labor movement in the thirties and forties was the keystone in inaugurating an era of reform that led to shorter work schedules, a fairer distribution of the nation's wealth, and a general improvement in the country's concepts of social justice. At this writing, organized labor is not participating in the progressive programs of our era.

There are those who believe that the white collar worker, who is now surpassing the blue collar worker in numbers, will eventually be unionized in impressive numbers and assume the role of leadership in the social, economic, and political fields which is today slipping from the grasp of organized labor. However, the problems of organizing the white collar worker are enormous for the reasons C. Wright Mills set forth in his best book, *White Collar*. For one thing, the white collar worker feels no such hostility to the boss as typifies management-employee relations in large manufacturing. Nor are class distinctions emphasized in office work as they are in a factory. The white collar worker is apt to have enjoyed a better education than his blue collar brother, and in the case of the many women clerical workers, job security and permanent employment are of secondary interest. Young women are working until they get married and begin to raise their families. Finally, the employment turnover in white collar areas makes an organizer's work a nightmare. In some stores, for example, where the majority of employees are women, it exceeds 40 per cent a year.

One thing is certain, the white collar worker will not join the production worker's union. Efforts by the United Auto Workers and other unions to enlist their white collar coworkers have failed totally. In England, a new type of labor figure, the well-educated business executive type, is emerging as leader of some of the white collar unions. Perhaps in this country, too, as scientific progress begins to pose the threats to the white collar worker that it presently does to the production worker, a demand for white collar organization will be felt. I doubt it.

If one could look ahead into the structure of our society after we have passed through the final and total stages of the industrial revolution, one might well see us emerging as a one-class society. Even today, employers are for the most part no longer owners; they are essentially hired managers employed in a supervisory role. Marx, Engels, and the other revolutionary thinkers of the nineteenth century could foresee only as far as a society in which the key segment was the proletariat. But it seems to me quite possible that within the next century the proletariat will be entirely absorbed in a one-class affluent society which [will] emerge from the completion of the industrial revolution.

3

LABOR DOMINATES THE DEMOCRATIC PARTY*

Raymond Moley

The following article suggests that the Democratic party is actually controlled by union leaders, who supply it with votes and funds. How accurate is this analysis? Are we rapidly moving toward a two-party system based on economic interests—capital v. labor? Or do both parties cut across party lines, blurring the economic cleavage?

Guileless, old-fashioned Democrats who believe that the candidate of their party represents the faith of their fathers and is capable of making that faith live once more in the White House should examine the reality behind the façade. Perhaps the name Stevenson stirs nostalgic memories of the days of Adlai's grandfather, of Grover Cleveland, Woodrow Wilson, and Alfred E. Smith.

But they need the sharp prod of truth to realize that, except in some parts of the South, their party is dead, its faith is forsworn, and its candidate is merely an empty urn, a vacant reminder of a vitality that has long since turned to dust and ashes.

The reality is the massive, disciplined, ruthless machine conceived and created by Walter Reuther and pleasantly designated as the AFL-CIO Committee on Political Education—COPE.

The proof of the identity of the political agencies of a few union bosses with the Democratic party in the 37 states outside the South is abundantly shown in the communication sent to 15 million union members, in which they are ordered to vote for or against members of Congress. This is called "How Your Senators and Representatives Voted, 1947–1956."

"ISSUES"

The people who compiled this culled, with deadly precision, only an average of two roll calls a year, numbering twenty for senators and nineteen for representatives. Only a third of these "issues" have to do directly with labor interests. Most are of general interest, which shows that COPE regards itself not as a mere labor agency but as a national political party. As far as the unions are concerned, these political bosses regard them as mere reservoirs of money and manpower to be used to further their political ambitions.

The descriptions of the "issues" should be an affront to the intelligence of the members to whom they are directed. For they reek with misstatements and prejudice. For example, the "tideland" vote in 1945 was "to override the Supreme Court and give offshore oil . . . to coastal states instead of using the revenue for schools or some other purpose of benefit to all U.S. citizens." The fact is that the

* Raymond Moley, "The Death of a Party," *Newsweek*, October 29, 1956, p. 120.

Supreme Court merely left the title to the "tidelands" in doubt after generations during which the states had legal possession. Nothing was "given" to anyone. Indeed, in the Court opinions in the case it was suggested that Congress should act.

If Walter Reuther had been pulling the strings directly, the Democrats in the 37 states outside the South could hardly have obeyed with more servility. For of all the 26 Democratic senators in those states, twelve had a perfect score and seven deviated only once. Of the 132 House members of those states, 77 had perfect scores, and 29 deviated only once. (A number of these single deviations were among New England members on the 1956 Democratic farm bill. Perhaps they were more loyal to labor than were its own leaders.)

IDENTITY

Thus there was 73 per cent identity between COPE and the Democratic party in the Senate, and 80 per cent in the House. In the next Congress the parity between COPE and Democracy may be nearer 100 per cent.

With COPE providing most of the money and manpower in senatorial and congressional races, the substance of power is with Reuther, et al., while the name "Democratic" is merely a convenient reminder of the past.

The Ohio situation is typical of industrial states. There are 23 Republican House members and six Democrats. All six have perfect COPE scores.

It remains to be seen whether in the years ahead those American citizens who have joined unions to serve their legitimate economic interests are going to be willing to serve as pawns—paying pawns—in this movement. For they are being exploited merely to serve the personal political ambitions of Reuther and others.

Unless they come to realize this and put a stop to it, there will develop much more powerful political forces to oppose them among the vast majority of Americans who are not members of unions. For the United States is hardly ready to be governed by a minority.

4

WHEN LABOR VOTES*

The role of union labor in American political life is interpreted variously, depending largely on the viewpoint of the observer. In an effort to get objective data, sociologists have recently turned to personal interviews. Results of a survey involving 800 union members are summarized in the article that follows.

Do union members resent political advice from their leaders? How much weight does a union's political endorsement carry with the rank and file? What factors most strongly influence the way union members vote?

To get specific answers to questions such as these, the United Auto Workers four years ago gave Wayne University of Detroit a grant for a study of how U.A.W. members in the Detroit

* Reprinted from the November 1956 issue of *Fortune Magazine* by special permission. © 1956 by Time, Inc.

area voted in the 1952 presidential election. The study was made by a group of Wayne University[1] sociologists, who interviewed more than 800 U.A.W. members shortly before the election and then went back and questioned many of them again after election day. The results of this survey have now been published as a book—*When Labor Votes* by Arthur Kornhauser, Albert J. Mayer, and Harold L. Sheppard (University Books). Some of the sociologists' findings suggest that a union's political influence on its membership, at least in the case of the U.A.W., is neither so strong as its leaders might wish, nor so slight as some businessmen would like to believe:

—Despite a vigorous union drive to get out the vote, about one out of five union members having the necessary qualifications for voting—e.g., American citizenship—either failed to register or for some other reason stayed away from the polls.
—Of those who did go to the polls, 75 per cent voted for Stevenson. But 25 per cent disregarded the advice of their leaders and voted for Eisenhower. This group included 60 per cent of the white collar workers in the sample, and 51 per cent of those whose fathers were Republicans.
—Only 5 per cent of the interviewees listened to radio or television talks by U.A.W. President Walter Reuther during the campaign, as against 83 per cent who listened to one or both presidential candidates.

[1] Now Wayne State University.

—Less than half the registered U.A.W. members were aware that the union had taken a stand on a local issue—state reapportionment—that the U.A.W. leadership considered of vital importance. Of those members who voted on reapportionment, however, a substantial majority sided, knowingly or unknowingly, with the union leadership.
—A whopping 78 per cent majority of the sample—including 53 per cent of those who voted for Eisenhower—agreed "it was all right for the unions to work to get Stevenson elected." But 14 per cent of this group didn't like some things the unions had done—e.g., "spent union dues and took men out of the shop to work for P.A.C."
—Campaign activity on the part of businessmen was also approved by 78 per cent of the union members interviewed. Out of this group, 15 per cent said business had done things they didn't like—e.g., "contributed too much money."
—Fifty-five per cent of the sample said they would like unions to have "more to say about the things the government does that are important to working people." Among the Eisenhower voters, only 27 per cent agreed with this statement, however, and 33 per cent thought unions should have less to say.
—When asked where they got most of their information about the candidates, only 7 per cent named the union. Forty-seven per cent named television and 65 per cent mentioned newspapers. But this doesn't mean that U.A.W. members necessarily believed what they read in the papers; 42 per cent named newspapers as a particularly untrustworthy source of political information.

5

CAUGHT ON THE HORN OF PLENTY*

W. H. Ferry

Traditionally, every dilemma has at least two horns. But the horn of plenty is generally regarded as a cornucopia, rather than one facet of a dilemma. Mr. Ferry suggests that the American horn of plenty does have a price tag attached. On the one hand it promises abundance for all; on the other hand it promises mounting unemployment, To solve this paradox will require more than "massage and Band-Aids." Instead, it will require a reordering of American society, with government intervening more and more in the nation's industrial life.

Strangely enough, Americans are having a hard time getting used to the idea of abundance. Abundance is not only a relatively recent state of affairs. There is also an idea current that it may not last very long. The barriers to general comprehension of the possibilities and demands of abundance are numerous. There is, for example, tradition, and a mythology that seeks to confine the growing abundance of this country inside the old political and social enclosures. Happily there is also the beginning of a less dusty literature on the topic.

As consumers, Americans are joyously sopping up affluence, quarter after quarter sending private debt for consumer goods to record levels, and inventing new categories of services. But the lesson of abundance is even here ambiguous; for while there is enough to go around for all, not all are sharing. There is enough in our ever-swollen granaries so that no American need to go to bed hungry. Yet millions do, while millions of others are vaguely uneasy and feel guilty about so absurd a situation. The American farm is technology's most notorious victory. That the disaster of abundance on our farms has so far resisted solution is a portent of greater dilemmas in other areas.

For the country may soon be in the same fix with regard to consumer goods and services—more than enough for all, but without the political wit to know how to bring about a just distribution. We may, in fact, be in that situation at present. There is evidence that something like 30 per cent of our productive facilities are standing idle most of the time. Much of our machinery is obsolete. Everyone knows that the steel industry spent about a year in the doldrums of 50 per cent of capacity production. Planned obsolescence, which is the design and sales strategy of many manufacturers, is latent abundance, just as the fields left unturned by wheat and barley and rice farmers are latent abundance. It is not only what is produced that counts up to a total of abundance, but what is capable of being produced.

* W. H. Ferry, "Caught On The Horn of Plenty," *Bulletin*, Center For The Study of Democratic Institutions (Santa Barbara, Calif., January 1962).

Not the least of our troubles occurs over definitions. Abundance of this self-evident variety, for example, is not the opposite of the classical idea of scarcity. And what are resources? How do you tell when a resource is scarce? Or not scarce? Are people resources? Are people without jobs or skills resources? What is prosperity? This is a particularly hard definition. The recession is said to be past. Newcomers by the millions are thronging into the stock market. The gross national product is at a 3.4 rate. And around 5,000,000 people are out of jobs. Is this prosperity? What are today's definitions of work, leisure, play, affluence? Our vocabulary is tuned to yesterday's industrial revolution, not to today's scientific revolution. Abundance might, for instance, be defined as the capacity—here meaning resources, skill, capital, and potential and present production—the capacity to supply every citizen with a minimum decent life. We have the capacity, so this makes us an abundant society. Yet some 30,000,000 Americans are living below the poverty line.

This paper focuses on a disagreeable abundance—the ironic and growing abundance of unemployment. Radical technological change is producing a surplus of labor, and radical measures will be required to deal with it. Since no such radical measures have been, or seem likely to be, proposed by the federal government, technological unemployment may soon grow to the proportions of a crisis. For generations the dictum that Machines Make Jobs was demonstrably valid. Now the dictum is losing its force and generality. Machines are replacing workers. Some part of the 50,000 new jobs that have to be provided weekly to keep the American economy going are, to be sure, being supplied by new machines. But what the machine giveth at one place it taketh away at another: hence, structural unemployment.

The prospect is that through the 1960's the gross national product will continue to rise. Current predictions are for an economic boom in 1962–63. Profit and dividend levels and stock market prices will continue upward. So will the total number of employed. But the likelihood is that the absolute and relative number of unemployed will also be growing, as will the number of distressed areas.

How will this state of affairs be described? There is no word or combination of words at present to define such economic sunshine-and-shadow. We are used to thinking of major economic phenomena moving in roughly parallel lines. But it might turn out that the number of unemployed in the United States is at the lowest point today—around 6.5 to 7 per cent—that it will reach again. Current attacks on technological unemployment have produced more disappointment than results. The labor force is growing at a rate of 1,250,000 annually, and technological progress permits the discharge of another 1,250,000 each year. The dimensions of the situation are becoming plain. The next three years ought to suffice to determine whether a liberated margin is in fact in the making. If by 1964 the unemployment rate is close to 10 per cent, despite the use of all conventional medications, we may be ready to agree that once again, as in the Thirties, the nation is in a radical dilemma, a dilemma of abundance.

The question is whether jobs can be manufactured fast enough to approach full employment, using the present definition of jobs and the means of providing them that are presently regarded as acceptable. The essential contention of this paper is that the answer is no. An apparently unavoidable condition of the Age of Abundance is increasing structural unemployment and underemployment.

The novelty of this proposition is that the majority of victims of technological displacement will be *permanently* out of work. They will not just be "resting between engagements." They will not just be waiting for the next upturn, or for expansion of the industry or company in which they were working. They will no longer be the objects of unemployment insurance plans, for these plans are designed to fill the gap between jobs, not to provide a permanent dole.

The rapidly emerging fact is that every year from now on we shall be able, because of accelerating technology, to produce the goods and services needed by the nation with fewer and fewer of the available hands—say 90 per cent or less.

I use the phrase "90 per cent or less" advisedly although it does not comport with the 6.5 to 7 per cent unemployment figure mentioned earlier. It is a delicate way of bringing in the touchy issues of featherbedding and underemployment. Everyone knows what featherbedding means. Underemployment describes workers who continue to hold jobs after it has been established that the jobs can be done as well or better by machines or people who work only part-time. The underemployed, according to some authorities, total as high as 25 per cent of the labor force. The underemployed include also a million or more agricultural workers who stay on the farm because there is no work in industry for them, 5,000,000 women who would like jobs, and 2,000,000 part-time workers. Note must be taken also of double-job-holding—"moonlighting"—by hundreds of thousands of workers.

The unemployed and underemployed are no longer almost exclusively the unskilled, the recent immigrants, the colored, the groups at the end of the economic scale, who have customarily borne the heaviest weight of economic slides. White collar workers are joining this group as automation reaches the office. There is some reason for thinking that white collar workers will after a few years comprise most of the growing category of technologically displaced. Herbert Simon has observed that by 1985 machines can do away with all of middle management, "if Americans want it that way." Since middle management is considered the ultimate destination of much of middle-class America, Simon's words have an air of clammy prophecy about them.

Senator William Proxmire commented recently on the assertion that there is nothing really novel about the present situation:

"I call for a frank recognition, especially among our experts on economic policy, that we do not have the answers to the perplexing problem of unemployment in a rapidly-automating, work-force-growing free economy. A vigorous search for answers consistent with economic freedom is urgently needed."

Harvey Swados remarked some time ago in a brilliant essay that the question of work would be the biggest domestic political issue of the 1960's. Part of his argument was that accelerating technological displacement would harden into an established economic pattern; the country would sooner or later be driven to the knowledge that it is not dealing with a regrettable but transient phenomenon. And, Swados said, there is a serious question whether Americans can accommodate themselves either to the idea or to the use of abundant leisure. The revolutionary consequences of leisure in a nation committed to economic dynamism and to work, any kind of work, as a good in itself have found no radical echoes yet in public policy. The likelihood is that the country will stay for a while with the policies that the administration has chosen.

These will be accompanied by spread-the-work campaigns, by union demands for shorter hours, union-management agreements to retrain employees or to share the shock of automation (as West Coast shippers and the longshoremen's union have done), early retirement schemes, and more public works programs by local and regional authorities. There is nothing wrong with stop-gaps of this nature. It is only wrong to think of them as solutions instead of palliatives.

Mention of the word "planning" rouses instant suspicion. When coupled with the word "national"—that is, national planning—it sends editorial writers headlong to their typewriters. Yet national planning is indispensable if the United States is going to make sense out of its future. Can anyone imagine an unplanned transition from war to peace production, or an unplanned highway program? For those willing to acknowledge that free enterprise is not a divine dispensation and capitalism not a dictate of natural law, the need is evident everywhere. Such is the acceleration of technical and social change that international planning may be expected within the next decade or so.

The essential elements of the program proposed here are: First, national planning authorized by Congress, and not national planning administered by a bureaucratic ogre to be appointed by the CIO, the NAM, or the ADA. . . . Second, a scheme based on what W. Arthur Lewis calls "planning by inducement," by which he means the use of politics and persuasion, in their various guises, to achieve a more reasonable utilization of resources and a better distribution of income. . . . Finally, recognition of today's economic order for what it is, an enormously complicated piece of machinery which cannot be run by the instruction manuals of the eighteenth and nineteenth centuries. National hypocrisy has in few places as many facets as it has in the simplistic rhetoric of the opponents of planning. The most violent antiplanners are the same men who expertly plan the future of their corporations for ten to thirty years, and who rely on planners to keep their suburbs from infestation by junkyards and filling stations.

National planning will be recognition that the government bears the final responsibility for the quality and content and prosperity of the nation. This may perhaps be called modern mercantilism. Those who construe these proposals as some dark version of new and unholy economic doctrines are advised to refer to economic planning in sixteenth and seventeenth century England or, even better, to the economic history of the Eastern seaboard of this country in the eighteenth and early nineteenth centuries.

In an abundant society the problem is not an economic one of keeping the machine running regardless of what it puts out, but a political one of achieving the common good. And planning is one of its major means.

But whether or not we can figure out some such way of taking systematic advantage of the bewildering fact of abundance, we shall within a short while have to discard attitudes that grew up in the dog-eat-dog phase of capitalism and adopt others suitable to modern mercantilism. For example, we shall have to stop automatically regarding the unemployed as lazy, unlucky, indolent, and unworthy. We shall have to find means, public or private, of paying people to do no work.

This suggestion goes severely against the American grain, and it will have to be adopted slowly. The first steps have been taken. Unemployment insurance and supplementary unemployment benefit plans reached by company-union negotiations are examples. As these have come to be accepted as civic-industrial policy, so may plans for six-month work years, or retirement at 50 or 55 at full pay until pension schemes take hold. So may continuation of education well into adult years, at public expense. So may payment from the public treasury for nonproductive effort, such as writing novels, painting pictures, composing music, doing graduate work, and taking part in the expanding functions of government. Is a physicist more valuable to the community than a playright? Why? The responsibility of the individual to the general welfare runs far beyond the purely economic.

Abundance will enable a reversal of the old order of things. Modern mercantilism will remove the economic machine from the middle of the landscape to one side, where, under planning by inducement, its ever more efficient automata will provide the goods and services required by the general welfare. Humanity, with its politics and pastimes and poetry and conversation, will then occupy the central place in the landscape. Management of machines for human ends, not management by them, is the true object of industrial civilization.

This is the promise of modern mercantilism, and if the time is not yet, it is yet a time worth striving for. Meanwhile, the chief necessity is to revive respect for law and government as the proper instruments of the general welfare. Without this respect the economic future of this country and that of other nations linked to it will be determined, and stultified, by the accidents of private ambition and the hope of private gain. With this respect the Age of Abundance can be made into the Age of the General Welfare, and the United States can become in fact the moral commonwealth it has always claimed to be.

6

AUTOMATION: FALLACIES AND FACTS*

Victor R. Fuchs

Is there a middle position with respect to the questions posed by automation? Must we choose between the prophets of doom and those who forsee a cloudless future? The following article attempts to sift conflicting claims.

The current debate over automation tends to be dominated by the "alarmists"—those who can only see the warehouses filling up with goods and the streets filling up with unemployed—and the "do-nothing" school who find automation an unmixed blessing. This debate is marked by exaggeration, illogical reasoning, and other

* Victor R. Fuchs, "Automation: Fallacies and Facts," *The New York Times Magazine*, April 7, 1963 (abridged). © by The New York Times Company. Reprinted by permission.

fallacies. These are the principal fallacies indulged in by the "alarmists":

1. The rate at which labor is being displaced by technological change is more rapid now than in the past.

This particular fallacy lies at the heart of the "alarmist" position. It is the fundamental premise; the rest is elaboration. But the fact is that there is no economic evidence to support this premise.

If technological innovations were replacing labor at an increasing rate, one would expect to find evidence of this in the output obtained per man hour of labor. The figures show no such trend.

For the period 1947–60 output per man-hour in the private sector of the economy grew at an annual rate of 3 per cent. This is a slightly higher rate than the average for the entire twentieth century but it is not an unprecedented rate for the United States, and it is far below the pace achieved in Japan, Russia, and several West European countries.

2. Automation makes it possible to produce more goods and services than we can possibly use.

Most of the talk about our having the ability to produce more goods and services than we need or want, now or in the foreseeable future, is nonsense.

We need more rapid growth, not less. Consider the demands for helping to raise the living standards of the underdeveloped two thirds of the world. Consider the problem of removing the deep pockets of poverty that still exist in our rural areas and urban slums. Finally, consider the simple fact that to bring up the average American family to the level of living currently enjoyed in the more prosperous suburbs surrounding New York City would require 25 to 30 years of very rapid growth at full employment.

To argue, as some do, that the problem is primarily one of distribution, is completely in error. If income were divided absolutely equally in the United States, each family would have about $7000 per year—an income that falls far short of producing satiety.

The ultimate scarce resource is manpower. At the present time about 6 per cent of our labor force is unemployed. Some 2 or 3 per cent more would probably seek work if it were available, while short work weeks for those currently employed represent perhaps an additional 2 or 3 per cent of involuntary unemployment. One must subtract, however, about 3 per cent for frictional unemployment—that which is built into a dynamic economy—this being about the minimum level consistent with efficiency and the right of workers to change jobs whenever they wish. On balance, the removal of all involuntary unemployment would raise labor input by 7 or 8 per cent.

3. Automation will result in mass unemployment because there will not be enough purchasing power to buy the increased output.

This is a more sophisticated version of the "overproduction" fallacy. It is not factually false, but it is illogical. It is based on a circular argument that runs as follows: no purchasing power-unsold goods-unemployment-no purchasing power.

This could happen. Indeed, it did happen in the 1930s. But it is incorrect to argue that it must happen. Whether it does or not will depend primarily on whether we are able to manage our monetary and financial affairs in a sensible manner. Our tools of monetary and fiscal policy are admittedly imperfect, but most economists are prepared to bet that they are not so imperfect that we need suffer mass unemployment because of a shortage of purchasing power.

Not all of the exaggeration and illogic

can be found on the alarmist side. A smaller but equally vociferous group sings the praises of automation in arguments that do not stand up well under inspection. This group voices three major "do-nothing" fallacies:

1. Automation automatically creates at least as many new jobs as it eliminates.

The key word here is "automatically." Of course, it is possible for automation to create new jobs. Automation typically results not only in a cheaper and better way of doing what was done before, but also in the possibility of doing and producing new things.

Thus, the job-creating potential of automation is present, but there is nothing automatic about it. It depends upon many things—price policies, wage policies, investment policies, and the maintenance of a high level of demand in the economy.

2. Automation always results in more interesting jobs, requiring greater skill and training.

If this is meant to apply to the specific factory or office situation it is incorrect. Professor James Bright of Harvard and others who have looked at particular examples of the introduction of superior machinery report that the effects of automation vary greatly.

3. Any problem created by automation can be solved by the individual firm concerned or by local government.

Efforts by individual firms, unions, and local governments to deal with the problems created by automation are to be commended. We should not, however, blindly put our trust in them simply out of fear or dislike of the federal government. Some federal activities are warranted on economic grounds, and might obviate the necessity for the government to assume a much larger role.

Given the fact that automation does pose some problems, that our national economy is highly complex and the parts are intimately related, and given the inability of state and local governments to deal adequately with many of the social and economic difficulties now before them, it is reasonable to conclude that the federal government must play an important and positive role.

What should this role consist of? First and foremost, the economy must be kept operating at a high level so that output can expand and workers displaced by technological change can seek jobs in a buoyant economy. Second, the costs of change should be distributed fairly throughout the economy. Third, strenuous efforts should be made to facilitate re-employment of displaced workers.

In the short run, this means support of retraining and relocation programs, an expanded employment service and the removal of artificial barriers to employment such as racial prejudice. In the long run, it calls for a large-scale shoring up of our educational system, a revolutionary improvement in our approach to vocational education and technical training, and the development of attitudes and institutions appropriate to the concept of education as a life-long process—not one that terminates with a "drop out" or a diploma.

There is need to face the problems with coolness, sympathy, intelligence, and determination. A "do-nothing" attitude is unwise and unjust. The greatest danger is not that technological change will come too quickly, but that our institutions will adapt too slowly to the problems and the promise of automation.

7

THE NATIONAL GOVERNMENT ATTACKS TECHNOLOGICAL UNEMPLOYMENT*

Howard M. Gamser

Inevitably, the rise of technological unemployment has been accompanied by demands for government programs to alleviate it. Some critics have protested that federal action is unnecessary. Others have declared that measures taken thus far are midget attacks against a giant threat. In the article that follows, Mr. Gamser, a member of the National Mediation Board, summarizes national policies to combat technological unemployment.

* * *

I have been asked to comment on the role the national government can play in attacking technological unemployment. Our difficulty today is the inordinately high supply of manpower engulfing us in the Sixties. This great supply is the result of several causes: large numbers of workers are no longer able to find profitable employment on our farms. This fact is obvious, I am sure, to the members of this community. Due to advances in technology, one farmer can meet the demands for food and fibers today to satisfy the needs of 25 people where it took seven farmers to turn out the same amount at the turn of the century. In the last 16 years, farm productivity has increased 30 per cent while farm employment has dropped by three million. It is now quite clear that only one out of every ten boys now living on a farm will find full-time work in agriculture in the future. We must look to other sectors of our economy to use the productive energies of those displaced by the technological revolution in agriculture.

A floodtide of youths will sweep into the labor market in the 1960's. Our postwar baby crop has now completed its schooling and is ready for jobs. Altogether in the 1960's we will have 26 million new young people ready for work. Job seeking will be a frustrating and heartbreaking experience for many of them. Already workers under the age of 25, although they comprise less than one-fifth of the labor force, constitute more than one-third of the unemployed. The problem of finding employment opportunities for our young people is complicated by the fact that they must seek work in an economy where an increasing premium is being placed on higher education and more sophisticated skills and many of our youths, as they are presently equipped, are just not employable.

The long-term trend in American industry has been toward the expansion of occupations which require college education or technical training. Our school drop-out rate today is still four out of every ten. Thus, it is becoming

* Excerpts from an address delivered at the Fifth Public Affairs Forum, State College, Indiana, Pennsylvania, March 29, 1963.

increasingly difficult for youth to secure a job and to maintain continuous employment without adequate educational preparation. Today, while the nationwide rate of unemployment is about 6 per cent, the rate of the 16 to 21 age group is over 13 per cent. Putting it another way, one out of every 14 in the present labor force is in the 16- to 21-year age group; however, that group accounts for almost one out of every five of the unemployed.

If we break these statistics down further we find that nonwhite youths and youths who have dropped out of school present an even more alarming rate of unemployment. A situation has evolved which Dr. James B. Conant, former President of Harvard University, who has studied the problem, calls, "the most dangerous social condition in America," and then he added that it is a problem laden with "social dynamite."

Another major source of our present supply of available manpower, under more detailed examination at this meeting, is the rationalization and dislocations in our industrial economy caused by the application of new scientific knowledge to the production process. In the eighteenth century came mechanization and the factory system. In the early twentieth century we saw the advent of mass production and the assembly line. Since World War II, a new application of scientific knowledge to production has added automatic communication and control which we know by the shorthand name of "automation."

By whatever name we call it, no matter what great benefits mankind is deriving and will derive from this almost miraculous stimulant to productivity, it is, at this moment, a mixed blessing. Although our capacity to produce has moved forward at a remarkable rate, it has left in its wake a multitude of human problems which we face and will continue to face in the years ahead.

Examples could be taken from almost everywhere of the numbers of jobs that have disappeared and job opportunities that have dried up because of automation. The Holland Committee, in its study of the Impact of Automation on Employment, concluded that in just this one year over 1,800,000 persons would feel the effects of technological change, and in the immediate years ahead it could conservatively be estimated that over 2,000,000 workers would be displaced each year because of rising productivity in existing industry.

Let us get no farther away from home than the boundaries of your own state for specifics. The bituminous coal industry, for example, employed well over 400,000 production workers just 15 years ago. Since then we have seen the development of mechanized loading, the expansion of strip mining, the adoption of automatic mining equipment. These changes in technology have led to a doubling of hourly output; and these, and other developments, have contributed to a decline in employment in this industry in the last 15 years so that under 120,000 miners are presently required.

Look at your rail yards and terminals, such as still exist, near at hand. Railroad workers too have suffered sharp declines in employment as a result of the introduction of the diesel, the improvement in automatic signal and track maintenance equipment—as well as advances made in other forms of transportation. Railroad employment figures for this same period also have to be examined. In 1947, the Class I railroads of this country employed nearly 1,400,000 workers. That total now has been cut nearly in half.

Your neighboring steel industry also

has been hard hit by declining employment. Again, largely due to improved technological innovations with no marked decrease in productive potential. The basic steel industry, as late as 1957, employed 600,000 production workers—but it is now employing some 450,000, representing a drop in employment of some 150,000 in this one industry in the space of just five years. I am not unaware of the foreign competition and the alleged low domestic demand for this product that has kept many mills from working anywhere near capacity during this period, but even if there were to be a marked and remarkable increase in demand, the sad but realistic fact is that many an unemployed worker, who still proudly calls himself a steel worker, will never be needed in that industry again.

Lest it be said that I am painting the gloomiest of pictures and am overlooking the new postwar industries, the remarkable growth in electronics, rocketry, services of all kinds with the attendant need for new employees—I hasten to acknowledge that in some sectors of our economy a new demand for manpower has arisen. But these dreary statistics still furnish us with undeniable evidence that on the horizon there is no growing demand as yet for the services of over 2,000,000 Americans who will be seeking employment opportunities each year.

There are several other factors contributing to the manpower situation of the Sixties which must be mentioned before discussing our attack upon the problems at hand.

More women are entering and remaining in the labor market longer. Even here, labor-saving devices at home give women the time and energy to increase their availability for gainful employment—I must charge here tonight that the manufacturers of the TV dinner have added a further complicating factor in our calculations of manpower availability.

There are also more older workers who still possess the physical capacity, thanks to advances in medical science, to give a good day's work for a day's pay—these good people are experiencing great difficulty in finding acceptance among many employers.

The job location difficulties experienced by Negro workers must also be placed on the record. Regardless of skill and availability of facilities for training, many work opportunities and avenues of employment still remain closed.

And finally, the unfortunate people who live in communities where work opportunities have dried up to such an extent that we must label them distressed areas—here, too, is presented a particularly acute and perplexing manpower problem.

The point has come, in these remarks, to put into a more humane perspective the true dimension of the problem we have been discussing. It is well and good to illustrate and expostulate with statistics, but if one is to design a legislative program or a course of action to combat a problem, true inspiration cannot come from bare statistics. A federal program might be launched to combat unemployment; but if the perniciousness of the problem were only visualized by the innovators in terms of "structural unemployment" or "man-days of idleness" or in percentage terms, a solution worthy of a democracy would not be found. Behind these technical terms are human faces, and these must be seen by those who would draft our legislation or chart our course. In the report of the Secretary of Labor to the Congress, which is required by the

Manpower Training and Development Act, and which was released last month, the Secretary talked about these faces in the following terms:

. . . The perplexed face of a man whose job has been eliminated by a machine.

. . . The cynical face of the school drop-out who has discovered that a high school diploma is necessary for most jobs.

. . . The bitter face of a 50-year-old job-seeker who has been told time and again that he is too old.

. . . The sometimes resigned, sometimes challenging face of the Negro who sees no way out of the occupational ghetto.

. . . The pinched face of the coal miner who has been on relief for over a year because many consumers of fuel have shifted to gas or oil or because fewer miners are required when modern equipment and techniques are utilized.

. . . The sunlined face of the dirt farmer or farm wage worker who has been "tractored" off the land into the rapid-paced world of concrete and asphalt.

The President of the United States was in Chicago last week and was talking about these faces, and about some of the figures which I cited earlier. He had this to say:

"The trouble is that each of these figures grows worse after each recession—and each one is bound to grow worse in the Sixties as the labor force increases even faster, unless we take actions to reverse these trends and make the most of our manpower. Unless we step up our rate of growth—unless we create a supply of jobs that is more equal to the demand —our rate of unemployment will steadily and swiftly climb to the recession level of 7 per cent, even without a recession.

"Without full employment, consumer markets are below their potential. Without stronger consumer demand, plant capacity is not fully in use. Without full plant utilization, profit margins are reduced. Without higher profits, investment lags behind. And so the sagging spiral continues.

"Our task is to reverse this spiral—and no single magic solution will solve all of our manpower problems."

I believe that there has been a practical and pragmatic realization on the national level that, as the President said, "no single magic solution will solve all of our manpower problems." A host of bills attacking various aspects of the problem were tossed into the legislative hopper in the 87th Congress. Some of them became law. Other proposals were renewed again in this Congress and are now under active consideration. I would like, in the brief time remaining, to attempt to outline some of the provisions of the legislation which have already been passed, and also to discuss briefly some proposals presently undergoing scrutiny in the halls of Congress.

The mandate to initiate federal programs which will provide for the maximum use of our manpower potential is to be found in the Employment Act passed in 1946. This statute calls upon the government "to promote maximum employment, production, and purchasing power." Of course, nowhere in this statute nor in any other is there set forth an inflexible blueprint which must be slavishly followed to achieve these ends. It was contemplated in this legislation, as it has been in all enacted subsequently, and in the proposals now on the drawing board, that such action as is taken will be coordinated with and responsive to the combined efforts and the results of a host of programs, policies and decisions made by individuals, private institutions, and state and local governments. We are not prepared to meet this challenge with a totalitarian, closed society, response. We are committed to a belief that our principle of voluntarism need not be sacrificed to achieve the ends which we seek.

The obvious keystone in the construction of any federal program to stimulate an increase in job opportunities is the encouragement of the rate of economic growth in the country. The first imperative is to release and stimulate those consumer and investment forces that create the demand for work. Major tax changes have been proposed this year with this end in view. It has been proposed by the administration that $10 billion in tax savings be placed in the hands of the consumer and investor to stimulate new markets, new equipment, new payrolls, new jobs and then still more investment and consumption. Last year Congress passed liberalized depreciation regulations and investment credit measures to also stimulate investment. Other economic measures that must be mentioned are the trade expansion legislation and the stimulus to housing and urban redevelopment in the 1961 housing legislation. All other programs can do no more than supplement our efforts to increase our rate of economic growth.

In the last two years, two federal programs have been initiated to help counteract certain structural aspects of unemployment.

Area development assistance for our distressed regions was passed in 1961. A range of federal services are offered to labor markets with excessive unemployment rates; loans to create new private enterprise and expansion of existing firms, financial aid for the improvement of public facilities, and technical aid to develop new products, markets and resources for the area concerned. This act also introduced the concept of the training of the unemployed in needed skills—training periods, up to 16 weeks with training allowances for a limited number of unemployed are provided in this legislation. Already over 300 such programs have been initiated involving about 18,000 workers throughout the country.

To further assist these areas of substantial unemployment, the Public Works Acceleration Act was passed in 1962. Congress originally authorized $900,000,000 for this program. $400,000,000 of this was appropriated last year and the remaining one-half billion has been requested.

The large scale effort to help workers meet the job requirements of the Sixties was initiated in the Manpower Development and Training Act passed last year. This pioneering effort, called by some the most important piece of social legislation since the New Deal, adds several training innovations not found in the Area Redevelopment Act. The training is not limited to certain areas of the country, training allowances are authorized for periods up to 52 weeks, and training will also be provided for the underemployed farm worker as well as a limited number of unemployed youths. Finally, this statute also imposes upon the government the task of appraising, "the manpower requirements and resources of the nation, and to develop and apply the information and methods needed to deal with the problems of unemployment resulting from automation and technological changes and other types of persistent unemployment."

The Secretary of Labor recently reported to the Congress, as required by this law, that in the first six months of operations under this law over 600 training programs have been started and nearly 30,000 unemployed are in training. It should be noted here that these 30,000 unemployed are being trained for existing jobs and for skills currently needed. Congress is being asked to provide more funds for the next fiscal year to increase the number of trainees who may be enrolled under this program.

The Trade Expansion Act, which I mentioned earlier also contains adjustment features to assist those workers who are displaced as a result of a liberalized trade policy. These workers who are the victims of foreign competition are provided with training, special income protection during their unemployment and relocation assistance, if necessary.

Any program to help fit workers to existing job opportunities and to cushion the hardships of displacement requires that our placement services through the United States Employment Service and cooperating State Employment Services upgrade the skill and efficiency with which they operate. Our unemployment insurance system must also be re-evaluated and benefits as well as length of periods of assistance revised in the light of current needs. Recommendations to the Congress for such measures have been made. Public welfare measures and minimum wage legislation, too, fit into the arsenal of weapons required to sustain our attack upon unemployment.

This year new legislative proposals are before the Congress to meet the manpower crisis which has been described. Already reported out by the House Education and Labor Committee, as well as the Senate Committee on Labor and Public Welfare, is the Youth Employment Act. It is designed to provide useful work experience for those of our youths who are out of work and out of school. The program envisages two types of employment experiences for these youths. Under Title I, work camp experience similar to that provided in the old CCC will be available, and under Title II, state and local government would be assisted with grants to provide job opportunities in local community service activities. This program is an expensive one. It has been estimated that an effective start could only be made if $100,000,000 were available for the first year of operations. Some voices have been raised about the wisdom of such an expenditure in a year when a tax cut has also been proposed. In view of the explosive problem we are facing with our youth today, about which I spoke earlier, can we afford *not* to undertake this effort?

As a further means of upgrading our skills to meet the needs of today's technology and tomorrow's even more sophisticated requirements, many federally sponsored and assisted educational programs have been proposed. In the Omnibus Educational Bill sent by the President to the Congress, specific proposals have been made to expand the availability and quality of education. People presently in the labor force need to, as a minimum, read well and calculate correctly. A little recognized problem is the adult illiterate and his job placement problems. A federally assisted program of basic illiteracy elimination through the cooperation of state educational agencies has been proposed. Our present vocational and technical education programs, already receiving large sums from the federal government creak along applying yesterday's methods to yesterday's needs in many states and localities. Again, in this omnibus measure, federal stimulation of our vocational and technical education programs has been advanced. Higher education and graduate study need also be encouraged, if we are to meet the challenge of tomorrow's world of science and technology. We will need in the future, as we need now, more engineers and scientists to keep abreast with our adversary in the cold war and provide the technical "know how" to provide our country with all the benefits available from scientific progress. In this Omnibus Education measure, about which I have spoken, proposals have been advanced to meet current problems faced by today's adult job seeker as well as tomorrow's infusion of youths into a technologically oriented world of work.

Many more approaches, many more methods of attack, could be and should be mentioned. To many of you the present legislation and further suggestions may be overwhelming, utopian, visionary, expensive—and many other less than flattering adjectives could be added. But the President summed up the scope and seriousness of the problem last Saturday in Chicago when he said:

"But if this tide continues to flood our labor markets with pools of idle men, then, I must warn you, this nation faces a decade of chronic trouble and recession —characterized by the economic waste and the human tragedy of unemployment, by higher welfare payments and weaker consumer markets, by recurrent problems of crime and delinquency and unstable labor relations . . .

"That is why our No. 1 domestic concern is, and must be, jobs—jobs for the Sixties, jobs for the tidal wave of men and women now flooding our labor market. It is a concern which requires the best efforts of us all—federal, state and local governments—management and labor leaders—builders of education and moulders of opinion."

Properly channeling and controlling this human tide of energy—manpower, our most precious resource—harnessing the energies of our swelling labor force so that our living standard remains the envy of the rest of the world and so that each individual may reap the rewards of a full and useful life is the challenge of the Sixties. Our democracy must make the decisions and plot the course which will permit this. Democracy is now put to the test to meet the challenge of joblessness.

Will we use automation as a "device with which to displace and dispense with men, or as a means to increase his stature"?

I hope that the programs in operation and those being presented will demonstrate that this country will again meet another challenge successfully.

XIV

The Government and Welfare

The term "welfare state" describes a wide range of government activity designed to protect the individual from economic disaster. It includes minimum wage legislation, old age assistance, unemployment insurance, assistance for the physically and mentally handicapped, and programs for public education, housing and health. The controversy over these measures has many facets. Sometimes they are challenged as unwise public policy—an attempt of government to do for its citizens what they should do for themselves. Not only do these programs waste tax dollars, so the argument runs, but they erode the foundations of American capitalism and prepare the way for one version of socialism. This tendency is branded as "statism" and welfare-state advocates are sometimes described as bureaucrats with a lust for power that causes them to believe that they can manage other peoples' lives.

Defenders of the welfare state are apt to stress the growth of economic insecurity in the modern world. Our industrialized, urban society assigns to each worker a highly specialized job. A regular pay check is his only guarantee of such basic necessities as food, clothing and shelter. If the pay check stops because of unemployment, or if it is not large enough, the average man can do little to close the gap. Therefore, the organized community (government) assumes responsibility for providing certain minimum living standards as they relate to housing, health, education, food and clothing.

Fundamentally, the debate over the welfare state is closely linked to the issue of national poverty, its causes, and proposed cures. Middle income and well-to-do people are not pressed to the edges of an adequate living standard. In a sense, under the welfare state concept, these people assume responsibility for the mitigation and eradication of poverty through government action. Some programs are geared directly to the individual, as in the case of aid to dependent children. Other programs are only indirectly concerned with individuals, as are the attempts to promote prosperity and high living standards through credit control and government spending policies. Still other programs blend the two approaches, as in the case of unemployment insurance that maintains national purchasing power and makes payments directly to individuals.

In this chapter we will first examine the issue of poverty and the role that modern government should properly play in relation to the impoverished. Next, we will look at one of the most hotly debated aspects of the welfare state program—public health policy as it relates to physicians and patients.

American Poverty: Chronic or Curable?

Should poverty be regarded as evil and un-American—a kind of virus in our economic bloodstream that should be pursued and exterminated? Or should it be regarded somewhat complacently as an individual challenge—a necessary handicap that spurs men to action? Is the eradication of poverty an individual problem or is it more properly the concern of government?

Such questions as the foregoing are basic in considering the arguments of defenders and critics of the welfare state. What causes poverty? Who are the poor? Do they tend to reproduce themselves? If so, why? Is poverty the result of a lack of opportunity? Mental incapacity? Physical handicaps? Illness? Racial prejudice? Lack of education? Unproductive work? Poor development? If these are the basic components of poverty, can they be erased through government action? Or are the causes more sophisticated—perhaps a combination of moral, physical and mental decadence? Are the poor the inevitable by-product of our industrial society—a kind of national slag pile that must necessarily be associated with a productive nation?

If the elimination of poverty is accepted as a proper function of government, other problems remain. Should our major effort be directed toward raising general productivity and living standards? If we raise the national standard of living, will the impoverished be benefited automatically? Or does this group represent a peculiar, isolated segment of our people, whose life is outside the mainstream of the American economy? Perhaps the impoverished should be regarded as charity cases, and tax dollars should be diverted to them as a salve to the national conscience? Or is the welfare of these people directly bound up with general prosperity? By aiding the physically and mentally handicapped, the unemployed, and the aged are we not actually taking out an economic insurance policy for the nation? In other words, are the charity aspects of the case secondary to the general welfare?

A final set of questions centers around the question "How?" Assuming that the reduction of poverty is accepted as a national goal, how can it be achieved? What role should education be assigned? Medicine? Housing? How should these various conditioning factors be blended? How can a static acceptance of poverty ("The poor ye have always with ye") be replaced by an aggressive, positive policy?

American Health: Public or Private Responsibility?

The boundaries between public and private health programs are constantly shifting in the United States. Conflict between those who demand extensive governmental programs and those who fear such programs is a part of the welfare state debate.

All of the arguments against government action are mustered with special force as they apply to health. Since the well-being and very existence of the individual may be at stake, charges of slovenly, mechanical service have great relevance. On the other side of the issue, the inadequacy and high cost of medical treatment are argued forcefully. Probably the issue is not really a choice between black and white as the extremists would insist. In the time-honored tradition of compromise, Americans appear to be moving toward a system of medicine that combines public and private medical care.

Among the unresolved issues are such questions as the following: Should state and federal funds be used to subsidize medical education, hospital construction, and medical research? How can American health standards be advanced most successfully? What medical responsibility should government assume toward members of the armed forces, veterans, and members of their families? Are group medicine and industrial medical plans a step toward the future or do they threaten the foundations of private medicine? Are private insurance plans adequate? If they are expanded, what direction should this expansion take? How can we shift from curative to preventive medicine? Who should be responsible for the medically indigent? What special provisions, if any, should be established for care of the growing number of aged people?

1

THE MITIGATION OF POVERTY*

John K. Galbraith

Having denied that the automatic functioning of our economy will solve the problem, Galbraith suggests an over-all pattern of governmental action that will break the poverty cycle. How do slum clearance, health facilities, and education fit into this program?

An affluent society that is also both compassionate and rational would, no doubt, secure to all who needed it the minimum income essential for decency and comfort. The corrupting effect on the human spirit of a small amount of unearned revenue has unquestionably been exaggerated as, indeed, have the character-building values of hunger and privation. To secure to each family a minimum standard, as a normal function of the society, would help insure that the misfortunes of parents, deserved or otherwise, were not visited on their children. It would help insure that poverty was not self-perpetuating. Most of the reaction, which no doubt would be almost universally adverse, is based on obsolete attitudes. When poverty was a majority phenomenon, such action could not be afforded. A poor society, as this essay has previously shown, had to enforce the rule that the person who did not work could not eat. And possibly it was justified in the added cruelty of applying the rule to those who could not work or whose efficiency was far below par. An affluent society has no similar excuse for such rigor. It can use the forthright remedy of providing for those in want. Nothing requires it to be compassionate. But it has no high philosophical justification for callousness.

Nonetheless any such forthright remedy for poverty is beyond reasonable hope. Also, as in the limiting case of the alcoholic or the mental incompetent, it involves difficulties. To spend income requires a minimum of character and intelligence even as to produce it. By far the best hope for the elimination, or in any case the minimization, of poverty lies in less direct but, conceivably, almost equally effective means.

The first and strategic step in an attack on poverty is to see that it is no longer self-perpetuating. This means insuring that the investment in children from families presently afflicted be as little below normal as possible. If the children of poor families have first-rate schools and school attendance is properly enforced; if the children, though badly fed at home, are well nourished at school; if the community has sound health services, and the physical well-being of the children is vigilantly watched; if there is oppor-

* John K. Galbraith, *The Affluent Society* (Boston, Mass.: Houghton Mifflin Company, 1958), pp. 329–33. Reprinted by permission of the publishers.

tunity for advanced education for those who qualify regardless of means; and if, especially in the case of urban communities, law and order are well enforced and recreation is adequate—then there is a very good chance that the children of the very poor will come to maturity without grave disadvantage. In the case of insular poverty this remedy requires that the services of the community be assisted from outside. Poverty is self-perpetuating because the poorest communities are poorest in the services which would eliminate it. To eliminate poverty efficiently we should invest more than proportionately in the children of the poor community. It is there that high quality schools, strong health services, special provision for nutrition and recreation are most needed to compensate for the low investment which families are able to make in their own offspring.

The effect of education and related investment in individuals is to enable them either to contend more effectively with their environment, or to escape it and take up life elsewhere on more or less equal terms with others. The role of education as an antidote to the homing instinct which crowds people into the areas of inadequate opportunity and frustration is also clear. However, in the strategy of the attack on insular poverty a place remains for an attack on the frustrations of the environment itself. This is particularly clear in the case of the slum. Slum clearance and expansion of low and middle income housing removes a comprehensive set of frustrations and greatly widens opportunity. There is a roughly parallel opportunity in the rural slum. By identifying a land use which is consistent with a satisfactory standard of living, and by assisting with the necessary reorganization of land and capital, public authority can help individuals to surmount frustrations to which they are now subject. The process promises to be expensive and also time-consuming. But the question is less one of feasibility than of will.

Nor is case poverty in the contemporary generation wholly intransigent. Much can be done to treat those characteristics which cause people to reject or be rejected by the modern industrial society. Educational deficiencies can be overcome. Mental deficiencies can be treated. Physical handicaps can be remedied. The limiting factor is not knowledge of what can be done. Overwhelmingly it is our failure to invest in people.

It will be clear that to a remarkable extent the requirements for the elimination of poverty are the same as for social balance. (Indeed a good deal of case poverty can be attributed to the failure to maintain social balance.) The myopic preoccupation with production and material investment has diverted our attention from the most urgent questions of how we are employing our resources and, in particular, from the greater need and opportunity for investing in persons.

Here is a paradox! When we begin to consider the needs of those who are now excluded from the economic system by accident, inadequacy, or misfortune—we find that the normal remedy is to make them or their children productive citizens. This means that they add to the total output of goods. We see once again that even by its *own terms* the present preoccupation with material as opposed to human investment is inefficient. The parallel with investment in the supply of trained and educated manpower discussed above will be apparent.

But increased output of goods is not the main point. Even to the most intellectually reluctant reader it will now be evident that enhanced productive efficiency is not the *motif* of this volume. The very fact that increased output offers itself as a by-product of the effort to eliminate poverty is one of the reasons. No one would be called upon to write at such length on a problem so easily solved as that of increasing production. The main point lies elsewhere. Poverty—grim, degrading, and ineluctable—is not remarkable in India. For few the fate is otherwise. But in the United States the survival of poverty is remarkable. We ignore it because we share with all societies at all times the capacity for not seeing what we do not wish to see. Anciently this has enabled the nobleman to enjoy his dinner while remaining oblivious to the beggars around his door. In our own day it enables us to travel in comfort through south Chicago and the South. But while our failure to notice can be explained, it cannot be excused. "Poverty," Pitt exclaimed, "is no disgrace but it is damned annoying." In the contemporary United States it is not annoying but it is a disgrace.

2

OUR INVISIBLE POOR*

Dwight Macdonald

Much of the contemporary literature on poverty in the United States starts with the bland assumption that it is a kind of anachronism that survives temporarily in the midst of general abundance. In the article that follows, Mr. Macdonald denies this pleasant assumption and portrays present and future American poverty as a tough, unyielding blight that encompasses one-fourth of the nation. Rather than being a temporary phenomenon, he believes that American poverty will require Herculean efforts to dislodge it.

In his significantly titled "The Affluent Society" (1958) Professor J. K. Galbraith states that poverty in this country is no longer "a massive affliction [but] more nearly an afterthought." Dr. Galbraith is a humane critic of the American capitalist system, and he is generously indignant about the continued existence of even this nonmassive and afterthoughtish poverty. But the interesting thing about his pronouncement, aside from the fact that it is inaccurate, is that it was generally accepted as obvious. For a long time now, almost everybody has assumed that, because of the New Deal's social legislation and—more important—the prosperity we have enjoyed since 1940, mass poverty no longer exists in this country.

Dr. Galbraith states that our poor have dwindled to two hard-core categories. One is the "insular poverty" of those who live in the rural South or

---

* Dwight Macdonald, "Our Invisible Poor," *The New Yorker*, January 19, 1963, pp. 82, 84, 91, 92, 94, 96, 98, 128–32. As adapted by the Sidney Hillman Foundation.

in depressed areas like West Virginia. The other category is "case poverty," which he says is "commonly and properly related to [such] characteristics of the individuals so afflicted [as] mental deficiency, bad health, inability to adapt to the discipline of modern economic life, excessive procreation, alcohol, insufficient education." He reasons that such poverty must be due to individual defects, since "nearly everyone else has mastered his environment; this proves that it is not intractable." Without pressing the similarity of this concept to the "Social Darwinism" whose fallacies Dr. Galbraith easily disposes of elsewhere in his book, one may observe that most of these characteristics are as much the result of poverty as its cause.

Now Michael Harrington, an alumnus of the *Catholic Worker* and The Fund for the Republic who is at present a contributing editor of *Dissent* and the chief editor of the Socialist party bi-weekly, *New America,* has written *The Other America: Poverty in the United States.*[1] In the admirably short space of under two hundred pages, he outlines the problem, describes in imaginative detail what it means to be poor in this country today, summarizes the findings of recent studies by economists and sociologists, and analyzes the reasons for the persistence of mass poverty in the midst of general prosperity.

In the last year we seem to have suddenly awakened, rubbing our eyes like Rip van Winkle, to the fact that mass poverty persists, and that it is one of our two gravest social problems. (The other is related: While only 11 per cent of our population is nonwhite, 25 per cent of our poor are.)

[1] Michael Harrington, *The Other America: Poverty in the United States* (New York: The Macmillan Company, 1962).

What is "poverty"? It is a historically relative concept, first of all. "There are new definitions [in America] of what man can achieve, of what a human standard of life should be," Mr. Harrington writes. "Those who suffer levels of life well below those that are possible, even though they live better than medieval knights or Asian peasants, are poor. . . . Poverty should be defined in terms of those who are denied the minimal levels of health, housing, food, and education that our present stage of scientific knowledge specifies for life as it is now lived in the United States." His dividing line follows that proposed in recent studies by the United States Bureau of Labor Statistics: $4,000 a year for a family of four and $2,000 for an individual living alone. (All kinds of income are included, such as food grown and consumed on farms.) This is the cutoff line generally drawn today.

Mr. Harrington estimates that between 40 and 50 million Americans, or about a fourth of the population, are now living in poverty. Not just below the level of comfortable living, but real poverty, in the old-fashioned sense of the word—that they are hard put to it to get the mere necessities, beginning with enough to eat. This is difficult to believe in the United States of 1963, but one has to make the effort, and it is now being made. The extent of our poverty has suddenly become visible. . . .

THE LIMITS OF STATISTICS

Statistics on poverty are even trickier than most. . . . It is not, therefore, surprising to find that there is some disagreement about just how many millions of Americans are poor. The point is that all recent studies[2]

[2] The studies, all of which are referred to by the author, include Dr. Gabriel Kolko,

agree that American poverty is still a mass phenomenon.

The model postwar budgets drawn up in 1951 by the Bureau of Labor Statistics to "maintain a level of adequate living" give a concrete idea of what poverty means in this country—or would mean if poor families lived within their income and spent it wisely, which they don't. Dr. Kolko summarizes the kind of living these budgets provide:

> Three members of the family see a movie once every three weeks, and one member sees a movie once every two weeks. There is no telephone in the house, but the family makes three pay calls a week. They buy one book a year and write one letter a week.
>
> The father buys one heavy wool suit every two years and a light wool suit every three years; the wife, one suit every ten years or one skirt every five years. Every three or four years, depending on the distance and time involved, the family takes a vacation outside their own city. In 1950, the family spent a total of $80 to $90 on all types of home furnishings, electrical appliances, and laundry equipment. . . . The family eats cheaper cuts of meat several times a week, but has more expensive cuts on holidays. The entire family consumes a total of two five-cent ice cream cones, one five-cent candy bar, two bottles of soda, and one bottle of beer a week. The family owes no money, but has no savings except for a small insurance policy.

One other item is included in the B.L.S. "maintenance" budget: a new car every twelve to eighteen years.

Wealth and Power in America (New York: Frederick A. Praeger, Inc., 1962); "Poverty and Deprivation in the U.S.," Conference on Economic Progress, April 1962, Washington, D.C., 1001 Conn. Ave., N.W.; Dr. James N. Morgan, et al., *Income and Welfare in the United States* (New York: McGraw-Hill Book Company, Inc., 1962); "Poverty and Deprivation" (pamphlet), Conference on Economic Progress, Leon H. Keyserling and others.

This is an ideal picture, drawn up by social workers, of how a poor family *should* spend its money. But the poor are much less provident—installment debts take up a lot of their cash, and only a statistician could expect an actual live woman, however poor, to buy new clothes at intervals of five or ten years. Also, one suspects that a lot more movies are seen and ice-cream cones and bottles of beer are consumed than in the Spartan ideal. But these necessary luxuries are had only at the cost of displacing other items—necessary, so to speak—in the B.L.S. budget.

The distinction between a family income of $3,500 ("poverty") and $4,500 ("deprivation") is not vivid to those who run things—the 31 per cent whose incomes are between $7,500 and $14,999 and the 7 per cent of the topmost top dogs, who get $15,000 or more. These two minorities, sizable enough to feel they *are* the nation, have been as unaware of the continued existence of mass poverty as this reviewer was until he read Mr. Harrington's book. They are businessmen, congressmen, judges, government officials, politicians, lawyers, doctors, engineers, scientists, editors, journalists, and administrators in colleges, churches, and foundations. Since their education, income, and social status are superior, they, if anybody, might be expected to accept responsibility for what the Constitution calls "the general welfare." They have not done so in the case of the poor. And they have a good excuse. It is becoming harder and harder simply to *see* the one-fourth of our fellow-citizens who live below the poverty line.

> The poor are increasingly slipping out of the very experience and consciousness of the nation [Mr. Harrington writes]. If the middle class never did like ugliness and poverty, it was at least aware of them. "Across the tracks" was not a very

long way to go. . . . Now the American city has been transformed. The poor still inhabit the miserable housing in the central area, but they are increasingly isolated from contact with, or sight of, anybody else. . . . Living out in the suburbs, it is easy to assume that ours is, indeed, an affluent society. . . .

Clothes make the poor invisible too: America has the best-dressed poverty the world has ever known. . . . It is much easier in the United States to be decently dressed than it is to be decently housed, fed, or doctored. . . .

Many of the poor are the wrong age to be seen. A good number of them are sixty-five years of age or better; an even larger number are under eighteen. . . .

And finally, the poor are politically invisible. . . . They are without lobbies of their own; they put forward no legislative program. As a group, they are atomized. They have no face; they have no voice. . . . Only the social agencies have a really direct involvement with the other America, and they are without any great political power. . . .

Forty to fifty million people are becoming increasingly invisible.

These invisible people fall mostly into the following categories, some of them overlapping: poor farmers, who operate 40 per cent of the farms and get 7 per cent of the farm cash income; migratory farm workers; unskilled, unorganized workers in offices, hotels, restaurants, hospitals, laundries, and other service jobs; inhabitants of areas where poverty is either endemic ("peculiar to a people or district"), as in the rural South, or epidemic ("prevalent among a community at a special time and produced by some special causes"), as in West Virginia, where the special cause was the closing of coal mines and steel plants; Negroes and Puerto Ricans, who are a fourth of the total poor; the alcoholic derelicts in the big city skid rows; the hillbillies from Kentucky, Tennessee, and Oklahoma who have migrated to Midwestern cities in search of better jobs. And, finally, almost half our "senior citizens."

PERPETUATING POVERTY

It seems likely that mass poverty will continue in this country for a long time. The more it is reduced, the harder it is to keep on reducing it. The poor, having dwindled from two-thirds of the population in 1936 to one-quarter today, no longer are a significant political force, as is shown by the Senate's rejection of Medicare and by the Democrats' dropping it as an issue in the elections last year. Also, as poverty decreases, those left behind tend more and more to be the ones who have for so long accepted poverty as their destiny that they need outside help to climb out of it. This new minority mass poverty, so much more isolated and hopeless than the old majority poverty, shows signs of becoming chronic. "The permanence of low incomes is inferred from a variety of findings," write the authors of the Morgan survey. "In many poor families the head has never earned enough to cover the family's present needs."

For most families, however, the problem of chronic poverty is serious. One such family is headed by a thirty-two-year-old man who is employed as a dishwasher. Though he works steadily and more than full time, he earned over $2,000 in 1959. His wife earned $300 more, but their combined incomes are not enough to support themselves and their three children. Although the head of the family is only thirty-two, he feels that he has no chance of advancement partly because he finished only seven grades of school. . . . The possibility of such families leaving the ranks of the poor is not high.

Children born into poor families today have less chance of "improving themselves" than the children of the pre-1940 poor. Rags to riches is now more likely to be rags to rags. "Indeed," the Morgan book concludes, "it appears that a number of the heads of poor families have moved into less skilled jobs than their fathers had." Over a third of the children of the poor, according to the survey, don't go beyond the eighth grade and "will probably perpetuate the poverty of their parents." There are a great many of these children. In an important study of poverty, made for a congressional committee in 1959, Dr. Robert J. Lampman estimated that 11 million of the poor were under 18. "A considerable number of younger persons are starting life in a condition of 'inherited poverty,'" he observed. To which Mr. Harrington adds, "The character of poverty has changed, and it has become more deadly for the young. It is no longer associated with immigrant groups with high aspirations; it is now identified with those whose social existence makes it more and more difficult to break out into the larger society." Even when children from poor families show intellectual promise, there is nothing in the values of their friends or families to encourage them to make use of it. Of the top 16 per cent of high-school students—those scoring 120 and over in I.Q. tests—only half go on to college. The explanation for this amazing—and alarming—situation is as much cultural as economic. The children of the poor now tend to lack what the sociologists call "motivation." At least one foundation is working on the problem of why so many bright children from poor families don't ever try to go beyond high school. . . .

The federal government is the only purposeful force—I assume wars are not purposeful—that can reduce the numbers of the poor and make their lives more bearable. The effect of government policy on poverty has two quite distinct aspects. One is the indirect effect of the stimulation of the economy by federal spending. Such stimulation—though by war-time demands rather than government policy—has in the past produced a prosperity that did cut down American poverty by almost two-thirds. But I am inclined to agree with Dr. Galbraith that it would not have a comparable effect on present day poverty:

> It is assumed that with increasing output poverty must disappear [he writes]. Increased output eliminated the general poverty of all who worked. Accordingly it must, sooner or later, eliminate the special poverty that still remains. . . . Yet just as the arithmetic of modern politics makes it tempting to overlook the very poor, so the supposition that increasing output will remedy their case has made it easy to do so too.

He underestimates the massiveness of American poverty, but he is right when he says there is now a hard core of the specially disadvantaged—because of age, race, environment, physical or mental defects, etc.—that would not be significantly reduced by general prosperity. (Although I think the majority of our present poor *would* benefit, if only by a reduction in the present high rate of unemployment.)

To do something about this hard core, a second line of government policy would be required; namely, direct intervention to help the poor. We have had this since the New Deal, but it has always been grudging and miserly, and we have never accepted the principle that every citizen should be provided, at state expense, with a reasonable minimum standard of living regardless of any other considerations. It should not depend on earnings, as does social security, which continues the inequalities and inequities and so tends to keep the poor forever poor. Nor should it exclude millions of our poorest citizens because they lack the political pressure to force their way into the welfare state. The governmental obligation to provide, out of taxes, such a minimum living standard for all who need it should be taken as much for granted as free public schools have always been in our history.

"NOBODY STARVES"

It may be objected that the economy cannot bear the cost, and certainly costs must be calculated. But the point is not the calculation but the principle. Statistics—and especially statistical forecasts—can be pushed one way or the other. Who can determine in advance to what extent the extra expense of giving our 40,000,000 poor enough income to rise above the poverty line would be offset by the lift to the economy from their increased purchasing power? We really don't know. Nor did we know what the budgetary effects would be when we established the principle of free public education. The rationale then was that all citizens should have an equal chance of competing for a better status. The rationale now is different: that every citizen has a right to become or remain part of our society because if this right is denied, as it is in the case of at least one-fourth of our citizens, it impoverishes us all. Since 1932, "the government"—local, state, and federal—has recognized a responsibility to provide its citizens with a subsistence living. Apples will never again be sold on the street by jobless accountants, it seems safe to predict, nor will any serious political leader ever again suggest that share-the-work and local charity can solve the problem of unemployment. "Nobody starves" in this country any more, but, like every social statistic, this is a tricky business. Nobody starves, but who can measure the starvation, not to be calculated by daily intake of proteins and calories, that reduces life for many of our poor to a long vestibule to death? Nobody starves, but every fourth citizen rubs along on a standard of living that is below what Mr. Harrington defines as "the minimal levels of health, housing, food, and education that our present stage of scientific knowledge specifies as necessary for life as it is now lived in the United States." Nobody starves, but a fourth of us are excluded from the common social existence. Not to be able to afford a movie or a glass of beer is a kind of starvation—if everybody else can.

The problem is obvious: the persistence of mass poverty in a prosperous country. The solution is also obvious: to provide, out of taxes, the kind of subsidies that have always been given to the public schools (not to mention the police and fire departments and the post office)—subsidies that would raise incomes above the poverty level, so that every citizen could feel he is indeed such. "*Civis Romanus sum!*" cried St. Paul when he was threatened with flogging—and he was not flogged. Until our poor can be proud to say "*Civis Americanus sum!*" until the act of justice that would make this possible has been performed by the three-quarters of Americans who are not poor—until then the shame of the Other America will continue.

3

THE ESSENCE OF LIFE IS STRUGGLE*

Samuel B. Pettengill

Conservative Americans, alarmed at the extension of the welfare state concept, have often attacked the tendency on philosophical grounds. Are not fear and the struggle for existence basic ingredients in human progress? Without ulcers, hypertension, and poverty would not mankind stagnate?

STRUGGLE IS A BLESSING TO BE SOUGHT FOR, NOT AN EVIL TO BE AVOIDED

In recent years, society has gone "nuts" on the pusillanimous cult of "security," guaranteed by government; in short, a nation of parasites. The illusion of the age is that people can vote themselves rich. It is a superstition that "social security" depends on the promises of politicians, not on the character, competence and courage of men. It is a fable and a fraud that the output of society can be greater than the input of individuals.

It is a universal complaint that nobody *wants* to work any more, or only enough to "get by." Employers are frantic for dependable employees. Labor unions have the laudable desire to improve the position of their members, but they overplay their hand when they say "Stretch it out. Take it easy. Do no more than enough to stay on the payroll."

When young people apply for their first job, they ask, "When will I begin to draw a pension? How many coffee breaks in a day? How many paid holidays? How long and frequent are the paid vacations? And if I work more than 40 hours in the 144 in six days, do I get time-and-a-half?"

The young men who ask none of these questions are sure to get and hold a job. In fact, this sort of young men have a golden age ahead of them. They will have less competition than that kind of men have ever had—and greater rewards.

When I was at Vermont Academy, Theodore Roosevelt was President. He attracted national attention when he said: "I wish to preach not the doctrine of ignoble ease, but the doctrine of the strenuous life." He said of himself, "Let me wear out, not rust out." He told young men to hit the line hard. He told women not to shirk their prime function to bear children. He said this at a time when any woman who had more than two children was considered subhuman, if not a little indecent.

Theodore Roosevelt dreamed nobly of his country, and by the fire of his example, lit other fires in millions of homes. It was said that Washington founded the nation, Lincoln saved it, and T.R. revitalized it. He appealed to the strong side of men as is now done chiefly by Marine sergeants and

* Samuel B. Pettengill, "The Essence of Life Is Struggle," *Vital Speeches*, August 15, 1957, pp. 665–66.

the coaches of athletics like my old friend, Knute Rockne.

But today, the general appeal is to the soft side of men—envy, self-pity, covetousness, class hatred. Our elections have become auctions in which rival politicians of both the old parties outbid each other by opening the door of the treasury in exchange for votes.

"Come and get it" is the slogan as people become the vandals of their own country and "bread and circuses" the formula for political advancement.

In the educational field, men like John Dewey have tried to eliminate struggle from the classroom. No required subjects! No examinations! Children develop inferiority complexes, rather than the challenge to do better. Never punish a child. Children should be wholly free. And so forth. With the result that employers despair because "Johnny can't read and Mabel can't spell."

So we have cities with few citizens, but many who wish to share the blessings of liberty, but shirk its burdens.

This is not the Spirit of 1776, nor of the great chess master, nor of Theodore Roosevelt. America needs a rebirth of "the strenuous life" and I know I am talking to young men who will take their part in it.

It was said of those who crossed the Appalachians down into the valleys of the Ohio, the Mississippi and the Missouri and pushed the frontiers of freedom to the Pacific shore that "The cowards never started and the weak never arrived. With no capital save courage and no resource except resourcefulness they built the American empire."

Here are the hundreds of miles of stone walls of Vermont—every stone dug from the ground and moved to where it now lies by ox-power and human muscle alone. We think of the pyramids of Egypt, and the tens of thousands of slaves who dragged the huge stones across the desert under the whips of their masters. It is my guess that the stone walls of Vermont represent more toil than the pyramids. But the walls were laid by the free choice of free men. "They scorned delights and lived laborious days."

Avoid struggle and life becomes sterile, vapid and meaningless. Our mental hospitals are being filled with thousands of neurotics, many of whom feel inadequate to meet life because they were protected from taking the bumps in childhood.

No man was ever greater than the difficulties he overcame. Great difficulties, great men. Small difficulties, small men. From struggle comes strength—and physical and mental health.

"I dream no dream of a nursemaid state
"That spoons me out my food.
"No, the stout heart sings in its strife with fate,
"For the toil and the sweat are good."

4

WELFARE LEGISLATION: NATIONAL ECONOMIC STABILIZER*

Neil H. Jacoby

Rather than detracting from individual incentive, the author finds social legislation to be a stimulus for personal advancement. In contrast with a preceding article, that praises fear as a motivating force, this selection reports that personal security is the foundation for economic progress. Which argument has greater validity? What does our national experience since 1930 prove?

A firm "floor" of personal and family security is one foundation stone of a high-incentive economy. To some, this assertion may appear strange. Until recently, many Americans have believed that there is a conflict between individual enterprise and individual security. Many have lightly assumed, without thinking about it deeply, that the more "security" the individual has, the less will be his enterprise. How easy it is to conclude that people become enterprising only if they, and they alone, are compelled to provide for their own future.

Political controversies and party alignments of the past have fostered the notion that one who favored a vigorous free enterprise economy must necessarily oppose federal old-age pensions, unemployment benefits, or aids to slum clearance. On the other hand, those who emphasized the need of the individual family for a measure of economic security in a complex industrial society have often been considered poor friends of individual enterprise. The New Deal of President Roosevelt put emphasis on "security" and built into the United States economy many bulwarks against personal misfortune. The administrations which preceded it had more concern for personal opportunities and individual advancement in a growing economy.

A *distinguishing feature of the Eisenhower economic program has been a synthesis of the best elements of the New Deal and of preceding administrations*. The discovery has been made that, far from negating each other, personal security and personal enterprise complement each other. In an urban, industrialized society, the individual needs assurance of a minimal income, an assurance that was unnecessary in an earlier time. As President Eisenhower said in his *Economic Report* of January 1954: "Because the floor of security to the individual has been built primarily upon welfare considerations, its contribution to the economic progress of the United States has not been adequately appreciated. Yet the worker is likely to be fully productive only if he feels reasonably safe against

* Neil H. Jacoby, *Can Prosperity Be Sustained?* (New York: Holt, Rinehart & Winston, Inc., 1956), pp. 79–84. © 1956. Reprinted by permission of the publisher.

want from unemployment, old age, or misfortune."

Far from weakening the "social security" measures initiated during the Thirties, the Eisenhower administration has significantly strengthened and extended them. At the same time, it has widened the individual's opportunity and incentive for personal betterment. It has understood that, to release the full energies of people for their tasks, it is necessary first to free them from the nagging anxieties of want that might come from sickness, old age, or joblessness.

Of course, provision of a "floor" of security is only the foundation for vital private enterprise. The individual wants also a ladder of opportunity wherewith to climb above the floor. This, too, it is a responsibility of government to maintain. A necessary balance should be maintained in governmental action to foster progress.

The contemporary government of the United Kingdom likewise has been synthesizing elements of divergent economic philosophies in Britain's past. Just as the Eisenhower administration in Washington merged two divergent streams of economic thought into a unified policy for progress, so it became the task of the Churchill-Eden administrations in Britain to weld together many sound Labor measures for protection of the worker and his family and the competitive enterprise policies that date from the Manchester School. *The London Economist* put the matter succinctly: "The task of the next few years is to press on with the construction of the 'two-decker' economy—a firm base of welfare and social justice to ensure that no citizen is deprived of his economic and social rights, with a superstructure of the greatest possible freedom for enterprise and efficiency."

The United States has come a long way in protecting the individual against privation through governmental action. Government—federal or state—provides old-age and survivors pensions, unemployment insurance, aid to dependent children, aid to the blind, and general assistance to those not qualifying for special types of aid. Government insures and guarantees home and farm loans. It provides low-rent housing for low-income families and supports slum clearance and neighborhood redevelopment. It offers educational and other benefits to those who have served in the armed forces, and does a multitude of other things to promote health, education, and personal welfare.

A technologically advancing nation is wise to build into its economic legislation measures that will help people adjust themselves to changes. The more dynamic the economy is, the more necessary are such buffers to individual incomes. In a rich economy like ours, individuals provide most of these buffers for themselves through private insurance, pension and savings programs. In a poor nation the government must provide a larger part of them, in the form of unemployment insurance, programs for retraining workers whose skills have become obsolete, assistance to families in moving to more promising areas of employment opportunity, and the like.

In the whole field of personal health, education, and welfare, the job of government is to assure that a "floor" of minimum benefits is built under every person to forestall privation and hardship. Upon the individual rests the responsibility for providing, through his own savings and investments, something more than a bare living in old age, sickness, or idleness. The line separating the public minimum from the higher standard of private comfort is sometimes difficult to draw; but an acceptable division can usually be made in practice.

5

THE CHALLENGE TO AMERICA*

A recent full-dress analysis of American economic and social problems is embodied in Report IV of the Rockefeller Brothers Fund. Members of this panel represented a cross-section of American business and professional leadership outside government circles, and owe politcal allegiance to both major political parties. The program presented here represents consensus on our national policy for the next 10–15 years.

Human betterment is primarily achieved directly through increased individual and family income. The capacity to live in a better home, to buy more nutritious food, to provide better health care for one's family, to acquire life and health insurance protection, to widen educational and cultural horizons—these are all basic aspects of individual and family welfare which increased income can make possible. It is for this reason that individuals and families presently outside the mainstream of our economic growth must be enabled to the fullest extent possible to become more productive and thus participate in the general economic advance of the nation.

A healthy and expanding private economy means far more in terms of individual and family well-being than any reasonable expansion of government services and social programs. In the period from 1929 to 1952, for example, a period of great expansion in government's participation in welfare programs, the absolute increase in purchasing power afforded to all workers through their regular wage and salary payments amounted to eight times the increase in social welfare payments made available from public and private sources combined.

The distribution of national income in 1957 showed about 70 per cent of it went to employees in the form of wages and salaries, about 11 per cent to the self-employed, and about 18 per cent to the owners of property in the form of corporate profits, interest in indebtedness, and the rental of real estate. The realization of the growth potentials we have found in our economy should double real wages in the next 30 years. This will make possible a tremendous advance in human welfare.

INDIRECT BENEFITS OF ECONOMIC GROWTH

There are certain aspects of human welfare which are not a direct concomitant of economic growth alone. Some areas of need require action through social institutions, as distinct from action by individuals or even by employers and employees. Medical research, for example, cannot be furthered by individual workers and their families nor even in any significant way by most employers.

* Rockefeller Brothers Fund: *The Challenge to America: Its Economic and Social Aspects.* Special Studies Project Report IV (New York: Doubleday & Company, Inc., 1958), pp. 49–52, 59–60. © 1958 by Rockefeller Brothers Fund, Inc. Reprinted by permission of the publishers.

Similarly, education for all cannot practicably be provided through individuals or collective employer-employee action. Certain groups in society, which have not been effectively integrated into our working economy, also need special public attention. In these instances, we need institutional provision for channeling economic growth toward human betterment.

The social institutions to achieve this may be either private or public in nature, i.e., nongovernmental or governmental.

a. Private Institutions: Private philanthropy in this country has been and will continue to be a very substantial factor in our social welfare structure. Its expenditures from contributions alone (exclusive of endowments) aggregate at least $6.7 billion annually, and serve many functions which public institutions cannot. These expenditures fit specialized and local requirements more effectively than government's, and can be quickly channeled toward new and pressing needs. Perhaps most important, private philanthropy has provided in many fields the leadership and pioneering spirit so essential to meet changing needs in human welfare.

Charitable contributions by individuals have risen to unprecedented levels. In addition a fairly recent development in private philanthropy is the increase in corporate giving for education and for general welfare purposes. However, corporate giving in the aggregate averages only slightly over 1 per cent of taxable income, while the federal income tax law permits deductions for charitable purposes up to 5 per cent of taxable income. We should give every impetus to accelerating the upward trend of corporate giving in the next decade.

b. Public Institutions: In many areas of human welfare government action is clearly necessary, as a complement to private action. Through the use of tax revenues and its legislative powers, government can assure that a portion of our increased national product goes to achieve those human welfare purposes which would not otherwise be adequately served.

Whether the institutions to promote human welfare are sponsored privately or publicly, they are dependent for their continued effectiveness on a growth economy. All over the world there are examples of social legislation and private welfare endeavors that remain "paper programs" or which badly fail of their objectives because the communities or countries that establish them are not sufficiently productive to support them. Our social welfare policies in this country must recognize clearly the fundamental importance of an expanding economy toward furthering human welfare.

At the same time, successful social welfare policies will help to advance our economy. A society characterized by rising standards of living, and by physical and intellectual vigor, and in which each person is helped to achieve his maximum potential as a productive human being, is important to maintaining a dynamic economy.

AREAS OF WELFARE CONCERN

Some of the basic elements of individual and family welfare which we shall examine are the opportunity for a good education, economic security, good health, and the opportunity to expand cultural horizons. We shall also discuss the special problems of the lowest income groups in our population and the welfare problems which have been created by the weakening of family life and the tensions of an urbanized society.

Reference to government programs will predominate. By this we mean to de-emphasize neither the role of individual action nor of private institutions. We intend rather to give special focus to those matters which present questions of public policy, as distinct from questions more appropriately for private decision. At all times public policy should be so formulated as to encourage and foster expansion of individual and private institutional effort.

LOW INCOME GROUPS

Studies have indicated that there were in 1955 about 4 million families with a year's income of less than $2,000. These represented some 9 per cent of all the families in the United States. In addition, several million single persons were in a comparable income bracket.

Many in the low-income category are in jobs where the pay is below reasonable standards. We believe that the coverage of the minimum wage laws should gradually be broadened, and that continuing study be given to the proper level of minimum wages with the regard for efficiency and productivity. We recognize the complexity of this problem, and its implications for the expansion of employment opportunities in some industries and areas. Nevertheless, adequate minimum wage standards for all workers must be our ultimate goal.

However, low earnings for regular, full-time employment are not the primary cause of the distress of the majority of lowest-income families. A large segment of our population is outside the mainstream of the economic growth of the nation as a whole.

Many in the low-income category are aged persons, and opportunities for restoring them to an economically productive status are limited. The long-range solution for their problem is largely the maturing and strengthening of our old-age, survivors, and disability insurance program. Many are physically or mentally ill or disabled; they can be helped through the combined force of improved social insurance, health and rehabilitation programs. Some, even in times of high employment, are unemployed for a variety of reasons; they can be helped by improved unemployment insurance and vocational counseling and retraining programs. Many are members of broken families lacking the support of a husband and father; here the long-range solutions lie largely in the strengthening of the role of the family in our society. Many are in rural areas and working on uneconomical farms; they can be helped by vigorous prosecution of an agricultural policy along the lines suggested in the previous section. Many are in areas of urban blight, and can be helped by comprehensive urban redevelopment programs or, in the case of persons newly arrived in cities from rural areas, by efforts at preparation for urban life.

For the employable, there are sometimes specific impediments to movement into better paying jobs, such as discrimination in employment against minority groups. Indeed, herein lies perhaps the most dramatic example of waste of manpower in our economy. Other impediments are the costs of geographical movement to better jobs and lack of education or vocational training to meet the needs of our technologically advancing economy.

Where all else fails, public assistance must continue to serve as the ultimate economic backstop. Public assistance payments must be kept adequate to achieve the purpose of providing basic subsistence. At all times there should be vigorous pursuit of the objectives legislated into the federally aided public assistance programs in 1956—that of helping individuals on the relief rolls to achieve self-support and self-care.

In conclusion, the economic status of many low-income families can be raised through programs focused specifically on their individual problems. While the initial leadership should come from the federal government, only through cooperative effort on the part of both public and private organizations can an intensive attack be successful. Launched perhaps through the selection of pilot communities, such help ought to be extended as its effectiveness is demonstrated.

6

THIS NONSENSE ABOUT "SOCIALIZED MEDICINE"*

Arthur S. Flemming

Mr. Flemming, who served as Secretary of Health, Education and Welfare under President Eisenhower, in this article describes current government health insurance proposals for the aged. He flatly rejects the American Medical Association charge that these plans constitute "socialized medicine" and warns that the cry of "wolf" when there is no wolf is always a mistake.

Just what do we owe our senior citizens?

I think we would all agree that we owe them our continued love and a full measure of privacy—but, in more practical terms, we also owe them a chance to live out their lives free from the fear—or worse, the reality—of the crippling costs of a major, catastrophic illness.

How this can be accomplished is one of the most urgent problems of our times and, specifically, of the present session of Congress.

Why is the issue so important? Take the case of Mr. A.

He is 69 years old. His total annual income is $960, and he has no health or medical insurance.

In 1958, 1959, and 1960, his medical expenses averaged $177 a year—a heavy enough burden. In 1961, he had a heart attack, and his medical expenditures rose to $750—an impossible one.

Although Mr. A. deprived himself of many of the necessities of life to meet his medical bills, he was hardly able to pay all of them. So, to help him, his son and daughter-in-law were forced to withdraw $600 from the savings earmarked for the education of their children.

Mr. A. is typical of the majority of our senior citizens. Approximately 10 million of the more than 16 million people aged 65 and over have incomes of $1,000 or less, or about $3 a day. Three-fourths of this group have incomes of less than $2,000 a year. It is true that some have husbands or wives

---

* Arthur S. Flemming, "Care for the Aged . . . and This Nonsense About 'Socialized Medicine,'" *Good Housekeeping*, April 1962, pp. 42, 45, 46, 49. © 1962 by The Hearst Corporation. Reprinted by permission of The Sterling Lord Agency.

with incomes of their own. As a group, however, they have pitifully limited resources. About half have some kind of health or medical insurance. But very few can afford policies that protect them against the costs of major or long-term illnesses.

When such illnesses occur, and when their own or their family's resources are not sufficient to meet them, they are forced on relief.

Recently, the National Association of Blue Shield Plans and the American Medical Association announced a nationwide program to pay the full cost of medical and surgical services for single persons 65 and over whose annual income is $2,500 or less and for couples whose income is $4,000 or less. But as Abraham A. Ribicoff, present Secretary of Health, Education and Welfare, points out, this private program (which would cost about $3 a month per person) fails to answer the principal problem—hospital care of the aged.

Millions of older people, and tens of millions of their sons and daughters, are demanding an end now to this intolerable situation. Most of them feel that the government should take the lead in establishing a system that will insure the aged against a large percentage of their medical and hospital bills. They believe that everyone who benefits from such a system should also contribute to it.

I firmly agree with them.

At present there two bills before Congress proposing such a system. One is the official administration plan supported by President Kennedy. The other, which I believe is the sounder, is backed by Senator Jacob Javits of New York.

The subject of medical care for the aged has been made to sound very complicated. It has been further confused by the irresponsible charges of the American Medical Association, which also opposed the introduction of social security in the 1930s, that the Kennedy administration's proposal amounts to "socialized medicine."

Actually, the issues are very simple. Here are the basic differences between the administration and the Javits plans.

The administration plan (King-Anderson Bill, HR 4222) would be open to persons 65 or older who are covered by either the social security or railroad retirement systems. It would pay some of the costs of hospital and nursing home care, diagnostic services and the services of such persons as visiting nurses and technicians. It would be financed entirely through the social security system.

The Javits plan (S. 2664) would be open to all persons 65 or older who are retired. In addition to paying some of the costs of hospital or nursing home care, laboratory tests and other auxiliary services, it would pay some of the cost of medical care in the home or physician's office. This plan would be financed partly through social security, partly through general government revenues.

I believe Senator Javits' proposal is the better because:

It covers an additional two to four million senior citizens who are not under social security or railroad retirement.

The plan would be administered by the states, rather than the federal government. (However, the states would have to conform to minimum federal standards.)

By making some provision for the costs of preventive medical care in the home or physician's office, the plan could be expected to reduce major illnesses and their heavy costs.

Older people could choose between insurance that would pay the initial costs of any illness and the insurance that would help pay costs of a major or long-term illness.

Those who preferred to take out individual or group health insurance policies from private companies or prepayment organizations like Blue Cross or Blue Shield instead of participating in the government plan would be given help in making the premium payments.

Though I am concerned about the omission of these provisions in the Kennedy administration plan, I realize that reasonable people can differ about the merits of the two bills. If Congress debates them on their merits, I am sure a sound plan will emerge.

What would such a plan mean to Mr. A.? If it had been in effect at the time he had his heart attack, for which he was hospitalized for 20 days, it would have provided him with from $500 to $600 to pay his total costs of $750. Mr. A., and the millions like him, would no longer have to become a burden to their families, or be added to the nation's relief rolls.

Why, then, does the American Medical Association oppose such a plan? And why is the form their opposition has taken not only unsound but shockingly unfair?

The AMA contends that the needs of the aged in the medical-care field can be met by legislation already in existence—the Kerr-Mills Law. This law makes provision for government help for emergencies after they arise. As such, and in lieu of something better, it is a good law, and I supported it when I was Secretary of Health, Education and Welfare. This is what it does:

It provides additional federal funds for the medical-care provisions of the Federal-State Old-Age Assistance program. This program uses public funds to help support elderly people whose incomes are below the minimum levels specified by their respective states.

It provides for a federal-state program to care for the needs of senior citizens whose income is too high to permit them to qualify for the Old-Age Assistance program, but too low, in the judgment of their respective states, to enable them to meet their medical bills.

Many of our older citizens, however, do not want to wait for a medical emergency to arise and then be completely dependent on government. Nor do their sons and daughters—in their parents' behalf now, in their own later, when they themselves are old. They want insurance against emergencies. This the Kerr-Mills Law does not provide. It is misleading, therefore—and insulting—for the AMA to claim that this public assistance law is the final answer to the costs of medical care for older people.

Even worse, however, are the AMA's efforts to discredit the administration proposal ("this compulsory health-care program") by labeling it "socialized medicine." In paid advertisements in newspapers and magazines, the AMA has alleged that ". . . when the federal government enters the privacy of the examination room—controlling both standards of practice and choice of practitioner—the cost includes loss of freedom. Your doctor's freedom to treat you in an individual way. Your freedom to choose your own doctor. When the doctor is socialized, his patient is socialized as well."

This is irresponsible nonsense. It is simply not the truth!

Under socialized medicine, all hospitals and health facilities would be owned and operated by the government. All doctors, nurses and other health workers would be on salaries paid by the government and would be under direct government supervision.

The administration proposal includes a specific prohibition against government interference in the practice of medicine. The patient chooses his own doctor, his own hospital or nursing home. He pays the doctor himself, regardless of where his services are performed. For hospital and other services, he would simply be provided with the means of paying a part of the costs.

The same freedom of choice is offered by the Javits plan.

There is thus no basis whatever for the AMA's charges. By persisting in labeling as socialized medicine something that is not socialized medicine, the AMA does a disservice to the nation. It weakens, rather than strengthens, the possibility of defeating proposals that can legitimately be placed in that category. Crying "wolf! wolf!" when there is no wolf is always a mistake.

The AMA's charges are simply an effort to block intelligent discussion of a major issue by arousing unjustified fears, and, as such, are not worthy of argument.

Instead, let's focus our attention on the merits of the administration and Javits proposals, or any other plan that would insure our senior citizens against the economic hazards of illness.

Since these medical-care proposals, if passed, will have a positive impact, sooner or later, on almost every American family's welfare, it might be wise for you to try to learn more about them.

Make up your own mind about them—and then make your views known by writing to your congressman.

May the best plan win!

7

MEDICARE—BAD MEDICINE FOR EVERYBODY*

Dr. Edward R. Annis

Opposition to the administration's health program for the elderly (Medicare) has been spearheaded by the American Medical Association. The basis of this opposition is set forth in the article that follows. Questions that Dr. Annis attempts to answer include these: What motivates the proponents of Medicare? Why is it necessary? How can opposition to Medicare be regarded as part of a general philosophy of government?

Some of us are Democrats, some of us are Republicans and some of us are political independents. We are interested in helping spread the faith in freedom which is shared by millions of Americans in both parties.

Unfortunately, our faith is not shared by some people in this country—and we find them, too, under a variety of political labels. There is a hard core of Fabian socialists, government bureaucrats, social and economic planners, and political opportunists who believe that there is just one basic answer to any and all national problems. That answer is more and more government programs, bigger and bigger federal

* Excerpts from an address delivered by Dr. Annis, president-elect, American Medical Association, at the Fifth *Human Events* Political Action Conference at Washington, D.C., January 11, 1963.

budgets to carry out the programs, and higher and higher taxes to finance the budgets to carry out the programs.

Unfortunately, also, this behind-the-scenes group of social architects has been able to influence large numbers of sincere, well-meaning people. Over the years—through artful propaganda, clever distortion of facts, easy generalities and falsely emotional appeals cloaked in humanitarianism—they have managed to mislead many Americans who did not perceive the ultimate design of the completed fabric, the eventual cost in both money and freedom.

Fortunately, however, the pendulum seems to be swinging the other way. More and more of our fellow citizens are becoming concerned over the increasing costs of government, the mounting threat of governmental controls and regulations, the shrinking purchasing power of their paychecks, the growing loss of freedoms.

They are becoming less vulnerable to the blandishments of fantasy, as compared with the facts. They are becoming less gullible about promises of pie-in-the-sky, as compared with the facts. They are becoming more realistic in their viewpoint toward grandiose federal panaceas, as compared with the facts.

I think I can say, honestly and with pride, that my profession—the entire medical profession—has played a major role in bringing about this trend. More than any other single group, and for many years, we physicians have been threatened—persistently, doggedly and closely—by the various legislative proposals of the social planners. So far, we have resisted them with courage and success, and in so doing I believe we have caused a lot of people to think twice about a lot of things.

The courage we can claim as our own. But the success was achieved only by going to the American people with the facts, and thereby gaining millions of allies through the avenues of communications and public opinion. In these efforts—first against the Murray-Wagner-Dingell bill in 1949–1952, then against the Forand bill which first came up in 1957, and more recently against the King-Anderson bill of the past two years—we have had great help from organizations and individuals . . . who share our opposition to creeping socialism.

This year, next year, and for as long as necessary, we intend to continue with courage and success—and without compromise on basic principles. To spell it out, that means no compromise in our opposition to the idea of financing health care through the social security system.

And we shall continue to go to the American people with the facts—not only the facts about why we oppose the King-Anderson type of legislation, but also the even more important facts about the progress and potential of existing, voluntary mechanisms.

THE FACTS ABOUT MEDICARE

1. The great majority of Americans over 65 are not poor, ill and without proper health care.
2. Both the health and finances of our senior citizens are far better than they have been pictured, and they will be improving constantly in the years ahead.
3. The medical cost problems that do exist among the aged are problems of individuals, not of an entire age group.
4. Those problems can be met most efficiently and economically by methods which fit individual needs and the great variety of state and local situations.
5. Our nation already has voluntary, flexible programs to accomplish that purpose. Our job now is to expand and improve them.

6. One of those programs is the Kerr-Mills law, which Congress passed in 1960. This law enables the states to provide medical assistance for all low-income people over 65, regardless of whether or not they are covered by social security.

7. As of today, under the Kerr-Mills law, 38 states and territories had improved their Old Age Assistance medical programs, and 31 had established new medical assistance programs for old people who are not on public assistance. The medical profession is working actively to promote full, efficient use of the Kerr-Mills law in all states which need it.

8. The other existing method is voluntary health insurance and prepayment plans which already protect 55 per cent of our senior citizens. New plans and ideas are developing at a fast pace, and within the next three years voluntary plans will be protecting 70–75 per cent of the people over 65.

9. By promoting full use and development of these tools already at hand, we can solve the problem and avoid the faults and dangers of the King-Anderson type of program.

10. The King-Anderson type program, for example, would meet neither the medical nor the financial needs of the old people who really need help.

11. It would scatter certain limited benefits, at public expense, to millions of people over 65 who neither need nor want such help.

12. It would raise social security taxes on all workers—including young people just starting out in their careers—to provide these limited benefits for only one age group.

13. It would radically alter the whole purpose and nature of our American system of social security.

14. It would be the first major step toward national compulsory health insurance for our entire population.

15. Its enactment would have a far-reaching influence on the social, economic and political future of our nation.

Federalized hospitalization for the aged was exposed before the last Congress and the people as a hoax and a fraud. It was demonstrated again and again that the program would do what the proponents piously denied it would do: namely, permit government intervention in the practice of medicine in this country for the first time and begin destruction of the twin traditons of freedom of the patient's choice and freedom of the doctor's practice which have made American medicine one of the wonders of the modern world.

At the same time, it was shown that the cost of the program would be staggering and the end result would have little real meaning for the needy aged. The measure provided only 25 per cent of complete medical care; physicians' fees were not covered; no drugs were included; about four million elderly citizens were arbitrarily excluded because they are not on social security.

But bureaucrats with a mission are a tireless breed. They can lose time and again, and keep coming back and coming back, confident that they will at last wear down their opposition and win their way. Those against them can lose only once. For them there is no second chance.

Americans must recognize this peril as the stage is set for another struggle over Medicare.

FREEDOM UNDER ATTACK

If they surrender a fragment of freedom under the guise of compromise or because they weary of the fight, that fragment of freedom is gone—never to be retrieved. Or, stated another way, a federal government takeover is like poured cement. If you do not struggle as it is being poured, but wait until it is an accomplished fact, it hardens and you never escape.

Medicare is not an isolated issue. Far from it. Medicare is part of a greater struggle which has as its goal the surrender of individual freedom and self-respect on promise of unearned government handouts. The people's votes and control of their personal lives and destinies would be purchased with their own money, collected in higher taxes and doled back to them by an all-knowing bureaucracy which claims to have a monopoly on sympathy and good will. A more vicious or cynical combination of forces striking at the keystone of liberty would be impossible to imagine.

Whatever form these welfare schemes assume, the aim is the same—complete centralization of authority in Washington, corruption of a truly independent franchise and the end of democratic government in this country.

Whatever alternative proposals or purported Medicare compromises are put forward in the months to come, Americans should see them all as merely different routes to the same destination—government control of the practice of medicine.

Only a resolute and clear-thinking electorate, proud of its heritage and determined to hold to its principles of self-reliance and personal integrity, stand between the administration and its objective in this fight.

Have no illusions about it. It will be a brutal fight. With a presidential election standing at the trail's end of the next Congress, the White House will use every pressure resource, every power device at its disposal, to force passage of a medical care bill to purchase support at the polls to stay in power. The gigantic propaganda campaign of the past and the "arm twisting" of members of Congress by the administration lobby will undoubtedly be remembered as only the beginning of what is to come.

The opponents will have to draw heavily upon their arsenal of truth and fact to meet the drumfire of distortions, innuendo and half-truth which has marked the campaign for Medicare from its inception. We must be as tireless and unswerving as the bureaucrats in striving to reach the consciousness of all Americans, young and old alike.

We cannot, because of fatigue or exasperation over the seemingly endless controversy, allow ourselves to get trapped into a compromise which merely means surrender and loss of freedom by the salami method—a slice at a time.

THE REAL ISSUES

The real issues are unmistakable when light is shed on them:

Should wage earners and their employers be compelled to pay for medical care for millions of Americans who can well afford to take care of themselves?

Should a hired employee of the federal government be empowered to interpose himself in the normal doctor-patient relationship?

Should a new and possibly ruinous burden be imposed on the social security system?

To their everlasting credit, the people have responded to the facts when these and the array of related questions have been examined in the open forum. There is no reason to suppose the great majority will not continue to resist the blandishments of the do-gooders, the uplifters and the political schemers if they have the facts; if they understand that an end to freedom of medicine can only mean other freedoms are in jeopardy.

This is the real nature of the challenge confronting the nation today. It can be met only if all Americans determind to preserve a free society fight this proposal from the day it is introduced.

Write to your senators and congressman and make clear to them that there must be no compromise on principle. Let the editors of your local newspapers know that you believe in helping those who need help, but that you reject any form of health care which is compulsory and which would squander millions of tax dollars on people who are willing and financially able to take care of themselves.

Arm yourselves with the facts so that in your home community you can overcome deceitful and false arguments with the truth. Promote discussion groups and get the Medicare question raised before civic organizations in your area to counter the gigantic propaganda mill in Washington. For only by spreading the truth to reach Americans in every corner of the land will this fight be won.

In conclusion, I want to emphasize one fundamental point:

We physicians, in opposing the King-Anderson type of legislation, are not simply trying to defeat a bill in Congress.

We are not simply defending the medical profession or protecting our own personal interests.

We are fighting for basic principles which underlie the American system and which have made our nation great.

Medicine, in order to continue to progress in the future as it has in the past, must continue to operate under a free enterprise system which fosters competition, the striving for excellence, the never-ending attempt to "build a better mousetrap."

For the benefit of the American public, we shall welcome and appreciate the vigorous support of all those who believe in initiative, self-reliance, progressive action within the framework of the American way of life—and, above all, personal freedom.

8

MUST WE CHOOSE BETWEEN EXTREMES?*

Irving Kristol

As Mr. Kristol points out in the article that follows, much of the debate over the welfare state poses two choices—either exclusive private enterprise or a government monopoly. Kristol argues for a middle position, and illustrates his point by reexamining the debate over health programs in the United States.

Ever since John Kenneth Galbraith, in *The Affluent Society*, popularized the distinction between the private sector and the public sector of our economy, these two categories have been the shuttlecocks of ideological debate. On the one hand, the liberals think it a scandal that this nation

---

* Irving Kristol, "Is the Welfare State Obsolete?," *Harper's Magazine*, June 1963. © 1963 by Harper & Row, Publishers, Inc. Reprinted by permission of the author.

should spend as much on cosmetics as on space exploratoin (including missile development) . . . that automobiles should flourish while civic transit decays . . . that private vanities predominate over the public welfare. On the other, there are the conservatives for whom the contrast between private and public sectors is between "productive" and "nonproductive" expenditures, between the "voluntary" and "coercive" areas of American life, between individual, rational self-interest and public folly.

I think this debate is anything but insignificant or sterile, but I also think the terms in which it is defined are profoundly misleading. I would even say they are deliberately intended to mislead. Beneath this rhetorical controversy is a rather crude struggle for political and social power. The liberal community—i.e., the teachers, the journalists, the civil servants, the trade unionists, the leaders of minority groups, etc.—envisages the welfare state as the one institution through which it can exercise a power and authority over the nation's affairs which it does not otherwise possess. The conservative community—i.e., businessmen and their associates—sees the welfare state as a *parvenu* authority that usurps its traditional power and prerogatives, obstructs its habitual freedom of action. Each party doubtless sincerely believes that its sovereignity is most conducive to the common good. Whom the gods would make power-hungry, they first make sincere.

In some significant respects, of course, this conflict has already been decided in favor of the liberals. The need for huge government defense expenditures, the sheer massive complexity of our industrial society and the consequent necessity for increased regulation, the simple fact that businessmen are an electoral minority—these have made it inevitable that a modern democratic state will be a strong state, not a weak one. There is not much point in lamenting this development; and, so far as I can see, no reason to do so.

But true strength knows its own limits; and there is a real question as to whether the welfare state, as it is taking shape in America today, is not exhibiting delusions of omnicompetence.

The terms "public sector" and "private sector," as commonly used, are summary answers to the question: Who spends the nation's money? Not: For what purpose? Not: With what consequence? Merely: Who?—government, or private associations and individuals?

A more relevant response would be to concede the desirability of the ends pursued while focusing attention on new methods of achieving them. We might then find that the idea of a welfare state does not necessarily imply that the state should itself always dispense all welfare. Perhaps it would suffice for the state to establish a legal framework for a society in which individual welfare is recognized as a *social* responsibility without at the same time necessarily being a direct responsibility of the *state*.

ILLUSIONS ABOUT MEDICARE

For instance, the President's Medicare bill might possibly be the best way of dealing with the problem created by the dual fact of medical care costing so much more than it used to and people living longer than they used to. On the other hand, it might not be—we shall require a couple of decades to find out. Would it not, therefore, be prudent to establish that governmental medical insurance will not buy the *only* way? Monopolies are sometimes necessary evils, but we ought not to concede the necessity prematurely. We already have a nongovernmental pattern of medical insurance—two-thirds of the American population is now covered by surgical and hospital insurance issued by nonprofit organizations such as Blue Cross or Blue Shield or by private insurance companies. Why not encourage this natural growth, parallel to any state insurance scheme that is set up? Why not give individuals the option to choose among a plurality of insurers? It is one thing to make medical insurance compulsory; it is quite another to make only one *kind* of medical insurance compulsory.

Any medical insurance program is going to cost the taxpayer money. The mute appeal of a state-run monopoly is the illusion that over a period of time, and in some undefined way, people may get more than they put in, either because the federal government will magically "close the gap" or because "someone else" (the rich or the employers or whoever) will be called upon to make up the difference. This idea is appealing, but baseless. It is as appealing, and as baseless, as the notion that government money is something additional to the people's money, instead of being identical with it. It is as appealing, and as baseless, as the belief that the steeply progressive income tax significantly reduces the tax burden of the average citizen. In a society and economy such as ours, where government expenditure is so infinitely greater than the ability of the rich to pay for it, such egalitarian fancies are mischievous and deceitful. Just because most people, most of the time, feel poorer than they think they ought to be, it does not follow that they are "underprivileged." Indeed, it is this very majority who will have to subsidize medical care for the truly poor—under whatever program is instituted.

The question of how much the American people wish to spend on medical care, as against other things (such as education, leisure, etc.) is something the American people are in the process of deciding. But if, as seems likely, they decide to compel themselves to spend more than they are now doing, it does not follow that only the federal government is competent to spend it for them—and certainly not for all of them.

What holds for Medicare may hold for other areas of the public sector as well. Public-welfare outlays by federal, state, and municipal governments have doubled since 1955, and now amount to more than $40 billion a year. (This excludes expenditures on education by states and municipalities.) This money has not been "wasted"—but can anyone claim that it has been spent as efficiently as it might have been? Or that we have nothing to learn from the experience of these years?

It is right for the government to see to it that public needs are adequately met. It is not always necessary for the government to do the job itself.

Once one gets into the swing of thinking along these lines, all sorts of intriguing possibilities emerge. Would it not be interesting to explore these possibilities instead of persisting in the sterile argument over the relative merits of the private and the public sectors? It is always the taxpayer's money that is going to be spent for purposes of improving his welfare. But it does not always follow that it is the tax collector who can spend it most wisely or efficiently.

The important thing is that welfare be improved and enlarged. The means by which we proceed to do this may be as various and as flexible as we wish them to be. And the more various and flexible—the more open to innovation, the more susceptible to reform and revision—the better. Waste and inefficiency there will always be, but the less monumentally it is institutionalized, the less incorrigible it is. Surely a good motto for an open society is: keep it open.

9

A PROGRAM FOR FUTURE HEALTH AND MEDICAL CARE*

Conservative Americans commonly defend the present status of America's health and medical organization. Pointing with pride to the past, they argue that future progress is assured if present trends are continued. Critics of the existing system are apt to picture it as obsolete and in need of major reform, probably through governmental action. Because we can never be certain of the direction of change, it is interesting to note the recommendations offered by the Rockefeller Brothers Panel IV, concerning changes in the American pattern of health and medical care during the next 15 years. Since the panel represents a consensus of prominent industrial, financial and academic leaders, it may well be a shadow cast before the main body of change.

Health in its broadest aspects has an importance to our nation second only to our national security. The advances in this field during the past few decades have been remarkable. The gradual extension of the average lifetime offers ample evidence of the results of medical research, preventive medicine, and health education. The infectious diseases have ceased to be major causes of death; the hazards of childbirth have been largely overcome.

But the more rapid our progress is, the greater the necessity that we think ahead in the field of health. The broad national policies which such a "look ahead" suggests are outlined below.

MEDICAL RESEARCH

The toll of today's leading killing and crippling diseases, such as cancer, cardiovascular diseases, and mental illness, is staggering in both human and economic terms. In addition, many new types of health problems and opportunities are emerging today which demand intensive investigation.

The acquisition of new knowledge is basic to advancing national health. We recommend, therefore, continued expansion of our medical research programs as rapidly as the supply of scientific talent will permit.

As we step up medical research efforts, equal strides must be taken toward putting their results to use more rapidly. We recommend that public health authorities and private medical groups join in a study analyzing the extent of the time lag between the acquisition of new medical knowledge and its practical availability to the gen-

* Rockefeller Brothers Fund, *The Challenge to America: Its Economic and Social Aspects*. Special Studies Project Report IV (New York: Doubleday & Company, Inc., 1958), pp. 56–59.

eral public, identifying the causes of delay, and delineating measures to reduce it.

MEDICAL MANPOWER

We are short of doctors in many parts of the country and also of many categories of medical specialists. The number of doctors should increase in relation to total population, whereas it appears now to be constant or declining in relation to population. We urge immediate steps to overcome this trend including maximum possible utilization of the facilities of existing medical schools and immediate planning for the inauguration of new medical schools.

The existing medical schools are having serious financial difficulties. If private fund-raising efforts and indirect government aids prove inadequate, we would recommend consideration of a federal-state program of assistance to the operational budgets of the medical schools.

Federal and state loan and scholarship programs, in addition to increased scholarship funds from private sources, commend themselves as a means of helping the student to overcome the high cost of medical education, which is not recouped by the student for many years. Similar measures to encourage the training of more professional and practical nurses should be continued and expanded.

MEDICAL FACILITIES

Subject to the limitations imposed by personnel shortages (particularly nursing and technical personnel), we need in most areas of the country more hospitals and other health facilities of many kinds. The increase in chronic disease and the needs of an aging population highlight the necessity for substantial expansion of facilities for long-term care, particularly of high quality nursing homes for the care of the aged with moderate impairments.

We recommend the use of a portion of available hospital construction funds for developing radically new types of medical facilities such as hospitals permitting maximum self-help, and community care centers offering diagnostic services and extensive outpatient treatment and homemaker services.

At the same time, modernization and rehabilitation of existing hospitals —particularly older ones in large cities —must be a major target of the next decade. We suggest consideration of low-interest state loans for this purpose.

PAYING THE COSTS OF MEDICAL CARE

As medical practice has become more complex and specialized, it has become apparent that cooperative efforts among practicing physicians can enhance the quality of care given. The first question is how best to achieve this. The second is how to pay for high quality medical care so as to spread costs among a large group of individuals and families, and over years of high and low health costs for each individual or family. The increasing costs of hospital and medical care lend urgency to this question.

One approach, adopted effectively in some communities, is group medical practice, affiliated with a common hospital, and with essentially all costs prepaid by the subscribers through family health insurance premiums. The range of physician services covered by the fees should be comprehensive in scope. The resulting incentives tend to emphasize preventive care and early diagnostic services, and to minimize unnecessary hospitalization. We believe that this group practice prepayment approach, although by no means suited to all communities, could be advantageously adopted by more communities.

Health centers established by industry and labor in connection with a place of employment also offer great possibilities for improved health care.

Irrespective of the form through which physician's services are provided, we urge as a major objective of prepayment plans over the next decade the coverage of doctor's and nursing care outside the hospital. Such coverage can serve as a real encouragement to early discovery and treatment of physical defects and illness, thereby resulting in better health and lower costs, and to shorter periods of hospitalization.

More people should be covered by the newer "catastrophic illness" plans, designed to help meet extraordinary costs of accident or illness over and above the costs met by a comprehensive basic plan. The cost of this protection, when spread over a large group, is relatively small—provided that the underlying basic plan is broad in the scope of services covered and encourages rather than discourages early use of diagnostic services and facilities.

For the present needy aged and for the "medically indigent" who cannot afford to pay for protection even under basic health prepayment plans, financing from general tax revenues—federal, state or local, or a combination of the three—seems essential.

XV

Foreign Affairs: America, Russia, and Some One Hundred Other Nations

So far this book has dealt with the kind of America we are and are becoming and can and ought to become, in terms of what Americans want and need. But we live in a world with more than 100 other nations and 2,000,000,000 other people. Continued American survival, prosperity and freedom in the kind of world we want depend on what the rest of the world is and wants to be. What the rest of the world is and wants to be, and the hard choices this requires of us, are what this chapter is about.

In foreign policy and defense policy four snarled skeins of thought are interwoven. These four turn up again and again as problems. They are: (1) The question "will the Russians become any nicer?" or must we go on and on, spending $50,000,000,000 a year and the time and effort of 2,000,000 men opposing them at every turn. (2) The fact that there is no world police force nor world army and each major nation must carry its gun on its hip or find a Big Brother to protect it. Is this gun-happy behavior the only language we and they understand? How can a major nation arm itself for its defense without, by its very choice of weapons, scaring its adversaries and its allies into irrational and dangerous behavior? (3) The need to further the slow development of world community and institutions for peaceful settlement of conflicts. And (4) the need and duty to do something for the undeveloped peoples, yet the seeming endlessness of it.

Will the Russians Get Any Nicer? or at Least Easier to Live with?

For two decades we have been caught in a grinding drive to check Russia all over the world. Will this go through our lifetime and our children's lifetime? During the 1930's and 1940's America's enemies were Germany and Japan, both now allies, and Russia, now an adversary, was our ally. Are they really dedicated to burying us? Or are they changing and becoming easier to live with? Will their revolutionary zeal run down? Will we ever pull so clearly ahead of them that they'll recognize the fact and quiet down?

The Competition in Weapons: A Long, Hard Struggle Toward Peace? or a Compulsive Race Toward War?

In our own country we come and go every day and feel safe. The police are there and back of them are the courts. Between nations there is no such web of protection. Each nation carries its gun on its hip. The United States, for example, is wearing a $50,000,000,000-a-year gun. In International disputes there is always the possibility of resort to force. Any nation big enough to threaten another *must* be assumed to be likely, one time or another, to threaten the other, and must be considered to be the other's potential enemy. What is "big enough"?—Having a large population *and* a large land area *and* a heavily industrialized economy. National safety has the utmost priority. A big nation therefore seeks bases near its potential enemy and far from its own shores because any resort to force is likely to cause terrible destruction where it takes place, however localized and brief. In defense nobody wants to play any home games; if one must fight one wants to fight over there and away from here. The result is a complicated network of world-wide alliances and military bases and a complicated world-wide race between the U.S. and its allies and the U.S.S.R. and its allies. It is a race in weapons development and production, in economic production, and in applied science and technology. Each seeks to be bigger, and each scares the other into greater efforts. Each seeks to keep its techniques of military defense secret but the race is a race in invention and innovation and an idea can't be locked up. Each wants to "get ahead" in the race, so clearly ahead that it will scare the other into behaving, but it is hard to keep secrets when the object in having a weapon is to show it to the "enemy" in order to give him pause. Consequently the pace of the world race quickens and quickens. This is the situation. It is the state of the world and of the U.S. and the U.S.S.R. today and as far into the future as we can see.

In this part of this chapter we will take a brief look at American defense and the risks it involves today—defense by infantry advisers in a brush fire war, defense by stand-by intercontinental missiles just in case the Big War ever starts. Then we'll take a look at the next decade's problems if we and Russia continue by the same rules of the game. Then we'll discuss alternatives. We Americans are fabulous technicians, splendid at engineering and organizing our way out of a problem of the moment, but not inclined to theorize and think our way out of the basic situation. Not surprisingly we spend almost all of our efforts redesigning missiles to cut delivery time by say 8 minutes and none of our efforts trying to get out of the hole of having to go on, underground, redesigning billion dollar, 30,000,000-ton-of-TNT missiles. "Everybody is for disarmament, but nobody believes anybody," remarks Paul Goodman. It is fashionable to ignore possibilities of controlling the arms race and get on with the job of the next city buster—the neutron bomb (which not only destroys all life but leaves machines and buildings uncontaminated. But uncontaminated for whom? Gophers?)

Can the same inventiveness provide us adequate safeguards and freedom from self-inflicted wounds at the same time? Few would accept or advocate a unilateral end to the cold war at our exclusive expense, but are accommodations totally out of the question? If some agreement now seems feasible when is the danger line reached? It is over matters such as these that the debate rages.

America and the United Nations: The Only Consensus the World Has? or Declamation Without Action?

Alliances and regional associations of nations of similar interests exist. NATO, SEATO, OAS, ANZUS, CMEA, the Warsaw Pact and the Arab League are examples. But alliances and regional associations are organized *against* some other nation or group. They require an enemy.

A long-run problem in American foreign policy is how to further the development of *universal* international organizations and institutions, how to further the slow growth of world community so that eventually disputes can be settled peacefully.

The only major institution capable of sometimes transcending the bipolar struggle between the U.S. and the U.S.S.R. is the United Nations.

Some Americans cannot stand the U.N. Consider the following:

> *United Nations a gigantic fraud.* . . . in spite of all the propaganda, and the tons of paper and ink devoted to making black appear white, the fact remains and is growing clearer every day that the "United Nations" is a fraud. It is neither an avenue toward international amity and cooperation nor an instrument for peace. It is a mechanism for fastening upon the world an international collectivism which, if it prevails, will destroy human freedom. . . . And, in the process, in the quest for world uniformity at the expense of individual and national freedom it will plunge us into another cycle of wars.[1]

[1] From Merwin K. Hart, in *Economic Council Letter* No. 192, June 1, 1948, p. 1.

or this:

"UNESCO," the United Nations' Educational, Scientific and Cultural Organization, is a subversive association. It is consciously furthering a campaign calculated to pervert the teaching profession in this country, and so destroy the worth and integrity of America's first bulwark of freedom—our tax-supported public schools.[2]

[2] From the October 1951 issue of *Philadelphia Newsletter*. Quoted from Gordon D. Hall, *The Hate Campaign Against the U.N.* (Glencoe, Ill.: Beacon Press, 1952), pamphlet.

To such people and such groups the U.N. is internationalist and therefore un-American. To them the U.N. is collectivist and therefore un-American.

Others celebrate U.N. Day the way Americans used to celebrate Independence Day. Consider this:

The people in our town—Asheville, North Carolina—arranged an impressive celebration last October 24th, twenty days after Sputnik No. 1 burst upon an astonished world. First there was a parade with several bands, interesting floats, pretty drum majorettes, National Guard units and a retired three-star general as master of ceremonies. Then the mayor presided at a program in the municipal auditorium attended by members of the Chamber of Commerce, civic clubs and such national organizations as the League of Women Voters. Students came from all our higher schools.

The celebration marked the 12th birthday of the United Nations, and the people of Asheville were observing this anniversary on a city-wide scale for the first time. All this had been planned before the Russians produced an earth satellite, but the conquest of outer space did make the occasion seem more significant. Obviously peacemaking efforts had become more urgent. Asheville's demonstration of "grass-roots" support for the U.N. was duplicated in many other cities and towns across the United States, and in other countries and continents. . . .[3]

[3] Demaree Bess, "Is the U.N. Old and Tired?," *Saturday Evening Post,* February 15, 1958, p. 25.

To most of the citizens celebrating the U.N. it stands for action for peace; to "take a matter to the U.N.." is good, and to win a vote of support in the U.N. means we won.

Neither of these groups' points of view helps much in the difficult matters of trying to decide what the U.S. should do in, for, and to the U.N. Between nations, to *do things* usually takes men, money, guns, or some combination. The U.N. has almost no money, and no armies or arms. It cannot do much. Between nations, to do things also takes the consent and support of other nations. And this is difficult to get outside of the U.N.

We seek to show the folly of setting our expectations of the U.N. too high and to show the impossibility of trying to do certain things without U.N. support.

America and 1,000,000,000 Living in Poverty: A Plain Case of Need for Help? or an Impossible Burden?

Since 1948, the first "delivery year" of the U.S. Marshall Plan for West Europe, the United States has put about $5,000,000,000 each year into aid to other countries. In the first postwar decade this aid was used in Western Europe, and now Western European countries by and large are splendidly prosperous and self-supporting. In more recent years this aid is being put into underdeveloped countries of Asia, of the Middle East, of Africa, and of Latin America.

It is bewilderingly complex. One reads about U.S. projects to build roads in Sumatra, to initiate a job classification system in Spain, to send experts in ground-cover crops to the Philippines to try to improve coconut culture, and so on. One often hears cries of outrage about this. Some call it waste, "money down rat holes," "glob-aloney," and want it stopped. Others concentrate their criticism upon the Americans who are trying to do these things—the "technical experts" or artists in "overseasmanship." Others talk about the urgency of the *needs* of the underdeveloped peoples, and about the kinds of assistance the U.S. should give.

Why are we involved? What are we trying to do? Are our efforts merely token efforts? Is this our job? Can we do it?

1

THE SOVIET MIND AND WORLD REALITIES*

George F. Kennan

George Kennan (former Ambassador to Russia and to Yugoslavia, distinguished historian of Russia) takes a dim view of the dream of many Americans and Europeans that the Russians are becoming like us and that Russia's leaders will suddenly discover that their interests are close to ours. A few minor civil liberties, a slight rise in the standard of living—these have occurred within Russia, yes. But the Russian Marxist view of America, particularly of America's motives, is a condition, a habit of mind.

We are all familiar with the posture of irreconcilable hostility, ostensibly only toward the Western governments but in effect toward the Western peoples as well, which has at all times animated the Soviet leaders. We have learned to expect at their hands an unremitting effort to undermine our world position, to disrupt our relations with those who have formerly been our friends, to destroy our confidence in ourselves and the confidence of others in us, to reduce us, in short, to a state of isolation, helplessness and impotence in the affairs of the world. . . .

The rationale for this posture on the part of the Soviet government has, as we all know, invariably been expressed in ideological terms—in the characteristic jargon, that is, of Marxist-Leninist thought. There has been a common tendency here in the West in recent years to dismiss this ideological posture as mere window dressing, to ignore its political content and implications, and to see behind it nothing more than a primitive lust for military conquest—usually envisaged as a determination to overrun Western Europe, in particular,

* George F. Kennan, *Russia, The Atom and the West* (New York: Harper & Row, Publishers, 1958), pp. 16–31. Copyright 1957, 1958 by George F. Kennan. Reprinted by permission of the publishers.

by force of arms, as soon as military conditions might prove favorable.

. . . This is a dangerously inaccurate view of what we are up against. . . . The hostility has been there, certainly; and it has been a deadly hostility, aimed at a destruction of all that we most intimately cherish—a destruction no less sweeping, no less final than that which would be occasioned by an outright war. But the threat has not been one of all-out military attack. It has been a combined political and military threat, but more political than military—a threat intimately associated with the weaknesses of our Western civilization itself—looking to these weaknesses, in fact, rather than to the strength of the Soviet arms, to constitute the main instruments of our undoing. The Soviet design has consisted, in other words, primarily of a determination to exploit every element of disunity, of confusion, of short-sightedness in our society, with a view to causing us to eliminate ourselves as rivals to Soviet power and influence everywhere. . . .

One of the most serious evils of this overmilitarization of thinking in the West on the nature of the Soviet threat has been that it has confused people badly about the question of what could be done to meet this threat. Assuming that the ideological foundation for Soviet policy was simply disingenuous, many people have tended to suppose either that the Soviet leaders were genuinely suspicious of Western purposes, and that this was the real cause of their hostility; or that they were simply evil men, who wanted power for its own sake and believed that they could outpace us in the military competition to a point where we could safely be attacked and disposed of. And taking one or the other of these views, people assumed that if only we could prove ourselves strong enough to discourage military aggression, or, correspondingly, if we could lay to rest the Soviet suspicions about our motives, this whole situation could be suddenly cleared up—an entirely new outlook could suddenly be induced in the Soviet mind—and the cold war would be terminated at a stroke. And as the culmination of this happy process, people usually envisaged some sort of a summit meeting, at which the last misunderstandings would be removed and agreements would be arrived at for a peaceful collaboration in the future. . . .

These tendencies naturally received a certain fillip in recent years from the death of Stalin. His successors appeared to be men of greater moderation and good will and even humanity; and in some respects they really were—and are. Stalin, of course, also talked peace in his day, as Khrushchev does now. . . .

We have now had four years in which to study the political personality of this post-Stalin regime; and I am afraid that the time has come when we can no longer comfort ourselves with any of these illusions. . . .

From the time of their seizure of power, 40 years ago, the Russian Communists have always been characterized by their extraordinary ability to cultivate falsehood as a deliberate weapon of policy. They began by adopting an attitude of complete cynicism about objective truth, denying its value if not its existence, declaring the lie to be no less useful and respectable than the truth if only it serve the purposes of the party. Departing from this premise, they have systematically employed falsehood not just as a means of deceiving others and exploiting their credulity, but also as a means of comforting and reassuring themselves. It has seemed to them at all times easier, and in no way improper, to operate a militant political movement on the basis of convenient falsehood than on the basis of awkward truth.

. . . The effects of this systematic abuse of the human intellect are deep-seated and troublesome. Forty years of intellectual opportunism have wrought a strange corruption of the Communist mind, rendering it incapable of distinguishing sharply between fact and fiction in a single segment of its experience, namely in its relationship to any external competitive power.

In everything that can be statistically expressed—expressed, that is, in such a way as not to imply any judgment on our motivation—I believe the Soviet government to be excellently informed about us. I am sure that their information on the development of our economies, on the state of our military preparations, on our scientific progress, etc., is absolutely first rate. But when it comes to the analysis of *our motives,* to the things that make our life tick as it does, I think this whole great system of intelligence-gathering breaks down seriously. It breaks down because over all these 40 years the Communist party has made it impossible for the people who collect the factual information to accompany that information with any really objective analysis of the nature of Western society. Some of the fictions dearest and most basic to Russian Communism's view of itself would be jeopardized at every turn by that sort of analysis. The Soviet diplomatic representative or journalist abroad has no choice but to cast his analytical report in the terms of Marxist-Leninist ideology whether this is applicable or not in the given instance. In this way the Soviet leaders find themselves committed to a badly distorted image of the outside world.

Being thus committed, they are able to apprehend everything about us but the main things. They view us as one might view the inhabitants of another planet through a very powerful telescope. Everything is visible; one sees in the greatest detail the strange beings of that other world going about their daily business; one can even discern the nature of their undertakings; but what one does not see and cannot see is the motivation that drives them on these various pursuits. This remains concealed; and thus the entire image, clear and intelligible in detail, becomes incomprehensible in its totality.

The fact is that the Soviet leaders are the first and leading victims of the abuse they have practiced for so long on the freedom of the mind. I would not wish to maintain that they believe everything they say; I am sure they do not. But I would submit that their habitual carelessness about the truth has tended to obliterate in their minds the distinction between what they do believe and what they merely find it convenient to say. It would be easier for us if they either believed things entirely or spoke them in utter cynicism. In either case, we would know where we stood. As it is, our problem is very difficult indeed; for we can never know, when we encounter their statements and reactions, whether we have to do with the substructure of sincerely held error which does indeed exist in their minds, or with the superstructure of contrived and deliberately cultivated untruth to which they are so committed. . . .

We must accept, first of all, the fact that there is nothing anyone can do in any short space of time to alter this situation, to correct this corruption of thought, to make out of the Soviet leaders men capable of seeing world realities as we do. It is no good trying to argue them round to our point of view on any one occasion. They are men who can be directly influenced by situations, but not by words expressed in any terminology other than their own. There is nothing that can be said to Mr. Khrushchev on any one occasion by any Western figures, however illustrious, that would suddenly dispel this obscurity of vision. What we are confronted with here is not just misunderstanding, not just honest error, but a habit of the mind, an induced state, a condition. . . .

2

THE GREAT SLOWDOWN*

Harlan Cleveland

The power of Communist Russia (argues Harlan Cleveland) is on the wane. They've botched things in Asia, the Middle East, and Africa; Castro in Latin America is a Russian embarrassment and liability. We are far ahead of them in space technology. The Communist camp is divided into those who follow Russia, those who follow China, and those who follow neither. Internal Russia is half modern, half slum. Therefore, he argues, tough it out. We will find that their leaders can (as Kennan admits) "be directly influenced by situations." They will slowly grow more rational and easier and less expensive to live with.

TURNING OF TIDES AGAINST WORLD COMMUNISM

As we look back now we can see that the attractive power of communism on a global scale reached its peak in the years immediately following World War II.

At the close of the war Europe and Japan were smashed; the colonial empires were due to crumble; Southeast Asia, the Middle East, and Africa were about to catch fire; and Latin America was slumbering deceptively under obsolete, and therefore flammable, economic and social systems.

The Soviet Union had been victorious in the war against nazism and fascism; the Red army had covered itself with glory; the Communists throughout occupied Europe had supported and often led the underground resistance movements and thus became national heroes; Communists were taken into the cabinets of postwar European governments to represent large, flourishing, and well-financed national Communist parties; and elsewhere in the world Communists were as active as they could be in the national independence movements about to sweep the world.

Much of the world looked ripe for the kind of violent change and political chaos which sets the stage for Communists to play their classic role of scavengers.

In the name of international communism Stalin started things off by putting the clamp on Eastern and parts of Central Europe—by keeping territory already overrun by the Red army.

---

* Harlan Cleveland, "A Most Dangerous Time," *Department of State Bulletin*, December 10, 1962, pp. 877–81.

Then came the great windfall for communism with the collapse of Nationalist China and the consequent resounding impact of the Chinese revolution on Asian affairs and Asian thinking. The call went out from a meeting in Calcutta for Communist uprisings throughout Asia, and soon China was launched on that apparently spectacular "great leap forward" which many began to see as the model for modernization.

For a while communism really began to look to many—including some of our homegrown havoc-criers—like the wave of the future. But suddenly it passed its peak. Soviet pressures on Iran and Turkey, the Communist insurrection in Greece, the Berlin blockade, and unremitting hostility evoked countermeasures from the West. Interference in the Italian elections, the campaign to sabotage European recovery, and most of all the rape of Czechoslovakia, produced a moral revulsion in Europe. By about 1950 the bloom was off the rose. The tide of communism in Western Europe began to ebb, and it has been ebbing ever since.

The turn came somewhat later in Asia as the "great leap forward" ground to a noisy halt and then went into reverse—as one disaster of Communist mismanagement folowed another until the refugees swarmed into Hong Kong, as insurrections were put down in Malaya and the Philippines and the call to revolution went unheeded elsewhere, and as Asians learned from Korea, from Indochina, from Tibet, and finally from the invasion of India, what the Europeans learned from Czechoslovakia.

Weakened Communist parties in Asia are now torn between loyalty to Moscow or Peiping—or to some national variant of communism; and the tide may now be ebbing for the Communists in Asia as it did for those in Europe a dozen years ago.

Meanwhile in the Middle East the famous Communist "penetration" of the mid-Fifties ran out of gas as the Communists typically overplayed their hands and, also typically, bumped their heads against nationalism and a stubborn rejection of alien doctrine. Whatever social forms evolve in the Middle East, they will be in the name of local nationalisms, not proletarian internationalism; and in most countries it will be sanctified by Moslem, not Communist, prophets—by Mohammed perhaps, but not by Marx.

In Africa the Soviets leapt at the chance opened for them in the Congo. But they played their hand badly at the United Nations, voting three times in the Security Council for a Congo operation that cut right across their own plans for penetration. They showed their cards carelessly by flying in those big Ilyushins with conspicuous aid and "ugly Russians"; they apparently thought the levers of power needed only to be grasped, not realizing they first had to be created; they bet heavily and clumsily on an ineffective effort to prop up [Antoine] Gizenga; when they took out their frustrations in the Congo on Dag Hammarskjold, they succeeded only in lining up against their Congo policy nearly all the small nations, who would not brook an attack on the U.N. itself.

Elsewhere in Africa the Soviets had their knuckles rapped when they tried some heavy-handed meddling in other people's politics. The leaders of Africa, like those of Asia and the Middle East, clearly prefer to make their own independent mistakes without outside guidance. The struggle for Africa has only begun, but from the Communist standpoint it is not going too well.

The last chance for communism to

look like the wave of the future was in Latin America, but that chance has now been reduced by the sordid story of Dr. Castro and his sellout to Moscow. The Communists still have plenty of capacity for disruption and general mischief, but the prospects for the Soviet push into the hemisphere don't look so bright after the unanimous determination of the Organization of American States to shoo them off. Now much depends on what we Americans do in our own hemisphere, starting with redoubled efforts to make the Alliance for Progress hum with the noises of progress and reform.

The turning of the tides against world communism has been brought about mainly by a whole series of U.S. and Allied moves which made it abundantly clear that freedom was much more than a wave of the past—the Truman Doctrine, the Marshall Plan, the Berlin airlift, Korea, NATO, the Rio Treaty, ANZUS, Point 4, the Alliance for Progress, the Common Market, our aid to South Vietnam, and many more—the sum of postwar moves by the Western world, with U.S. leadership, to contain the outward thrust of Soviet communism and to develop the inward thrust of economic strength and defensive power in the non-Communist world. And the turning of the tide was also greatly helped by the deepening schism in the Communist church and the spin-off of rival denominations.

Thus communism as a world movement, reaching its crest in the immediate postwar years, began to ebb first in Europe, then Asia, the Middle East, and Africa, and now—with those departing missiles—in Latin America. Communism as a worldwide revolution is not stone dead. The wave can again surge forward but with lesser strength and more backwash. And as he has recently demonstrated, Chairman Khrushchev is a man who can see the holes in the ladder.

SLOWDOWN OF COMMUNIST ECONOMY

What of communism as a social system in the Soviet Union? What became of that image of unblemished success that was to have exerted so powerfully attractive an influence on the young nations of Asia, Africa, and Latin America?

The Soviet Union, as a Communist society, reached its peak of prestige and influence after the world Communist movement was already in decline—with Sputnik I or perhaps with Major Gagarin's flight. But here, too, the ebb tide has begun.

After World War II the Soviet Union engineered a most remarkable recovery from the worst punishment any nation has ever suffered in war. When Chairman Khrushchev came along he looked like a new kind of Communist—an extroverted political executive more interested in getting things done than in reciting the scriptures. The internal teror was lifted, and Soviet society seemed on its way to more liberal days; the Soviets were starting to move about in the outside world and to dish out aid and trade; the internal economy was booming and was beginning to look like a patented prescription for rapid modernity; the Soviets were riding the nationalist revolutions for all they were worth—and then along came evidence that, by the measure of rocket thrust, the Soviet Union has surpassed the United States in outer space.

That peak of prestige, too, now is past. The current successes and future prospects of the U.S. outer space program—including Telstar and meteorological satellites as well as manned flight and deep probes—have wiped out the mirage of over-all Soviet scientific leadership. They are good—in some fields superb—but they are not the best.

Even as the world was gasping at sputniks and orbiting cosmonauts, a lengthening inventory of internal problems suggested that Soviet Communist society might not, after all, be the answer to man's fondest aspiration.

A slowed-down Soviet economy seems to be faced with a clear need for rather drastic reforms if it is going to maintain growth on the same scale—and the miserable record of agriculture in many Communist states is a well-known scandal wherever planners discuss the advantages of alternative economic "systems." Most recently the Communist planners in Peiping, reading woodenly out of that same dog-eared book on agricultural economics that has ruined the farm production of half a dozen other Communist countries, have managed a great leap backward in Chinese agriculture too. With the entire underdeveloped world looking on—a world which is 75 per cent rural—Communist planners have come face to face with the impossibility of growing food efficiently by police-state methods.

Meanwhile, in the democratic world the miracle of Germany was followed by the miracle of France, the miracle of Japan, the miracle of Italy, and now the miracle of the Common Market with the U.K. perhaps included and with an Atlantic economic partnership on the horizon. Our mixed economy does not seem to be collapsing from internal contradictions or anything else; the so-called "capitalist camp" is not going to civil war over dwindling world markets or anything else; and the European Common Market now embraces an industrial complex so impressive that our Soviet critics, having failed to prevent it from coming about, are now trying to create their own common market with Eastern Europe and calling rather defensively for freer trade and economic cooperation between the Eastern apostles of autarky and the Western practitioners of liberalized trade.

SOME FACTS ABOUT THE SOVIET UNION

If communism as a revolutionary world movement is in partial eclipse—and if Soviet society is no longer so bright a magnet—what of the Soviet Union as a nation-state? The U.S.S.R. is and will remain a great power. But these things must also be said:

The Soviet Union is half modern and half rural slum. If the modern half is to continue to grow at the same pace, it must adopt more adequate substitutes for a price-and-profit system, which indeed it appears to be moving toward—and trying to invent some modern Marxist language to describe. If the slum half is to become modern, the Russians will have to alter Communist agricultural doctrine some more, which will change quite a lot of other things.

The Soviet Union is now run by a man who took one of the most risky and radical steps conceivable to change life in Russia—the total destruction of the reputation of a Soviet idol—and in the process clearly implied that the Communist system cannot protect a people against brutality, error, sin, and incompetence at the top. The lesson can hardly have been lost on the Soviet people.

Before long the Soviet Union will come under another generation of leadership (though still without a mechanism for orderly transfer of power). For better or for worse, the new men will see things somewhat differently than the present leadership; how they see things will much depend on how vigorously *we* have been using *our* opportunities around the world.

State controls in the Soviet Union are being slowly eroded by writers, painters, jazz buffs, beatniks, juvenile delinquents, black marketeers, and nylon stockings—probably an irreversible process—further testimony that all the propaganda in the world cannot undo the cussed determination of modern man to seek his own kind of freedom, wearing his own collar.

Let us look at a few more facts:

The Soviet Union is a not-quite-so-closed society at a time when science and technology are making closed societies increasingly hard to keep shut off from the turbulent, interesting world of pluralism and variety outside the wall.

The Soviet Union clearly does not possess the exclusive patent for rapid industrialization and economic growth, given the "miracles" of Germany, France, Italy, and Japan—or Israel or Puerto Rico for that matter. And so the developing countries are passing up the temptation to copy the faded Soviet blueprint.

The Soviet Union is suzerain of a group of European states in which nationalism will not die, which also are being de-Stalinized, which are all having trouble with their agricultural sectors, and whose centrifugal pull probably may someday result in the creation of a much looser commonwealth—which was briefly offered to them, you will remember, at the height of the Hungarian crisis. And a looser commonwealth is the beginning of the end of that antique Communist dream, the closed and monolithic empire.

The foreign policy of the Soviet Union is frustrated by U.S. initiative, by prolonged stalemate, by the undependability of Communist China, by nuclear inferiority, by the failure to capture the world nationalist revolution, and now by pullback in the Caribbean.

The Soviet Union is a member of the United Nations, which it will not support, cannot control, but dares not quit.

The Soviet Union is engaged in a prestige race for achievement in outer space which is a serious drain on resources and competes for funds with the armed forces and the need for heavy investment in agriculture and some sectors of industry.

PROSPECTS OF A WATERSHED IN THE COLD WAR

It is hard for an American, or any Western man, to compensate for the special prisms imposed on the vision of a Communist. But to Western eyes, trying to look at things from where Soviet man sits, it is difficult to resist the conclusion that a point has been reached at which the wisest, indeed the only sensible, course of action for the Soviet Union is to seek some basis for living more safely on the same planet with the non-Communist nations—some live-and-let-live formula, some set of explicit or tacit ground rules for non-military competition.

This would have been a rational conclusion for Soviet leaders to reach before the recent events in the Caribbean and along the Sino-Indian frontiers. But in the wake of these crises the Soviet leaders would be justified in finding that such a conclusion is not only rational but imperative: They have played out their hand of nuclear blackmail and failed; the West looks more formidable than ever; the danger of putting nuclear weapons in the hands of too many nations is now to obvious; the vision of unity in the Communist world has turned out to be illusory; the nonaligned states are showing signs of clearer thinking about where their national interests really lie; the East European satellites can be excused for certain apprehensions about the future; and the mythical goal of a Communist world revolution begins to look more and more expensive, more and more unlikely of achievement.

If Soviet leaders are prepared to finish the job of liquidating the Cuban crisis, we may find ourselves at an important turning point in history, at a watershed of the cold war as we have known it. For the Soviet leaders hold in their hands one of the world's most powerful weapons: the simple decision to live at peace with their neighbors, to stop fighting the United Nations and gradually join it in fact as well as name, to start down the road toward disarmament, to enter piecemeal into cooperative scientific and technical projects, and, in time, to become so enmeshed in international organizations and obligations that it becomes inescapably clear to them—as it is already clear to the rest of us—that there is much more to be won in this world by cooperation than by coercion. But there is a problem in discussing the prospects of a watershed in world affairs. It is this: People immediately jump to the conclusion that we shall wake up some fine Friday morning and discover that the horrors and threats and sweat and struggles of the past decade and a half were no more than bad dreams; all of a sudden, the tensions will go out of international life, and we can all return to those more private and more placid pursuits which we all claim to yearn for. And the United Nations, of course, will take care of any unpleasantness that might intrude on the new "normalcy" in world affairs.

This, of course, is bottled-in-bond mythology. There will be no Friday morning awakening.

The tattered remains of Communist ideology, including the mad dream of a Communist one-world, will die hard in the minds of reactionary dogmatists and will haunt new generations of Communist leaders. . . .

And a Soviet Union in a more nationalistic frame of mind could conceivably be as troublesome as a Soviet Union promoting an illusory world revolution of the proletariat. In any event a Soviet Union which had abandoned the military confrontation with the United States would shift to the field of economic competition; it would still cling to totalitarian principles; it would still for a time cling to the foreign real estate kept as booty from World War II; it would still be warped by inherited dogma; it would still be fearful of the open society, addicted to the secrecy that antedates communism in Russia; it would still be suspicious of the motives of that noisy and various world community which the Communists insist on calling the "capitalist camp." Living at peace with its neighbors will not come easy to a state with so many phobias and neuroses. Yet it would make sense for the Soviet Union today.

So what I mean by a turning point in contemporary history is far from a 180-degree turnabout—more like an evolutionary mutation, changing subtly and with massive deliberation but—we can hope—moving in the direction of peace through complex forms of cooperation, rather than war, through simple appeals to pride and prejudice. . . .

3

OUR G.I.'s FIGHT A "PRIVATE WAR" IN VIETNAM*

David Halberstam

One aspect of defense of America is helping an ally way out there on the perimeter where Communist power intrudes upon U.S. allies. This is part of the diplomacy of defense too, and we do well at it.

SAIGON

In the mountainous territory north of here, where the brush seems to grow in three thick levels—foot-level brush, shoulder-level brush and tree-level brush—there is a tendency for Communist guerrillas to consider the terrain their own and a tendency for Vietnamese officers to agree. It is nightmare country, a scenic, brutal haven for the irregulars, but hated by government regulars who sense ambushes all around them. Recently American and Vietnamese officials, in an attempt to change the pattern of the war in the north, designed a new tactic: The idea was to strike quickly into the heart of the mountains, defy the laws of guerrilla warfare (the laws say you don't attack the enemy unless you have a 7-to-1 manpower edge, but here it should be more like 10-to-1), hit a larger enemy force by surprise, tear him up—and run like hell.

The first of these operations, with Vietnamese troops ferried into the mountains by American helicopters was a glowing success. The rice, said one officer, was still warm in the enemy's rice bowls when the government forces were counting the Vietcong dead. The second of the operations was a bit trickier. . . .

At any rate, in the late afternoon as the choppers were coming in to pick up the Vietnamese, the Communists opened up extremely heavy fire. . . . Circling up above in a gas-turbine chopper, Capt. Ray Vining and Capt. Joseph Josh were flying rescue and evacuation for the raid. They had already rescued a crew from one downed chopper. . . .

Now, as they circled above, they saw the last aircraft take off under particularly brutal fire. . . . [they] suddenly saw a ball of orange flame hit the body of the chopper. They watched it autogyrate to a point . . . where there was no protection. . . . They landed 50 feet from Gray's craft . . . sitting in an open area exposed to the fire from the ridge up above. . . . Finally they were all inside. "We had been on the ground too damn long—about four minutes when 30 seconds would have been better," says Vining. . . .

"But you know it wasn't much different from a lot of missions or risks

* David Halberstam, "Our G.I.'s Fight a 'Private War' in Vietnam," *The New York Times Magazine*, November 4, 1962, pp. 19, 108–12.

taken by all the other boys." . . . "just another day in Vietnam."

* * *

There will probably never be a Hollywood spectacular on this war. Each day it continues its grinding, unrewarding way. For the Vietnamese, it has been going on since World War II. . . . For the Americans . . . this war has its own particular significance: America is not at war and . . . these men—7,000 to 8,000 of them—have become engaged in their own private war. . . .

They do not seem to doubt that they ought to be here, although they are extremely aware of their limitations as advisers and the difficulties ahead. . . .

"The longer you stay here the more you become a part of this war; the more you see them as a threat to you and your buddies' survival; the more they become your enemy," one officer said. . . .

The Americans . . . are advisers and not commanders. It is one thing . . . to give good advice and it is quite another thing to have that advice accepted by a Vietnamese who may be extremely conscious of "face" and indeed have political problems far beyond the ability of an American officer to understand. . . .

This is not to say that the Americans and the Vietnamese do not get along well together. The opposite is closer to the truth; in general, they get on quite well. And the further you get down the ranks and the less the political involvement and the greater the human involvement, the better the relationship, until at the bottom you find some captain living in the swamps with a company of Vietnamese.

The Americans are impressed with the willingness of a 100-pound Vietnamese (pronounced "Veet Nmees" in Army terminology) to shoulder a 20-pound automatic rifle and walk 15 miles in a swamp without complaint. The Vietnamese, in American eyes, are an inordinately cheerful and generous people. The Vietnamese in turn tend to be impressed by what good fighters and bad colonialists Americans are (indeed, had Americans settled here instead of the French, it is extremely likely that the Vietnamese would have colonized the Americans) and it is to their eyes a decent and honorable combination. They are impressed by American willingness to share their swamps and their food but most of all they are impressed by American insistence on sharing the ultimate danger, noting that on patrols and in choppers Americans seem to be in the most dangerous positions.

This especially impressed a German photographer. Even when a particular assignment seemed impossible, "they still went at it 100 per cent. They always do the job. I can't imagine European troops would work like that except in actual combat."

* * *

4

WEAPONS OF THE LATE 1960's*

Hanson W. Baldwin

Nobody knows exactly what is beyond the next turn of the road in defense technology. We do know we'll discover it (whatever it is) and build it and test it. And we also know it won't make the world any safer. The neutron bomb (which only kills all living things) is just around the corner.

. . . Two other potential developments, probably far away, loom as a possible result of resumed testing [of nuclear weapons].

One might be the so-called "neutron bomb," a weapon deliberately designed to maximize the killing flux of neutrons released at the instant of explosion, but to minimize (and perhaps eliminate entirely) the residual and persistent aftermath of radioactivity now associated with any nuclear explosion, particularly one in which fission products predominate.

Such a weapon would unquestionably provide any nation possessing it a considerable enhanced battlefield flexibility; enemy troops in a specific area, for instance, could be destroyed without extensive contamination of the area and without the danger of radioactive fallout over far wider areas.

The other possible development might expedite the production of an antiballistic-missile weapon. . . .

* "To Test or Not to Test?," *The New York Times*, June 26, 1961, p. 3.

5

WEAPONS TECHNOLOGY IN THE 1970's AND THE ARMS RACE*

Herman Kahn

Already the U.S., the U.S.S.R., Britain, France, Israel, and possibly Egypt have achieved atomic explosions, and Communist China is working zealously at her first atomic pile. President Kennedy put it this way:

> *Personally I am haunted by the feeling that by 1970 . . . there may be ten nuclear powers instead of four, and by 1975, fifteen or twenty.*†

What happens when these continent-busters really get around? Shall we consider trying to change the rules of the game now, *while we are still alive?*

I would like to deal with some of the possibilities for the . . . late Sixties and early Seventies. . . . We have to consider the possibility of "breakthroughs" and other surprises. . . . Since one can almost guarantee that many startling and unexpected developments will occur. . . . I will consider: cheap, simple bombs; cheap, simple missiles; cheap satellites; controlled thermonuclear reaction; other sources of cheap neutrons; other sources of nuclear fuels; californium bullets; ground-effect machines; reliable sensors; supercalculators; cheap calories; medical progress; advanced materials; cheap, fast transportation (for limited wars); reliable command and control; Doomsday Machines, and disguised warfare. . . .

* * *

Under the current programs, 1969 may be a little early for the diffusion of these devices to other than "advanced" nations. It is very difficult to predict the rate at which the technology, materials, and information will be disseminated. Even without explicit controls, it might be the mid-1970's or even a later period before they become cheap and simple for the majority of "developed" nations. But there are many things that could accelerate this dissemination process: the use of nuclear weapons in a limited war; successful programs for the peaceful uses of nuclear explosives in the mid-1960's might at least make nuclear "devices" widely available; the deliberate diffusion of nuclear technology, by either the United States or the Soviet Union, to enough allies so that there will be no more secrets; a break-

---

* Herman Kahn, "The Technology of the 1970's and the Arms Race," in *Arms and Arms Control*, ed. Ernest W. Lefever (New York: Frederick A. Praeger, Inc., 1962), pp. 21–25. (Originally printed in *Daedalus*, journal of the American Academy of Arts and Sciences.)

† Presidential press conference, March 22, 1963.

through in technology or materials, etc.

As an example of this last possibility, consider the fusion reactor. It is improbable that this device will be practical by 1969. . . . Let us, however, go ahead . . . by assuming not a qualified, but an outstanding success —such a success that even relatively primitive nations will find it possible either to build or buy a fusion reactor and thereby acquire a virtually unlimited source of cheap power. This spectacular gift of technology has a significant side effect: it gives off neutrons very copiously, so copiously that it may not be exaggerating to state that the neutrons are for all practical purposes free.

Free neutrons would mean that many kinds of nuclear fuels would be very cheap. With these nuclear fuels and with the kind of technology that is likely to be available in 1969, it may literally turn out that a trained and technically minded person, even one who is a member of a relatively primitive society, would be able to make or obtain bombs. This would raise forcefully the question of the illegal or uncontrolled dissemination of bombs. (One can today buy machine guns, artillery, tanks, and fighter aircraft on the grey market.) Thus, the 1969 equivalent of the Malayan guerrillas or the Algerian rebels or the Puerto Rican nationalists, or even less official groups, such as gangsters and wealthy dilettantes, might be able to obtain such bombs.

Even if the controlled thermonuclear reaction does not prove to be a success by 1969, there are other possibilities for the cheap production of neutrons. For example, many of the commercial uses of nuclear devices would release neutrons as a by-product. This might lead to either the clandestine or open production of weapon-grade nuclear fuels. . . . It is also possible that we and others will learn how to make bombs using only or mostly materials already widely available, such as deuterium and lithium. . . . Briefly, 1969 . . . may see the advent of the era of the conventional nuclear bomb, in which (in the absence of adequate controls) any "legitimate" nation can get some illegitimate groups or governments may also get access to nuclear weapons. . . .

I have scarcely been able to touch upon the complexities of the technological arms race and the stability of the United States-Soviet balance of terror. I have tried to point out that technological process is so rapid that there are almost bound to be doctrinal lags. These doctrinal lags will in themselves be dangerous, leading to important gaps in our preparations, the waste of badly needed resources on obsolete concepts, the neglect of possible strengths, the excessive use of especially glamorous tools, and, possibly most important of all, heightened possibilities of serious miscalculations or accidents because we have not had time to understand and make provisions for the requirements of the newly installed systems. To the extent that arms-control measures are supposed to alleviate dangers or costs by allowing the current "balance of power" status and military competition to be conducted, by agreement, at cheaper or safer levels, or to the extent that one hopes to increase each state's objective capability to prevent surprise attack or other disaster, this inability to understand "the military problems" introduces almost intolerable complications. (The reason for the adverb "almost" is that we have these complications, whether or not we have arms control.) I have almost ignored the even more complex problem of the conduct of international relations in a world in which force is becoming both increasingly more available and increasingly less usable, a problem that is complicated by the spectacular increase in the number of sovereign nations, by increased nationalism, militarism, and "ambitions" in these new nations and governments, and by the revolution of rising expectations.

Anyone who attempts to control the arms race must be able to live with all the stresses and strains that the above problems will create. It is most unlikely that all of these problems will be solved in an atmosphere of good will and common fellowship, or by the use of ad hoc committees and intuitive judgments derived from experience in almost irrelevant situations. And we may not have much time in which to work.

6

WE'LL HUFF AND WE'LL PUFF . . .*

The Editors of The National Review

Many Americans agree with this writer that military readiness, military posturing, military acts, are the only language our adversary understands. We have spent almost 20 years negotiating with the U.S.S.R. and its allies at "disarmament talks," yet nothing, absolutely nothing, has been agreed to.

This editorial was written when the problem was whether the U.S. should or should not resume nuclear testing. The U.S.S.R. resumed testing A-bombs. Then so did we. And there was no result from the tests either, other than further radioactive pollution of the atmosphere. Is there no way out of this race?

Once more, and yet once more, bold words have been launched from the eloquent pads of the New Frontier toward Moscow and the four quarters of the earth: this time to trumpet Mr. Kennedy's stand on the grave topic of nuclear tests. The United States' note of June 17 accurately reviews the "almost three years of painstaking effort on the part of the United States and the United Kingdom to work out an effective agreement with the Soviet Union." It recounts the long (much too long) series of generous (far too generous) concessions that the West has made to the Soviet viewpoint. It carefully explains why the "proposals and position taken in the Soviet *aide memoire* [of June 6] negate the entire concept of effective international control."

The Soviet proposals, the note bluntly continues, "would leave the Soviet Union, with its closed society, its government unaccountable either to a parliament or to an informed public opinion, and its actions shrouded in a veil of secrecy, free to conduct nuclear tests without fear of exposure.

* "We'll Huff and We'll Puff . . . ," *The National Review*, July 1, 1961, pp. 405–406.

For almost three years, the United States has been willing to assume the risk of not testing nuclear weapons without the certainty that the Soviet Union has likewise stopped its testing. The national security and defenses of the free world do not allow this risk to be assumed indefinitely."

All such being manifestly the case, the government of the United States has of necessity, for the sake of the nation's survival, to . . . , to. . . . To resume tests, surely? Whoa, there, citizen, let's not fly off the handle. To . . . , to . . . , well, "to face an increasing need to take whatever steps may be necessary" and . . . , and to point out to everybody that for "the failure to agree . . . the U.S.S.R. . . . would have to take the responsibility" and . . . , and, well: "An effective test ban treaty should be signed without delay." Period. End of document.

Well, that's the kind of stuff that will make old Khrushchev tremble in his boots, all right. From laughing, that is. Unless he's getting just plain bored with the repeats of this Kennedy turn. What a statement it was three months ago on Laos! The United States would never let Laos run down the Communist drain, no Sir! An immediate cease-fire, or else! And then—though Thailand, the Philippines, South Vietnam and Taiwan were ready to send the troops needed for actual resistance in the field—there was no cease-fire, and the rush down the drain has been uninterrupted, and the United States has done nothing except to offer (through Mr. Harriman at Geneva, two days after the note on nuclear testing) to withdraw from Laos all its military personnel. What is to be sequel, then, of these intelligent, informative and frequently brave words . . . ? As in each preceding case, there is only one conceivable conclusion that can complete the logic: an *act*, a firm and unhedged act.

Khrushchev, of all men, knows the meaning of these practical syllogisms. Without the act, the words are smoky wind and bombast. The President went to Vienna, we are told, to make sure that Khrushchev would not press too hard from "a miscalculation" of our strength of purpose, to show Khrushchev "our determination" to defend our rights and obligations, above all in the decisive matter of Berlin. But how will the President prove to Khrushchev our strength and determination—if these indeed exist or can be summoned into being? Never, certainly, by words, however brave or loud. Khrushchev judges men by their acts; he scorns their words. As everyone realizes, he has been for the past five months of investigating *the will* of the new United States leadership. In every experiment so far made he has uncovered beneath the words, confusion, floundering, withdrawal, retreat. By the evidence, why should he suppose that he cannot advance with as little serious risk in Berlin as in Laos or Cuba?

Do we want to save Berlin? To call a halt?

Enough of talk, then. Let the nuclear tests resume. They, or rather the act of decision that triggers them, will speak a language to which Khrushchev will begin to listen.

7

EVIDENCE OF MATURITY IN U.S. REACTION TO CRISIS*

Harlan Cleveland

Harlan Cleveland, who, in an earlier piece in this chapter, argued that we are beginning to break ahead in this race against the U.S.S.R., here argues that a cool head, steady nerves, and "the restrained use of power" will enable us to weather each international crisis as it occurs, as we always have in the past. Tough it out, he says.

We find the advice comforting and are personally resolved to do our utmost to emulate Steve Canyon, but what if these infernal machines and the Button, in a decade or less, are also in the hands of Castro or his successors, or some very un-Steve Canyon types in places like the upper Malay peninsula or central Africa?

. . . I can, I think, suggest a few lessons that can be drawn from recent exposure in the world political area . . . several things are very clear from the busy days and nights of the past months:

First: Crises never develop in quite the way—or at quite the time—the experts expect them to develop. All planning is contingent, and most action is extemporaneous.

Second: The restrained use of power, the application of the gentlest form of power that serves the purpose, is the most difficult and demanding exercise of power. We therefore must learn how to clench our teeth and maintain in combination a degree of restraint and a degree of simple courage that has never before been asked of a democratic people.

Third: Each problem or crisis in world affairs is unique and therefore demands its own solution—its own mix of power and diplomacy, force and restraint; its own instruments of action or leverage, instruments military, political, economic, or persuasive; its own choices between national action, bilateral diplomacy, action by regional allies, and the use of the United Nations as forum, mediator, and policeman; or, as in the Cuban case, a judicious mixture of all of these. We therefore must refrain from generalizing from the particular—refrain from assuming, for example, that what worked in the Caribbean last month necessarily will work the same way anywhere else. And we also must create and build and learn to work these complicated and fascinating instrumentalities of our great but limited power, including the 51 international clubs of which we are paid-up members.

Fourth: There is no single or simple answer to the woes of the world at any

---

* Harlan Cleveland, "Evidence of Maturity in U.S. Reaction to Crisis," in "A Most Dangerous Time," *Department of State Bulletin,* December 10, 1962, p. 881.

given time, no fundamentalist theory or formula with the whole solution, no one blinding insight into the meaning of it all. The better one understands that human affairs are almost infinitely complex, the clearer will be the vision. There is hardly an issue in in world affairs worth discussion which is not interrelated with other issues; which does not involve a mix of strategic, political, economic, and other factors; which does not involve some elements which we control and other elements which we do not control; which does not involve contradictions between domestic politics and international politics—for ourselves and for everyone else party to the issue. And this is why we have to search, untiring and unfrustrated, not for the simple answer which is always wrong but for the answer which is complex enough to be right.

And fifth: We have seen clearly, I think, that real toughness in world affairs is best seen as maturity. Maturity requires a cool head, steady nerves, unflagging patience, tiresome restraint, and the sheer capacity to repeat ourselves until we are sure we are understood—which is sometimes long past the point of extreme boredom. It also requires that ready confidence, that calm faith in the future of freedom and variety in human affairs, and that healthy pinches of optimism which help us to see that the deep tides of history are moving in our direction and impel us to seize the opportunities while facing up to the dangers. . . .

8

THE COMING POLITICS OF DISARMAMENT*

Fred J. Cook

Fred Cook's concern is that our fantastic input ($50,000,000,000 per year) into extra *weapons is bleeding us poor. You can't take that much (including many of our best brains and skills, most of our research and development work) out of the economy just to throw it away or to pop it into new holes in the ground and* not *suffer. And we are. We have a low rate of economic growth and growing unemployment. We have plenty of weapons margin over our adversary so we don't need most of these things we manufacture for a year or two's use in military display. Economics, he says, is beginning to reinforce moral and humanitarian pleas for a slowing down or stop in the arms race.*

In . . . a year in which the military budget has so escalated that even $50 billion seems like the piddling commitment of a simpler past, it may seem the height of paradox to suggest that the basis is being laid for a politics of disarmament. But such is the reality.

While no politician worth his salt at the ballot box would, as yet, dare to embrace disarmament, the hidden forces that eventually move even poli-

* Fred J. Cook, "War at the Arms Trough: The Coming Politics of Disarmament," *The Nation*, February 16, 1963, pp. 131–35.

ticians to rationality are beginning to operate. The fact is that the prolonged arms race has started at last to commit a form of economic hara-kiri. Recessions come with increasing frequency; unemployment rates continue disturbingly high; the growth rate limps. These are symptoms that clearly say all is not well, and the inquiring mind, probing behind them, quickly discerns two facts: (1) military spending is a drag on the over-all economy of the nation; (2) it represents a financial drain to most of the states and awards its beneficences only to the few.

These are hard, economic facts, only now becoming apparent. . . .

The first hard fact favoring the new politics is that the billions spent on arms do not build up the domestic economy; in the long run, they debilitate it. Of course, military expenditures have provided millions of jobs, and still do. But the end-products of these jobs are mostly waste: Minuteman, once finished, is sunk in its silo and there it sits, waiting for Doomsday. The billions spent to produce it and its kindred flock are dead; they have not created useful goods, they have not opened up new lines of endeavor, they have not stimulated and regenerated the economy. Economists, analyzing the prosperity of Western Europe, where the growth rate outstrips ours, where unemployment runs far lower, have been struck by the fact that this prosperity seems to bear a direct ratio to the proportion of the national income that is plowed back into the domestic economy instead of being buried in the silos of modern war.

Coupled to this first fact is the second: Though an entire nation is being bled by onerous taxes to finance armaments, the immediate economic benefits are distributed with gross inequality. A Department of Defense analysis of the distribution of procurement contracts, issued September 29, 1962, tells the story.

. . . 57.2 per cent was distributed among just seven states. California . . . led all the rest, gobbling up 23.9 per cent of all major orders. New York . . . benefited to the extent of . . . 10.7 per cent of all contracts. Only five other states . . . managed to wangle their way into this exclusive billion-dollar club. . . .

The armament race is keeping a select few of the states in a style to which they never previously were accustomed; the rest are getting only crumbs. In many of the latter, unemployment has become endemic; businesses fail; hard times clamp down cruelly in the midst of the bounty of the Warfare State. The picture spells the potential. For years, these comparatively deprived states, their businessmen and their politicians, have tried to cut for themselves a larger slice of the munitions pie. They failed; and it must soon dawn upon them that they must continue to fail, for the bulk of military procurement will continue to go to the states that already have the vital installations, the major research centers, the key production plants.

These two facts, then, offer the broad economic base for a new politics of disarmament. One foundation stone is being laid by the dragging national economy, hampered by its abnormal devotion to military interests; the other, and politically the more explosive, lies in the inevitable—and inequitable—economic consequences of military procurement: the rich getting richer, and the poor poorer, and there is nothing much that can be done about it.

* * *

Gardner Ackley, a member of the President's Council of Economic Advisers, testifying before the Senate Committee on Banking and Currency last July, was asked by Senator William Proxmire (D., Wis.) to explain why Western European economies were growing at a much faster rate than ours. The witness replied:

I would certainly also stress the fact that in the United States we have been devoting a very substantial chunk of our resources to military purposes during this period. Those same resources in most of Europe are being devoted to productive investment, and it is not surprising that this productive investment should permit a much more rapid growth of total output than we have.

Senator Hubert H. Humphrey (D., Minn.), in a hearing last August 29 before the Senate Small Business Committee, noted that, in America, the government finances about 65 per cent of all research and development and that by far the larger portion of this is devoted to the needs of military and space. On the other hand, as the Senator pointed out:

In Germany, 85 per cent—85 cents out of every research dollar—is private, and less than 15 per cent goes into military and space. Eighty-five cents of that goes into the civilian economy, so that today the German plant competition for world markets of civilian goods is being automated, modernized, equipped in the latest and best fashion, and new products are developing, while we are developing new wrappings. We are the greatest packagers in the world. . . . In Japan, it is about 85 to 15 again. . . . In England, which also has a low rate of economic growth, as does our country, 60 cents out of every research dollar is governmental and goes into military and space, atomic energy. . . .

What is happening to our civilian economy as we plow more and more of our scientific personnel, our brains, into the military and into space and into atomic energy for military purposes? Where are we going to end up in this trade competition with these Belgians and these Dutch, who are clever, and the Germans who are very clever, who are spending more money for civilian aspects and will develop products cheaper, better and more serviceable?

It was a good question, and it is significant that it is being asked, even if it is not yet being answered. For it is becoming increasingly clear that our economy is beset with deep-seated problems that are not being tackled, much less solved, while our brains and energies and resources are devoted to the creation of new and more ghastly implements of war. The new world of electronics is bursting upon us like a cataract. Its flood is such that not even multibillion-dollar boosts in the already bloated military budget can prime the economic pump. For not only are military end-products an economic waste; they are also now being produced in an automated world that calls for ever fewer workers. Analyzing this trend, Gerard Piel, publisher of the *Scientific American*, said in delivering the Phi Beta Kappa oration at Harvard last June:

The arms budget is losing its potency as an economic anodyne. It is concealing less and less successfully the underlying transformation of our economic system. Progress in the technology of war, as in all other branches of technology, is inexorably cutting back the payroll. . . . Expenditure on armaments has begun to yield a diminishing economic stimulus.

Yet our fixation with the cold war and military demands has so hamstrung us that we have not even recognized the true nature of our economic problem, much less considered what to do about it.

* * *

Even such a veteran and ardent cold-warrior as the ultra-conservative columnist David Lawrence sees the issue. In a column last July, Lawrence wrote:

> How can the armament expense of the United States . . . be materially reduced so that an era of business growth and a sound economy can be achieved in America?
>
> This question is more important than a tax cut or any other "gimmick" being advanced as a cure for the stagnant economy of today. For the truth is America cannot absorb the present-day expense for armament and grow productively at the same time.

Here then is the first basis, only now beginning to be perceived and discussed, for the eventual creation of a politics of disarmament. Given time, it may perhaps be highly persuasive, for business itself, which has been committed ideologically and financially to the aims and rewards of the cold war, must come to see that this commitment no longer serves—that the economic welfare of the nation demands a civilian, not a military, employment of the nation's best brains and resources.

* * *

Such is one face of the Warfare State. The question arises: Can we keep the Warfare State and change the face?

* * *

In a single edition last November, for example, the *Los Angeles Times* ran 14 solid pages of advertisements from major aviation-space-electronics firms pleading with scientists, engineers and technicians to flock to "lotus land" and partake of its lucious fruit. "The Sky's the Limit for Scientists, Engineers & Technicians," screamed an eight-column banner over one such page of advertisements. "Reach New Heights in the Space Age—Enjoy a Challenging Future," proclaimed another.

There is no disposition here to challenge the thesis that this country needs an adequate defense system. But the fact is that our swollen military budget is only partly related to legitimate defense needs. . . . The upshot has been that we have achieved, and are constantly adding to, a *needless overkill capability* at the expense of our national economy.

This is the issue as it is beginning to present itself to some, at least, of our politicians and economists. And it is aggravated by the fact that the largess of military procurement is distributed in such a way that those who already have much, get more, while those who have little get less. Economics, in other words, has begun to throw its powerful arguments behind the idealistic and humanitarian pleas of those who are seeking to stop the arms race.

9

CLOSE-UP OF A "PEACE STRIKER"*

Alvin Shuster

Mrs. Wilson was just a housewife and mother, like your mother or the lady next door, till she became angry at the way we put anti nuclear-bomb demonstrators in jail. Now 150,000 women are organized to pressure the government (ours and *the U.S.S.R.'s) to keep its eye on, and some of its brain power busy at, the main task—trying to find a means of agreement with each other. Their demand is "You keep trying!" Their conviction is that each government is in the habit of assuming that the other is totally untrustworthy, and each is in the habit of ignoring the dangers not only of war but of the arms race itself. Do you want your kids to drink radioactive milk?*

Thousands of women, of many kinds and all over the country, have joined a loosely organized group, "Women Strike for Peace"—a sort of direct-action campaign reminiscent of female activities in the suffrage and prohibition fights of years ago.

One of its prime movers is Mrs. Dagmar Wilson, a petite 46-year-old mother of three teen-age daughters, and a person of some versatility. She is an illustrator of children's books and a designer of amateur-theatre sets and costumes. A "nonjoiner," she is a political neophyte, though with quite a cosmopolitan background. . . .

Her crusade is in many ways informal and it started almost casually. The idea came to Mrs. Wilson one day last September while she was sitting with her husband Christopher (an aide at the British Embassy) and some friends in the backyard of her house in Georgetown. They were talking about the jailing in London that day of Bertrand Russell for his part in antinuclear-bomb demonstrations.

"I realized this was a man who had worked all his life for peace and no one listened to him," she recalls. "Finally he had to resort to civil disobedience. This shocked me. I felt like chartering a plane and going over to picket the jail. I thought it was a disgrace. He was speaking out for humanity. I called up a few friends and the next thing I knew we had this women's movement. They called their friends. And they in turn called others. And they all wrote letters to friends in other cities."

A couple of meetings were called around town and out of them grew . . . the movement. . . . Another decision was to call for a general demonstration on November 1 throughout

---

* Alvin Shuster, "Close-up of a 'Peace Striker,'" *The New York Times Magazine*, May 6, 1962, pp. 32, 68, 72.

the country. The result was that 50,000 women in 60 cities turned out to demonstrate for disarmament, against resumption of atmospheric testing by the United States, and for peace in general.

"We were amazed by the response and while we had been looking only to the November 1 demonstration we decided to keep going," she says.

Keep on going it did. One hundred and thirty contacts for Women Strike for Peace have now been set up in some 40 states. No one knows for sure, but the contacts in turn probably keep in touch with another 100,000 women who at the simple mention of "Christmas Island" stand ready to write their Congressmen, picket stores selling war toys, come to Washington to parade in front of the White House, man tables at public libraries to line up signatures on peace petitions, attend discussion groups on the dangers of fallout, hand out leaflets at supermarkets urging a ban on fresh milk for one week after each U.S. atmospheric test, or even—as 50 of them did a while back—fly to Geneva to apprise the delegates to the disarmament conference of their view.

The Geneva group . . . told the heads of both the United States and Soviet delegations to their faces that they were both too inflexible over disarmament, handed them bundles of petitions with 50,000 names, and dispatched a wire to President Kennedy asking that a U.S. military base near Russia be turned over to them for disarming and conversion into a "cultural exchange center."

If the women haven't succeeded in altering any official policies, they have at least managed to draw some official attention. They met with all the delegations to the 17-nation meeting at Geneva.

* * *

Groups in various cities make suggestions to each other. Some agree and some don't. And those who do disagree do not leave the movement because there is "nothing to leave." For example, after the President announced plans to resume nuclear tests, the strike leaders called for a period of mourning, but there were many who were reluctant to participate in the demonstrations because they felt the President knew best.

"I think that is naïve," Mrs. Wilson says. "There is no justification for testing under any circumstances. We are polluting the air for our generation and for future generations. As far as I can see, there is no military need to resume testing on our part. I don't care what the reasons given are. We don't recognize a military need. Let's face it. Wars can no longer be won. Wars are antediluvian. We simply have to abolish them."

. . . Mrs. Wilson does not agree that one effect of the women's activities is to obscure the basic issues between the United States and the Soviet Union. Rather, she feels that the politicians of the world are obscuring them. She believes, for instance, that the delegates at Geneva seem to be "trying to avoid reaching agreements."

"It's all rather reminiscent of some of the games our six-year-olds play. They make the rules as they go along and when they are not winning they change them. We can tolerate this with our six-year-olds because we know they are going to be eight in a couple of years and they will learn to stick to the objectives of the game and agree to abide by the decision of an umpire whether they like it or not. The men in Geneva are not six-year-olds. . . .

Thus, while the movement was started in part to support President Kennedy's "peace race," . . . the women . . . are increasingly critical of the presentation by the United states of disarmament plans "with elements we know will be unacceptable to the Russians."

"I don't know why we Americans do this, but we do," Mrs. Wilson says sharply. "We'll make a suggestion and they don't take it up. They make a suggestion and we don't consider it. It's really very hard to say who is making it more difficult on the other. But I don't think we can blame it all on the Russians. . . ."

. . . She believes this country is pushing the principle of inspection too far in its negotiations on a nuclear-test-ban treaty.

"There are enough stations—I don't know what kind they are—all over the world able to tell what they're testing," she says. "And the Russians don't want us on their territory. . . . Frankly I believe inspection would expose their weaknesses rather than their strength. I think they are diffident to show us their marbles. And I think it is unfair for us to say we want to go in and look at them.

"In short, I think that if we show signs of giving a little, the Russians will, too. I believe the Russians want to disarm. They really have everything to gain by disarming. They do not have private money tied up in the armament industry so they don't have the vested interests profiting from the arms race. If they could, they obviously would like to provide more for the material needs for their people."

. . . Mrs. Wilson thinks one thing that would impress the Russians considerably would be the disarming of that base near Soviet borders.

"That would really impress them," she says. "They are very sensitive about the bases surrounding them. They are aware of our building of military might more and more each day. They think we are getting substantially stronger than they. . . . I sense in Geneva the Russians are intensely fearful and terrified of war and I believe they have no intention of starting one. They simply can't stand the thought of being second in power to the United States. It's their fight for recognition that is making them rigid, and not their aggressive intentions."

As part of the movement's activities, Mrs. Wilson says the women are now trying to work out a way to increase their contacts with Soviet women . . . there is a "Soviet Women's Committee." . . .

. . . Mrs. Wilson says, ". . . we might be able in the exchanges to point up what each of our governments is doing right and wrong in working for peace."

After all, she says, Soviet and American women . . . "have a common concern, the welfare of our children."

10

HIDE AND SEEK: SOME DOUR THOUGHTS ON INSPECTION*

Charles Burton Marshall

Since 1946 the Great Powers have sought agreement to check the arms race. The obstacles have been varied and profound, political even more than technical. The problems are here set out by a negotiator of many years' experience—problems which have hampered the reaching of any agreement in the past and might well limit developments in the future.

Some key terms relevant to arms control and disarmament . . . have been mauled about . . . I feel compelled to offer, on behalf of rigor, some simple definitions. I begin with the generic term "verification."

One kind of verification can be carried out without the acquiescence or cooperation of the government subject to check . . . this kind of verification is "monitoring."

A second kind of verification requires grant of access by a government whose actions or capabilities are assessed. . . .

One sort of access is that conceded by a government for a specific limited occasion. Outside authority is permitted to enter an area to confirm that the inviting government has done what it claims to have done (e.g., dismantled a missile pad). The visitors have no warrant to ferret out unreported matters. In effect the government is host, the outside authority is guest. An appropriate term here is "authentication."

A contrasting sort of access is exercised when a government vests an outside authority with power not merely to check matters admitted . . . but also and essentially to determine . . . what may have been left undone or done covertly. The correct term here is "inspection." Such is its sense in official parlance generally—in banking, postal operations, military outfits, and so on. An inspector comes around, welcome or not, with warrant to poke and to raise issues—not merely to nod through a prearranged checklist.

* * *

. . . The main parties to negotiation at [disarmament talks at] Geneva are the governing groups in the U.S. and the U.S.S.R. . . .

The governing groups in the U.S. and the U.S.S.R. are aware of the chances of calamity. A shared desire to get armaments under control may be assumed without arguing. . . . Arms control and disarmament, however, . . . overlap and interact with a great range of other considerations. The rub

---

* Charles Burton Marshall, "Hide and Seek: Some Dour Thoughts on Inspection," *The New Republic*, November 24, 1962, pp. 14–17.

is . . . with respect to these other matters.

A bargain, if and when arrived at, must be a *political* one, in the broadest sense. Each party is under constraint to ensure terms which will preserve the order of values basic to its polity. . . .

This gets close to the heart of the inspection issue. Each side—with reason—attributes to the other ultimate desires and preferences incompatible with its own. . . . Authentic spokesmen for the U.S.S.R. articulate international goals entirely incompatible with the U.S. order of values. Spokesmen on our side articulate world goals which could be realized only after a frustration of the U.S.S.R. amounting to historic defeat. That the articulated goals of both parties may lie beyond reach is beside the point. Each side makes plain enough what preferences it would establish as purposes of policy if it could. . . .

* * *

The mode of thought underlying the U.S. approach, whether or not recognized and acknowledged, rests on ideas of natural law. A unified Creation, with a pattern of right reason inherent, is postulated. Good is identified with it. Principles are held as reflections of this good. What opposes good is ascribed to aberrant free will. Interests are seen as colored with such aberrant imperfections associated with misguided free will. Principles thus transcend interests. Social good inheres in upholding principles impartially. The concept of authority—which is to say, power to bind in conscience—is based on devotion to principles unswayed by interests, impartially applied. Facts are items of information developed impartially by authority and are an objective basis on which to apply principles. Such are the justifying, if not always reigning, concepts in state life.

In the U.S. view, an inspectorate in connection with arms control comprises institutional arrangements for projecting onto the world scene, and especially onto the U.S.S.R., a fact-finding function based on the conception of authority described above. It must be above interests, impartial in endeavor—its authority acknowledged, permitted scope, facilitated in operations, submitted to without cavil or hindrance. Its existence and functions, thus serving as both a substantive and symbolic substitute for trust between the great adversaries, would gradually evolve a basis for confidence. It would serve to assemble and to verify facts to bolster assurance or to confirm doubt. In extremity—that is, in event of the need to abrogate an agreement in face of unacceptable violations by others—the system would provide warrant and vindication. In sum, the U.S. plan for a disarming or disarmed world is congenial to the U.S. view of legitimacy.

The U.S.S.R. view is different. The U.S.S.R. asserts a total claim on the future, based on its dialectic concepts of history. An essential aspect of this claim is that history progresses by inherent momentum toward a final perfection perceivable only through Communist doctrine. Concepts of legitimacy are derived from the law of history which ordains eventual universal triumph for Communist interests and purposes. All other interests and purposes are deemed deviant and devoid of legitimacy. The ruling Communist party is considered sole interpreter and custodian of legitimacy. Bearers of party authority are constrained not to concede legitimacy to any authority beyond their control.

No thread, I contend, has been

more consistent in Communist conduct than this sensitivity to making any concessions to external authority. . . .

* * *

Soviet willingness to *invite* an authenticating agency *on occasion* is quite conceivable but has no bearing on submitting to inspection. The U.S.S.R. persistently says inspection is out—a stand consistent with Communist dogma. In fact of this, it is difficult to explain lingering U.S. hopes that the U.S.S.R. really does not mean it, and that obduracy can some day be overcome by adjusting details. The U.S. may indeed exaggerate the efficacy of inspection. In this connection, the notion that inspection has a potential for guiding the U.S.S.R. toward becoming an open society may be laid aside as inherently too marginal and speculative for serious consideration. . . .

One question pertains to inspection as a way of ensuring compliance with any agreement . . . formal acceptance does not necessarily mean cooperation. The Korean armistice pattern might well be repeated—continuous frustration, postponement, avoidance, and administered ambiguity. The level and quality of information afforded might well be less than attainable through monitoring—that is, verification by means available to the U.S. irrespective of Soviet cooperation. The international inspectorate would probably provide small, if any, assurance of compliance.

A second question concerns the qualities of an international inspectorate. To gain necessary respect and credit even under favorable conditions, such an inspectorate would have to have high motivation and technical competence. Yet presumably an inspectorate would have to draw heavily on people from uncommitted countries. Most of these countries are—and will remain for a long time—short on technicians. They will need to keep their best men at home.

Third, a question is in order concerning the integrity of findings by an international inspectorate. U.S. expectations are based on the assumptions that everyone can divorce "truth" from its consequences. The U.S. envisages an international inspectorate disciplined and constrained to rigorous, exacting attitudes toward empirical data, irrespective of preconceptions and preferences. Yet the U.S. doubts the detachment of Communists in an inspectorate . . . neutrals may prove equally self-interested.

United States expectations overlook a disposition, basic in the cultures of many of the neutralist countries, to view magisterial functions as intended not so much to forward the triumph of good over evil as to keep contention between them from getting out of hand. This calls for temporizing, mitigating, hoping always to work out arrangements to save something all around, but in a pinch favoring concessions to the more intransigent. . . .

I recall an illustrative instance. Representing the government of the United States at an International Red Cross Conference during 1952 I was forced to the limit of my patience in trying both to avoid a donnybrook and to preserve national prestige in the face of outrageous attacks from Chinese Communist delegates. At intermission, a delegate from a leading neutralist country, after praising me for reasonable forbearance, added, "These men are mad dogs. You should have let them have their way"—a *non sequitur* to me but obviously plausible to him.

To expect unequivocal findings by

an international inspectorate which has neutrals in the swing position—especially with respect to crucial considerations likely to precipitate renewed competition on armament—is probably too much. . . .

* * *

In this perspective, limits, difficulties, and doubts regarding inspection recede to academic import. Questions of confidence and dependability are not merely technical. They never were. . . .

I see little in recent events to nourish the mystique of trust. An uninspected arms control compact seems out for the calculable future. The outlook is dour—indefinite impasse on formal terms, with abatement of the problems restricted to unilateral steps and to informal and tacit agreements, with or without more such crises as the one over Cuba [in late 1962].

11

"A SHAFT OF LIGHT IN THE DARKNESS"*

John F. Kennedy

In the summer of 1963, relations with the Soviet Union seemed to take a decisive turn. Faced with Chinese intransigence and nuclear developments in several countries, the U.S. and U.S.S.R. agreed to a test ban. The achievement of this ban came with full cognizance of the problems set out by Marshall. Awareness of the obstacles to further agreement and the risks involved were almost as evident in President Kennedy's explanation of his action as his guarded optimism and reasoned hope.

Good evening, my fellow citizens:

I speak to you tonight in a spirit of hope. Eighteen years ago the advent of nuclear weapons changed the course of the world as well as the war. Since that time, all mankind has been struggling to escape from the darkening prospects of mass destruction. In an age when both sides have come to possess enough nuclear power to destroy the human race several times over, the world of communism and the world of free choice have been caught up in the vicious cycle of conflicting ideology and interests. Each increase of tension has produced an increase in arms; each increase in arms has produced an increase in tension.

Yesterday, a shaft of light cut into the darkness. Negotiations were concluded in Moscow on a treaty to ban all nuclear tests in the atmosphere, in outer space and under water. For the first time, an agreement has been reached on bringing the forces of nuclear destruction under international control—a goal first sought in 1946 when Bernard Baruch submitted our comprehensive plan to the members of the United Nations.

* * *

---

* John F. Kennedy, "A Shaft of Light in the Darkness," *The New York Times,* Western Edition, July 27, 1963, p. 2.

But the achievement of this goal is not a victory for one side—it is a victory for mankind. It reflects no concessions either to or by the Soviet Union. It reflects simply our common recognition of the dangers in further testing.

This treaty is not the millennium. It will not resolve all conflicts, or cause the Communists to forgo their ambitions, or eliminate the dangers of war. It will not reduce our need for arms or allies or programs of assistance to others. But it is an important first step —a step toward peace—a step toward reason—a step away from war.

Here is what this step can mean to you and your children and your neighbors.

First, this treaty can be a step toward reduced world tensions and broader areas of agreement. The Moscow talks reached no agreement on any other subject, nor is this treaty conditioned on any other matter. . . .

No one can predict with certainty, therefore, what future agreement, if any, can be built on the foundations of this one. It could include controls on the preparations for surprise attack, or on numbers and types of armaments. There could be further limitations on the spread of nuclear weapons. The important point is that efforts to seek new agreement will go forward. But the difficulty of predicting the next step is no reason to be reluctant about this one. . . . If both sides can by this treaty gain confidence and experience in peaceful collaboration, then this short and simple treaty may well become an historic mark in man's age-old pursuit of peace. . . .

* * *

I do not say that a world without aggression or threats of war would be an easy world. It will bring new problems, new challenges from the Communists, new dangers of relaxing our vigilance or of mistaking their intent.

But those dangers pale in comparison to those of the spiraling arms race and collision course toward war. . . .

A war today or tomorrow, if it led to nuclear war, would not be like any war in history. A full-scale nuclear exchange, lasting less than 60 minutes, could wipe out more than 300,000,000 Americans, Europeans and Russians, and untold numbers elsewhere. And the survivors, as Chairman Khrushchev warned the Communist Chinese, "would envy the dead." For they would inherit a world so devastated by the explosions and poison and fire that today we cannot even conceive of all its horrors.

* * *

The treaty can be a step freeing the world from fears and dangers of radioactive fallout. Our own atmospheric tests last year were conducted under conditions which restricted such fallout to an absolute minimum. But over the years the number and yield of weapons tested have rapidly increased —and so have the radioactive hazards from such testing. Continued unrestricted testing by the nuclear powers, joined in time by other nations which may be less adept in limiting pollution, will increasingly contaminate the air that all of us must breath.

Nor does this affect the nuclear powers alone. These tests befoul the air of all men and all nations, the committed and the uncommitted alike, without their knowledge and without their consent. That is why the continuation of atmospheric testing causes so many countries to regard all nuclear powers as equally evil; and we can hope that its prevention will enable those countries to see the world more clearly, while enabling all the world to breathe more easily.

Third, this treaty can be a step toward preventing the spread of nuclear weapons to nations not now possessing them. During the next several years, in addition to the four current nuclear powers, small but significant number of nations will have the intellectual, physical and financial resources to produce both nuclear weapons and the means of delivering them. In time, it is estimated, many other nations will have either this capacity or other ways of obtaining nuclear warheads, even as missiles can be commercially purchased today.

I ask you to stop and think for a moment what it would mean to have nuclear weapons in many hands—in the hands of countries large and small, stable and unstable, responsible and irresponsible, scattered throughout the world. There would be no rest for anyone then, no stability, no real security, and no chance of effective disarmament. There would only be increased chances of accidental war, and an increased necessity for the great powers to involve themselves in otherwise local conflicts.

If only one thermonuclear bomb were to be dropped on any American, Russian or other city—whether it was launched by accident or design, by a madman or an enemy, by a large nation or small, from any corner of the world—that one bomb could release more destructive force on the inhabitants of that one helpless city than all the bombs dropped during World War II.

Neither the United States, nor the Soviet Union, nor the United Kingdom, nor France can look forward to that day with equanimity. We have a great obligation—all four nuclear powers have a great obligation—to use whatever time remains to prevent the spread of nuclear weapons, to persuade other countries not to test, transfer, acquire, possess or produce such weapons.

This treaty can be the opening wedge in that campaign. It provides that none of the parties will assist other nations to test in the forbidden environments. It opens the door for further agreement on the control of nuclear weapons. And it is open for all nations to sign. For it is in the interest of all nations—and already we have heard from a number of countries who wish to join with us promptly.

Fourth, and finally, this treaty can limit the nuclear arms race in ways, which, on balance, will strengthen our nation's security far more than the continuation of unrestricted testing. For in today's world, a nation's security does not always increase as its arms increase, when its adversary is doing the same. And unlimited competition in the testing and development of new types of destructive nuclear weapons will not make the world safer for either side.

It is true that the Soviets have tested nuclear weapons of a yield higher than that which we have thought to be necessary; but the 100-megaton bomb of which they spoke two years ago does not and will not change the balance of strategic power. The United States has deliberately chosen to concentrate on more mobile and more efficient weapons, with lower but entirely sufficient yield; and our security is not, therefore, impaired by the treaty I am discussing.

It is also true, as Mr. Khrushchev would agree, that nations cannot afford in these matters to rely simply on the good faith of their adversaries. We have not therefore overlooked the risk of secret violations. There is at present a possibility that deep in outer space that hundreds of thousands and millions of miles away from the earth illegal tests might go undetected. But we already have the capability to construct a system of observation that would make such tests almost impossible to conceal, and we can decide at any time whether such a system is needed in the light of the limited risk to us and the limited reward to others of violations attempted at that range.

For any tests which might be conducted so far out in space which cannot be conducted more easily and efficiently and legally underground would necessarily be of such a magnitude that they would be extremely difficult to conceal.

We can also employ new devices to check on the testing of smaller weapons in the lower atmosphere.

Any violation, moreover, involves along with the risk of detection, the end of the treaty, and the world-wide consequences for the violator.

Secret violations are possible, and secret preparations for a sudden withdrawal are possible. And thus our own vigilance and strength must be maintained as we remain ready to withdraw and to resume all forms of testing, if we must.

But it would be a mistake to assume that this treaty will be quickly broken. The gains of illegal testing are obviously slight compared to their cost, and the hazard of discovery. . . .

While it may be theoretically possible to demonstrate the risks inherent in any treaty and such risks in this treaty are small, the far greater risks to our security are the risks of unrestricted testing, the risk of a nuclear arms race, the risks of new nuclear powers, nuclear pollution, and nuclear war. . . .

There is no cause for complacency. We have learned in times past that the spirit of one moment or place can be gone in the next. We have been disappointed more than once. And we have no illusions now that there are short cuts on the road to peace.

At many points around the globe, the Communists are continuing their effort to exploit weakness and poverty. Their concentration of nuclear and conventional arms must still be deterred. . . .

Nothing could more greatly damage our cause than if we and our allies were to believe that peace has already been achieved and that our strength and unity were no longer required. But now for the first time in many years the path of peace may be open . . . history and our own conscience will judge us harshly if we do not now make every effort to test our hopes by action, and this is the place to begin.

According to the ancient Chinese proverb a journey of 1,000 miles must begin with a single step.

My fellow Americans, let us take that first step. Let us, if we can, step back from the shadows of war and seek out the way of peace. And if that journey is 1,000 miles, or even more, let history record that we, in this land, at this time, took the first step.

Thank you, and good night.

12

WHY THE UNITED NATIONS?*

Dag Hammarskjold

Here we see that, although the U.N. is far from a world government, it is a developmental or evolutionary stage between the stage of sovereign nations and the ultimate stage of international coordination and peaceful resolution of all conflicts. Here we see that the U.N. can do things which no nation or coalition can do outside of it.

Why the United Nations? That such a question can be posed and deserves to be answered, demonstrates how short a distance we have traveled in developing organized forms of international coexistence. Who asks today why we have parliament, or why we have an organized diplomatic representation? . . .

The United Nations is necessary because the classical forms of bilateral diplomacy are no longer sufficient in the world that has become ours. The organization is necessary, moreover, because regional organizations alone cannot satisfactorily make up for these shortcomings of bilateral diplomacy. The organization is necessary, finally, as a phase in the evolution toward those more definitive forms of international cooperation of universal scope which I, for one, am convinced must come, but which cannot be brought into being without many experiments and long preliminaries.

It often happens, both among friends of the United Nations and among its critics, that its so-called successes or failures are discussed as though the organization were independent from the governments and disassociated from them in its efforts. This, for instance, appears to be in the background when it is said that it was—or that it was not—the United Nations that brought the Suez crisis under control. This is also the sense in which appeals are made for "support of the United Nations."

To yield to the temptation of regarding the United Nations in this manner is to overlook the basic character of the organization. It is no way a kind of independent, state-like entity, least of all a "supergovernment." It is a platform, or more accurately a constitutional framework, for specific negotiations between governments in forms which have been added to those offered by traditional diplomacy and with similar methods but with geographical delimitations in various regional associations of states.

The organization has offered the opportunity of developing new forms of negotiation, advancing further than bi-

* Dag Hammarskjold, "Why the United Nations?", *United Nations Review,* July 1958, pp. 14–17. Mr. Hammarskjold was Secretary-General of the United Nations until he was killed in an airplane crash in the Congo.

lateral or regional contacts. In this, it has responded to a need which has made itself increasingly felt as the international system of states has been transformed. New nations in Africa and Asia have come into being and have had to be integrated in world politics. At the same time, the ties between various parts of the world have become so strong as to entail worldwide consequences for almost any international conflict, no matter how limited it may seem at the outset. . . .

The technique which has primarily attracted attention, is of course, the public debate in the Assembly or the various Councils. It represents a public diplomacy added to the private diplomacy that used to be the rule. The transition to public diplomacy allows public opinion to follow the unfolding of diplomatic operations and, conversely, it offers an opportunity for public opinion to influence the positions taken in the course of the negotiations.

Next, I should like to mention the introduction of voting as a form of resolving diplomatic conflicts. In interstate politics we are still only at the beginning of an evolution toward a system where a minority is presumed to bow to a majority. . . . The influence of this older attitude has prevented the voting technique within the United Nations from reaching full efficiency. On the one hand, agreement between the five permanent members of the Security Council remains a condition for achieving a decision of the Council in questions of substance. On the other, as is well known, all the decisions in the General Assembly, and most decisions of the Councils are only recommendations, the effect of which may depend mainly on how well they are believed to reflect world opinion.

A third innovation within the United Nations, as far as diplomatic techniques are concerned, stems from the fact that all member states maintain permanent representation in New York and accredit ambassadors to the organization. This has created what actually amounts to a standing diplomatic conference at United Nations headquarters. The new and broader opportunities of negotiation which have thus been opened are being used increasingly. Aside from those debates and votes which figure in the press, there is thus a continuous, intense and fruitful diplomatic activity of the multilateral type, which had led to a coordination of positions, to reconciliations and to planning which would have been far more time-consuming and complicated if conducted in traditional forms—if they had then been possible at all. It is dangerous to overestimate the importance of personal contacts, but on the other hand it is unrealistic to underestimate the importance of the fact that qualified representatives of opposing camps live together, sharing their problems, and at the same time are in continuous touch with representatives of "uncommitted" governments. In these respects, as far as I am able to judge, things have developed further in New York than in any international center in the past.

Finally, and as a fourth new technique added to the arsenal of classical diplomacy, I should like to mention the utilization of the diplomatic functions of the Secretariat. Over the years, the weight of the work of the secretary-general has increasingly moved from what are conventionally regarded as political and administrative tasks to the diplomatic ones. This has not stemmed from any directed or planned development; it has happened under the pressure of practical needs which have increasingly made themselves felt. The diplomatic activity of the secretary-general and his assistants is exercised in forms and for purposes which in many ways resemble those typical of the activity of an ambassador on behalf of his government, whether he is exercising "good offices" or operates as a negotiating party in relation to some other country. In this connection, the position of the Secretariat is unique in that, of course, it does not represent any country. Nor has it, as has the representative of a government, the means of putting force behind its words. When diplomatic efforts by the secretary-general are increasingly demanded by member governments this must be taken as evidence that they have found it useful, in their relations with other states, to have available an outside party representing what might be called the common denominator. Often the secretary-general has had to go into action where formerly a third government would have functioned, but where in this day and age, with present complex relations between governments, it has appeared simpler and more effective to turn to the Secretariat of the United Nations.

VALUE OF UNIVERSAL APPLICATION

It is difficult for those on the outside to evaluate the evolution of diplomacy within the United Nations which I have just described. The touchstone of its importance should not be the superficial classifications of "success" or "failure." At the present state, it must rather be whether the governments cooperating within the United Nations have felt the need of such new techniques—and use them. What has governed their attitude in this respect is probably, not least, their view of how things would have gone if they had not had access to these new possibilities . . . so far no state has even considered leaving the United Nations, and . . . the Great Powers have found reason; not only in words but also in action, to support in their foreign policy the new diplomatic techniques which the United Nations has made available.

Much of what I have said naturally applies also to regional associations such as NATO. It is evident, however, that the value of these new techniques has a special meaning when given universal application. It is all right to play the new instruments within the framework of a limited, relatively homogeneous association of states. But what is to be done concerning the relations between such associations if they are pitted one against the other? Each group may rejoice in the development of cooperation among the states belonging to it, and feel safer in the strength yielded by this cooperation. But where is the possibility of finding ways toward a reconciliation with other groups?

The prevailing differences will hardly be lessened if one group or the other maintains its strength, no matter how valuable this may be to its defense of shared values, while in other respects it simply adopts a waiting attitude in the hope of some more or less automatic improvement in the general situation in the course of time, perhaps following a breakdown within a competing group. Present risks being what they are, even an advocate of such a course must recognize that it is necessary at the same time to preserve the best possibilities available for understanding and reconciliation between the groups. This is so, quite apart from the fact that those forms of universal organization are also motivated by the need of solving the thousand and one lesser differences which are reported daily by the newspapers and which are objects of almost daily activity by the United Nations.

SERVING AN APPRENTICESHIP

. . . It is often said that the solution of the problem of international coexistence must be world federation. Unfortunately, it is necessary to learn to crawl before one can walk. And it is rather risky to refuse to move at all just because one has not learned how to walk.

It is difficult to see how a leap from today's chaotic and disjointed world to something approaching a world federation is to come about. To attain such a goal, elements of organic growth are required. We must serve our apprenticeship and at every state try to develop the forms of international coexistence as far as is possible at the moment if we are to be justified in hoping some day to realize the more radical solutions which the situation may seem to call for. We must, for instance, feel we are along the road of majority voting and get to know its political and psychological possibilities and difficulties in international life. We shall have to create a corps of administrators and diplomats who know, from within, the questions facing an international organization with political tasks. For such a development, the United Nations offers a framework which appears as good as the world situation permits at present.

The road toward more satisfactory forms of organization for a world community of states does not lead through publicized "successes" of the United Nations. It leads through a series of good or bad experiences with the specific techniques made possible by the United Nations. It goes via the conclusion we are able to draw, in action, about these experiences. In this respect, the continuous, but unsensational and therefore little-known work on current tasks which is conducted within the United Nations is also of importance. Each conquest of new ground for diplomatic activity and international cooperation is a lasting gain for the future. Its value is not nullified if the tested techniques, in spite of their continued developments, should prove incapable of any particular movement of coping with one of the crises facing us.

These new techniques have already yielded important results, apparent to everybody. Without discussing the decisive importance of the national policy of various member states for the solution of, let us say, the Suez crisis [of late 1956], I should like to recall that the success of the policy followed was predicated on the specific possibilities of shaping an organized cooperation within the universal United Nations framework. Furthermore, only through this organization was it possible to create the police force—the UNEF—without which things would have developed quite differently, and probably catastrophically.

What I have now said refers, of course, primarily to the diplomatic and political tasks of the organization in the narrow sense. It applies also to the technical, economic and social assistance activities of the United Nations, particularly in relation to the so-called underdeveloped countries. These activities, however, deserve attention in their own right, as another important element in evaluating the United Nations.

It is unnecessary to dwell on the need of aid to underdeveloped countries. Two-thirds of the world's population live under economic conditions in sharpest contrast to the relatively high standards enjoyed by the remaining third. Unfavorable economic conditions prevail in areas strongly influenced by the new nationalism which is such a prominent feature of the present situation. This should be enough to demonstrate the importance of this general problem for political developments in the world as a whole.

In various forms, those countries which have the capabilities have launched an extensive aid activity in underdeveloped countries. Like the Marshall Plan in its day, this activity is not a form of charity but rather an effort of enlightened self-interest to enable the underdeveloped countries, by exertion of their own, to improve their economic and social conditions. Experience has shown that such technical assistance faces certain typical difficulties when conducted bilaterally. If the country offering financial means and experts is small enough for its activity to be without political overtones, there is the risk that its resources are too small for its contribution to be adequate. In the case of a Great Power, on the other hand, it is difficult to avoid giving a political overtone to its technical assistance, even though all such conditions may be expressly waived. The beneficiary tends to feel his economic dependence as a political liability. Political considerations apart, the fact remains that the beneficiary country—often a newcomer on the world scene—feels the burden of maintaining relations of indebtedness and gratitude to another country.

Because of these political and psychological factors, multilateral forms of assistance have emerged as superior to the bilateral ones in important respects. If aid is channeled from the giver country to the beneficiary country through the United Nations or one of the specialized agencies within the United Nations framework, the political accent is avoided and psychological pressure is eased in other ways at the same time. It is not my contention that the multilateral form should supplant the bilateral one. Both are needed. What I want to stress is that bilateral forms are insufficient and face difficulties which make it urgent to pursue the multilateral course further and fully utilize its potentialities. This focuses attention from another side upon the question of the necessity of the United Nations. The United Nations itself, the World Health Organization, the Food and Agriculture Organization, and the other agencies within the framework of the charter offer forms for states to "multilaterize" their assistance activities, thus by-passing the difficulties attendant on assistance in the bilateral form. . . .

13

DEPOLITICALIZE THE U.N.*

The Editors of The National Review

The thing that bothers many of us about the U.N. is not that it has a world organization to try to eradicate malaria or that it has a large number of technical agencies investigating and reporting on everything. It is the brass trumpet it provides for all those tiny nations who have nothing, nothing but a seat and access to the microphone. This is representation without taxation, representation without responsibility (to invert an old American slogan.)

An example of this point of view follows.

. . . Most of the U.N.'s *political* functions are not merely useless, but fraudulent, mischievous and often gravely injurious to the major goals—international peace and order—that the U.N. Charter proclaims. As a technical organization we are, if not unqualified *for* the U.N. at any rate prepared to accept it. As a political organization, we are against it, and strongly so. We therefore conclude that the U.N. ought to be, to the maximum extent possible, *depoliticalized.* If this proves to be impossible, then—since the political aspect has in the past year dropped to an intolerable badness—the U.N. as a whole ought to be liquidated.

Rapid communication and transport on a world scale along with other developments of modern technology, the population explosion, mass literacy and mobility, pose technical problems that can be handled only on an international scale: problems of disease control, allocation of radio-TV channels, air, and soon, space navigation rules, weather information, the assembling of many sorts of statistics, combatting international food pests (such as locusts or plant rusts) are examples. International agencies, for all their inevitable faults, are often the best and sometimes the only way to deal with many of these matters. Moreover, partly because of the sheer practical difficulties of staging international conferences and sustaining continuing international bodies, it is probably most efficient to have the various agencies linked through an over-all international organization.

* * *

But there is no necessary reason why these international communications must include political decisions. Far from promoting peace, order and harmony among nations, the political motions, resolutions and acts of the U.N. have exacerbated bitterness, made compromise and negotiation more difficult, exaggerated minor differences into major crimes, helped create artificial blocs and splits, and actually brought chaos and war to

* "What About the U.N. Bonds?", *The National Review,* January 30, 1962, pp. 48–49.

regions that were doing all right while the U.N. kept out of their affairs.

These evils have been thrice compounded since the U.N. axis shifted from the Security Council to the General Assembly. It is inconceivable that a pow-wow of 104 diverse nations, each with full voice and vote, more than half of them weak, disorderly and immature, should conduct itself responsibly. Even the U.N.'s greatest admirers throw up their hands in despair, nowadays, when they talk about the behavior of the Assembly. . . .

The fundamental reason for the monstrosity of the U.N. as a political organization lies in the fact that a fraud—or, more gently, an illusion—is embodied in its essence: the illusion that there exists a consensus of some significant sort among all nations of the world, leading them to seek peace, justice, freedom, well-being and what not, and serving as trustworthy foundation for an international law. The truth is otherwise. . . .

14

FIVE CHEERS FOR THE NONALIGNED!*

Carl Soule

They may be poor but they have ideas, argues Carl Soule. Are we afraid of new ideas? Ideas are what the U.N. is for. Where they can they do their share of the world's work. Consider the job they've done in salvaging the Congo from chaos.

Some people in the United States are worried about the presence of so many new nations in the United Nations. They have in mind the new members from Asia and Africa—especially those from Africa, which have sent delegates "whose grandfathers were not only illiterate but cannibals." . . .

A certain columnist summed up this attitude last November in an article headed "Primitive Nations Ruin U.N." He wrote: "We have degenerated a lofty ideal by the inclusion of raggedy-seat nations whose vote is equal to nations of ancient standing, parliamentary savoir-faire, and liability to taxes and law and order. . . . We are hip-deep in midgets in the U.N. . . ."

The nonaligned—that is the name many of the new U.N. members prefer to be called. . . .

. . . Five cheers for the nonaligned! Our first cheer is prompted by the fact that their presence there is making the U.N. truly universal in its membership. . . .

At first, when the U.N. was formed, almost all its member nations were from North America, South America and Europe; there was a mere handful from Asia. After ten years most members were from those four continents, with a handful from Africa. Now there are between 20 and 30 members from each of the five major conti-

* Carl Soule, "Five Cheers for the Nonaligned!", *The Christian Century*, May 30, 1962, pp. 683–84.

nents. North and South America together have the least (22) and Africa has the most (29). To people who are worried about African nations' membership we would say bluntly that before 1970 their number will probably increase to about 40.

The newly born nations are eager to join the U.N. The day after their independence they are in New York with hat in hand, as it were, knocking on the nickel-plated doors of the building by the East River.

* * *

Our third cheer is for the sweep toward independence in Asia and Africa. Who among us wishes to repudiate the American revolution? . . . What is wrong with independence for other parts of Africa? The fact is, you can hardly educate people—teach them French or English and have them study French history or British or American history—without giving them ideas about self-government.

* * *

Our fourth cheer is for the spirit in which so many of the new and small nations from Asia and Africa are nonaligned in the cold war. They refuse to become rubber stamps for either East or West; they listen and make up their own minds. . . .

. . . A delegate from the Central African Republic declared:

> My country, like so many other small nations, is profoundly disappointed by the incapacity shown by the Great Powers for finding an area of understanding. Instead of finding guides in them, we come to consider them as the possible authors of our early annihilation.

A member of the mission from Guinea expressed the feeling of many people when he said:

> If we had the power, we would immediately, completely, and unconditionally disarm all states, large and small. Unfortunately we do not have that power. . . . By their presence, their moderation, their objectivity, and their sincerity the representatives of the nonaligned nations should facilitate a rapid agreement between the views of the Soviet and American governments.

A speaker for Nigeria said:

> Leave our continent alone. Do not bring these ideological conflicts to our continent. Take your rockets to your own homes. Test your atom bombs in your own kitchens. . . . The great powers do not have all the greatness in them at all. They are great in some aspects, but in others they are very small. . . . By the intervention of the smaller states we may bring sanity in the midst of insanity and save humanity from total destruction.

Because of such convictions the 16th Assembly passed ten resolutions on disarmament, sometimes by small margins, sometimes by large margins, sometimes unanimously, sometimes even against the vote of the Soviet Union or the United States. Specifically, the resolutions were (1) against the Soviet test of a 50-megaton bomb; (2) against further nuclear tests by any nation; (3) for a test ban treaty; (4) for a denuclearized Africa; (5) against the use of nuclear weapons in any situation, as contrary to the Charter; (6) for agreement on disarmament between the Soviet Union and the United States; (7) for the establishment of a nonnuclear group of nations; (8) against the spread of the possession of nuclear weapons; (9) for the creation of a new disarmament committee; and (10) for the application of international law to outer space.

East and West tacitly acknowledged the providential role of the nonaligned nations when they agreed on the composition of the new disarmament committee. . . .

Our fifth cheer is for the solid and intelligent support which the nonaligned nations of Asia and Africa and the neutral nations of Europe have given the cause of unity and order in the Congo. Not only have they served on the Congo advisory committee of the secretary-general and voted in the Security Council for sound resolutions but out of fine loyalty to the United Nations their isolated soldiers have courageously faced primitive barbarism, sophisticated cunning, anarchy, demagoguery, torture and even death. What troops from the larger, "aligned" powers could not do in the Congo, the few battalions from India, Ireland, Ethiopia, Sweden and other neutral and nonaligned nations have done and are doing. . . .

15

THE NON-EUROPEAN WORLD*

George F. Kennan

Many, like George Kennan, have serious doubts about jumping into large developmental programs all over the world and trying to remake age-old cultures in the image of the Ohio valley or the modern American city. Have we the answers to these peoples' problems? In terms of costs, we are very well-off compared to others and we can afford to carry a considerable number of such programs, but can 64,000,000-some American taxpayers support 1,000,000,000 people, even in part or even only initially? And what makes anyone think it would be only initially? Politically, technical assistance programs will involve us in these countries' most internal politics. Do we want to stimulate revolutions abroad and then have to try to stay on top of them? What makes us think such programs would make peoples like us?

. . . In that great arc of territory that runs from China's southern frontier around through southern Asia and the Middle East to Suez and the north of Africa . . . things have generally been moving in recent years in a manner favorable to Soviet interests and unfavorable to our own. . . .

Now there are significant differences between the situation in this southern band of states and the situation in Europe or in the area of Japan or Korea. . . .

In the southern band of states . . . the formal status of the respective countries is not generally at stake, and there is little substance for negotiation between ourselves and Russia. Our problem in that part of the world is primarily one of the attitudes of the peoples who inhabit it. The things Moscow has been doing there—whether it be shipping arms or giving technical aid or making offers of trade or sending delegations around—how-

* George F. Kennan, *Russia, The Atom and the West* (New York: Harper & Row, Publishers, 1958). Copyright 1957, 1958 by George F. Kennan. Reprinted by permission of the publishers.

ever disturbing they may seem, are not things to which we can take formal objection. They are ones that are technically within the limits of international propriety. . . .

What are these attitudes which have played so powerfully into the Soviet's hands? . . . Their origins lie in such diverse things as the emotional legacy of colonialism, resentments arising out of the color problem, jealousy over the material successes and outward affluence of certain Western countries, notably the United States, frustrations experienced by people who are for the first time bearing the responsibilities of power, an easy acceptance of Marxist clichés and symbols, and various prejudices and misapprehensions relating both to Russian society and to our own. Added to this are the impulses of a violent and sometimes irresponsible new nationalism—a nationalism which Moscow, having little to lose, has not hesitated to encourage whereas the Western powers, having more at stake, have been obliged to view it with concern and even to oppose it on a number of occasions. And, finally, because all political reactions are in a sense cumulative, there has been a widespread impression throughout these regions that the West, whatever its merits or deficiencies, was in any case on the decline, whereas the star of Moscow was rising; and this has not failed to impress that sizable portion of mankind which has more respect for power and success than it has for principle. In this bundle of impulses and reactions there is, in fact, something for everyone, something to appeal to every type of mind; and it is small wonder that it has all added up to a massive anti-Western complex, a complex in which a sneaking admiration for Western institutions and a desire to emulate them are mixed with a special, irritated sensitivity, an instinctive longing to see Western nations shaken and humbled, and a frequent inability to balance with any degree of realism the advantages of association with the West against those of association with Moscow. It is these states of mind, not what Moscow is doing to take advantage of them, which lie at the heart of our problem.

. . . I did not mention our own mistakes. . . .

. . . We have expected too much. Many of us seem to have believed that Russian influence could and should be excluded completely from this entire area. This attitude is surely unrealistic. . . .

. . . This anxiety about Russian influence is often either unnecessary or exaggerated. Some of us seem to believe that no country can have anything to do with Moscow, even in the most normal ways, without at once losing its independence. Such a view exaggerates the sinisterness of Moscow's immediate purposes. . . . It also involves an underestimation of the talent of Asian and African statesmen for seeing through the more dangerous long-term aspirations of international communism and protecting their countries against them. Left to themselves, many of these statesmen would surprise us, I am sure, by their ability to take the measure of Moscow's motives and methods and to find resources of their own with which to protect the integrity of their national life. . . .

We have sometimes contrived to give them the impression that they would be reasonably safe, in fact, in playing close to the edge of danger, because if they got too close we could always be depended upon to come rushing in and rescue them with one sort of aid or another. We have even created a situation here and there where people believe they can exploit the threat of an unwise intimacy with Moscow as a means of bringing pressure to bear upon us. . . .

When suggestions are made to us that if aid of one sort or another is not forthcoming, people will, as the saying goes, "go Communist," surely there is only one answer: "Very well then, go. Our interests may suffer, but yours will suffer first."

The demands frequently made upon us by the independent countries in parts of the world seem to me to run something like this: "We," they say, "are determined to have economic development and to have it at once. For us, this is an overriding aim, an absolute requirement; and we are not much concerned about the method by which it is achieved. You in the West owe it to us to let us have your assistance and to give it to us promptly, effectively, and without conditions; otherwise we will take it from the Russians, whose experience and methods we suspect anyway to be more relevant to our problems." In response to this approach, a great many people in my own country have come to take it for granted that there is some direct relationship between programs of economic aid on the one hand and political attitudes on the other—between the amount of money we are willing to devote to economic assistance in any given year and the amount of progress we may expect to make in overcoming these troublesome states of mind I have been talking about. . . .

Why all the urgency? It can well be argued that the pace of change is no less important than its nature, and that great damage can be done by altering too rapidly the sociological and cultural structure of any society, even where these alterations may be desirable in themselves. In many instances one would also like to know how this economic progress is to be related to the staggering population growth with which it is associated. Finally, many of us in America have seen too much of the incidental effects of industrialization and urbanization to be convinced that these things are absolute answers to problems anywhere, or that they could be worth *any* sacrifice to obtain. . . .

I must also reject the suggestion that our generation in the West has some sort of a cosmic guilt or obligation vis-à-vis the underdeveloped parts of the world. The fact that certain portions of the globe were developed sooner than others is one for which I, as an American of this day, cannot accept the faintest moral responsibility; nor do I see that it was particularly the fault of my American ancestors. . . .

To those who come to us with requests for aid one would like to say: "You tell us first how you propose to assure that if we give you this aid it will not be interpreted among your people as a sign of weakness or fear on our part, or of a desire to dominate you."

These are not the only psychological dangers of foreign aid. There is the basic fact that any form of benevolence, if prolonged for any length of time (even in personal life this is true), comes to be taken for granted as a right and its withdrawal resented as an injury. There is the fact that any program of economic development represents a change of the terms of competition within a country and brings injury to some parties while it benefits the others. It is hard to give aid to any other country economically without its having an effect on internal political realities there—without its redounding to the benefit of one political party and the disadvantage of another. . . .

Finally, I do not think for a moment that the Soviet Union really presents the alternative people seem to think it represents to a decent relationship with the West. Moscow has its contribution to make to what should be a common task of all the highly industrialized countries; and there is no reason why this contribution should not be welcomed wherever it can be really helpful. But Moscow is not exactly the bottomless horn of plenty it is often held to be; and it is rather a pity that it has never been required to respond all at once to the many expectations directed to it. We ourselves should be the last, one would think, to wish to spare it this test. The results might be both healthy and instructive. . . .

16

HELPLESSNESS IN THE TROPICAL WORLD*

Pierre Gourou

It is all very well to shrug off the burden. But take a look at the extent of human helplessness.

Malaria is the most widespread of tropical diseases. . . . The malarial patient knows quite well that a bout of fever may be the unpleasant reward for hard work. In a period of six months a hundred workmen from a healthy district suffered the following casualties . . . : between 15 and 25 were eliminated by death or evacuation; those remaining had . . . lost 25 per cent of their capacity for work; and the capacity for work of the group had fallen off by 50 per cent . . . one death from malaria corresponds to at least 2,000 days of illness. . . .

Intestinal diseases . . . anyone who harbors plasmodia in his blood and a rich collection of amoebae and dysenteric bacilli, hookworms, tape-worms, schistosomes of bilharziasis, and various other parasites in his intestines—as do most of those who dwell in the hot, wet regions—must certainly be debilitated, unfit for hard physical work, and incapable of great mental effort. . . .

THE MAN WITH THE HOE

. . . Throughout the hot, wet regions, with the exception of certain parts of Southern Asia, none of the cultivators has progressed beyond the hoe. Either for lack of draught animals or of inventive minds, they have not adopted the use of the plough. . . .

. . . They belong to a "vegetable civilization." . . . The diet does not contain the quantity of calories needed by a manual worker. . . . Being underfed, the people of the tropics often focus their attention on the food-

* Pierre Gourou, *The Tropical World: Its Social and Economic Conditions and Its Future Status,* trans. by E. D. LaBorde (London: Longmans, Green & Co., Ltd., third edition, 1961), pp. 6–7, 9, 29, 67, 68, 73.

supply. The chief topic of conversation in the villages is what has been or will be eaten. . . . The low yield from labor in these regions is clearly as much bound up with undernourishment as with tropical diseases. . . .

17

A HOPEFUL LETTER TO FOWLER HAMILTON*

John Fischer

Mr. Fischer was writing the then new head of the U.S. Agency for International Development and telling him his (and many of our) reasons for dissatisfaction with U.S. foreign aid in the past.

Agreed, most of the underdeveloped world needs help. Agreed, we can help some. But watch all those rich fat cats who in the past have had their hands in the till inside the recipient governments! Useful aid requires more than money; it requires skill and purpose.

Dear Fowler:

As a taxpayer, I was delighted to hear that you will be taking over the job of running our foreign-aid program.

* * *

Moreover, as the head of the new Agency for International Development, you will be taking on what may well be the toughest management job in the world. You inherit a staff which is, in many places, badly demoralized, cluttered with deadwood, and not at all sure what it is supposed to be doing. . . .

But these administrative details will, of course, be the least of your problems. What makes me really cheerful about your appointment is the fact that you have had a good deal of experience in economic warfare. You will know how to use foreign aid as a weapon.

So long as you use it that way—as the best weapon we have in the not-so-cold war that we'll be fighting for so long as anybody can see into the future—then I'm pretty sure that most taxpayers will be willing to give you whatever money you need, for as long as you need it. But if you fritter it away for other purposes—to prop up shaky dictators, for example, or in a heartwarming effort to abolish poverty where poverty is inevitable—then you will have an eruption on your hands. If I read the seismograph correctly, the public's annoyance with that kind of waste has just about reached the explosion point.

For some of your predecessors didn't know just what they were meant to accomplish with all that money. Buy friendship? Strengthen allies? Feed everybody who is hungry? Undermine the Soviet empire? Carry out a senator's pet project? Industrialize Africa? Arm Vietnamese guerrillas? Clinch a few doubtful votes in the United Nations?

---

* John Fischer, "A Hopeful Letter to Fowler Hamilton," *The Editor's Easy Chair, Harper's Magazine*, November 1961, pp. 12, 14, 16, 21. © 1961 by Harper & Row, Publishers, Inc. Reprinted by permission of the author.

Since in recent years the White House seldom specified precise objectives, the poor administrators tended to dribble out the cash for a little of everything. Usually with no strings attached. That has been the No. 1 fetish—for we were never, never meant to "interfere with the internal affairs" of the countries who got our money. Even when everybody knew that El Presidente was a thief, we dared not insult him by asking for a look at the books. . . . I trust you will abandon our traditional hypocrisy, tie a chain on every dime—and yank hard if it isn't spent in the clearly defined interests of the United States.

That will offend a lot of our benefactees, of course, especially the so-called neutral nations. Don't let that give you grey hairs. We have worried too much about what they think of us; let them worry a while about what *we* think of *them*. Besides they have finally taught us . . . that being nice to them gets us nowhere. . . .

* * *

Dealing with our enemies is, of course, the easy part of your new job. We taxpayers hope you are also tough enough to say "No" to some of our friends.

You might start with the Europeans. Just after the war we started supplying them with arms, to hold back the Communist pressure toward the West. That made a lot of sense in those days, when Europe was in ruins. But it makes no sense today, when Western Europe is enjoying the biggest boom in history. Our partners in NATO can well afford to pay for their own planes and tanks—but they still let us pick up the tab. Nearly a half-billion dollars a year is earmarked, in the current aid program, for military help to Western Europe. How come?

* * *

Our Latin friends could do with a few plain words, too.

For example, when Cheddi Jagan was elected prime minister of British Guiana a few weeks ago, he announced that he would condescend to accept our money. He is against "Yankee imperialism," of course. After all, he is an acknowledged Marxist, who plans to follow "a policy of neutralism like Nehru and Nasser." But since Tito, Nehru, and Poland get American aid, he wants his share of the gravy.

Perhaps Dr. Jagan should be told these facts of life:

There isn't enough gravy to go around. Even if the United States—and Russia and Western Europe—cut off their own economic growth and poured *all* of their savings into the underdeveloped countries, they still couldn't provide enough capital to industrialize all of those nations as fast as they demand. The aid which actually will be available from all sources, East and West, won't begin to meet the expectations of Dr. Jagan and his 60-odd rival claimants. Some will have to do without; none will get all he wants.

Many of the underdeveloped countries will always be poor. They just don't have the resources to support a modern industrial society—nor the land to feed their already hungry and fast-growing populations. . . .

* * *

What the Latins (and most other underdeveloped areas) need more than money—or anything else—is birth control. But for domestic political reasons, on this problem we can offer no help.

Given these facts, it makes sense for us to concentrate our help in those countries where it is likely to produce really worthwhile results—both economic and political. (India may be the prime case. It has a fighting chance to build both a stable economy and a democratic government; and its race with China may well determine the future of all Asia. Annoying as Nehru may be from time to time, this looks like a good place to put our blue chips.) But the hopeless cases will have to go to the end of the queue. . . .

Your big trouble—as I am sure you know—will not come from the young rebels like Jagan. It will come from men who look just as respectable as you—the bankers, generals, and landowners who have long formed the traditional ruling class in much of Latin America.

They are the rich Guatemalans who won't let their Congress pass an income tax—even though social injustice in their country is so flagrant that they had to be rescued from a Marxist regime only a few years ago, and may soon be threatened by another. They are the Brazilian millionaires who put their money into real estate speculation (and Swiss banks) instead of industrial development. They are the twelve families who own El Salvador, and don't believe in either education or shoes for their peasants.

* * *

The smart ones realize, of course, that such empires can't last much longer. They have seen them crumble already in Mexico, Venezuela, Costa Rica, Cuba. They are likely therefore to steal all they can—from their countrymen, and from your aid funds—and then to skip out just before the revolution pops. After all, that plan worked fine for Perón, Batista, Jiménez, Patiño, most of the Trujillo family, and plenty of other strong men who are now living it up in St. Tropez and Miami Beach.

The only way you can beat their game is to side with the Good Revolutionists—the democratic ones like Figueres, Muñoz-Marín, Gallegos, and Betancourt. In the long run, such men are the only workable alternative to the other kind of revolutionists, of the Castro, Jagan, Arbenz, and Guevara variety.

For genuine social revolution—as contrasted with the old-fashioned palace coup, which changed nothing but the hand in the till—is probably inevitable in most of Latin America. It offers the only hope for even those modest gains, in living standards and human dignity, which the Alliance for Progress can honestly promise. Your job is to preside over that revolution—to guide it, nudge it along, and make it work. . . .

* * *

If it is any comfort, you can look forward to dealing simultaneously with a different kind of pressure: blackmail. Your new clients are expert at it, because most of them have been using it on us for years. All they have had to say is: "Give me what I want"—it may be a hydroelectric project, or a flock of tanks to keep the army happy, or a few million to replace what The Boys stole out of the last budget—"or I will go to Moscow."

Nearly always they have been getting away with this kind of bluff. . . .

At some point, you too will have to say "No"—simply because you won't have enough money to pay off all the blackmailers who will be calling on you. When some sheik or generalissimo wants another $39 million to build a palace for his latest mistress, you will have to tell him to send the bill to Mr. Khrushchev.

* * *

Hopefully yours,
JOHN FISCHER

18

THE CLAY REPORT: ECONOMIC AID ONLY WHERE JUSTIFIED*

Committee to Strengthen the Security of the Free World

Aside from the border areas where our defense and our friends' safety is the overwhelming question of the moment, U.S. aid should be given only to those who make effective *use of it in terms of their and our (the Free World's) common goals. No performance, no money.*

. . . There has been a feeling that we are trying to do too much for too many too soon, that we are overextended in resources and undercompensated in results, and that no end of foreign aid is either in sight or in mind.

. . . It is clear, for example, that economic and social growth can be achieved only if it is based on an internal expression of will and discipline, without which external aid is of little value. Yet, many of the countries which have received our aid have not fully performed their part of the assistance bargain with their own resources. Moreover, we have not adequately conditioned our aid in many cases on the achievement of such performance. Indeed, we may find ourselves, in effect, granting a number of continuing subsidies because it is argued that their denial would create instability and lose us good will.

It is obvious, also, that the process of economic development is a long one and will be limited at the outset by the absence of trained manpower and adequate local institutions. . . .

PRESENT STATUS AND FUTURE GUIDELINES

. . . We cannot believe that our national interest is served by indefinitely continuing commitments at the present rate to the 95 countries and territories which are now receiving our economic and/or military assistance. Substantial tightening up and sharpened objectives in terms of our national interests are necessary. . . .

There should be no doubt, however, of the great value of properly conceived and administered foreign aid programs to the national interest of the United States and of the contribution of the foreign assistance dollar in such programs to the service of our nation's security. We live in a world in which poverty, sickness, instability and turmoil are rife and where a relentless Communist imperialism manipulates this misery to subvert men and nations from freedom's cause. A foreign aid program is one instrument among many which we and other developed countries adequately can afford and

* From the Report of the President's Committee to Strengthen the Security of the Free World, to President Kennedy, March 28, 1963. (General Lucius D. Clay, chairman; members Robert B. Anderson, Eugene R. Black, Clifford Hardin, Robert A. Lovett, Edward S. Mason, L. F. McCollum, Herman Phleger, Howard A. Rusk and George Meany. Mr. Meany, however, dissenting.)

vigorously must use in the defense and advancement of Free World interests.

* * *

We are convinced that the United States must take more risks for the purpose of obtaining performance from foreign governments, be more willing to live with charges that it is insensitive to other countries' needs, and accept the consequences that in some countries there will be less friendly political climates.

THE BORDER AREAS [ASIA]

. . . Several of these nations are carrying defense burdens far beyond their internal economic capacities. These countries are now receiving the major portion of United States foreign assistance but are also providing more than two milion armed men ready, for the most part, for any emergency. While their armies are to some extent static unless general war develops, they add materially to Free World strength so long as conventional military forces are required. Indeed, it might be better to reduce the resources of our own defense budget rather than to discontinue the support which makes their contribution possible.

. . . [But] we are convinced that in several of these countries, indigenous forces are larger than required. . . . There, phased reductions of a very substantial order appear practical. . . . This would not only lessen the cost of military assistance but reduce related supporting economic assistance as well. . . .

There are a few other border countries whose military forces presently are of value largely for internal security purposes . . . we believe the present level of support to these forces, particularly with sophisticated weapons, cannot be considered as essential to the security of the Free World . . . significant reductions of military and economic assistance are in order.

In addition there are other countries in this border area, particularly in Southeastern and Western Asia, to which we provide economic assistance and, in some cases, military equipment, though they are neither Allies nor members of alliances with which we are associated. We believe most of this military assistance is not essential. . . .

* * *

In any review of front line countries, special attention must be given to India, even though it is not an ally. . . . Together with our ally, Pakistan, it is the only area of South Asia able to offset the Red Chinese colossus. Unless their freedom and economic growth continue, there can never be a balance of power in Asia and our own involvement in this area could be indefinite and infinitely more costly. Thus, we believe that in the interest of our own and Free World security, economic and military assistance to India, as well as to Pakistan, must continue. . . .

We cannot leave this area of the world without special reference also to Indonesia. Because of its population, resources and geographic position, it is of special concern to the Free World. However, we do not see how external assistance can be granted to this nation by Free World countries unless it puts its internal house in order, provides fair treatment to foreign creditors and enterprises, and refrains from international adventures. . . .

On the western end of the bloc periphery, Greece and Turkey are moving toward increased security and well-being. Both of these important nations, however, are still in need of military assistance and economic support, and Turkey will require both forms of assistance for some time to come. . . .

AFRICA

. . . Immediate security interests [in Africa] are less evident than in countries adjacent to the Communist bloc. . . . The committee regards Africa as an area where the Western European countries should logically bear most of the necessary aid burden. . . .

It can always be said that in fragile, new, developing countries, the United States must provide aid lest they accept it from Communist nations with resulting political penetration and eventual subversion. We cannot accept this view . . . our aid programs in this area are generally new [and] experience has shown they tend to increase . . . the United States cannot undertake to support all of the African countries. . . .

. . . In general, future economic aid to countries in this area should either be curtailed as existing commitments are fulfilled or substantially reduced, except for technical assistance—the primary present need—and PL-480 shipments of agricultural commodities.* . . .

* * *

The Congo merits particular mention. . . . We believe the United States . . . has contributed proportionately more than its share . . . the United States should attempt to maximize the economic assistance of other nations to the Congo. . . .

LATIN AMERICA AND THE ALLIANCE FOR PROGRESS

. . . The Alliance for Progress—predicated on a joint endeavor to achieve for the Latin American peoples economic progress and social justice with free institutions and political liberty—was born in the face of a formidable inheritance: Political and economic instability, habits of government, and social rigidity in Latin America, ambivalent emotions toward United States power and influence in the Hemisphere, deteriorating Latin American terms of trade, vacuums of political leadership and technical skill, the absence of United States and Latin American institutional structures adequate to deal with these problems, and increasing Communist efforts to exploit them. These and other conditions combined to argue for both the urgent necessity and short-term impossibility of the Alliance.

Our offer of a multilateral Alliance and our performance subsequent to that offer should have proved the strength of our commitment to this program. Latin American understanding of and willingness to fulfill the undertakings of leadership, self-help, and self-discipline agreed to . . . however, with notable exceptions have yet to be proved.

. . . We believe the United States should increase its efforts to achieve greater Latin American performances. . . .

The United States should continue to make unmistakably clear that the Alliance for Progress is a long-term venture of extraordinary complexity and scope, demanding a decade or more of sustained effort by all involved to attain truly significant results. . . .

The United States should indicate it expects the achievement of certain attainable goals over the next few years, with continued assistance meanwhile conditioned on reasonable progress toward that end.

The United States should be increasingly more specific on the self-help and reforms it seeks and do so on a country

* "PL-480": Public Law 480 authorizes the U.S. government to ship abroad surplus cotton, wheat, and other products purchased by it in the U.S. to sustain American farm prices, and to sell them for soft (nonconvertible) foreign currencies.

by country basis. At the top of such a list are the goals of monetary stability, sound financial and social budgeting, reductions and eventual elimination of subsidies to government enterprises, tax systems and administration which contemplate raising local revenue levels, stimulating private local and foreign investment and distributing the tax burden more fairly, and measures for the better utilization of land designed to increase agricultural productivity and credit, expand and diversify agricultural exports, encourage rural development, and increase income on the lower levels of society.

. . . Proper incentives to the private [enterprise] sector are required for dynamic growth [and this] must be accompanied by sustained United States and Latin American efforts and decisions at all levels of government policy and action. . . .

. . . The United States must employ the judicious withholding of funds as well as their timely award to encourage necessary internal reform. . . .

SHARING THE ASSISTANCE EFFORT

. . . The burden of sustaining foreign assistance to the developing countries is falling unfairly upon the United States . . . the industrialized countries can and should do more than they are now doing. . . .

TECHNICAL ASSISTANCE

The most serious obstacle to growth in many less developed countries is the inability of their people to effectively utilize the resources at their disposal. Technical assistance should be directed primarily at the removal of these obstacles. . . . In many ways . . . our technical assistance programs are the most direct evidence to the people . . . of our intent to help them advance. These programs need to be of high quality. Also, they should be undertaken only if deemed of sufficient value to be accepted and continued by the recipient country out of its own resources within a reasonable period of time. Such programs should be of specific and limited duration, fixed as they are started and scheduled for completion or turnover. . . . We recommend that new program starts be sharply limited. . . .

THE PRIVATE SECTOR

AID has shown increasing awareness of the vital role played by local and foreign private investment in the development processes, but fuller cognizance is required . . . based . . . on the practical realization that it is the private sector, operating with the cooperation of . . . democratic labor movement and enlightened management . . . which will make the greatest contribution to rapid economic growth and over-all development. . . .

FUTURE U.S. ASSISTANCE PROGRAMS

. . . Reductions are in order in present military and economic assistance programs. . . .